THE HISTORY OF THE FOURTH WAY:
SCHOOL REALIZED

Other books by Hugh James

The Life and Work of Plato

The Story of Man:
A History of the Great Spiritual Traditions

The History of the Fourth Way: School Realized

Hugh James

OREGON HOUSE
2025

Copyright © 2025 by Hugh James

All rights reserved. No part of this book may be used or reproduced in any manner whatsoever without written permission except in the case of brief quotations embodied in critical articles and reviews.

For information, address:
Apollo University Press, PO Box 1037, Oregon House, CA 95962

Published in the United States by Apollo University Press
www.apollouniversity.org

Hugh James
The History of the Fourth Way: School Realized

First Edition
ISBN 978-1-7335653-5-6
Printed in the United States of America
Book Design by William Bentley

*This book is dedicated to all those who,
over more than a century, have given their lives
in support of the five teachers whose stories
are recounted in these pages.*

Acknowledgments

Thanks to:

The late Lucas Cambridge, for the initial encouragement to write this book, and to Apollo University for its patient support over many years.

My wife Tamara, for reviewing the manuscript, and for enabling me to put in the time and effort that was necessary to complete the project.

Guinevere Ruth Mueller, Jonathan Parks, Christopher King, Patricia Chancellor, Paola Igliori and Thomas Hart, for their good memories and for their willingness to share.

Robert MacIsaac, a student of Fourth Way history, who — throughout the time of writing — suggested ideas and additional readings, made available manuscripts and documents, caught errors of fact, and added material from his personal memory. Last but not least, he edited and proofread the entire manuscript.

Margaret Campbell, Pauline Stuart, Paul Harvey, Hugh Lusted and Solee MacIsaac, for accepting the role of readers: living with the book for many weeks in their already busy lives and providing insightful feedback. Their input has significantly guided the final draft.

Michael Jackson, Paulina Herrara, Dominique Reale, and Luis Lombo for their help with the images.

Hugh James

Table of Contents

ACKNOWLEDGMENTS .... *vii*
INTRODUCTION .... *xi*
OVERVIEW OF THE WORK .... *xxv*
   The Study of Man's Possible Evolution .... *xxv*
   Self-Remembering, Self-Observation, and Divided Attention .... *xxxiii*
   The Centers Comprising Human Psychology .... *xl*
   The Different Worlds .... *xlviii*
   Different Levels of School: The Conscious Hierarchy .... *liv*
PROLOGUE IN HEAVEN .... *lix*

CHAPTER 1
   GEORGE IVANOVITCH GURDJIEFF: THE SEARCH YEARS 1
   Youth and Years of Search 1
   The Teaching Found 32
   The Formation of the Teacher 70

CHAPTER 2
   GEORGE IVANOVITCH GURDJIEFF: THE YEARS OF TEACHING ... 89
   Moscow to Constantinople: 1912-1921 89
   Gurdjieff at Fontainebleau 117
   From the Motor Crash to All and Everything: 1924-1935 141
   The Turning Point and the Paris Apartment Teachings: 1935-1949 162
   Conclusion 203

CHAPTER 3
   PETER DEMIAN OUSPENSKY 205
   Formative Years: 1878-1915 205
   Ouspensky and Gurdjieff: 1915-1917 213
   Ouspensky's Awakening: 1917-1919 228
   The Young Teacher: 1919-1921 235
   Early London Years: 1921-1924 242
   Going it Alone: 1924-1934 256
   The Prime Years: 1934-1941 273

  The Mendham Years: 1941–1946 290
  The Final Months: 1947 305
  Ouspensky's Work 335

CHAPTER 4
 RODNEY COLLIN 341
  Early Life and Marriage 341
  Rodney Meets Ouspensky 345
  The Outbreak of War and the Move to Mendham 346
  The Return to Lyne: Ouspensky's Last Eight Months 353
  From Lyne to London 372
  The Move to Mexico 376
  Rodney As Teacher 383
  At the Center of the Maelstrom 396
  Aftermath and Final Thoughts 402

CHAPTER 5
 ALEXANDER FRANCIS HORN 407
  Years of Apprenticeship: 1947–1956 409
  Journeyman Years: 1956–1965 435
  Alex as Teacher: 1965–1988 441
  How Things Went Forward: 1966–1978 456
  New York and Boston: 1979–2007 475
  The Passing of Alexander Francis Horn 484

CHAPTER 6
 ROBERT EARL BURTON AND THE FELLOWSHIP OF FRIENDS 487
  Early Years and Work with Alex Horn: 1967–1969 487
  The Beginning of the Fellowship: New Year's Eve 1969 492
  The Founding of the Ranch: 1971 498
  The Move to Carmel: 1972 506
  Return to the Ranch: 1973–1975 511
  A Global School Begins: 1976 519
  The Goethe Academy and Europe 536
  The Centered Whole: Renaissance, Community, and School 540
  The Inner Work Changes: 2004 560
  Created Light and Uncreated Light 576
  Postcript 580

EPILOGUE IN HEAVEN *583*
BIBLIOGRAPHY *585*
IMAGE CREDITS *593*

Introduction

The Fourth Way is a line of spiritual teaching that was initiated by George Ivanovich Gurdjieff in Russia in 1912. The term Fourth Way describes a path of spiritual development which takes place in the medium of everyday life. Its aim is awakening, or the achievement of objective consciousness. The Fourth Way distinguishes itself from three other spiritual ways: the way of the monk, the way of the yogi, and the way of the fakir. The way of the monk is a way of devotion, based on emotion. It requires retreat. The way of the yogi is based on the understanding of cosmic laws, combined with rigorous meditative practice. It is an intellectual way, and it also requires retreat. The way of the fakir involves the transformation of physical suffering into a heightened experience of the present moment. It requires strict control over sensations and the motor function. Each of these ways requires either complete retreat, or some degree of isolation from the conditions of everyday life. The Fourth Way, by contrast, takes place in the midst of everyday life, and develops all the functions in a balanced way: emotion, intellect, sensation, and motor function. With reference to the other three ways, the Fourth Way *combines* devotion, understanding, and the transformation of suffering. Students of the Fourth Way master a specific set of tools that allows them to achieve, the awakened state in everyday life.

Clear evidence of this kind of teaching can be found throughout history, but it only became known as the 'Fourth Way' when George Gurdjieff introduced it as a distinctive teaching in Moscow and St. Petersburg. In so doing, he initiated a lineage of Fourth Way teachers that has continued down to the present day. It is this lineage that our history traces. It includes the teachings of George Gurdjieff, Peter Demian Ouspensky, Rodney Collin, Alexander Francis Horn, and Robert Earl Burton. If there are other

Fourth Way teachers, or other lineages of teachers, hopefully other authors will write about them.

The tools and techniques that Gurdjieff originally introduced in Moscow and St. Petersburg provided a foundation for each of the teachings to follow. These tools are often taken to be what defines the Fourth Way and taken together they are known as 'The System.'

But we must be clear from the beginning that the system does not work by itself. Each teacher must give conscious life to this set of tools in their own special way. The system is many elements brought into a working unity by how the teacher perceives the needs of his students and responds to them. In other words, the priorities and points of emphasis will vary according to circumstance. Ouspensky once called this system "Fragments of an Unknown Teaching."[1] These fragments are made whole by *a vision*, which molds the elements together in a certain way, at a certain place and time.

George Gurdjieff presented such a vision in Russia, which he then tried to actualize in Fontainebleau, France in the early 1920s. Each of the other teachings drew from that vision. But, while the teachings of Peter Ouspensky, Rodney Collin, Alexander Horn, and Robert Burton are connected to this original vision, they did not develop out of it in a continuous line — but unexpectedly, and not according to plan. In fact, each of these teachings was effectively a re-start. And thus, we shall have to recreate the vision level of each teaching as best we can. Of course, it will be impossible to replicate the vision of each teacher's group exactly as it was. But because of the value these teachings have, and because they are all fast fading into the grey-on-grey of secondary social history, we feel called upon to make the attempt. Therefore, in these pages we are focused not on 'special experiences' with charismatic spiritual teachers, but the actual aims of their groups and the extent to which these aims were realized.

This brings us to an important point. *In this book, we shall present a 'top down' view of the Fourth Way*. We do not begin — as many accounts do — with the experiences of the students, or the 'adventures of the way,' but

---

1. This was the original title of Ouspensky's book *In Search of the Miraculous*, which records the original teachings given by Gurdjieff.

with the aims of the teachers. Their aims come from a higher level than the system: they are set *in relation to* a level where higher states of consciousness are understood for what they are in themselves, and not for what they might mean to the person who experiences them. Peter Ouspensky once referred to this level as "the invisible source of the system." It is a level beyond the 'personal' or 'individual,' at least as we know it. It is connected with something much larger. Each teacher is originally tasked from this higher level, and the success or failure of their Work is in relation to it.

Thus, the measure of a Fourth Way teaching is not how many followers it attracts, or how many publications it generates, or how many successful theater or dance companies it produces. It can succeed in all these things and still fail. The measure of the teaching is given from an objective level that is beyond human understanding. The teacher was originally tasked from this level, and that task is a cross that they bear, for their understanding will always be partially human. Evidence of the Fourth Way teachers having been tasked in this way, is given by the fact that each one of them made efforts beyond any human expectation until the last day of their respective lives. While the author does not pretend to know the objective measure of any of these teachings, he knows that such a measure exists, and he has enough evidence and experience to recognize its traces: to see where teachers are referring to the higher and when they are guided by the higher.

However, our presentation is not only a view from the top down, but also a view *from the inside out;* in the sense that it looks at the history of the Work *through the lens of the Work ideas*. The practitioners of the Fourth Way think in terms of the Work ideas and make their decisions in relation to them. We must therefore make a clear presentation of this system of ideas to be able to interpret their actions. Such a presentation is best done all at once, at the beginning of the book, rather than piecemeal throughout. This is the aim of the section Overview of the Work.

There are three points to keep in mind when considering a view that is both 'from the top down' and 'from the inside out':

1. Objective, or 'cosmic,' context of the Work.
2. Link between school on earth and Higher School.
3. Aims of the individual teachings.

INTRODUCTION

THE COSMIC CONTEXT OF THE WORK

The universe that we inhabit — which is only partially described by the sciences of chemistry, astronomy, and astrophysics — is alive: it is sentient. It is a living unity possessed of consciousness, conscience, and will. This sentience is not some all-embracing background presence or pantheistic unity. It is actualized at a single point, possessed of ultimate authority. This is the Absolute. Beneath the Absolute is the graded scale of Creation, in which each lower level is created out of and contained within the level immediately above it. In the terminology of the Fourth Way, it is a *hierarchy of cosmoses,* a *Macrocosm*. Each level of the hierarchy is the domain of sentient beings, capable of developing themselves within this graded scale, and through this development of moving from one level to the next.

Upward movement in the graded scale is, ultimately, the emulation of the Absolute, or the state of being that the Absolute represents. What this means practically is different at each level of the scale. But the point to be made here is that *there is a cosmic center,* and from that center radiates an authority which is felt at every level. At each stage approaching the center the authority is clearer and more distinct. Thus, to evolve is, at every level, to recognize and acknowledge the authority of a level higher than your own.

The Fourth Way teachings that we speak of in this book can only be *understood* with reference to the level that they serve. These teachings cannot be understood as one would understand a corporation or a nation state, which can indeed be understood on the level that they are on. With respect to the Fourth Way, when you have lost the view 'from the top down,' you have surely lost your story!

A Fourth Way teacher begins from some contact with the level of objective consciousness, where the graded scale of Creation is seen for what it is, and where there is real understanding of the requirements of a teaching. Without that they do not have a real teaching mandate. Each one of the five teachers had such a mandate, and it was from this perspective that they understood the requirements of their teaching. Each teacher, then, must communicate these requirements to their students in the way that best fits their circumstances. They cannot communicate them directly, because only consciousness can understand the level of objective consciousness, and the students are not yet fully conscious. Throughout our narrative, we will see each of the teachers making extraordinary demands upon themselves and upon their students. By the standards of humanity at large, these may sometimes seem extreme, but they reflect the teacher's awareness of a measure that humanity cannot see. Rightly understood, there is compassion in their demands.

THE LINK BETWEEN SCHOOL AND HIGHER SCHOOL

The practitioners of the Fourth Way understand their Work to awaken as the first responsibility of man. It is what relates the individual human being to the sentient whole that contains them. Mankind was originally created to add consciousness to the life of the Macrocosm; that is its objective measure. The link between the life of the Macrocosm and the individual human microcosmos is *conscious presence*. That is, being present and knowing that you are present while you are present. Presence fully *self-aware*. This is not an idea, it is a state. The teaching of the Fourth Way is a means of first evoking, then deepening, and finally making permanent that state.

There are different degrees of presence. When an individual man or woman connects deeply with the present, to the extent that their normal thought processes cease, and their personal reference points in the past or the future dissolve, then the immediate context of their 'external world' may also begin to dissolve. In other words, the whole solid, tangible theater of outer life may begin to disappear. It fades just as the images projected on a movie screen fade when the lights are turned up in the theater. Consciousness shows itself, step by step, to be *more real* than created matter. And then — in a certain moment — the world of form and matter disappears. One finds oneself in a vast sounding space of Being, without limit or boundary in any direction. It is filled with radiant light. It is as though one had been newly born into a world that is silently singing with deeper consciousness: fresh, pristine, immaculate, and totally alive. It is a sphere that pre-exists the cycle of birth and death; and when one enters this sphere, one may feel that an old and long-forgotten wound has been healed.

This radiant space is peopled with luminous entities, who are part of it and who function naturally within it. These entities are without cellular bodies, of the kind that we possess. In relation to embodied men and women we might call them Gods. Human beings may visit the domain of the Gods, but only for a limited period of time. They may enter as guests, in the company of an adept guide, or they may force entry as intruders, through artificial stimulants. But *to establish one's identity in this sphere,* in a form which can be permanently sustained, requires a lifetime — or even several lifetimes — of the most rigorous preparation and training. The transition to this sphere is not without its dangers, and the student needs expert guidance to succeed. It is, after all, a matter of changing *everything that you are*. In the Work it is said that this transition involves the development of a second, or molecular, body, which ultimately replaces the physical body, allowing for its permanent release at the end of a given lifetime. There is no comparable transition in the normal course of a human life.

It is in this space of radiant light that the great esoteric teachings of the past have been grounded: the lineages of Vedic Rishis, the generations of the Egyptian temple priests, the four orders of Tibetan Buddhism, the monastic orders of the Catholic Church, the monastic lineages of the Orthodox Church, and the many Sufi Orders of Islam. It is the space in which school engages Higher School. Recognizing and acknowledging this space allows us to represent the link between school on earth and higher levels of school — for in the highest reaches of the way there is overlap between the two.

Each of the Fourth Way teachers has represented this space in a different way, for it has different aspects, and each teacher emphasizes those aspects most relevant to their students: Gurdjieff spoke of the *Inner Circle of Humanity*; Ouspensky, the *Source of the System*; Collin, the *One Hierarchy*; Horn, the *Kingdom of Consciousness*; and Burton, simply, *Higher School*. In these pages we shall use a generic term, calling it the *Sphere of Sentient Being*. This luminous realm is accessed through a certain connection between Worlds 6 and 12 in a person's being. Moments of access may occur naturally in a person who has practiced the Work for many years. But access by one without experience in the Work can only be achieved through life-changing shocks or through the use of stimulants. In their practical work schools do not focus on this sphere, because it is best for students to achieve presence, and to learn to sustain that presence, in the context of the time and space that they are in. It is nonetheless within the Sphere of Sentient Being that the direct interactions between the Gods and the most conscious members of humanity occur. By 'direct' we mean not through reading symbols, hearing voices, or having dreams, but, as the Apostle Paul put it, "seeing face to face."

We must emphasize that the space we have just described is the beginning, not the end, of human development. Just as the everyday world that we inhabit is integrally linked to the Sphere of Sentient Being, so the Sphere of Sentient Being is grounded in a yet more concentrated sphere, and that sphere in a sphere more concentrated yet. This series of nested spheres is, ultimately, the set of cosmoses that comprises the Macrocosm of Creation.

The greatest schools of the past—the schools of Zoroaster, Moses, Buddha, Christ, Confucius, and Muhammad—deeply penetrated the levels above the human. These schools had connections running far into the system of nested spheres that comprises the Macrocosm. In the connection between each of these spheres there is always the work of school on a higher level. When there is upward movement in the higher levels of school, that affects the levels immediately below. It creates a chain of possibilities; a lift-on-lift upward movement that runs throughout the whole.

Having said all of this, our connection to these higher levels must be stably grounded on planet Earth. The obstacles to our development—which the Fourth Way identifies as negative emotions, imagination, identification, lying, psychological features, and inner considering—are internal to each one of us, and it is only within time, space, and matter that we can be taught to confront them. There must be an established and limiting context where help is given, or our energies will be dispersed.

THE AIMS OF THE INDIVIDUAL TEACHINGS

Fourth Way practitioners understand their Work in the cosmic context depicted above. If men like Gurdjieff, Ouspensky, Collin, Horn, and Burton are viewed outside of this context, as discrete individuals with private agendas and rather colorful personal histories, they cannot be understood. To view them as individual men, independent of the Higher Worlds to which they have become connected, and to which they are held accountable, is to view them 'on the flat.' Yes, each of them do have a life on the flat, and each of them are subject to human weaknesses, but we must be able to see them in their vertical dimension — *because this dimension exists,* and because their life within it is the core of their being as Fourth Way teachers.

Moving, then, from the teacher to the teaching, we see each one of the five teachings not only as it exists in the stream of time, but in its relation to a Higher Level, and in relation to its original aim, or vision, which was established with respect to that level. Our reference point — with respect to establishing the vision of each of these teachings — will be its 'golden hour.' What is meant by this?

When an individual man or woman — who is fated to become a teacher — makes the transition to the awakened state, they are given to understand something of what is wanted of them *from that level*. They may also be given to understand something of what is not wanted of them. We can make an analogy here to what any professional person goes through when they are hired to fill a position. They are hired to perform a function for which they have been deemed suitable, and not some other function. As a consequence, they are given a certain freedom of action within their area of competence and limiting parameters outside of it. This is to ensure that they produce the right result for the company that hired them. Just like the professional person, the awakened being does not work in a void: there is always someone on 'the next level up,' to whom they are held accountable, and there are always people on 'the level one below,' for whom they are responsible. Each newly minted teacher is thus given to understand something of the context of his role.

But the parameters defining a conscious role are not spelled out, as in a job description. They are understood in the moment — for they issue from a state of consciousness that has both great depth and disarming immediacy. Insight from this level, when it comes, is like "the clear ringing of a crystal glass that shatters when it rings."[1] It combines the sudden penetration of the ringing crystal with the remarkable stillness that follows. In such a

---

1. The words of the conscious poet Rainer Maria Rilke, in his *Sonnets to Orpheus,* Part Two, 13.

moment the fledgling conscious being may be given to understand what kind of teacher they are to be: whether, for example, they are to raise humanity through a particular art form (like Leonardo da Vinci, Jalal-ad-Din Rumi, Johann Sebastian Bach), teach by exercising governance (like Muhammad, Queen Elizabeth I, Marcus Aurelius), or teach principally through direct psychological contact (like Moses, Jesus Christ, George Gurdjieff).

This moment of insight may be followed by specific indications of the next steps to be taken: publish a book, erect a cathedral, start a theater, begin a lecture series, establish a retreat center, or sail tomorrow for Guadalajara. Again, these steps are not spelled out in words; they follow naturally from the initial insight, like the ripple-effects of a stone thrown into a pond. An opportunity presents itself and the newly formed conscious being knows with certainty that their name is written on it. Once the initial steps have been taken, they may — at a certain point — find themselves surrounded by a group of other people, who recognize something of what has taken place, and who seem ready to support them in their endeavor. When this response evokes response in turn, the teaching has begun. The teacher then begins to focus more specifically on the task they have been given. As they proceed, they come to understand it more clearly. Once the group itself has been through some initial testing, the teacher may share in greater detail the exact nature of their 'teaching mandate.' This might include the possible conditions for more serious group work or even an actual historical task to be carried out. The teacher's initial commitment to what is outside of space and time starts to become a shared commitment within the line of time. It is as though the sound of the ringing crystal, still reverberating out from the initial moment of contact, suddenly extends into the group.

Some members of the group will immediately see the teacher's aims and the teacher's vision *as being their own*. For these people the commitment to the teaching will be sacred: a matter of first or most precious things. They sense that this commitment will form, or re-form, the whole of their lives. These people, then, become *the inner circle* of the group. The individuals in question are not chosen, but choose themselves by their response. Some, whom the teacher may have cultivated as promising candidates, may have only a superficial response, while others, who were only in the room by accident — such as relatives or spouses — unexpectedly respond with understanding. With the teacher's presentation of his mandate, and the assent of the inner circle, the group begins to take form. It begins to shape itself into a kind of body around the energy field of the teacher. This is not a loss of individuality on the part of those involved, but the beginning of a higher kind of individuality.

This critical moment, including the people who are gathered into it, with all their capacities and all of their weaknesses, is a moment of destiny in the life of the group or school. The vision that is shared in this moment *will never be perfectly realized in the line of time,* but it is — for that reason — no less real. The fact that it will never be perfectly realized reveals the 'tragic aspect' that is part of the life of every school. Nevertheless, that original vision will drive the individuals involved for the remainder of their lives, for this kind of phenomenon does not happen twice in a lifetime. This is the *truth* of their school. Thus, if we do not have some sense of the golden hour of a school, we will not be able to understand the behavior of its members.

The great esoteric teachings of the past — the Vedantic, the Judaic, the Buddhist, the apostolic Christian — left clear records of a core vision, and the teachings evolved on that basis for centuries. The note sounding from the ringing crystal is clear in the Vedas, the Upanishads, the Buddhist Sutras, the Torah, and the New Testament. The teachers had a living connection to Higher School, and their respective inner circles recorded this, under supervision, in a way appropriate to the civilizations of their time. The visions of these schools have been obscured by the passage of time, and by the inevitable sectarian conflicts that followed in their wake, but they remain clear for one who has eyes to see. The span of each of these teachings, *as living teachings,* was many centuries. Within each of them were continuous and successive lineages of enlightened beings, with multiple teachers in each generation. In short, there was an environment which simply does not exist today. The lineage of Fourth Way teachings has not yet stabilized in this way. For this reason, the teachings existed as groups, preliminary to school. Each of the five teachers referred to their circle as a group when they wanted to emphasize the serious requirements of the Work, and then as a school when they wanted to include their students in the wider vision of the great schools of the past. It matters not, the groups or schools are both connected to the Sphere of Sentient Being and to the Gods, although not quite in the same way.

A problem in writing about the Fourth Way teachings is that the core vision of each group was not carefully recorded. This was not something intended by the teachers, it just happened. The original vision was impressed on the inner circle, but the inner circle, for the most part, did not write. They were challenged just to support their teacher and to do their own Work. The teachers themselves wrote teaching material, but they did not write the story of their own teachings. The outer circle wrote, but wrote in a journalistic way — without the guidance needed to produce a clear record of the vision level. Because of all this, we have a work of reconstruction before us.

In trying to understand a teacher and to reconstruct his Work, we keep in mind the following:

1. No embodied being is perfect. No one who functions from a cellular body is unaffected by the form of their embodiment and by its characteristic limitations. The very highest teachers have flaws. Additionally, the higher the teacher, the greater the pressure they are under, which tends to bring any flaws they have into relief.

2. Higher beings are free of the need to make a favorable impression on other people because their sense of identity is not dependent on other people's feedback, whether positive or negative. They are answerable to a higher standard; they follow the beat of a different drummer.

3. Higher beings perceive humanity, in its present condition, as being dominated by habit and by conventional morality — which is in turn based on a combination of fear, the need to be liked, and the need to sustain a credible personal identity. A teacher is committed to act in such a way as to liberate students from these psychological limitations. This means that their actions will often defy conventional morality.

4. Finally, and most importantly for interpreting the secondary literature on the Fourth Way, there is a marked tendency — at every level of Creation — for the lower level to reduce the higher level to its own terms. This is a cosmic law. For the lower level to feel good about itself, it must suppress the view that the higher level has of it. It does this by discrediting or otherwise reducing the teacher, to show that "he is not much different from me."

Almost all the material that has been published on the five teachers of the Fourth Way comes from people who were either: 1) never in a real teaching, or 2) left a real teaching and felt unresolved about having done so, or 3) were only peripherally involved in such a teaching, and so not in a position to understand the teacher's aims.

Incomparably the best presentation of George Gurdjieff's teaching is found in Peter Ouspensky's *In Search of the Miraculous,* though this was mainly an attempt to represent the content of Gurdjieff's teachings in 1916 and 1917, under the circumstances in which they were given, and not an attempt to convey the teacher's aims and vision. Ouspensky tells us that Gurdjieff disclosed his vision of the Work in the Essentuki workshop of June 1917, but he does not tell us what it was. Incomparably the best reportage on Peter Ouspensky's teaching is found in the remarks scattered throughout excerpts from the letters of Rodney Collin in *The Theory of Conscious Harmony.* But these remarks are fragmentary at best. In each case the quality of this material is given by the fact that the writer was not writing from any of the motives listed above, and so is able to *see more*. The entire history of the Fourth Way deserves such treatment.

With these thoughts in mind, we have not weighted all our sources equally. The direct report of conscious beings outweighs, for example, the reports of Rom Landau and Louis Pauwels on George Gurdjieff, or the reports of Claude Bragdon and Marie Seton on Peter Ouspensky. The reports of these people are little more than the workings of the cosmic law by which the lower is driven to reduce the higher to its own level. Even students who leave us with a valuable record of different aspects of the Work, such as Stanley Nott or Robert de Ropp, may fail to interpret certain actions of a teacher and may report negatively on them — simply in order to feel comfortable with decisions they had made in their own lives. Having said that, much of what they have recorded is taken into account.

The reader will notice that the reporting on the different teachings varies. For some teachings there already exist many secondary sources, and it is a matter of collating and interpreting those sources. For others, where there are fewer sources, there is a correspondingly greater labor of reconstruction. The narrative may, at times, have an analytic quality. The record of Alexander Horn's teaching is based principally on oral history and interview, which gives it a different tone. Additionally, the chapter devoted to each teaching will have its own body of contextual material. The Gurdjieff chapter includes the whole historical background of the system that he introduced to the West. The Ouspensky chapter explains the theory of cosmic processes that he developed. The Horn chapter includes an overview of mid-20th century theater, necessary to understanding Alex Horn's aims and Work.

Because there is such a large body of support material, this book is in some ways like a textbook. For that reason, the contextual material is shaded in gray and set in a smaller font. The reader is free to skip past these discussions, or perhaps return to them at a later time.

Another detail: there is no strict convention in the use of teacher's names. Gurdjieff and Ouspensky are often Mr. Gurdjieff and Mr. Ouspensky. Alexander Horn, Rodney Collin, and Robert Burton are often Alex, Rodney, and Robert — but there is never a breath of George or Peter. This relates to the conventions that were used within the different groups. The use of one or another name is simply the author's feeling for 'rightness' in the context, and we hope it does not offend. You can't always call somebody 'Mr.,' and most people did and do call Alex, Rodney, and Robert by their first names.

And who is it, then, who takes the pains to write all of this? One who has given his life to the endeavor. One who, as of this writing, has worked for forty-six years in the fifth of the five teachings under study.

In sum, whatever the nature of the source material, or the manner of presenting it, or the conventions used, the overriding aim of this book is to salvage the essential vision of each of these teachings and to interpret their history in light of it. Once this has been accomplished, we can, at long last, begin our history — going back to the dusty streets of Alexandropol, in the year 1866, to begin tracing the remarkable life of George Ivanovitch Gurdjieff.

But we shall start it all off with a mythic reaffirmation of our top-down, vision-oriented approach ...

Overview of the Work

In the Introduction we stated that unless the context of the Work is understood the motives of those practicing it will not be clear, and it will be impossible to write a real history of the Fourth Way. So we begin our history with this overview. We shall present the principal Work terms, in their right relation, and then use them freely throughout the book. We shall do this by summarizing the contents of a short pamphlet written by Peter Ouspensky, which outlines the basic ideas of his teaching. It was first circulated in the 1920s as *Psychological Lectures*. The content was refined over the years, and finally published, after his death, as *The Psychology of Man's Possible Evolution*. It brings together the core teaching ideas, rightly prioritized, in an order that makes them accessible. In presenting these ideas we will include the advances and amendments that have been made in ninety years of continuous application. This set of ideas will be used to *interpret* the histories of the five teachings to follow.

The Study of Man's Possible Evolution

The Psychology begins with the statement that *man, as we know him, is not a completed being*. Contemporary society — by contrast — takes 'man as we know him' as the ultimate reference point. It interprets both the individual and society from this perspective. *The Psychology* states that the true measure of man is *man as he was created*, with the potentials for development that were implanted in him at the beginning. These potentials, which have been known and understood at different points in history, are unknown to contemporary society.

Ouspensky emphasizes that, *before a man can realize these potentials he must see his present state. Man is actually a machine,* in the sense that none of his movements, thoughts, or impulses are initiated from himself. He is "brought into motion by external influences and impacts."[1] All movements, actions, words, ideas, and emotions are produced in him by external stimuli. "He is a marionette pulled here and there by invisible strings."[2] However, man is different from his own mechanical creations in one way: *he can know that he is a machine*; he can understand in what way he is driven by these stimuli, and on this basis cease to be subject to them.[3] Only when this has been done can he address his hidden potentials.

The first step in this process is for a man to realize that *he does not possess unity; he does not have one permanent and unchangeable 'I.'*[4] The sense he has of possessing a unified identity is an illusion. He is actually a collection of different impulses, thoughts, and emotions which are unconnected in their origin. The illusion of unity is created by 1) the sensation of a single physical body, 2) the fact that he has been taught to answer to a single name, and 3) the repeating patterns of mechanical habit that make his behavior recognizable to others. *In fact there is not one 'I' but many separate 'I's which follow one upon the next.* "Every thought, every feeling, every sensation, every desire, every like and every dislike is an 'I.'"[5] And here we come to the capstone of the Fourth Way teaching: *Man is many 'I's, and there is no 'I' that has the 'I's.*

A, B, AND C INFLUENCE

Man comes under three orders of influence, which we refer to as A, B, and C Influence.

---

1. Ouspensky, P.D., *The Psychology of Man's Possible Evolution*, Alfred A. Knopf, New York, 1979, p. 12.
2. *Ibid.*, p. 13.
3. *Ibid.*, p. 13.
4. *Ibid.*, p. 13.
5. *Ibid.*, p. 14.

A Influence: Interests and attractions created by the medium of life itself: the desire for food, shelter, rest, and sex; interests in career, social position, and material possessions; relations between parents, children, spouses, and friends; the influence of society and culture.[6]

B Influence: Interests aroused in a man by ideas which were not created in the general medium of life, but which came originally from schools. "These influences do not reach a man directly. They are thrown into the general turnover of life, pass through many different minds and reach a man through philosophy, science, religion and art — always mixed with A influences."[7]

While B influences originate from a conscious source they cease to qualify as Influence C as soon as they lose their direct connection to that source. Over time B influence will slip down to the level of A influence, but at the same time schools can make use of the B influence that circulates in life for their own purposes.

C Influence: Influences coming from a higher level of creation. While B influence is conscious in its origin, *C influence is conscious both in its origin and in its action, or in the way it takes effect.* This can be the direct influence of a conscious teacher, or the direct action of the Gods themselves.[8]

CONSCIOUSNESS

As sensation, feeling, thought, and motor activity are the 'material' of the four lower centers, so consciousness is the 'material' of the two Higher Centers. The lower centers are functions, in the sense that they operate in the stream of time, in a pattern of stimulus and response. Consciousness is not a function. It simply is. It relates to what is *behind* the four lower centers, and to what is *outside* the stream of time. The concentration of consciousness in our being connects us to the all-encompassing ground of Being that sustains the created world. We have called this the Sphere of Sentient Being.

---

6. *Ibid.,* pp. 66-67.
7. *Ibid.,* pp. 66-68.
8. *Ibid.,* pp. 68-69.

As our body is the vehicle for our physical life, so the latent Higher Centers are the vehicle for our conscious life. While the physical vehicle comes fully formed, the Higher Centers must be activated through great labor.

Why the great labor? The reason is that, while the purpose of the Work is to enable consciousness, it must begin from the functions; from efforts made from the functions. Consciousness is, in itself, beyond the functions. It has a speed of vibration that the functions cannot comprehend. This makes things very difficult for us. Like sex energy, conscious energy can be known by its effects on the four lower centers. But fortunately — at a certain point of concentration — it can know itself for what it is. It can become self-aware. All the techniques of the Fourth Way are designed to enable this moment. Consciousness is the awareness of one's existence in the present, independent of any learned sense of identity; of any idea of past or future; or of anything existing in our environment. It is a quality and intensity of presence that brings us directly into the mysteries of existence.

Ouspensky further clarifies that consciousness has degrees, and he gives three measures of degree:

- Duration — how long one was conscious
- Frequency — how often one became conscious
- Extent and penetration — of what one was conscious, which can vary very much with a man's level of being.[1]

The Work begins with the capacity to distinguish consciousness from functions.

Consciousness can be aware — *at the same time* — of:

1. The functions working internally: our thoughts, feelings, and sensations,
2. The many and varied impressions of the outer world, and
3. A presence that remains constant as both the external and the internal impressions cycle by.

---

1. *Ibid.*, p. 18.

For the purposes of practical Work, we can say that there are four states of consciousness: sleep, the waking state, self-consciousness, and objective consciousness. The first two states are actually beneath the level that we have described as consciousness, but as they comprise the greater part of human experience, it is necessary to include them. The second two states, when we begin to experience them, each show a much greater range than the first two states.

The First State: This is what we call sleep. It is a purely subjective and passive state where there is "no logic, no sequence, no cause, no result."[2] In deep sleep the centers refresh themselves, and we do not dream. Dreams, when they come, are re-workings of the unresolved experiences of the day, combined with confused perceptions of the moment: sounds, temperature changes, bodily sensations, etc. What happens in this state leaves little or no trace in memory.

The Second State: The second state of consciousness comes when one awakens from sleep; it is our normal waking state. Ouspensky makes the point that "the first state of consciousness does not disappear when the second state arrives."[3] Dream activity continues, with all its vague irrational impulses. It is just that the dreaming becomes invisible — just as the stars and the moon become invisible in the glare of the sun. In the second state, however, our senses are directly connected to a world that exists outside of our dreams. There is a more critical attitude towards outer impressions, there are more connected thoughts, and there is more discipline of action.[4] Nevertheless, there is no actual self-consciousness or presence attending our experience of the second state, and for this reason it is called the state of waking sleep.

In the second state one is still largely controlled by the dreaming-level: hopes, fears, desires, imaginings, and subjective longings. A person in the third state can actually see this process occurring in other people. It appears

---

2. *Ibid.*, p. 31.
3. *Ibid.*, p. 32.
4. *Ibid.*, p. 33.

that people in the second state are 'turned in on themselves' in a certain way. Their vision appears clouded, or it seems that little cloud formations are running across their eyes.

The Third State: This is the state of self-consciousness.[1] When a person in the second state suddenly comes to self-consciousness, they experience a quality of presence to which they are unaccustomed. Everything is more vivid, and the moment is unique. Suddenly there is no reference to past or future. The unprepared person does not know what this state implies, and they have no control over the flashes of it that may occur in a lifetime. When the third state is sustained, the Higher Emotional Center may become active. When it does, all the outer impressions become vivid and precise, our usual sense of self dissolves, and there is the sense of being or existence on another level. It is possible for a man or woman to develop control of consciousness on this level and to become completely conscious of themselves in this way.

Genuine moments of self-consciousness leave vivid memories which survive in pure form, not in the confused or distorted form of memories created in the second state.

The Fourth State: This state is what Ouspensky calls "objective consciousness."[2] It is a function of the Higher Intellectual Center; in other words, when we experience it, the Higher Intellectual Center has momentarily become active. This can occur as the result of a life-threatening shock, or when a person has been under extreme pressure for an extended period of time, or when a person has been able to remain in the third state for an extended period of time.

In the fourth state a person can have an objective perception of reality, entirely independent of their subjective dreams and illusions. In it they can know the truth, both about themselves and the universe. With the fourth state comes a complete acceptance of things as they are, and a complete indifference to the 'I's that cycle through the four lower centers. You are

---

1. *Ibid.,* p. 35.
2. *Ibid.,* p. 35.

completely outside your normal sense of self. In this state one has truly transcended the limitations of time and space.

In each state of consciousness you have glimpses of the state one above. The Higher Emotional Center and the Higher Intellectual Center are latent in us, and under the right conditions may become active. It is our life's calling, then, to bring the both of them permanently into the active state.

ESSENCE AND PERSONALITY

Ouspensky states that "It is impossible to study man as a whole, because man is divided into two parts: one part which, in some cases, can be almost all real, and the other part which can be almost all imaginary."[3] These two parts are called essence and personality. Essence is lighter and more emotionally open. It is what we are born with; it is the natural state of a child. Personality is like a heavy outer shell, which builds around essence, sometimes protecting it — but more often encasing and stifling it. Either one or the other is ascendant in any given moment, and this affects the working of all the centers, particularly the emotional center.

A person is born in essence, yet very quickly the four lower centers accumulate new and often quite artificial material. From the moment of birth, a child imitates the acts and gestures of those around them, and their lower centers soon become infected with the negative emotions that are generally accepted in their culture. Gradually they learn the whole complex pattern of socially acceptable behavior. In particular, the child will be taught to present itself as though it were always one single 'I.' This is the basis for what the system calls personality. A child of three months is essence without personality. The average man of forty years is personality, with very little essence. Most men of forty, however, still have a connection to essence. They may experience it directly, for example, with loved ones, in nature, or in the presence of great art. Essence is what is genuine in a man and what must serve as the basis for real growth and development. Personality, at its best, is a protective filter for essence, and at worst a kind of criminal deformation.

---

3. *Ibid.*, pages. 41-42.

Personality is based on: 1) the unconscious conviction of one's uniqueness, and 2) the fear that is created when that conviction is threatened. While personality is formed through imitation, it combines a number of 'generic' aspects. For example, everyone is subject to vanity, and everyone knows the impulse of fear. Other universal impulses include the will to power, the need to control one's circumstances, and the tendency to resist initiatives coming from without. Different people have these impulses in different degrees, but they are elements of all human behavior. At the level of essence they are tendencies only. But in personality they become fixed, and can become crystallized in quite undesirable ways.

Let us be more specific: personality is formed of a set of generic reaction patterns in a certain balance. The Fourth Way calls these reaction patterns 'features': the features of dominance, power, vanity, fear, non-existence, willfulness, naiveté, greed, destructiveness, mechanical goodness, and so on. Each person has a 'chief feature' which acts as a pivot point for the other features that comprise their personality. It is the hub of the wheel so to speak. A person cannot know their own chief feature without outside help; it is something too much 'under your skin.' It acts upon you unawares and it permeates the energy field of your being. You see the world through it.

To conclude the subject of essence and personality, it is an important part of schoolwork to develop essence, because we cannot develop Higher Centers except on this foundation. There is a natural relation of essence to presence. When a person is in essence, presence is *deeper* and more stable. Gurdjieff was an expert at evoking essence in his students. We think of the Arabian Nights enchantment of his ballet *The Struggle of the Magicians*, the exotic dinners, the spectacle of the movements, the toasts to the idiots, the steam baths at the Preiuré. More generally, schools throughout history have used the arts to evoke essence: theater, music, dance, the visual arts, monumental sculpture, and architecture.

Self-Remembering, Self-Observation, and Divided Attention

Gurdjieff presented the principal tools for awakening as self-remembering, self-observation, and divided attention.

Self-Remembering: Self-remembering is the effort to be aware of one's existence in the present moment, and to sustain that awareness in the constantly changing conditions of outer life. Self-remembering has been defined as the attempt to penetrate the present. When one has succeeded in penetrating the present, one's identity comes free from any thoughts or feelings concerning the past or the future. One is where one is and nowhere else. There are many lines of effort that lead to this: the attempt to control negative emotions, the attempt to be out of imagination, the attempt to not-identify, the attempt to stop the 'I's, the attempt to control features, and so forth.

Self-Observation: Self-observation begins with one center observing another, for example, the intellectual center classifying emotions, or the emotional center observing the sterility of ceaseless intellectual activity. But in its depth self-observation is a kind of magic. We are connected to a deep internal mirror, that can observe intellect, emotion, sensation, and motor activity just as they are. With practice, you begin to see what goes on inside yourself. You *see yourself* initiating conversations, arguing with colleagues, being attracted to members of the opposite sex, reacting to changes in a schedule of events, and so forth.

Divided Attention: Divided attention is an intentional effort to sustain the awareness of two or more things at one time. Efforts to divide attention begin at the level of the lower centers, expanding their field of attention in different ways, and holding it for longer periods of time. Through practicing divided attention, one becomes able to hold the awareness of one's inner state (one's thoughts, feelings and sensations) and of the outer environment *at the same time*. We may ask, then, what is simultaneously aware of one's inner world *and* the environment? This is consciousness itself. The final phase of divided attention includes consciousness self-aware.

MAGNETIC CENTER, DEPUTY STEWARD, AND STEWARD

When a person begins to be attracted to ideas of spiritual development, they are attracted to Influence B, and it concentrates within them. This concentration is called a 'magnetic center,' and when it forms it naturally seeks a school. If the person is born in the right time and at the right place, it may lead them to a conscious school — which is, ultimately, Influence C. On meeting the school the magnetic center, which was based on subjective attractions, is gradually replaced by the objective teachings of the school. Priorities change. Many old things must be left behind and many new things acquired. As the person works according to school methods a deputy steward forms, monitoring the process of their development. It begins to distinguish things that pertain to the new Work, and things that pertain to everyday life. It disallows mixing things that relate to different levels. It begins to distinguish between what is mechanical and what is conscious. Finally, as the student begins to experience moments of Higher Centers, and as those moments become more frequent, a steward takes form. At this point the student begins to have a directional center *within* themselves. The steward regulates the machine in relation to its aim to awaken, and, as the movements of Higher Centers become more frequent, it enters into service to them.

To clarify how the terms 'deputy steward,' 'steward,' and 'master' were used in traditional society, we recount a short story told by Peter Ouspensky.

> There is an Eastern allegory which deals with the creation of 'I.' Man is compared to a house full of servants, without master or steward to look after them. So the servants do what they like; none of them does his own work. The house is in a state of complete chaos, because all the servants try to do someone else's work, which they are not competent to do. The cook works in the stables, the coachman in the kitchen, and so on. The only possibility for things to improve is if a certain number of servants decide to elect one of themselves as a deputy steward and in this way make him control the other servants. He can do only one thing: he puts each servant where he belongs and so they begin to do their right work. When this is done, there is the possibility of the real steward coming to

replace the deputy steward and to prepare the house for the master. ... This allegory helps us to understand the beginning of the possibility of creating a permanent 'I.'[1][2]

A steward develops in a man number four and this enables a greater frequency and consistency of effort. Increasingly everything is taken in terms of the Work, and no opportunity is missed. With the transition to man number five the steward must perform a difficult balancing act. It functions in a different way. The Higher Centers are actually making their appearance, and they become aware of many things. They have their own initiatives, and, at the same time, they become more aware of what needs to be changed in the machine. The steward of a man number five is between two worlds. *It must learn to actually support the Higher Centers.* Every evolving being on the planet, through to man number eight, needs a steward to keep on course. Slips of different kinds are possible at every level. So work on the steward is very much a part of the Work of school on every level.

THE STEWARD

We have noted that the latent Higher Centers are helpless in their present state. However, the microcosmos man has not only been given Higher Centers, but *the means of activating them.* This possibility exists because the most refined energies generated by the lower centers can vibrate at the speed of the Higher Emotional Center. We are speaking here of energies that reside in the king of hearts. Thus, there is an overlap between the range of energies with which the planetary body functions and the range of energies that fuel the Higher Emotional Center. On this basis we can be taught to enable the Higher Centers.

---

1. Ouspensky, P.D., *The Fourth Way*, Routledge & Kegan Paul, London, 1967, p. 33.
2. For further material on the traditional vocabulary, as used by schools, see Gurdjieff, G.I., *Views From the Real World: Early Talks of Gurdjieff*, E.P. Dutton, New York, 1973, pp. 96-100, concerning the parable of the horse, the carriage, and the driver.

The normal function of the king of hearts, taken as a whole, is to address the difficult decisions of our lives; decisions that may lead to acts of sacrifice, to the acceptance of suffering, or to making a serious commitment to another person, or to a cause. The king of hearts is also the part in us that can recognize and appreciate great art — not simply art that stimulates or gives pleasure, but art that is significant and gives meaning to life. This part, and this part only, can recognize and remember the experience of Higher Centers.

Most people have glimpses of Higher Centers during their lives, and they carry traces of these experiences in memory. Sometimes the traces are buried or overlaid, sometimes they are still accessible. When we are able to remember a higher state of consciousness, it is because the king of hearts registered its significance and took the impress. You can have a higher state of consciousness without being able to remember "just how it was." This might be the impact of higher consciousness on, for example, the intellectual center. But to retain some sense of "how it actually was" is the king of hearts. This part can be trained to recognize presence and to value consciousness, and — beyond that — to actually enable consciousness in our being. In describing these specialized abilities, we move from the king of hearts to its emotional part, the nine.

The nine of hearts can be strengthened and trained to deploy the work 'I's that come from the other centers and other parts of centers. For example, the work 'I's can say, "Separate from this negative emotion," or "Control your moving center," or "Do not identify with how hot it is in this room," or "Gather your thoughts." It can refine these 'I's, and the observations that are behind them. It can deploy them, not randomly — like a cowboy firing a pistol at a rodeo — but in relation to the perceived needs of the moment. It sees the need, chooses the appropriate tool, and acts with a clear aim. Gradually this activity concentrates into a steward. As the nine of hearts deploys work 'I's more frequently and more efficiently, it creates an environment that enables the Higher Centers to come more frequently, and even to sustain themselves for periods of time. When this begins to occur, the whole process becomes yet more centered and effective. The steward learns to pause (to be passively alert) in the moments when the Higher Centers arrive.

The degree of development of the steward represents a man's *level of being*. It might be argued that level of being is simply 'degree of consciousness,' but — as any degree of consciousness must be secured by the action of the steward — the two are effectively the same. People at different levels of being will respond differently to the same stimulus; an insult that sends one man into a rage does not affect another. It is inevitable that people understand the teaching in terms of their level of being, and so there are different levels of understanding. The level of being of a man number five encompasses understandings of the Higher Emotional Center. The level of being of a man number six encompasses understandings of the Higher Intellectual Center.

THE OBSTACLES TO AWAKENING

We have described something of what man is and something of what is possible for him. We must now look at the concrete obstacles that stand in the way of his achieving what is possible. In studying these obstacles, we are studying the veil that separates us from the Sphere of Sentient Being. Ouspensky lists six principal obstacles:

Lying: Lying, as Ouspensky speaks of it, is not simple distortion of the truth, but pretending to know the truth when you do not. And we actually know very little. Indeed, the more important a matter is, the less anything certain is known about it. Man does not know about God, or the universe, or the reason for his existence, or what will happen when he dies, or how he should make use of his life while he is still alive. Above all he does not know himself. We usually speak as though all of these things were taken for granted, and this produces a false sense of complacency and allows a feeling of self-importance to develop. Any sense of self-importance makes self-remembering impossible.[1]

---

1. Ouspensky, P.D., *The Psychology of Man's Possible Evolution*, Alfred A. Knopf, New York, 1979, p. 40.

Another way in which people deceive themselves is in believing the things that they *want to be true* to be actually true, and then speaking and acting as though they were.

Imagination: The continuous — and entirely involuntary — formation of thoughts and images in the mind. There is an unceasing succession of thoughts and images related to what one is going to do next, who one is going to see, what one will eat for the next meal, fears about what might happen tomorrow, or recriminations about what happened yesterday. These thoughts and images are "the undigested byproducts of past perceptions which flow in a meaningless and unbroken stream — as though the waste clippings of a great cinema-studio were stuck together at random and the result run continuously day and night through some forgotten projector in a back room."[1]

The Expression of Negative Emotions: This refers to emotions of anger, irritation, self-pity, suspicion, fear, irritation, boredom, mistrust, jealousy, and the like. These emotions are generated from within ourselves, yet we invariably attribute them to external causes, and particularly to the actions of other people. Actually they are a malfunction of the machine: a wrong connection between 1) the emotional center, 2) the instinctive center, and 3) the imaginary sense of 'I.' We give negative emotions credence every time we express them. And once we have expressed them their effect is compounded by the impact they have on others, and the negative reactions that others may have towards us. In the moment we give expression to negative emotions, we have lost the possibility of separating ourselves from them, and so not identifying with them. Without resisting the expression of negative emotions we cannot awaken.[2]

Ouspensky points out that ... "In the emotional center there is no natural negative part. The greater part of negative emotions are artificial; they do not belong to the emotional center proper and are based on instinctive

---

1. Collin, Rodney, *The Theory of Celestial Influence,* Watkins, London, 1976, p. 204.
2. Ouspensky, P.D., *The Psychology of Man's Possible Evolution*, Alfred A. Knopf, New York, 1979, p. 49.

emotions which are quite unrelated to them but which are transformed by imagination and identification."[3]

Unnecessary Talk: This can be described as talking for the sake of talking: passing on undigested or only partially digested experiences. Unnecessary talk is usually connected to the need to draw attention to oneself. One cannot make accurate observations of oneself (or of anything else) while engaged in this talk, for the observations evaporate immediately as the talk continues.[4]

Identification: In the state of identification a man allows his identity to rest in either: 1) the 'I's being generated by his four lower centers, 2) the objects of the outside world, or 3) the events which he is caught up in. All of the other mechanical manifestations described above — lying, imagination, the expression of negative emotions, and unnecessary talk — are byproducts of the state of identification. Man "identifies with everything — with what he says, what he feels, what he believes, what he does not believe, what he wishes, what he does not wish, what attracts him and what repels him. Everything absorbs him, and he cannot separate himself from the idea, the feeling, or the object that absorbed him."[5]

Inner Considering: A form of identification with other people, whereby a man worries about what others think about him; whether they give him his due, or whether they admire him enough. All emotions of worry, doubt, and suspicion are based on, and reinforced by, inner considering.[6]

Features: In presenting the ideas of essence and personality we introduced the idea of features.[7] These are mechanical tendencies in a person's nature that take definite form as personality develops. The personality of an adult is centered around a chief feature, such as dominance, vanity, power, or

---

3. *Ibid.*, p. 84.
4. *Ibid.*, p. 50.
5. *Ibid.*, p. 51.
6. *Ibid.*, p. 52.
7. *Ibid.*, pp. 47, 62, 91.

non-existence. Chief feature gives a certain order to the several subordinate features and becomes the basis of the illusion of a unified identity.

Features bind us deeply to the second state of consciousness. Chief feature is like a distortion in the glass windowpane through which we view the world. A man number four is aware of his chief feature but cannot work on it directly. A man number five does work directly on chief feature. No embodied being has perfect control over their chief feature.

In reviewing the obstacles to awakening we have outlined a very difficult situation. Now we must begin to look at the way out — for with the latent Higher Centers we have been given the keys to a Higher Level. It would have been perverse if we had been given this connection with no means of actualizing it, and the Gods are not perverse!

The Centers Comprising Human Psychology

Not only does man have many 'I's, but these 'I's actually arise from four different brains or 'centers,' which function independently, each for itself.[1]

Intellectual center: Generates thoughts, concepts, rational activity, affirmation and negation, comparison, and the use of words generally.

Emotional center: Generates different feelings and emotions, positive and negative: joy, sorrow, fear, love, anger, astonishment, amusement, and so on.

Moving center: Regulates our motor functions, such as walking, driving, swimming, washing the dishes, and the host of other motor activities required to get through the day.

Instinctive center: Gives us both the world of our senses and our instinctive sensations. It is also concerned with all the inner work of the organism: the digestion and assimilation of food, the circulation of blood, the building of new cells, the elimination of waste material.

---

1. *Ibid.*, pp. 23-30, pp. 59-61, and pp. 76-114.

A careful study of the four centers shows us that man does not have unity. The system, however, speaks of three additional centers, which function at a speed that we cannot properly observe. These are the sex center, the Higher Emotional Center, and the Higher Intellectual Center. The sex center generates an energy that affects all of the lower centers. While we cannot observe it directly, we can observe its effects on the other centers. The two Higher Centers, then, correspond to the states of higher consciousness that are possible for us. When these states appear, they transcend the many 'I's, and exist quite distinctly from them.

Sex center: The sex center is most directly experienced in sexual attractions and in the sexual act. The sexual act itself is an instinctive function, which is connected to intense feelings of desire through the finer and more intense energies of the sex center — and in this way the reproduction of the species is ensured. What we call sexual desire is not the sex center, but the effect of sex energy on the instinctive center.

The effect of sex energy on the other three centers is connected, in exactly the same way, with a heightening of desire. In the moving center it can be behind extreme physical efforts. In the emotional center it can be behind extreme fears or fanatical hopes and desires. In the intellectual center it can be behind lunatic and unreasonable convictions. Normally our supply of sex energy is exhausted in these usages.

A right use of sex energy — not connected to desire — is to bring harmony to the external environment and to our lives. It can be used to heighten and enrich our entire experience of life, and this use can be directly connected — as we shall later see — to the pursuit of presence.[2]

Higher Emotional Center: The Higher Emotional Center is associated with heightened presence: not flashes of presence, but presence stable and concrete — knowing itself for what it is. There is a certain experience of ... "I am here now" that is sustained — in simplicity and wonder. This is true self consciousness.[3]

---

2. *Ibid.*, p. 25.
3. *Ibid.*, p. 24.

When the Higher Emotional Center becomes active there is a different feeling of 'I'. There is a sense of identity which is rooted in presence itself, without reference point or qualification of any kind. From this place the world around us may appear quite differently; one can suddenly see the animate quality in inanimate things. One's relation to everything becomes direct and emotional.

Higher Intellectual Center: The Higher Intellectual Center brings a state of unity that is beyond any distinction of I and not-I. There is no longer an 'I' that is "here now," but a state that transcends the duality of self and other. The very idea of 'I' loses its meaning. In this state one begins to see the manifestation of universal laws. We may begin to see, in the unfolding pattern of the world around us, the expression of the laws that govern a higher level. Indeed, it is as though these universal laws begin to know themselves through us. Ouspensky stated that the workings of the Higher Intellectual Center can yield objective knowledge of the Universe.[1]

When the four lower centers are tied to — and limited by — the imaginary sense of 'I,' they work together to create a veil that separates us from Higher Centers. The Higher Centers are actually there, but do not receive the quality of impression they need to come to life. The lower centers, infected by the self-reflexive illusion of 'I,' filter everything that comes to them. They act like the interference on a radio channel that does not allow the message to come through. Having said that, the lower centers are important for the Work. A knowledge of the divisions of the four lower centers, and of how they can be used in relation to the Work, is necessary to connect with the Higher Centers.

In summing our situation Ouspensky emphasizes that as long as man credits himself with unity, consciousness, and will, he has no hope of change, because "as long as he believes that he possesses these qualities he will not make the right efforts to acquire them."[2] Ouspensky further stip-

---

1. *Ibid.*, p. 24.
2. *Ibid.*, p. 16.

ulates that "the most important thing man lacks is consciousness," and this can be seen as the focal point of all activity on the Fourth Way.

THE SPECIALIZED STUDY OF THE FOUR LOWER CENTERS

The four lower centers are integrally connected. Within each center there are subdivisions based on a combination of the energy of that center with the energies of the other three. For example, within the emotional center, there is an intellectual part, an emotional part, a moving part, and an instinctive part. Each one of these parts is again divided into parts of parts. Further, each center, and each part of a center, is divided into positive and negative halves — which communicate the positive and negative experiences of that center. For the emotional center this would be positive and negative emotions; for the instinctive center, the sensations of pain and pleasure; for the moving center, the experience of motion and of stasis; and for the intellectual center, the experience of affirmation and negation.[3]

The Tarot deck — which comes to us from the schools of ancient Egypt — provides a complete breakdown of all seven centers: the lower centers, the Higher Centers, and the sex center. It shows, for each of the lower centers, the divisions, and the divisions within divisions. Surprisingly, the normal deck of playing cards still carries the imprint of this knowledge, to the extent that it can be used as a teaching tool for the study of the centers. We can illustrate the parts and divisions of the four lower centers using the normal deck of playing cards, with its four suits.

The suit of hearts can be used to represent emotion, the suit of diamonds intellect, the suit of spades motor function, and the suit of clubs instinct. The two Higher Centers are symbolized by the two jokers, which are usually the first cards lost.

The breakdown of the four suits into face cards and number cards can be used to represent the breakdown of the centers into their component parts. In each one of the four lower centers there are intellectual, emotional, instinctive, and moving parts.

---

3. This depth of study of the divisions comes from the work of Robert Burton. This presentation is related to the author's presentation of the same subject matter in *The Story of Man*, Apollo University Press, Oregon House, CA, 2019, pp. 62-107.

Figure 1. Face cards of the common playing deck.

The three face card divisions of the common deck of playing cards are, respectively: *the kings,* which can be used to represent the intellectual divisions of centers; *the queens,* which can be used to represent the emotional divisions; and *the jacks,* which represent *both* the instinctive and moving divisions. Why are the jacks used to represent both the instinctive and the moving divisions? In the original Tarot deck each jack is separated into the page (instinctive part) and the knight (moving part). This is technically correct. The conflation may have occurred because the instinctive and moving parts are so closely knit that they often act as one, and it can be very difficult to distinguish them in actual observation. And, in most people, if the kings and queens are in order, the jacks do their job. They are executants. It is not necessary to 'work on' the jacks, other than not letting them do the work of the kings.

Each of these face card divisions — king, queen, jack — is again broken into intellectual, emotional and moving parts. The divisions of the king (the intellectual part of the center) are the 10, 9, and 8; the divisions of the queen (the emotional part) are the 7, 6, and 5; and the divisions of the jack (the instinctive/moving part) are the 4, 3, and 2.

The diamond face cards shown below represent the primary divisions of the intellectual center: the king (the intellectual part of the intellectual center), the queen (the emotional part of the intellectual center), and the jack (the instinctive/moving part of the intellectual center).

In these cards we see illustrated the idea that each center (and each part of a center) has a positive and a negative half. Each of the face cards can be reversed, right-side up or upside down, according to whether the perception is positive or negative.

To the extent one is able to observe the centers impartially, one is able to understand — in quite a practical way — that there is not one 'I' but many 'I's, and that these 'I's change in relation to changing circumstances.

We have seen something of the complexity of the centers that, together, give us our experience of life. But how do they add up to a unified experience? The seven centers do not themselves have unity — there is no 'I' that has the 'I's — yet every adult man and woman believes that they possess unity.

How is it all held together? Each of the four lower centers spontaneously and continuously communicates its experience — its needs, its desires, its hopes, and its fears — so that we live in an ongoing stream of thoughts, images, sensations, and motor impulses. The utterances of the four centers continually rush together to create the vague and general sensation of 'I.' We are taught not to question this 'I,' for it is an illusion that we need to function normally. It is sustained through a kind of internal discourse that becomes continuous in each one of us, from about the age of three. It is, in other words, "Me thinking about myself." This internal discourse will pattern itself around the dominant 'I' of the moment: "I got mad at Henry." "I stubbed my toe." "I went for a walk." And so forth. This, then, becomes, "I got mad at my brother Henry this morning (emotion), and as a result I accidentally stubbed my toe (sensation). I felt so bad I went for a walk to clear my head (motor function)." But the 'I' is, in each case, an addendum. Through the action of the internal discourse each impulse that comes to the surface — whether intellectual, moving, emotional, or instinctive — is able to represent itself as the whole, and the intellectual center translates for each one.

Why, we may ask, is this sense of 'I' so strong and so persistent? Because it is based on something very old; something that we have inherited from the animal world: *the instinct for survival*. This instinct is rooted in the intellectual part of the instinctive center, or the king of clubs. The king of clubs has an omnidirectional awareness that picks up on any threat to our life or well-being, and in a moment can focus every capacity of the four lower centers on whatever that threat might be. It operates even when we are asleep. The king of clubs will be highly developed in a commando or a martial arts expert, and these people often radiate the coolness and self-control characteristic of that part of a center. When you seriously threaten a person's sense of 'I,' showing them to be a fool in front of other people, this deeper instinctive force may suddenly assert itself. You see a change come over the person. They may become aggressive and will strike back as they can. The negative connotation of the term 'ego,' as it is used in popular psychology, reflects the character of the king of clubs. It is not just 'I,' but 'I' with a certain self-assertion and self-importance behind it. It may possess force, but it has behind it all the fears and insecurities which are its other face.

The resistance to awakening is based in this part of the instinctive center. We noted that the king of clubs has the role of ensuring the well-being of the machine, and higher consciousness — in whatever form — is a threat to its solid, animal sense of well-being. The Higher Centers open up a high-energy world that is, in some sense, 'behind the machine.' These higher energies threaten the false sense of unity on which our normal identity is based. The resistance to these energies is based specifically in the *emotional part* of the king of clubs, or the nine of clubs. In the terminology of the playing cards, it is known as the Black Queen. It is the nine that *feels the threat* and will focus on eliminating what caused it. Connected as it is to the instinct for the preservation of life, the nine of clubs is capable of manipulating all our hopes and fears in relation to its own ends.

In the Work, the nine of clubs is countered by the *emotional part* of the king of hearts, or the nine of hearts. The opponent of the Black Queen is sometimes called the White Queen. This part of the king of hearts recognizes and remembers the experiences of Higher Centers. It can organize the other parts of centers to struggle against sleep. This part, and this part alone, can recognize and counter the impulses of the nine of clubs.

The roles of the nine of clubs and the nine of hearts were not originally presented by Gurdjieff and Ouspensky, but they came to light in the further practice of the Work. Yet both Gurdjieff and Ouspensky were clear about the nine of clubs as an internal denying force to awakening. They just did not classify it as a part of a part of a center. At different times, they each referred to this part in ourselves as "the devil." The devil, then, is not an external entity, but something inside of us.

On the 9th of February 1923, in the Salon of the Prieuré, Gurdjieff spoke to his students about the devil:

> It is said in some ancient teachings that on the day God created man he also created for each man two spirits — the spirit of good and the spirit of evil, or as they are called, an angel and a devil, and placed the angel on the right side of man and the devil on the left. .... This teaching says the following about the angel and the devil: Every action of a man, every step, every moment, every movement, emanates either from the one or from the other. Emanations from both are equally deposited in the human organism in the form of certain crusts of real tangible matter, which one can examine and distinguish whether the crust is of one kind or another. Each crust obeys certain laws, leads to certain consequences. And in the case of man things whispered by the devil have greater effect.[1]

There is an imperfect recording of Peter Ouspensky speaking to his students about the devil in 1944 in New York:

> Devil is very important ... He works through inner considering, negative emotions, imagination. But if you fight against these dangers you are safe. Devil is the embodiment of evil, but with purpose ... No devil can keep you from self-remembering, if you work. The Devil has so many faces. ... He is real, quite real. ... Devil's object is man's soul ... In relation to the Devil, or with the help of Devil, there is possibility of conscious evil ... Can devil have any function in organic life apart from man? No. Animals, insects, fishes, bacteria? No. Devil can manifest only through help of man. Man has the possibility of evolution. Devil can stop him; create conditions

---

1. Azize, Joseph (compiler) *Gurdjieff's Early Talks 1914-1931*, Book Studio, 2014, pp. 229-230.

against it. ... when man was invented, the Devil was invented also.[1]

Despite the existence of the nine of clubs, we must point out that her counterpart, the nine of hearts — the emotional part of the king of hearts — plays the most significant role in awakening. We will explore her role in relation to the development of the steward.

The Different Worlds

What is a 'world?' In a general sense 'the world' refers to everything within the scope of our experience: both the events of our personal lives and everything that is external to us. Our world, the human world, is not the world of an amoeba or the world of an archangel. It is an intermediary world, but it is a world of experience that coheres and provides a locus of meaning. Each world is such. Gurdjieff presented the Ray of Creation as a hierarchy of interlocking worlds; the higher worlds under a fewer number of laws, the lower worlds under a greater number.[2] The worlds are named by the number of laws that they are under. The worlds relevant to the human experience are Worlds 6, 12, 24, 48, and 96.[3] Man was originally centered in World 24, but this is not something fixed. His center of experience can

---

1. Patterson, William Patrick, *George Ivanovitch Gurdjieff*, Arete Communications, Fairfax California, 2014, p. 412.

2. There are different laws, and different sets of laws, that pertain to each world at each level of Creation. The laws governing the higher levels of Creation are not those known to our sciences. The laws known to the sciences are subsets of those higher laws, operative on the level we are on. There are laws within the Macrocosm that are operative from the 'top down,' which the human intellect does not have the capacity to understand. It is the higher centers that can understand these laws. Each lower level of Creation is subject to all the laws that apply to the levels above it, plus the laws that apply on its own level.

3. The author does not pretend to understand what the numbers represent, but accepts that they represent the degrees of freedom that correspond to each world. In the range of worlds, the numbers seem adequate to express the difference between them.

easily slip down into the lower worlds or up into the higher worlds. Ultimately, he has access to all the worlds.

World 1: The Absolute as he is, in himself. As such, he is unknowable to man and even to the archangels. Gurdjieff's teachings of 1916 present World 1 as being comprised of three forces:

1. What we might think of as the deity (God),
2. Something that negates the deity (Not-God, the Void, or meaningless entropy), and
3. Something which transcends and contains both God and Void: the Absolute *as he is in himself*.

In internalizing the Void, the Absolute produced Creation. He did so because he needed to neutralize the effects of the Void within himself. Creation neutralizes the entropy of the Void by generating consciousness out of created matter. The aspect of World 1 that gave form to Creation — as a cosmos of cosmoses — was its substantial component (God). It is this aspect that faces Creation, and is, indeed, the God of the great religions.

World 1 is the only world of experience that includes everything. At the same time, it exists outside of and above the system of laws that governs all the other Worlds.[4]

World 3: World 3 is the first World created out of the triadic Absolute. World 3 is, if you will, between the Absolute and Creation. It is close to the Absolute — as he is in himself — and at the same time it can experience the unity of the Created Macrocosm. It knows the unity of Creation and at the same time it is somehow present in Creation.

While World 3 (which is also the first world of Creation) transcends the structure of Creation, it also sustains it. It is energy with very little form or matter.

---

4. For a more complete discussion of the Absolute see James, Hugh, *The Story of Man*, Apollo University Press, Oregon House, CA, 2019. Chapter 2, Man and the Absolute, p. 131-156.

World 3 is accessible to a conscious being, and this is an enigma. While we are connected to World 12 by the Higher Emotional Center and World 6 by the Higher Intellectual Center, World 3 does not correspond to a center latent in the human body. Yet a man who has both the Higher Emotional Center and the Higher Intellectual Center fully developed can enter World 3. Mankind can only have a relationship to World 3 through those rare individuals. These are the prophets of history (see the reference to Man Number Eight above). While the relationship to World 3 is distant, it is nevertheless part of our common destiny, just as the prophets are part of our common destiny.

World 6: The world of experience that corresponds to the Higher Intellectual Center. When a man is centered in World 6, he feels such a degree of unity with Higher Centers that his mortal vehicle — his body, heart, and mind — seem external to him. The usual sense of 'I' is entirely transcended. When an unprepared man experiences World 6, he feels himself near to the death of his body.

World 12: The world of experience that corresponds to the Higher Emotional Center. This is presence sustained, knowing itself for what it is. In World 12 one is relieved of all restrictions of thought, feeling, and action that occur when the lower centers are subordinated to the false sense of 'I.' It is this sense of 'I' that ties us to feelings of guilt, fear, recrimination, and aggression that are the unspoken backdrop of human existence. World 12 is without a shadow. It is presence stable and concrete, knowing itself for what it is. There is a certain experience of ... "I am here now" that is sustained — in simplicity and wonder.

Energies of the level of World 12 (which the system specifies as hydrogen 12) also exist in the world outside of us. They may be experienced in art, in music, and in the highest moments of human love. This is why many schools have used art to evoke the Higher Emotional Center, or to produce experiences of the Higher Self.

World 24: This world is the world of essence. In a pure state of essence there is no trace of negativity, but childlike spontaneity and joy. It is life on the planet at its best. It is the natural state of people in love. The fusion of essence (World 24) with the Higher Emotional Center (World 12) is necessary for the right formation of the Higher Self.

World 48: This is a specifically human world; a practical clear-headed state of mind, capable of calculating risk and assessing difficult situations. It is a specifically human intelligence, and it is common sense. World 48 is not independent of (not subject to) either strong emotion or strong sensation. It is the source of what we normally call discipline.

World 96: A world of experience comprised of the vital energies that we share with the animals. These energies are of a coarse nature, and this World is dominated by instinctive sensations: aggression, pain, pleasure, fear, greed, lust, jealousy, competitiveness. These coarser energies are quite capable of overriding human emotion (World 24) and human intelligence (World 48) and subordinating them. In an adult human being, they connect with the shell of personality, weighting it towards false personality. Humanity is fundamentally connected to World 96. Below World 96 there are Worlds 192 and 384, which reach into the even more limited experiences of the vegetable and mineral realms.

THE SEVEN LEVELS OF MAN

This nomenclature of the seven levels of man is awkward, because the first three levels are not actually levels, but three variations of a single level. Gurdjieff and Ouspensky often used the shorthand of man number 1-2-3 for the first level, and then spoke of man number four, five, six, and seven as separate levels.[1]

Man Number 1: "A man in whom the moving or instinctive centers predominate over the intellectual and emotional, that is: physical man."

Man Number 2: "A man in whom the emotional center predominates over the intellectual, moving, and instinctive: emotional man."

---

1. Based on Ouspensky, P.D., *The Psychology of Man's Possible Evolution*, Alfred A. Knopf, New York, 1979, p. 53-54.

Man Number 3: "A man in whom the intellectual center predominates over the emotional, moving, and instinctive: intellectual man."

Man Number 4: A man who is the product of school Work. He differs from man number 1, 2, and 3 in his self-knowledge; in his ability to recognize consciousness; and in his consistent line of effort to separate consciousness from functions. He has an aim. His lower centers are in a more balanced condition, and his essence begins to predominate over his personality. At the same time man number four does not possess any special powers, and he can easily lose everything he has acquired.

Man Number 5: A man who has achieved unity and self-consciousness, and in whom the Higher Emotional Center is active. A man number five knows himself objectively and has many functions and powers that the ordinary man does not. He may have periodic workings of the Higher Intellectual Center, but this function is not fixed or established in him. A man number five must still struggle actively with features and false personality, and if he is lax in this, he may yet lose everything he has won.

Man Number 6: A man in whom both Higher Centers are active and in whom the Higher Emotional and Higher Intellectual Centers have fused. This process of fusion is called crystallization. Such a man has faculties and powers far beyond those of a man number five. He has achieved permanent immortality and is a celestial being still possessed of a cellular body.

We could say that while a man number five is transparent to himself, a man number six begins to become translucent — so that the light of a higher level shines through him.

Man Number 7: We noted that a man number six has both Higher Centers open and awake. Not only are they active, but they are integrally linked. What, then, lies beyond this? The range of development of the fused Higher Centers is greater than anything which preceded it. A complete man number seven is more different from a man number six than a man number six is from a man number five — but it is impossible to represent this difference in words. A man number seven has permanent 'I,' free will, and can control all states of consciousness within himself. He cannot lose anything he has acquired.

Man Number 8: Gurdjieff spoke occasionally of a man number eight, referring to the level of a prophet: Moses, Jesus, or Muhammad. A man number eight is distinguished from a man number seven, not so much in relation to what can be known and understood on this level, but in the quality of his connection to a higher level. There is something in him that transcends the entire scale of Creation. He is connected to the deity.

THE THREE LINES OF WORK IN SCHOOL

A Fourth Way teaching provides three lines of work, for work on one line alone will not produce the desired result. Work on any one line will come to a standstill, unless it is reinforced and fortified by work on the other lines. The lines of work are as follows:

First Line: The study of oneself and the study of the system. All attempts at self-remembering, self-observation, internal separation, divided attention, and non-identification. Working on this line one works for oneself.[1]

Second Line: Work with other people in the school. In the second line one learns to work for other people in the same way, and in the same spirit, that one works on oneself. The second line includes both giving and receiving. Real second line of work must always, in one way or another, be useful to the school.[2]

Third Line: Work for the school. In order to work for the school, one must first understand the school itself, the aims of the teacher, and the needs of other students in relation to those aims.[3]

The first line, taken by itself, is not sufficient to free us from the selfishness that is so deeply ingrained in human nature: ultimately, the iron grip of the

---

1. *Ibid.,* p. 70-72.
2. *Ibid.,* p. 70-72.
3. *Ibid.,* p. 70-72.

instinctive center. The larger aims of the school help us to connect practically with something that is greater than 'just ourselves.' The experience of other people in the Work, coming from different backgrounds, and with different psychological characteristics, is necessary to give us additional outside perspective on ourselves. The three lines of work together create the context in which our line of effort can become continuous; work on each line reinforcing the others.

We have now collected enough material to distinguish the different levels of school that have existed through history. To distinguish these levels is important, because it will help to clarify the respective aims of Gurdjieff, Ouspensky, Collin, Horn, and Burton. For the most part the Work of these men was connected with groups aspiring to become schools, but school was always the ultimate aim, and understanding the different levels of school is necessary to understanding the aims of these men.

Different Levels of School: The Conscious Hierarchy

The first level of school is that of a man number five teaching men number one, two, and three to become man number four. Technically this is better called a group, preliminary to schoolwork, because it is engaged only in partial awakening.

The next level of school adds another level of work. Peter Ouspensky described this added level in a lecture in 1937:

> ... in the beginning of our work, in 1916 in St. Petersburg, we were made to understand that a school, in the full sense of the term, must consist of two degrees, that is, it must have two levels in it: one level, where men 1, 2, and 3 learn to become No. 4, and the other level where men No. 4 learn to become No. 5. If a school has two levels it has more possibilities, because a double organization

of this kind can give a larger variety of experience and make the work more quick and more sure.[1]

This second level requires the presence of a mature man number six. While a man number five may have gone through the eye of the needle and become conscious himself, he lacks the breadth of experience to guide other different types of people through this difficult transition. A man number six has a more objective vision. He completes, in a special way, the circle of people that forms around him. The 'all possibilities' of the students are in some way stimulated by the realized 'all possibilities' of the teacher. Additionally, the added level of "men number four learning to become men number five" changes the whole character of the group. A high man number four is often a better teacher to new students than a man number five or six, being closer to their level. Additionally, several experienced men number four may represent different approaches to the Work, and can help free people from the impulse to slavishly imitate their teacher. Peter Ouspensky, who had achieved the level of man number six by 1937, had this second level of school as a goal when he gave the lecture quoted above. He was, exactly, trying to add the second level of Work that he had described.

However, there is yet another level of school. The great schools of the past — the Vedantic, the Tibetan Buddhist, the Sufi Orders of Islam, the apostolic Christian schools — have all been based on what could be called *a conscious hierarchy*. In these schools a number of men number five are guided by a man number six or seven, who is himself under the guidance of Higher School. It is thus — from top to bottom — a hierarchy of service. When conscious service *to the level above the human* has been achieved, everything else falls into place.

The teacher of such a school — a man number six or seven — acquires a breadth and competence, through direct connection with the level above his own. The development of the men number five is accelerated by working contact with a teacher whose Higher Intellectual Center is engaged in active service to the entities that inhabit the Sphere of Sentient Being. The

---

1. Ouspensky, P.D., *The Fourth Way*, Routledge & Kegan Paul, London, 1972., p. 101.

men number five are then able to instruct and to guide a larger number of men number four. The development of the men number four is immeasurably enhanced, not just by the quality of the teaching they receive, but by the *example* of the men number five who have entered their apprenticeship to the Gods. The men number four are able to sense something of what their actual motivation is. The men number five are not torturing themselves to awaken, they have an essentially *positive* motivation and make sacrifices in relation to this. Additionally, under these circumstances, the men number five are capable of interpreting the often wordless teachings of the men numbers six and seven, and so create a kind of chain effect linking all the levels. And finally, those working to become man number four are able to give a motivating example to the men number one, two, and three who are trying to find their way in the Work. When all of these levels of Work are occurring simultaneously, the school is brought into an ever deeper connection to the Sphere of Sentient Being and to the entities who dwell therein.

Each level works better when it works in the light of a higher level: in other words, when it is exposed to the higher kind of Work that would naturally develop out of the Work that it is doing. In this regard the hierarchy of the Work is exactly the same as the hierarchy that exists in the training for a particular sport — where the novice gains by playing the journeyman, and the journeyman gains by playing the master. The conscious hierarchy also helps to break the identification of the student with the person of a particular teacher. This is a distinct problem for the first level of school. This interaction of different levels opens the way to what Rodney Collin and Alexander Horn called *The Great Work*.

Gurdjieff spoke of the highest level of school — schools having a direct, working link with Higher Forces — as the Inner Circle of Humanity:

> The inner circle is called the 'esoteric;' this circle consists of people who have attained the highest development possible for man, each one of whom possesses individuality in the fullest degree, that is to say, an indivisible 'I,' all forms of consciousness possible for man, full control over these states of consciousness, the whole of knowledge possible for man, and a free and independent will. They

cannot perform actions opposed to their understanding or have an understanding which is not expressed by actions. At the same time there can be no discords among them, no differences of understanding. Therefore, their activity is entirely coordinated and leads to one common aim without any kind of compulsion because it is based upon a common and identical understanding.[1]

We see only the traces of such a level in history. A school with such leadership would be capable of bearing all the pressures that the Gods apply, and for that reason would be capable of interpreting and implementing the will of Higher School in history. Such schools may occur in the time of a Prophet, or in circumstances where the Gods intend to effect change in a civilizational order. A school of this kind can serve the level below it — serve humanity — not in relation to humanity's subjective needs, but in relation to its objective needs and the aims of Higher School. This is what humanity needs more than anything else: this kind of service is objective compassion. It is what the Apostle Paul called αγάπη, or charity, the highest form of love. Once this tenuous link has been secured, the links connecting Higher School to the Absolute are all already in place.

There is a final thought to consider. According to the Fourth Way teachers, the medium of organic life on earth, and on other planets like the earth, is presently the only source of new conscious beings in the universe. Those that have graduated into Higher Schools remain, in a strange way, dependent on their source, for to rise within the Macrocosm they must replace themselves on the level they are vacating. As they move upwards, they must put new conscious beings in their place. Thus, the most developed cells of humanity participate in a lift-on-lift movement that runs throughout the universe to the Absolute, and these most developed cells redeem the larger body of Mankind, by making it into a living whole.

---

1. Ouspensky, P.D., *In Search of the Miraculous,* Routledge & Kegan Paul, London, 1977, pp. 310-311.

Prologue in Heaven

With Apologies to Johann Wolfgang von Goethe

We find ourselves looking into what appears to be a vast floodlit amphitheater, open at either end. It is the vault of creation. We see — at a great distance — a procession moving from one end of the amphitheater to the other. This is the longer life of humanity stretched out before us: the forty-five thousand year span of *homo sapiens sapiens*. Four of the Archangels — Michael, Gabriel, Raphael, and Uriel — are looking down upon the procession of Mankind.

The Archangels have been working for several ages in the middle sections of the span. They are modelling individual schools and whole spiritual traditions. They work the unrefined base material of the human experience into matrices of light, which expand, shine brilliantly, and then disperse ... leaving myriads of sparks — a few of which shimmer back into life. Within the matrices there are moments of great concentration, which radiate an intensity of light and understandings of many different kinds. These moments of concentration involve, and deeply affect, innumerable human lives. They are usually followed by a sudden splitting or fragmentation, and then a gradual dispersion. There may or may not be a re-concentration to follow. It is apparent that certain of the matrices have a kind permanence. While they may flicker off, they tend to recur.

It goes on and on. The lives of thousands of individual men and women play themselves out. It is like a 'theater of light,' and the individual men and women sometimes seem little more than counters to be used in this conscious art. A paladin of light may suddenly turn into a prince of darkness, an obscure bit part player may suddenly become radiant. Sadly, for the majority of the players, the light begins to emerge and then simply fades or goes out altogether. In this great play of light and shadow, a few of the rôles are clearly preordained; it is as though they were given in the beginning and remain reference points throughout. These are the rôles of the great prophets and avatars of Mankind.

The background pattern of it all is the sequence of civilizations itself: the Sumerian, the Egyptian, the Taoist, the Confucian, the Vedic, the Minoan, the Judaic, the Greek, the Roman, the Christian, the Islamic. The pattern of each individual civilization is a symphonic unity, with themes and counter themes and complex patterns of thematic development that may be taken up by more than one civilizational order. Each Archangel is focused in a particular area, and wherever they work one senses an emergent pattern in the vast tapestry of schools and civilizations.

There are three things then: the base material on which the Archangels work, the pattern of civilizational order which forms the backdrop of their work, and the emergent matrices of light. The base material is — in itself — inert, merely organic, yet it is surprisingly responsive to their influence. At points it actually facilitates the emergence of the matrices. When several matrices of light appear simultaneously, one begins to sense the phrasing of a civilizational symphony.

The Archangels work, each at their given point and at the same time in relation to all the other points. They are working in concert in a way we cannot understand. While we are looking at the line of time, somehow everything is all happening at once.

The great labor of the Archangels requires speed, accuracy, and intuitive sense — because the quality of their matter is so uncertain. The raw material that they work with is, in its inert state, dim: neither liquid nor gaseous. It is thick and murky and seems possessed of a resistant will. With such base material humanity's being seems uncentered, it is an alchemical substance alive with all kinds of possibilities — both for good and ill. While on the one hand it can be dark and sulfurous, on the other it can become pliable and translucent. But when it begins to become translucent, the resistance of its darker side becomes more focused. The darkness knows how to preserve its own — and it has great intelligence of a certain kind. There is an almost perverse instability in all the experiments, and in each individual experiment on whatever scale. All of this is in the nature of the base material. One thinks of Goethe's *Faust*: "For man must strive, and striving he must err." The potentiality and the instability are related; the resistance that is generated from the base material is somehow essential to producing the transparency and the brilliance. It just depends on how that resistance is handled.

Another aspect of this situation is that the potentials that exist in the medium are not completely known to the higher level, yet they have a determining effect on the result. The Archangels themselves are never — even momentarily — affected by even the most tragic dispersals of the light. They never falter, and never miss an opportunity; for they know the Absolute, and they are, in their innermost being, a continuous movement towards the perfections that He indicates.

The Archangels work tirelessly, without a trace of expectation, without a glimmer of hope, without a shadow of resentment. Their creativity is too strong, for their satisfaction in their work is in the quality of service they give to the Absolute, whatever its results.

There is a pause. The Archangels draw back. It is a time to let things play themselves out for a while, and for man to prove or disprove himself in the stream of events. The Archangels look to each other and then look up and down the forty-five thousand year span of *homo sapiens sapiens*. They also look deeply into the beginnings and endings of things, which are obscure to us.

Raphael: There is a darkness and a confusion that calls our service.

Michael: I see good things in the nearer range: Abraham, Zoroaster, and Moses freeing humanity from the slow descent of the prehistoric religions. The Buddha making a statement of remarkable purity. Jesus demonstrating the equality of all men through love, and the apostles supporting him so well. Yet in each case, after a time, there is a slipping back into the primordial state. The prophetic religions — that follow from each of the prophetic teachings — are reabsorbed into the pattern of life, just like the ancient religions which had preceded them.

Gabriel: Yes, and even the Spiritual Traditions connected to the prophetic religions do eventually fail. Yet they, unlike the religions themselves, have a significance beyond the span of their life in time, for some part of them is actually outside of time. Recrudescence of their original light may follow at much later points in time: the full flowering of the classical world comes centuries after the initial illuminations of Pythagoras, Socrates, and Plato; the faith of the high Middle Ages comes more than a millennium after Jesus' teaching; and the delicate bloom of the High Renaissance in Italy comes even later, arising out of a confluence of these two streams.

Uriel: (*Looking further down the line.*) We see the great religions introduced by the prophets becoming themselves ancient, covered over with layer upon layer of debate and contention. On the one hand they are dispersed into theology and on the other transformed into simple belief or constricting superstition. They lose their sacred quality; they pass their special moment and enter the time when one truth is in competition with others. And with the descent of the religions, the self-created gods of humanity come to the fore: the political ideologies, the popular forms of science, the images artificially generated out of an emergent mass media.

Raphael: (*Follows Uriel's gaze to focus on the late 19th early 20th century.*) Yes, the great religions have finally returned to the original medium: clouded and opaque. Sad, but not surprising, for humanity is incapable of sustaining such a level of activity over such a long period. But finally, even the regenerative light of the inner Spiritual Traditions, connected with each of the religions, fades. Once so strong and vital the bright lights of the Vedantic Schools, of Catholic and Orthodox monasticism, of the Tibetan Buddhist Orders, of the Sufi Orders of Islam, flicker and fail.

Gabriel: Yes, the inner Spiritual Traditions founder with the rise of the industrialized nation-states. It is difficult for them to sustain themselves without patronage in a medium of intense commercial life with an expanding popular culture.

Michael: (*Moving closer to the twentieth century.*) The medium itself — the base material — becomes darker and more resistant, while at the same time showing a strange profusion of color. It is suddenly, at a certain point, infused with a kind of electronic waste material. New technologies render the coarse matter fascinating, so that few look beyond it. Yet at the same time the medium itself becomes more violent and explosive.

Uriel: You are seeing the "night" that the Absolute had the early Prophets foretell: what Vishvamitra called the *Kali Yuga,* what Zoroaster called *the Age of Angra Mainyu,* what the Buddha called the time of *the Decline of the Dharma,* what John of *Revelations* called *The Apocalypse,* and what Muhammad called *the Dark Age*. In this time the religions merge with the original state of the medium, and the spiritual traditions slip down into the place that the religions had vacated. They are now institutions only. Human intelligence has become fascinated with itself. The eternal teaching that we have so striven to inseminate has descended to the level of words and gestures only, spoken but not practiced, yet ...

All the Archangels now look directly into the 'change of the age' that follows the end of the Napoleonic Wars: the definitive displacement of religion and the full fruition of the first industrial revolution. They see the two global conflicts of the 20th century, and the creation and deployment of weapons of mass destruction. Yet lights still flicker and shimmer on the horizon.

Michael: There are the few, as there have always been, that look up — for man is a microcosm and Mankind a created cosmos. There will always be conscious cells in the body of Mankind. Yet in this age they are deprived of the Spiritual Traditions we so labored to create.

Raphael: Look, there, further on, there comes one — a Greek. And there another, a Russian. And several others beyond: a lanky

Englishman, a robust American who seems a replication of the Greek, and a second American who resembles the Englishman. We must see what is possible with these men. They each have flaws, and they each will have great difficulty in forming — out of the unstable matter — a second tier of awakened cells around themselves. But they *are* the light in the darkness; they have a great and strange beauty as they themselves labor in the darkness of the last age. Let us shift ourselves into this arena and begin again.

And so the play begins anew. The spheres begin to revolve, the phosphorescence shines.

Gabriel: I'll meet the Greek at the artillery range in Kars, follow up at the oasis at Yanghi Hissar, and then bring him through to the ancient monastery just north of Bokhara, where the last light of the spiritual traditions still shimmers.

Michael: I'll meet the Russian at his sister's death in Moscow, then on the ship in the Sea of Marmara, and then at Essentuki.

Gabriel: I'll meet the Englishman where he joins the Russian on the liner in the mid-Atlantic …

The rhythmic labor of the Archangels begins again. At whatever point they engage the medium, little sparks are drawn and attracted. Connected forms begin to emerge. But then also there is a tremendous release of toxins from the resistant medium: revolution, war, genocide, atheism, a degenerate popular culture. Yet the Archangels are unfazed, for they sense only the potential, and see in the resistance only the means to an end. But for the human being looking in on the scene, it is terrifying.

CHAPTER 1

George Ivanovitch Gurdjieff: The Search Years

Youth and Years of Search

George Ivanovitch Gurdjieff was born in the Greek quarter of Alexandropol in Russian Armenia on the 23rd of April 1866.[1] This was a garrison town on the Russian border of Ottoman Turkey. In the year 1866 the Ottoman Empire was in its decline, and Russia was reasserting her influence in the disputed areas of the Caucasus.

George Gurdjieff's father, Ioannas Giorgiades, was — by vocation — a bard (an *ashokh*), who made his living as a grazier. He could trace his

---

1. Gurdjieff had no birth certificate. The range of passports that were found in his Paris apartment after his death give birthdates from 1864 to 1877. James Moore makes a compelling argument for 1866, citing the recorded notes of his Paris meetings, where - on several different occasions - Gurdjieff mentions his age, each time giving a figure which corresponds to an 1866 birthdate. (See Moore, James, *Gurdjieff: The Anatomy of a Myth*, Element, Longmead, Shaftesbury, Dorset, 1993, p. 338). John Bennett records that Gurdjieff told him directly that he was born in 1866. (See Bennett, J.G., *Witness: The Story of a Search*, Dharma Book Company, Inc., New York, New York, 1962, p. 64.) The record of events given in *Meetings with Remarkable Men* contradicts, in one way or another, both the 1866 birthdate and all of the passport birthdates. So the direct testimony of Gurdjieff himself - who presumably knew his own age - seems the most reliable indicator. In the *Third Series* Gurdjieff gives his birthday as April 23rd, see Gurdjieff, G.I., *Life is real only then, when "I am"*, All and Everything, Third Series, E.P. Dutton, New York, 1978, p. 43.

ancestry back to a Byzantine Greek family that had fled Constantinople when it fell to the Ottomans in 1453. The name Gurdjieff is a Russification of the Greek Giorgiades, and it is probably what the young George was called by his childhood friends and schoolteachers.

Ioannas (John) had inherited from his father herds of cattle and seigneurial obligations for the grazing land on which he kept them. He was a practicing Orthodox Christian. While his faith gave him Russian — as opposed to Ottoman — sympathies, his poetic culture, as an *ashokh,* connected him deeply to the heritage of the pre-Islamic, pre-Christian Middle East. In mid-19th century Russia, such an overlay of Christian teaching and ancient wisdom was not seen to be a contradiction, just as it was not seen to be a contradiction by the Church Fathers of ancient times.

As a practicing bard Ioannas had a vast repertoire of stories, songs, aphorisms, and myths, which were drawn from a reservoir of folk wisdom that had existed for millennia in the Middle East. There were stories of princes, beggars, gods, heroes, enchantments, and high adventure. When, in his maturity, George Gurdjieff encountered the translations of the Sumerian Gilgamesh epic (newly excavated by German archaeologists), he realized that his father had told him these same stories in his childhood. In their origins these Sumerian myths were more than 6,000 years old. Thus, Ioannas drew on a reservoir of traditional wisdom that reached long back before the coming of Christianity. He often travelled to give public recitations, and would bring his young son along as a travelling companion.

One of Ioannas' stories had a great impact on the young George; it was a legend of the now forgotten Inner Circle of Humanity: the Imastun Brotherhood. This brotherhood had been created in our pre-history, in the foreknowledge of a great flood which preceded Noah's flood. The flood was intended by God to destroy a decadent humanity. The brotherhood prepared themselves for this event, preserving all that had been previously understood, along with a knowledge of the errors that had caused humanity to be so harshly judged. The most important thing the Imastun preserved was an understanding of the objective measure of man and his place in the living universe. When the flood came, only a small population survived. As humanity gradually repopulated different parts of the earth, the members of the brotherhood dispersed, taking up residence in the major population centers as they developed. The Imastun were able to remain in communication through telepathy, and so formed an active network overseeing and guiding the affairs of man and the renewal of the human race.

In 1873, when George was seven years old, a cattle plague exterminated the Giorgiades herds in Alexandropol, and Ioannas was left without a living. He sold the household furniture and opened a lumberyard, making planks from freshly cut timber brought in from nearby forested lands. The business gave the family just enough to get by. Through this difficult time the elder Gurdjieff maintained a calm detachment and a complete acceptance of what fate had allotted him. This made a deep impression on his son.

In the year 1876 the Ottoman Empire drew the attention of all Europe with its brutal suppression of nationalist uprisings in Herzegovina and Bulgaria. Fifteen thousand unarmed Bulgarian Christians, including women and children, were systematically massacred. At the same time the Ottomans refused to recognize the Constantinople Accord of 1856, which allowed equal rights for religious minorities in all nations. The Accord had been specifically designed to alleviate the situation of the many millions of Christians living within Ottoman territories. On the 24th of April 1877, Tsar Alexander II of Russia, as the leader of a Christian Empire bordering the Ottoman Empire, declared war on the Ottomans. The Caucasus, where the Georgiades family lived, was one theater of this war.

Gurdjieff's parents, whose Greek and Armenian ancestors had been persecuted by the Ottomans, were encouraged by the prospect of a Russian victory. In November of that year, the Russians occupied the town of Kars, a key military position, which — from that moment — became a new center of administration and commercial life. The lands surrounding Kars were relatively fertile and ensured the city's prosperity. Ioannas, now with seven mouths to feed, promptly moved to Kars, fifty miles west of Alexandropol, in what is now Turkey. Here he established himself as a carpenter.

At the time of the Russian conquest, Kars had a population of over 20,000.[1] A large part of this population was Turkish, and many of the Turks left the city to resettle in the Ottoman-controlled lands to the South. The Russians then encouraged non-Turkish peoples to settle in the growing tracts of vacant land: Armenians, Tartars, Kurds, Turko-Persian Qarapapaqs, Daghestanis, and Aisors (the last descendants of the ancient Assyrians). Additionally, there came the peoples of the non-conformist churches seeking religious freedom: Molokans, Dukhobors, and Lutherans. Finally, there were the Yezidi — a Kurdish people with a religion linking Zoroastrianism with the ancient Mesopotamian myths.

It was a collection of people, which — taken as a whole — preserved the myth-pool of the ancient Middle East. There were cultural strands running back to the most ancient cultures of the Tigris-Euphrates river basin. The Russian population was rooted in Orthodox Christianity, which in the 19th century still had direct links to the great Russian Monasteries and to Mount Athos itself. A substantial Turkish population represented Islam, with connections to the still existent Sufi Orders. Thus, the traditional culture Ioannas had acquired as an *ashokh* was mirrored in the population of Kars. The myths and stories that the young Gurdjieff heard from his father were reflected in the cultures that immediately surrounded him.[2]

Gurdjieff, as the eldest son of his family, would have been trained, from his earliest years, to help his father with his carpentry, and his mother with the raising of four younger brothers and sisters. His upbringing occurred at a time of financial insecurity, and this made for extra demands in both areas. As an adolescent he often found himself doing the heavy work of a man.

Yet his cultural life was rich. From his mother he learned Armenian and from his father the Cappadocian Greek dialect and the Turko-Tartar tongue that he used as an *ashokh*. In the city of Kars, the young George

---

1. For details on 19th century Kars see Bennett, J.G., *Gurdjieff: A Very Great Enigma*, Samuel Weiser, Inc., York Beach, Maine, 1973.
2. The Hermetic teaching that Gurdjieff was to inherit in his mature years, and the mythic presentation that he made of it in *Beelzebub's Tales*, registers directly the background of the Mesopotamian and Zoroastrian myths.

was able to pick up Ottoman Turkish. To complete his linguistic education the Giorgiades family hired a priest to teach him Russian. With these languages the young George was equipped to penetrate the complex overlay of traditional societies that made up the Russian Caucasus, and the lands of Central Asia that lay beyond. He was to have the opportunity of travelling these lands in the last years before they were changed forever by the industrial revolution.

In Kars the young George attended the Russian Municipal School. This, in combination with a succession of private tutors, gave him a background in mathematics, geography, history, and the basics of modern science. Within weeks of arriving in Kars he auditioned as choir boy at the Kars Military Cathedral. His boyhood participation in the Orthodox choir was both sincere and passionate, and throughout his life he retained a deep connection with music. George's voice drew the attention of Dean Borsh, who was the highest Orthodox spiritual authority in the region. The Dean became a friend of the Giorgiades family, forming a close personal relationship with both George and his father. He became George's first tutor and took his confessions for two years. At the same time the Dean, as a person with a deep interest in the mythologies of ancient Mesopotamia, attended Ioannas' bardic recitations. The Dean would often walk into Ioannas' carpentry shop, where the young George was at work, and begin a dialogue with the father. The two men would play at a game of questions and answers. One of them would unexpectedly ask the other a question, and the other, without haste, would calmly reply: "Where is God just now?" "God is just now in Sari Kamish." "What is God doing there?" "He is making double ladders and on the tops of them he is fastening happiness, so that individual people and whole nations might ascend and descend." A thread of deeper meaning was concealed beneath these questions and answers. The game recreated a mythical context that was thousands of years old.[3]

The Dean had hoped to prepare the young George to become a physician and a priest, capable of healing both body and soul. He understood that the mind and the body are intimately connected, and that a priest must

---

3. Gurdjieff, G.I., *Meetings with Remarkable Men*, E.P. Dutton & Co. Inc., New York, 1963, p. 38.

be able to relate to the whole person. In this he was successful, as George was to study healing throughout his life, and as a mature teacher he retained the role of healer.

As Dean Borsh grew older, he recommended a tutor to succeed him: an Orthodox seminarian named Bogachevsky. Young Father Bogachevsky was to confess Gurdjieff for two years, and carefully instructed him in the difference between subjective and objective morality, and the place of conscience. Bogachevsky later became established as a chaplain at Mount Athos, and in his maturity joined the Essene Brotherhood, first in Egypt, and then in Jerusalem. Gurdjieff remained in touch with him into his own teaching years. As a result of this upbringing and education, the young Gurdjieff knew the rituals of the Orthodox Church intimately, and was able to connect with their underlying meaning.

There is a particular episode from Gurdjieff's youth in Kars that was a formative part of his development, and that suggests the involvement of C Influence. In his early teens, George and one of his friends, Piotr Karpenko, fell in love with the same girl at the same time. They agreed to decide their rivalry by engaging in a form of Russian roulette, with the survivor free to pursue the girl. The two boys hid themselves on an artillery range, close to where the targets were placed, at the very time firing practice was to be held. Fate would then determine which of the two would survive. Gurdjieff said that, once the shelling began, "there arose in me for the first time the whole sensation of my self, which grew stronger and stronger," as he sensed the nearness of death. It was the first appearance in him of Real 'I.'[1] He was changed and reformed by this experience. Fortunately, both boys survived, and became firm friends thereafter. The romance that triggered the duel was forgotten.

From the time he was fourteen or fifteen, Gurdjieff began to make excursions outside of Kars. At the age of seventeen (in 1883) this adventurous young man moved to Tiflis in the central Caucasus (now in present day

---

1. *Ibid.*, p. 207.

Georgia) and worked as a stoker for the Transcaucasian Railway Company. The Transcaucasian railways ran the entire length of the Caucasus, from the East coast of the Black Sea to the West coast of the Caspian Sea. These were the lands of the old Safavid and Qajar Khanates, and they gave Gurdjieff an immediate exposure to many cultures: Georgian, Armenian, Persian, and Azerbaijan. In the years 1884-9 he travelled yet more widely. In the course of these travels, he stayed at several monasteries, in the status of a novitiate or guest. While he was attracted to the idea of retreat, and to the discipline of monastic life, the monasteries themselves did not seem to have the answers that he sought. He began to feel that there was "a religion behind the religions" that he knew, and wondered what this might be.

By the time Gurdjieff had reached the age of eighteen, in 1884, he had formed an aim that was to direct his activities through his early adult life: what we shall call his 'journeyman years.' Gurdjieff mentions this aim in both the *Third Series* and the *Herald of Coming Good*.

> [This aim] consisted in what I would now term an 'irrepressible striving' to understand clearly the precise significance, in general, of the life process on earth of all the outward forms of breathing creatures and, in particular, of the aim of human life in the light of this interpretation.[2]

> ... the aim of my inner world had been concentrated only on my one unconquerable desire to investigate from all sides, and to understand, the exact significance and purpose of the life of man.[3]

At the age of eighteen George Gurdjieff had already seen too much to accept the explanations of creation put forward by either Russian Orthodox Christianity or Ottoman Islam. At the same time, he had seen enough of the world to wonder at the miracle of creation itself, independently of any theology. He had enough science, and enough experience of agriculture and animal husbandry, to appreciate the complex system of mutually

---

2. Gurdjieff, G.I., *The Herald of Coming Good*, Sure Fire Press, Edmonds, Washington, 1988, (reprint of Paris 1933), p. 13.
3. Gurdjieff, G.I., *Life is real only then, when "I am"*, All and Everything, Third Series, E.P. Dutton, New York, 1978, p. 26.

dependent life forms that has developed on our planet. Within this system of life forms, the higher levels of organization and intelligence have been literally built out of the lower levels, so that man — taken as the culmination of this hierarchy — contains all of the elements that comprise the system as a whole: animal, vegetable, and mineral. The young Gurdjieff had already understood on the artillery range at Kars that this hierarchy culminates in man's experience of Higher Centers. Thus, a higher, more simple, and infinitely deeper awareness completes the series of more limited forms of awareness, that somehow have that end implicit in them. And this convergence — as finally realized in man — occurred over an immensely long period of time. It began with a succession of meteoroids and asteroids bringing complex organic molecules to the planet's surface, four thousand million years ago. The completed system as we know it is clearly not an accident, and at the same time it is clear that this system did not create itself.

Why does it exist? More specifically — for Gurdjieff — *what purpose does it serve?* Is Mankind, taken as the end result, in any way distinct, in its destiny and potentials, from all the other forms of cellular life which have preceded it? This question would have been meaningful for Gurdjieff, given that he had been raised in an agricultural community where animal life serves the human, and vegetable life serves the animal. Humanity should serve a life form higher than itself, yet human life often appears as rough and meaningless as that of most of the domesticated animals. Only a minute portion of Mankind, at any point in time, has been able to recognize the higher and more simple states of consciousness that Gurdjieff had experienced on the artillery field at Kars. And yet these higher states of consciousness are latent in every single human being, and must have been the intended outcome of the whole process. Where does individual human destiny stand in all of this? It is part of the enigma of our species that it proceeds in the ignorance of first things, and is not particularly bothered by this fact. Humanity is hypnotized by the magic-lantern show of its own common life; focused on gratifying immediate desires, responding to immediate threats, and seizing immediate opportunities. The young Gurdjieff found that traditional religion, for which he had the deepest respect, did not provide adequate answers to these questions, and that modern science, with which he was fascinated, was unable to pose them in a meaningful way.

Having looked at the young Gurdjieff's personal aim, we are now ready to examine his adult life. But before doing so we must take our bearings with respect to his own autobiographical writings, particularly *Meetings with Remarkable Men,* which covers the period from 1866 to 1900.[1] Most of those who have studied this text carefully take it to be, at least to a degree, symbolic. Certainly much of the material is not intended to be taken literally. And it is, in some ways, more remarkable for what it does not say than for what it does — for it does not record *any* of the several accomplished spiritual teachers that Gurdjieff must have encountered before he began to teach himself. John Bennett remembered Gurdjieff telling him that, "Every man must have a teacher. Even I, Gurdjieff, have my teacher."[2]

Having said this we must add that *Meetings with Remarkable Men* certainly does portray something of Gurdjieff's life, from his childhood through to 1900. All of the places, some of the dates, and many of the people in *Meetings* are probably real. But in interpreting *Meetings* we must keep in mind that the sixty-one-year-old man who wrote this document wrote it as a teaching tool, to produce a certain effect on his students.

There is a particular aspect of *Meetings with Remarkable Men* to which we must draw attention, the narrative of the *Seekers for Truth.* We remark on it because it conceals aspects of Gurdjieff's life that are of interest to us.

---

1. A clarification is needed with respect to Gurdjieff's writings. In the 1970s Gurdjieff's three principal written works were published as the three parts — or series — of a masterwork entitled *All and Everything.* The three series remained three separate books, and the numbering (first, second, third) does not refer to the order in which they were written. *Meetings with Remarkable Men,* which is subtitled the 'First Series,' was the second of the three books to be written. It was written in 1927-1928 and published in 1963. The first book that was written, *Beelzebub's Tales to His Grandson,* was drafted in the years 1924-1927 and eventually published in 1950. For some reason it was subtitled the Second Series. The third book, in the order of writing, is *Life is real only then, when "I Am".* It is subtitled the Third Series. It is comprised of meeting notes compiled by Jeanne de Salzman and finally published in 1974. To add to the confusion the third book is usually called just by its series name, the *Third Series.*

2. Bennett, J.G., *Gurdjieff: Making a New World,* Turnstone Books, London, 1973, p. 80,

THE SEEKERS FOR TRUTH

The story of the Seekers for Truth is used to organize the narrative of *Meetings with Remarkable Men* between the years of 1884 and 1900. Something like the Seekers for Truth probably did exist, but it is unlikely that it played such a prominent role in Gurdjieff's life for such a long period of time. The history of the Seekers for Truth conceals deeper, more formative themes in the life of George Gurdjieff: 1) his connection to real schools and real teachers, and 2) his connection with the Romanov government (which we shall document in the pages to follow). Gurdjieff was almost certainly under vow not to reveal the teacher and the school that was his principal esoteric source. And it was expedient for him to conceal the nature of his connection with the Romanov government. (He was to travel in Soviet Russia a few years after completing *Meetings with Remarkable Men*.)[1]

Fortunately Gurdjieff has provided us with other references for this period in the *Third Series* of *All and Everything* and in the *Herald of Coming Good*. Both of these works were written after *Meetings with Remarkable Men*, and without its peculiar narrative devices.[2]

Finally, before continuing with the story of Gurdjieff's life, we must recreate the international context of his search years.

THE GREAT GAME

From the close of the Napoleonic Wars, in 1815, Britain, France, and Russia became involved in a contest to establish spheres of influence in the Near East and in Asia. This was called, at the time, 'The Great Game.' The stakes in the game increased considerably with the coming of the first industrial revolution and the consequent creation of a world economy. Each of these countries had many agents active throughout the Eastern world. Materially, all parties — Asian and European — stood to benefit from the creation of economies of scale, and the availability of new markets for their goods. Culturally, however, it was the beginning of the end of the colorful traditional societies of Asia, Central Asia, and the Near East. The sudden expansion of the industrialized

---

1. Gurdjieff's record as an agent of the Romanov government has been given as one reason why the British Home Office refused him residential status in the U.K. in 1922.

2. We shall refer frequently to the Third Series for biographical references. The publication of the *Third Series* we have used is E.P. Dutton, New York, 1978.

West opened these traditional societies to the outside world, and this was, ironically, the reason why Gurdjieff was able to penetrate so many of them. He was able to glimpse their inner life before the candle flame flickered and went out.

In the context of the Great Game, Russia had slightly different motives than France and Britain. The Romanov government had a genuine respect for, and interest in, 'ancient wisdom.' The records of the Russian agents' assignments show that they not only assessed the political climate of different regions, but penetrated secluded monasteries, researched ancient teachings, recorded sacred ceremonies, and studied occult rites. The agents themselves were people very like Gurdjieff: multi-lingual, cosmopolitan, and — for the most part — of indeterminate Asiatic ethnicity. The government records of many such individuals survive: Ushe Narzunoff, Shamzaran Badmaieff, Ariuna Tserempil. But behind these shadowy figures were senior members of the Romanov court, such as the great orientalist, Prince Esper Esperovitch Ukhtomsky. These people were all part of the world to which Gurdjieff himself belonged from 1889 to 1911.[3] Gurdjieff was himself, almost certainly, such an agent. People of this class might be presented to the Tsar — as Gurdjieff himself was in July of 1901 — and they were generally connected with the pattern of court life, as, within the court, there was an active interest in their work.[4] Gurdjieff's wife, the Countess Ostrowska, was a lady-in-waiting to the Tsaritsa, and Gurdjieff's status as an agent would explain how he could have met and courted her.[5] John Bennett stated that, over the quarter century he knew Gurdjieff, "he always spoke warmly of Nicholas II and once described him as a good man and very compassionate."[6]

It appears that, from 1890 onward, Gurdjieff was continuously connected, in one way or another, to the Romanov Government. In *Meetings with Remarkable Men* he lists a number of political involvements. He was, at one time or another, a courier of the Armenian Protectionist Society, a representative of the Armenian Social Revolutionary Party, and an agent of the Ethniki Hetaira (a Hellenist Spartacist society). The Russian Government had a direct interest in each of these political organizations.

---

3. This context was carefully researched by James Webb. See the opening chapters of Webb, James, *The Harmonious Circle*, Shambhala, Boston, 1987.

4. Gurdjieff mentioned his presentation to the Tsar to John Bennett. See also pp. 614-617 of Gurdjieff, G.I., *All and Everything, First Series, Beelzebub's Tales to his Grandson*, E.P. Dutton & Co., Inc., 1964. Here Gurdjieff describes a presentation to the Tsar which probably reflects his first-hand experience.

5. Bennett, J.G., *Gurdjieff: Making a New World*, Turnstone Books, London, 1973, p. 117.

6. *Ibid.*, p. 116.

> He admits that he acted as a Tsarist agent during his three years in Tibet. Needless to say, the coming of the Bolshevik Revolution in 1917 brought to an end that phase of Gurdjieff's career.

Gurdjieff's two decades of active search (1884-1908) culminated in an encounter with a great teaching, somewhere in Central Asia. In *Meetings with Remarkable Men* Gurdjieff referred to this teaching as the Sarmoun Brotherhood.[1] Both the events that led up to this encounter and the encounter itself changed Gurdjieff profoundly. To understand the nature of this change we must understand Gurdjieff's relation to the occult powers that he developed within himself in the early years of the twentieth century. It had not been his aim to acquire occult powers, but he had a predilection towards them, and he was in a position to feed that predilection. For a spiritual aspirant the possession of such powers is a difficulty, because when you are in possession of powers, *you are the life of those powers*. And they wish to experience that life *through you*. Gurdjieff renounced his powers (conditionally) during a personal and spiritual crisis that occurred in 1904. To some extent his life between 1884 and 1904 is the story of the development of these powers, which possessed him as much as he possessed them.[2] Occult powers — while they involve the concentration and control of the invisible energy fields connected with the human body — are distinct from consciousness, and from spiritual development as such. It was only after Gurdjieff's contact with this unknown Central Asian teaching, at the end of the 19th century, that he achieved a permanent focus on consciousness itself, which connected him in a more genuine way to the great teachings of the past. In the body of teaching that Gurdjieff presented to his groups

---

1. In *Meetings with Remarkable Men* this is spelled Sarmoung. This spelling reflects the Armenian pronunciation of the Persian term Sarman. In Persian it has several meanings: (1) "he who preserves the doctrine," (2) the "bee," as one who collects the honey of traditional wisdom, (3) "the chief repository of the tradition." The balance of usage over time seems to have been Sarmoun. See Bennett, J.G., *Gurdjieff: The Making of a New World*, p. 56-57. We have kept to the Persianate pronunciation here.

2. Gurdjieff himself acknowledges this. See Gurdjieff, G.I., *Life is real only then, when "I am"*, All and Everything, Third Series, E.P. Duttpon, New York, 1978, p. 8.

in Moscow and St. Petersburg in the years 1915-1916 there is an extraordinary understanding of the work of schools over the centuries. However Gurdjieff acquired these teachings, he had succeeded in making them his own. He had studied them thoroughly, had been tested on his knowledge of them, and had prepared his own being as an adequate vehicle for their transmission.

We plunge again, then, into the line of time. In the summer of 1885, at the age of 19, Gurdjieff travelled to Constantinople (present day Istanbul) to see the great dervish centers — Mevlevi, Bektashi, Rufaii, Kadiri, and Naqshbandi — in what was then the capital of the Ottoman Empire. There he found a friend and patron in the person of Prince Yuri Lubovedsky, who kept a house in the Pera district, which was in the immediate neighborhood of the great Sufi tekkes. He was to connect again with Prince Lubovedsky at several points later in his life. In the fall of 1885 he visited his parents, who had, in his absence, moved from Kars back to Alexandropol. While staying in Alexandropol he met Sarkis Pogossion, a young man who shared many of his interests. The two of them worked together on researching ancient Armenia, and other civilizations of the ancient Middle East. They found references to a brotherhood called the Sarmoun, whose work appeared to span many centuries. Studying all the texts they were able to assemble, Gurdjieff concluded that this ancient brotherhood had been formed in Babylon in the third millennium before Christ. It had apparently possessed Great Knowledge; direct knowledge of the place and fate of humanity.[3] Gurdjieff found evidence that the Sarmoun had been based in Izrumin, near the town of Nivsii, in about the 6th century AD, before the Byzantine conquest of Mesopotamia (in 626 AD) drove them out. On the basis of these leads, Gurdjieff and Pogossian made plans to travel in these areas to seek further evidence.

---

3. Gurdjieff mentions references to an ancient 'school behind schools' in the pages of the Merkhavat. This he equated with the Sarmoun Brotherhood. It is not certain what historical document or sacred text the Merkhavat refers to.

These plans were interrupted in 1887 when Gurdjieff (aged 21) accepted work as a courier of the Armenian protectionist society, the Armenakans. Gurdjieff does not tell us the context for this connection to the Armenakans, but the job was probably a way of financing his further travels. We speculate that it was his first assignment as a double agent for the Romanov government. Later that year, this assignment completed, he set out with Pogossian for Kurdistan (part of present day Syria and Northern Iraq), where the valley of Izrumin was located. By chance, however, he discovered a map of pre-sand Egypt. This was enough to divert both Gurdjieff and Pogossian from their pursuit of the historical Sarmoun, and sometime in 1887 Gurdjieff and Pogossian travelled to Alexandria.

During his time in Egypt Gurdjieff studied both the ancient Egyptian civilization and the Coptic Christian teachings, which were still alive in Alexandria. By this time, however, the interests of the two young men had begun to move in different directions. Gurdjieff left Pogossian in Alexandria and travelled to Cairo, where he met two men who were to be his colleagues and travelling companions for the next thirteen years: his Istanbul patron Prince Yuri Lubovedsky, and Professor Skridlov, a Russian archaeologist.

In relation to Gurdjieff's Egyptian studies, a few things must be taken into account.

GURDJIEFF'S VIEW OF ATLANTIS, SUMERIA, AND EGYPT

Gurdjieff's references to Atlantis, Sumeria, and Egypt are not uniform, and his statements concerning them are often combined in different ways. Helena Blavatsky's *Isis Unveiled* was first published in Russian in 1877, when Gurdjieff was eleven. It caused an immediate sensation in a culture that respected traditional wisdom. By the time Gurdjieff was twenty he had studied the text carefully, as it touched on all his principal areas of interest — particularly Atlantis, Sumeria, and Egypt. Later in his life he remarked that he had worked very hard to divest himself of, and to correct, "certain theosophical ideas."[1] Despite these efforts Gurdjieff retained traces of the Theosophical packaging of history, specifically Helena Blavatsky's presentation of the story of

---

1. In 1949 Gurdjieff told his students in Paris that he had met Helena Blavatsky personally. See Bennett, J.G. & Elizabeth, *Idiots in Paris*, Weiser Books, N.Y., 1991, p. 88.

Atlantis — which is a modification of Plato's Atlantis myth. Helena Blavatsky believed that Atlantis was a parent civilization to Egypt, and this notion determined her approach to the study of Egyptian history. Blavatsky, like the young Gurdjieff, had the idea of celestial beings guiding history, in direct communication with chosen human agents. But this communication, in the Theosophist view, was not based on a development of Higher Centers in the human agents, but on spiritualist methods. The mature Gurdjieff was able to re-think this material on the basis of his direct understanding of Higher Centers, but he retained the idea of Atlantis.

In *Beelzebub's Tales* (and only in *Beelzebub's Tales*) Gurdjieff spoke of a "school of Atlantis," the Akhaldian Society, that was formed in Atlantis and inseminated civilizations to follow. Its aim was "the striving to become aware of the sense and aim of the Being of beings".[2] It carried out the study of both cosmic laws (what we would call Hermetical studies) and of cosmic substances (what we would call alchemical studies) and achieved a competence in both fields that has not been matched since.[3] When the continent of Atlantis sank, the Akhaldian society was destroyed but individual members survived and preserved certain of its understandings, bringing a legacy (over a vast span of time) to Egypt, China, and Mesopotamia. Gurdjieff has Beelzebub say that the Egyptian Sphinx strongly reminded him of the statue appearing opposite the original headquarters of the Akhaldian Society in Atlantis. The presentation of the Akhaldian Society thus shadows the idea of the Inner Circle of Humanity, but does not directly represent it. In sum, there is the image of a prior civilizational order that seeded the first civilizations known to modern history — and this suggests the work of an Inner Circle of Humanity (as Gurdjieff presented that idea in Moscow and St. Petersburg in 1915-1916).

The source of the myth of Atlantis (in the form that it took in the 19th and 20th centuries) derives entirely from the writings of Plato and Helena Blavatsky. Blavatsky took Plato's reference to the continent of Atlantis as historical fact and greatly elaborated its history. The few other classical references that exist are all derivative of Plato's *Critias,* and all of the many modern references (e.g. Ignatius Donnelly, Rudolf Steiner, and Edgar Cayce) were originally triggered by Blavatsky's *Isis Unveiled*. In a word *all ultimately originate from Plato's vivid mythic presentation in the Critias*. Having made this point, Plato's Atlantis myth is not a 'real' myth; rather, Plato used it as a heuristic device, to measure the value of the civilizational orders of his own time. At the end of the *Critias* Plato promised a further dialogue describing a war between a pre-historic Athens and Atlantis. The state of war would be used to represent, in action, the

---

2. See Gurdjieff, G.I., *All and Everything, First Series, Beelzebub's Tales to his Grandson*, E.P. Dutton & Co., Inc., New York, 1964, p. 297.

3. See *Ibid.,* p. 299-300 and 303.

archetype of different kinds of civilizational order: to show how people cooperated, what core values were alive in them, and what the nature of those values were. Neither Plato nor his students would have expected this presentation to be historical.

No trace of an Atlantis myth or of an Atlantis story comes from the material that has been excavated in Egypt. Madame Blavatsky accepted Plato's date of 10,000 BC for the sinking of the continent of Atlantis. Gurdjieff, in his version of the Atlantis myth, pushed the date much further back in time — 17,735 years before the "second Transapalnian perturbation." While we do not have a definite reference point that allows us to fix this date, it could not be less than 40,000 years ago. In considering possible timelines we must keep in mind that civilizations the size of the mythical Atlantis require developed agriculture, with settlement, villages, and animal husbandry. It is only on the basis of developed agriculture that cities can be formed. Networks of multiple villages may, over an extended period of time, become cities capable of supporting a more advanced division of labor, which allows for the development of crafts and ultimately industries. Plato and Blavatsky's date of 10,000 BC (for the termination point of Atlantis) requires that a highly developed urban civilization (as part of a family of highly developed urban civilizations) had emerged *before* the end of the last Ice Age. This is in a time before we have any record of agricultural settlements, and in a period in which modern archaeology estimates the total population of human beings on the planet to have been less than one million.

Gurdjieff's much earlier date requires that the development of agriculture (with the domestication of plants and animals, the formation of villages, and the development of a division of labor) occurred somewhere in the midst of the last Ice Age. From this same period modern archaeology has retrieved the skeletal remains of migrant stone age peoples, and the traces of Paleolithic civilizations, advanced both spiritually and artistically, but founded on a shamanic culture and on a hunting and gathering lifestyle. That we should be able to trace some branches of this shamanic civilization — and not a family of civilizations — each with a population of many millions capable of supporting huge cities, is extremely unlikely.

While we are skeptical of the myth of Atlantis, it is quite possible that, in the period between the end of the last Ice Age and 5,000 BC, there emerged a civilization (or civilizations) that achieved an advanced division of labor, with developed craft and industry, comparable to (and even possibly superior to) that of Dynastic Egypt or ancient Sumeria. Such a civilization could easily have been based on a population of 500,000. (The population of ancient Sumeria is estimated to have been between 500,000 and 1,500,000, while the population of Old Kingdom Egypt is estimated to have been between 1,000,000 and 2,000,000.) The idea of such an 'anterior' civilization also fits with the myths of 'ancient parentage' that exist in most of the early civilizations known to history. And here we speak of the traditional idea of civilization: a social order recognizing and encouraging, not the advantage of an individual or a social class, but the highest development possible for man. In other words, a social order based on real values. There is no reason why such a lost civilization (or lost civilizations) might not have supported an Inner Circle of Humanity, or have represented a higher level of civilization than anything that has appeared since. Indeed, that would explain how both Dynastic Egypt and ancient Sumeria appear to have arrived on the scene fully formed.

So there could easily have been a forgotten civilization, on a cultural level higher than Sumeria or Dynastic Egypt, in the period between 10,000 BC and 5,000 BC. We could think of it as Atlantis, but the name now carries with it so many contradictory associations that it is better to lay it aside. We remark that Plato did not view his Atlantis as an advanced civilization, but as an overly developed one, which had problems with its core values. He would have placed the civilization of Archaic Greece (as idealized in the *Republic*) above that of Atlantis. There is no reason at all why a paleolithic/shamanic civilization might not surpass the spiritual level of the Atlantis depicted in Plato's *Critias*.[1]

Thus, we take Gurdjieff's attempt to trace a possible Inner Circle of Humanity, and his speculations as to which historical civilizations may have provided the basis for it, to be legitimate. On the basis of his studies of mythology, he sees civilizations behind the civilizations known to history, and he has grounds for these speculations. The validity of this work is not dependent on Helena Blavatsky's theory of Atlantis. An Inner Circle of Humanity may have been based in one of several prehistoric civilizations that developed out of the shamanic/tribal civilizations that existed during the last Ice Age. We recall that Heinrich Schliemann successfully excavated the cities of Mycenae and Troy on the basis of ancient myths. Gurdjieff had a unique understanding of many ancient myths.

It is likely that the schools of ancient Sumeria (via the Mesopotamian family of civilizations that followed from them) made their contributions to the system that

---

1. In closing this subject we note that estimating population movements before 5,000 BC is a speculative activity, because a hunting and gathering people can, simply in the course of following the migrations of animals, move thousands of miles in a century, and then in the next century move back. When we speak of millennia, in the plural, we are speaking of spans of time in which people might move anywhere on the planet. Determining that a particular population moved from here to there is very difficult.

the mature Gurdjieff taught. We shall explore this possibility later in the chapter. We have questioned the historical myth of Atlantis.[1] What, then, of the place of ancient Egypt?

Gurdjieff once told Solita Solano (his secretary from 1936 to 1940) that he had been initiated into the Egyptian Mysteries four times. When Gurdjieff was in Egypt in 1887-1888, he was 21 or 22 years old. In seeking these initiations, he was almost certainly inspired by the Theosophical literature. He was as yet — by his own later admission — unable to distinguish true esotericism from the pursuit of instinctive powers. And, beyond this, it is doubtful that there would have been any continuity between the Egyptian cults in Cairo in 1887 and the ancient Egyptian teachings. There was a definite popularization of the Egyptian religion in Ptolemaic times, and Egyptian mystery cults appeared in all the major cities of the Mediterranean. Their teachings were quite unrelated to the great teaching lineages of the pre-Ptolemaic Egyptian priest caste at Thebes or Sais. The mystery cults specialized in spirit possession, the creation of talismans, and different forms of clairvoyance. Indeed, this popularization probably corresponded to the passing away of the great Egyptian School. While the ancient teachings may have been able to sustain themselves behind the scenes for some centuries, the classical records that we have of the late mystery cults show no relation to the content of Gurdjieff's system. When Gurdjieff visited Egypt, it was a devoutly Islamic country, and most people with a monastic vocation would have joined the Egyptian Sufi Orders. It would have been naive to have expected truth from the Egyptian mystery cults of Cairo in the late 19th century.

A further clarification is in place with respect to Egyptian influence on Gurdjieff's system. The cosmological material presented in Moscow/St. Petersburg in 1916 is what is called a Hermetic teaching, and Hermeticism is often traced to Egypt. Gurdjieff's system is Hermetic in the sense that it is focused on the understanding of cosmic laws; it places man in relation to the different levels of laws in a sentient universe. The aim for the students, then, is to put themselves under the laws of a Higher Level and to subordinate the lower levels of their being to the higher. Essentially it is a non-mythical presentation of the structure of the universe, based on the very carefully assimilated experience of Higher Centers. This kind of Hermeticism may be, and often is, backed by myth. But the non-mythical side of Hermeticism *did not exist before the second century AD*. In that century it first appeared under the name of Hermes Trismegistus, with a fusion of Greek cosmology and the proto-science of alchemy, as that had developed in

---

1. Here we note that the references to the Inner Circle of Humanity in relation to Babylon/Sumeria from *Meetings with Remarkable Men* (begun in 1927) were written after the material in *Beelzebub's Tales* (dictated 1924-7) connecting Egypt to Atlantis.

Egypt. The Hermetic cosmology represented the *form* of the universe (cosmos, Macrocosm, transcendence, harmony) and the Hermetic alchemy represented the *substance* of the universe (the different vibrational levels of matter). The fusion of the two was seamless and produced something more than was in either of the component parts. In the first Hermetic teachings this study of cosmic law was backed by myth, principally but not entirely Egyptian. But, as the Hermetic side of the teaching developed, the myth-base became optional. Hermetic teachings were later used in conjunction with the myths of both the Christian and the Islamic religions. In the Hermetic teachings myth and religion are used to give dramatic background to the cosmology. But the true dramatization of the cosmology should be the application of its methods to produce the lived experience of the different cosmic levels it describes.

There was a marked revival of Hermeticism in Europe in the late Medieval/early Renaissance period. There were also Sufi forms of Hermeticism, which to some degree developed in parallel. Gurdjieff's presentation of the system in Moscow in 1916 shows some relation to each of these, but the strongest cosmological roots run back to ancient Mesopotamia.

In *Meetings with Remarkable Men,* Gurdjieff tells us that in 1888-1889 he went with Prince Lubovedsky to Thebes, and with Professor Skridlov to Abyssinia (present day Ethiopia), the Sudan, and the recently excavated remains of Babylon. During the years 1888-1889 Gurdjieff also visited Mecca and Medina. In 1889 he returned to Constantinople where he met Prince Lubovedsky's associate Vitvitskaya. No family name is ever given for this Polish-born woman, who had connections to the Russian aristocracy. Vitvitskaya was an authority on music, music theory, and music in relation to different vibrational levels. She was in her sixties when Gurdjieff met her. Gurdjieff escorted her to Russia, and after this visit he undertook a series of political assignments, all related to Russian areas of interest. It is possible that the well-connected Vitvitskaya recruited the young, multi-lingual and widely travelled Gurdjieff as a Russian agent at this time.

In the years 1890-93 (aged 24-27), Gurdjieff acted as a political envoy for the newly constituted Armenian Social Revolutionary Party, the Dashnakzutiun. In that status he visited Switzerland, and based himself for a period in Rome. In *Meetings with Remarkable Men* Gurdjieff tells us that in 1895 he returned again to Alexandropol, where, at the age of 29, he founded the Seekers of Truth, which had at least 21 members, including Skridlov,

Lubovedsky, and Vitvitskaya. The organization formalized a project of search which was, in fact, already well underway. In that same year (1895) Gurdjieff obtained a letter of introduction which gave him access to the Russian monastery of Saint Panteleimon, on Mount Athos, allowing him to visit the center of Orthodox Christian monasticism. More generally, in his years of search, Gurdjieff was able to study many variants of Christianity, always striving to reach back to the apostolic Christian teachings.

In 1896, as an agent of the Ethniki Hetairia, a Hellenist Spartacist society, Gurdjieff went to Crete, where the Greek population was in revolt against their Turkish rulers. Here Gurdjieff, looking like an Asiatic Greek, and circulating in a Greek crowd, was shot. He was taken by his colleagues — unconscious — to Jerusalem to recuperate. While in Jerusalem, he obtained a letter of introduction from his childhood confessor Father Bogachevsky (now Father Evlissi), which allowed him to spend some time with the Essenes. On his recovery he returned to his family home in Alexandropol.

Gurdjieff tells us, in *Meetings with Remarkable Men,* that in 1897 he travelled again with members of the Seekers of Truth, journeying through Turkestan to Tabriz and Baghdad, and then through Central Asia. Later in that year, independently of the Seekers, he established a connection with Agwhan Dorzhiev, the Tibetan diplomat who was the official liaison to the Romanov Court. At some point in the year he rejoined the Seekers, travelling with them to Siberia. The text of *Meetings* does not make it clear what, specifically, the Seekers hoped to find in Siberia.

The year 1898 finds Gurdjieff in Bukhara, in present day Uzbekistan, where a dervish acquaintance informs him of a contact that he had met who belonged to a brotherhood, known to the local Sufi Orders as the Sarmoun. Gurdjieff is suddenly reminded of the discoveries that had originally inspired his travels twelve years earlier. Through the dervish acquaintance Gurdjieff is able to secure a meeting with this contact, who, as it turned out, already had knowledge of him. Their meeting is presented as a fateful event. Through this contact Gurdjieff and his travelling companion at that time, Igor Soloviev, were given permission to visit the remote and carefully concealed Sarmoun monastery.[1] Here — to his great surprise — Gurdjieff met his companion Prince Lubovedsky, who had already found and joined the order. At the end of the two weeks, Gurdjieff and Soloviev are invited to meet the Sheikh of the order, who is 275 years old.[2] Nothing is said about this person, or about what he said to the two young men. However, following the conversation with the Sheikh they "entered into the life of the monastery." Again, just what comprised the life of the monastery is not described. Gurdjieff teasingly adds that he will perhaps recount it, "at some time in a special book." But this is exactly the "meeting with remarkable men" that we would like to know about!

At the end of three months Prince Lubovedsky came to Gurdjieff and Soloviev with the information that the Sheikh told him that he (Lubovedsky) has only three more years to live. He is advised to visit a particular monastery in the Himalayas for his final retreat. Lubovedsky must now pack his bags and make his travel arrangements, and Gurdjieff and Soloviev

---

1. In *Meetings with Remarkable Men* Gurdjieff called this the monastery of the Sarmoun Brotherhood, and presented it as an Asiatic organization. The teachings associated with this Central Asian source, which are outlined in *In Search of the Miraculous,* combine material of Eastern and Western origin. For these reasons we shall refer to it simply as an ancient Central Asian teaching. Peter Ouspensky gave his opinion on the matter on a meeting given on 4th November 1937, recorded in the Yale Papers (p. 32). "Question: Where did the schools come from that taught Gurdjieff's school? Ouspensky: It is possible to understand that it was somewhere in Central Asia. But what it was, I don't know. Gurdjieff gave several descriptions, and one of them was very interesting and possible. You must understand the situation: after the Revolution, the possibility to go to that country disappeared. If life were normal, I would go there and try to find this school, but as it is there was no possibility to go there. And probably now everything has disappeared. One school he described was near Kashgar in Chinese Turkestan. But round it there has been war ever since, so probably nothing remains of it now, if there was such a school." Kashgar is just east of the origins of the Syr Darya and Amu Darya river systems. It is now part of China.

2. According to Gurdjieff the members of the Sarmoun Order had developed techniques to extend human life, in an attempt to compensate for the tragic shortness of our species' memory, with each generation repeating the errors of the one before. Gurdjieff was absolutely consistent in his refence to this longevity throughout his life. It is doubtful he meant it literally, but it is hard to determine what he did mean.

are ready to help. Suddenly, somehow, they too are packing their bags. But why they have decided to pack their own bags at this time we are not told.

More generally, we must ask why Gurdjieff decided to leave this teaching after so short a time, when the Brotherhood had apparently known of his coming, and expected him? Gurdjieff had found what was apparently the object of his search, and he is leaving because his friend is sick. The friend himself is being well cared for and does not need Gurdjieff's assistance. In the narrative of *Meetings with Remarkable Men* this unknown teaching is presented as an ancient lineage, descending directly from a teaching that was initiated by the Inner Circle of Humanity in Babylon, some 2,400 years ago. Why would you leave such a teaching after three months?

At this point we make a hypothesis: it may be that the brotherhood, as a condition of transmitting its full teachings to Gurdjieff, made certain requirements of him. Perhaps the teachings would be given only if they were applied in a certain way, or only if Gurdjieff was prepared to take certain vows. Gurdjieff may not have felt himself ready to accept these conditions; he may have needed some time to think. We hypothesize that during his three month visit Gurdjieff established a relationship with the Central Asian Order, with the idea of considering its formal conditions of entry at a later point in time. It may be that the Gods who were engineering the play of the Fourth Way wanted to expose Gurdjieff to this option, as one stage in preparing him to meet those requirements — completely and without reservation — at a later point in time.

Whatever Gurdjieff's reasons for leaving the monastery, on leaving it he and Soloviev rejoined Professor Skridlov, and the other members of the Seekers for Truth, with the aim of exploring a certain region of the Gobi Desert. They were searching for a buried city, for which Professor Skridlov had found significant indications. We note that this represents a considerable step down from the direct contact with the monastery of the Sarmoun Brotherhood! Having explored the Gobi Desert without significant results, Gurdjieff then (in 1899) travelled through Central Asia with Skridlov and made studies of Persian magic. In 1900 Gurdjieff and Skridlov made contact with an Italian monk, Father Giovanni, who belonged to a 'World Brotherhood.' Father Giovanni gave them a discourse on universal religion and provided teachings on the inner and the outer life of man. The presentation of these teachings caused Skridlov to feel that his search was at an end. He prepared to spend the remainder of his life focused on self-realization, with the knowledge that Father Giovanni had given him. This is the beginning of the end of the Seekers for Truth. In *Meetings with Remarkable Men* the episode with Father Giovanni may stand as a critique of the Search mentality, and its preoccupation with adventure and romance. While Father Giovanni is spoken of with the greatest respect, he remains, somehow, a two-dimensional figure.

In 1900 (in the chronology of *Meetings with Remarkable Men*) Gurdjieff set out with the Seekers for Truth from Chardzhou (in Turkmenistan) east across the Pamir Mountains and then south into India. The expedition, while lengthy, brought little result. The group then disbanded and its members went their separate ways.

While the Seekers for Truth dissolved, Gurdjieff's connection to the Tsarist government remained quite intact. On the 23rd of July 1901 Gurdjieff was presented to Tsar Nicholas at Livadia Palace, the Tsar's summer residence in the Crimea. Here the Tsar would meet with various Oriental rulers and Eastern political operatives. According to John Bennett this was the first of several audiences Gurdjieff had with the Tsar. Shortly after his first official connection with the Tsar, Gurdjieff entered Upper Tibet, travelling as a Russian agent. The Russian government had quite definite interests in that country. Tibet, under threat of invasion from Manchu China, had submitted — at different times — for the status of protectorate to both Russia and Britain. Russia was in intense competition with both Britain and China for a sphere of influence on the Tibetan plateau.

Gurdjieff's Tibetan contact was Agwan Dorzhiev, a senior Tibetan official who had a working contact with the Tsar and regularly attended the meetings at Livadia. He was a multilingual political operative who spoke Tibetan, Chinese, and the various Mongolian dialects — while being fluent in both French and Russian. He had the reputation, in some circles, of being a double agent, who worked both for the Tsar and for the 13th Dalai Lama. He was born a Buryat Mongol in 1850 in Russian controlled territory near Lake Baikal. In his youth he entered the great Tibetan monastery at

Ganden, and later transferred to Drepung in the Tibetan capital of Lhasa. He succeeded in establishing himself in the theocratic politics of Tibet, and became one of its governing monastic officials acting as a tutor to the 13th Dalai Lama. He clearly understood the threat that China posed to Tibet and actively promoted alliance with Russia. In a remarkable coup, he managed, with Romanov support, to have a Buddhist temple constructed in the very heart of Orthodox St. Petersburg. As the 13th Dalai Lama began to look more favorably on an alliance with Britain, he came at cross-purposes with Dorzhiev, who, in 1908, told the American Minister in Peking that the Dalai Lama was corrupt, self-seeking, and "willing to abandon Tibet to China."[1] This statement was contradicted by the 13th Dalai Lama's actions, when, in 1912, he proclaimed Tibet's complete independence from China and the European Powers and expelled all Chinese officials from Tibet. In 1914 the Dalai Lama announced that Dorzhiev "did not have the authority to speak for Tibet," and asked that henceforward he "merely work for the benefit of the Buddhist religion." Shortly after this Dorzhiev returned to Russia and established himself in the Buddhist monastery at St. Petersburg, where he remained until 1937, when — during a Stalinist purge — he was charged with treason. He died in police custody in 1938.

Gurdjieff stated that, while in Tibet, he had studied with the "red hat lamas," which is a general term referring to all lamas from the Nyingma, Sakya, and Kagyu Orders. The one Order not included is the "yellow hat" Gelugs-pa Order, to which the Dalai Lama belonged.

GURDJIEFF AND TIBETAN BUDDHISM

It is unlikely that Gurdjieff formally entered one of the Tibetan Buddhist Orders, as they only accepted candidates who were prepared to make a lifetime commitment on the basis of a lengthy novitiate. Gurdjieff may well have worked with lamas connected to the independent sects of the Nyingma Order, of which there were many.[2] With these qualifications, Gurdjieff seems to have had a positive experience of Tibetan

---

1. Sir Charles Temple, *Portrait of a Dalai Lama*, p. 78.
2. Gurdjieff's contact, Agwan Dorzhiev, while highly placed in the Tibetan theocracy, was not a spiritual teacher, but a political operative. In the years 1901–1904 contact with Dorzhiev would not have given access to the 13th Dalai Lama.

Buddhism, as he consistently distinguished 'Lamaism' (Tibetan Buddhism) from 'Buddhism,' and rated it amongst the few highest teachings in the history of Mankind. In *Beelzebub's Tales* he classified 'Saint Lama' (Padmasambhava) as one of the most developed conscious beings in the history of the human race, putting him on a par with the Buddha, Jesus, Moses, and Muhammad.

Gurdjieff came to Tibet at a time when the country was undergoing an internal transition. In the 18th and 19th centuries there had been (from the Buddhist point of view) an aberrant development of the shamanistic/occult side of spiritual practice, particularly within the renegade sects of the Nyingma Order. Most of the authentic teachers of that age (including the 13th Dalai Lama) were connected with an anti-sectarian movement of reform, known as the Rimé movement. This movement came to embrace all four of the Tibetan Orders, and it gave a clear priority to direct work on consciousness, over the acquisition of occult powers. Gurdjieff makes no mention of this movement — which was exactly contemporary with his stay — or of the teachers involved in it. The remarks that Gurdjieff made, at different points in time, about the excesses of Tibetan Buddhism do not apply to the practices that were standard in the major Tibetan Orders at the time of his visit.[3] To take one example, in *Beelzebub's Tales* Gurdjieff describes the Tibetans walling an aspirant into a small enclosed space without light for many years, until the death of the aspirant.[4] This could refer only to an aberrant practice. The longest retreat in the monastic regimen of the Tibetan Orders was seven years, and this occurred at an established location, where the aspirant was supported by a team of observers who made sure he had supplies and was not in any danger. There did exist, within the Kagyu lineage, the practice of one month's sensory deprivation (where the aspirant was walled into an enclosed space) but this was undertaken only with the most careful preparation and oversight. Gurdjieff's comments about Tibetan Buddhist practice suggest that his contact with the red hat lamas was outside of the formal structure of the Tibetan Orders.

Given the prevalence of the study of the occult in Tibet, and given the young Gurdjieff's active interest in that area, it is likely that he acquired the occult powers that he was later to forsake in Tibet.

More generally, it is unlikely that any teaching Gurdjieff received in Tibet had a formative effect on his mature teachings. Tibetan Buddhism emphasizes voidness (Śūnyatā) over the idea of a deity, and the principle of no-self over the principle of a self. Gurdjieff presented a triadic Absolute, which he quite comfortably referred to as

---

3. All of the Tibetan Orders have since published material on their traditional teachings and practices.
4. Gurdjieff, G.I., *All and Everything, First Series, Beelzebub's Tales to His Grandson*, E.P. Dutton & Co., Inc., New York, 1964, p. 260.

> God, and spoke of the Self (or Real 'I') in the same way that the Hindu speaks of the Atman. The Higher Self, or Atman, approach is common to both Sufism and Orthodox Christian monasticism. The no-self non-theistic approach of Tibetan Buddhism fits naturally with the extended periods of sitting mediation that are not, by definition, part of the Fourth Way. The mature Gurdjieff's Fourth Way teaching explicitly did not section off one part of time for self-remembering. It was something you did all the time. Having said this, the movements exercises that Gurdjieff later developed were deeply influenced by his understanding of Tibetan sacred dance, and particularly the Cham dances.

In 1902, after perhaps a year in Tibet, Gurdjieff was shot during a local skirmish of the Tibetan mountain clans. He received care from three European and two Tibetan doctors. The immediate availability of the three European doctors suggests again his status as a government agent. After receiving medical attention, he went into retreat to heal and recover at an oasis at Yangi Hissar in southwest China. This location was renowned for its air and climate. After several months he returned to Tibet to continue his work; that is, his work for the Russian government which allowed him to pursue his personal interest in the practices of Tibetan Buddhism.

In the year 1904, after about three years in Tibet, Gurdjieff was obliged to leave the country, because he had developed hydropsy (edema — the accumulation of fluid beneath the skin and in the cavities of the body). He returned to his family home in Alexandropol to recover, and this probably marked the end of the diplomatic mission that had financed his stay in Tibet. Once he recuperated, Gurdjieff set out for Central Asia, almost certainly with the aim of reconnecting with the monastery he had visited in 1898. At the very beginning of this journey, in what is now Georgia (near the Chiatura railway tunnel), he was caught in a skirmish between Cossacks and Gurians, and received a third bullet wound. He was given immediate medical care, but his recovery proved incomplete. Concerned for his physical health, he decided to return to the oasis at Yangi Hissar, where he had memories of a unique healing experience. He made the long journey under conditions of great hardship, and arrived (in late 1904) on the verge of an internal crisis, brought on by his weakened condition.

At Yangi Hissar Gurdjieff found himself unable to summon the level of consciousness which he had taken to be his own, and which he had previously been able to summon at will. He reached a nadir of self-questioning and despair. He saw clearly the place that the desire for food and the desire for sex had taken in his life, and he saw within himself an uncontrolled tendency for vindictiveness.[1] At this very moment, and in the depth of his despair, an experience of Higher Centers came to him.

> And here also is God!!! Again God! ... Only He is everywhere and with Him everything is connected. ... He is God of all the world, and also of my outer world. I am God also, although only of my inner world ... Whatever is possible or impossible in the sphere of His great world should be possible or impossible in the sphere of my small world.[2]

This experience was something in the line of his fate, and probably both the crisis and the moment of renewal were the result of the intervention of the Gods in his life. In light of this radical separation of consciousness from functions, Gurdjieff was able to make a review of his motives and decisions over the previous few years:

> I, in the process of general life, especially for the last two years, had been spoiled and depraved to the core.[3]

We note that these last two years were the ones spent in Tibet. Gurdjieff concluded that he required, "some kind of continuous perpetuation of the reminding factor" to keep the principle of consciousness separate from the desires and impulses that arise from the functions. He took the vow to "intentionally stop utilizing the exceptional power in my possession ... never to make use of this inherency of mine and thereby to deprive myself from satisfying most of my vices."[4]

Following this oath, *he went directly to a monastery in Central Asia for a retreat of two full years* (c. 1905-1907). In *The Herald of Coming Good*

---

1. Gurdjieff, G.I., *Life is real only then, when "I am"*, All and Everything, Third Series, E.P. Dutton, New York, 1978, p. 21.
2. *Ibid.*, p. 22-23.
3. *Ibid.*, p. 25.
4. *Ibid.*, p. 25.

Figure 2. The Tiger of Turkestan.

Gurdjieff refers to this as "a certain Dervish monastery ... where I had already stayed."[1] John Bennett believed this to be the same monastery that he had visited with Soloviev some six years before.[2] In this view the Dervish monastery of *The Herald of Coming Good* and the Sarmoun Brotherhood mentioned in *Meetings with Remarkable Men* are the same organization — that Gurdjieff was under oath not to reveal. We note this same ambivalence of Dervish and Asiatic terms in reference to the Sarmoun monastery in the text of *Meetings with Remarkable Men,* where Gurdjieff uses the Sufi term 'Shaikh' to refer to the head of the Brotherhood — which is explicitly not a Sufi organization.

---

1. Gurdjieff, G.I., *The Herald of Coming Good*, Sure Fire Press, Edmonds, Washington, 1988, (reprint of Paris 1933), p. 20.
2. Bennett, J.G., *Gurdjieff: Making a New World*, Turnstone Books, London, 1973, p. 64

What reinforces Bennett's theory is that, according to the narrative of *Meetings with Remarkable Men,* Gurdjieff spent only three months at this monastery in 1898, and he mentions only a single short meeting with the Shaikh. A full transmission of the teachings that are recorded in *In Search of the Miraculous,* would — under normal circumstances — require several years. Such a transmission is not simply a matter of sharing information, but involves a testing of the novice's understanding and — on the part of the novice — a willingness to accept certain standards and requirements.

What is decisive in our acceptance of Bennett's theory — equating the Dervish monastery of 1905-7 with the Sarmoun monastery of 1898 — is a reference in Gurdjieff's *Third Series*. Here Gurdjieff states that his program for the *Institute for the Harmonious Development of Man* had been worked out by "honorable and impartial people" who had "already overcome two centuries of their existence."[3] This is a direct reference to the members of the Central Asian monastery described in *Meetings*. Nowhere else does Gurdjieff mention people of more than 200 years old. The working out of the program for the Institute implies an understanding and accord between Gurdjieff and the members of this monastery that did not exist at the time of his 1898 visit. In 1898 he was 1) not ready and 2) not there for long enough.

Following the vow of 1904 at Yangi Hissar, Gurdjieff did feel ready to accept the conditions that had been given in 1898. It is really from the time of his emergence from the second retreat (1905-1907) that Gurdjieff appears as a man under obligation, held accountable to a Higher School. J.G. Bennett describes his impression of the mature Gurdjieff:

> We can see that Gurdjieff was pursuing a clear and consistent plan. ... he was evidently driven by the conviction that his mission was important for mankind, and that the Higher Powers would provide the means to fulfill it ... He gave me the impression of a man who had a well-defined program. He said that he was able to call on help from people who knew the importance of his task. It is impossible to convey the complete assurance with which he threaded his

---

3. Gurdjieff, G.I., *Life is real only then, when "I am",* All and Everything, Third Series, E.P. Dutton, New York, 1978, p. 78-79.

way through the complications of countries devastated by war and revolution.[1]

Through the period 1912-1924 Gurdjieff many times abandoned a particular teaching scenario, and then re-grouped his people in the months following. He constantly tested those around him. But he conveyed very centrally the sense of being *a man with a mission,* a man tasked with a great project.[2]

Gurdjieff was certainly not focused in this way after his first visit to the Central Asian monastery. In his own words, he was, from 1902 to 1904, "spoiled and depraved to the core." One of his nicknames was 'the Tiger of Turkestan.' As we have noted, it is likely that he spent part of his time in Tibet developing his occult powers. But, after 1907, he is the Gurdjieff that we know from *In Search of the Miraculous*. Perhaps, then, he had had his first contact with an authoritative teacher in 1898, was able to establish his personal aim to awaken at Yangi Hissar in 1904, and actually received the major teachings in 1905-7. We could look at the three bullet wounds Gurdjieff received (in Crete in 1896, in Tibet in 1902, and in Georgia in 1904) as a means by which the Gods prepared a physically powerful and independently minded young man for the transmission of a great teaching — that he would be obligated to share with others for the rest of his life. We note that each of these three wounds came from a stray bullet, and each was followed by a positive spiritual experience: the first in Jerusalem was his reunion with Father Evlissi and the Essenes; the second was the healing experience at the oasis at Yangi Hissar; and the third his oath at Yangi Hissar that led ultimately to his return to the monastery in Central Asia. Gurdjieff was not to receive the teaching until he was prepared to be its servant.

When Gurdjieff finally left the anonymous Central Asian monastery in 1907, he established himself in Tashkent (then the capital of Russian Turkestan). In that same year he received the news that his colleague Vitvitskaya was on her deathbed, and he immediately went to Samara, in Southern

---

1. Bennett, J.G., *Gurdjieff: Making a New World,* Turnstone Books, London, 1973, p. 132.
2. *Ibid.,* p. 230.

Russia, to be with her for the last weeks of her life. This visit drew the curtain on his years of search, and Gurdjieff returned to Tashkent to start a new chapter of his life. The years in Tashkent were not years of search, but years of focused preparation for the teaching stage of his life.

In reviewing the years 1884-1907, Gurdjieff had significant contact with: 1) Christian monasticism, 2) Sufism, 3) Tibetan Buddhism, and 4) an unknown source in Central Asia that carried teachings passed down from ancient times. While he did not have a significant contact with Vedantism that we know of, the generalizations that he makes about the Vedantic schools in the record of *In Search of the Miraculous* are accurate. It is likely that the teachings Gurdjieff received from Central Asia were based on a careful assimilation of the teachings of the Vedantic schools. Let us make a brief review of the major sources of Gurdjieff's mature teaching.

Orthodox Christianity gave Gurdjieff the spirituality of his essence: his feeling for Self, Real 'I', and God. In later years, at the Prieuré in France, he regularly invited an Orthodox priest to perform religious observances for the community, and his funeral was held in a Russian Orthodox Church. Orthodox ritual was to remain important for him throughout his life.

The Sufi Traditions gave Gurdjieff exposure to a wide range of Fourth Way techniques applicable to the conditions of everyday life; in other words, the practical side of self-remembering. Additionally, Gurdjieff was well versed in Sufi dance technique. Much of his knowledge of healing, and of the detailed working of the four lower centers, came from Sufi sources.

Tibetan Buddhism gave Gurdjieff exposure to a fully formed theocracy, and an environment in which esotericism was pursued at a high level. In a different way, and from a different point of view, he was no doubt interested in the accumulation of the occult knowledge that existed in Tibet. It was here that he saw, at first hand, both the use and the abuse of occult powers. The positive application of these powers was in the area of healing, and he had a great respect for Tibetan medicine. He himself worked his whole life as a healer. He also studied the sacred dances of Tibet, and his own dance company later replicated several of these dances in Paris and New York.

The Unknown Central Asian Teaching was probably the direct source of: 1) the system that Gurdjieff taught, 2) the general guidelines for the kind of teaching organization he tried to create, and 3) certain aims behind his whole teaching project that were never made public.

Clearly, we must assess the legacy of the Central Asian school in a different way than we do the others. To that end we shall now examine what Gurdjieff so adroitly skirted in *Meetings with Remarkable Men*: the source of the system that he received.

The Teaching Found

THE SOURCE TRADITION

The remarkable body of teaching material contained in *In Search of the Miraculous* had been thoroughly internalized by Gurdjieff, but it almost certainly did not come from him — and he would never reveal where it did come from.[1] In the previous section we have suggested that Gurdjieff was under oath not to reveal his source. If the Brotherhood were as prescient as Gurdjieff suggests they were, they might have seen trouble coming their way, which would have heightened their desire for invisibility.

What is common in Gurdjieff's references to this unknown source (in *Meetings with Remarkable Men*, the *Herald of Coming Good*, and the *Third Series*) is that he felt that it was a great and ancient school in the final phase of its existence. It appears that this school reinforced the personal aim he

---

1. Both Peter Ouspensky and John Bennett, who knew Gurdjieff well and were familiar with his manner of thinking and expression, were certain that the system itself did not originate from him. Bennett states, "If Gurdjieff invented this cosmology, he was a prodigious original genius. His power was in his quest and his determination to fulfil his mission. That he was not a trained thinker is quite clear from the unfinished state of so many of his speculations." See Bennett, J.G., *Gurdjieff: Making a New World*, Turnstone Books, London, 1973., p. 265.

Figure 3. Gurdjieff in Kashgar, China.

had established at Yangi Hissar and gave him direction as a teacher. It also provided him with the teaching material that he was to use for the remainder of his life.

We shall argue here that the cosmological system Gurdjieff received has clear roots in European Hermeticism. Yet Gurdjieff's depiction of the monastery, and of the teaching lineage, is consistently Asiatic. How did an Asiatic/Mesopotamian teaching find its final cosmological expression in Western Hermetic terminology? Let us review the material that is available to us.

The Asiatic/Mesopotamian heritage is always connected, in Gurdjieff's mind, with the idea of an Inner Circle of Humanity. This is, indeed, a theme in Gurdjieff's life: from his boyhood exposure to the myth of the Imastun Brotherhood; to the references to an ancient 'school behind schools' in the pages of the Merkhavat; to the Byzantine manuscripts he later unearthed at Ani. All of these refer to an organization of Mesopotamian origin, which pre-dated the prophets by many centuries. As Gurdjieff's researches continued, it seemed to him that a school of Mesopotamian origin had survived the Persian Conquest of Mesopotamia in 539 BC, the Byzantine Conquest in 626 AD, and the Islamic Conquest in 633 AD, shifting its base to Central Asia in the 7th century, and networking with the Khorasanian Sufi Orders. It was almost certainly from this organization (whatever its real name) that Gurdjieff received his mature concept of the Inner Circle of Humanity. Let us review this idea, as Gurdjieff presented it to his students in 1916.

> This circle consists of people who have attained the highest development possible for man, each one of whom possesses individuality in the fullest degree, that is to say, an indivisible 'I,' all forms of consciousness possible for man, full control over these states of consciousness, the whole of knowledge possible for man, and a free and independent will. They cannot perform actions opposed to their understanding or have an understanding which is not expressed by actions. At the same time there can be no discords among them, no differences of understanding. Therefore, their activity is entirely coordinated and leads to one common aim without any kind of compulsion because it is based upon a common and identical understanding.[1]

It seems that only the great prophets of history could have met such a standard. Did Gurdjieff believe that such an inner circle has always existed? Has it existed intermittently, only in certain times and places? Or is this what the Inner Circle of Humanity would have to be, if it did exist? Is the inner circle — and the level of work described — inclusive of the disembodied conscious beings who work with humanity?

Gurdjieff leaves the matter open. Probably he saw the Inner Circle of Humanity as having existed intermittently through the history of the species. The real 'control center,' in relation to microcosmos man, is C Influence. But humanity has seldom risen to the point where there has been an inner circle capable of sustaining an open connection to C Influence. What

---

1. Ouspensky, P.D., *In Search of the Miraculous*, Routledge & Kegan Paul, London, 1977, pp. 310-311. Here the esoteric circle of humanity is equated with the Inner Circle of Humanity.

we can be sure of is that Gurdjieff felt the Inner Circle of Humanity, in whatever form it appeared in history, had to have a working connection to C Influence.

Our interpretation of Gurdjieff's view is that the Inner Circle is a latent potential in humanity, which has, at certain points, and for certain periods of time, become active. This Inner Circle is latent in man in the same way that Higher Centers are latent in man. Higher Centers are ready to appear at any time, but, for the most part, man is not ready for them.

Gurdjieff pursues this analogy and describes this latent potential in the most striking way in one of his 1916 talks.

> The process of evolution, of that evolution which is possible for humanity as a whole, is completely analogous to the process of evolution possible for the individual man. And it begins with the same thing, namely, a certain group of cells gradually becomes conscious; then it attracts to itself other cells, subordinates others, and gradually makes the whole organism serve its aims and not merely eat, drink, and sleep. This is evolution and there can be no other kind of evolution. In humanity as in individual man everything begins with the formation of a conscious nucleus. All the mechanical forces of life fight against the formation of this conscious nucleus in humanity, in just the same way as all mechanical habits, tastes and weaknesses fight against conscious self-remembering in man.[2]

If we follow the historical narrative of *Beelzebub's Tales,* it does not present such an inner circle as being active through the longer life of the species. It is rather that, because man has been created from a Higher Level, there is a certain tendency — under optimal circumstances — for such an inner circle to come into being. This tendency has been realized in greater or lesser degree in different times and places. If one views the Inner Circle of Humanity as *being* C Influence – in the manner of Theosophy – then, of course, it is always active and always existent, but if one views it as *a working link between C Influence and school on earth,* we cannot presume that it is always, or even usually, there.

---

2. *Ibid.,* p. 308.

What is clear from all that Gurdjieff writes about the organization he contacted in Central Asia is that it was not, at the time he contacted it, a direct expression of the Work of the Inner Circle of Humanity. It may have carried something of the legacy of the Inner Circle of Humanity, but it was not, in 1898, functioning as an invisible 'spiritual center' for the world — understanding the purposes for which all its different civilizations were created, monitoring the development of all different schools, and directly connected with the level above the human. Here we pause to make another distinction. While not *being* the Inner Circle of Humanity, it may yet have had a connection to Higher School, for there are individual schools — that are not the Inner Circle of Humanity — that have achieved a working contact with C Influence. These schools are given a particular task, such as the creation of a religion or a new civilization. They are often barely able to get the job done before the link with Higher School dissolves, and all is once again absorbed into the level one below.

It is possible that the ancient school that Gurdjieff contacted in Central Asia had been, in Babylonian and Chaldean times, an actual realization of the Inner Circle of Humanity, and had sustained itself in that role for some centuries. When it ceased to function as the Inner Circle of Humanity it continued as a C Influence school, maintaining both its contact with the level one above, and the memory of what it once had been. The fact that it ceased to function as the Inner Circle of Humanity may have been no reflection on the work of its members, but a reflection on the state of humanity as a whole. Even after the Islamic invasion it remained a special 'school behind the schools' in Central Asia. Gurdjieff probably encountered this organization in the last decade of its existence, and met the last generation of its members who had known direct contact with Influence C.

So what, more specifically, is the history of this unusual school that was once a vehicle for the Inner Circle of Humanity? Where are the historical traces of its greater influence and centrality? Let us review what we might call our 'Mesopotamian inheritance.'

A study of the Mesopotamian family of civilizations, beginning from ancient Sumeria, explains the centrality of the Tigris-Euphrates river basin for the work of an Inner Circle. We know historically that a single priest caste was in place in that region for five millennia, from the historical origin of ancient Sumeria until — at least — the time of the Persian invasion of Mesopotamia in 539 BC. This same priest caste sustained itself, in different forms, through many successive regimes. In its final iteration as the Chaldean priest caste, it made a remarkable synthesis of the Mesopotamian, Egyptian, Vedic, and Zoroastrian teachings. Many of the Great Schools of humanity of that time, including the Egyptian, the Vedic, and the Zoroastrian, had a presence in Mesopotamia.

THE MESOPOTAMIAN CURRENT

Ancient Sumeria is the earliest developed civilization of which we have record. There are architectural and ceramic remains dating from 5500 BC. It provides us with the earliest evidence of written language on the planet. The Sumerians had a developed mathematics, with a combined base-ten/base-sixty number system. They had a profound knowledge of astronomy and astrology, and they were the first people that we know of to map the constellations. The universal conventions of 24 hours to the day, 60 minutes to the hour, and 360 degrees to a circle are inherited directly from the Sumerians.

Gurdjieff pursues this analogy and describes this latent potential in the most striking way in one of his 1916 talks As we noted, Gurdjieff believed that both Sumeria and Dynastic Egypt were sourced from a prior civilization that has been lost to history. In *Beelzebub's Tales* Gurdjieff referred to the parent civilization of the Sumerian Civilization as the Tikliamishian Civilization, which he described as being located in what is now the Karakum Desert, east of the Caspian Sea, in present day Turkmenistan. It was bordered on the northeast by the Amu Darya River. Indeed, there are extensive unexcavated archaeological sites in this area.[1]

At whatever point the Sumerians originated, as a people they make their appearance in recorded history at about 5500 BC: a theocratic civilization

---

1. When Gurdjieff sources both Sumeria and Egypt in a prior civilization (which in *Beelzebub's Tales* he gives as Atlantis), he is referring to a civilization that existed millennia before, during the last Ice Age. The Tikliamishian civilization is presented as having existed *immediately before* the Sumerian, and *long after* the Atlantian.

ruled by a priest caste, and without a developed military caste. Ancient Sumeria existed without outside interference for 3,000 years, until about 2500 BC. From the very first traces we have of this civilization they show a developed art and architecture. They were the carriers of a great mythology, which, in different forms, became the mythology of all the peoples to follow them in the Tigris-Euphrates river basin: the Akkadians, the Assyrians, the Amorites, the Babylonians, the Kassites, and the Chaldeans. That is a lifespan of approximately 5,000 years, outlasting Dynastic Egypt by two full millennia. A single priest caste continued intact through all of the different conquests and changes of regime that occurred. In some centuries it ruled directly and in others it was involved in rule through its influence on a ruling dynasty. The original myths continued, and were reconstituted, millennia after millennia. Let us briefly review the chronology.

ANCIENT MESOPOTAMIA

As we noted, the Sumerians inhabited the mouth of the Tigris-Euphrates river basin from at least 5500 BC. In about 2500 BC the Akkadians entered the Southern reach of the river basin, and the Assyrians the Northern. The Akkadians conquered the Sumerians, and there was a fusion of the Akkadian and Sumerian peoples, with the politically dominant Akkadians absorbed into an essentially Sumerian culture. This pattern of political dominance and cultural absorption was to be repeated in the later arrival of the Amorites, the Kassites, and the Chaldeans.

After the fusion of the Akkadian and Sumerian peoples, the Amorites entered the Southern basin, and in about 1780 BC they led the Sumero-Akkadians against the Assyrians. From this time we see the rise of Babylon. The 6th King of Babylon, Hammurabi (1810-1750 BC), established an empire which included the greater part of the Tigris-Euphrates river basin, pushing the Assyrians into the Northern Arm of the Tigris River. The Babylonian Empire had an ecumenic quality, and it was Hammurabi who formulated the first code of law in human history.

The Assyrians reasserted themselves in 911 BC, creating the empire of the greatest physical extent in the Mesopotamian cycle, known to modern scholars as the Neo-Assyrian Empire.

Gurdjieff placed special emphasis on the Mesopotamian Tradition because he felt that in Babylon, in the 9th century BC, under the Neo-Assyrian Empire, there was a synthesis of the understanding of the Egyptian and the Mesopotamian schools. Between 912 BC and 612 BC the Neo-Assyrian Empire included Babylon and *all of Egypt,* and many Egyptians relocated to Babylon as a great cultural, religious, and administrative center. Even during the Neo-Assyrian Empire, the Assyrian capitol of Nineveh never rivalled Babylon as a cultural center.

At the end of the 6th century BC the Babylonians, under Chaldean leadership, overthrew the Assyrians, and the Babylonian-Chaldean priest caste became authoritative both in a religious and in a political sense. In the Chaldean phase of the Babylonian Empire (626-539 BC) there was an assimilation of the Vedic and Zoroastrian teachings. The Chaldean priest caste became a center for the Great World Religions of its time. It is in this period that Babylon becomes known as one of the wonders of the ancient world.

With the Achaemenid conquest of Mesopotamia in 539 BC (under Cyrus II) there was a fundamental change in the balance of power in the region, and while the city of Babylon was not sacked, and continued prosperous under Persian rule, its role as a religious center gradually declined.

We see here, between the 9th and the 5th centuries BC, a historical context in which there is the potential for an Inner Circle of Humanity to function.

Generalizing from Gurdjieff's writings in *Beelzebub's Tales,* and translating its torturous language, he believed that a single school, pre-existing the Biblical flood, worked actively behind the scenes — first with the Sumerians, then with the Babylonians, then with the Chaldeans, and then — following Cyrus II's conquest of the area in 539 BC — with the Persian Magi. At some point it shifted north, into the general area of what is now Kyrgyzstan/Uzbekistan/Tajikistan. Finally, after the Islamic conquest in 650 AD, it worked with the emergent Sufi schools. It began with and it retained a 'universalist' perspective: it was a school for Mankind. Gurdjieff believed that this school was a locus, at different points, for the Inner Circle of Humanity. As the centuries followed, and as the world changed around it, it gradually ceased to function as such. It nonetheless retained its integrity. It is this school that Gurdjieff represented as the Sarmoun Brotherhood in *Meetings with Remarkable Men.* At the turn of the 20th century the members of this Order probably realized that they were in their last generation. Peter Ouspensky later pointed out that, after the outbreak of the First World War and the Bolshevik Revolution, the area radically destabilized, and has been a locus of war ever since. Indeed, it is as much a locus of war now as it was at the time of Ouspensky's death.

We shall briefly review how this school is presented, in the final phase of its existence, in *Meetings with Remarkable Men*. We take into account that this presentation is more symbolic than descriptive.[1] The monastery itself is likened to a medieval fortress, with three courts, one within the next. These are probably symbolic of the exoteric, mesoteric, and esoteric circles of the Order — in the higher definition of those terms given in *In Search of the Miraculous*. Here the exoteric would be "the outer circle of the inner part of humanity" which is, at the very least, the level of Man Number Four.

On their arrival at the Order's Monastery, Gurdjieff and his travelling companion Soloviev are given food and lodging in the outer court. There Gurdjieff receives a message from his erstwhile patron, and fellow member of the Seekers for Truth, Prince Lubovedsky. The Prince, Gurdjieff, and Soloviev meet daily in an inner court. After two weeks Gurdjieff and Soloviev are invited to the third or innermost court of the monastery, to meet the head of the order, who is called the Sheikh. Nothing is said about this person, or about his conversation with the two young men. However, following the conversation with the Sheikh, they "entered into the life of the monastery."

Gurdjieff is here presenting himself as a member of the exoteric circle. Lubovedsky, who has accepted all the requirements of the Order, is of the mesoteric circle, and the Sheikh is a member of the esoteric circle of humanity.

The only substantive description Gurdjieff gives of life in the inner court relates to the dances that are performed there. These are performed by priestesses, who are selected from childhood, and consecrated to the service of God. They are taught the sacred dances — which are examples of ancient objective art — from the time of their arrival at the monastery. The sacred dances are performed daily in the innermost court. We may note that this population of resident priestesses, trained from childhood to sacred dances, sharply distinguishes the Sarmoun Brotherhood from any Sufi organization, Naqshbandi, Mevlevi, or Bektashi. Gurdjieff takes great pains

---

1. See Gurdjieff, G.I., *Meetings with Remarkable Men*, (All and Everything, Second Series), E.P. Dutton & Company, New York, 1963, pp. 159-161.

to describe the "dancing apparatuses" — created in ancient times — which are used to train the priestesses.

> Each apparatus consisted of a smooth column, higher than a man, which was fixed on a tripod. From this column, in seven places, there projected specially designed branches, which in their turn were divided into seven parts of different dimensions, each successive part decreasing in length and width.[2]

This suggests an imbrication of the law of three and the law of seven, resulting in a hierarchical structure, with each of the seven branches consisting of seven parts. We find a parallel interpretation of human movement, attributed to an ancient Babylonian school, in *Beelzebub's Tales*.

> The learned beings of this time had already long been aware that every posture and movement of every being in general, in accordance with the same Law of Sevenfoldness, always consists of seven what are called 'mutually-balanced-tensions' arising in seven independent parts of their whole, and that each of these seven parts in their turn consists of seven different what are called 'lines-of-movement,' and each line has seven what are called 'points-of-dynamic-concentration;' and all this that I have just described, being repeated in the same way and in the same sequence but always on a diminishing scale, is actualized in the minutest sizes of the total bodies called 'atoms.'[3]

Both here, and in his descriptions of the sacred dances, Gurdjieff attributes an understanding of the law of seven to this ancient Sumerian/Babylonian teaching.[4]

It is clear that Gurdjieff needed contact with this school to launch his own Fourth Way project. He was not ready to be a teacher before his contact with the brotherhood. The contact thus represents a fateful moment in

---

2. *Ibid.*, pp. 163-164. Gurdjieff replicated these apparatuses for training in the movements, and the replicas still exist with the Institute G. I. Gurdjieff in Paris.

3. Gurdjieff, G.I., *All and Everything, First Series, Beelzebub's Tales to his Grandson*, E.P. Dutton & Co., Inc., New York, 1964, p. 476.

4. For the law of seven see The Hermetic Teaching below.

the history of the Fourth Way. But, while the contact may have had some relation to the designs of Higher School, it was not — we have argued — a direct contact with Higher School itself. The Central Asian school Gurdjieff connected with had once had a direct connection to Higher School, but in its last years this connection probably only existed in the memory of its older members. To clarify: any connection with Higher Forces exists *outside of time*. The surviving members of this school (whom Gurdjieff always represents as being extremely old) may have *had* a direct connection with Higher Forces in their earlier years. For them, of course, this point of contact is permanent, and they are able to represent it to others. But this does not mean Higher Forces are *still actively managing* the organization itself, and working directly with the new people who come to it (for example Prince Lubovedsky). If the active role of the school, as a working link between Mankind and Higher School, has been completed in the line of time, then the Gods will not actively engage the new people coming to it. If the Gods have withdrawn their involvement, then the next generation of students (who will still have conscious teachers) will know of C Influence only from the report of those who did have contact with them. And the generation following will have only the written record.

Having said all of this, Higher School probably did preside over the meeting of Gurdjieff and the Central Asian brotherhood — without directly revealing themselves. The Hermetic system used by the brotherhood would originally have been the result of direct contact with Higher School itself. And so the transference of that system to another school (and thus its survival in a different context) would likely be monitored by Higher School. The conscious beings of the brotherhood would have been aware of this, and this would have disposed them to extend themselves to Gurdjieff.

We have noted that nothing in the 1898 contact with the brotherhood, described in *Meetings with Remarkable Men*, suggests the conditions necessary for a transmission of the system to Gurdjieff. The Sheikh simply has a brief personal meeting with Gurdjieff and Soloviev, after which they "enter into the general life of the monastery." The references to the 1905-7 contact in the *Third Series* (1930) do suggest such a transmission.

> ... many years ago, before the organization of the Institute, when I planned and worked out this program in detail ... I had to address myself for advice and direction ... to honorable and impartial people ... who, by the way ... had already overcome two centuries of their existence and some of whom were bold enough to hope to surmount even the third century ...[1]

As we noted, Gurdjieff only ever referred to people several hundred years old in relation to the Sarmoun Brotherhood. There is a second mention of such an agreement with "honorable and impartial people" in Central Asia in *The Herald of Coming Good* (1932).

> At the very beginning, when I had finally decided to organize the Institute on the principles mentioned in this booklet, and was looking for a suitable country in which to put this into practice, I foresaw certain possible changes in the conditions of ordinary life and decided therefore, in any eventuality, to confide my intentions to a "brotherhood" (a kind of monastery existing in the very heart of Asia), with a view to securing in certain ways their future cooperation.
>
> As a result of long discussions about all sorts of mutual obligations which, on my side, were chiefly on the grounds of my future religious and moral actions, and, on their side, were on the grounds of guiding, in strict accordance with the means indicated by me, the inner world of people whom I would confide to them, we came to a certain agreement.[2]

The obligation on the side of the brotherhood is unclear, and Gurdjieff does not offer further explanation. He does say that after his arrival in Tashkent he sent some people to visit the brotherhood's monastery.[3] These would

---

1. Gurdjieff, G.I., *Life is real only then, when "I am"*, All and Everything, Third Series, E.P. Dutton, New York, 1978, p. 78-79.
2. Gurdjieff, G.I., *The Herald of Coming Good*, Sure Fire Press, Edmonds, Washington, 1988, p. 59.
3. *Ibid*. In this reference Gurdjieff says that he arrived in Russian Turkestan in 1911. (Tashkent was the capital of Russian Turkestan.) Gurdjieff is often contradictory with respect to dates. In *Meetings with Remarkable Men* he states that he

have been his early 'experimental' students, but we hear no more of them. Certainly none of the students in Moscow or St. Petersburg (where Gurdjieff relocated in 1912) were sent to a monastery in Central Asia. This apparent lapse of the brotherhood side of the obligation may relate to changes that were occurring in the part of Central Asia where the brotherhood had its base (Kyrgyzstan/Uzbekistan/Tajikistan). The area was destabilized during the period 1914-1917, due to World War I and the Russian Revolution. We know from Bennett's references that through the 1930s and 1940s Gurdjieff maintained contact with individuals in this area, and sought advice from them.[1]

The program of work of Gurdjieff's Institute was, then, an implementation of what had been decided in Central Asia in 1907. This would have included: the principle of developing exoteric, mesoteric, and esoteric circles; the means of doing that; the application of three lines of work; the actual work tools used; and the cosmology.

THE HERMETIC TEACHING

Before beginning this section, we must pause to say that if you, the reader, are not fascinated by things like the enneagram, the table of hydrogens, and the food diagram (as the author is, perhaps to excess) you can skip on to the following section without losing the narrative line of this book.

While we can say little about the source tradition Gurdjieff contacted in Central Asia, the cosmological system he received from that tradition is Hermetic. Hermeticism is an approach to human evolution based on the study of cosmic laws, and, on the basis of an understanding of those laws, subordinating the lower parts of one's being to the higher, bringing oneself, progressively, under a fewer number of laws and liberating one's higher faculties. In ancient times Hermeticism was known for its combination of faith and reason.

---

spent five years in Tashkent, and we know he arrived in Moscow on or near New Year's Day 1912. (See Gurdjieff, G.K., *Meetings with Remarkable Men*, All and Everything, Second Series, E.P. Dutton & Company, New York, 1963, p. 270.).

1. Bennett, J.G., *Gurdjieff: Making a New World*, Turnstone Books, London, 1973, p. 111 and p. 132.

Hermeticism made its appearance in or about the second century AD as a result of the fusion of ancient teachings related to the proto-science of alchemy and Greek cosmology:

Ancient teachings related to the proto-science of alchemy developed, in parallel but connected lines, in Mesopotamia and Egypt. The core of this science is the study of the transmutation of matter, from coarser substances to more refined substances, in the context of a living universe, where — ultimately — the finer matters regulate the coarser matters. The ancient alchemical teachings were originally related to experimentation made in the development of medicines, the creation of dyes, and glassmaking. But in the inner teachings of the alchemical schools, the reference to visible or physical matter is largely analogical. The ancient alchemists were most directly concerned with the invisible energy fields that are the context of human life. This would include the matter of human perception, and more refined matters that lie beyond our immediate sense-perception. From the ancient science of alchemy comes the representation of the universe as a hierarchy of interpenetrating energy fields of different densities.

Greek cosmology includes particularly the ideas of cosmos, microcosm, and macrocosm, and the Orphic, Pythagorean, and Neo-Platonic conceptions of a cosmic harmony uniting the different levels of the universe. Greek cosmology presents us with the principle of self-transcendence, linking the different levels of a living whole.

The Hermetic teachings presented in *In Search of the Miraculous* include the more recent understandings of Renaissance Hermeticism, and register the influence of modern western science. Peter Ouspensky said that, in his opinion, the source of this system was Oriental, but the presentation Western.

The similarities of the cosmology Gurdjieff received from the brotherhood to certain of the cosmological speculations of Renaissance Hermeticism are undeniable. Yet even the most developed of the Renaissance cosmologies lack the remarkable integration of Gurdjieff's system. The enneagram itself is unique. It is the seamless synthesis of the law of three and the law of seven, describing the self-contained system of cosmoses which comprises the Macrocosm of Creation — sourced in a triadic Absolute. It places man, and his potentials, precisely within this framework. This material, in such a complete state of synthesis, *comes from a Higher Source.*

We noted above that Gurdjieff believed that the law of seven came from the Sumerian/Babylonian line of transmission. But the teaching presented in *In Search of the Miraculous* goes beyond the law of seven. In the legacy of the Mesopotamian family of civilizations there is no enneagram, no system of cosmoses comprising a Macrocosm, and no table of hydrogens. No trace of such a synthesis has been found in the Sumerian, Babylonian, Chaldean, or Sufi teachings. Where, then, did this material come from?

To make a meaningful search for the precursors of this system, we must review the system itself. Here we are not trying to explicate its finer points, but just to suggest the general nature of its content, and the essential connectedness of the different diagrams and symbols. We begin with the enneagram.

The enneagram shows a circle with two figures inside of it: a triangle, and a star-like figure. In Figure 4, the triangle is depicted in a serrated line and the star-like figure in a solid line. The circle shows nine points of contact with the two inner figures. These are numbered, in a clockwise direction, beginning from one o'clock.

Six of the nine points of contact come from contact with the star-like figure. These are numbered 1, 2, 4, 5, 7, and 8. Three of the points of contact come from the triangular inner figure. These are numbered 9, 3, and 6. As you move clockwise round the circle from point 1, the six points of contact of the star-like figure represent the critical or transitional moments in the life of a cosmos. These six transitional moments thus represent the unfolding of the life of a cosmos in the line of time. In the movement through these six points there is normally no transcendence, as most cosmoses — at least on our level — do not realize their potential. The three points of the inner circle add the movement towards transcendence. If this movement does occur, the cosmos will connect with the life of the higher cosmos that contains it. These three points appear only in the life of an ascending being. The combination of the inner and the outer figures thus shows the universal pattern of upward and downward movement, which links all cosmoses

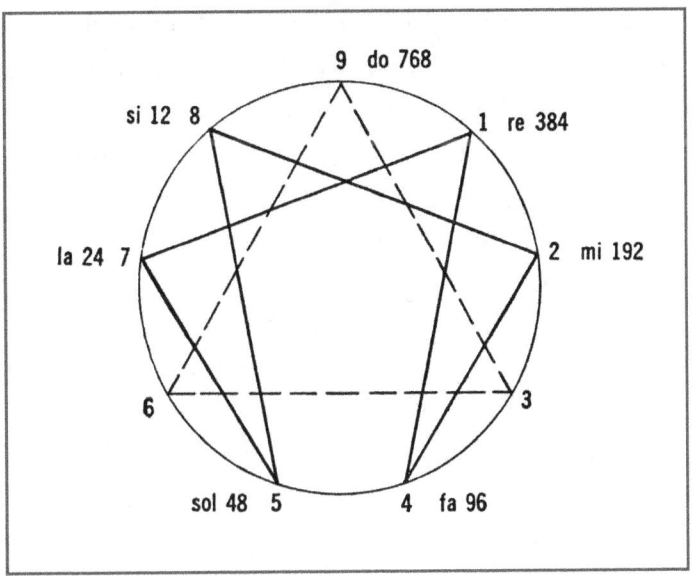

Figure 4. The Enneagram.

comprising the Macrocosm. At the same time, it shows the potential path of development for the entities inhabiting each level of the Macrocosm.

The figure can also be used to represent the life of the Macrocosm as a whole. Viewed from the top down (beginning at point 9) it reveals the pattern of Creation that gives form to the multiple cosmoses comprising the Macrocosm. Viewed from the bottom up (beginning at point 1) it reveals the successive densities of matter at different levels of the Macrocosm, and the moments of transcendence that link those levels. The image shown above has, added to it, the hydrogen numbers of the different substances that comprise the human experience. But you can apply the hydrogen numbers of any created being in the universe to the nine points of the enneagram.

As we noted the inner figure touches the circle at three points, and the outer figure touches it at six. If you add the point at the apex of the triangle to the six points created by the star (the pattern of life-in-time) you have seven points. These seven points represent the Mesopotamian law of seven. The seventh point is connected to the six points of the star-like figure, not as one of them, but as linking the six points (showing the line of time) to what is outside of time: the moment of birth and death. In an ascending being, however, this seventh point is not the mechanical moment of birth-and-death. It is the moment of transcendence into a higher cosmos: not birth but *rebirth* on a higher level. The vehicle that carried the evolving entity through the six points is shed (or dies) but the transcendent entity directly continues.

The apex point, taken as a moment of transcendence, cannot come into being without the enabling shocks that come at the two base points of the triangle. These two shocks come from without, introducing additional energy, or finer hydrogens. When these shocks have a right effect (when they are rightly used by the entity who experiences them), they enable the moment of transcendence at the apex, making the life a total of nine points. When there is no transcendence, there are only the six points of the outer figure, plus the mechanical moment of birth-and-death. The two base point shocks are thus related *only* to the potential transcendence at the apex. If these shocks fail to produce the required effect (if they are not used, or transformed, by the entity experiencing them), then the six points describe the life of that entity in time, and the seventh point signals either: 1) the repetition of that life, 2) the experience of an equivalent life, or 3) the cycling down into a more limited life form. The first and second alternatives occur if the two shocks have not been used. The third alternative might occur if either of the shocks had been used in the *wrong* way. If both shocks are used in the *right* way, they produce transcendence, and the apex point becomes the birth of a cosmos self-realized. The total of nine points represents the pattern of *the law of three and the law of seven working together*.

In sum, in the life of an ascending being in the line of time there are two enabling shocks, which are shown at the two base points of the triangle. These come at gaps, or intervals, in the series of contact points of the six-pointed star and the containing circle. They are, if you will, pauses, in which the forward momentum of the life is interrupted. In these pauses energy is liable to slip back to its original level. When these intervals are bridged (by the effort of the entity who receives the shocks), the vibrational level increases, allowing for transcendence at the apex point.

The combination of the law of three and the law of seven is also known as the law of octaves, because the placing of the two intervals corresponds exactly to the placing of the intervals in the heptatonic musical scale. In the system, reference to the law of octaves focuses attention on the timing of the intervals and the requirement of bridging them. When you are thinking of the intervals you are thinking in terms of completion.

Taking all of this into account, we could say that the enneagram itself describes *the dynamic of upward and downward movement* within the Macrocosm. This is complemented by the table of hydrogens, presented by Gurdjieff to the St. Petersburg Group in 1916, which describes *the substantiality of the different levels* of the Macrocosm.

The table of hydrogens is an alchemical table, combining the graded hierarchy of the Macrocosm with the substances corresponding to each level. These substances are represented as sets of interpenetrating vibrational levels. In the science of alchemy, substances are defined by their stability and their consequent ability to interact with and influence other substances. A substance can be an individual element (for example, gold), a stable chemical compound, or a stable system on a larger scale. The table of hydrogens presents the traditional esoteric teaching of the 'quaternity of matter.' In this view a substance — on any scale — is the product of the interaction of three vibrational levels. The substantial unity that results represents the fourth aspect. It is this unity which enables interaction with other substances. Within the dynamic of the macrocosm, all of these substances, as they exist on many different scales, and all of the interactions they support, are required to sustain the whole. They are, if you will, the interdependent links in a chain. They are similar, in principle, to the alchemical cosmic substances. In the system the three components of the triadic interaction are represented in a generic way, with reference to element names: Carbon, Oxygen, Nitrogen. The interaction of C/O/N is represented in its unity by H, or Hydrogen, which is again a generic reference. The vibrational level of the substance is then given by a number connected with the Hydrogen, e.g., H_{12}. Thus matter, at any level, is four things: the interaction of C/O/N plus the averaged resultant H. It is significant for our theory of the origin of Gurdjieff's cosmology that all of these elements (C/O/N/H) were discovered before the outbreak of the Napoleonic War. At that time scientists saw the understanding of these elements as a key to understanding substances on every scale.[1][2]

Figure 5 shows the relation of the hydrogen levels that comprise the universe (the three columns on the right) to the law of octaves (the column on the left). The three columns of hydrogens show, on each single horizontal line, the interactions characteristic of a particular level.

---

1. The elements Oxygen and Nitrogen were discovered by Rutherford in 1772. Hydrogen was discovered by Cavendish in 1776. Carbon by Lavoisier in 1789.

2. We note that the hydrogen numbers (3, 6, 12, 24 and so forth) correspond to the numbers of the Worlds, given in the Overview. This correspondence needs clarification. We shall summarize some points given in detail in *In Search of the Miraculous*. The list of Worlds and their properties is given on pp. 76-86. The list of cosmoses and their properties is given on pp. 205-211. To summarize what is said in those pages: Hydrogens are not Worlds, but they correspond to Worlds. To understand the idea of Hydrogens you must understand the theory of Cosmoses in relation to the theory of Worlds. Worlds are general (universal) levels in the Ray of Creation; the Ray of Creation is a hierarchy of Worlds. Cosmoses give form to the different levels of the Ray of Creation; the Ray of Creation is also a hierarchy of cosmoses. The levels of Worlds and the levels of Cosmoses correspond down to the level of World 12. For example, the Protocosmos is formed in World 1, the Megalocosmos is formed in World 3, and so forth. After World 12 (the site of the Deuterocosmos, which corresponds astronomically to our sun) things become complicated. There is a cosmos connected to the relation of the earth to the sun's other planets (the Mesocosmos), and there is a cosmos connected to the relation between organic life on earth and the other planets and the moon (the Tritocosmos). There is a complicated downward transition of cosmoses through to the microcosmos man. (This is what Gurdjieff called the lateral octave of the Ray of Creation.) The cosmoses following the Deuterocosmos do not correspond to Worlds in a one-to-one relationship. They are composite: that is, they each function on a range of energies drawn from different Worlds. These energies are present in them as hydrogens. So, for example, man, a microcosmos centered in World 24, processes hydrogens derivative of both higher and lower Worlds. A man, centered in World 24 may experience hydrogen 12, which is for him a special or elevating experience. But he does not, for that reason, enter World 12; he just gets a taste of it. This taste can take many forms. His experience is still centered in World 24. Man has access to a wide range of hydrogens. At the same time man can also experience different Worlds, but this is a different thing. The change of Worlds is a general change of state that affects his entire experience at once.

We can relate this 'schema of the macrocosm' to the scale of an individual psychology. In other words, we can relate the numbered vibrational levels of matter (the different hydrogen numbers) to the enneagram's movement of transcendence, to produce a view of the inner workings of the human microcosm. This has been analyzed on the basis of the incom-

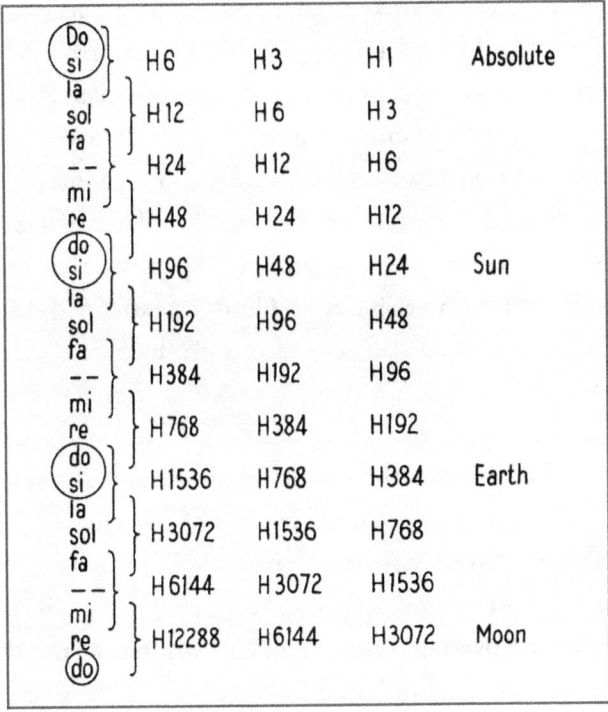

Figure 5. Table of Hydrogens.

ing substances/vibrations through which the microcosm constitutes and reconstitutes itself. There are three different levels of incoming substances: food, air, and impressions. These three sets of incoming substances are processed in such a way as to sustain the human organism. Gurdjieff represents each of the three intake systems as a story in the three-storied house of man. The intake of impressions is shown in the top story, the intake of air is shown in the middle story, and the intake of food is shown in the lower story. Collectively these are known as the three foods, and this visual representation is called the Food Diagram.

The food that we eat enters at do 768 in the lowest story of the food diagram. Air enters at do 192, in the middle story, and impressions enter at do 48 in the upper story.

In Figure 6 we notice that the incoming impressions (at do 48) produce related effects and new chemical combinations that impact all three stories. They can generate hydrogens as high as 6 and 12. Unfortunately, this series of effects does not usually occur. It requires that a special quality of attention be brought to the incoming impressions (at do 48) so that they go deeply into us, and are not dispersed in the fog of imagination that is continuous in the second state. Once the impressions have penetrated deeply, other processes can occur. The diagram thus represents the three stories of a person who is working on themselves. Gurdjieff explained that the special effort brought to the intake of impressions produces the "first conscious shock." In the Work a "second conscious shock" can, with special training, be applied to the negative emotions that are produced in the human machine when the first conscious shock is applied over time. The second conscious shock, with its related effects, is not represented in any of the diagrams Gurdjieff shared with his group.

In the version of the food diagram shown above, the effects of the first conscious shock are overlaid on the regular workings of the three-storied food factory. This shock is initiated by the effort to bring presence to incoming impressions, to be out of imagination, and so to allow the impressions to go deep and create emotion.

In fact, the diagram above shows two shocks, which are represented by the two serrated horizontal lines, one in the upper section (impressions), and the other in the middle section (air). As we noted, the former represents the first conscious shock. The latter is a mechanical shock that occurs in all human beings, without volition. But the mechanical shock that comes from the intake of air produces materials that are needed for the first conscious shock, and so it must be understood.

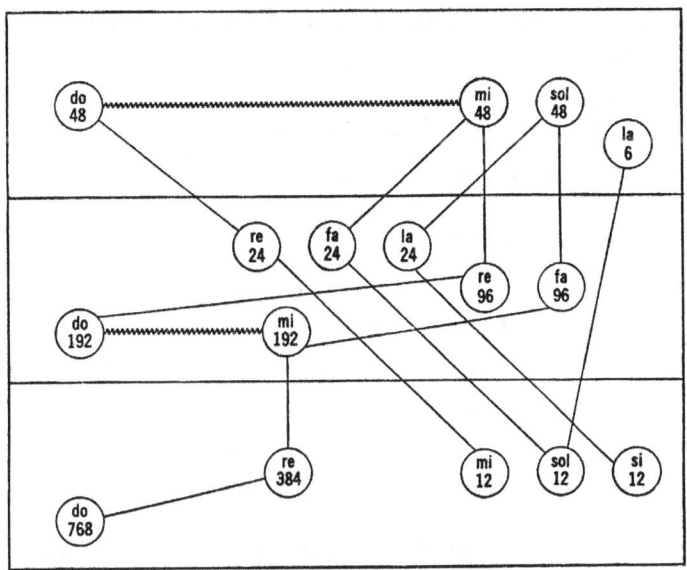

Figure 6. Food Diagram with the three foods and first conscious shock.

The shock that comes from the intake of air initiates two causal sequences.

1. The serrated line in the air intake (middle section) connects the incoming do 192 to the mi 192, which has been generated out of our food intake. This in turn generates fa 96, sol 48, la 24, and finally si 12. This is the finest energy that the machine produces under normal circumstances; it is associated with 1) sex energy, 2) the energy associated with extreme emotions and psychotic states, and 3) energies connected with extreme athletic exertion.

2. There is a second (non-serrated) line beginning from the do 192 of the air intake, which represents the production of mi 48. This is an energy necessary to our thought processes. It is this energy that we must learn

to bring to incoming impressions, in order to produce the first conscious shock.[1]

When the first conscious shock occurs (when mi 48 is successfully brought to do 48) two additional causal sequences are initiated.

1. Firstly, there is the causal chain generated from the serrated line connecting the re 96 of the incoming impressions to the mi 48 (e.g., the effort to divide attention). The interaction of re 96 with mi 48 produces fa 24, sol 12, and la 6. This is shown in the line beginning in the top (impressions) section with mi 48, descending to the middle section with fa 24, moving to the lower section with sol 12, and returning to the top section with la 6.

2. Secondly, there is the causal chain shown by the non-serrated line running laterally downwards, which shows the production of re 24 and mi 12.

The first conscious shock thus produces three hydrogens that can directly be used as food by the Higher Centers: mi 12, sol 12, and la 6. Sol 12 and mi 12 are both finer than the si 12 produced from the air octave. (They are the ideal fuel for consciousness to become aware of itself independent of functions.) Nevertheless, si 12, sol 12, and mi 12 can all be used as fuel for the Higher Emotional center. The la 6 is the beginning of the accumulation of material that will be needed to fuel the Higher Intellectual center.

Here we note that the Higher Centers can operate on a range of fuels. The only requirement is that there must be enough fuel to produce combustion. But the different fuels give different qualities of experience, so that conscious beings have different characteristics and may pass through different stages of development.

Let us now move to the second conscious shock, which is not depicted in the diagram. The mi 12, sol 12, and la 6 that are generated by the first conscious shock represent more potent fuels than are normally processed

---

1. In some schools in Tibet and India special work was done to amplify the shock that takes place at the intake of air, in order to produce a better quality of material for the first conscious shock.

by the food factory. They have the effect of igniting the more primitive si 12, so that it becomes directly a part of our experience. With si 12 everything becomes more intense: both our positive emotions and our negative emotions. The second conscious shock involves disengaging consciousness (accumulated via the increasingly frequent application of the first conscious shock) from the more powerful negative emotions generated from si 12. In other words, as a person works on themselves, their machine begins to function on more volatile fuels, and as a result they may begin to experience kinds of negative emotion they did not experience before. Fortunately, these finer fuels can *also* be used to separate from the machine itself, and the separation effected under these conditions is much deeper and more complete than the separation that can be effected through mi 48.[2] That is why the second conscious shock is termed "the transformation of negative emotions." The second conscious shock produces a range of effects, including an increase of the mi 12, sol 12, and la 6 already shown, and possibly beyond that fa 6, do 6, la 3, and sol 3. The mastery of this technique requires a life dedicated to this purpose. Doubtless the school in Central Asia had another diagram detailing these effects.

In sum, by working on himself a man can introduce two shocks, additional to the mechanical shock that takes place at the intake of air. These shocks initiate processes that refine the incoming energies to a further stage, generating a higher range of energies and higher states of consciousness that correspond to them. This would be like adding the inner triangle to the six-pointed star of the enneagram, turning a man from a simple organism into a cosmic entity capable of upward movement in the universe.

The symbol of the enneagram mirrors with mathematical precision all of the processes shown in the food diagram.

- The six-pointed outer figure represents the natural functioning of the machine in the line of time. It is the food diagram without the two

---

2. Taking this into account, we can see why the history of the Fourth Way is so colorful.

additional lines of effects produced from the first conscious shock. It is the life of a cellular being.

- The addition of the three-pointed inner figure produces the mi 12, sol 12 and la 6 which are the material of transcendence. This connects man to eternity.

The version of the enneagram shown in Figure 7 shows the entry of food, air, and impressions, with the mechanical shock at the intake of air, but without the first conscious shock being applied to the incoming impressions.

A second enneagram diagram (Figure 8) shows, in schematic form, the substances produced when the first conscious shock is applied. Point 8 shows the finest hydrogens generated by this process, which constitute the materials for the next highest octave. We note that it actually produces hydrogen 6 in the form of la 6. The inner triangle shows the context, with the hydrogens that are introduced from the entry of food (do 768), air (do 192), and impressions (do 98).

With the second conscious shock fa 6, do 6, la 3 and sol 3 could probably be added.

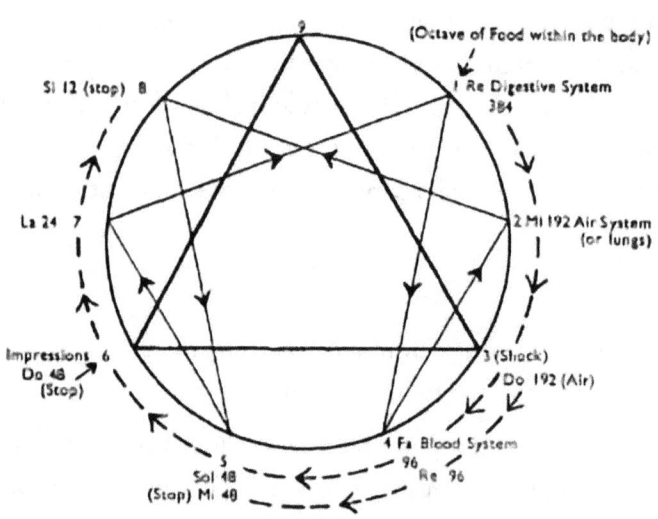

Figure 7. Enneagram and the processing of the three foods.

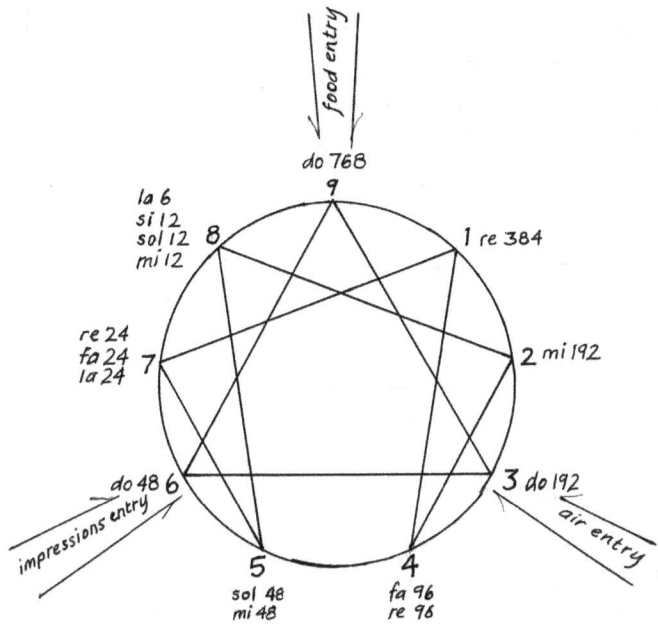

Figure 8. Enneagram and the first conscious shock.

We shall now return to our first presentation of the enneagram, looking *only* at the inner triangle of man's self-completion (Figure 9 on page 58). We factor out the intake of food and air (at 9 and 3) and show instead the first and second conscious shocks. We are thus representing a process within a process. In this version of the enneagram, we show the two intervals (at the base points of the triangle) as having been successfully bridged. The triangle thus shows the first conscious shock introduced at (3) and the second conscious shock introduced at (6), but not achieving its resolution until (9). In other words, the second conscious shock is carried through four points of the outer circle. We are therefore able to show the seven notes of a completed octave on the outer ring. This represents the work on the scale of a person's life. It is the image of a human microcosm transcending itself.

Now let us look at the intervals given by the law of octaves. The mi-fa interval is between points (2) and (4), while the si-do interval occurs between points (6) and (9). The mi-fa interval skips point (3), because that is a shock point. The shock from the inner triangle at (3) neatly bridges the mi-fa. The shock bridging the si-do, however, cannot fall between the notes

GEORGE GURDJIEFF: THE SEARCH YEARS   57

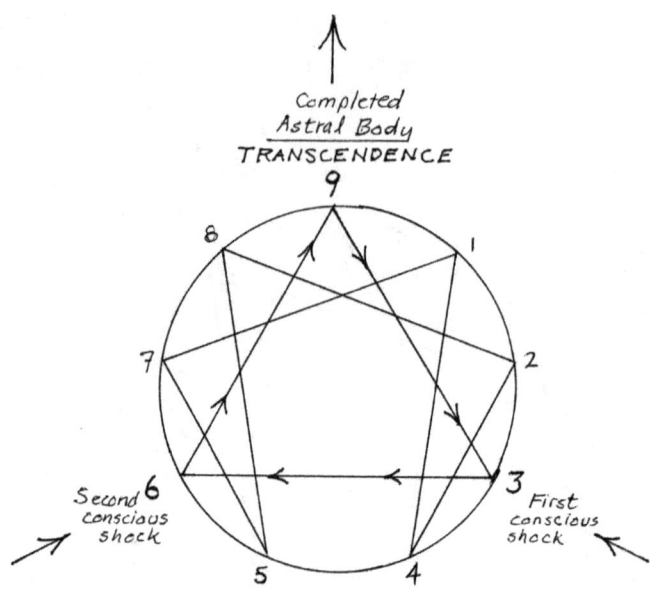

Figure 9. Enneagram and the two conscious shocks.

si and do, as there is no space for it to do so. The note do, borrowed from the inner triangle, already fills the space of an interval. The shock that initiates the work *to bridge the si-do interval comes between the notes sol and la, at point (6)*. This begins a process which continues through the following three notes, to complete itself at the final do. Thus, while the bridging of the mi-fa hits point (3), the bridging of the si-do interval is a much more complex movement. The shock at (6) develops through points (7), (8), and (9) — and this difference is of great significance. The second conscious shock — as we noted above — is termed in the system "the transformation of negative emotions." It is our struggle to transform the more volatile fuels that are introduced into the food factory by the first conscious shock. The transformation of intense negative emotions into finer substances is the highest function of which man, as man, is capable. There are three stages in the transformation of negative emotions:

1. **Internal Separation.** You strive to separate your identity from the intense negative emotions now circulating within your being. You

discipline yourself to see these emotions as something happening in you, which is external to what you really are.

2. **The Lower Approximates The Higher.** The steward, struggling against these negative emotions, tries to approximate the standpoint of Higher Centers. There are a number of different lines of effort. You study the kind of imagination that the negative emotions generate. You study the ways in which you manifest these emotions in your outward behavior. On the basis of these observations, you determine how *not* to act out the negative emotions. You intentionally adopt alternative patterns of behavior that correspond to a more a more enlightened state of mind. At the same time, you replace the imagination that is connected with these emotions with simple presence. The attempt to act on these aims creates an intense internal struggle. The negative emotions that follow from the first conscious shock may burn with the intensity of si 12. We could say that, when this occurs, the very devil has been released into your system. In the aspirant who is prepared, seeing the devil face-to-face initiates an unceasing struggle to separate consciousness from the functions. This combines with the attempt to bring the 'poisoned' functions out of imagination and into the present. All of these efforts are the attempt of the lower level to emulate the Higher Level. In the system this is called regeneration. This quality of effort, sustained through the four points of the outer circle of the enneagram (points 6-9), creates a condition where the Higher Level can actually enter into the lower level.

3. **The Higher Infuses The Lower.** Once the internal struggle has weakened our sense of a unified 'I,' and created a field of tension at a high vibrational level, influence from the Higher Level can enter. This enables the moment of transcendence. From the standpoint of the lower level this happens suddenly and spontaneously: something more than what it is suddenly appears. When the higher infuses the lower, it reorganizes the matter below it to more perfectly reflect its presence. It does so naturally, just as a magnet reorganizes randomly placed iron filings on a cardboard surface. It can do this, however, only because it

is acting in an *already prepared* environment. And so, ultimately, the infant Self perfects its servant, the steward.

At the si-do interval our internal work organizes potent hydrogens (both negative and positive) in a form approximating that of a higher being. The result is that the *outward-looking presence* of the lower centers is superseded by the *self-aware presence* of the Higher Centers. Thus, the enneagram, scaled to the appropriate point on the table of hydrogens, produces a graphic image which exactly represents the experiences that monks and anchorites have undergone for many centuries.

There is an interesting point to keep in mind with respect to bridging the si-do interval.

AS ABOVE, SO BELOW

In examining the extended effort needed to bridge the si-do interval, we have focused on a critical process within the human microcosm and represented it through the enneagram. But the enneagram represents all processes occurring at all levels of the universe. As the ancient Hermeticists put it: "As above, so below." We can go to the top end of the universe and use exactly the same tools to analyze the long mi-fa interval at the beginning of the descending movement through which the Absolute initiated Creation. This is an exact mirror to the movement just described. Because we are moving in reverse, the descending mi-fa corresponds to the four-point movement of the extended si-do. In looking at the moment of Creation, we are, just as with the transformation of negative emotions, isolating a process within a process. When the Absolute engendered the Macrocosm of Creation, he was moving energy from a Higher Level into a lower level. But *at the same time* he was anticipating that the Macrocosm so created would generate conscious energy that did not previously exist. There is, thus, a regenerative dimension to this first downward thrust.

What caused the Absolute to will Creation?[1] In Gurdjieff's view the Absolute became aware, at a certain critical point, of a negative entropy, that was outside of him, and that was acting upon him — subtly and continuously. This negative 'other' would, over an immeasurable period of time, undermine the Absolute's integrity, and the universe itself would be spoiled. In a critical moment the Absolute accepted this 'negative other' into himself, allowing it to become one with himself. This made the

---

1. In considering the moment of Creation we use the language of temporal sequence, although this moment is outside of time as we know it: pre-existent, if you will. All that we can really say is that it is in the being of the Absolute.

Absolute — for the first time — truly universal, but it did not eliminate the fundamental condition of entropy. The Absolute neutralized this condition of entropy (now internal) by generating the structure of Creation, which was intended as a mechanism to engender consciousness. Thus, in the moment of accepting the negative 'other' into himself, the Absolute became truly universal, and Creation appeared. At the same time, and in this single act of will, the Absolute transcended himself. His will became something beyond Being and Not-Being, beyond God and beyond the Abyss.

The Absolute's crisis moment, his decision to internalize an unknowable and ultimately destructive dimension of Being, is the same confrontation with the devil that we saw in the second conscious shock. From one point of view Creation represents the intentional transformation of the unimaginable suffering of the most intelligent being in existence.

The last diagram Gurdjieff presented to his students in St. Petersburg in 1916 (Figure 10) is a generalization of all of the above. It is the Vision of the Macrocosm represented by the Diagram of Everything Living. (This was called by his students the Step Diagram.)

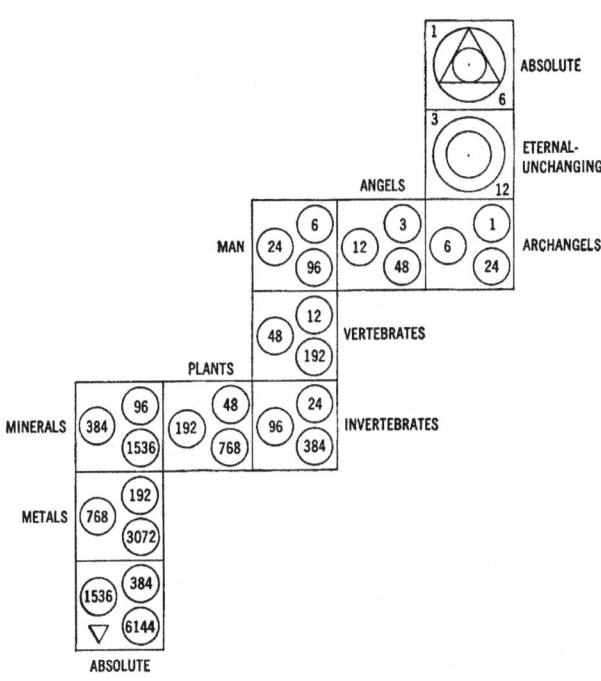

Figure 10. Diagram of Everything Living.

The range of each level is very great, yet each level is limited tightly by its 'center of gravity' point. The human level contains both the mineral and the divine, yet the everyday experience of a human being occurs within an exceedingly narrow band of vibrations. The expansion of sentience at the high end of the step diagram is exponential. What spans Angels, Archangels, and the Eternal Unchanging is well beyond the experience of the greatest prophets known to history. It is quite beyond both the speculative and experiential powers of our species.

In summary: the enneagram, the table of the hydrogens, the food diagram, and the diagram of everything living are totally integrated with one another. What is seamlessly incorporated into the enneagram is remarkable: the laws of three and seven, the six cosmic processes, the theory of microcosm and macrocosm, the triadic Absolute, the quaternity of matter. It reflects the enigmatic quality of the Absolute's Creation.

Now let us review the Western precursors to this teaching.

THE WESTERN PRECURSORS

We provide here an overview of diagrams created by two Western Hermeticists: Raymon Lull (1232-1316), and Robert Fludd (1574-1637).

The Franciscan Hermeticist Raymon Lull was one of the alchemical forerunners of modern science, influencing Leibniz and pioneering computation theory. In Figure 11, the image on the left shows Lull's combinatory

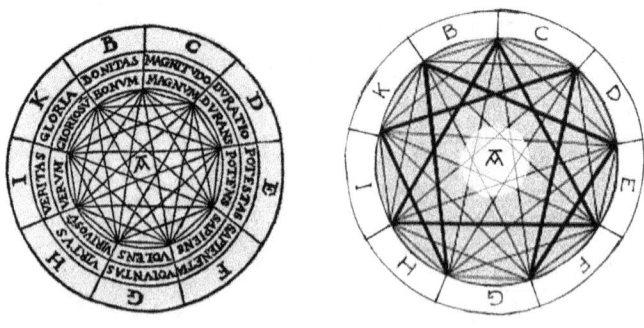

Figure 11. Enneagram: Raymon Lull 1305 precursor.

Figure 12. Step Diagram: Raymon Lull precursor.

wheel, which represents the pattern of life in the macrocosm. The image on the right shows the enneagram inked over Raymon Lull's diagram.

Lull's diagram shows all the possible connections between nine points, and so contains the enneagram — as shown in the enhancement on the right.

Lull also provides a clear precursor of the diagram of everything living (the step-diagram, Figure 12), replicating almost exactly the image Gurdjieff presented to his students in 1916. It lacks only the vibrational numbers.

We see a clear precursor of the table of the hydrogens in the work of the English Paracelsian physicist Robert Fludd (Figure 13 on page 64, c.1625), who connected the law of octaves (Pythagorean version) with the different self-contained concentrations of matter, each under their own laws, that comprise the Macrocosm. There are seven interior circles (curved lines with lettered names) and two intervals, one starred and one banded.

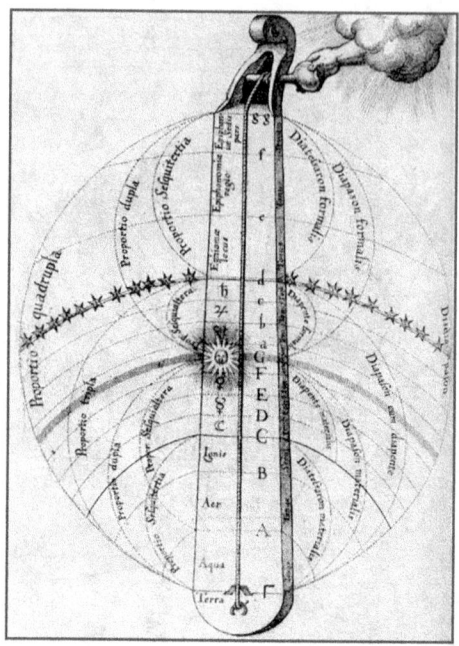

Figure 13. Harmony of the Spheres: Robert Fludd.

There is a clear precursor of the Food Diagram in Fludd's representation of the intake and processing of food, air, and impressions. In Figure 14 on page 65 there are representations of the first and second conscious shocks, and their transcendence through the pineal gland (see the starred image of the Mundus Intellectualis). While there is not the precise classification of the substances comprising the different levels of matter, it is clearly moving in the direction of Gurdjieff's 1916 diagram.

To emphasize the unacknowledged Western side of Gurdjieff's cosmological inheritance, the expanded form of the Table of the Hydrogens (Figure 15 on page 66) — presented by Gurdjieff in St. Petersburg in 1916 — incorporates the quaternity of each of the matters involved (C, O, N — H).

We note in passing that the content of this diagram is quite compatible with the content of the periodic table of the elements.[1] But the point we wish to make in presenting the expanded table is that it is: 1) not the work

---

1. See Collin, Rodney, *The Theory of Celestial Influence,* Watkins, London, 1980, Chapter VII, The Elements of the Earth, pp. 92-104.

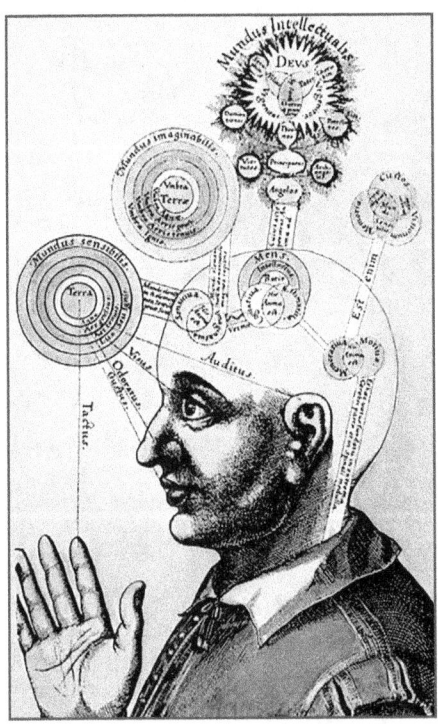

Figure 14. Food Diagram: Robert Fludd precursor.

of George Gurdjieff, and 2) not the product of an oriental mind. Nor can it be inferred from the Epic of Gilgamesh or any surviving Sumerian, Assyrian, and Babylonian tablets. It is the product of a Western mind, yet it is an exact and profound synthesis of many very ancient ideas.

HOW COULD THESE TWO CURRENTS HAVE COME TOGETHER?

An ancient school, stemming from the Mesopotamian family of civilizations (which Gurdjieff called the Sarmoun Brotherhood), seems to have converged with a hidden stream of Renaissance Hermeticism. At a certain point the understanding of the Mesopotamian lineage (which includes the law of seven, and the understanding of an interpenetrating set of vibrational levels as the expression of single cause) came into contact with a current of European Hermeticism (which includes the ideas of Cosmos, Macrocosm,

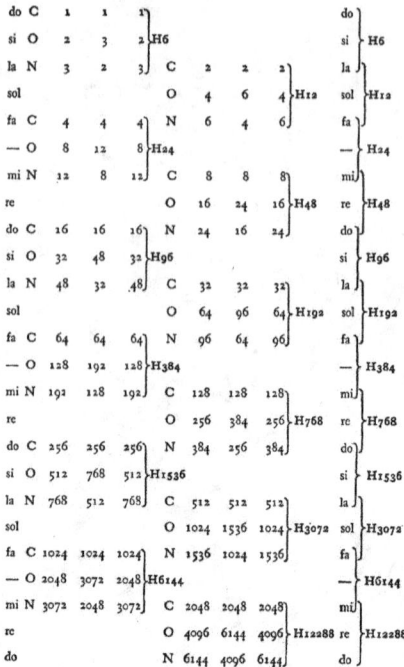

Figure 15. Table of Hydrogens (expanded).

and Microcosm — with a process of transcendence uniting all levels of the Macrocosm).

How could this have happened? There was no context in which such a meeting could have taken place before the late 18th century. In Europe, in the latter half of that century, there developed a marked interest in Eastern Wisdom, which paralleled the development of the global colonial empires.

The British presence in India dated from 1757. A French presence in Southeast Asia and China began from 1855. The Russo-Persian treaty of 1813 established a Russian sphere of influence in Persia. As the Napoleonic Wars drew to a close, Britain, Russia, and France engaged in a struggle for the partition of Asia: the Great Game. As we have already noted, each of these nations had agents continuously circulating throughout the different countries of Asia, gathering information and negotiating alliances of different kinds. Spheres of influence and control were quickly established: the

British in China and India, the French in China and Southeast Asia, and the Russians in Central Asia.

In the late 18th century European interest in Eastern Wisdom suddenly awakened. This was the age in which Sanskrit was first translated into German, French, and English. In 1787 Abraham Anquetil-Duperron published a French translation of fifty Upanishads. In 1791 Johann Ith made the first German translation of the Upanishads. English translations of the Buddhist texts began from the 1830s. Between 1844 and 1874 Max Müller made excellent translations of the Upanishads, the Vedas, the Rig Veda, and the Bhagavad-Gita into both German and English. His translation of the Buddha's Dhammapada appeared in 1869. The German Philosophers G.W.F. Hegel (1770-1831), Friedrich Schelling (1771-1854), and Arthur Schopenhauer (1788-1860) quickly realized the quality of wisdom in the Vedic/Vedantic corpus. Indeed, these teachings were probably better understood — in their spirit — in the early 19th century than they are today.

Given the physical penetration of the European nations into Asia, and the growing appreciation of Ancient Eastern Wisdom in the West, it is natural that a Western school should seek sources of Ancient Eastern Wisdom. Schools in the Hermetic Tradition, with their roots in ancient wisdom — perhaps Masonic or Rosicrucian — would be the most likely candidates.

Of the European nations it was Russia that showed the most direct interest in Eastern Wisdom. Some of the records of the Tsarist foreign agents survive, and — unlike their French or English counterparts — they *were equally encouraged to research ancient wisdom*: Tibetan, Sufi, Central Asian, Taoist, and Vedic or Vedantic.

We know that the Russian aristocracy supported innumerable Hermetic Lodges: Masonic, Rosicrucian, and occult. The Masonic and Rosicrucian groups were so prevalent in the late 18th century that there was the suggestion made that the new religion of Illuminism should succeed the teachings of the Orthodox Church. From the late 18th century onward there were different centers within Russian society trying to integrate wisdom from the traditional societies of Asia and Central Asia. Some of these organizations worked hand in hand with the Romanov civil service, while others, like Helena Blavatsky's Theosophists, worked independently.

We can imagine, then, a conscious Hermetic school, based in Romanov Russia, searching both the Near and the Far East in the years immediately following the Napoleonic Wars. It discovers an organization in Central Asia whose transmission was continuous through ancient times. Both schools (the Russian and the Asian) are gifted in Hermetic formulation, and the result is an extraordinary synthesis. This sounds a bit far-fetched, but when we consider the pattern of C Influence involvement, as depicted in the Prologue in Heaven, it is eminently possible.

In a playful spirit, then, let us imagine a member of the Romanov court circle, in the period just after the Napoleonic Wars (1803-15), setting out to seek ancient wisdom. This would be in the reign of either Alexander I (1801-25) or Nicholas I (1825-55) – which allows the Great Game to get well under way, and for modern science to make a decisive appearance.

Our conjectural Russian aristocrat has received Hermetic teachings in a conscious Rosicrucian or Masonic lodge and has himself awakened. He knows well the science of his own time, and has — like Peter Ouspensky — a marked interest in mathematics. Let us say that he sets out in 1820, under the reign of Alexander I, and travels through Central Asia, Tibet, and India, eventually locating a school in Central Asia. Here he finds awakened beings with a unique understanding of the history of school, and a great cosmological legacy.

The anonymous Russian aristocrat is fluent in Turkish, and this gives him a common language with the Asiatic schoolmen. He is able to speak openly with people who have a profound understanding of the law of seven, a familiarity with the Sumerian sexagesimal number system (which combines base 60 with base 10), and a mastery of the Chaldean science of vibrational levels. On his side, he has a firm grasp of both Classical and Renaissance Hermeticism, a knowledge of mathematics, and a knowledge of the fledgling science of chemistry.

The men of the East are aware that — after five millennia — they are facing a crisis of the forward transmission of their teachings, and of all the understanding they have acquired. The Russian works together with his

Turko-Persian hosts to assess their common inheritance and compile their understandings. We must consider here what would have been required, in the quality and level of observation, to accurately assemble the material that comprises the food diagram, and to link it to the law of three and the law of seven. What being would have been capable of making all of the fine distinctions between mi-12, sol-12, si-12, and la-6? The diagram itself explains so much: the different ways; the different paths to awakening; the different kinds of conscious beings; the different kinds of awareness conferring different powers, insights, and capacities. The material later presented in *In Search of the Miraculous* shows a profound understanding of the history of school.

We note that, while these great syntheses (the table of the hydrogens, the food diagram, the step diagram) are the result of analytic work by a community of awakened beings, they remain *a report on experience*. In other words, the cosmology of the system *is not simply a theoretical construct*, but an attempt to use concepts to give expression to the understandings of Higher Centers. And the concepts which provided the base material for this synthesis had already been refined by many generations of conscious beings.

The third of the five Fourth Way teachers in our series, Rodney Collin, speculated on the Hermetic source of Gurdjieff's system. He conducted spiritualist research, which he chose not to publish. His students, however, preserved some of the papers documenting this research, and passages have been quoted. While we do not take this material at face value, as Collin himself did not, it is of some interest, in that it portrays exactly the Russian Hermeticist that we have imagined above.

In answer to the question, "Who was the Teacher of Gurdjieff?" the medium working with Rodney Collin responded that one of his principal teachers was a Russian.

> Ivan Ivanovitch was one of the teachers of Gurdjieff, very tall and blonde, wore a blue tunic buttoned high at the neck, had very blue eyes. ... [He] ... was a mysterious figure who came from Tibet early in the 19th century, who moved unseen behind the schools in Sicily, in Florence and in Rome, who inspired Ibsen and Stevenson

and Nietzsche, who returned to Russia about 1885, gave Krylov his fables, helped Philemon translate the Philokalia, molded the Russian ballet, and disappeared whence he came on the eve of the 1914 war.[1]

While this passage does not mention Central Asia, Central Asia stands directly between Tibet and Europe. As a Russian during the early years of the Great Game, this individual would have known of the esoteric and historical significance of Central Asia, and would have traversed this region in his search for truth.

Having completed our speculations on the source of the system, we can return to our story, examining Gurdjieff's aims as a teacher — at least as he has revealed those to us. At this juncture we shall shift perspective, then, viewing Gurdjieff as a teacher rather than as a seeker. To do so we must begin again from the oasis at Yangi Hissar, with George Gurdjieff recovering from a bullet wound, and then continue the historical narrative through Tashkent and Moscow.

The Formation of the Teacher

To understand Gurdjieff's aims as a teacher, we must review the events connected with his awakening, and see how, in that context, he received the teaching that he was to transmit for the remainder of his life. We noted that between 1905 and 1907 Gurdjieff received a great teaching, which he internalized carefully and completely. He could only have absorbed this teaching in the presence of a person with developed Higher Centers, for it is not data, and the understanding of it is not an intellectual exercise. Internalizing such a teaching requires receiving both the information and the states of consciousness that make sense of that information. Beyond this, the Order transmitting the teaching would have ensured that the young Gurdjieff was prepared to be its carrier. A real teacher is the servant of a Higher Level, and this is a most exacting service. Service to a Higher Level has two aspects:

---

1. Collin-Smith, Joyce, *Call No Man Master*, Gateway Books, Bath, 1988, p. 79.

1. The will to hold the lower level in subjection. One must be able to place the higher over the lower, repeatedly, moment by moment, for the duration of one's earthly life.
2. The will to affirm the Higher Level in action. The Higher Level exists not just 'for oneself,' but it has implications for humanity. Higher Centers exist to serve. One must be able to place the service proper to Higher Centers over one's personal interests and concerns.

We have seen Gurdjieff *being prepared* for this. He would never have wished the three bullet wounds upon himself, yet they were necessary to change his life. The oath he took to forswear his powers was directly a result of the third bullet wound, and its timing was precise. That oath in turn preceded the teaching transmission of the Central Asian Brotherhood. Gurdjieff was only ready to properly receive this teaching after having understood that the acquisition of powers does not yield the only thing of real value: consciousness.

This brings a qualification. In traditional societies a teacher *used* powers, as part and parcel of their work with students. It appears that Gurdjieff did continue to use powers in that way: as a teacher of the dance, as a healer, and as one examining the minds and hearts of others. He certainly used his psychic powers with Ouspensky, who leaves us with a clear record of this in *In Search of the Miraculous*.[2] In fact, immediately after taking the oath at Yangi Hissar Gurdjieff states, "I made a reservation that my oath should not concern the application of it (special powers) for scientific purposes." He did use his powers in healing and in "the study of centers" in Tashkent, where he tried to understand the "hypnotic suggestibility" of man.[3] "Scientific purposes" almost certainly included, in Gurdjieff's mind, the teaching of esoteric truth and the transmission of higher states of consciousness. This was for the benefit of the recipient, not for the benefit of the one wielding the special powers. The governing principle would be, that

---

2. See Ouspensky, P.D, *In Search of the Miraculous,* Routledge & Kegan Paul, London, 1977, p. 261-2.
3. Gurdjieff, G.I., *Life is real only then, when "I am"*, All and Everything, Third Series, E.P. Dutton, New York, 1978, p. 26.

the lower must serve the higher: the use of powers must serve man's higher possibilities.

Thus Gurdjieff's self-formation really begins at Yangi Hissar, with the most definite step in the process being *his return to the Central Asian monastery,* and his acceptance of its conditions. It is from his second contact with the monastery that Gurdjieff prepares himself to be a teacher; makes specific demands on himself, takes vows, and sets specific aims. It was a characteristic of Gurdjieff that he took vows 'before his essence' and rigidly adhered to them. Usually these vows were given a definite time frame, for example — ten years. Indeed, it is impossible to understand Gurdjieff's behavior as a teacher without some understanding of these vows and the aims that were derived from them.

GURDJIEFF'S AIMS

We will list Gurdjieff's principal aims (at least those that we know of) in order that we can refer back to them in examining the later stages of his life — for often the 'timing out' of an aim produces a critical change, which is otherwise difficult to understand.

The Aim of Search had crystallized by 1884 when Gurdjieff was age 18. It would have been displaced, in 1898, by his first contact with the Central Asian monastery. [Time frame: Gurdjieff age 18 to 32.] In the *Third Series* Gurdjieff describes this aim as "my one unconquerable desire to investigate [organic life] from all sides, and to understand, the exact significance and purpose of the life of man."[1] The pursuit of this aim prepared him to receive and to rightly assimilate the theory of the Ray of Creation when it came.

The Aim to Awaken crystallized in 1902 at the oasis of Yangi Hissar and remained permanent until Gurdjieff's death. [Time frame: Gurdjieff age 36 to 83.] Initially this was the aim to renounce the unintentional use of occult powers, but on a deeper level it was the aim to subordinate functions to consciousness: ultimately to have the machine serve Higher Centers.

---

1. *Ibid.*

Gurdjieff continued to reformulate this aim on ever deeper levels throughout his life.

The Teaching Aims given Gurdjieff by the Brotherhood in Central Asia [Time frame: Gurdjieff age 39 to 58.] While these aims were quite specific when they were given, we can only reconstruct them in an approximate way. Gurdjieff wanted to initiate a school with three connected levels: exoteric, mesoteric, and esoteric. He wanted to consolidate the esoteric level in such a way that the school might link to the level one above the human, as certain great schools of the past had done. In Gurdjieff's mind the esoteric level was related to the standards that defined the Inner Circle of Humanity. He hoped to create a school that would, over a longer period of time, enable a reformation of the Inner Circle of Humanity, and so the cosmos of man. Another guiding principle was that the Work would have to begin in essence — not in personality — and take permanent root there.[2] Yet another aspect of Gurdjieff's task was that his teaching should take place in the West. It was to be a Western path, that would have to succeed without extended periods of retreat, and without the kinds of institutional support that were common to monasticism in the East. Gurdjieff often advised his students to combine the understanding of the East with the knowledge of the West. This was, indeed, exactly what the originator of the system had done.

These teaching aims were displaced by another set of aims after Gurdjieff's automobile accident, and the consequent closing of the Institute in 1924.

Practical Teaching Aim — To Understand the State of Sleep: formulated in 1907 on Gurdjieff's arrival in Tashkent, and held until his death in 1949 [Time frame: Gurdjieff age 41 to 83.] In the *Third Series* Gurdjieff describes this aim: "I must discover, at all costs, some manner or means for destroying in people the predilection for suggestibility which causes them

---

2. See Bennett, J.G., *Gurdjieff: Making a New World*, Turnstone Books, London, 1973, pp. 134-135.

to fall easily under the influence of 'mass hypnosis.'"[1] Gurdjieff qualified this aim after his car accident of 1924, but the evidence is that, on his recovery, he was quite consistent with it for the remainder of his life.

Practical Teaching Aim — Conscious Acting: formulated in 1911 during his preparation to teach in Moscow, on the basis of the observations of human nature that he made in Tashkent. Gurdjieff held this aim rigorously for 21 years until 1932. [Time frame: Gurdjieff age 45 to 66.] In the *Third Series* he refers to this as the aim "to lead in some ways an artificial life" or to "always act." He does not specify the kind of acting involved, but the aim had an undeniable effect on his students. The aim had at least two aspects: 1) that Gurdjieff have the will to subordinate his own mechanical behavior patterns, and 2) that he be able to defuse the kind of adulation that he naturally attracted. The latter, of course, complimented his aim to destroy the hypnotic state in his followers.

Following his automobile accident in 1924 Gurdjieff reconsidered his teaching aims, and produced a new set of aims.

Personal Aim — To Push Away Those Who Make Life Too Comfortable: formulated in 1928 and held for seven years until 1935 [Time frame: Gurdjieff age 62 to 69.] This aim was taken after Gurdjieff had set himself the practical aim to complete the writing of *Beelzebub's Tales*. The aim to push away others was implemented in order to: 1) raise his internal state, which had been adversely affected by the accident of 1924, and 2) allow him to achieve the required focus to complete *Beelzebub's Tales*. In the *Third Series* Gurdjieff formulated this as the aim "to remove from my eyesight all those who by this or that make my life too comfortable." This aim came to an end in 1935, and it is quite important for understanding Gurdjieff's behavior in the years between 1928 and 1935. In a certain way it extended the aim of "always acting" (which timed out only in 1932) in that it made his behavior — at least in some respects — artificial and hard to understand.

---

1. Gurdjieff, G.I., *Life is real only then, when "I am"*, All and Everything, Third Series, E.P. Dutton, New York, 1978, p. 27.

Reformulation of Gurdjieff's Teaching Aim. The second set of teaching aims were made in 1935 and held for the remainder of Gurdjieff's life. [Time frame: Gurdjieff age 69 to 83.] Gurdjieff came to a turning point in 1935, after his seventh visit to America and the failure of his plan to recreate the Institute there. We do not know the content of this second set of teaching aims, but they certainly existed. At the time of their formulation Gurdjieff returned to Central Asia (sometime between May and October of 1935) to reconnect with certain individuals from the Order from which he had originally received the system. He would have wanted to review both the original project and his own relation to it. We noted that, in 1924, Gurdjieff had placed his original teaching aims of 1905-1907 in suspension. In other words, he stopped teaching in the way he had done from 1912. From 1935 he does begin to teach again, in quite a different way, but with a very clear focus. In this second phase he is not sorting through many candidates to find a few whom he can pressure into becoming members of an esoteric circle. He relates to all his students exactly as they are — in the fashion of a traditional Sufi Shaikh. This new phase of teaching involved a complete and unqualified demand made upon himself, but this demand was concealed from his students.

Now let us focus on Gurdjieff's plan for his life's project: the Institute for the Harmonious Development of Man. This plan is derivative of 1) the aims given by the Central Asian Order and 2) the initial period of teaching experimentation in Tashkent.

A general aim, which almost certainly came out of the Central Asian brotherhood, is related to the kind of hierarchy that a real school requires. We come again to the principle of the four circles of humanity: esoteric, mesoteric, exoteric, and outer.

THE FOUR CIRCLES OF HUMANITY

The four circles of humanity can be understood either:

1. On the scale of humanity (this would be a humanity in which the process of regeneration governs the other six processes, or a cosmos of man).
2. As applied to the work of a particular school.

The former presumes an Inner Circle of Humanity, whether latent or active. But as an Inner Circle is so rare in history, this idea has more frequently been applied to individual schools. Understanding the ideas of the esoteric, mesoteric, and exoteric circles *without reference to an Inner Circle of Humanity* involves a step down of each category.

When there is an Inner Circle, the topmost level, or the esoteric level, links with Higher School, whereas on the scale of individual schools, the pyramid need only complete itself in the understanding of a single conscious teacher. It could then be adjusted to the level of the teacher and the level of the school.

The original schema given in *In Search of the Miraculous* is framed on the scale of humanity and implies a more developed civilizational base than presently exists. It appears to have been distilled from older Vedic/Egyptian/Chaldean schemas.[1]

The Esoteric Circle consists of those who have both Higher Centers active in unison. They have objective knowledge, both of themselves and of the living universe. The members of this circle thus have a shared base of understanding in relation to a Higher Level. This shared base is very close to the understanding of Higher School, and the esoteric circle is in communication with Higher School. This would include man number seven, and perhaps a high man number six. The esoteric circle functions on the level of what Gurdjieff called the Inner Circle of Humanity.

The Mesoteric Circle includes men and women in whom Higher Centers are active. They have realized their invisible Selves, but their understanding of their place in the vertical structure of the Macrocosm is more theoretical. Their understanding of the principles of the Work, and of man's place in the universe, is identical with that of the esoteric circle, and between them there can be no discord or misunderstanding. But the mesoteric circle may have understood things that have not yet found expression in their actions. This would be a beginning man number six, a man number five, and — with relativity — a high man number four.

The Exoteric Circle is "the outer circle of the inner part of humanity." These are people in a group or a school, connected to a teacher, but in the early stages of the work. They have the same knowledge, and much of the same understanding, that belongs to the esoteric and mesoteric circles — but their knowledge is more conceptual. In other words, it is much more based on the understandings of the king of hearts and

---

1. Ouspensky, P.D., *In Search of the Miraculous,* Routledge & Kegan Paul, London, 1977, pp. 310-311. We have paraphrased it below to incorporate the knowledge of the different levels of man from the Overview. This allows us to reflect on the presence of the Inner Circle of Humanity in history and to make a comparison to the step-down version of the schema of the four circles that Gurdjieff used when opening the Prieuré.

the king of diamonds, guided by periodic glimpses of Higher Centers. Their understanding may not be expressed in their actions. Nevertheless, they are deeply committed to the principles of school work. This represents the level of man number four.

The Outer Circle of Humanity includes all those people who have no exposure to the Work, which would include, in our own age, almost all of humanity. Here there is no common understanding, "everybody understands things in his own way and all differently". This is what, in the Bible, is called the 'confusion of tongues.'

This schema leaves us with those working to become man number four in an undefined place. Depending on their level of commitment they might be classed with the exoteric circle. If their interest in awakening is only a passing phase they might be classed with the outer circle. The thinking appears to be that it is a transitional place and does not merit a category of its own.

Before moving on to the step-down version, we would like to clarify the idea of the esoteric circle in its highest form, as the Inner Circle of Humanity. We introduced the idea of a distinction between latent and active forms of the Inner Circle of Humanity. We can approach this same distinction from the standpoint of the Prologue in Heaven.

THE INNER CIRCLE OF HUMANITY: LATENT AND ACTIVE FORMS

Latent Form: Known to History

History shows us examples of a developed school, with either a man number six or a man number seven as a teacher, and several men number five under him. These conscious beings are the regenerative cells of a small, self-contained cosmos that illuminates the sleeping civilization of which it is a part. The fully conscious beings are like shining stars that light up the networks of conscious influence running through the school. These networks and these lines of conscious light may even enter the larger, more opaque body of the civilization. The life of this school includes contacts with the Gods. The Gods are aware of the school, and the school has living memory of its contacts with the Gods. Such a school can produce a certain quality of influence in a civilizational order. The contact with the Gods helps the school to integrate itself and to concentrate its work. In a phase of civilization where schools are more available, this school will link easily with other schools and other groups, and facilitate their work. This gives the schools and groups which do not have the same kind of a connection with the Gods a more universal aspect, so that their work resonates more easily in the centers of civilizational order.

There is thus a connection of the most developed school with the other schools on the planet, and so with the civilizations of that time. Yet this connection is ephemeral, and it may disappear at any moment. Men and Gods are indeed within the same magnetic field, which is sometimes weaker, sometimes stronger. When it is slightly stronger, little systems of light flicker into life in the nervous system of the cosmos of man. Little patterns and forms momentarily reveal themselves, and then dissolve.

Active Form: Potential in History

Now we consider a school with several teachers having reached the level of man number six, and one of these a man number seven or man number eight. There may be quite a number of men number five. Each member of this conscious circle understands the others completely in relation to first things. We could say that "they have their heads above the water." The Gods are aware of them, and there are quite a number of points of contact. There is almost what you could call *a shared space* between the Sphere of Sentient Being which the Gods inhabit and the school. When this school knows other schools within its sphere, it knows the truth, or measure, of those schools. It also knows the truth or measure of the civilizations that they serve. In other words, it knows these schools and these civilizations *as they are known from a Higher Level*, and so can provide guidance and leadership in relation to first things. This is the active form of the Inner Circle of Humanity. Something in the pattern of heaven is reflected in the pattern of life on earth. Many lights are switched permanently on in the illuminated network of the cosmos of man.

The critical difference between the latent and the active forms of the Inner Circle of Humanity is the more active involvement of the Gods with the latter. When the active form is achieved, the Gods are able to influence Mankind. Mankind has shown itself a vessel capable of both receiving and retaining conscious influence. Why, then, does this not occur more frequently? One reason is that the emergence of the active form evokes its own opposite. When such a configuration begins to occur, those social forces aligned with the Black Queen resist more actively, and do not hesitate to engage in the most direct forms of persecution. In fact, in history, great good and great evil are often found in close proximity. It is inevitable that the higher the school, and the more directly it confronts sleep, the more it is perceived as a threat by the unregenerate dimension of Mankind. Note that the unregenerate dimension of humanity does not perceive the involvement of Higher School at all; it simply feels threatened, or actively de-legitimated, and tries to eliminate the source of that threat.

Closing Reflections

While the present writer can find no historical evidence of an active Inner Circle governing humanity, we do see evidence of an Inner Circle existing in latent form. The

> historical study of ancient Sumeria, early dynastic Egypt, and Medieval Tibet provides very interesting material. We also have the example of the circles of men and women surrounding each of the prophets: Zoroaster, Moses, Buddha, Christ, and Muhammad. Plato has provided us with a sketch, in the *Republic*, of how an Inner Circle might function in relation to an individual city-state. We also consider that a direct connection between Higher School, a particular school on the planet earth, and the civilizational order which supports that school, may have existed for periods of time without having properly stabilized.

But, given that we are not, in the *History of the Fourth Way*, examining a phase of history where the Inner Circle is in existence — in either its active or its latent form – how does this understanding apply practically?

The idea of the Inner Circle of Humanity may guide a teacher in establishing the hierarchy that a school needs to develop. Why is hierarchy necessary? When a teacher deals with a circle of students, each according to his or her individual needs, he is in effect reaching down to them. In the first years of a teaching a degree of this is inevitable. But ideally, the teacher asks the students to step up to his level. For, in a connection with the Gods, a teacher himself is constantly being asked to step up to a standard higher than his own. If he spends all his time accommodating the level below himself, he fails to keep the standard of the level one above. Thus, a real school does not — within limits — cater to individual students, but places a pressure on all its members, at all their different levels, to release the illusion of individuality that is derived from their culture, circumstances, and psychological type.[1]

In sum, each student must always be reaching a bit beyond themselves, and what they think is possible. But the pressure to ascend cannot, on balance, be negative. If the students are able to *see themselves* in the goal they are striving towards, it is positive. When a certain number of students understand the teacher on a deeper level, he must invest his energy in those students. He has, after all, only so much conscious energy — and he must use it well. And he can only deal intimately with so many people at a time. When an inner circle has formed around the teacher, the new students

---

1. This is not to deny genuine individuality, or character, of a kind which exists even on this level.

coming into the teaching can relate to the students in whom the teacher has already invested energy. The new students see that the older students have achieved something of value, and they can respect their presentation of the Work. And so a circle forms *around* the teacher's circle that is able to practice the Work in the way that the teacher has advised. It needs much less contact from the teacher to lift one of these prepared students, in the moment that he sees they are ready, than it does to prepare a first generation of students. Then, when a large middle circle has come into being, an outer circle can safely form around them — without diminishing the standards of the school. When a school expands too rapidly it dilutes the Work. The existence of a right hierarchy means that the school can expand without diluting, and that, at the same time, people can work at different paces. The outer circle might include those who presently face demanding circumstances in their lives, so that their participation is limited for the time being. It might include the children of students, who are connected to the group, but are yet too young to join. It might include those who have a real interest, but who need more time and experience. Once the three circles are established, the members of each circle face a continuous challenge to move up from the level they are on. But no one is asked to do what is impossible for them. There is, then, a working lift-on-lift hierarchy. When a person moves a level up, they create a space on the level one below for another to move into, and — because of the teacher's connection with the Gods — this lift-on-lift principle extends upward into the celestial hierarchy. The networks of personal relationships that naturally develop between the members of any group, do not then obscure the "stairway to the stars" that has been established.

In Essentuki, in Tiflis, in Constantinople, and most particularly at the Prieuré at Fontainebleau, Gurdjieff tried to apply a step-down version of the three circles, as applicable to the new teaching in an environment where other schools did not exist. At one point Gurdjieff placed all of his students, individually, in relation to the three circles. The Prieuré step down version is given programmatically in the *Third Series*.

Exoteric — "all those who had newly entered [the group], as well as those who had not yet acquired by their subjective merits the right to belong to the mesoteric group."

Mesoteric — all those who were "as yet initiated only theoretically."

Esoteric — all those who "were to be initiated not only theoretically ... but also practically, and to be introduced to all the means for a real possibility of self-perfection, but ... only after having been for a long time experimentally tried and verified in quite exceptionally planned circumstances."[1]

The esoteric circle in the stepped down version would be students whom Gurdjieff had worked with directly and intensively, who had some direct experience of Higher Centers, and who had a memory of those experiences that never entirely disappeared. In other words, a memory that could guide their Work. Ideally this would include some who were near the level of man number five. We notice that the teacher, who must at the very least be a high man number five, is not included in this schema. Neither the exoteric nor the mesoteric circles imply even a fully developed man number four. While this schema is much reduced from the original schema, it does create places for students to step up and function beyond their level, with the hope they will grow into the new level.

Part of Gurdjieff's driving motivation, from Tashkent forward, was to generate an esoteric circle around himself. To this end he tried to: 1) quickly determine who could Work and who could not, and 2) place immediate pressure — both negative and positive — on anyone who showed themselves capable of responding to his Higher Centers. He would then move the advanced students towards a confrontation with their own Black Queen/Chief Feature. This would be both to help the student to become conscious and to place the understanding of this area in the body of the school.

As the esoteric, mesoteric, and exoteric circles take form it becomes clear, for those entering the esoteric circle, that they must serve both the

---

1. Gurdjieff, G.I., *Life is real only then, when "I am"*, All and Everything, Third Series, E.P. Dutton, New York, 1978, p. 77.

circle one below and the circle one above. This creates the lift-on-lift structure that allows for the upward movement within the group. As other circles form in relation to the inner circle, each circle begins to operate more in relation to living examples of the level it aspires to. Things become more practical. If even a single man number five were established in Gurdjieff's inner circle, this would give him much greater latitude to work on the scale of the school itself.

Gurdjieff never presumed that his group had a working connection to the Gods. He nevertheless saw his Work in relation to the standards required of the Inner Circle of Humanity. In 1916 Gurdjieff was himself *already in* the space in which an inner circle is created ... but he was in it *by himself*. He wanted to bring others into that space, and he tended to be forceful about doing so. He had little time to achieve his aim, and so he was always moving quickly. Moving into this space with Gurdjieff was, then, a bit like sharing a space with a tiger. Yet he also existed in the space beyond this space, and there was that dimension to him.

Having explored the idea of esoteric, mesoteric, and exoteric circles, there were certainly other teaching aims that Gurdjieff had. One such aim was to combine the wisdom of the East with the knowledge of the West to found a new order of teaching in the West. This would require finding forms of Work that could be implemented in a non-monastic environment, without reliance on the faith of the traditional religions. Thus his emphasis on the dance.

TASHKENT 1907–1911

On having completed his two-year stay at the unnamed monastery in Central Asia, Gurdjieff moved to Tashkent, where he based himself for the next five years. The Tashkent phase was clearly a preparation for the launch of the Institute in Moscow/St. Petersburg in 1912. Gurdjieff went into it with aims that *he did not have* in his years of search. He focused on: 1) accumulating the capital he needed to function as an independent teacher, and 2) studying the four lower centers in relation the second state of consciousness. Gurdjieff understood the second state of consciousness — the state of waking sleep — as a hypnotically induced state, rather than a natural state.

He attempted to understand how this state has acquired such a hold on Mankind and how the hypnotic spell can be broken.

The first three years in Tashkent were focused principally on the aim of accumulating capital. Gurdjieff launched multiple business enterprises. He mentions contracts for the supply and construction of railways; starting up and then selling stores, cinemas, and restaurants; investing in oil wells and fisheries. His most prosperous ventures involved trading in carpets and antiques (particularly cloisonné). Gurdjieff remained connected to certain of these enterprises through the 1920s, 1930s, and 1940s. As a result of these activities, he was able to bring to Moscow approximately one million rubles and a valuable collection of carpets and antiques.[1]

Beginning in 1909, and particularly in 1910-1911, he began to put more time into the study of human psychology. In pursuit of his second aim Gurdjieff actually worked as a professional hypnotist, helping people to overcome substance abuse problems. For the most part he worked with people in groups. Gurdjieff ascertained that man can be hypnotized by a professional hypnotist because he already exists in the hypnotic state. In Mankind itself the hypnotic state is continuous. If we are suddenly awakened from it, we immediately return to it, as the norm of our experience. Following the Tashkent period Gurdjieff referred to this hypnotic state as the state of identification — with everything that is external to one's Self.

On the basis of his Tashkent studies Gurdjieff made a clear distinction between essence and personality. Man's deepest and most significant feelings are in his essence, and not in his personality. Man's mental activity and decision making take place principally at the level of personality. The hypnotic state that has such a grip on modern man is reinforced by the division of mind and heart that occurs when personality dominates essence. For the Work to produce proper results in a human being, it must begin from essence.

Additionally, Gurdjieff studied and integrated systems of human types, which he in turn connected to the study of physiology and to the state of

---

1. Gurdjieff, G.I., *Meetings with Remarkable Men*, (All and Everything, Second Series), E.P. Dutton & Company, New York, 1963, p. 270.

the different internal organs. In applying these understandings he combined healing with direct esoteric work.[1]

By 1911 Gurdjieff had added to the teachings he had received from the Central Asian monastery a special understanding of the state of sleep *in the form it takes in modern Western man*. This was then combined with his specialized understandings of human types and physiology.

On the 13th September 1911, as a final preparation to teach, Gurdjieff renewed his oath to abjure the use of powers, and made a second oath to bind himself for 21 years to lead an 'artificial life'. In *The Herald of Coming Good* he clarifies this:

> "... according to the special oath I took, I ... bound myself in my conscience to lead in some ways an artificial life, modelled upon a programme which had been previously planned in accordance with certain definite principles."

The purpose of this oath was twofold, firstly:

> ... to prevent ... in relation to me ... a natural process in the communal life of people as an outcome of a conjunction of the evil actions of so-called 'common people' and lead to the destruction of both him that tries to achieve something for general human welfare and of all that he has already accomplished to this end.[2]

Here Gurdjieff is suggesting a process in the 'collective unconscious' of the sleeping masses, whereby they experience higher consciousness as a threat, and are prepared to take action against conscious beings. In the *Herald of Coming Good* Gurdjieff gives several historical examples of this. Gurdjieff

---

1. This combination of healing and regeneration is clearly represented in the record of Gurdjieff's work with his students in the 1930s. See Solano, Solita and Hulme, Kathryn, *Gurdjieff and the Women of the Rope: Notes of Meetings in Paris and New York 1935-1939 and 1948-1949*, Book Studio, 2012. Gurdjieff had studied under a Sufi Order specialized in healing and he had extensive exposure to Tibetan Medicine, for which he had the greatest respect.

2. Gurdjieff, G.I., *The Herald of Coming Good*, Sure Fire Press, Edmonds, Washington, 1988, p. 12.

felt that the 'always-acting' oath would somehow deflect this destructive tendency.

The second purpose of the oath was:

> ... counteracting the manifestation in people with whom I came in contact ... of the feeling of enslavement, paralyzing once and for all their capacity for displaying personal initiative.[3]

These principles would have Gurdjieff: 1) act intentionally at all times and 2) avoid appearing like a saint. J.G. Bennett noted that he gave the feeling of 'always acting' in a way that radiated strength. He was, then, ready to appear in Moscow on New Year's Day 1912.

WHAT KIND OF A TEACHER RESULTED?

In the course of his travels George Gurdjieff had been subjected to harsh tests and trials of many kinds. Because these trials had produced a positive result in him, he did not hesitate to impose harsh trials on his students. But at the same time it is true that he made a profound commitment to his students, to his family, and to humanity at large. He showed a depth of generosity throughout his life and, ultimately, served those who were around him. The priest at the Russian Church where his funeral was held said that he had "never seen such a demonstration of mass grief."

We note, in all of this, Gurdjieff's total lack of pretension to any kind of sanctity or holiness. What made Leonid Stjernvall think that Gurdjieff was "Jesus Christ himself" was simply the depth and force of his presence. Gurdjieff did not hesitate to appear as an unsavory character, a black magician, or a ruthless manipulator. He discouraged worship or reverence in his students because he had studied human suggestibility in its depth. Mankind will reverence a saint without any reference to Higher Centers, and this reverence will be of no more value than the reverence given to a movie actor.

Gurdjieff was a master of the direct transmission of consciousness, *and* he was a master actor; in him the two were directly connected. He could

---

3. Ibid, p. 12.

in one moment show a terrifying severity, and in the next be completely casual. He could create his own emotions according to the requirements of the moment. As a teacher he could, under the right circumstances, evoke higher levels of consciousness in his students. He could also bring out the darkest side of human nature, in order to show his students what it was they had to deal with. He could do this by showing the dark side of his own nature, that the 'animal' in the other might react, and then — in the moment they did react — show them what had occurred. It was up to the student, then, to put the pieces together, and up to the teacher to see that the process was balanced.

Finally, we may ask, what kind of an impression did the mature Gurdjieff make on the people around him? Who was the person who appeared on the streets of Moscow and St. Petersburg in 1912? Some of his students give their first impression.

Peter Ouspensky describes his first meeting:

> We arrived at a small café in a noisy though not central street. I saw a man of an oriental type, no longer young, with a black mustache and piercing eyes, who astonished me first of all because he seemed to be disguised and completely out of keeping with the place and its atmosphere ... this man with the face of an Indian raja or an Arab sheik ... seated here in this little café ... in a black overcoat with a velvet collar and a black bowler hat. ... I gathered that G. had traveled widely and had been in places of which I had only heard and which I very much wished to visit. Not only did my questions not embarrass him but it seemed to me that he put much more into each answer than I had asked for. I liked his manner of speaking, which was careful and precise.[1]

> I liked his movements, which had a great deal of a kind of feline grace and assurance; even in his silence there was something which distinguished him from others.[2]

---

1. Ouspensky, P.D., *In Search of the Miraculous,* Routledge & Kegan Paul, London, 1977, p. 7-8.
2. *Ibid.,* p. 10.

Figure 16. Gurdjieff in the 1910s.

Jean Toomer first saw Gurdjieff as a dancing master touring with his performers.

> I saw this man in motion, a unit in motion. He was completely of one piece. From the crown of his head down the back of the head, down the neck, down the back and down the legs, there was a remarkable line. Shall I call it a gathered line? It suggested co-ordination, integration, knitness, power ... I was fascinated by the way the man walked. As his feet touched the floor there seemed to be no weight on them at all — a glide, a stride, a weightless walk.[3]

Henriette Lannes met Gurdjieff through Mme de Salzmann's Sèvres Group, which she joined in 1938.

> I was struck by the impact of his force, very quiet, calm and controlled, yet almost frightening, but more than anything by the degree of his total presence, a presence which I felt extended to the tips of his fingers. It gave meaning to all his movements, which

---

3. Quoted by Webb, James, *The Harmonious Circle*, Shambhala, Boston, 1987, p. 282.

seemed so much more alive than ours. As alive as those of a cat or a tiger. I also felt very strongly his vast generosity — a generosity which I would call superhuman.[1]

Solange Claustres also met Gurdjeff through Mme de Salzmann, in Paris, in the early 1940s:

> What left the deepest impression upon me was that profound look when he was listening to someone, silently listening with his whole being. Answering with words only the question put in words and, through a particular attitude in the tone of his voice, by a smile, a look, he conveyed to one's feelings something which the ordinary mind could neither hear nor understand ... I sensed and saw in him a quality of attention that nothing escaped.[2]

---

1. From Henriette Lannes' essay "To Recognize a Master" in Jacob Needleman and George Baker, eds., *Gurdjieff: Essays and Reflections on the Man and His Teaching*, NY, Continuum, 1996, p. 363.
2. Solange Claustres "The Dessert" in Jacob Needleman and George Baker, eds., *Gurdjieff: Essays and Reflections on the Man and His Teaching*, NY, Continuum, 1996, p. 400.

CHAPTER 2

George Ivanovitch Gurdjieff: The Years of Teaching

Moscow to Constantinople: 1912–1921

Gurdjieff pursued this task and this vision directly and without pause for twelve years, from his arrival in Moscow in January 1912 — through Essentuki, Tiflis, Constantinople, and Hellerau — to Fontainebleau, where in July 1924, he was seriously injured in a motor crash.

On leaving Tashkent Gurdjieff immediately travelled to Moscow, where he renewed the connection that he had with the Romanov court circle. This connection was through the Imperial civil service, where he had recently served as an intelligence agent. There were two aspects to the new connection.

1. He considered putting himself forward to replace Grigori Rasputin as spiritual healer to the Tsarevich, Alexei Nikolaevich.[3] He may have sensed an open door, through the Romanov circle, to furthering his long-term aim of establishing school in the West. Gurdjieff had acquired good references as a spiritual healer in Tashkent, and in early 1912 the members of the Octobrist Party were taking every measure to push Rasputin out of the Romanov circle. Gurdjieff was already

---

3. See Bennett, J.G., *Gurdjieff: A Very Great Enigma*, Samuel Weiser, Inc., York Beach, Maine, 1973, p. 70, and Bennett, J.G., *Gurdjieff: Making a New World*, Turnstone Books, London, 1973, p. 116-117.

known to the Octobrists (and to the Tsar) as being highly accomplished in the healing skills that Rasputin possessed. When Gurdjieff decided not to follow this path, or found that it was not open to him, he turned away from court circles, ending a more than twenty-year involvement with the Romanov Government.

2. In these same first months in Moscow Gurdjieff courted and married Julia Ostrowska, a lady-in-waiting to the Tsaritsa. They were married in St. Petersburg in 1912.[1] Julia Ostrowska was twenty-two and Gurdjieff forty. She was a beautiful and talented young woman whom Gurdjieff later trained to a very high level of proficiency in the dance. Thomas de Hartmann said of her, "She was tall of stature, exceedingly finely formed: a very beautiful woman .... We grew to love her deeply and sincerely."[2] She was with Gurdjieff until the end of her own life in 1926. That he loved her is without question, and he never married again after her death. While Gurdjieff had many sexual partners, Julia Ostrowska was always "my uniquely beloved wife." He treated her with the full respect and regard given a matriarch in a traditional extended family. To his students she was always Madame Ostrowska.

We shall focus now, more particularly, on Gurdjieff's pursuit of the tasks he had been given at the end of his second retreat in Central Asia in 1907. Gurdjieff arrived in Moscow just after New Year's Day 1912. He almost immediately attracted his first student, his cousin Sergey Mercourov. Shortly after that his first English student, Paul Dukes, joined them. He began to accept students, and a group began to form around him. We know little of Gurdjieff's activities during his first two years and ten months in Moscow, from January 1912 to November 1914. The Gurdjieff of these years is vividly depicted in the opening essay of *Views from the Real World*, entitled Glimpses of Truth.[3]

---

1. Bennett, J.G., *Gurdjieff: Making a New World*, Turnstone Books, London, 1973, p. 117
2. de Hartmann, Thomas and Olga, *Our Life with Mr. Gurdjieff*, Harper & Row publishers, San Francisco, 1964, p. 11.
3. This essay is anonymous but was probably authored by Paul Dukes.

Figure 17. Julia Ostrowska.

In November 1914 (after at least two years of preparation) Gurdjieff's group made a first public appearance in Moscow, with the performance of his ballet, *The Struggle of the Magicians*. As the ballet reveals something of Gurdjieff's teaching, and as it was later performed by the Institute in Tiflis, in Cairo, and in Paris, we shall provide a brief overview.

THE STRUGGLE OF THE MAGICIANS

The ballet takes place in early 19th century Central Asia. A beautiful young Indo-Persian woman, Zenaib, is the student of a great White Magician. A wealthy Parsi aristocrat, Gafar, falls in love with her, and wants to possess her as his wife. This would require detaching her from the influence of the White Magician. Gafar attempts to engage Zenaib's interest with lavish gifts, promises, and flattery, but fails. He also attempts to conquer his love for Zenaib, but cannot. Finally he contacts a Black Magician and asks him to put a spell on Zenaib to give him control over her. The Black Magician says that there is a spell that will deprive Zenaib of all that she has developed in her work with the White Magician. The Black Magician casts the spell — which his students enact in a dance sequence — but the White Magician, who is aware of what is occurring, produces a counterspell. This too is enacted in a dance sequence. The counterspell must, like the spell it is intended to neutralize, affect both Zenaib and Gafar. The White Magician not only frees Zenaib from the Black Magician's spell, but momentarily frees Gafar from his own identifications. This is possible because the love for Zenaib, which Gafar was unable to divest himself of, was ultimately the love of the truth in her. In the catharsis that follows both Zenaib and Gafar become students of the White Magician. There are many dance scenes throughout the ballet, each one enhancing its theme in different ways.

Peter Ouspensky recorded some of Gurdjieff's comments on the ballet:

> An important place in the ballet is occupied by certain dances. I will explain this to you briefly. Imagine that in the study of the movements of the heavenly bodies, let us say the planets of the solar system, a special mechanism is constructed to give a visual representation of the laws of these movements and to remind us of them. In this mechanism each planet, which is represented by a sphere of appropriate size, is placed at a certain distance from a central sphere representing the sun. The mechanism is set in motion and all the spheres begin to rotate and to move along prescribed paths, reproducing in a visual form the laws which govern the movements of the planets. This mechanism reminds you of all you know about the solar system. There is something like this in the rhythm of certain dances. In the strictly defined movements and combinations of the dancers, certain laws are visually reproduced which are intelligible to those who know them. Such dances are called sacred dances.[1]

And Ouspensky left us with these comments of his own:

> The important scenes represented the schools of a Black Magician and a White Magician, with exercises by pupils of both schools and a struggle between the two schools. The action was to take place against the background of the life of an Eastern city, intermixed with sacred dances. Dervish dances, and various national Eastern dances, all this interwoven with a love story which itself would have an allegorical meaning.
>
> I was particularly interested when G. said that *the same* performers would have to act and dance in the White Magician scene and in the Black Magician scene; and that they themselves and their movements had to be attractive and beautiful in the first scene and ugly and discordant in the second.
>
> "You understand that in this way they will see and study all sides of themselves; consequently the ballet will be of immense importance for self-study," said G.[2]

---

1. Ouspensky, P.D., *In Search of the Miraculous,* Routledge & Kegan Paul, London, 1977, p. 16.
2. *Ibid.*, p. 17.

A study of the script of the ballet shows us something of the size and nature of Gurdjieff's group. *The Struggle of the Magicians* has 45 performers onstage, all but a few of whom dance. Ouspensky noted the duplication of dancers who perform as the students of the two Magicians. This would take the total down to about 35. Then there would have been at least five musicians, and a host of set design people, setup people, ticket collectors,

Figure 18. Sergey Mercourov.

and ushers. This takes the total number of people involved up to an absolute minimum of 50. Given the capital Gurdjieff had acquired in Tashkent, and his need to have expert performers in the lead roles, he probably hired some professionals. The Moscow papers reporting the performance at the time noted the appearance of "certain well-known ballet dancers."[3] The performance of *The Struggle of the Magicians,* and its positive reviews in the Moscow Papers, give evidence of a large and active group. When Ouspensky met Gurdjieff, in April 1915, Gurdjieff told him that he had two groups

---

3. *Ibid.,* p. 17. However, even given the hired help, this ambitious project was not the work of a small study group.

in Moscow unconnected with one another and occupied in different work "according to the state of their preparation and their powers." Each person paid a thousand rubles a year and was able to work with the group while pursuing ordinary activities in life.[1]

In reviewing this initial period of teaching, we see that Gurdjieff rapidly expanded his group after his arrival in Moscow, drawing students from several different social circles. Many of the first-generation students proved inadequate to his purposes, and there was an exfoliation that occurred just before Peter Ouspensky's arrival.

Six months after *The Struggle of the Magicians* opened in Moscow, Gurdjieff accepted Peter Ouspensky as his student. Ouspensky was a journalist and lecturer based in St. Petersburg, with a large audience in that city. He and his circle rapidly became a second generation of students, combining with the core members of the first generation.

Soon after Ouspensky joined, there came Dr. Leonid and Elizaveta Stjernvall, Thomas and Olga de Hartmann, Andrei Zakharov, and Anna Bukovsky, later Bukovsky-Hewitt. (When the de Hartmanns joined they were living at Tsarskoye Selo, the summer palace of the Tsar.) Between April and December of 1915 the St. Petersburg group grew to forty members. As the group enlarged, Gurdjieff began to lead meetings in that city. Ouspensky noted that, "from all of those who came to our lectures a small group of people was gradually formed who did not miss a single opportunity of listening to G., and who met together in his absence."[2] In response to this interest Gurdjieff planned a series of lectures, which ran from February 1916 to February 1917, in which he presented the entire system of ideas that are recorded in *In Search of the Miraculous*. The center of gravity of the teaching gradually shifted from Moscow to St. Petersburg.[3]

The text of *In Search of the Miraculous* gives us a record of these meetings, and of the activities of this group. It is the most reliable record that we

---

1. *Ibid.*, p. 12. A 1917 ruble was worth about twenty dollars in 2025 dollar value, so each person was paying a considerable sum to work with Gurdjieff.
2. *Ibid.*, p. 33.
3. St. Petersburg was called Petrograd from 1914 to 1924, and Ouspensky later referred to this group as the Petrograd group.

have of any part of the history of the Fourth Way, and this is all the more remarkable because Gurdjieff disallowed taking notes during his lectures. The content of this teaching, as that is relevant to this book, has already been presented in the Overview. Many of the specific teaching experiences of 1916 are recorded in Chapter 3 to follow, which documents the life of Peter Ouspensky.

We note that Gurdjieff kept his groups to a size where he could work intensively with each member. He gave each student tasks, tested them in different ways, showed them their features, and created states of higher consciousness for them. But the group was not yet large enough to be separated into different levels with different kinds of roles. Students were either a part of it, or they were not. And if people were not actively following Gurdjieff's program of teaching, it was very difficult for them to stay in.

In March-June 1917, just after the forced abdication of Tsar Nicholas II — during the period of the Kerensky government — Gurdjieff travelled to the Caucasus to visit his family, then resident in Alexandropol. He knew that if Russia entered a state of civil war, Turkey would attempt to re-take Alexandropol, and his family would be in danger. After a few weeks he set out again for St. Petersburg, but decided to stop at Essentuki, not quite a third of the way to his destination. Essentuki was a resort town on the northern edge of the Caucasus, out of the reach of the Turks, and, at the same time, distant from any pending political upheaval. Then, in July-August 1917, he summoned all those of his Moscow and St. Petersburg students, who were able to make the journey, to come to Essentuki for a six-week intensive workshop.

Thus, in the seven-month lull between the overthrow of the Romanov Dynasty and the outbreak of the Bolshevik revolution, when the future of Russia was entirely up in the air, Gurdjieff gathered the core members of his group for a phase of spiritual work, the intensity of which would make everything happening outside of it seem an illusion. Gurdjieff was a consummate master at making use of situations; he was without fear, and he viewed life on this level as a theater for producing consciousness.

During the Essentuki workshop of 1917 Gurdjieff worked with his students "day and night for six weeks with unparalleled intensity."[1] Ouspensky stated that "G. unfolded to us the plan of the whole work. We saw the beginnings of all the methods, the beginnings of all the ideas, their links, their connection and direction ... "[2] In retrospect Ouspensky said, "Whenever I chance to speak with one of those who were there, they can hardly believe that it lasted only six weeks. It would be difficult in six years to find room for all that was connected with this time, to such an extent was it filled. The intensity of work was such that the passage of time was relative."[3] It was a time when everything seemed possible, and so a timeless moment in the history of the Fourth Way.

The participants slept for four, or at most five hours a night. Gurdjieff taught his students the principle of 'super-effort': effort beyond what is normal or necessary. And yet the work was paced. In the course of the six weeks Gurdjieff arranged excursions to Kislovodsk, Zheleznovodsk, Pyatigorsk, and Beshtau. Additionally, "G. superintended the kitchen, and often prepared dinner by himself. He proved to be a wonderful cook and knew hundreds of remarkable eastern dishes. Every day we had dinner in the style of some eastern country, we ate Tibetan, Persian, and other dishes."[4]

For many of the participants it was a special time, when possibilities that do not exist in the normal course of life suddenly opened up. There was a vision of what a great Fourth Way school might be. Yet there was also the great tension of functioning at that level. A dispute broke out between two members of the group. Gurdjieff immediately ended the experiment, holding all members of the group responsible for the dispute. It seemed extreme, or out of scale. People made of it what they could, but almost all presumed the work would continue in some different form. In August

---

1. Bennett, J.G., *Gurdjieff: Making a New World*, Turnstone Books, London, 1973, p. 120
2. Ouspensky, P.D., *In Search of the Miraculous*, Routledge & Kegan Paul, London, 1977, p. 346.
3. *Ibid.*, p. 346.
4. *Ibid.*, p. 346.

Gurdjieff travelled — with Julia Ostrowska, Andrei Zakharov, and the de Hartmanns — to Tuapse on the eastern coast of the Black Sea.

On the 26th October 1917 the Bolshevik revolution brought V.I. Lenin into power, and the Imperial Russian Empire was transformed into a single Communist regime.

In January 1918 Gurdjieff returned from Tuapse to Essentuki. Believing Alexandropol to be under the immediate threat of Turkish invasion, as in fact it was, Gurdjieff asked his family to join him in Essentuki, and everyone — with the exception of his father and his eldest sister and her family — did so. In early February a cart arrived with ten members of his extended family: his mother, his brother Dimitri with his wife Asta and their three daughters, and his younger sister Sophie Kapanadze with her husband George and their two children. Despite his growing responsibilities as *paterfamilias,* on the 12th February 1918, Gurdjieff summoned his students from Moscow and St. Petersburg to begin a second workshop.

From St. Petersburg there came Peter Ouspensky with his new wife Sophia Grigorievna, Leonid and Elizaveta Stjernvall, Alexander Petrov, and a few others. Since his arrival in Essentuki Gurdjieff had begun recruiting local people, and this increased the numbers of the group. By the beginning of March some forty people were assembled. John Bennett recorded that the workshop began "with a different system involving external activities of the most varied kind ... Gurdjieff for the first time introduced the group to the rhythms and dances which were mainly of dervish origin." In addition to exercises, dances, gymnastics, talks, lectures, and housework, special work was organized for those "without means."[5] The rhythmic movements and sacred gymnastics were Sufi exercises directly focused on separating consciousness from functions. When Gurdjieff later developed his own movements, these movements were used as warmups, fitting into a category known as the six obligatories.

Meals were eaten in common, without dishes. Participants took their food from large, shared serving bowls. Gurdjieff gave tasks every day to each person and questioned them about their progress with the tasks.

Bennett, J.G., *Gurdjieff: Making a New World,* Turnstone Books, London, 1973, p. 121-122.

These tasks were often related to a person's chief feature, and the questioning might be severe. Sometimes Gurdjieff would send everyone away and give special tasks to only a few. The 'stop exercise' was first implemented at this time; students were to freeze the moment Gurdjieff cried out "Stop," and hold that position for a set period of time. At one point Gurdjieff divided the entire waking day into hours, with each hour devoted to different exercises. We keep in mind that the new people that Gurdjieff had recruited in Essentuki were without any background in the Work at all. This meant that the aims of the Work itself could not be a point of focus as they had been in the first workshop. The many new arrivals created a tension, as the participants of the workshop were working at different levels and had different aims. This discontinuity had clearly been intended by Gurdjieff, but with what aim we can only guess.

In early May, Peter Ouspensky, who had been hoping for an extension of the Work of the previous workshop, left the group and took his own quarters. This was probably not a surprise to Gurdjieff, who continued to visit with him.

At the end of May Gurdjieff provoked one of his oldest students, Alexander Petrov, to the point where he could not control himself, and Petrov answered Gurdjieff in anger. Gurdjieff brought the workshop to an end. "Everyone felt a profound sense of guilt ... We all passed through a very acute emotional crisis."[1] It is impossible for us now to know what Gurdjieff's aims for this workshop were, and to what extent he achieved them. When the workshop ended, he remained in Essentuki, along with a nucleus of his students.

In that same month (May 1918) Alexandropol fell to the Turks, as Gurdjieff had anticipated. In mid-July the remainder of his extended family came to Essentuki. This included his eldest sister Anna Anastasieff and her family — including nephews, nieces, and their children. They came as

---

1. de Hartmann, Thomas and Olga, *Our Life with Mr. Gurdjieff*, Harper & Row publishers, San Francisco, 1964. People felt that something of great value had been lost, and that they were all implicated. If it happened to Petrov, it could happen to any one of them.

refugees, bringing news of the death of Gurdjieff's father, whom the Turks had shot on his own doorstep.[2]

From that moment forward, as well as being a teacher, Gurdjieff was the central figure in a traditional extended family. For the remainder of his life, he was to sustain a host of personal dependents. He always kept his family employed and always created opportunities of many different kinds for them. Over time, some of the children of his own students (and some of his own children by his students) became a part of this extended family. When it came time for any one of the family members to go their own way, Gurdjieff would always ensure they had some means of taking care of themselves. Increasingly, too, the people of his Work became family, and he would sometimes refer to them as being those "near to me in blood" — even when they were not personal relatives. In this regard George Gurdjieff always remained in the world of the 19th century. He had a fundamental sense of the responsibility of one human being for another.

As the conflict between the White Russians and the Bolshevik forces spread to include Essentuki, it posed a direct threat to Gurdjieff's group, which included known Tsarists and men of military age who might be recruited by either side. Gurdjieff decided to organize a prospecting expedition to Mount Induc in the Caucasus, with the aim of extricating himself and his students from this situation. The nominal aims of the expedition were: 1) prospecting for gold and 2) researching ancient dolmens that were to be found in the area. It was an expedition which could bring wealth to the Provincial Government, and so would be viewed favorably by either side in the conflict.[3] The expedition had to be organized in every detail without knowing what the outcome of the struggle between the Whites and the Reds would be. Ouspensky's family (Sophia, her widowed daughter Lenotchka, and Lenotchka's newborn child) and Gurdjieff's extended family were to remain in Essentuki.

---

2. Between 1913 and 1923 the Ottomans massacred between 750,000 and 900,000 Caucasian Greeks and 1,500,000 Armenians.

3. de Hartmann, Thomas and Olga, *Our Life with Mr. Gurdjieff*, Harper & Row publishers, San Francisco, 1964, p. 51.

The group of fourteen that comprised the expedition already had their Tsarist papers and passports, but — to their complete surprise — Gurdjieff demanded of them that they acquire Soviet passports and papers. This they succeeded in doing, with carefully crafted cover stories. The group then acquired all the equipment that would be needed for the expedition.

Thomas de Hartmann made an interesting observation:

> ... our stay with Gurdjieff (in the Caucasus) had never been associated in our thoughts or feelings with the idea that all the past was lost or that through Gurdjieff we could escape the Bolsheviks. That the Bolsheviks would really stay in power in Russia never entered anyone's head.[1]

This shows the extent to which Gurdjieff, through the intensity of his Work, had separated the group from the world around them. Yet the hour of the Russian Empire had passed, and Gurdjieff knew it. He made a firm requirement on all those going with him.

> He told us everyone would have to think very seriously before deciding to go; we were no longer to be husbands and wives, or brothers or sisters, to one another; we had to accept for the duration of the expedition unquestioning obedience to the leader. As the expedition would involve us in deadly peril, we had to fulfill every order exactly: disobedience would be punishable even by death, and saying this Gurdjieff put a large revolver on the table.[2]

In anticipation of the hardships on the journey, Gurdjieff began a program of physical training for his students. Elizaveta Stjernvall recalls:

> Gurdjieff ordered all the men of our group, in poor shape physically, to carry each evening a sack of some forty-five pounds on their shoulders and to race at high speed through the house for an hour. Also, without putting down the weight, they had to climb the stairs to the attic and then down to the cellar.[3]

---

1. *Ibid.*, p. 55.
2. *Ibid.*, p. 54.
3. Stjernvall, Nikolai, *My Dear Father Gurdjieff*, Bardic Press, Dublin, 2013, p. 61.

On August 6th 1918, Gurdjieff left Essentuki with a party of fourteen, including Julia Ostrowska, the de Hartmanns, the Stjernvalls, Zakharov, Zhukoff, and Petrov.[4] Over a two-month period the party travelled through the Caucasus mountains to Sochi, on the shore of the Black Sea, arriving in Sochi at the end of September. During this period, they moved between the lines of the warring White and Red armies *five times!* They were fired upon by bandits, and the de Hartmanns were robbed at gunpoint. The group often found themselves travelling through countryside where, due to the breakdown of the distribution system, the inhabitants themselves were in want. Thus, they would come into a village seeking shelter and supplies from people who had nothing to give. They often had to forage for food, sleep in the wild, or put themselves up in outbuildings or empty schoolhouses. They might go without food for more than a day, and they went without sleep for as long as two days. The environment and the changes of altitude brought extremes of heat and cold. The group slept in their clothes for the duration of the trip, so that at its end all of them had to make a thorough cleansing of fleas, lice, and other insects.

Gurdjieff made direct use of this situation to teach. He became the embodiment of the Fourth Way principle that, "We always make a profit." Throughout the journey he demonstrated his consummate professionalism as a guide, displaying the skills that he had learned from his travels in the wilds of Central Asia, China, and Tibet. He showed a complete acceptance of the chaos that was unfolding all around them, using each situation to teach and to demonstrate a state of non-identification. Every other member of the expedition was, at one time or another, at the limit of his or her endurance. Gurdjieff demonstrated what can be seen when one passes beyond the limits of the learned sense of self. It was a virtuoso performance and it permanently changed all of those involved.

The records of both the de Hartmanns and Elizaveta Stjernvall show a constant alternation between states of duress and exhaustion, and states of

---

4. This journey was recorded by Thomas and Olga de Hartmann in their book *Our Life with Mr. Gurdjieff*. See also Elizaveta Stjernvall's essay "Across the Caucuses with G.I. Gurdjieff," in Stjernvall, Nikolai, *My Dear Father Gurdjieff*, Bardic Press, Dublin, 2013, pp. 55-80.

exaltation — as though they were moving from a lower world into a kind of hyper-reality filled with enchantment and wonder. To take an example from Elizaveta Stjernvall's diary:

> The return (to the base of Belaya Mountain) was effected under the most deplorable conditions. During the ascent I kept stumbling and stepping on stones which broke under my feet. I had several falls, each time dropping from my hands the twelve kilos of meat I carried on my shoulder. To complete my mishaps the heat was unbearable and we sweated profusely. Finally, after unspeakable effort, we found the trail ... the countryside all around us was a constant enchantment which moved us to exclamations of wonder.[1]

It is clear that during Elizaveta's journey down the mountain, she had been transforming suffering, and the hydrogens generated from her efforts accumulated internally. When the instinctive pressure was removed, they suddenly ignited. Referring to the effect of the trip as a whole Elizaveta states, "I felt I was alive in all senses of the word. I came out of the demoralizing torpor in which I had indulged myself. Furthermore, our life had sense now. We had ceased to grope in the shadows."[2]

Both sets of records, Elizaveta's and the de Hartmanns', show people reaching the limit of their endurance *without giving way to the emotional parts of centers*. They describe how the members of the group created their own self-contained world, holding to their own aims, in face of the cataclysmic upheaval that was all around them. The experience brought them closer to one another and to their teacher.

On arrival at Sochi at the end of September the group was disbanded, as Gurdjieff needed to reorient himself to the ever-changing situation. But the connection between the people involved remained intact.

In January 1919 Gurdjieff took a core of students, including Mme Ostrowska, the Stjernvalls, and the de Hartmanns, to Tiflis, the capital of Georgia, where they settled. Gurdjieff then summoned his entire extended family, whom he considered unsafe at Essentuki. They appeared in Tiflis as

---

1. Stjernvall, Nikolai, *My Dear Father Gurdjieff*, Bardic Press, Dublin, 2013, p. 74.
2. *Ibid.*, p. 65.

a band of penniless refugees.[3] Gurdjieff quickly organized a carpet business, which was an immediate success. Through this he was able to involve and to support both his own followers and the twenty-odd members of his extended family. The size of Gurdjieff's business, and his own apparent role in helping refugees, drew the attention of the Georgian Government – which allowed them to use a two-story government building for their activities. It was here that Gurdjieff formally launched, for the first time, the *Institute for the Harmonious Development of Man*.

Gurdjieff immediately opened his new Institute to the general public, and once again invited all his former pupils to join him. Thomas and Olga de Hartmann encountered, in the street in Tiflis, two friends they had known from their earlier studies at the Dalcroze School in Hellerau, Germany: Alexandre and Jeanne de Salzmann. The couple joined the group, and soon after the de Salzmanns' friends Elisabeta Galumian and Olga Hinzenberg also joined. The four new arrivals included three professional dancers, and one of the most gifted stage set designers of his generation. Gurdjieff did not fail to recognize the potential in this situation. It was the beginning of a new phase of his teaching.

Let us review how the new phase began. When Jeanne de Salzmann joined the group, she had just given birth to her first child. To earn extra money, she began to give Dalcroze lessons to a group of young women in Tiflis. Jessmin Howarth recounts:

> It was this class that G.I. Gurdjieff came to watch, asked to experiment with "to give them some exercises of attention." Although for some time G. had been giving his followers examples of what he called "gymnastics," accompanying them with his guitar, here, with Jeanne to improvise at the piano, the [Dalcroze] Movements developed further.[4]

---

3. Only Gurdjieff's older sister, Anna Anastasieff, her husband and family, remained in Essentuki. All of them, except Gurdjieff's nephew Valya, lost their lives.

4. Howarth, Jessmin & Dushka, *It's Up To Ourselves*, Gurdjieff Heritage Society, copyright, Dushka Howarth, 1998, p. 31

After making a series of experiments with Jeanne de Salzmann's group, Gurdjieff introduced the Dalcroze movements to his own students and began working intensively on them. The Dalcroze movements Jeanne de Salzmann had been teaching developed the feminine or receptive side of human nature. In the beginning Gurdjieff added active elements from the sacred gymnastics that he had taught at the Essentuki workshop. He then deepened the receptive/expressive side with various dances from the Far East. These later became the 'women's dances,' the 'sacred eastern dances,' and the 'prayer movements.' In Tiflis Gurdjieff began to develop a system of exercises, movements, and dances that drew on all of his twenty years' experience in Central Asia and the Far East.

He was to develop these dances and exercises into a working whole over the next three years. As the system evolved, students began to call the totality of these activities "the movements," and we will use that term here – although it was not actually used in Tiflis in 1919. In his life Gurdjieff was to create some 250 of these movements. In collaboration with Thomas de Hartmann he composed over 200 musical pieces to accompany the movements. Where Dalcroze had used pieces from the repetoire of classical and romantic music, Gurdjieff composed his own music to create specific effects for each of the dance movements.

All of the movements – whether dances or exercises – required a concentration of attention that can be achieved only in the presence of a conscious teacher. The movements themselves were combined with Gurdjieff's application of mime technique to produce a heightened emotional state. This state, when achieved, gave the student control over his or her body, as a unit. Thought, feeling, sensation, and motor function were united in what John Bennett called a "single integral act of expression."[1]

Having initiated the movements, Gurdjieff announced that the group would now produce a re-choreographed version of *The Struggle of the Magicians*. Work immediately began on the music, costumes, sets, and promotion. Gurdjieff began the staging of the ballet by teaching his students the first movement-exercises, along with a number of Eastern ethnic dances.

---

1. Bennett, J.G., *Gurdjieff: Making a New World*, p. 130.

Before going further let us look at what comprised the Gurdjieff movements, for they were to become a permanent part of Gurdjieff's teaching.

THE INSTITUTE'S PROGRAM OF MOVEMENTS SACRED DANCE, AND DRAMATIC PERFORMANCE

We shall begin by looking at the background of the six principal Institute movement instructors.

Gurdjieff had made an intensive study of sacred dance in Turkestan, Afghanistan, Kafiristan, the Chitral, Transcaspia, India, and Tibet. He had a deep knowledge of the Dervish Dances, the Tibetan Cham Dances, and the Indian Temple Dances. To see, to know, and to internalize dance movements was, for Gurdjieff, a life's passion: he had a photographic memory for things of this kind. Through his mastery of occult and yogic technique, he had achieved a complete control over his own moving center. He exhibited no random movement, and all of his movements were accurate, precise, and compelling. He was a thoroughly accomplished dance master, and his company was comprised of able and dedicated performers. Gurdjieff and his students produced, as a by-product of their inner work, a dance company that was later acknowledged as world class by Sergei Diaghilev of the *Ballets Russes*.

Julia Ostrowska's background in the dance is unknown, but she, like her husband, developed a complete control over her moving center. Fritz Peters said of her, "I remember being fascinated by the way she moved; she walked without any perceptible movement of her head and without the slightest jerkiness in her movements; she was never hurried, but at the same time she worked at incredible speed; every movement she made in whatever she was doing was absolutely essential to that particular activity."[2] She had a presence which enabled her to integrate movement and stillness, and so to perform the difficult 'still' parts of *The Initiation of the Priestess* with complete naturalness.

Jeanne de Salzmann had studied piano, orchestral conducting, and music composition at the Conservatory at Geneva. She taught dance and rhythmic movements at the Dalcroze School at Hellerau. She took Gurdjieff's instruction completely into herself and practiced and taught the movements for the remainder of her life.

Olga Hinzenberg was an associate of the de Salzmanns from the Dalcroze Institute. She was a Montenegrin dancer of considerable natural ability, who met Gurdjieff at a point in her life where she was able to take full advantage of his teaching.

Elisabeta Galumian was an associate of the de Salzmanns at the Dalcroze School. She mastered the movements and was a gifted performer.

---

2. Peters, Fritz, *Boyhood with Gurdjieff/Gurdjieff Remembered/Balanced Man*, Bardic Press, California, 2005, p. 73.

Jessmin Howarth was a Dalcroze associate of the de Salzmanns who joined the group at the Prieuré in 1922. Like Jeanne de Salzmann, she taught dance and rhythmic movements at the Dalcroze School. She developed a rapid mastery of the Gurdjieff movements and became, with Jeanne de Salzmann, one of the two principal teachers of the movements at the Prieuré. In the years in which Gurdjieff did not practice the movements (1924-1938), she worked with Ouspensky's students, teaming with Nadine Legat, who had been the prima ballerina for the Russian Imperial Ballet and later the head of the Legat School of Dance in London.

Émile Jaques-Dalcroze, the founder of the Dalcroze School, was a Swiss composer, musician, and music educator. He studied under the composers Léo Delibes, Gabriel Fauré, César Franck, and Anton Bruckner. He realized that most people were limited in their capacity to receive and to respond to music. Just as perfect pitch is rare, so is the "innate rhythmic ability" which gives us the capacity to respond to music. The limitations of our ability to receive and respond come from learned patterns of behavior, which are connected to our subjective sense of identity. Because these patterns of behavior are not innate, they can be corrected. Dalcroze used a combination of different methods to teach his students to experience music directly through movement. He called this discipline Eurhythmics. He established a school at Hellerau, which became a world-famous center for the performing arts that focused on the education of the complete human being. As a mature educator Dalcroze worked with Rudolf Steiner, Konstantin Stanislavski, and Sergei Diaghilev. The school at Hellerau closed with the outbreak of World War I, which explains the sudden availability of so many of its faculty to Gurdjieff.[1]

Dalcroze taught that the human body was the *original instrument,* through which everyone realizes music, both apprehending it and expressing it. The movements a student makes in a Eurhythmics class are not made to convey a choreographic picture to an audience, but *to convey information back to the mover himself.* The movements are to set up a circuit of incoming impression and response, moving continuously between brain and body. With training and experience this circuit rises to ever higher levels of precision, coordination, and expressive power.[2] Dalcroze believed that both the receptive and the communicative capacities of the 'original instrument' could be

---

1. With the outbreak of the war, Dalcroze himself returned to Geneva, where he founded the Émile Jaques-Dalcroze Institute, which is active throughout the world to this day.

2. See Jaques-Dalcroze, Émile, *The Eurhythmics of Jaques-Dalcroze*, Nabu Press, Charleston, 2010, p. 65.

enhanced almost without limit. Gurdjieff's movements certainly embraced the expressive aspect of the Dalcroze system, but they went further in contributing to the individual control of the four lower centers.

While Dalcroze used the music of known composers, Gurdjieff composed music specifically for each of his movements. Pauline de Dampierre says of Gurdjieff's music:

> Its structure, its harmonies, its melody, and its rhythm must accompany not only the outward movements but also the inner impulses which develop progressively in the course of the exercise. If the quality of vibration is right, it will awaken its counterpart in the dancers; it will not carry them away nor distract them. It constantly brings them back to themselves and to their need to be open.[3]

The Dalcroze program is based on a concentration of attention, which is the same principle on which the Gurdjieff movements are based. The difference is that the Gurdjieff movements are based on an exact understanding of the working of the four lower centers, of the nature of the connections between those centers, and — above all — on a knowledge of the latent Higher Centers which constitute the original ground of our experience. In Dalcroze language Gurdjieff looked very deeply into the 'learned patterns of behavior' that spoil the workings of the 'original instrument.' For Gurdjieff these 'learned patterns of behavior' are the repertory of different acts and features, which, taken together, comprise our personality. In each one of us, the lower centers are wrongly programmed and wrongly connected. They function in relation to an artificially formed identity. In right order, each center should be liberated from the effects of this artificial identity, so that it can think directly for itself. The coordination between the centers should come, then, not from the acquired personality, but from the intellectual parts of centers. The wrong connections between the centers (or the conglomerate of learned acts which comprise our personality) are principally established at the level of the moving-instinctive and emotional parts of centers. These parts of centers continuously impact one another in many ways that we do not intend. With emotion, instinct, and motor function inextricably tangled, the intellectual center then provides an ongoing — and entirely involuntary — commentary. It constantly inserts itself as the 'I' which is the source of our behavior. This 'I' is, then, our life-illusion. The movement exercises teach one to isolate and activate the centers independently of the repertory of acts that constitutes the personality. One learns to see the intellectual center as one of four independent brains, and not as the source of "me

---

3. Pauline de Dampierre studied the movements with Gurdjieff in Paris in the 1930s and 1940s. She wrote the article, "Sacred Dance: The Search for Conscious Harmony."

thinking about myself." Only then can one place the connection between the centers in their intellectual parts, which means responding to each moment, not according to a set of pre-programmed attitudes, but according to its own unique requirements.

In *Views From the Real World* Gurdjieff explains how each individual's physical postures and movements are inextricably linked with his or her thoughts and feelings:

> We do not recognize to what an extent the intellectual, emotional and moving functions are mutually dependent, although, at the same time, we can be aware of how much our moods and emotional states depend on our movements and postures. If a man assumes a posture that corresponds, in him, to a feeling of grief or dejection, then within a short time he will actually feel grief or dejection. Fear, indifference, aversion and so on may be created by artificial changes of postures. Since all the functions of man — intellectual, emotional and moving — possess their own definite repertory of postures and are in constant reciprocal action, it follows that a man can never depart from his own repertory.[1]

Gurdjieff worked directly with students, and most of the interaction was non-verbal. There was an intuitive spontaneity in his instruction, as students succeeded in breaking from the elements of their repertory. To the extent they did break the repertory, the position of every member of the body — head, hand, or foot — became related to the positioning of the body as a whole, and excess movement fell away.

The mastery of the Gurdjieff movements leads to the emergence of a presence, existing independently of the activity of the four lower centers. When this presence is extended in time, and concentrated in itself, it becomes the unified will behind the four lower centers.

This changes one's relation to one's own body. Suddenly the body seems like something existing outside of oneself; it is no longer resistant, it is not something you have to force. It is no longer connected with heavy, complicated systems of personal fears and personal desires. It is just there: light, supple, and responsive. Thought is clearer, motion more deft and accurate. Entering this state is like being suddenly cured of a terrible disease; you see what life was really meant to be.

In this state the four lower centers may be used to communicate many things: emotions of awe, reverence, joy, fear, or sorrow — in simple, powerful, uninhibited form. In the Sufi orders of Islam, and in the orders of Tibetan Buddhism, sacred dances were actually used to communicate emotions which correspond to the reality of Worlds 6

---

1. Gurdjieff, G.I., *Views From the Real World: Early Talks of Gurdjieff*, E.P. Dutton, New York, 1973, p. 157

and 12. According to Gurdjieff the art of the dance could even be used to communicate cosmic laws. He had been exposed to this dimension of the dance at the monastery in Central Asia where he acquired the cosmology of his system.

In speaking of emotion we are moving from dance to drama, and it is the ballet which is a seamless combination of these two. Gurdjieff's ballet, *The Struggle of the Magicians,* contains dance sequences which convey powerful emotions related to both spiritual ascent and psychological degeneration.

The Black Magician and the White Magician struggle for the soul of Zenaib, and the two sets of students working under them enact spell and counter spell in dance sequences. The dance sequence of the Black Magician depicts a criminal deprivation of will, while the dance sequence of the White Magician depicts the lifting of the veil that separates human existence from World 12. There is, on the one hand, the darkest crime, and on the other transcendence and the renewal of life. The tensions in the relationship between Zenaib and Gafar are taken to the level of Love of Self (the Atman). In performance these elements were combined with Thomas de Hartmann's performance of Gurdjieff's music and Alexandre de Salzmann's brilliant sets and lighting.

The group that Gurdjieff first collected around himself in Tiflis was fully competent to realize his artistic vision. Where the ballet had achieved formal expression in Moscow, it was realized in spirit in Tiflis. When John Bennett, who had studied the performances of the Mevlevi, Yesevi, and Rufai dervishes, saw this ballet performed by Gurdjieff's troupe in Constantinople, he said he "had never seen anything like it". He was not, at that time, a student of Gurdjieff.

However, the so-promising projects of the fledgling Institute were soon to be interrupted. By the spring of 1920 the rising tide of the Bolshevik revolution had reached Georgia. The collapse of the Social Democratic Government seemed imminent, and Gurdjieff began to look for other safe havens. He might go west to Europe, or east into Turkestan and Persia. According to John Bennett, he went, with one companion, into Persia, nominally to examine the situation in that country, but actually — Bennett suggests — to "consult with people in whom he had confidence."[2] When Gurdjieff returned from his journey the decision had been made. He went to the Institute's studio in Tiflis and, in full view of his students, began to dismantle the ballet sets. It was a sharp lesson in work against identification. By May of

---

2. Bennett, J.G., *Gurdjieff: Making a New World*, Turnstone Books, London, 1973, p. 126

1920 Gurdjieff had liquidated his affairs in Tiflis and the group embarked for Constantinople.

We find no evidence that Gurdjieff had brought any of his family to Constantinople. It appears that, before leaving Tiflis, Gurdjieff found a stable situation in Russia for his family members. It may be that friends of the Gurdjieff family, who remained in Russia, and who were no longer threatened by the Turks, were able to provide for them. Whatever the case, Gurdjieff remained in close contact with his family, and three years later — in December of 1923 — he invited them to Fontainebleau.

On arriving in Constantinople, which was then the capital of the Ottoman Empire, Gurdjieff took an apartment in Koumbaradji Street, in the Péra district. Here he designed a prospectus for the Institute and outlined a complete program of activities — including ancient oriental dances, gymnastics, mime, and music. There were to be lectures on religion, science, psychology, philosophy, and art. The group was to give regular public performances as part of its Work.

Also during Gurdjieff's arrival, there occurred a strange play of fate. Thomas de Hartmann reports that "On the day after our arrival we found that Mr. and Madame Ouspensky were living in Prinkipo, half an hour by boat from the city."[1] The Ouspenskys, driven by the tide of struggle between the White and Red Armies, had moved from Essentuki to Ekaterinodar, and then, in February of 1920, left Russia for Constantinople. On arriving in Constantinople Peter Ouspensky had established himself at Prinkipo, an island district in the Sea of Marmara, just south of the city. He supported his family by teaching mathematics and languages in the Pera district. He had also started to give public lectures on the system, and to lead a small group in the Work. In June of 1920 he realized that Gurdjieff and his company had arrived in the city. It must have been quite a surprise for both men.

Gurdjieff made overtures to Ouspensky, and Ouspensky — acknowledging the fate that had brought them together again — was willing to work with him. He consigned all of his own students to Gurdjieff. We see

---

1. de Hartmann, Thomas and Olga, *Our Life with Mr. Gurdjieff*, Harper & Row publishers, San Francisco, 1964, p. 99.

Ouspensky, then, in the role of attracting students and presenting the principles of the Work, while Gurdjieff initiates the activities of the Institute, instructs in dance and the ballet, and works individually with students on the first line.

Gurdjieff soon rented a second set of rooms for the Institute at 13 Yemeneci Abdullatif Sokak, near the Galata tower, which gave the group space for lectures and presentations of different kinds.

He also rented a much larger space for the performance of the movements in a synagogue immediately adjacent, at 21 Yemeneci Abdullatif Sokak. This was popularly known as the Grand Rabbinate. After a few weeks Gurdjieff's students began to give regular Saturday performances of the sacred dances at this location. The Institute was beginning to take external form once again. Gurdjieff now had a small but totally dedicated and thoroughly professional troupe. John Bennett, then resident in Constantinople, attended one of the performances before having had any connection with Gurdjieff. He was taken aback by what he saw, and felt that, in order to produce such a result, a person would have to "completely dedicate his life."

Gurdjieff wanted to perform *The Struggle of the Magicians* at the Grand Rabbinate. He set to work with Ouspensky, Thomas de Hartman, and de Salzmann on the text, scenario, and music for the ballet. As part of their research Gurdjieff, Ouspensky, and Alexandre de Salzmann studied the dances and ceremonies of the Mevlevi dervishes, which were regularly performed at the nearby Mevlevi lodge. We recall that, in 1920, Constantinople, as the capital of the Ottoman Empire, was the greatest single center for the Sufi Orders of Islam. Ouspensky outlines Gurdjieff's project, as he saw it.

> G. gave to the ballet the central position of his work at that time. Besides this he wanted to organize a continuation of his Tiflis Institute in Constantinople, the principal place in which would be taken by dances and rhythmic exercises which would prepare people to take part in the ballet. According to his ideas the ballet should become a school. I worked out the scenario of the ballet for him and began to understand this idea better. The dances and all the other "numbers" of the ballet, or rather "revue," demanded a

long and entirely special preparation. The people who were being prepared for the ballet and who were taking part in it, would, in so doing, be obliged to study and to acquire control over themselves, in this way approaching the disclosure of the higher forms of consciousness. Into the ballet there entered, and as a necessary part of it, dances, exercises, and the ceremonies of various dervishes as well as many little known Eastern dances.[1]

After a period of time, however, Ouspensky had difficulty in working with Gurdjieff. The same problems that had surfaced in the second Essentuki workshop came up again.[2] In October of 1920 Ouspensky withdrew from the activities in the Galata district and began to teach again in Prinkipo. He continued with a longer-term plan to relocate in London, where he had some connections who might be prepared to finance his journey. He nevertheless remained on quite friendly terms with Gurdjieff and his students.

While all of this was occurring, Gurdjieff's personal situation became ever more dangerous. The Ottoman Caliphate, itself threatened from several different quarters, and fearing the betrayal of its non-Islamic nationals, was accelerating acts of genocide against its populations of Armenians and Cappadocian Greeks. Gurdjieff saw that he could not stay in Constantinople, yet he did not have the capital to move his small army of personal dependents. At just this point opportunity presented itself. Through a connection of Alexandre de Salzmann, Gurdjieff received a letter of invitation from Émile Jaques-Dalcroze, in Geneva, inviting him to settle at the Dalcroze Institute site at Hellerau, near Dresden. Gurdjieff accepted the offer without having the means to transport his dependents. He immediately made a large sum of money by curing a young man from a wealthy family of drug addiction. With the help of a tip from John Bennett, he was able to use this sum of money to purchase a British naval vessel, which he promptly resold at a very considerable profit. This gave him enough money for the

---

1. Ouspensky, P.D., *In Search of the Miraculous,* Routledge & Kegan Paul, London, 1977, p. 382.

2. We shall review Ouspenky's side of this experience in the chapter to follow.

move. On the receipt of the necessary visas, in August of 1921, Gurdjieff and his entourage travelled by train from Constantinople to Berlin.[3]

And so, in August of 1921, both Gurdjieff and Ouspensky left Constantinople — parting ways for a second time. Yet this second separation, which both men must have viewed as being potentially final, only set the stage for another, deeper phase of involvement. Peter Ouspensky's move to London proved, in the course of time, to be an indispensable prerequisite to the final establishment of the *Institute for the Harmonious Development of Man* in Fontainebleau. Immediately upon his arrival in London, Ouspensky — through his journalistic and literary connections — was given the opportunity to present the system to a wealthy and literate audience. With his unpretentious solidity, his logical clarity, and his ability to present the system clearly, he connected very well with the English. He quickly established an interested group of students, and found several wealthy patrons. These, then, were the people who made the down payment on the property at Fontainebleau and became the first generation of visiting students.

On arriving in Germany, Gurdjieff began to give lectures in Berlin, where he hoped to find a receptive audience — but the situation in Weimar Republic Germany was difficult. By December of 1921 he had moved from Berlin to Hellerau, and settled — with his entourage — at the Dalcroze Institute. He was strongly attracted to the property, and took steps to establish ownership. There were, however, some legal issues, and in June of 1922 Gurdjieff lost a civil action to acquire the property. Gurdjieff and his group still had the use of the facility, and could probably have established ownership over time, but other considerations came to the fore. It was apparent that Germany itself was becoming politically unstable. The German Communist Party was the largest Communist Party in Europe and was seen as the leading party in the International Communist movement outside of the Soviet Union. There had been attempts to overthrow the German government in 1919 and 1920, and, at the same time, the decadent, nihilistic side of Weimar culture had begun to reveal itself. We keep in mind that Gurdjieff had, in the previous four years, been run out of Moscow, Essentuki,

---

3. Bennett, J.G., *Gurdjieff: Making a New World*, Turnstone Books, London, 1973, p. 131.

and finally Tiflis by the Communists. He did not want to lose his labor once again. From early 1922 Gurdjieff had begun to investigate — through the multilingual Olga de Hartmann — possibilities that existed in Paris and London. Ouspensky and his English followers had also shown themselves willing to support a move of the Institute to the United Kingdom. Ouspensky's group quickly located a large house in Hampstead that would be suitable for a launch of the British branch.[1]

In February of 1922 Gurdjieff had visited London and addressed Ouspensky's students. He made a very trenchant presentation, speaking of the necessary foundation for work to engage Higher Centers, and why special circumstances and objective understanding were necessary. He explained that what we call 'will' is presently based in personality, and personality, as we find it, is not our own, and not in itself unified. It has been acquired through accident and imitation. Real Will — the basis for the things you really want — can only begin from essence. As Gudjieff put it, "The desires of essence are *your own* desires, but they are not conscious ... they arise automatically in you because you are like that. Essence and personality are even in different parts of you. Nearly everything that belongs to personality is in the formatory apparatus. Essence cannot use this material, and so it has no critical mind. ... Until essence begins to experience for itself, it remains as it always was. ... With most people essence continues to receive impressions until it is five or six years old. As long as it receives impressions it grows, but afterwards all impressions are taken by personality and essence stops growing. ... You cannot tell how essence can be changed and take a normal part in your life until you have more knowledge. Long study is needed, not only by oneself, but with others. This is how it is arranged for people in the Institute."[2]

Gurdjieff here outlines objective bases of school Work; he explains to the English why they need to establish a starting point to implement all that Ouspensky had taught them. He revealed objective things, that cannot be properly understood outside of schools. He then promised the controlled circumstances needed for serious work. He was also, very clearly,

---

1. *Ibid.*, p. 132
2. *Ibid.*, pp. 134-135.

treating Ouspensky as his student or protégé; in effect he was taking command. This made Ouspensky's students accessible to him, and placed him in a position where he could ask them for financial assistance. Ouspensky did not in any way resist Gurdjieff's initiatives, he just continued to be who he was. Gurdjieff made a second visit to London on March 15th, which further consolidated his connection to Ouspensky's students.

Gurdjieff then sought residential status in the U.K., and Ouspensky's students did everything they could to facilitate this. But with all the influence that Ouspensky's patron, Lady Rothermere, could bring to bear, the Home Office would not give Gurdjieff and his entourage visas for more than one month. Both the number of dependents (between 20 and 30) and the British records of Gurdjieff's activities as a Tsarist agent stood against him. By June it was clear that Gurdjieff had been refused resident status.

Having failed both to obtain a visa for the U.K. and to acquire the property in Hellerau, Gurdjieff decided to relocate to Paris. He soon determined that the group could achieve resident status in France, and, on July 14th, 1922, he brought his entourage directly to Paris from Hellerau. The costs of transportation and lodging were considerable, and it was Ouspensky's group that provided the financial backing. Gurdjieff himself was fluent in neither French nor English, and had to depend on those around him, especially Olga de Hartmann, to communicate. It was characteristic of Gurdjieff to walk into most situations with complete confidence — giving an object lesson in non—identification to all those around him.

Shortly after the group's arrival in Paris, Gurdjieff and Jeanne de Salzmann were taking a walk around the city when Jeanne suddenly recognized one of her old Dalcroze associates, Jessmin Howarth. Jeanne had studied with Jessmin at Hellerau in the late 1910s. It was a fateful reunion, exactly paralleling the reunion of the de Hartmanns and the de Salzmanns three years before in Tiflis. Jessmin was able to help Jeanne and Gurdjieff make the arrangements to rent some very reasonably priced rooms at the Dalcroze Institute, at 52 rue de Vaugirard. Beyond this Jessmin allowed Gurdjieff's company to use the Dalcroze studio, free of charge, at certain hours of the week. The movements were underway again! Almost on their arrival in Paris Gurdjieff's students were set to work making costumes and practicing the movements for twelve or thirteen hours a day.[1]

The months slipped by, and with so many personal dependents, Gurdjieff's financial reserves began to dissipate. He received significant support from Ralph Philipson, an industrialist, who was one of Ouspensky's circle. He also showed his own usual initiative in generating funds. John Bennett tells us that, "He undertook the cure of drunkards and drug addicts. He was able to start various business ventures, including a project connected with the Azerbaijan oilfields, which were still under the nominal control of private owners. He helped two groups of Russian emigres start restaurants in the Montmartre which later became famous."[2]

In the meantime, the ever-industrious Olga de Hartmann managed to locate a suitable property at the Prieuré des Basses Loges, a large château near Fontainebleau. It was an hour's drive south of Paris.

On October 1, 1922 Gurdjieff secured the château. The money for both the down payment on the property and the first mortgage payment came from Ouspensky's students, Lady Mary Rothermere and Ralph Philipson. The grounds of the Prieuré covered 200 acres, including open fields and forested land. There were various auxiliary buildings, including an enormous orangery built almost entirely of glass, and a smaller house in the garden known as "Le Paradou" (Paradise). The Prieuré was fully furnished, but had not been inhabited since 1914, and the grounds and gardens were considerably overgrown.

Shortly after the purchase of the property the group was able to move into what then became known as "the Château". The moment this occurred Gurdjieff borrowed on his ownership of the property to develop both the Château and its grounds. The group traveling with Gurdjieff were installed in Le Paradou, while the Prieuré itself was restored in preparation for the expected guests from London. Gurdjieff retained, as his Paris office, an apartment at 9 rue Commandant Marchand, and used it to manage his

---

1. Howarth, Jessmin & Dushka, *It's Up to Ourselves*, Gurdjieff Heritage Society, copyright, Dushka Howarth, 1998, p. 74.
2. Bennett, J.G., *Gurdjieff: Making a New World*, Turnstone Books, London, 1973, p. 136.

multiple business ventures. Through these ventures he was able to support the majority of the resident Russians, and, when they arrived, his extended family.

Gurdjieff at Fontainebleau

The project launched at the Prieuré des Basses Loges was the final realization of the task which had been given Gurdjieff in Central Asia fifteen years before. As we have noted, an important aspect of this task was to establish different circles of students with different levels of understanding. Gurdjieff presented the students assembled at the Prieuré with a schema of three levels: exoteric, mesoteric, and esoteric. It was a stepped down version of the schema presented in Moscow in 1916.

Exoteric: "All those who had newly entered, as well as those who had not yet acquired by their subjective merits the right to belong to the mesoteric group."

Mesoteric: All those who were "as yet initiated only theoretically."

Esoteric: All those who "were to be initiated not only theoretically ... but also practically, and to be introduced to all the means for a real possibility of self-perfection, but ... only after having been for a long time experimentally tried and verified in quite exceptionally planned circumstances."[3]

Gurdjieff did not include himself in this schema. The esoteric circle represents the senior students, with no suggestion that they are conscious beings. The mesoteric circle has taken in all the system teaching, without yet having made it their own. The exoteric circle is comprised of people without any background at all, coming to participate in the group. This schema is unpretentious, but at the same time it reflects exactly what was there. It is a working beginning. It does emphasize that, in relation to the Work, not

---

3. Gurdjieff, G.I., *Life is real only then, when "I am"*, All and Everything, Third Series, E.P. Dutton, New York, 1978, p. 77.

all people are the same. A school, whose aim is to achieve change in being, must acknowledge different levels of being.

Gurdjieff's hope was that, with the development of the teaching at Fontainebleau, new levels would be added to the top of the step-down version, which would produce a lift-on-lift effect, running through the mesoteric and exoteric circles. Eventually the step-down version would begin to resemble the original 1916 version. According to the 1916 definitions, Gurdjieff himself would have been a member of the mesoteric circle, aspiring to the esoteric circle (which would include the direct connection to Higher

Figure 19. The Prieuré in 1924.

School). According to the step-down version, he himself would be *above* the esoteric circle, lifting the entire esoteric/mesoteric/exoteric chain, and in so doing attempting to establish the connection with Higher School. As Gurdjieff himself moved from the mesoteric circle (of 1916) to the esoteric circle (of 1916), certain of those under him (presently in the esoteric circle of 1922) could rise into the mesoteric circle (of 1916), becoming fully conscious men number five. With this level of development achieved, the exoteric circle would rise to the level of 1916, being comprised of men number four, or people close to the level of number four. For these people it is important — before moving on to the more advanced stages — to ground their being in essence and develop will from that place (as Gurdjieff had explained to Ouspensky's students in London in February). In May 1922 Gurdjieff went so far as to say "Essence is germ of astral body, astral body germ of mental."[1]

Gurdjieff's immediate purpose in 1922 was to create an esoteric circle that could lift and form the circles below it. Once this circle had been created, he could focus on those students capable of responding directly to Higher Centers and rely on these students to give guidance to those who were not yet capable of responding directly to Higher Centers. This aim was *prior to* his aim of working with each of the individual men and women who came to join his group. He was looking to the life of the organization itself; he was trying to establish an objective standard in it.

Gurdjieff's hope was that once this lift-on-lift structure had been established it could be replicated. He stated in the Third Series that, "having established the main section of the Institute," he would at once begin to organize sections "in every big city of the continent of Asia, Europe, and North America."

Almost as soon as the Prieuré was occupied, people from London began to visit. Ouspensky represented the Prieuré as a special opportunity and encouraged his students to visit. John Bennett, who was in London at the time, records:

> Dr. Maurice Nicoll and Dr. Alsop, two very successful doctors and leading exponents of Jungian psychology, sold their practices and went with their wives and children. A.R. Orage sold the New Age [magazine] ... Several of our lady members, including Dr. Bell, also a psychoanalyst, Miss Crowdy, Miss Gordon, and Miss Merston, went with the same determination to go and see it through to the end.[2]

---

1. Azize, Joseph (compiler) *Gurdjieff's Early Talks 1914-1931*, Book Studio, 2014, p. 140.
2. Bennett, J.G., *Gurdjieff: Making a New World*, Turnstone Books, London, 1973, p. 136-7.

Each person who came to the Prieuré was entering a high-pressure wonderland – where the laws that govern the normal pattern of life no longer apply. In the years 1922-1923 there were between 60 and 70 residents at any one time, and there was a strict supervision of admission. At least half the residents were Eastern Europeans, and at any given time there were thirty or so English residents.

Gurdjieff had arranged a full program of work for the incoming students. The renovation of the Château and its very extensive grounds was only the beginning. The kitchen staff had to prepare three meals a day, and manage the purchasing and food storage necessary to support this. An extensive vegetable garden was planted to supply the kitchen. There was a metalwork shop and a carpentry shop, and there was the continuous work of creating the costumes, stage sets, and decorations necessary for the ballet performances. In addition, there was a stream of special projects: putting in irrigation lines, acquiring livestock, building fences. The construction of a Turkish bath was begun at the end of October 1922, and by late November Gurdjieff had secured a huge Zeppelin hangar from the French Air Force. This provided a stage for the ballet and seating accommodation for more than 300 people. This structure was to become the 'cultural center' of the Institute; it was here that the movements were rehearsed, here that the public performances were given, here that Gurdjieff gave his discourses, and here that open weekend festivities occurred. It was called simply the Study House, and it was carefully decorated in a Persian Sufi style. Gurdjieff had the entire structure insulated, and several stoves were put in place. The floor was covered with oriental carpets, and large electric lamps were set into the rafters to create the necessary lighting effects. A fountain was installed in front of the stage, which, during the events, was set to display in a sequence of changing colors. There were smaller fountains on either side of the doorway, filled with gold and silver fish. Around the walls ran a continuous low divan covered with oriental carpets. Behind the divan there were raised seats for the spectators. Alexandre de Salzmann covered the windows with designs in stained glass, rendered in harmonious colors. Around the eaves hung banners, lettered with aphorisms in a Persianate calligraphy: "Remember that work here is not for work's sake, but a means."

Figure 20. The Director of the Institute.

"Only he is just who is able to put himself in the position of others." "Remember yourself always and everywhere." It had the atmosphere of a sacred place. Gladys Alexander recalls that, "here, after the day's work, the practice of movements continued, often till the small hours of the morning, when, as the warmth from the stoves died down, the winter cold drove us back to the slightly lesser chill of the Prieuré."[1]

With the Study House established, the grounds prepared, and the first generation of students installed at the Prieuré, Gurdjieff then invited Jessmin Howarth and her pianist Rosemary Lillard to move from the Dalcroze Institute in Paris to the Prieuré. They were to work with Madame de Salzmann on the movements. It was the opportunity of a lifetime for these two ladies. Jessmin became expert in the movements and — with Madame de Salzmann — one of the two principal dance instructors of the company.

---

1. From the unpublished notes of Miss Gladys Alexander, quoted by Bennett, J.G., in *Gurdjieff: Making a New World*, Turnstone Books, London, 1973, p. 141.

What then was the pattern of the day? The kitchen staff began at five in the morning, and the getting-up bell for the rest of the house rang at half past six. Breakfast consisted of thick toasted bread, with butter and coffee. In the morning came the work of the day: putting in gardens, digging trenches, felling trees, sawing timber, building, painting, or scrubbing floors. There was a break from half past twelve to two, when a light lunch was served: stew with vegetables and a dessert. This was followed by a rest period. Tea was then served at four, and after this the group would work on the movements and selected exercises until about half past six. Then came dinner: meat with vegetables and pie to follow. When the weather was fine people dined outside at tables, when it was colder in the Russian Dining Room.[1] Gurdjieff would dine with students, except when there were guests, which was often. He then ate with the guests in the Main Dining Room, where the more formal Saturday Dinners took place. Describing what took place after dinner John Bennett wrote: "Every evening after dinner, a new life began. There was no hurry. Some walked in the garden. Others smoked. About nine o'clock we made our way alone or in twos and threes to the Study House. Outdoor shoes came off and soft shoes or moccasins were put on. We sat quietly, each on his or her own cushion, round the floor in the center. Men sat on the right, women on the left; never together."[2] Then began the focused work on the movements and sacred dances, which might continue for three, four, or even five hours – until all were exhausted.

Sometimes Gurdjieff would accelerate the work for days on end, or even a week consecutively. During such a period one worked almost around the clock; there was literally no time to oneself. One might fall asleep at night with one's work boots on, waking suddenly, only a few hours later, to coax one's stiff body into action once again. And on occasion Gurdjieff would rouse the whole household in the early hours of the morning to perform

---

1. At the Prieuré there was an informal dining room, sometimes called the Russian Dining Room, and a Main Dining Room, also called the English Dining Room. People would dress formally for the Main Dining Room.
2. Bennett, J.G., *Witness: The Story of a Search*, Dharma Book Company, Inc., New York, New York, 1962, p. 119.

some specially devised task. At any point he might impose a fast, lasting a day, or even several days, during which all work would continue.

As Thomas de Hartmann put it, "We were given minimal hours of sleep, just enough to give strength for the following day. Instead of abstinence, there is spending of forces to the utmost, attentive work renewing energies as they are spent, in the manner of a rhythmic flywheel."

Gurdjieff might break this routine at any time to give a lecture at the Study House, and throughout the day he would have personal talks with individual students. These Study House lectures were, for most students, the high point of their life at the Prieuré. They were a direct exposure to the teacher's Higher Centers. The content of each lecture would be tailored exactly to the circumstances of the Prieuré at that time. And one could never anticipate when they might occur.

Saturdays had the quality of a celebration. It was the day of the weekly banquet, and it was the day that guest performances were sometimes given. In the morning students were usually involved with preparations for one or another of the evening's activities. The first — and not the least important — activity of the day was the ritual of the Turkish Bath. The women had their baths in the afternoon, and the men began from 7:30 in the evening. Stanley Nott relates that, after an intense session in the steam room, where many jests and observations were exchanged, "We climbed down from the benches and flicked each other with bundles of twigs. Back in the hot room we shampooed and massaged each other on benches. Hot and cold shower. After washing and massaging, we drifted back one by one into the cooling room and smoked or dozed."[3] After the Turkish bath came the Saturday dinner. For this event everyone ate in the more formal English Dining Room. There was a large, central table, with long tables flanking it on either side. Older students and guests were seated at the central table, with younger students on one side, and children on the other. Stanley Nott describes the event, as only a participant could:

---

3. Nott, C.S., *Teachings of Gurdjieff: A Pupil's Journal*, Arkana, Penguin Books Ltd., London, 1990, p. 58

> These Saturday evening dinners and other special occasions were patriarchal feasts. At the beginning of the meal people sat quietly, then conversation began, but it never rose to an unpleasant pitch. In all my travels I think I have never eaten food so delicious as at these dinners — food from every quarter of the world. There was soup, meat with spices, poultry, fish; vegetables of all kinds, most wonderful salads whose juice we drank in glasses; puddings and pies, fruit of all sorts, dishes of oriental tid-bits, fragrant herbs, raw onions, and celery. Calvados and slivovitz for the elders to drink, and wine for the young and the children. A specialty was sheep's head after the meat course, done in Caucasian style, delicious and very rich. ... All the food supplies and the cooking were supervised by Gurdjieff, and there seemed no end to his recipes. He himself was a wonderful cook, and knew how to prepare hundreds of oriental dishes, though he himself never ate a great deal. ... dinner over, he would get up and lead the way into the salon, where coffee and liqueurs were handed round. He would talk — and there was almost always teaching in his talk. After the coffee, de Hartmann would play music.[1]

As the meal progressed some kind of spirits – Vieux Marc, Armagnac, or Vodka – was served and the ritual of the Toast of the Idiots began — usually going for seven rounds.

John Bennett describes what occurred after the Saturday dinner, on an evening when guests from outside of the Prieuré were invited to a staged performance:

> At the weekends the Prieuré received many visitors from Paris and elsewhere, and on Saturday evenings some of the local inhabitants of Fontainebleau and Avon were invited to watch demonstrations of the movements and exercises. These occasions were staged, as it were, in full dress. The Russian bath and supper over, the day's labours set aside, we donned our white costumes, keyed to the tension of a public performance. Those summer evenings, fading into nights spiced with the aroma of the forest, are unforgettable. I can

---

1. *Ibid.*, p. 55-57.

still hear the clanging of the entrance bell as the people streamed in, passing by the long flower beds to the study house, with the garden fountain playing a coloured rhythm of changing lights to the fitful dancing of the glow worms.[2]

On Sunday there was no work, except for the kitchen staff — who always made sure that meals were available for those who needed them. Gurdjieff would lunch in the English Dining Room and then travel to his Paris apartment at 9 rue Commandant Marchand. He would always take two or three students with him. After having done whatever business he needed to do in the city, he would meet in the evening with people at the Café de la Paix near the Paris Opera House, or sometimes at the restaurant l'Écrivisse in Montmartre. There were weeks when he would stay a few extra days in Paris to complete some business. Every couple of weeks Gurdjieff would drive, with a small group of students, in his Citroen into the French countryside.

This describes the general routine of life, which in fact varied greatly week by week. We shall now examine more closely two of the principal teaching tools Gurdjieff used at the Prieuré: 1) the practice of the movements, and 2) the Toast of the Idiots.

THE PRACTICE OF THE MOVEMENTS

The movements (and the applications of the movements in dance and in the ballet) occupied five to six hours of the day, five days a week. On the guest weekends this was six days a week. Under these circumstances the practice of the movements evolved considerably. Gurdjieff broke the movements into seven different categories. These categories were complementary, working together to produce an overall effect: firstly, in raising the performers' state of consciousness, and secondly, in preparing the performers to execute complete, choreographed, sacred dances. The seven categories were:

---

2. Bennett, J.G., *Gurdjieff: Making a New World*, Turnstone Books, London, 1973, p. 146-47

The Six Obligatories: Preliminary exercises of attention and coordination, as used and refined for centuries in the Sufi tekkes of Central Asia. These were proven aids to the control of attention.

Work Movements: Deft, precise movements which reflected the movements of work in a traditional society: harvesting, weaving, shoemaking, and the like.

Dervish Dances: Active, vital movements with dynamic rhythms, executed in an atmosphere of controlled intensity.

Women's Dances: Soft, gentle movements; embodiments of the feminine principle.

Sacred Eastern Dances: Movements of a slow tempo, executed in a reverent atmosphere. Most were drawn directly from Eastern rituals.

Prayer Movements: The lower level passively acknowledges and so invokes the Higher Level.

Multiplications: Calculated representations of the laws of three and seven, in which the group itself incarnates or embodies a cosmic principle, making it come alive. In his work with the movements in later life, Gurdjieff put an ever-greater focus on the Multiplications.

Figure 21. The Sacred Eastern Dances.

Figure 22. The Dervish Dances.

At any time during the practice, or even the actual performance of the movements, Gurdjieff might suddenly invoke the stop exercise and shout "Stop!" The effect was to suddenly freeze the dancers in unfamiliar postures. This helped to break down each person's fixed repertoire of postures and gestures. It also ensured that the performers did not lose themselves in the movements, but maintained their inner focus.

A total of twenty-seven complementary movements were developed at the Prieuré. They were treated as a working whole. A student had to learn them all in order to achieve the intended result.

Madame de Salzmann, Jessmin Howarth, Julia Ostrowska, Olgivanna Hinzenberg, and Elisabeta Galumian were the instructors — or répétiteurs — in the practice of the movements. With this intensive training Gurdjieff was preparing his group for public performance. This began with the invitation of visitors to the Prieuré on Saturday nights, and culminated, in 1924, with performances in Paris, New York, and Chicago.

THE TOAST OF THE IDIOTS

Gurdjieff had been exposed to a ritual toast used by the dervishes of the Persian Khorasan, and he felt that this ritual would be useful for his own people at the Prieuré. It became a permanent part of his teaching. For the dervishes, the student's inner community was not their family, or their clan, but their school. The Khorasanian schools did not suppress the sensual aspects of human nature; suppression would have produced a polished 'student act.' Their aim was to bring presence to all sides of human nature. Thus, the Sufi Orders had their celebrations and their festivals – but these were equally, and even especially, theaters of the Work. The Sufis had developed a 'science of idiotism' to show people where they stood in the Work: to celebrate a student's gain; to show a student what their sticking point was; to caution a student who overestimated their place. Basically, to help students to see themselves from the outside.

The 'science of idiotism' was based on a double meaning of the word idiot. On the one hand, an idiot is a person of limited intelligence, who may be viewed with contempt. On the other hand, the word can be related to genuine individuality. The root of the English word idiot is the Greek word 'idios' (ιδιος) which means 'pertaining to oneself' or 'uniquely one's own.' If a person with both the Higher Emotional and the Higher Intellectual Center active (a person who had something uniquely their own) behaved spontaneously, he or she would be perceived as a madman by those around them. People who live in a world of illusion are threatened by someone who does not share those illusions. The person who is without illusion might therefore be labelled an idiot. A person in the Work is an idiot from both points of view. Viewed from the level one below he is an idiot in the positive sense (a person without illusions), while viewed from the level one above he is an idiot in the negative sense (a person with a very limited view of things).

The ritual by which a person's idiot was determined was based on toasting and drinking, usually Armagnac or vodka. Alcohol loosens the inhibitions and encourages simple speech. In most people it weakens personality (which feels threatened by Higher Centers) and brings essence more to the fore. People may become more like children and more receptive to Higher Centers. Gurdjieff also remarked that, in relation to the teaching, alcohol can be used to "strengthen student's wish."

According to Gurdjieff there were twenty-one gradations of reason in the universe, representing twenty-one categories of idiot, from the ordinary man to the Absolute. The Absolute is, in himself, unknowable. The greatest prophets known to history — Abraham, Zoroaster, Moses, Buddha, Jesus Christ, and Muhammad — are in the nineteenth and twentieth gradations of reason (degrees of idiot). Gurdjieff referred to them as the "Sons of God". The aim of every person entering the work must be, ultimately, to reach the highest development a normal human being can reach, which is the eighteenth degree of idiot.[1] The list of the idiots that Gurdjieff normally toasted is as follows: 1. ordinary idiot, 2. super idiot, 3. arch idiot, 4. hopeless idiot, 5. compassionate idiot, 6. squirming idiot, 7. square idiot, 8. round idiot, 9. zigzag idiot, 10. enlightened idiot, 11. doubting idiot, 12. swaggering idiot, 13. born idiot, 14. patented idiot, 15. psychopathic idiot, 16. polyhedral idiot.

The first twelve idiots are all related to differentiations of type and feature. In other words, they represent different kinds of life-illusion. At the toast each new pupil was required to choose his or her own idiot from among the first twelve. They were questioned about their choice, and then Gurdjieff would assign an idiot to the person according to his own observations. There are some differentiations of development in the first stratum: for example, a hopeless idiot might develop into a compassionate idiot — but this would be something peculiar to that person's path of development.

Idiots 13-16 are one gradation up in their development. In other words, people reached this level only by working on themselves. They are, if you like, 'idiots in the Work.' While there is some differentiation of development at this level, the difference between idiots is still very much related to differences in human character and typology.

Idiots 17-21 constitute a spiritual hierarchy. They do not reflect differences of type and character, but gradations of objective reason. Of these, only 17 and 18 are possible for someone not born a prophet. Gurdjieff apparently never toasted higher than 16.

Understanding one's idiot is clearly related to understanding chief feature: how chief feature manifests in different types, and how its

---

1. *Ibid.*, p. 157-158

manifestation changes at different levels. John Bennett describes Gurdjieff's practice of the science.

> Gurdjieff had a fixed ritual in proposing the toast of the idiots. The Director started with ordinary idiots, going on to the super idiot, then the arch idiot. The fourth, the hopeless idiot, is satisfied with himself and does not see he is a 'candidate for perishing like a dog!' The true hopeless idiot has seen his own complete nothingness, but does not realize that this 'death of self' is the guarantee of his resurrection. From this stage he becomes a compassionate idiot, whose reason has opened to enter into the sufferings of others. The sixth is the squirming idiot who is not yet ready for help. There are then three 'geometric' idiots — square, round, and zigzag — who represent stages in the establishment of true reason, at first only momentarily, then comes the discovery of one's own identity and third the desperate struggle to break free. ... At the Saturday evening meals, the toasts seldom went beyond the zigzag idiot, unless he (Gurdjieff) wished to associate someone present with the characteristics of one of the next series. These are the enlightened, the doubting and swaggering idiots. Beyond these again are idiots whose characteristics are deep in their essential nature. At each stage there is a death and resurrection before a new gradation of reason is attained.[1]

The determination of a student's idiot was often accompanied by special tasks or exercises, to help the student address the obstacles connected with their place. This ritual, initiated at the Prieuré, was further developed in the Paris Apartment years, when it was performed almost every day. Gurdjieff created a range of roles to support the ritual: the Director, the Verseur (Pourer), Monsieur Egout (Sewer), Monsieur Poubelle (garbage can), Bouche d'Egout (sewer mouth), and Egout pour Sweet (sewer for sweets).[2]

---

1. *Ibid.*, p. 157-158.
2. Bennett, J.G. & Elizabeth, *Idiots in Paris*, Weiser Books, N.Y., 1991, p. ix.

We have outlined the general pattern of life and the different forms of Work that were practiced at the Prieuré. But at the heart of it there was something more essential: Gurdjieff's capacity, as a teacher, to directly transmit higher states of consciousness. When Gurdjieff noticed a student in a receptive state, or under pressure of a certain kind, he might focus all his attention on that person, and create a situation for them where their Higher Centers might ignite.

John Bennett describes such an experience. He had been suffering from a bad case of diarrhea, but had decided, nonetheless, to go and attend the movements classes. He found that, on that day, new and difficult movements were being introduced. As the session progressed, he found himself exhausted, and with each new exercise promised himself that "At the next change I will stop." But somehow he managed to continue.

> Gurdjieff stood watching intently. Time lost the quality of before and after. There was no past and no future, only the present agony of making my body move. Gradually, I became aware that Gurdjieff was putting all his attention on me. There was an unspoken demand that was at the same time an encouragement and a promise. I must not give up — if it killed me. ... Suddenly, I was filled with the influx of an immense power. My body seemed to have turned into light. I could not feel its presence in the usual ways. There was no effort, no pain, no weariness, not even any sense of weight.[3]

The movements training ended and the exercise class was dismissed. The other students went off to the house for tea. Bennett, wanting to test the new power that had been given him, went out alone into the garden, took a spade, and began to dig.

> I felt no fatigue and no sense of effort. My weak, rebellious, suffering body had become strong and obedient. The diarrhea had ceased, and I no longer felt the gnawing abdominal pains that had been with me for days. Moreover, I experienced a clarity of thought that I had only known involuntarily and at rare moments, but

---

3. Bennett, J.G., *Witness: The Story of a Search*, Dharma Book Company, Inc., New York, New York, 1962, p. 123.

which now was at my command ... The phrase 'in my mind's eye' took on a new meaning as I 'saw' the eternal pattern of each thing I looked at: the trees, the plants, the water flowing in the canal and even the spade, and lastly my own body. I recognized the changing relationship between 'myself' and 'my pattern.' As my state of consciousness changed, 'I' and my 'pattern' grew closer together or separated and lost touch. Time and eternity were the conditions of our experience .... Now I was living in Eternity and yet I had not lost my hold on Time. I was aware that Life itself is infinitely richer and greater than all that our thinking mind can possibly know about it.[1]

As the pupils began to return to the garden to begin the evening watering, I left my digging and wandered into the forest. I went past the stone quarry, past the saw-pit, along a path that led up the hill behind Avon. The great trees, the grey rocks, the cloudless sky and the murmur of evening insects all blended with my inner life. There was no distinction of outside and inside: everything was where it was, and so was neither inside nor outside of anything else. I no longer wished to test anything or prove anything; I was satisfied to be just as I was. ...

Turning a bend in the path, where there was a big grey rock, I met Gurdjieff. Our meeting seemed inevitable, although I had never been in that part of the Forest before. Without any preliminaries, he began to talk about the energies that work in man.[2]

Having explained something of the range of energies accessible to man, Gurdjieff told Bennett that he had become momentarily connected to a 'cosmic accumulator' of energy. He stated: "Those who have this quality [of access to the accumulator] belong to a special part of the highest caste of humanity. It may be that one day you will become such, but you will have to wait for many years. What you have received today is a taste of what is possible for you."[3] Gurdjieff told Bennett that he could become part of his

---

1. *Ibid.*, p. 123-124.
2. *Ibid.*, p. 124,
3. *Ibid.*, p. 124.

longer-term plans for the Institute if he wished, and that he would speak to him about it in a few days' time.

So, behind the spectrum of activities we have described, this level of activity was also occurring. Peter Ouspensky described similar experiences, at an earlier stage of the work, in Finland and in Essentuki. Gurdjieff's inner circle was bonded to him at this level. And yet this is only a first stage, in relation to forging a connection to the Inner Circle of Humanity. Should Gurdjieff move to the level above the level he was on, and a number of his students move into the level that Gurdjieff promised Bennett, then the step-down model of esoteric, mesoteric, exoteric would move up one notch, bringing them one step closer to the original schema of 1916.

We step back, then, to consider the effect that this whole experience — from scrubbing the kitchen floor to special contacts with the teacher — would have on a student. It is hard even to imagine. The pressure of work is high and unrelenting: through certain hours of the day your knees are weak and you feel giddy. In certain moments you actually struggle to keep your eyes open. At other times you feel a magical renewal of life, and in particular moments you may glimpse a world outside of time and space. The scheduled sequence of events that comprises the day is punctuated by moments of primal intensity. Such moments may come with the teacher's discourse at the Study House, the performance of the Sacred Dances, or the Toast of the Idiots. Or they may come unheralded: a fire in the kitchen, an unexpected drive with Gurdjieff into Paris, a painful observation of one's chief feature that catches one off guard. There are times when you feel you are actually living a tale from *The Arabian Nights*. But these moments alternate with moments of aridity, exhaustion, and despair. You are directly challenged in your areas of deepest identification. You cannot hide anything from anybody. Your learned sense of individuality is shaken to the core. You experience the searing fires of self-deprecation. As the days lengthen into weeks and months you begin to see yourself as exactly equivalent to all the other players around you, in a kind of other-worldly drama. You come to know your fellow students as formative characters in your own life — and in fact you do form one another. This is life lived to the hilt: lived as if there were no tomorrow and no yesterday. It is the intensity of the gladiatorial arena, but more is at stake — for the different levels of your being are being separated out in an alchemical process for which there is no going back. In this context you are able to understand, in an entirely different way, the standards of the Inner Circle of Humanity. The Inner Circle is no less distant, *but the measure that defines it is no longer abstract*. You see that the students of the group have been gathered – magnetically attracted as it were – into a kind of mystery play. And the whole bundle of roles that comprises the play is wound up tight, like a living connected organism. Gurdjieff had created a "great living thing" that abstracted the limiting circumstances of contemporary civilization. The Institute at the Prieuré was an approximation of the great living laboratory that humanity *is supposed to be*.

And what did the *students* understand the aim of all of this to be? Gurdjieff said, at one of his lectures at the Prieuré:

> We have an ark, in which we can take refuge from the flood. The teaching, based on ancient objective knowledge, is an ark; and in this ark are preserved the seeds of that from which a real culture, a real civilization could grow.[1]

John Bennett leaves us with his own statement.

> One day he (Gurdjieff) took me in his big car for a drive in the forest of Fontainebleau, ending up in a clearing from which we could look down on the Prieuré. He sat on a fallen tree, and he told me how he intended the Institute to develop, how it would become a center of training and research not only into the powers of man himself, but into the secrets of the solar system. He said he had invented a special means for increasing the visibility of the planets and the sun, and also for releasing energies that would influence the whole world situation. Looking back, I can see how, in my naiveté and inexperience, I accepted all these claims and was ready to devote myself to helping Gurdjieff to realize them. Soon after this, Gurdjieff did indeed show me how to release energies such

---

1. Nott, C.S., *Journey Through This World*, Routledge & Kegan Paul, 1969, p. 113.

as I had never before experienced and to know things I could not possibly have known otherwise. I believe that, with all the exaggerations and absurdities, Gurdjieff was seriously planning a great undertaking and moreover intended to do this on his own initiative and responsibility.[2]

Having attempted to provide some overview of what life in the Institute at the Prieuré was like, we return to our narrative. In December of 1923 Gurdjieff's family — after four years of separation — arrived from Russia. He had summoned them to come, and he found quarters for them in Le Paradou. The Turks had taken their home in Alexandropol and the Bolsheviks their refuge in Russia. The family group included his mother; his brother Dmitri with his wife Asta and their three daughters; his sister Sophie with her husband George Kapanadze and their daughter Lucia; and finally his nephew Valentin Anastasieff. Young Valentin was the only surviving member of Gurdjieff's eldest sister's (Anna Anastasieff's) family. As Valentin matured, he became his uncle's student, and remained with him through the Paris apartment years until Gurdjieff's death.

In that same month, after fourteen long months of preparation, Gurdjieff decided to present the Sacred Dances to the world at large. We have described the effect of the movements on the state of the individual performer. But the movements are *group activities,* and when executed by a group they can generate a shared force field that enters into the experience of the audience. The unfolding movements of the individual dancers on the stage give expression to special inner relationships that are inscribed in the essence of the dance. The movement is, then, a kind of hieroglyph. As the dancers move through their positions together, the group is charged with an influence that is transmitted to the audience; they are revealed as the bearers of cosmic forces.

---

2. Bennett, J.G., *Gurdjieff: Making a New World*, Turnstone Books, London, 1973, p. 148.

The performances at the Study House had already drawn public attention. Sergei Diaghilev, a friend of Thomas de Hartmann's, had attended several of the performances and had asked Gurdjieff if the company would appear as an item on a billing with the *Ballets Russes*.[1] Gurdjieff refused, but he eventually received an offer for an exclusive billing at the Théâtre des Champs-Elysées. The prospect of performing at such a venue must have been both a surprise and a challenge to his students. On December 16th 1923, the Sacred Dances premiered at the Théâtre des Champs-Elysées.

The reviews of the performance were mixed. All the reviewers were greatly impacted: some very favorably, while others were shocked and repelled. For the movements revealed, not only something of man's relation to a Higher Level, but also something of the illusion of human individuality. In other words, in certain moments, all the performers seemed to be the moving expressions of a single mind. Gurdjieff himself showed not the slightest interest in the reviews. He just proceeded with his plans.

Only two weeks later, on 4th January 1924, he set sail for America with a company of thirty-five students to make public demonstrations of the movements in New York, Philadelphia, Boston, and Chicago. The effect was electrifying, on both the audiences and the performers. Stanley Nott had his first contact with Gurdjieff and his group at one of the New York performances. He describes the performance as follows:

> ... never in the East or West had I seen anything to compare with the loveliness, the grace, the charm of these. The names were given as The Sacred Goose, The Lost Loves, The Prayer, The Waltz, and so on. ...
>
> All though the evening thoughts and feelings had been stirring within me, reminding me by association of vivid emotional experiences — of dances of men and women I had seen in India and China; of the incredibly sweet singing of women in temples; of the drums; of the Taj Mahal, the Sphinx, and the Pyramids; the images of Buddha; the singing of choirs and the pealing of the organ in old cathedrals at Easter; all that had most deeply touched me in

---

1. Nott, C.S., *Teachings of Gurdjieff: A Pupil's Journal*, Arkana, Penguin Books Ltd., London, 1990, p. 48.

religion, music, and art had been gradually waking. Now the music of the Big Group began in a slow and solemn measure, almost of warning. As it proceeded, rising and falling in waves of sound, a sense of joy pervaded my feelings; at the same time my mind was fixed on the complicated movements of the pupils. But with the feeling of joy was blended a sense, not of sadness, but of deep seriousness. It was as if it were saying something to me and I was trying to understand — a script that I was trying to decipher. Then, as the music swelled to a triumphant crescendo, a light broke. 'This,' I felt, 'is what I have always been searching for. Here is what I went to the ends of the earth to find. Here is the end of my search!'[2]

It was during this trip, on 8th April, 1924, that Gurdjieff founded the New York branch of his Institute, based on the contacts established during the tour. These contacts were to be important for the future of his work. The first students included Stanley Nott, Margaret Anderson, Muriel Draper, Jane Heap, Gorham Munson, and Jean Toomer. Many of these people were part of a literary circle based in an avant-garde bookshop called *The Sunwise Turn*. It is interesting that Gurdjieff was drawing from exactly the same social stratum that Ouspensky had drawn from in London: relatively well-to-do literati. In the autumn of 1924 Gurdjieff sent one of his first students from London, A.R. Orage, to New York to supervise the group and to share what he had learned at the Prieuré. Orage had been through the kind of initiation described by Bennett, and was himself a literary figure. He was well equipped to relate the values of an avant-garde pseudo-esoteric culture to the realities of the Work.

We note here that Jeanne de Salzmann, Gurdjieff's principal instructor in the movements, was unable to participate in the demonstrations — at either the Théâtre des Champs-Elysées or later in America. She had become pregnant by Gurdjieff, and their son Michel was born on 31st December, 1923. Jessmin Howarth, who stood in for Jeanne de Salzmann, realized on the tour that she too was pregnant by Gurdjieff.[3] To be clear: Gurdjieff

---

2. *Ibid.*, p. 11.
3. Howarth, Jessmin & Dushka, *Its Up To Ourselves*, Gurdjieff Heritage Society, New York, New York, 1998, p. 68. Jessmin Howarth informed Gurdjieff of the

had sex with his students. Both Jeanne de Salzmann and Olga Hinzenburg spoke of sex with Gurdjieff as a natural part of their relation to their teacher, and something that had a beneficial effect on their evolution. Elizaveta Stjernvall also had a son by Gurdjieff in 1919. For the most part, sex with Gurdjieff was a consensual act between adults, but there were also unfortunate incidents.[1]

John Bennett speaks of Gurdjieff's relationship with women.

> With some there was no sexual element, with others a very strong sexual element. His sexual life was strange in its unpredictability. At certain times he led a strict, almost ascetic life, having no relation with women at all. At other times, his sex life seemed to go wild and it must be said that these unbridled periods were more frequent than the ascetic. ... Quite a number of his women pupils bore him children and some of them remained closely connected with him all their lives. Others were just as close to him, as far as one could tell, without the sexual relationship.[2]

He then elaborates on Gurdjieff's teaching concerning sex.

> He was very insistent that sex should be separated from the intellectual and emotional life of man. Sex was sex and, if treated as such, was not only a legitimate but even a necessary part of the process of our development. ... His teaching about the transformation of the sexual energy [into the energies associated with consciousness] is

---

pregnancy, and told him of her plan to manage the situation. She recorded that: "Gurdjieff vetoed my plan of going to live with friends in Italian Switzerland, and went off (to France) without leaving me a return ticket." Within weeks of his return to France Gurdjieff had a near-fatal auto accident, which interrupted whatever plans he may have had for Jessmin Howarth's future. She had to fend for herself, and only reconnected with Gurdjieff (with her daughter) after the war.

1. One of these is recounted by James Webb (see Webb, James, *The Harmonious Circle*, Shambhala, Boston, 1987, pp. 333, 362, and 384). A different perspective on the same incident is given by Jessmin Howarth (see Howarth, Jessmin & Dushka, *It's Up to Ourselves*, Gurdjieff Heritage Society, New York, New York, 1998, p. 68-69).

2. Bennett, J.G., *Gurdjieff: Making a New World*, Turnstone Books, London, 1973, p. 231-232.

very personal and he was emphatic that there are no general rules that can be given. In some cases he regarded abstinence as desirable, in others encouraged strong sexual activity ... In some cases, he demanded at least for a time a completely promiscuous sexual life in order to rid a man of obsession with sex. This variety of advice as regards sex leaves one with the feeling that Gurdjieff did not wish to give any rules that people would take to be universally valid and that could lead not only to misunderstanding but even to disaster.[3]

More generally, the concentration of higher energies in Gurdjieff's circle made them, in a way, closer than family. The intensity and depth of commitment that defines school Work is the most intimate connection that can exist between human beings, for school is a living connection to a Higher Level. This intimacy makes sex energy between people more difficult to deal with, not less difficult. People may find themselves intensely sexually attracted for no apparent reason, and certainly people are more prone to falling in love. A teacher may choose an ascetic path for their school, or they may incorporate sex into the school in one of several different ways. Because of the potency of the energies involved, sex will always remain a challenge for human beings. It is never something we tidily resolve. It is the responsibility of a school to help each student address their identification with sex, and the sexual aspect of their identity, just as it is the responsibility of school to help each student address their identifications with money, food, and social status.

And there is another aspect to sex. The energies connected with the sexual act, in its purity, correspond to the level of the energy with which the Higher Emotional Center functions. They are not *the same as* the energies with which the Higher Emotional Center functions, but they are *related to* that energy, and they can evoke that energy. They both involve what Gurdjieff called hydrogen 12. (Technically sex energy is si-12, and the Higher Emotional Center functions more directly with mi-12 and sol-12, which develop from the intake of impressions.) Because of this connection

---

3. *Ibid.,* p. 233-234.

sex can be used to bring students into higher states of consciousness. This was a known practice in the tantric Buddhism of Tibet, which was otherwise an ascetic path. It is likely that Gurdjieff helped some of his students through having sex with them, and made mistakes with others. It is not our place to assess his performance in this area, but to acknowledge that it was another part of the amazing composite experience that was the Institute at the Prieuré.

When Gurdjieff returned to Paris from the six-month American tour, in June of 1924, he exchanged his Paris apartment at Commandant-Marchand for a new apartment at 47 Boulevard Peréire (just east of the Place de Wagram by the Porte d'Asnières). Activities were reaching a crescendo. Gurdjieff was managing and administering the Prieuré, acting as a teacher to students on two continents, giving regular lectures on the system, arranging dance performances, managing restaurants in Paris and business investments in Central Asia.

Despite this phenomenal level of activity, all was not going quite according to plan. The Work of the Institute was not conforming to the template Gurdjieff had originally worked out in consultation with 'respected individuals' in Central Asia. In the summer of 1923, before the tour, there had been several internal shakeups, and on the 21st August 1923, Gurdjieff stated the following at one of his meetings:

> For one section of the people here their stay has become completely useless. If this section were to be asked why they were here, they would be completely unable to answer or they would answer something quite nonsensical, would produce a whole philosophy, themselves not believing what they were saying. A few may have known at the beginning why they came but forgot it later. ...
>
> There is only one salvation: to remember day and night that you are here only for yourself and everything and everyone around you must either not hinder you or you must act so that they do not hinder you. You must make use of them as means for attaining your aims. Yet everything is done here except that. This place has been turned into something worse than in ordinary life. Much worse. All day long people are either occupied with scandal, or they blacken one another, or they think things inwardly, judge and consider

with each other, finding something sympathetic, something antipathetic; they strike up friendships, collectively or individually play tricks on each other, concentrate on the bad sides of each other.[1]

This observation describes what is *below* the level of the exoteric. It describes the level of the uninitiated who are outside of any teaching. At the same time, it affirms the standards of the exoteric: being able to hold a line of Work for yourself, and not being affected by the sleep of other people. We note that Gurdjieff is here describing *only one section* of his students, and perhaps only one aspect of that section. At the same time, he is describing a phenomenon that affected, and so limited, the level of development of the group as a whole.

In August 1923 Peter Ouspensky received a telegram from Madame Ouspensky, telling him to come to the Prieuré immediately. When Ouspensky arrived, he went directly to meet Gurdjieff. After a long silence Gurdjieff told him that he was "very dissatisfied with the work and attitude of several people in the Institute" and that "the momentum of the work was such that he could not control it in the same way." We do not have Ouspensky's response, but we note here that Gurdjieff is treating Ouspensky as a colleague, and as a fellow teacher, rather than as a student. Was he tacitly acknowledging that Ouspensky had awakened? But, in sum, as the level of activity accelerated, there were unresolved problems to be addressed.

From the Motor Crash to All and Everything: 1924–1935

In July of 1924 matters came to the breaking point. To understand what happened it is necessary to enlarge upon the context. A particularly stressful part of Gurdjieff's schedule had been his weekly commute to and from Paris. In order to make this journey he had taught himself to drive, at least to his own satisfaction — but his passengers found the experience terrifying. Kathryn Hulme notes, "He drove like a wild man, cutting in and out

---

1. Azize, Joseph (compiler) *Gurdjieff's Early Talks 1914-1931*, Book Studio, 2014, pp. 268-270.

of traffic without hand signals or even space to accommodate his car in the lanes he suddenly switched to ... the chances he took overtaking buses and trucks were terrifying."[1] Olga de Hartmann, as a single passenger in Gurdjieff's car, once reached a point where — after several comments about the driver's speed — she asked him to stop the car. Presuming Olga needed to use the washroom, he did so. But she got out of the car, went into an adjoining service station, and called for her husband to pick her up. Gurdjieff drove away, as if in anger, but returned in five minutes and said he would go any speed she wished if she would re-enter the car. After the two had returned to the Prieuré, Gurdjieff, passing through the kitchen, made some remark about Olga's behavior to Madame Ouspensky and Madame Ostrowksa. When Olga later came into the kitchen, the two ladies criticized her for daring to teach Gurdjieff to drive, and not trusting implicitly in the wisdom of the Master. She replied tartly that, "If he believed he could drive on clouds it was alright, but I did not want to be on such a trip."[2]

On the 5th of July 1924 Gurdjieff, returning alone from Paris, went off the road north of Fontainebleau and crashed into a tree. He was discovered, by chance, by a gendarme, lying unconscious by the side of the road, some twenty feet from the car, with a pillow under his head. How had he gotten away from the car? Who had placed the pillow under his head? Shortly after the gendarme's discovery of the body — and by sheer coincidence — an ambulance came by, and the gendarme hailed it. Gurdjieff was taken directly to the hospital with a severe concussion and remained there, in a coma, for five days. The doctors did not expect him to recover, yet — to their surprise — he did regain consciousness. By his own wish, and at the request of his students, he was released to convalesce at the Prieuré. For several weeks he could not speak and did not leave his room. When he was finally able to leave his room, he was a different man. It was to take him years to fully recover. This was to change everything.

Olga de Hartmann took over the daily administration of activities at the Prieuré. After several weeks Gurdjieff appeared in the gardens, his head

---

1. Quoted by Howarth, Jessmin & Dushka, *Its Up To Ourselves*, Gurdjieff Heritage Society, 1998, p. 233.
2. *Ibid.*, p. 233.

bandaged and his eyes concealed by dark glasses. He did not recognize students. Jean Toomer said, "My impression was that he took each walk as he took each step, deliberately and with unswerving determination. He did not speak to anyone — or show any recognition of their existence, if he saw them at all."[3] After several weeks of making periodic appearances, he gradually began to superintend activities from his chair.

Seven weeks after the accident, on 26th August 1924, Gurdjieff assembled everyone in the Study House and stated: "What happened to me, how it happened, I do not know. I remember nothing. I went to the place where it happened and imagined how it happened. ... In principle, I had to die, but accidentally I stayed alive."[4] Gurdjieff then told his students that he had decided to close the Institute. In explaining his action he said:

> First of all, there are very few close people who understand. I gave all my life for my Work but the result from other people in general was not good, and that is why I think it is not necessary for those few to sacrifice their lives here. And I don't wish to continue as I have done until now. All my life I gave up all my money to other people, but now I have decided to close the Institute. Forgive me. I wish now to live for myself and tell everyone that the Institute is closed. I will liquidate this house. There are many people here; they can live here as guests. I always received guests for two weeks, and now my house is also open for two weeks, but later I will ask everyone to leave. All the same, I cannot throw away all my Work ... In two weeks I will begin a new Work. The names of those who may stay will be posted. Others will have to leave.[5]

And from a different record of the same talk:

> Again, I repeat that the Institute is closed. I died. The reason is that I was disenchanted with people after all that I have done for them,

---

3. Quoted in Webb, James, *The Harmonious Circle*, Shambhala, Boston, 1987, p. 291.
4. de Hartmann, Thomas and Olga, *Our Life with Mr. Gurdjieff*, Harper & Row publishers, San Francisco, 1964, p. 140.
5. *Ibid.*, p. 140-1.

and I have seen how "well" they have paid me for it. Now inside of me everything is empty.[1]

With respect to this speech Thomas de Hartmann said, "My wife and I, and Gurdjieff's wife also, saw very clearly that he was not well ... that something had not yet come back to him."[2]

The visiting students were given two days to move out. A new 'post-Institute' direction of Work was not announced at the end of two weeks, but those who stayed continued to maintain the Prieuré and to keep up the principal Work activities.

There are several things to note about Gurdjieff's statement. When he said that "the result from other people in general was not good," he did not mean that people were not making a sufficiently rigorous line of effort, but that they had not internalized the Work in the right way. Then, implying that there were some who had internalized the Work in the right way, he stated, "It is not necessary for those few to sacrifice their lives here." This reveals how Gurdjieff saw his own "inner circle." It was to the degree of sacrificing one's own life.

Gurdjieff's ultimatum was not just a test or a teaching gambit; he was actually disbanding the Institute. This was not simply because, after the accident, he could no longer perform all the functions necessary to being its director, but because he saw problems with the way the Work had been developing. He took the motor accident as a fateful sign that the project of the Institute — as originally determined by himself and 'honorable individuals' in Central Asia — was off course. Gurdjieff felt that not only were there problems with the Institute, but problems between the project of the Institute itself and the social order of which it was a part. Reflecting on this in the *Third Series* Gurdjieff stated: "I am now quite convinced — it [the motor accident] was the last chord of the manifestation toward me of that

---

1. Azize, Joseph (compiler) *Gurdjieff's Early Talks 1914-1931*, Book Studio, 2014, p. 397.
2. de Hartmann, Thomas and Olga, *Our Life with Mr. Gurdjieff*, Harper & Row publishers, San Francisco, 1964, p. 141.

'something' usually accumulating in the common life of people."[3] This 'something accumulating in the common life of people' was, ultimately, the tendency to reject conscious influence. In *The Herald of Coming Good* Gurdjieff called this accumulative cause *Tzvarnoharno,* and related it to the many disasters that have befallen schools in history.[4] *Tzvarnoharno* is an overall outcome of the "evil actions" of a people and leads to "the destruction of both him that tries to achieve something for the general human welfare and of all he has accomplished to this end." A Vedantic teacher might have used the term 'karma' to describe such a cause: *Tzvarnoharno* would then be the result of a 'collective karma.' Gurdjieff felt that he himself (and so the Institute) had been subject to the working out of such a karma.

Nevertheless, life itself did go on.

> Little by little life in the Prieuré resumed its activity, but there was something new. Mr Gurdjieff began to travel through France and Switzerland, always taking several people with him. ...
>
> At the same time the work indispensable to the maintenance of the house went on. The composition of music, movements, talks by Gurdjieff in the Study House, and individual work with pupils — all this continued as before. And nothing, but nothing, was done at the Prieuré which was not intended to give experiences to one or another of us ...[5]

Gurdjieff did not sleep well after his initial recovery. Olga de Hartmann observed:

---

3. Gurdjieff, G.I., *Life is real only then, when "I am",* All and Everything, Third Series, E.P. Dutton, New York, 1978, p. 80.

4. On p. 21 of *The Herald of Coming Good* (Sure Fire Press, Edmonds, Washington, 1988) Gurdjieff describes Tzvarnoharno as the general social cause that defeated the work of King Solomon. Despite Solomon's dedicated labor to realize the Ark of the Covenant, as given by Moses, on his death the Kingdom of Israel split irreversibly into Israel in the north and Judah in the south. According to Gurdjieff, the cause for this failure lay not with Solomon, or with the aims he labored for. It was simply not in the being of the people of Israel to realize the covenant.

5. de Hartmann, Thomas and Olga, *Our Life with Mr. Gurdjieff,* Harper & Row publishers, San Francisco, 1964, p. 142.

> Mme de Salzmann and Mr. de Hartmann would sit with him. I generally knew about it and would bring them coffee.[1]

In the end, a number of Gurdjieff's inner circle, a number of dependent Russians, and all of Gurdjieff's family members remained. It is impossible to know exactly what determined who stayed and who went; it was not simply a matter of the level of inner Work. Madame Ouspensky moved to Asnières-sur-Seine in the north of Paris, and Olgivanna Hinzenberg went to New York, eventually marrying Frank Lloyd Wright and becoming a central figure in his organization at Taliesin.

Activities were to continue at the Prieuré estate for another eight years, until the mortgage foreclosed in May of 1932. At that time the remaining occupants were finally dispersed. But these activities did not represent a concerted attempt by Gurdjieff to create a hierarchy of esoteric/mesoteric/exoteric circles, capable of functioning in a direct relation to Higher School. What continued was an organization of sorts, centered around the Prieuré, with a conscious teacher inside of it. Gurdjieff did still occasionally refer to it as 'the Institute,' but he was no longer the "man with a mission" that his students had known between 1912 and 1924.

While Gurdjieff asked many of his closest students to leave the Prieuré in 1924, he did not sever contact with the American students who had joined in the wake of the American tour, six months earlier. Orage's partner Jessie Dwight and his student Jean Toomer were invited to stay at the Prieuré. Orage continued as the director of the New York branch of the Institute. Jean Toomer was eventually made the director of a Chicago branch. And new American students continued to visit the Prieuré on a regular basis. Madame de Hartmann was still administering the estate, and she would assign people to different projects, where there might or might not be oversight. In 1925 Jane Heap, a member of the New York branch, moved to Paris and visited the Prieuré. She was discouraged from permanently relocating at the Château and took an apartment in Paris. There she initiated — with Gurdjieff's approval — a group in Montmartre, which attracted students who were to become part of the later phase of Gurdjieff's work.

---

1. *Ibid.*, p. 142.

While Gurdjieff ceased to teach the movements himself, their practice continued nonetheless. Jessmin Howarth and Rosemary Nott taught movements classes to Ouspensky's students in London, and then later at his estate in Mendham. Olgivanna Hinzenberg initiated movements classes at Frank Lloyd Wright's estate at Taliesin, Wisconsin. Jeanne de Salzmann taught the movements in Sèvres, beginning from 1928. Gurdjieff was to become involved with the movements once more in 1938, when he connected with Jeanne de Salzmann's Sèvres group.

To return to Gurdjieff himself, the accident and the forced closure of the Institute was not the end of his adversity. In the spring of 1925, his mother contracted a liver disease, and she died in June of that year. That winter Madame Ostrowska was diagnosed with cancer, and she died on the 26th June 1926. Gurdjieff was certain that he could have helped both of these ladies — the two people closest to him — had his own health remained intact. In fact, he was obliged to watch both ladies die while he himself remained incapacitated. This was, for him, a private Golgotha.

As he slowly recovered his powers, he considered how he might put his energies to best use. He came to a definite decision: it began in this way. On the 16th December, 1924, Gurdjieff, the de Hartmanns and Alexandre de Salzmann were staying at the Paris apartment on Boulevard Péreire. It was late in the evening and Olga de Hartmann thought to bring Gurdjieff a cup of coffee.

> ... I took Gurdjieff coffee at night, I told him that both Mr. de Hartmann and Mr. de Salzmann had to get up early to leave for work in the morning. He asked me, "Could you write what I will dictate to you? Are you too sleepy?" I said, "I can, I am not sleepy. But I do not know shorthand." He said, "That's all right. Bring your notebook."
>
> He began to dictate in Russian a kind of melodrama where brothers killed each other and so on and so on. I wrote practically three pages before Gurdjieff stopped me and asked me, "Does it please you?" I told him in all sincerity that I felt it was awful, that it was terrible, and that I'd like to throw it away.
>
> Gurdjieff very quietly told me, "All right. Throw it in the wastepaper basket. We will write something else. Perhaps it will please

Figure 23. Thomas and Olga de Hartmann at the Prieuré.

you better." With great pleasure, I tore out the three pages and threw them away.

Gurdjieff began to dictate again: "It happened in the 123rd year after the creation of the World ... Through space flew the ship Karnak." He did not stop dictating till I had written three pages, and I sat there quite transported to another sphere. He asked, "Does it please you now? Do you wish to continue?" I could not even utter a word, but he understood from my face how happy I was.

... So "Beelzebub" was born, and on the first draft, from the beginning to the last page — which was written in the Café de la Paix in Paris on a little round marble table — he worked only with me.[1]

It is amusing to see how Gurdjieff elicited Olga de Hartmann's total allegiance in the vast project of *Beelzebub's Tales,* by making the decision to do it partly her own. Gurdjieff had determined to record, in writing, the understandings of his lifetime. In his own words:

> I decided to devote all the functions of my inner world to the end that somehow I might expound the very essence of all the material

---

1. *Ibid.,* p. 145-147.

elucidated by me for the welfare of humanity in the form of some kind of exposition.[2]

But he reached an impasse in late 1925. The students who were asked to review the draft manuscript had difficulty understanding it. Orage was summoned from New York to act as editor. He declared that the first draft of *Beelzebub's Tales* was unintelligible. Gurdjieff wrote: "I certainly and clearly understood, without doubt, that, of these writings of mine, people who did not know me personally could understand absolutely nothing."[3] He focused ever more determinedly on his task. Orage commuted from New York to review the manuscript with him. But Gurdjieff remained unsatisfied with his progress: what he had in him was not, somehow, coming across. Finally, he sought special means to motivate himself. On November 6, 1927 he made the following, rather drastic, aim:

> If unable to discover this means, then, on the evening of the last day of the old year [December 21, 1927], to begin to destroy all my writings, calculating the time so as, at midnight with the last page, to destroy myself also.
>
> From that day on, while trying outwardly to live and work just as before so that my unusual state should not be noticed by the people surrounding me, I directed my thoughts only to this question of how to emerge from my desperate situation.... I became perceptibly thinner and more feeble, and what's more, in addition to this, there for some reason began to reappear in me the consequences of my former ailments contracted many years before.[4]

He felt a shell of his former self. He thought carefully about what might help him to succeed with his writing aims. Shortly before the new year (with its drastic solution to the problem) he formulated three related aims:

---

2. Gurdjieff, G.I., *Life is real only then, when "I am"*, All and Everything, Third Series, E.P. Dutton, New York, 1978, p. 32.
3. *Ibid.*, p. 33.
4. *Ibid.*, p. 35.

1. To rewrite all of my expositions, but in a new form which I now already understood.
2. To make clear to myself some still obscure questions concerning the 'common psyche of man,' and make use of this information for my writings.
3. To renew my physical body and spirit, so that when my writings are complete, I can direct the spreading of them myself.[1]

With respect to the first aim, he had the conviction that the right use of conscious suffering would be a key to success: "Although it is possible to attain any self-imposed aim, it can only be done exclusively through conscious suffering."[2] Working at this pace, it was to take him another year — until late 1928 — to get a first draft.

Before going further we must ask: What was the all-consuming writing project on which Gurdjieff banked so much? In his personal life it was a replacement for the Institute, into which he had put all his life force for the previous eighteen years. The 'replacement task' had to be something that would sum up his life's work and allow him to contribute what he had understood to others.

ALL AND EVERYTHING: BEELZEBUB'S TALES TO HIS GRANDSON

Gurdjieff had a great deal of valuable material to put into a book. He had a unique vision of the place of man in the universe, and a special understanding of what it meant that Mankind existed in the state of sleep. He had acquired an extraordinary cosmology with which to interpret and classify his understandings. And he had a vision of the unfolding of human history that corresponded exactly to this cosmology. He was able, convincingly, to place the struggles of the Absolute — Our Common Father — at the center of the pattern of human history. Beyond this he had formulated a myth which would pull all of these pieces together. He had created his own ashokh song, just as his father had created mythic songs in Alexandropol, sixty years before.

Beelzebub's Tales is a myth that provides the backdrop for the emergence, the rise, and the fall of the great schools of history. It shows us the repeated appearance of an

---

1. *Ibid.*, p. 35.
2. *Ibid.*, p. 41.

Inner Circle of Humanity, and it shows its repeated dissolution. It conveys a sense of the truth of each of the great religions. And, in this context, it paints a vivid picture of the childish, self-preoccupied, and daemonic quality of the modern age, so strangely reminiscent of Babylon or Atlantis. It provides modernity with the critique it so badly needs.

We keep in mind that when *Beelzebub's Tales* was written — from 1924 to 1928 — it was the only record of the cosmology that Gurdjieff had acquired. A better and more complete record of the cosmology had been presented verbally in the Petrograd lectures of 1916-1917. Peter Ouspensky had recorded these in the draft of *In Search of the Miraculous*, which was only published in 1949.[3] While Ouspensky's record is much clearer and more complete than the cosmology of *Beelzebub's Tales*, the latter does contain cosmological principles that are absent from *In Search*: the elaboration of the triadic nature of the Absolute; the relation between the Absolute and Creation (as expressed in the law of the Merciless Heropass); and the structure of self-maintenance that is inscribed in the Macrocosm of Creation (what Gurdjieff called the trogoautoegocratic process). There is also interesting material on the different levels of school in the universe.

Having said this, there is an allegorical dimension to *Beelzebub's Tales*. There is cosmological material not intended to be taken literally, and, at the same time, there are buried truths that complete the cosmology given in the St. Petersburg talks.

Given the value of *Beelzebub's Tales*, we must say that it was not what its author believed it to be when he wrote it. Gurdjieff believed that his book would have a tremendous impact on the age. He believed that if he could make it readable it would sell, because he had put something of great value in it. But Gurdjieff was not a professional writer, and he did not know how to produce effects on English language readers. Ouspensky, who had assisted Gurdjieff on several writing projects, pointed out that while Gurdjieff could speak eight or nine languages, he was fluent in none of them. He had not mastered the forms of expression of any one language, and he constantly sought to combine a variety of forms that did not go together well. In *Beelzebub's Tales* Gurdjieff strove to produce a special result that would, in the right circumstances, awaken the reader. In the Introduction to *Beelzebub's Tales* Gurdjieff stated that his aim was to "destroy, mercilessly, without any compromise whatsoever, in the mentation and feelings

---

3. *In Search* was put forward for publication by Gurdjieff himself in the last year of his life, the manuscript having been given him by Madame Ouspensky, after Ouspensky's death. The two books, *In Search* and *Beelzebub's Tales*, were, in the end, published at almost the same time: 1949 and 1950 respectively. Having said this, we note that Ouspensky had circulated copies of *In Search* internally to some of his own people, as there is evidence that both Maurice Nicoll and Rodney Collin were familiar with its contents well before 1949.

of the reader, the beliefs and views, by centuries rooted in him, about everything existing in the world."[1] While he was a fully awakened being, and while he had the ability to do this in direct contact with his students, he had neither the writing skills nor the English language skills to accomplish this in a publication. No writer is born knowing the effect that his or her writing will have on other people; this is something learned. And Gurdjieff did not learn it. He once explained to Orage that the obscurity of *Beelzebub's Tales* was the result of his having created an intentional denying force for the reader by "burying the bone deeper." But when he set himself to "bury the bone deeper" it was already too far underground for the English reading audience.

Nevertheless, Gurdjieff believed in his book as he believed in himself and his task. Perhaps, in 1924, he had to believe in it. And the book certainly did have value, and this value is still accessible to us.

With the three aims of December 1927 Gurdjieff was able to proceed with his writing. After five months of working successfully with the supporting aim of conscious suffering, he was, on May 5th 1928, able to give his supporting aim a more specific form:

> In the future ... to remove from my eyesight all those who by this or that make my life too comfortable.[2]

Sometimes he referred to this as "banishing" all those who made his life too comfortable. This was a drastic aim. He was to separate himself from all those who were closest to him! He believed that this great friction, and the nervous energy generated from it, would help him towards physical renewal, and a recovery of the kind of presence he had known before 1924. There was also, however, a practical side to the "banishment" aim. It would stop him from receiving the "shocks upon my mental associations" that come from constantly adapting to questions coming from people of "different degrees of comprehension."[3] In other words, he did not want to be under the pressure of having to constantly adjust his thinking to the varied

---

1. Gurdjieff, G.I., *All and Everything, First Series, Beelzebub's Tales to his Grandson*, E.P. Dutton & Co., Inc., New York, 1964, p.v (introductory remark).
2. Gurdjieff, G.I., *Life is real only then, when "I am"*, All and Everything, Third Series, E.P. Dutton, New York, 1978, p. 43.
3. *Ibid.*, p. 60.

understanding of his students, while he was, at the same time, trying to develop the more consistent and objective usage demanded by his book. And so "I closed the doors of my house to all people."[4]

In the autumn of 1928, when the first draft of *Beelzebub's Tales* was nearly complete, Gurdjieff made yet another aim to propel himself forward. It was to "press the most sensitive corn of everyone I met." He later claimed that this refinement was "miracle working" for him.[5] He completed a draft of *Beelzebub's Tales* in 1929, but he continued with the difficult aims. There was, however, the suggestion that at some point in the future he might ease off on his followers.

> If I should attain my self-imposed aims, and should still survive, then I would live with a definite program, as follows: one third of all my waking state I shall devote to pleasures of my own body; the second third, exclusively to those by that time remaining near to me, in spirit as well as in blood; and the third part to science, that is, to all humanity.[6]

For Gurdjieff, in the situation that he was in, these were legitimate aims. While he still appeared the same formidable figure to his students, and while he was still an awakened being in a sleeping world, he was clearly having physical and psychological difficulties. If he could renew himself physically and mentally, he might find himself in a place where he could complete his projects. If the lower centers began to function normally, the Higher Centers might function as they had done before the accident. This was personal work, not "work for other people," and he himself admitted it. In the *Third Series* he stated, "Could this principle invented by me [stepping on other people's corns] be also, in all other surrounding conditions of ordinary life, such a vivifying factor? Frankly speaking, according to the opinion of my subconscious, I must say ... no. This could have happened only thanks to the general material crisis [i.e., the crisis created by

---

4. *Ibid.*, p. 61

5. *Ibid.*, see pp. 51-52. Here Gurdjieff describes the physical benefits that he received from this aim and how it helped him to understand human psychology.

6. *Ibid.*, p. 54.

the motor accident]."[1] The work of the Institute had been, by contrast, a "universal" work. We see that the accident changed everything!

Let us review, then, the longer-term consequences of the general change of direction that began in 1924 and continued through 1928.

PLACING GURDJIEFF'S CHANGE OF AIM

Beginning from 1924 the aim to realize the Institute was displaced by the aim to write and to publish *Beelzebub's Tales*. With this came the supporting aims to "remove from my eyesight all those who make my life too comfortable," and to "press the most sensitive corn of everyone I meet." As we can imagine, this had a devastating effect on Gurdjieff's old inner circle. These aims were necessary to Gurdjieff in the mid-nineteen twenties, but how can we place them in the full span of his life's work?

Yes, *Beelzebub's Tales* was important, but — as we have pointed out — it was not what Gurdjieff believed it to be when he wrote it. The myth that encodes his teaching does not quite come through, and most people do not spontaneously 'find themselves' in it. Gurdjieff was simply not equipped to produce an *Aeneid*, a *Divine Comedy*, or a *Paradise Lost*.

Yet the writing aims, the banishing aims, and the corn-stepping aims did help Gurdjieff to survive a chapter of his life when some part of his vital faculties had been taken from him. We cannot understand Gurdjieff's life between 1924 and 1935 without remembering that he had set these aims and that he adhered to them.

Having said all this it must be acknowledged that Gurdjieff never did give up his vision of the Institute. He considered re-starts with: 1) the banking heiress Mabel Dodge Luhan (*Taos Art Colony*, New Mexico 1934), 2) Frank Lloyd Wright (*Taliesin*, Spring Green Wisconsin in 1934), and 3) Senator Bronson Cutting (scheme to repurchase and develop the Prieuré 1935). He continued to mention a re-creation of the Institute in the postwar years in Paris, predicting that he would live to an age of 120 and complete the project. In the winter of 1948, he visited New York to raise money to purchase the *Château de Voisins* at Saint-Hilarion as a replacement for the Prieuré. In the last year of his life he actually purchased, with the same aim, a hotel by the name of *La Grande Paroisse* in the Champagne-Ardenne region of France.[2] The vision of the Institute remained a part of Gurdjieff until his dying day.

---

1. *Ibid.*, p. 53.

2. See Blom, Gert-Jan, (compiler and producer), *Gurdjieff: Harmonic Development, The Complete Harmonium Recordings 1948-1949*, Basta Audiovisuals, Netherlands, 2004, p. 83.

Having documented the radical turn in Gurdjieff's work, we must now look at the effect it had on his inner circle. Some of these people had followed him from St. Petersburg, through Essentuki, Tiflis, Constantinople, and Hellerau to Paris. They had been trained to cleave to their teacher at all costs, and they had been tested repeatedly. They presumed, of course, that this change of direction was another test. But it was not. The fact that Gurdjieff had already tested them many times made this sudden apparent rejection all the more difficult to understand. They looked at it as a reflection on their Work, a failure in relation to first things. But it was simply Gurdjieff's aim to push them away. Alexandre and Jeanne de Salzmann were sent away in 1928. They moved to Sèvres, southwest of Paris, where Alexandre took up set design work for the theater. He died of tuberculosis in 1934. The de Hartmanns went through an extremely difficult separation from Gurdjieff in 1930 and were never to see him again. Leonid and Elizaveta Stjernvall were finally asked to leave in 1932. They moved to Sotteville, Normandy to open a rooming house. Here Leonid died of cancer in 1938. These were people "near in blood and spirit" who had literally "sacrificed their lives."

By the mid-1920s Gurdjieff had entered a period of uncertainty with respect to his students. The Institute had been disbanded, but the Prieuré itself was still inhabited. Perhaps the Institute had not actually been disbanded, or perhaps Gurdjieff was contemplating some new teaching project? Perhaps the publications he was working on would signal a new phase of his Work? And so the post-Institute years began to slip by. Gurdjieff's health was not good, he had constant money problems, and he was surrounded by students and dependents with needs and expectations of different kinds. He was clearly not satisfied with the existing state of affairs, and he did not feel himself in a position to launch a new phase of his teaching. He was still very much in the mode of personal reconstruction.

In 1929 Gurdjieff made a second visit to America, opening contacts with the American students, but very much adhering to the aims of May-June 1928. They had a prickly time of it.

And Gurdjieff continued his writing after the completion of the 1929 draft of *Beelzebub's Tales*, although at a more relaxed pace. He completed

Meetings with Remarkable Men in 1931, although it was not published until 1963. In 1933 he published *The Herald of Coming Good*. A bundle of notes and writings from 1934 were published in 1974 as the *Third Series*.

In 1929 Gurdjieff began to speak to Thomas and Olga de Hartmann about reorganizing their lives in Paris independently of the Prieuré. They already had a room in Paris where Thomas composed and taught music, in order to generate a modest income. It was very difficult for the de Hartmanns to consider a permanent move from the Prieuré, as they had not been parted from Gurdjieff since he left Russia. Olga had been his personal secretary, arranging all his major moves, and, from the time of the accident, scheduling all the work at the Prieuré. Thomas had been Gurdjieff's collaborator in musical composition and his accompanist in the movements from the very first performance. They had never thought to leave him. However, Gurdjieff continued to press them, and eventually they took a house in Courbevoie, although — even then — they remained partly based at the Prieuré. Gurdjieff then asked them to take in, at the house in Courbevoie, Olga's aged parents, who were then in a Russian home for the elderly. Olga's parents had many friends at the home, and — having been at the very center of the Romanov Imperial circle — they were accustomed to a certain kind of life. Olga notes:

> Tension increased more and more. But we could not really believe he actually wished us to go as we had followed him for so long, in spite of every kind of hardship. Finally, Gurdjieff made conditions impossible, and one day, after a very strained and difficult conversation we could do nothing but go. I was very unhappy and nervous, and Mr. de Hartmann, who was so much more sensitive and individualistic by nature, could not endure it and was on the verge of a nervous breakdown.[1]

They made a permanent move to the house at Courbevoie. Olga did still carry out tasks and projects for Gurdjieff. One day Gurdjieff called by the house and was met by Olga's mother, who knew him, and received him very

---

1. de Hartmann, Thomas and Olga, *Our Life with Mr. Gurdjieff*, Harper & Row publishers, San Francisco, 1964, p. 153-154.

graciously. The de Hartmanns prepared coffee and sat together with Olga's parents and Gurdjieff. Then, as Olga describes it, quite suddenly Gurdjieff turned to Olga's parents, and said:

> "Look, come back to the Prieuré, leave this house; it will be much better for you." My mother said, "No, we are already settled here, and everything is done for us. We are old, and it is difficult for us to get into the life at the Prieuré." Then, without changing his tone, Gurdjieff said, "Well, if you don't come in a week's time, a coffin will be in this room, and your daughter will be in it." My father got quite pale, and I grasped his hand and told him not to pay any attention. But my father could not accept these kinds of things. My mother said, "Gurdjieff, why do you tell us such nonsense? We are not children!"[2]

Gurdjieff laughed and that was the end of it. Olga then had to explain to her parents that "Gurdjieff does this sort of thing to show you that one must not believe without understanding." Gurdjieff had humiliated Olga de Hartmann's parents in front of her, and had humiliated her — quite acutely — in front of her parents. It would have been hard to find a more sensitive corn to step on, or to step on it more deftly.

Sometime after this incident, in the autumn of 1929, Gurdjieff asked Olga to travel to Berlin with him, as his secretary, to help him with one of his projects. During the trip he made things very difficult for her.[3] On her return to Paris she went one evening to the Prieuré and Gurdjieff asked her to do something that she felt was simply impossible for her. She told him she couldn't do it. Sometime later that same evening Gurdjieff told her, in an icy tone, that if she would not do what he asked something bad would happen to de Hartmann. When she returned to Courbevoie on the first morning train, she was in the depths of despair. She found Thomas alive and well.[4]

---

2. *Ibid.*, p. 153-154.
3. *Ibid.*, p. 154.
4. *Ibid.*, p. 155.

In late December of 1929 Gurdjieff decided to go again to New York and Olga made all of the arrangements for the trip. On the day of his departure Olga went to his flat, at his request, early in the morning. They had a wonderful talk, "a talk which could occur only in exceptional moments. ... He told me that I was the only person who never had done what he demanded without wishing it myself."[1] She was very happy then. But suddenly Gurdjieff began to speak of how much he wanted Thomas and Olga in New York. He asked that they join him in a week's time. Olga replied that it was not possible, and that de Hartmann was not at all well. On his previous trip to New York Thomas had had a serious health crisis, and indeed he never returned to full health. It was now a great struggle for him to fulfill his contracts for music composition and to give music classes. Gurdjieff replied, "Come in a week's time, or you will never see me again." She replied, "How can you ask of me such a thing, you know I cannot do it." He replied, "Then you will never see me again." Olga then described the final parting: "The train moved. Gurdjieff stood motionless looking at me. I looked at him without moving my eyes from his face. I knew that was forever."[2] They never saw each other again.

Having described these difficult things, we must note that, seven years later, in 1936, Gurdjieff said of Olga de Hartmann, "She is first friend of my inner life, such thought she had for me."[3] Note the use of the present tense.

Gurdjieff arrived in New York in early January 1930. There he made things difficult for Orage and the New York group by engaging in forms of high-pressure fundraising. He demanded large sums of money in short periods of time, added special requirements, and made threats as to what might happen if the funds were not received. On 13th March 1930, he departed for France, leaving the group in relative disarray. He returned to New York on 13th November 1930, while Orage was travelling, and immediately

---

1. *Ibid.*, p. 155.
2. *Ibid.*, p. 156.
3. Solano, Solita and Hulme, Kathryn, *Gurdjieff and the Women of the Rope: Notes of Meetings in Paris and New York 1935-1939 and 1948-1949*, Book Studio, 2012, p. 64.

confronted the New York students with a virulent attack on Orage. He stated that Orage had come under the influence of his "left shoulder angel," and accused him of holding back money and of starting unauthorized classes in the movements. It was not immediately clear to the students why these judgements were so sudden and so severe. Gurdjieff selected five of Orage's followers as candidates for a new start in the Work. No one could join the new group who had failed to sign a "form of obligation," which forbade any member of the new group from associating with any member of the old. All were prohibited from associating with Orage himself. Gurdjieff stated that he would not meet with Orage unless Orage himself signed the obligation.

To the astonishment of everyone, Orage, on his return to New York, promptly signed the obligation, and he promised to break even from himself. He said that he had been aware of the contradiction between his own inner uncertainties and the part of an omniscient teacher he felt increasingly called upon to play. He took an oath to separate himself from his former self.[4] Gurdjieff was deeply moved by Orage's act of repentance. He created special conditions for Orage and for those students who had waited to sign the form of obligation after Orage had signed it, to join the new group. They all had to pay very substantial fines and to undergo a lengthy probationary period. If this seems confusing, it was so, for all concerned.

As this drama came to its conclusion, Orage was immediately caught up in issues related to the publication of *Beelzebub's Tales*. Gurdjieff had been unexpectedly harsh with Alfred A. Knopf, with whom he and Orage had been negotiating for the publication. Knopf ultimately turned the manuscript down. Gurdjieff, with Orage's help, took the manuscript to Doubleday, who, after lengthy negotiations, also refused the manuscript. Orage concluded that they would have to publish the book themselves. When Gurdjieff finally left New York, on 29th December 1930, Orage had to personally pay the large number of debts that Gurdjieff had incurred on his visit. By this time Orage was both exhausted and disillusioned. His role as the leader of the New York group had been taken away, he could no longer live off funds provided by members of the group, and his reserves had

---

4. Gurdjieff, G.I., *Life is real only then, when "I am"*, All and Everything, Third Series, E.P. Dutton, New York, 1978, p. 123.

been depleted. He decided to return to England, to re-create his career, and to digest all that had occurred. He felt that, after having done so, he might be able to return to Gurdjieff when they were both in a better state of mind. This never came to pass, as on the 6th November 1934 Alfred Richard Orage died unexpectedly of a heart attack.

To return to the timeline of our history, in the summer of 1931 Gurdjieff refused Ouspensky access to the Prieuré, creating a final rupture with his oldest student. In the winter of that year he made his fifth visit to America to raise funds, focusing principally on Jean Toomer's group in Chicago. He placed the American groups under great pressure. On the 11th of May 1932 there was a final, enforced closure of the Prieuré and a dispersal of its occupants. Gurdjieff took a room in Paris at the Grand Hôtel, adjoining the Café de la Paix.

The year 1932 was a critical year. We note that on the 13th of September of that year Gurdjieff's 1911 aim "to lead in some ways an artificial life" and to be "always acting" timed out. This aim had been made for a period of 21 years, anticipating the teaching phase of his life. It had been made to enable Gurdjieff to hold the standards needed to implement the exoteric/mesoteric/esoteric hierarchy that would be the condition for *Great School in the West*. The fact that the timing out of the 1911 teaching aim and the closure of the Prieuré happened *at the same time* was significant. What concealed the timing out of the 'always acting' aim was the implementation of the two aims of the 6th of May 1928: "to always step on the corns of others" and to "banish those closest to him." Both of these aims involved conscious acting, so it was not until these aims timed out — two years seven months later — on the 2nd April 1935 that we see evidence of Gurdjieff entering a new phase. But let us return to 1932 to see how all of this played out.

On his sixth visit to America, in October 1932, Gurdjieff made repeated demands on his students for money, often creating the impression of venality. This kind of pressure finally estranged Jean Toomer and the Chicago group. In September 1932, Gurdjieff began writing the *Herald of Coming Good*, which was published the following year. It was intended to raise funds, and while containing some interesting biographical material, it had a pompous and unrealistic tone. Gurdjieff himself repudiated it in 1934, and had it recalled.

In April of 1933, Alexandre de Salzmann, terminally ill, requested a meeting with Gurdjieff at the Café Henri IV in Fontainebleau. He was seeking a reconciliation with his teacher that would allow him to die peacefully. According to a student who was there, Gurdjieff was unrelenting in his aims to step on corns of others and to banish those closest to him. The meeting was devastating. It was the last time Alexandre de Salzmann ever saw Gurdjieff; on March 3rd 1934 he died of tuberculosis.

In the autumn of 1933, Gurdjieff made his seventh visit to America, which lasted nearly two years. He began by contacting Orage's old group in New York, and he remained there for nearly a year. In June-July of 1934 he visited Olgivanna Hinzenberg at Taliesin, Wisconsin, making a deep impression on her husband, Frank Lloyd Wright. Under Olgivanna's influence the organization at Taliesin increasingly took on the external form of the Work, as practiced at the Prieuré. On the 18th August 1934 Gurdjieff contacted Mable Dodge Luhan for the use of a ranch in New Mexico (that she had originally offered him in January of 1926). She refused. On the 5th November 1934, while still in America, Gurdjieff learned of Orage's death. This was a violent shock for him. In Orage Gurdjieff had sensed a candidate for the mesoteric circle, and the two men were, by nature and disposition, close friends. The depth of Gurdjieff's grief shows that, while he had pushed Orage away and made his situation in the group unbearable, he still expected him to return. He still thought of him as a student. It also shows a break in the hard persona he adopted at that time.

Gurdjieff then travelled to Washington, Boston, and Chicago, before returning to New York. In April, in New York, he gave a number of meetings to define the direction of his Work. These meetings are recorded in the publication *Life is only Real Then, When I Am*.[1] While Gurdjieff's seventh visit to America continued until May 1935, we must leave April-May of that year for the next section, for April of 1935 brought a major stage change to Gurdjieff's Work.

---

1. This was a draft for the Third Series of *All and Everything*, which Gurdjieff never completed. The meeting notes were reworked by Gurdjieff until 1945, and finally published after his death in 1974.

To summarize the period from July 1924 to March 1935, Gurdjieff cut a very somber figure. In France, he stalked the almost empty halls of the Prieuré, banishing one student after another from his sight. In America he made repeated demands for money, often giving a calculated impression of venality and stepping expertly and frequently on people's sorest corns.

The Turning Point and the Paris Apartment Teachings: 1935–1949

On the 2nd April 1935 the aims set on the 6th May 1928 (to press everyone's corns and to banish those closest to him) came to an end. On that day Gurdjieff wrote, "Today is the final time limit for my self-imposed aims. My health is good. The book is in finished form."[1] We sense, then, the beginning of a thaw. But this turning point, like most of the turning points in Gurdjieff's life, came with a violent shock.

During his two years in America, Gurdjieff had come into contact with Bronson Cutting, a United States Senator from New Mexico.[2] Senator Cutting was an unusual person. On having inherited a vast fortune, he took a vow to use that fortune, and his own life energies, to serve the common good — as he could best understand that — for the remainder of his life. He was a Republican who crossed the house to play a key role in Roosevelt's New Deal, and particularly in the important banking reforms which were a part of it. He donated generously to what he considered worthy social causes, and he apparently considered the Institute for the Harmonious

---

1. Gurdjieff, G.I., *Life is real only then, when "I am"*, All and Everything, Third Series, E.P. Dutton, New York, 1978, p. 46. The book Gurdjieff is referring to is *Beelzebub's Tales*, the Second Series of *All and Everything*, which had made such a physical demand on him. Keep in mind that the titles First Series, Second Series, and Third Series do not refer to publication order, but to a sequence numbering later imposed on three texts. By 1935 Gurdjieff had also completed the First Series, *Meetings with Remarkable Men*, and had drafted the Third Series, *Life is real only then, when "I am"*. This, indeed, was as much writing as he was going to do.

2. Bronson Cutting was part of Mable Dodge Luhan's group in New Mexico. One of Gurdjieff's students, Paul Anderson, who had a historical connection to that group, arranged the meeting between Bronson Cutting and Gurdjieff.

Development of Man to be one such cause. Under conditions that are unknown to us, Cutting promised Gurdjieff financial backing for both the repurchase of the Prieuré, and the recommencement of the work that had begun there. This arrangement was made sometime in late March 1935.

We can imagine what this must have meant to Gurdjieff, coming within a few days of the timing out of his 1928 aims. The agreement with Cutting had put the project of Gurdjieff's life — the opening of *Great School in the West* — back on the agenda with fresh impetus. We can be sure that in April 1935 Gurdjieff was actively working out plans for the reopening of the Prieuré.

Gurdjieff and Cutting agreed to meet in Washington on 7th May to discuss the details of the project. Gurdjieff arrived in the city on 2nd May and waited there for Cutting to arrive. On 6th May Gurdjieff received news that Cutting's plane, flying from Albuquerque to Washington, had crashed in bad weather near Atlanta, Missouri. The radio transmitter had died in the midst of a storm, the plane ran out of fuel in thick fog, and the pilot was forced to make an emergency landing. The pilot, Bronson Cutting, and three other passengers were killed instantly.[3] The impact that this shock had on Gurdjieff can hardly be overestimated. Its implications link directly back to the initial directions Gurdjieff had received from the Monastery in Central Asia in 1905-1907, and to the countervailing effect of the fateful motor accident of July 1924. The timing of Cutting's death is as precise as the timing of the three bullet wounds Gurdjieff received prior to his awakening. This pattern of shocks in Gurdjieff's life suggests a close involvement of C Influence.

After Cutting's death Gurdjieff disappeared for five months, from May to October of 1935. He informed no one — in America, Britain, or France — of his plans. John Bennett, who later saw Gurdjieff's passport, and the stamps made on it during those five months, determined that he had journeyed as far as the Caucasus and Central Asia. It was Bennett's belief that Gurdjieff reconnected, at this time, with the 'honorable and respected' individuals from whom he had received the project that was realized in the Prieuré. Presumably a few of them had survived. Such a connection would

---

3. Reported in *Time Magazine*, 13th May, 1935.

help to explain the radical change that we see in Gurdjieff on his return to Paris.[1]

We cannot now know what happened to Gurdjieff — externally or internally — during his months of travel, but we can know that, from this point forward, he accepted the people who came to him and worked with each one according to his or her individual needs. While Gurdjieff was always a forceful, and sometimes a frightening figure, the harsh artificiality, which had badly confused his students, was gone. From this time forward he adopted more the style of a traditional *paterfamilias*.

In October of 1935 he suddenly reappeared in Paris and took a room in the 17th arrondissement, in the Hôtel Napoleon Bonaparte.

THE LADIES OF THE ROPE

The motor accident and its aftermath could be viewed as a dark night of the soul for George Gurdjieff. The task that he had given his life to was taken from him; his wife and his mother died before his eyes; and in the decade to follow he became distanced from his old inner circle.

Toward the end of 1935 he began to teach again. But he was no longer the Gurdjieff of the early 1920s: rifling through candidates for the esoteric circle, initiating an amazing range of activities, trying to generate a lift-on-lift structure that would link humanity to Higher School. In the beginning he simply took the people who came to him and related to them individually. When older students gravitated back, he related to each one according to who they were and where they stood in life. He presented a certain consistent persona, even when physically weak or in great pain.

On his return to Paris — in the midst of the void that he himself had created — he made no attempt to connect with his followers. He contacted his family, and he contacted Jane Heap, asking her to teach in England. This left Jane's eight students unattached, knowing that Gurdjieff was in Paris. Three of them, independently, sought him out. They had each known him

---

1. See Bennett, J.G., *Gurdjieff: Making a New World*, Turnstone Books, London, 1973, p. 182. Bennett also claimed to have heard Gurdjieff make mention of a pre-war journey to Central Asia in his conversation.

from short visits to the Prieuré in the 1920s: Solita Solano, Kathryn Hulme, and Alice Rohrer. But here we must take a step back to provide context.

We will recall that, in 1925, Jane Heap had — with Gurdjieff's blessing — organized a group in the Montmartre district. She and Margaret Anderson had been the co-founders of a successful American literary journal, *The Little Review*. Both were lesbians, and both were connected to a talented literary circle of lesbian women. Other members of this circle included Solita Solano, Janet Flanner, Dorothy Caruso, Kathryn Hulme, Alice Rohrer, and Georgette Leblanc.

When, on his return from Central Asia, Gurdjieff asked Jane Heap to start a group in London, she did so, and remained there for the rest of her life, reporting back to Gurdjieff at regular intervals. Solita Solano, Kathryn Hulme, and Alice Rohrer immediately gravitated to the district where Gurdjieff had taken an apartment. They presented themselves to him at the lobby of the Hôtel Napoleon Bonaparte, and at an adjoining café that he frequented. Then he began, in a way, to court them. He might bait or test them, and then say, at a certain point, that he saw something special in them. He said to Solita Solano, "You very dirty but have something very good — many people have not got — very special." He would then tell them that he could help them, under certain conditions. The 'certain conditions' would imply a commitment of time and energy on their part. And from that point the dance would begin.

Gurdjieff himself contacted a lady from outside of Jane Heap's circle, Elizabeth Gordon, one of Ouspensky's students who had visited the Institute in 1922. She was a prim British lady in her sixties, not a lesbian, who gave a certain balance to the group. Although she had grown up in Victorian England, and was imbued with the values of that place and time, she had an unquestioned reverence for Gurdjieff that never left her.

The four ladies were invited to meet at the Hôtel Napoleon Bonaparte on 21st October 1935. This little circle then became Gurdjieff's first Paris group. Three other ladies from Jane Heap's circle joined: Margaret Anderson, Georgette Leblanc, and Louise Davidson. The group came to call itself *The Rope* — a lifeline thrown from a ship to people drowning in the sea. It was a much more relaxed and informal teaching than the teaching of the Prieuré. It was, for Gurdjieff, the beginning of a process of healing, and the beginning of the 'Paris Apartment' phase of his life. Solita Solano and Kathryn Hulme agreed to take daily notes, and as a result almost all of Gurdjieff's teaching over the next five years was recorded.[1]

Something had stabilized. Gurdjieff was no longer the somber, ruthless, and often frightening figure of the late-Prieuré period. The group regularly undertook motoring journeys outside the Paris *banlieue,* and to different parts of France. In December of 1935, to facilitate the work of the group, Gurdjieff quit his small room at the Hôtel Napoleon Bonaparte and took a larger apartment close by in 11 rue Labie, in the 17th arrondissement.

The Rope was, in one way, the opposite of the Institute at the Prieuré: it was a non-hierarchical organization. Each student was equal to the others, and Gurdjieff gave each one individual attention and followed their progress carefully. Gurdjieff did not try to force somebody through to the esoteric circle of humanity, yet the work of the group was intensive. It was always focused on the next step for each student, which was defined and even anticipated. At different points in the daily record of the teachings Gurdjieff remarks that his students' assigned exercises should occupy half or two-thirds of the day. Indeed, it is difficult to imagine how the ladies could have held full-time jobs. We know that Solita Solano worked as a journalist and that Margaret Anderson was publishing material throughout the 1930s. Most of the others appear to have had independent sources of income.

Gurdjieff gave the ladies "inner animal" names: Margaret Anderson was 'Yakina,' Alice Rohrer 'Theen One' or 'Boa,' Solita Solano 'Kanari,' Kathryn Hulme 'Krokodeel,' and Louise Davidson 'Sardine.' These names were related to physical type and feature, and also to the 'idiot type' of the person in question. Each of the ladies was carefully classified as one of the sixteen idiots of the toast, and that classification changed as they developed. Gurdjieff often said to one or another of them that he would pray for them to reach their next idiot. He used all of these tools to analyze the physical

---

1. See Solano, Solita and Hulme, Kathryn, *Gurdjieff and the Women of the Rope: Notes of Meetings in Paris and New York 1935-1939 and 1948-1949*, Book Studio, 2012.

and psychological energies of each lady: their attitudes to the world around themselves; their impulses to manifest; their possibilities to move to the next step.

Gurdjieff's analysis of each of the ladies is both psychological and physiological, bringing out the relation between the two aspects. He thus combines the functions of a healer with those of a teacher. Gurdjieff sees the points at which his students' centers (instinctive, moving, intellectual, or emotional) are closed: either undeveloped, subject to wrong work, or filled with useless forms of imagination. He then opens that center, or that part of a center, in the light of his own greater presence — so that the student becomes aware of a new side of themselves. Some aspects of their 'closure' may be physiological, and he addresses this side of it. There is quite an emphasis on diet, medicine, and special injections. Additionally, every time Gurdjieff gave one of the ladies an exercise, he realized that it would have a physical as well as a psychological effect, and he counseled them accordingly.

In the notes it becomes apparent that Gurdjieff was also healing people other than his seven lady students, and that the apartment at rue Labie served as a clinic. He returned to a trade that he had relied on ever since Tashkent. Patients come and go. There is an electrolysis machine in his apartment, he dispenses medicines, he gives injections, and he provides counsel.

In July of 1936 the ladies went with Gurdjieff to Vichy for a few days; a five-hour drive south of Paris. One day, after lunch, they all went out separately to shop or sightsee. Later in the afternoon Kathryn Hulme and Alice Rohrer were passing through a park, and they saw Gurdjieff sitting alone at a table. They sensed that he was in a special state. The notetaker of the day writes:

> In the Park café — his summer office. There we find him at five in the afternoon. He sits in a white wicker chair, his coat hung over the back, his Panama on the ground beneath. He seems absolutely immobile. ... We think we will not disturb him but he sees us and waves.
> "We hesitate to come up, Gurdjieff, because you have a look of such peace, we wish not to disturb." "Truth, is good place here."

He calls the proprietress, a stout white-haired lady and introduces us. "Friends," he says. Presently Miss Gordon comes. We are all so happy to see him in such a state of peace. He talks a little, tells how [in the years of the Prieuré] he always had children when he came to Vichy, and so chose this café near to where the donkeys could be hired for riding. "You can imagine how was," he says, "four, sometimes five small children come to me, run around, make cry …" His smile wishes they were all back and around him again. The trees are so beautiful, great lime trees, in blossom.

Miss Gordon: I cannot believe, Gurdjieff, that we sit here with you like this. I think about that chapter — Reflexes of Truth — how a great man was met for the first time, and how difficult it was to see him. And now here we sit.[1]

Gurdjieff: Yes, all is different since accident. Then I die, in truth, all die. Everything began then from new. I was born in that year, 1924. I am now twelve years old boy, not yet responsible age. I can remember how I was then — all thought, feeling. I was heavy, too heavy. Now everything is mixed with light.[2]

Here is an acknowledgment, by Gurdjieff, of what Thomas and Olga de Hartmann and Julia Ostrowska had said of him in 1924, just after he gave the speech disbanding the Institute:

… he was not well … something had not yet come back to him.[3]

---

1. Reflexes of Truth is an essay, probably by Paul Dukes, describing Gurdjieff in Moscow. It was intended as a representation to the uninitiated of what a teacher is. A prospective student becomes aware, in stages, of the state of consciousness that is behind the man who is in front of him. It was later published as Glimpses of Truth in *Views from the Real World*. The original wording can be found in Joseph Azize's *Gurdjieff's Early Talks 1914-1931*.

2. Solano, Solita and Hulme, Kathryn, *Gurdjieff and the Women of the Rope: Notes of Meetings in Paris and New York 1935-1939 and 1948-1949*, Book Studio, 2019, p 62.

3. de Hartmann, Thomas and Olga, *Our Life with Mr. Gurdjieff*, Harper & Row publishers, San Francisco, 1964, p. 141.

However, one detail of Gurdjieff's description of his rebirth is mistaken. He had not been reborn in 1924; he only, finally, shed his unnatural heaviness a few months before by making contact with the Ladies of the Rope. To place the date back a decade would have been reassuring for the seven ladies who had entrusted their lives to him. And, with them, then, he is much more a boy than ever he was before.

In order to better understand Gurdjieff's situation in 1936, we draw attention to a situation described in *Beelzebub's Tales,* written in the years immediately following his accident. In reviewing this text, we translate the highly personalized language of *Beelzebub's Tales* into the standard system terms used in the St. Petersburg lectures of 1916-1917.

In the chapter on "The Holy Planet Purgatory" Gurdjieff describes the situation of beings who have activated both the Higher Emotional Center and the Higher Intellectual Center and who have freshly shed their planetary bodies. In other words, fully conscious beings who have just died. What comes next? He explains that, in an earlier stage in the life of the universe, these beings would have proceeded directly to World 3, where they would have been in the presence of the Absolute and, under his sovereignty, begun to each fulfill their divinely preordained purposes. Unfortunately, an imbalance occurred in the working of the laws of the Ray of Creation, such that beings of this level—now without a planetary body—found themselves unable to enter Word 3 and experience direct contact with the Absolute. His presence was in some way obscured. They discovered that the cause of this obscuration was subjective flaws existing in their own nature. The change in the Ray of Creation had allowed impurities to enter the process of their evolution. Despite the active Higher Centers, and the shedding of the physical body, they still carried unresolved "sins-of-the-body-of-the-soul." Discovering this was confusing and brought remorse of conscience. They were, in effect, flawed angels. The Absolute, feeling compassion for these beings, created a place in the universe where they might work through, correct, and otherwise resolve these flaws. This was called the Holy Planet Purgatory. In Purgatory "… they are always deeply absorbed in their intense work in purifying themselves from those undesirable elements which have entered their presences from causes totally foreign to their individuality."[1] Note, these are beings with *both* the Higher Emotional Center *and* the Higher Intellectual Center active. On earth they would be considered demigods.

The Absolute frequently looks in on the labors of these beings, both to remind them what they are missing and to help them see — in his greater presence — the flaws they have within themselves. As Gurdjieff put it "... seeing our COMMON FATHER ENDLESSNESS HIMSELF so near and so often they have become aware that on account of the undesirable elements present in them, they are still unable to help HIM in the fulfillment of HIS most sacred tasks for the good of our whole Megalocosmos."[2] The most important part of this regenerative process is the performance of a certain kind of service, which Gurdjieff calls "being-Partkdolg-duty." They perform this service in relation to a substance (or hydrogen) called iraniranumange, which is made accessible to them in Purgatory. (The square brackets in the quotation are the author's clarifying insertions.)

> ...through being-Partkdolg-duty ... through their serving the purpose of the common-cosmic iraniranumange — [they] might become helpers in the ruling of the enlarged World [the Ray of Creation] and ... [receive] ... the sole possible means for the assimilation of the cosmic substances required for the [final] coating and perfecting of the higher being-bodies ...[3]

What, then, is this iraniranumange? We take it to be a cosmic substance at the level of Hydrogen 3. This substance is, as Gurdjieff puts it, an enabler of the "common-cosmic-exchange-of-substances." In other words, it is a substance in a live relationship with all other parts of the universe (as World 3 itself is). In the proximity of this hydrogen, you can see the presence of the whole in the part. Thus, as an angel, in responding to your immediate situation in Purgatory, you are responding to the whole, as that is present in your situation. In your place in Purgatory, you are able to perform

---

1. Gurdjieff, G.I., *All and Everything: Beelzebub's Tales to his Grandson*, E.P. Dutton & Co. Inc., New York, 1964, p. 801.
2. *Ibid.*, p. 805.
3. *Ibid.*, p. 792.

being-Partkdolg-duty in relation to all that is. And your own moments of self-transcendence in this struggle are moments in the life of the whole; they help the whole, and you are aware of this.

So the inhabitants of Purgatory had to learn to respond to the actuality of the whole and not to their own subjective hopes, fears, aspirations, and desires. This tutelage in being-Partkdolg-duty would require great attentiveness, great patience, and great persistence.

It is hard not to see the image of the inhabitants of Purgatory as an allegory for Gurdjieff's situation in the period that followed his car accident. Like the beings in Purgatory he had two Higher Centers active. The accident had come to him because of a subjective flaw in his nature, and so in his teaching. As a result of the significant damage done to his body and his nervous system, his spiritual vision was partially obscured. And there was even a period where he was in a coma, not directly connected to his physical body — exactly like the beings in Purgatory. He did still have the two developed Higher Centers, but he had lost a kind of clarity that he had had before. At the same time, he had not yet acquired the greater clarity that would result from the resolution of his subjective flaw. It would take him a long time to work this out. His engagement with the Ladies of the Rope was the beginning of a right relation to his external situation. We might say that this corresponded to his gaining a place in Purgatory where he could access the iraniranumange hydrogen. It signaled that the initial period of his physical and psychological healing was over — and so it was the beginning of his being-Partkdolg-duty. His execution of this duty over the remaining thirteen years of his life became ever more precise and more refined. Indeed, in reviewing the Paris years, we see a remarkable sense of duty reflected in all that Gurdjieff did: in the unfolding pattern of each day of his life. And — above all — he was not imposing his own vision on a resistant reality; he took whatever and whoever came to him and worked with that. He showed a much greater degree of patience, acceptance, and tolerance than the Gurdjieff of the Prieuré had ever done.

In the "From the Author" addendum to *Beelzebub's Tales* — which was written some years after the main text — Gurdjieff said of the first chapters:

> ... I wrote at a time when the functioning of my entire whole — a functioning which engenders in a man what is called "the-power-to-manifest-by-his-own-initiative" — was utterly disharmonized, that is to say, when I was still extremely ill ...[1]

He was still, at the time he wrote these words, freeing himself from this obscuration in slow stages.

In sum, Gurdjieff had been a bit "off the rails" from the time of his car accident until his trip to Central Asia. In the immediate wake of the accident, he knew that he had not properly come to himself, and he had initially thought to cure himself through an act of will. He recovered himself physically, but the psychological recovery was incomplete. In 1935, with the unexpected death of Bronson Cutting, there was a fundamental change in Gurdjieff, the causes of which we can only speculate. The journey to Central Asia that followed this defining shock could be likened to the imperfect angel's entry into The Holy Planet Purgatory. On his return to Paris, in early October 1935, he had clearly dropped the aims to "banish those closest" and to "step on the corns" of all who approached. He had found a new direction, and he was building a new outwardly facing self. He was re-creating himself as a teacher. It was as though he had somehow acquired the iraniranumange hydrogen needed to perform the being-Parltdolg-duty.

To illustrate the nature of the teaching given the Ladies of the Rope, we quote Solita Solano's 1973 description of the group's work:

> Gurdjieff's daily teachings and "exercises" could not have harmed the most delicate child — examinations of conscience, learning to seek God, how properly to pray, how to undeceive oneself, conquer feelings of pride and revenge, distinguish between the true and the false, care of one's health, clean out the stables before trying to cultivate one's soul, et cetera. Of course, all was not "holy;" he had an earthly side — food and drink, ribald humour at times, but he

---

1. *Ibid.*, p. 1,185.

was always a very religious man. ... He wanted only to help people make the best of themselves and avoid wasting wonderful life. In my simple thoughts, it is as simple as that.[2]

In the meeting notes for December 10th of 1936, several months after Gurdjieff had first spoken of his 'rebirth,' Kathryn Hulme recorded that after speaking to each of the ladies about their respective cures:

> "... Gurdjieff speaks of his own 'cure,' which is now half done, now half of his inner world is free, now he begins to feel like a man with a mustache."[3]

Where Gurdjieff had said, at Vichy, that he was a newborn child, he now acknowledges that he is still carrying some of the scars of the 'old man.' These are under control in a way they were not before, and the intimate, personal teaching situation allows him to neutralize their effects.

Gurdjieff made an interesting comment to one of the ladies during this same period. In a personal interview with Margaret Anderson, he learned that she was making extra physical efforts, beyond the exercises already given. He tells her that what she is doing is not necessary. What she needs is the right kind of inner friction. He continues:

> My special saint is St. George. He is very expensive saint. He not interested in people burning candles to him. He wishes suffering, an inner world thing, and only interested when I make something for my inner world. He always knows this suffering beyond price.[4]

What Margaret needs is the kind of inner friction that creates pressure to separate out the different levels of yourself, so that you can see and affirm

---

2. This description was given in defense of Gurdjieff, long after his death, in response to Louis Pauwels' virulent attacks on Gurdjieff in his book *Gurdjieff* (1972). It comes from an exchange of letters between Solita Solano and Margery West of Times Press.

3. Solano, Solita and Hulme, Kathryn, *Gurdjieff and the Women of the Rope: Notes of Meetings in Paris and New York 1935-1939 and 1948-1949*, Book Studio, 2019, p 103.

4. *Ibid.*, p 56.

he higher level over the lower level. It is a 'special friction' for the person lucky enough to have it. It cannot be 'found' or 'chosen;' it is unique to each individual's psychology, and it becomes part of the fabric of their inner life. It is something given. As long as you are working ("making something for your inner world") the friction does not go away. Gurdjieff says to Margaret ... "I pray for this for you." At this point we recall that in *The Herald of Coming Good* (1933) Gurdjieff had attributed his motor accident to *tzvarnoharno* ... "a manifestation toward me of that 'something' accumulating in the common life of people" ... which was ultimately the unconscious tendency to reject conscious influence. In this view the cause of the accident was a malfeasant force acting upon Gurdjieff from without. The attribution of the friction to *tzvarnoharno* is not an acknowledgement of the involvement of St. George; not an acknowledgment of necessary suffering to be accepted and transformed. The adoption of St. George as a patron saint (which probably occurred in 1935) is an unqualified acceptance of the great task of transformation.

At any rate, in this environment, the proper balance of a fully enlightened being is being reestablished. If we liken the human machine to a lens through which the higher centers view the world, the distortion in the lens (created in 1924) is being corrected. Within a few months of his having said the cure was "half done" things in his environment began to change. While in 1935-1936 Gurdjieff kept a gentle pace, and admitted, several times, that he was "not quite all there yet," in 1937-1938 the pace accelerated.

In January or February of 1937, while several of the Ladies of the Rope were travelling, Gurdjieff made a tentative first contact with Jeanne de Salzmann's Sèvres group. What a moment that must have been for her! He visited the group on several occasions, and, after that, Madame de Salzmann was occasionally invited to join the group at rue Labrie. On August 22nd 1937 Gurdjieff's brother Dmitri, who lived within half a mile of the teaching apartment, died of cancer. After the funeral, on 5th September, Gurdjieff moved into Dmitri's more spacious apartment on 6 rue des Colonels Renard. Almost magically a space had opened which could include both the members of The Rope and the Sèvres group. This was to remain Gurdjieff's base of operations until his death in 1949.

THE PARIS APARTMENT TEACHINGS

And the change of context continued. In December of 1937 Kathryn Hulme and Alice Rohrer had to return to America. Gurdjieff was now accommodating a wider range of students, and the form of his teaching began to change accordingly. In 1939 he made a trip to America reconnecting with Kathryn and Alice, making contact with some of the other American students he had known at the Prieuré, and renewing contact with Frank and Olgivanna Lloyd Wright.

From 1938, 6 rue des Colonels Renard became the center of what was effectively a new group, based principally on Jeanne de Salzmann's Sèvres students. It was also a new stage of Gurdjieff's teaching, where he begins to engage more completely as a teacher.

The de Salzmanns had moved to Sèvres after leaving the Prieuré in 1928. Alexandre was able to find employment designing stage sets for theater productions, and together he and Jeanne began a work group at 54 rue du Four. They had the additional responsibility of raising Jeanne's son, Michel, fathered by Gurdjieff. In 1930 the de Salzmanns were able to rent a handsome public building, where their group practiced the movements and gave readings from a draft copy of *Beelzebub's Tales*. Alexandre contacted tuberculosis sometime in 1933 and passed away in 1934. By the time he died the group was well established. From 1928 to her reconnection with Gurdjieff in 1937, Jeanne de Salzmann had pursued her line of Work with exceptional steadiness — while undergoing significant personal suffering.

The students of the Sèvres group had been well prepared to find a teaching. Most of them were people who had become disillusioned with life in France in the difficult years of the Popular Front government. Gurdjieff opened himself to them. Mme de Salzmann became, in effect, his deputy. By 1939 the members of that group — including Luc Dietrich, René and Vera Daumal, Philippe Lavastine, Henri and Henriette Tracol — had become the basis of a new group centered in the apartment at rue des Colonels Renard. This was the beginning of a second phase of the Paris teachings. Where the Ladies of the Rope had been principally American, Madame de Salzmann's students were all French. It was here that he positioned himself through the war and the German occupation.

The French students were to have the longest continuous student relation to Gurdjieff of any of his pupils, from 1938 through to 1949. The Americans, by contrast, had a more intermittent relationship. It takes many years of continuous effort to properly internalize such a teaching.

With the return Jeanne de Salzmann came the movements. Just as Gurdjieff had taken over Jeanne's movements group in Tiflis in 1919, he took over her movements group in Sèvres in 1938. This long-suppressed dimension of Gurdjieff's being suddenly came alive. The group rented the studios at the Salle Pleyel, a ten-minute walk from Gurdjieff's apartment along the avenue des Ternes. The Salle Pleyel was (and is) a magnificent concert hall capable of seating 3,000 people.

Movements classes were usually given four days a week. Gurdjieff impressed his students as not only a gifted, but an inspired teacher. From the moment Gurdjieff resumed the movements until a few weeks before his death in October of 1949 he continued to create new exercises. Pauline de Dampierre, a student of those years, writes:

> [We] were struck by his extraordinary sense of rhythm and precision in movement and by his suppleness and inventiveness. It was astonishing to discover so great a knowledge of this art in someone whose teaching was already so vast. Everyone had the feeling that they were in the presence of something unique coming from very far away and from very high: an ancient knowledge of the laws of the universe, of the laws governing movements and postures, and of the laws relating to the harmony of the body and to feelings of a higher order. Each gesture, each tempo, had to be executed with great precision. Gurdjieff often used the expression "to do exactly." When this "to do exactly" was there each posture resonated in us like the precise echo of something much higher. Forces long forgotten within sprang forth.[1]

When demonstrating new movements Gurdjieff rarely explained them; he taught by example. With the great strength of his presence students

---

1. Pauline de Dampierre "The Role of the Movements" in Jacob Needleman and George Baker, (eds.) *Gurdjieff: Essays and Reflections on the Man and His Teachings* (New York: Continuum, 1996), p. 294.

absorbed the movements directly, and in that presence they went into memory. He discouraged choreographic notes that might reduce the first-hand impression to an after-the-fact record. During the final two years of his life, Gurdjieff worked tirelessly to create literally hundreds of new movement 'exercises.' (A single movement may be comprised of many such exercises.) In the last phase the 'multiplications' — the representations of cosmic laws — become relatively more important. The movements of the last period are called the "39 Series," with thirty-nine complete and finished movements. Gurdjieff gave himself completely to the task at hand, as though he were existing through his students; as though he were moved by a sacred hydrogen.

With the re-centering of Jeanne de Salzmann's group around the person of George Gurdjieff, the apartment at rue des Colonels Renard became a little Alladin's cave, hosting a constant round of dinners, events, and meetings of different kinds. The preparation and cleanup for the many daily events turned the apartment into a perpetual hive of activity. On most days there was a reading, followed by a meal with the toasting ritual.[2] There were sometimes two such sessions in a day: a lunch session lasting from 1:30PM to 4:30PM and an evening session from 10:30PM to 2:00AM or 3:00AM. The dinners were work-meetings, with all of the elaborate protocols surrounding the toasts for the idiots. The teacher shared information with his students, took questions, gave tasks, and reviewed the results of tasks given. Following the evening meal Gurdjieff might bring out his portable harmonium, and play his compositions. He rested it on his knee, playing with one hand and working the bellows with the other, to produce the strangest and most wonderful music. It affected people both instinctively and emotionally, often bringing involuntary tears. Many dinners continued through the night and into the following morning.

The character of the apartment changed to fit its new role — as the banquet hall of a Khourasanian Sufi Khanquah. The little entrance hall to

---

2. Bennett, J.G. & Elizabeth, *Idiots in Paris*, Weiser Books, N.Y., 1991 p.vi-vii.

Figure 24. Number 6 rue des Colonels Renard.

the apartment was covered, from floor to ceiling, with paintings of widely varying quality, which Gurdjieff had purchased from the Paris street artists. This bizarre impression was the transition between the grey streets of wartime Paris to a world filled with the magic of ever-deepening presence. As the Khourasanian banquet chef Gurdjieff stocked a legendary pantry, filled with foods and spices from all over the world — which he maintained through both the German occupation and the postwar rationing.

Stanley Nott has left us with a description of the pantry.

> This store-room was overflowing with every kind of delicious food from every part of Europe and the Near East — fruits, dried meat, cold sausages and salami, sweets, preserved and canned food, and herbs. The room was permeated with the smell of lovage ... There

was a large refrigerator, a small table, and a chair for Gurdjieff and one for a visitor.[1]

John Bennett leaves us with his first impression of the apartment.

> As we entered the odours of Asia, saffron and tarragon and others less defineable, produced the impression of being transported into another world. The flat was a strange contrast to the Prieuré. Here all was small and dark and dingy, giving an impression of poverty of a kind that was neither European nor Asiatic. Recalling the magnificent salons and gardens of the Prieuré, the great Study House with its ornate decoration and the brilliant sunshine of 1923, it seemed that Gurdjieff had turned his back not only on splendor but on sunshine itself. It was early afternoon and yet all the shutters were closed and electric lights were burning.[2]

Elizabeth Bennett leaves us with hers.

> The flat looked exactly the same at all times; by day and by night the shutters were closed and the electric lights burning. After a time one ceased to know whether it was night or day. More than once after a meal I have emerged blinking into the hot summer sunshine in the street, when I had expected lamplit darkness, or been surprised by darkness when I had expected daylight. The exact repetition of the external framework left one free to attend to the shifting possibilities of the inner world. Every moment in Gurdjieff's presence was a chance to learn, if one was sufficiently awake to take the chance.[3]

From the meetings at 6 rue des Colonels Renard Gurdjieff organized and orchestrated the lives of all those around him. He gave his students tasks and took private interviews in the pantry. Madame de Salzmann was a key

---

1. Nott, C.S., *Journey Through This World*, Routledge & Kegan Paul, London, 1974, p. 107.
2. Bennett, J.G., *Witness: The Story of a Search*, Dharma Book Company, Inc., New York, New York, 1962, p. 245.
3. Elizabeth Bennett, from: Bennett, J.G. & Elizabeth, *Idiots in Paris*, Weiser Books, N.Y., 1991 p.x.

figure in this miniature world. Under Gurdjieff she led the practice of the movements, and she consistently provided supportive counsel for Gurdjieff's other students. When someone had been upset by one of Gurdjieff's more devastating remarks, she would help them to understand it in context. If a person was overwhelmed by a problem in their personal lives, she would help them to apply the Work to it. After the dinners small parties of students would meet at a nearby café to reconstruct what Gurdjieff had said, and to understand what he had taught. Madame de Salzmann was a constant presence at these gatherings.

On 26th August, 1924, at the time of the closing of the Institute, Gurdjieff had said: "All my life I gave up all my money to other people, but now I have decided to close the Institute. Forgive me. I wish now to live for myself."[1] And for a decade after that he gave priority to his own affairs over those of his students. We noted above that, in 1935, this changed — with Gurdjieff accepting a small number of students on their own terms, and working with each of them personally. With the opening of 6 rue des Colonels Renard Gurdjieff changed again. He gave of himself, without reserve, as in the days of the Prieuré, but this time he concealed his line of effort and responded to exactly what was before him. He gave each student what they could best work with: not more and not less. It was as though he was making payment in the Sacred Planet Purgatory.

The little apartment turned into an engine of Work, running day and night seven days a week. And Gurdjieff was now a much older man, whose body brought him constant suffering. The illnesses and accidents he suffered in the Paris apartment years were equivalent to anything he suffered at the Prieuré. But the students heard nothing of this. He was just the inscrutable 'Gurdjieff.' He had finally become invisible, his machine a pliant tool for producing presence in those around him.

Coming out of the 'dark night' of 1924 to 1935 his life found its mature expression — as a fundamental commitment to the sharing and enabling of the awakened state.

---

1. de Hartmann, Thomas and Olga, *Our Life with Mr. Gurdjieff*, Harper & Row publishers, San Francisco, 1964, p. 141.

❧

On 3rd September 1939 France and England declared war on Germany. On the 14th June 1940 German troops occupied Paris, and on 22nd June an armistice was signed between the French and the Germans. The Prime Minister, Paul Reynaud, resigned, and Marshall Petain formed a new government, which became known as the Vichy regime.

American and English residents caught in areas engulfed by the blitzkrieg were put into internment camps for 'foreign nationals.' The condition of the camps was not good. None of the Ladies of the Rope, except Georgette Leblanc, were French citizens. Louise Davidson, Solita Solano, and Margaret Anderson were all forced to return to America in 1940. Only Elizabeth Gordon was interned. She was in her seventies when this happened. She did retain some continued access to Gurdjieff.

Gurdjieff's French students encouraged him to relocate to the countryside, but he chose to remain at rue des Colonels Renard. The winter of 1940 was harsh and supplies were very limited. Gurdjieff, as if by magic, always had resources. He began to extend his charity to an extended family of needy neighbors, and there was often a little line at this door. He particularly helped the elderly who were alone. And it was not just food that he gave them. Fritz Peters, who visited Gurdjieff at the apartment just after the armistice, noticed the lines of elderly and destitute people, and also noticed the kindness and courtesy with which Gurdjieff treated them. He asked Gurdjieff about this.

> You notice all such people who come here are already old. Without me not have possibility to die properly. Except me, such people not have family, and for future can only look towards death. If I help such people die in right way, this can be very important and very good thing. Someday you understand this better, but you still young.[2]

---

2. Peters, Fritz, *Boyhood with Gurdjieff: Gurdjieff Remembered: Balanced Man*, Bardic Press, California, 2005, p. 239-240.

This brings attention to another aspect of Gurdjieff's teaching. To his students he would speak of humanity as a sleeping mass with no possibilities. But he himself never forgot the level of humanity, which includes the level of essence. He always, scrupulously, fulfilled his duties to the many members of his own family. In his last years he behaved towards humanity at large like a bodhisattva: one who places the enlightenment of every sentient being above their own. This was not because he had taken the bodhisattva vow, but because *Higher Centers are like that.* He did not, like an ambitious business executive, filter everything that was outside the sphere of his immediate interest. He had a universal awareness of *what is,* and he functioned out of the center of that.

In May of 1942 the Germans required all Jews to wear the Star of David. Gurdjieff immediately advised his Jewish students to leave their home addresses and stay with other members of the group. Starting in June a total of 76,000 Jews were deported from France, most of them from Paris, to the extermination camps in Poland. All of Gurdjieff's students were saved.

And here we see a direct resonance through time. We remember Gurdjieff in the first throes of the Russian revolution, acting to protect his students and his family, while creating a special environment that separated them all from the coarse crowd emotions of the time. He did exactly the same thing, twenty years later, during the Nazi occupation of Paris. To follow the journals of his students, and the records of his meetings, you have no sense of what is going on outside the little apartments at rue Labie or rue des Colonels Renard. Certainly his students knew and suffered the occupation, but their life-interest was engaged in pursuit of the eternal present.

On the 8th of May 1945 victory was declared in Europe. From that moment the insular world of 6 rue des Colonels Renard began to re-open. Gurdjieff's students all over the world began to realize — through phone calls and letters and travelling visitors — that he was still alive, still teaching, and resident in Paris.

From 1946 Jane Heap began to send her London students to Paris three or four times a year. In January of 1947 Gurdjieff heard of Ouspensky's return to England. He invited Ouspensky to Paris, but Ouspensky declined — not out of disregard for his teacher, but because he was in the

Figure 25. Gurdjieff in the Paris Apartment Years.

final months of his own life, working intensively with his own students. On 2nd October 1947 Peter Demian Ouspensky died. In June 1948 Gurdjieff sent an open letter to all Ouspensky's students, saying that he could provide them with a safe haven. Some, particularly those who had splintered off with Bennett, or who had been close to Madame Ouspensky, gravitated to Gurdjieff. But the groups that had formed around Francis Roles, Maurice Nicoll, and Rodney Collin continued on their own respective paths. Many people from Gurdjieff's past, and many people who had been taught by his students, came to rue des Colonels Renard.

All the Ladies of the Rope came to visit Gurdjieff in Paris after the war, with the exception of Elizabeth Gordon. Elizabeth had been released from her internment camp in early 1945, before the end of the war. She was not in good health and she died shortly after. She had been Gurdjieff's student for 25 years.

John Bennett later encountered the Ladies of the Rope on his own visits to rue des Colonels Renard. He said of them: "These ladies had a special relationship which continued right up to the end of Gurdjieff's life. When they came to visit him they were always treated as privileged people."[1]

---

1. Bennett, J.G., *Gurdjieff: Making a New World*, Turnstone Books, London, 1973, p. 232.

On 30th June 1948 Margaret Anderson and Dorothy Caruso returned after an absence of nine years. Margaret noted that the apartment at rue des Colonels Renard was shabbier, the colors faded, and the carpets worn through with patches, but ...

> Gurdjieff himself seemed to me unchanged. He was a little older, he was a little tired, but he was still as lavish as ever with his existence and his ceremony. ... He let no slight failing pass without signal or correction. Most of the old pupils felt that he was gentler than in the old years. I could only feel that his weariness with the human condition had reached the breaking point. But we knew that he would fulfill to the end his obligation to life. There were now so many new pupils ... that he transmitted much of his instruction through a person we had known in the old Prieuré days. After years of work with him her stature was now visible to everyone. Her name was Jeanne de Salzmann.[1]

Bennett himself, on hearing of Gurdjieff's presence in Paris, determined to re-establish his once-so-promising connection. (Since Ouspensky's death in 1947 he had established his own separate group at Coombe Springs, southwest of London.) On 6th August 1948 he arrived with his wife Winifred and his secretary (and wife to be) Elizabeth. Gurdjieff was prepared to renew his commitment to him: "Now you have much Knowledge, but in Being you are a nullity. If you wish, I will show you how to work, but you must do as I say."

Shortly after Bennett's arrival there came a significant turning point in Gurdjieff's life. On 8th August, Gurdjieff set out on a trip to Cannes with three companions. As he drove through the town of Montargis a small truck ran from a side road into the main street, hitting Gurdjieff's car on the driver's side. The driver, who was drunk, and his passenger were killed instantly. Bennett records: "Gurdjieff's car had buckled up, pinning him between the wheel and the seat. It had taken an hour to extricate him. He had remained perfectly conscious, and directed each move so as to avoid

---

1. Anderson, Margaret, *The Unknowable Gurdjieff*, Arkana, Penguin Books Ltd., 1991, p. 172.

fatal loss of blood. The three passengers in Gurdjieff's car had escaped with minor injuries."[2] Gurdjieff was taken immediately to the Montargis hospital, where, after an examination, he called Madame de Salzmann, insisting — in face of the staff's resistance — that he be driven home. Bennett saw Gurdjieff climbing out of Madame de Salzmann's car.

> His clothes were covered with blood. His face was black with bruises. But there was something more, that made me realize that I was looking at a dying man. Even this is not enough to express it. It was a dead man, a corpse, that came out of the car; and yet it walked. ...
>
> He walked into his room and sat down. He said: "Now all organs are destroyed. Must make new." He saw me and smiled, saying: "Tonight you come dinner. I must make body work." A great spasm of pain passed through him and I saw blood flowing from his ear. I thought: "He has a cerebral haemorrhage. He will kill himself if he continues to force his body to move." He asked Madame de Salzmann: "How is X?" I could not catch the name. She replied that he was in the American Hospital. He said: "Go and see him. How he is?" Then he added: "I wish watermelon. Buy watermelon when you come back." ...
>
> The doctor had come, and said that Gurdjieff must lie absolutely still, and that he was likely to die of pneumonia if not of the injury. Gurdjieff disregarded all advice and came in to dinner. He ate a few mouthfuls and listened to four toasts. Then at last he went off to bed. Bernard arrived with the morphia, having gone to one after another of his doctor friends before finding one at home. Gurdjieff said it was no longer necessary, as he had found 'how to live with pain.'[3]

Before the accident, he had been the enigmatic Gurdjieff that we had known, and of whom so many stories are told. For four or five days after the accident, it seemed that he either could not or did not feel the need to play a role, to hide himself behind a mask. We then

---

2. Bennett, J.G., *Witness: The Story of a Search*, Dharma Book Company, Inc., New York, New York, 1962, p. 250

3. *Ibid.*, p. 250.

felt his extraordinary goodness and love for humanity. In spite of his disfigured face and arms — he was literally black and blue from head to foot — and his terrifying weakness of body, he was so beautiful that we felt that we were looking at a being from another and better world. Bernard and Elizabeth, who had not seen him before, found it impossible to reconcile their impressions with all that they had heard and read about him. I believe that, for a few days, we caught a glimpse of the real Gurdjieff, and that all his strange and often repellant behavior was a screen to hide him from people who would otherwise have idolized his person instead of working for themselves.[1]

It is remarkable that an automobile accident closed the first phase of Gurdjieff's teaching and a second automobile accident opened its final phase. His response to the second accident was the opposite of the first. In the weeks after the accident, when any normal eighty-two-year-old man would have been in the hospital, he: 1) opened his doors to all who had known him, and 2) revived the idea of the Institute, seeking actively to rent a great estate. He must have known that in the time left to him he could not carry such a project through to completion. It is possible that, at the time of the accident, he had a vision of the time remaining to him and the possibilities contained within it. He simply went ahead with his new aims. We cannot know what his exact intentions were, but it is clear that — on the scale of Gurdjieff's lifetime — a certain archetypal form of school was trying to realize itself though him. He determined to share his Higher Centers, and his vision of school, as fully as he could.

On the day following the accident Gurdjieff asked Bennett how many people he had in England. Bennett answered about two hundred. Gurdjieff replied: "Let all come. Now my French group are away on holiday. Necessary not to lose time. Go home and bring whoever wishes to come."[2] This was the beginning. Within the next few days he issued a general invitation to people who had been connected to him through all the different phases of his Work, to congregate in Paris. His physical recovery was remarkable,

---

1. *Ibid.*, p. 250-251.
2. *Ibid.*, p. 251.

particularly considering his age. He still spoke of living another forty years, but, almost certainly, he didn't believe this.

When Bennett returned to Coombe Springs he said to his group, "Whereas I went to Paris convinced that self-remembering is both indispensable for man and impossible of attainment, I am now sure that it can be attained."[3] During August 1948 "Gurdjieff's pupils new and old from all over the world were beginning to flock back to him."[4]

Bennett has left us with his perception of the French core of students who had been with Gurdjieff through the years of German occupation.

> We of the English group were deeply grateful to the French, who did all they could to make our approach to Gurdjieff easy by withdrawing into the background. For seven years they had had Gurdjieff almost to themselves, and he had given them more consistent and continuous teaching than any of his pupils had previously received.[5]

The French demonstrated, by their charity, that they had internalized those teachings — and so Gurdjieff's activities accelerated.

> He never relaxed his efforts: every day from morning till night he was seeing individuals, listening to readings, presiding over midday and evening meals, giving classes in his rhythmic exercises and often ending the day improvising unearthly melodies upon a hand organ.[6]

Gurdjieff felt it was now the time to publish *Beelzebub's Tales*. He believed that its circulation would bring thousands of students, and he wanted to have a teaching venue capable of supporting a much larger organization. He sought out the Château de Voisins, forty miles southeast of Paris, which was for lease. He became quite fixed on this location. The Château had been constructed between 1903 and 1906, modelled on the architectural style of

---

3. *Ibid.*, p. 250-251.
4. *Ibid.*, p. 252.
5. *Ibid.*, p. 252-253.
6. *Ibid.*, p. 254-254.

Ange-Jacques Gabriel, the principal architect for Louis XV. It had been designed by René Sergent for the landscape architect Achille Duchêne. There were a total of 36 bedrooms and vast gardens surrounding. It had been used by the Vichy Regime for receptions, and had been visited — only a few years previously – by Petain, Hitler, and Ribbentrop. Bennett was asked to make a careful assessment of the running costs and of how many guests would be needed to cover those costs.

But, both the publication of *Beelzebub's Tales* and the lease of the Château would be costly. Gurdjieff decided to sail to New York, to connect with as many of Orage's and Ouspensky's old students as he could in order to raise the money.

Aware that Madame Ouspensky was still managing Ouspensky's estate at Mendham, and that Jessmin Howarth was directing the movements classes there, Gurdjieff sent — in advance of his own arrival — a young Frenchman, Alfred Etievant. Alfred was to teach the new series of 39 movements that Gurdjieff had created in Paris, in preparation for his own visit in December. Jessmin Howarth took Alfred to Mendham and showed him how the movements were being practiced — as the 'total set' of 1924. Madame Ouspensky made it possible for the Mendham people, including Jessmin, to go to New York and to work with Alfred there, in preparation for Gurdjieff's arrival.

On the 13th December 1948 Gurdjieff set out from Le Havre with Jeanne de Salzmann, Lord Pentland, and Aubrey Wolton. On arriving at New York on the 17th December he took a room at the Hotel Wellington. He used Child's Restaurant in Manhatten as his 'New York Office' and people were welcome to meet him there.

On the evening of his arrival in New York he went to oversee Alfred Etievant's movements classes. There was Jessmin Howarth, whom he had left pregnant with his child twenty-five years before. He asked her to come to his apartment to talk seriously. When she arrived he said: "And now I am not interested in many people (for the movements), only interested in a few young people. Your daughter also. You please give her to me while I am here. I am impartial parent, not kind, but I will teach her."[1]

On the next day Gurdjieff went to visit Franklin Farms, and the now invalid Madame Ouspensky. She recounted that, on seeing him again, "she felt the innocent joy of a baby recognizing its mother".[2] She gave Gurdjieff a manuscript copy of *In Search of the Miraculous,* which contained the only full record of his original Moscow and St. Petersburg teachings, in perfectly readable English. Gurdjieff had passages read to him at the apartment in New York. John Bennett, who had joined the party from London, recorded him saying: "Very exact is. Good memory. Truth was so." After hearing a particular reading, he said: "Before I hate Ouspensky: now I love him. This very exact, he tell what I say."[3] Gurdjieff saw the significance of what had come into his hands, and the project to publish *Beelzebub's Tales* was extended to include *In Search of the Miraculous.*

In New York Gurdjieff actively engaged in fundraising, showing pictures of the Château de Voisins, and offering permanent suites to anyone who would contribute $5,000 to the cost. He spoke of resuscitating the Institute for the Harmonious Development of Man, and of making the Château its headquarters.[4] In anticipation of this expansion he named literary executors for France, England, and America: respectively, Rene Zuber, John Bennett, and Lord Pentland.

In the meantime people were flooding into New York. Olgivanna Hinzenberg came to visit with her husband Frank Lloyd Wright and their 24-year-old daughter Iovanna. Edith Taylor, a student of the movements at the Château in 1923/4, brought her daughter by Gurdjieff, Petey. With this widening exposure to the second generation of his 'family' he had the idea of involving all of them in the movements at the Salle Pleyel in Paris. On Jessmin Howarth's recommendation, and in negotiation with their parents,

---

1. Howarth, Jessmin & Dushka, *It's Up to Ourselves,* Gurdjieff Heritage Society, New York, New York, 1998, p. 202.
2. *Ibid.,* p. 208
3. Bennett, J.G., *Witness: The Story of a Search,* Dharma Book Company, Inc., New York, New York, 1962, p. 260.
4. *Ibid.,* p. 261.

he asked six young ladies to join him in Paris, as the "first row" of the future movements demonstrations. This included: his own two daughters, Dushka Howarth and Petey Taylor; Iovanna Wright; Tania Savitsky (Madame Ouspensky's granddaughter); Patty Welch (the daughter of Mendham students William and Louise Welch); and Marian Sutta (the daughter of Mendham students Maurice and Evelyn Sutta). The six girls were affectionately known as 'the calves.'

Jessmin was initially reticent to allow Gurdjieff to suddenly take the full role of parent with her daughter. Jessmin had raised and educated Dushka entirely on her own, and was just now trying to save in order to provide her with a good education. She did not know if she could take Gurdjieff's sweeping promises seriously. However, shortly after she had refused Gurdjieff's first offer, she saw him, at a distance through her window – an old man picking his way across the street amidst the mud and melted snow. She saw what Bennett had seen after the accident at Montagris: his tremendous effort of service. The fear and distrust dissolved, and that night she went to him and told him that, if he wished to take Dushka to Paris, she would encourage her daughter to go.[1]

To the chagrin of the New York students, Gurdjieff spent a good deal of time with the Mendham people. In fact the New York followers had been working largely independently, and had little practical experience of group work. The people at Mendham had been subject to the full discipline of three lines of work, which Madame Ouspensky had tried very hard to preserve.

Eventually, reviewing the cost of the Château des Voisins against the results of his fundraising, Gurdjieff decided to focus instead on publishing *Beelzebub's Tales* and *In Search of the Miraculous*.

At the end of the New York trip Gurdjieff contacted Bennett at Coombe Springs, "Soon I return to Europe. You come to me, and I will show you how to work."[2] On 11th February 1949 Gurdjieff boarded the

---

1. Howarth, Jessmin & Dushka, *It's Up to Ourselves*, Gurdjieff Heritage Society, New York, New York, 1998, p. 215.
2. Bennett, J.G., *Witness: The Story of a Search*, Dharma Book Company, Inc., New York, New York, 1962, p. 263.

Queen Mary, with a large entourage, sailing for Le Havre. It is hard to believe that we are recording the activities of an 82-year-old man, who, six months earlier, had been described as "a walking corpse."

On his arrival in France he continued to search for a smaller and more affordable château, and soon made arrangements to purchase *La Grande Paroisse,* which had been the station-hotel for a French commune of the same name, situated a few miles east of Fontainebleau, on the banks of the Seine.

That summer Gurdjieff made a number of long car trips with the 'calves;' to Dieppe, to Cannes, to Vichy, and in July to Geneva. Whenever he stopped for lunch or dinner on these trips the full ritual of the toasts was observed. At Geneva he visited Dr. Stjernvall's widow Elizaveta and her 30-year-old son by Gurdjieff, Nikolai. Gurdjieff had maintained a contact with the Stjernvall's in the years after the Prieuré, and had visited Dr. Stjernvall frequently in 1938 when he was dying from prostate cancer. In visiting Elizaveta he was saying goodbye to one of his first disciples, and to one of the founding members of the Petrograd Group.

To his students Gurdjieff was the same as he had been before the accident at Montargis; the dinners, the day-trips, and the dance rehearsals all continued exactly as before. But internally he was often in pain, and experienced great fatigue. Dorothy Phillpotts, who went with him on the day-trips in 1949, observed:

> He would go for days on a very simple diet of dry rusks soaked in milk, cream and yogurt, with only one glass of alcohol. Often nowadays he ate practically nothing, for the food he so carefully prepared was all passed to others."[3]

Yet he welcomed all, invited all, and conveyed to all a tremendous sense of the future. He created an environment where people could feel that everything was possible. This was a great actor completing his role. To some, however, the growing weariness was visible. Bennett commented, "Gurdjieff

---

3. Phillpotts, Dorothy, *Discovering Gurdjieff*, AuthorHouse UK Ltd., Milton Keynes, 2008, p. 230.

was beginning to get very tired, and looked much older and moved with greater difficulty than when I had come to Paris a year before."

On 1st September Gurdjieff determined to make a day trip south to see the prehistoric cave paintings at Lascaux.[1] It was something he had wanted to do for a long time, and it was a profound experience for him — for he saw in the paintings a record of school reaching back deep into prehistoric times.

On the return journey the group made an excursion to visit *La Grande Paroisse,* and Gurdjieff spoke to them of his plans:

> "There will be a house at the top of the hill where I will rest from my labours, and to this only my nearest will come. Below will be a hall like Study House for movements, classes and lectures, and under that will be rooms where visitors will live. On each side of the hotel coming up from the outside street will be a path. This double path will be paved with mosaic. I will bring special architect to make this path, which will have many thousand stones of different colours." As he was saying this ... a young English architect ... interrupted him and said: "I can find you good mosaic artists here in Paris." Gurdjieff turned to him with majestic scorn saying: "Idiot! Such mosaic as I need no artists can make!" It was evident to all who were accustomed to his idiom that the mosaic represented his pupils from all countries and races and that the three houses stood for the three bodies of man.[2]

Throughout the return journey from Lascaux Gurdjieff treated Bennett — whom he had given the promise of special Work – with an icy disdain. Bennett, who had banked everything on this time with Gurdijeff, was deeply hurt. In a quiet moment during the return journey he took the opportunity to say to Gurdjieff, "I cannot thank you for what you have done for me. That I can never repay."[3] Gurdjieff was quiet for a long time, as though he had not heard, and then suddenly said:

---

1. Bennett, J.G., *Witness: The Story of a Search*, Dharma Book Company, Inc., New York, New York, 1962, p. 271.
2. *Ibid.,* p. 273.
3. *Ibid.,* p. 274.

Figure 26. La Grande Paroisse.

What you say about never repay — this is stupidity. *Only* you can repay. Only *you* can repay for all my labours. What you think is money? I can buy all your England. Only *you* — with great emphasis — can repay me by work. But what you do? Before trip I give you task. Do you fulfil? No; you do just opposite. Never once I see you struggle with *yourself*. All the time you are occupied with your cheap animal.[4]

How can we explain this? How could a person so long involved with the Work find themselves in such a position? We shall take this question as an opportunity to clarify the difference between group work and school work, and the nature of the work of the steward.

A CLARIFICATION OF LEVELS IN THE WORK

The first thing one learns in the Work is to make efforts to be present, and then to sustain those efforts through one's waking hours. As one gains proficiency, two things happen:

1. One comes to realize that the denying force to making these efforts is internal, and that what resists the Work has its own sleepless intelligence.

---

4. *Ibid.*, p. 274.

2. One understands that in order to combat this denying force one must learn not to identify with the success or failure of one's efforts. In other words not to identify with the very efforts that one makes, or the short term results that may come from them. One must continue to make efforts without any expectation and without any identification with the efforts themselves. One must trust that Higher Centers will come when they can.

Success in not identifying with efforts requires self-knowledge: knowledge of one's lack of unity; knowledge of the four lower centers; knowledge of one's features; knowledge of one's major areas of identification; knowledge of one's different moods and states of mind. As effort becomes ever more continuous one begins to see how little result most of the efforts have, and how — in the moment one's attention lapses — there is an immediate resurgence of imagination. And when the state of sleep regains its hold it is as though it had never not been there.

As one continues, one sees the nature and the depth of the resistance to awakening. This brings a new level of self-observation; one begins to have a sense of *the machine as a whole*. One is not struggling with this 'I' or that, with this feature or that, one is struggling to separate from the whole working mechanism. And the whole working mechanism fights back.

All of this forces a clarification of one's aim; it forces more intelligent effort, and a better quality of effort. Self-observation is no longer "what I have seen about myself" but snapshots of the machine as a whole, and accurate observations of the different levels of energy connected with it.

More importantly, one begins to distinguish the presence of the lower centers from the presence of the Higher Centers. What does this mean? A dog, when it is not distracted by food or play, can be present to what is around it. The dog is not in imagination, it is just there. But it is present only in its lower centers, for it has no Higher Centers. This is the simple presence of the lower centers to what is before them in the moment. But, when an adult human being has been trained to bring the lower centers into this open state, and when this state is prolonged through time, *a different kind of presence* can emerge. This is not just being "present to;" it is presence fully self-aware. It is a presence that knows itself for what it is. It is Higher Centers coming awake in the machine. When we learn to distinguish this quality of presence we see how rare it is. When the lower centers are in a right condition it is natural for them to look out. And, in a person trained in the Work, this is recognized, remembered, and acknowledged.

When one is capable of distinguishing Real I from the presence of the lower centers, one begins to understand, in a very basic way, that the efforts one has been making *have not been initiated from the level of Real I*. Efforts are initiated from the level of the functions in the anticipation of Real I. In the beginning Real I is utterly incapable of initiating itself, it just comes in certain moments. Our Work is, then, to remember the quality of 'presence self aware' and to clear the ground for it. And when it comes to let it run the show.

Having said this, the efforts that are made from the lower centers remain the essential building block of the Work. Continuous effort from the lower centers, guided by the memory of the past experience of the Higher Centers, is necessary to displace the control of the Black Queen. When the control of the lower level is broken, even for a moment, one can become aware of "the whole machine" as something outside of oneself. This is what the Black Queen fears, for to her it is an 'invasion' by something she cannot understand. On the basis of this fear she determines to hold her ground, and she works at this *twenty-four hours a day*.

The steward is here challenged to a conflict it can never win, because it cannot defeat the Black Queen on her own ground. All it can do is fight her. And if there is just fighting then the Black Queen wins, because all the battles take place on the scale of the many 'I's. So there is no space for the Higher Centers. Thus, there must be more to our Work than continuous effort! What is this 'more?'

Firstly, in the moment when Real I comes, we must be able to recognize it for what it is. When we experience that quality of presence we must immediately disallow the lower centers from displacing it, even with thoughts about the Work. *The steward learns to bow before what is higher than itself*. During this measured pause one must be poised to begin making efforts again in the moment that Real I disappears. For if one does not recognize the passing of this state the Black Queen will be there first, with an 'I' about the wonderful higher state one has just experienced, or a sudden fear that one has lost a state one may never recover.

This is the field of tension in which the Work of the steward develops. It is, in its highest phases, the science of establishing the right relation between effort and non-effort. It requires a sense of the machine as a whole: an awareness of the place and function of the Black Queen, accurate observations of Higher Centers, and accurate observations of presence 'timing out.'

What we have described here is the Work of a man number four trying to become a man number five. A man number five does exactly the same Work, except that the periods of extended presence become longer – as consciousness learns to sustain itself. In a man number five, there are moments when the Higher Centers themselves deploy the work 'I's to prolong their own presence. Then, for periods of time, an entirely different kind of identity is there. Also, for a man number five, the understanding of the denying force is more developed, and the external challenges that they face are greater.

We are describing here a level of Work that has been well-documented by the great schools of the past: the Sufi Orders of Islam, the monastic communities at Mount Athos, the Four Orders of Tibetan Buddhism.

When one reaches the stage where one is aware of the continuous presence of the Black Queen, one is not frightened, as Bennett was, by the prospect of 'perishing like a dog' because one is focused on an opponent who is always directly before one. The only thing one can be frightened of is losing presence in the moment, and that can always be corrected now.

Bennett came to Gurdjieff with some experience of the Work, and with clear memories of the experience of Higher Centers, but he did not come with the continuity of effort and the depth of self-knowledge that signals the Work of the steward. On returning to his students at Coombe Springs, after his first visit to Paris, he said, "I went to Paris convinced that self-remembering is both indispensable for man and impossible of attainment ..."[1] and later, "My idea of working on myself was merely to make life as unpleasant and exhausting for myself as I could."[2] These remarks show a two-dimensional view of the Work, for the Work of the steward *includes the moment of Real I* — which is outside the cycle of recrimination and despair. One may not be fully awake, but one has lost the right to believe in the level of 'I' that generates recrimination and despair. Bennett records that, after a few weeks of working in the proximity of Gurdjieff, "My second life beats ten times more strongly than before." Yet only a few hours after having made this observation he noted that his "second life" had receded. He records that ... "I was terrified that I had strangled it at birth."[3] Being 'terrified' about losing the state is the means by which the Lower Self re-takes the ground. The natural feeling of loss, which triggers the emotion of fear, should immediately be replaced by *effort without expectation*.

The discipline of the steward does not come from applying the spur ever more vigorously to erring flesh; it is both more subtle and more severe. It arises from our service to the emergent Self. And it brings with it the unquestioning concern that a pregnant mother has for her unborn child. On Bennett's first visit to Paris, Gurdjieff was able to bring him to this level of Work by his external presence. But Bennett was still unable to sustain it on his own, in relation to an internal presence. Then, after six months of working together, Bennett and Gurdjieff travelled with other students to Lascaux. On this journey Bennett lost himself in the other members of the group, and in his interest in the caves themselves.

---

1. Bennett, J.G., *Witness: The Story of a Search*, Dharma Book Company, Inc., New York, New York, 1962, p. 252.

2. *Ibid.*, p. 257.

3. Bennett, J.G., & Elizabeth, *Idiots in Paris*, Weiser Books, N.Y., 1991 p. 77

What Bennett had understood in Gurdjieff's presence in Paris, he lost in the context of the group travelling to Lascaux. He did not have an awareness of the constant presence of the Black Queen and he had not yet acquired a clear sense of what it was he was serving internally.

From this point of view the Work is not the practice of the movements, or the toasts to the idiots, or the cosmology, or the perfect submission of will to a teacher, or even having visionary experiences. It is the ability to separate out the different levels of yourself and make the lower levels serve the higher levels.

In October 1949 it appears that Madame de Salzmann had reached this level of Work, but Bennett had not. Although Gurdjieff's presence brought Bennett near to this level, he had not yet achieved it stably on his own. He kept identifying with his personal success or failure, his wish to be a good teacher to his own students, his role as the husband of Polly Beaumont, or his role as the mate of Elizabeth Mayall. Almost certainly others around Gurdjieff had reached this point of stability in the Work, but they were quiet about it. This is natural, because a person who reaches this point does not advertise; they simply get on with it.

One must know how to value a Higher Level for what it is, *on the basis of one's own experience*. For without this the Higher Centers will not come of themselves. Jesus said to his disciples, when he knew his hour had come: "It is expedient for you that I go away: for if I go not away, the Comforter will not come unto you; but if I depart, I will send him unto you."[4] The "Comforter" is the direct experience of one's own invisible Self.

Having made this point, we note that Gurdjieff did not abandon Bennett, as he had abandoned other students in the 1920s or 1930s. He followed through with him and encouraged him. In October of 1949, in the last month of Gurdjieff's life, Bennett questioned him about what he meant by 'real unchangeable I.' Gurdjieff replied with a metaphor about a taxi. The succession of passengers are the many 'I's. "This is real unchangeable 'I' — to keep one's own motor car. Now, you have only taste, but one day you will have such 'I,' and when you know it has come, you will have such happiness as you cannot imagine."[5] Shortly after, speaking to Elizabeth

---

4. Bible: John 16:7, King James translation.

5. Bennett, J.G., *Witness: The Story of a Search*, Dharma Book Company, Inc., New York, New York, 1962, p. 276.

Mayall — within Bennett's hearing – Gurdjieff said, "But he (Bennett) not *minister* yet — perhaps in one or two years."[1]

Gurdjieff was severe with Bennett yet he gave him every opportunity. And so he did with all those who came to him in the Paris years. He gave to everyone that asked, regardless of his own increasing physical weakness:

> The stream of visitors from all over the world grew in volume, and in the insistence of their demands for interviews with Gurdjieff. He refused no one. The atmosphere of unbearable tension was not confined to the flat, but spread out to the hotels where visitors were staying: the Belfast, the Réna, and the San Remo, and the cafes where we met and talked in the middle of the night, and to the studios of the Salle Pleyel, where movements classes were held several times a week, and which he rarely missed.[2]

Bennett cites the example of a Russian lady who had been raped by soldiers during the Russian Revolution, when she was only thirteen. She responded to the hard, objective side of Gurdjieff's teaching, which corresponded exactly to her view of a hard, meaningless life:

> Yet he accepted her; treating her as a daughter, and taking infinite pains to gain her confidence. He then set about convincing her that her life had a great meaning, providing only that she would allow that meaning to take shape. Her bitter feeling of the injustice of life prevented her from believing in the love of God. Gurdjieff was at pains to show that we as individual essences are not God's handiwork, but the results of heredity and the conditions of our conception … God is not responsible for this. He made man to be clean: if he is now dirty it is his own fault.[3]

---

1. Bennett, J.G. & Elizabeth, *Idiots in Paris*, Weiser Books, N.Y., 1991 p. 74.
2. Bennett, J.G., *Witness: The Story of a Search*, Dharma Book Company, Inc., New York, New York, 1962, p. 270.
3. *Ibid.*, p. 276.

Figure 27. Last Photo of Gurdjieff 1948.

THE FINAL MONTHS

Later in September 1949 Gurdjieff was able to complete the purchase of *La Grande Paroisse,* and, at the same time, began to plan another journey to New York. The first edition of *In Search of the Miraculous* was now selling well, and there was the general feeling that the publication of *Beelzebub's Tales* would bring a new stage in the work.

On October 7th 1949 Gurdjieff and seven students bundled into two Renaults and drove out to the new château. Elizabeth Bennett describes the visit. The group drove through the forest at Fontainebleau, past the old Prieuré, and continued a few miles on to the new property:

> This was much nicer than I had expected: a little house built above the railway on a steep slope of poor soil, with a view over the river. There is a patch of neglected kitchen garden, some good outhouses and a few scrubby fruit trees. Tall chestnut trees along the hedge by the road, a well and a few flowers, marigolds, unpruned rose bushes and what not. The house has a large room on the left where we lunched, a bar on the right and a good kitchen, easy to work in and keep clean, etc. Upstairs are four or five bedrooms. (The Entwhistles have moved in there to live, as he has to be there so much.)

> The attics, or rather one large attic, is accessible at present only by a ladder (G's *escalier* make chic up-house"), but this is where the outside double staircase comes in, with a terrace to be made on the slope behind the house, and the mosaic with the Enneagram, etc.[1]

A week later, on the 14th October, Gurdjieff collapsed at a movements class at the Salle Pleyel, and was taken back to his apartment where he was nursed by Lise Tracol. Doctors were called in, and his student Dr. William Welch in New York kept in constant touch. Gurdjieff's condition fluctuated. On hearing of what had happened to Gurdjieff Bennett flew in from London. As his taxi came up to the rue des Acacias, he saw Gurdjieff before the fruit stall at his favorite greengrocers. He quit the taxi and greeted Gurdjieff:

> I walked back with him to his café at the corner of the rue des Acacias and the avenue MacMahon. He had not been out of doors for a week and an endless stream of French beggars, and aged Russian and Armenian exiles, came up to his table for alms. Invalids — a young man paralytic — a woman evidently near despair — approached him. A few quiet words of advice — some medicine — or instructions to a doctor — and they left with an air of encouragement and fresh hope. Someone came in and paid him a large sum of money as a thank you offering for a cured paralysis. It was soon distributed among the beggars. Children came for sweets, old friends of the quartier to say a word of greeting. All rejoicing in the belief that he would now get strong again — none suspecting that they were seeing him for the last time.
>
> The last weeks of Gurdjieff's life were like that. It was as though he had decided to leave not a single loose end, nothing untidy behind him. Indeed in the weeks that followed his death, we became aware with growing astonishment of the meticulous care with which he had provided for everything.[2]

---

1. Bennett, J.G., & Elizabeth, *Idiots in Paris*, Weiser Books, N.Y., 1991, p. 109-110.
2. Bennett, J.G., (compiled by A.G.E. Blake) *Talks on Beelzebub's Tales*, Samuel Weiser, Inc. York Beach, Maine, 1988, epilogue.

He supervised the Toasts for the Idiots for the last time on Monday 24th October. Later that night, after the diners had left:

> ... he called in four people who happened to be sitting in the salon through the night — de Salzmann, Russell, Vera were three, I suppose Gabo was the fourth — and just looked at them for a long time, saying not one word. They believe he was saying goodbye.[3]

On the following day, the 25th October, Gurdjieff finally consented to Dr. Welch being sent for, from New York. When the doctor arrived on the 26th he explained to Gurdjieff that he could take much better care of him if he would allow himself to be hospitalized. Gurdjieff quietly agreed to this. And in the evening of the 26th he was taken to the American Hospital at Neuilly:

> The ambulance men brought the stretcher to his room, but he wouldn't have this, and walked out into the hall and got on to the stretcher there, sitting back, saying, "Oy!" as he always does. He did not dress, but wore pajamas, and his red fez on his head. He sat upright on the stretcher, and was carried away like a royal prince! All the family was clustered at the street door (the crusty old concierge was in tears!) and as they carried him across the pavement he made a little gesture, a sort of wave, with his hand and said. *"Au revoir, tout le monde!"*.[4]

On his arrival at the hospital Dr. Welch made an abdominal puncture and relieved him of 12 litres of water. Gurdjieff gave his final instructions to Jeanne de Salzmann on the following day. He told her to publish the *First* and *Second Series* when she felt the time was right. To publish the *Third Series* was not necessary, but she might do so if she wished. The most important thing, he told her, was to prepare a nucleus of people capable of responding to the demand which will arise from these publications. Madame de Salzmann visited Gurdjieff on the following day, when it appeared he was unconscious. Solita Solano remembers that:

---

3. Solano, Solita, *On the Death of Gurdjieff: October 29, 1949.*
4. Bennett, J.G. & Elizabeth, *Idiots in Paris*, Weiser Books, Boston, 1991, p. 129.

> ... on the day before he died Jeanne de Salzmann, standing by his bed, had spoken to him in Russian. He did not, could not reply, but he lifted his hand and held it out for her to take.[1]

On the 28th October Gurdjieff went into a coma, and died at 10:30AM on the 29th. The cause of death was given as cancer of the liver. William Welch, who was with him continuously from the 26th, said: "I have seen many men die. He died like a king." The funeral service was held at the Alexander Nevsky Cathedral, 12 rue Daru on the 2nd November. It was attended with a full high requiem mass. There was a one hour delay in the preparation of the coffin, and the congregation stood in silence for the entire hour ... "neither a footstep, a cough, a rustle or a breath. A remarkable quality of silence which is so rare as to be noted as unique."[2]

> Six men carried him in — Russell, Valya, Gabo, Michel, etc. Dim lovely lights, many flowers which had arrived early, vested priests and small choir for the service. Church was crowded even for that small ceremony, all golden under the incense-smoky high dome. The catafalque was covered with large black cloth, embroidered with silver.[3]

> The priest at the Russian church stated that there has never been such a funeral before, except Chaliapin's; that he has never seen such mass grief, or such a concentration of attitude, he said, on the part of the mourners.[4]

On the 3rd November Gurdjieff was buried in the family plot, with his wife and mother and brother Dmitri, at Fontainebleau-Avon.

---

1. Solano, Solita and Hulme, Kathryn, *Gurdjieff and the Women of the Rope: Notes of Meetings in Paris and New York 1935-1939 and 1948-1949*, Book Studio, 2012, p. 223.
2. *Ibid.*, pp. 223-224.
3. *Ibid.*, p. 234.
4. *Ibid.*, p. 236.

Figure 28. Gurdjieff's grave, Avon, Seine-et-Marne.

Conclusion

Gurdjieff never lost his connection to the vision that was established in him in 1898, and finally fixed in 1907. The grand experiment of the Prieuré, while it came to an early end, sounded a note that continued to resonate through the second half of the twentieth century. It was, for one golden hour, its own enclosed world — devoted to the tasks for which man was originally created. It was an 'ark' for Mankind in an age of conflict and of the overwhelming prevalence of materialistic values.

Looking back over Gurdjieff's teaching life, he began with a great task and an even greater vision. Yet — unlike the Sufi Shaikhs, or the Tibetan Lamas, or the Vedic Rishis – he had to start from scratch: to find unprepared people and to train them. Thus he rifled through different sets of candidates, looking for individuals whom he could bring to the awakened state, and then use to maintain the standards of his Work in a larger population. He started groups, shut them down, and restarted in another place. Whenever he dispersed his teaching he would allow the more dedicated to return, and created the opportunity for a 'new beginning.' Yet in the wake of the 1924 motor accident he questioned the original project. The years from 1924 to 1935 were a dark night of the soul, both for Gurdjieff and for his students. By the end of World War II he had reassessed his role. He would help all those to whom fate had connected him, and at the same time sow as many seeds for the future as he could. While he never let go his vision of the Great Work — the self-enclosed community totally dedicated to the realization of man's potentials — he accepted that this might be the achievement of another generation.

And so, from the infinitely adventurous youth, born in the twilight years of the great schools of Central Asia, to the compelling 'Tiger of Turkestan,' to the servant and inheritor of the Great Spiritual Traditions, to the severe teacher who tested men's souls in the alchemical fire, to the solitary and nihilistic figure of the early 1930s, to the wise and benevolent patriarch of rue des Colonels Renard: mage, dancing master, and host to the toast to the idiots. Himself an idiot with three zeros.

CHAPTER 3

Peter Demian Ouspensky

Formative Years: 1878–1915

Peter Demianovitch Ouspensky was born in Moscow on March 5, 1878. His father was a government land surveyor; he died when Ouspensky was only a few months old. This left Ouspensky's mother a widow with two children: a girl of two, and the baby Peter. After her husband's death Ouspensky's mother moved back to her parents' home on Pimenovskaia Street. Her father – Ouspensky's maternal grandfather – was a well-known church painter, who took contracts to paint religious subjects. Unfortunately, Ouspensky's grandfather died only a few years after the move, when Peter was only four. Yet there remained enough money in the family to support Ouspensky's mother and her two children. Ouspensky's mother was, like her father, an accomplished painter, and well read in both French and Russian literature. Ouspensky said of his family that it, "did not belong to any particular class and was in touch with all classes."[1]

Ouspensky was a precocious child, learning to read at the age of five, and, by his seventh year, he was able to make his way through the short stories of Mikhail Lermontov and Ivan Turgenev. By the time he was eight he had begun to take an interest in the natural sciences. At school he was not inspired by the routine of study, but as the boys were left very much to themselves he was able to spend a good deal of time reading on his own. By

---

1. These details come from Taylor, Merrily E., (compiler & editor), *Remembering Pyotr Demianovich Ouspensky*, Yale University Library, New Haven, CT, 1978.

the age of sixteen he had discovered and read Nietzsche. In a short autobiographical reference, written in 1936, he states:

> I particularly distrusted all forms of academic science and took a firm decision never to pass any examinations and never to take any degrees. At the same time, I worked very intensely on biology, mathematics, and psychology. I was enormously excited by the idea of the fourth dimension and, subsequently, terribly disappointed by the usual 'scientific' treatment of it.[1]

In 1898, at the age of twenty, Ouspensky visited Paris with his mother. He was strongly affected by the Cathedral of Notre Dame, and made a careful study of it. He understood that "the thought that created the cathedral was the same in the moment of his knowing it as it had been in the moment of its creation." He described it as a living being, and — at the same time — an expression of the inner history of humanity.[2] These are remarkable perceptions in one so young. Shortly after Ouspensky and his mother returned from Paris to Moscow she died, which was a great blow to him. From the time of her death, he began to travel to remote parts of Russia to experience the different cultures that could be found there. At the same time, he took up journalistic writing, usually writing for the left-wing newspapers. While he distrusted radical socialism, he preferred the socialist newspapers because the right-wing papers, in his own words, "did not smell well." In 1906, at the age of 28, he was working in the editorial office of the widely circulated Moscow daily, *The Morning*.

Ouspensky's sister, whom he was very close to, was involved in the general strike of 1905, which ended in the Bloody Sunday massacre. She was arrested as a conspirator, imprisoned, and died in prison a few years later. Her premature death, following the death of his mother, his grandfather, and his father, had a profound effect upon him.

---

1. Ouspensky, P.D., *A Further Record: Extracts from Meetings 1928-1945,* Routledge & Kegan Paul, Arkana Paperbacks, London 1986, p. 300
2. Ouspensky, P.D., *A New Model of the Universe,* Alfred A. Knopf, Inc., New York, 1969, p. 305-9.

In and around 1906 Ouspensky wrote his first novel, *Kinemadrama*, which was based on the idea of eternal recurrence. It was not finally published until 1910. Ouspensky redrafted the manuscript in the last years of his life, and it was this draft that was finally published in English in 1947 as *Strange Life of Ivan Osokin*. It is the work of a gifted writer, with the expressive capacities of a Tolstoy or a Dostoevsky. The passages describing Osokin's final expulsion from school depict an unknowing moment of World 6; a moment in which there is a complete transcendence of the unbroken stream of thoughts, emotions, movements, and sensations that run though our personal psychology.

In 1907 Ouspensky discovered Theosophy:

> In 1907 I found theosophical literature, which was prohibited in Russia — Blavatsky, Olcott, Annie Besant, Sinnett, etc. It produced a very strong impression on me although I at once saw its weak side. The weak side was that, such as it was, it had no continuation. But it opened doors for me into a new and bigger world. I discovered the idea of esotericism, and found a possible angle for the study of religion and mysticism, and received a new impulse for the study of 'higher dimensions.'[3]

Ouspensky began to publish and lecture to a Theosophical audience, and soon became prominent in Theosophical circles. He acquired a wide readership in a certain stratum of Russian society. It is hard for us now to imagine the impact that Theosophy had in the late nineteenth and early twentieth centuries. This was a time when, while formal religion was in question, there remained a deep respect for what was *behind* religion, and for the various traditions of "ancient wisdom."

While Ouspensky was educated by Theosophy to the world of esotericism, he soon began to think outside of the context of the Theosophical Society. But with respect to what was *beyond* the Theosophical Society he knew that he needed help. Theosophy had convinced him of the existence

---

3. Ouspensky, P.D., *A Further Record: Extracts from Meetings 1928-1945*, Routledge & Kegan Paul, Arkana Paperbacks, London 1986, p. 300-301

of real, esoteric schools. If these existed he had to find them, and if they had existed in the past he had to find the traces of them.

> I imagined ... the possibility of making contact with schools of the distant past, with schools of Pythagoras, with schools of Egypt, with the schools of those who built Notre Dame, and so on. It seemed to me that the barriers of time and space should disappear on making such a contact. The idea of schools in itself was fantastic and nothing seemed to me too fantastic in relation to this idea.[1]

Ouspensky's determination to seek out a direct connection to Higher Mind brought him to travel, and he found that he was able to combine travel with his journalistic work.

> In 1908 I was in Constantinople [Istanbul], Smyrna [on the Aegean coast of Turkey], Greece and Egypt. Early in 1909 I finally left Moscow and after that lived in St. Petersburg. I studied occult literature; made all kinds of psychological experiments by the Yogi and magical methods; published several books, *Tertium Organum* among them, and gave public lectures on the Tarot, on Superman, on Yogis, etc.[2]

In Constantinople he was able to see the Mevlevi whirling dervishes. He had expected to see dancers performing spectacular feats in a state of ecstatic possession, but the experience was quite different. He sensed, in the unfolding of the dance, the elucidation of certain cosmic principles, the representation of a unity which he could feel but not quite understand.[3] Ouspensky felt that these dervishes were somehow the 'soul' of old Constantinople, the center of a great living entity — which was to be displaced with the coming of Kemal Ataturk in 1923 and the banning of the Sufi Orders in 1925.

---

1. Ouspensky, P.D., *In Search of the Miraculous,* Routledge & Kegan Paul, London, 1977, p. 1.
2. Ouspensky, P.D., *A Further Record: Extracts from Meetings 1928-1945,* Routledge & Kegan Paul, Arkana Paperbacks, London 1986, p. 301
3. Ouspensky, P.D., *A New Model of the Universe,* Alfred A. Knopf, Inc., New York, 1969, p. 340.

Figure 29. Ouspensky in Ceylon.

In 1909 Ouspensky published *The Fourth Dimension*, which, while giving clear expression to his interest in Higher Mind, provided a sober balance to the romantic-spiritualist tendencies in Theosophy. In 1912 he published *Tertium Organum*, which was written in a period of his life when he was engaged in experiments with the use of stimulants. (This period is described in *A New Model of the Universe*, in the chapter Experimental Mysticism.) Through these experiments he gained first-hand experience of the 'invisible world' that is behind visible creation. He had an adequate conceptual framework – from his studies of Kant and mathematics – to give a balanced expression to what he had seen. In other words, he was able to indicate something of his experience, without forcing concepts to do what they are not designed to do. Additionally, given his great admiration for science, his experiments allowed him to see *in what way* a materialistically oriented science had fettered Western thought. *Tertium Organum* is lucidly written, with a clear understanding of the limitations of conceptual thought, in service of what is beyond thought. It is a masterpiece of its kind.

The book was an immediate success. Its first impact was accurately conveyed in Claude Bragdon's introduction to the 1920 English edition.

> Here is a book which will reorganize all knowledge. The *Organon* of Aristotle formulated the laws under which the subject thinks; the *Novum Organum* of Bacon, the laws under which the object may be known; but the Third Canon of Thought existed before these two, and ignorance of its laws does not justify their violation.[1]

He had accessed a 'mode of consciousness,' a 'world,' that was immeasurably more alive and connected than the world that we know, and promised to explain the world we know "from the inside." The difficulty was in establishing a viable bridge between the two worlds. Ouspensky now had an experience of both sides, *but no bridge at all*. If he were to continue on that path there would be ever deepening chaos. "I came to the conclusion that without the help of those who know another approach it is impossible to do anything."[2] This was a seminal decision. Ouspensky had the instinct to know that, while these states are a part of our inheritance, they should not be accessed by artificial means. While narcotics open a door on one level, they close it on another.

In 1913 Ouspensky published the *Symbolism of the Tarot*, which was quite popular with the readership he had established. While Ouspensky's writings were no longer explicitly Theosophical, they were of direct interest to a Theosophical audience. We see, in all of Ouspensky's early works, a steady struggle to place concepts at the service of what is more than conceptual: to preserve conceptual rigor in its right place, stabilizing insight rather than obscuring it. This has been the fundamental impulse of Hermetic thought through recorded history.

---

1. Ouspensky, P.D. (transl. Nicholas Bessaraboff with an introduction by Claude Bragdon), *Tertium Organum*, Manas Press, New York, 2nd edition, 1928.
2. Ouspensky, P.D., *A New Model of the Universe*, Alfred A. Knopf, New York, 1969, p. 304.

Following the publication of *Tertium Organum* in 1912 Ouspensky convinced several of the newspapers that he worked for to finance a trip to the Far East. In 1913 and 1914 he was able to travel to India and Ceylon [Sri Lanka], and there found teachings that were of considerable interest to him: the Advaita Vedanta teachings as presented by the followers of Ramakrishna, and the Mahayana Buddhist teachings that he found in Ceylon. But he did not feel that these teachings possessed 'real knowledge.' At the same time he heard rumors of schools that had such knowledge, but required a complete and unqualified commitment at the moment of entry. Such a commitment would have forced Ouspensky to remain in India and to make a complete break with his former life, becoming a dependent being in a context that was completely foreign to him. This he was not prepared to do. In summarizing his experience in India, he wrote:

> I did not like, or trust, devotional schools. In many ways it was cultivation of imagination. All these trance states, Samadhi, etc., are imagination in higher emotional center (or ordinary emotional center). This leads to a blind alley from which it is impossible to pass to any higher experience. So I realized that real work must be work on being, and that without work on being nothing can be done. But work on being requires understanding of aim, methods and the necessary conditions. There are two chief conditions in the work:
>
> 1. One must not believe anything, one must verify everything.
> 2. An even more important condition that refers to 'doing' — one must not do anything until one understands why and for what purpose one is doing it.[3]

In Egypt he found clear traces of the great schools of the past, but little that was of interest to him in the present.

On the basis of what he had learned on this journey, he decided to make a second journey into Persia and Russian Central Asia. However, before

---

3. Ouspensky, P.D., *A Further Record: Extracts from Meetings 1928-1945,* Routledge & Kegan Paul, Arkana Paperbacks, London 1986, p. 132

his return to Russia, the First World War broke out. August of 1914 found Ouspensky in Ceylon, and he was forced, by the conditions imposed by the war, to return to Russia through London, Norway, and Finland, finally reaching St. Petersburg in November 1914. While in London he made a number of literary and journalistic connections, including Carl Bechhofer Roberts and A.R. Orage, who were both involved with the journal *New Age*. Ouspensky maintained a correspondence with both of these men, and they were both to be important to his future.

During his Far Eastern journey he drafted a novelette, *Talks With A Devil*, which was finally published in Russian in 1916.

In the years before the war, it had seemed to Ouspensky that the esoterically oriented intelligentsia that had sprung up in Europe since the 1880s might be the harbinger of a new age, and perhaps even the nucleus of a new world order. In writing and in lecturing he felt himself the servant of that world order. When the Great War came it was a stark denial of this possibility; it represented a forceful reassertion of all that was base, animal, and materialistic in man. It shattered the hopes that had sheathed the young Ouspensky's life in a radiant glow. In so doing it forced an internal adjustment, which matured Ouspensky and made him more focused.

In early 1915 Ouspensky began to give public lectures in St. Petersburg. These lectures regularly drew audiences of over a thousand. Ouspensky was now 'reporting back' to a growing audience that was already familiar with his work. He could rely on his lectures being well attended and he could rely on his publications producing an income.

During this period he noted a newspaper reference to a ballet called *The Struggle of the Magicians*, which was being performed in Moscow. In April he went to Moscow to begin a lecture series there. After one of the lectures two of the men in the audience engaged him in conversation, and told him that they were part of the group that had produced *The Struggle of the Magicians*. They convinced him to meet the leader of the group, George Ivanovich Gurdjieff.

At this point we must ask: who was the Peter Ouspensky who met George Gurdjieff in April of 1915? He was a thirty-seven-year-old journalist, who had travelled extensively through Europe, India, and Southeast

Asia seeking ancient knowledge. He was a published author with an established readership. He felt acutely the crisis of Russia, and the crisis of Western Civilization as a whole, at the beginning of the First World War. He had realized deeply in his being that mankind lives in a waking dream; that our species is under the hold of a collective illusion. He had seen that there is "a thin veil that separates us from a completely different perception of the world," and he had, on occasion, drawn back that veil. He knew, from direct experience, of the existence of Higher Mind in the universe, and he understood that he had — in himself - no control over experiences of this level.[1] It was this combination of insight, with the understanding that he could not control the deeper moments of insight, that distinguishes Peter Ouspensky. All that he had achieved was only a point of departure; he needed methods and he needed direction.

Ouspensky and Gurdjieff: 1915-1917

In April of 1915 Ouspensky went to see what promised to be a very interesting ballet, *The Struggle of the Magicians*. It was, of course, produced by Gurdjieff's group. He spoke with members of the troupe, and they invited him to meet with their master. Ouspensky responded to the invitation and the two men met alone at a small café in Moscow. On the basis of this first meeting Ouspensky went on to meet with Gurdjieff every evening for a week. Recognizing an authentic teacher, and understanding that strict requirements would be made on him, Ouspensky worked out conditions acceptable to both parties under which they might work together. Ouspensky emphasized that he was a writer, and that he must be able to decide for himself what he would write about. Gurdjieff agreed, on the condition that Ouspensky not write about his own work without understanding it first.[2] This requirement had implications that Ouspensky did not fully understand at the time. Gurdjieff knew that Ouspensky would have to reach a

---

1. *Ibid.*, p. 131.
2. Ouspensky, P.D., *In Search of the Miraculous,* Routledge & Kegan Paul, London, 1977, p. 11.

certain level of being first. In fact, he would have to awaken. It was a fateful moment for both men — as it was to be Ouspensky who ultimately put Gurdjieff's teachings into writing for posterity. Had Ouspensky not done this, we would not have a record of the core of these teachings.

Some months later, in the autumn of 1915, Gurdjieff came to St. Petersburg, and from then on he visited the city regularly. Ouspensky invited many of his Theosophical connections to Gurdjieff's meetings, and a St. Petersburg group soon began to form. The original group included Andrei Zakharov, Anthony Charkovsky, Dr. Leonid Stjernvall and his wife Elisaveta Grigorievna, and the lady that Ouspensky was courting at that time, Anna Butkovsky. Within a few months Thomas and Olga de Hartmann joined the group. To this small circle of people Gurdjieff delivered – between February of 1916 and February of 1917 – the bulk of the material recorded in *In Search of the Miraculous*. During that year the group increased from seven to thirty, largely through Ouspensky's recruiting efforts.

In June of 1916 Gurdjieff moved to St. Petersburg and took an apartment at the corner of the Nevsky Prospect and Pushkinskaia, quite close to Ouspensky's apartment. With Gurdjieff's presence in the city, the group met almost every night at the home of Mme. E.N. Maximovitch.

In August of 1916 members of the group made a weekend retreat to the Finland dacha of Mme. Maximovitch. Here Gurdjieff placed a great deal of pressure on Ouspensky, creating a unique experience for him. Prior to the retreat Ouspensky had shared an observation with Gurdjieff in confidence about Leonid Stjernvall; to the effect that his thinking was formatory. At the retreat Gurdjieff repeated the observation in front of the group, humiliating both men. From this point Gurdjieff continued to pressure and humiliate Ouspensky in different ways, bringing him into a very receptive state. Then, suddenly, while Gurdjieff was speaking to the group, Ouspensky found Gurdjieff's voice speaking inside of his own chest, making certain very difficult requirements on him. These requirements were the conditions for his remaining in the group. Ouspensky immediately accepted the conditions, and an exchange followed. To the other students it appeared that Ouspensky was speaking sharply out of turn, and that Gurdjieff was for some reason tolerating and even encouraging him. Then, later

Figure 30. Ouspensky in 1912.

in the evening, when he was alone, Ouspensky heard Gurdjieff's voice in his chest again, making a yet-more-difficult requirement, which he had to either accept or leave the group. Again Ouspensky accepted, but Gurdjieff would not accept his response, asking him to think about the requirement carefully and speak to him at a later date.

Ouspensky records that, on the following evening, Gurdjieff said something to him which affected him deeply. He sprang from his chair and walked out of the dacha into the forest, "wholly under the power of the most extraordinary thoughts and feelings."[1] He was experiencing emotions, both positive and negative, infused with hydrogen 12. "Finally, at the moment of what felt like the climax of contradictions and of inner turmoil ... I saw that G. was right; that what I had considered to be firm and reliable in myself in reality did not exist."[2] The specific issues and conditions that had been discussed on the previous evening were no longer at the center of

---

1. *Ibid.*, p. 269
2. *Ibid.*, 270.

this heightened experience, for ... "I had found something else." The crisis had evoked his Higher Self.

> We stayed in Finland three days longer. During those three days there were very many talks about the most varied subjects. And I was in an unusual emotional state all the time which sometimes began to be burdensome. "How can this be got rid of? I cannot bear it anymore," I asked G. "Do you want to go to sleep?" said G. "Certainly not," I said. "Then what are you asking about? This is what you wanted, make use of it. You are *not asleep at this moment!*"[1]

Reflecting back on the experience he wrote:

> It was at this time that certain very definite changes began in my views on myself, on those around me, and particularly on 'methods of action' if this can be said without more precise definition. ... they were not in any way connected with what *was said* in Finland but they had come as a result of the emotions I had experienced there. The first thing I could record was the weakening in me of that extreme individualism which up to that time had been the fundamental feature in my attitude to life. I began to see people more, to feel my community with them more. And the second thing was that somewhere very deep down in me I understood the esoteric principle of the impossibility of violence ... violent means and methods *in anything whatever* would unfailingly produce negative results ..."[2]

There are two things to note about Ouspensky's digestion of the experience in Finland. Firstly, he speaks of a weakening of the "extreme individualism" that had been characteristic of him. We can take this moment as the beginning of Ouspensky's work on becoming a man number five, which developed in stages up to mid-1919. The extreme individualism he describes would have to be displaced for his steward to function with the consistency that is needed to support Higher Centers. The second thing to note is that Ouspensky speaks of the impossibility of violent methods in esoteric work.

---

1. *Ibid.*, 271.
2. *Ibid.*, p. 273.

This conviction almost surely relates to Gurdjieff's methods. It is unlikely Ouspensky is referring here to physical violence, but to a confrontational style of teaching: for example, putting a student on the spot, with the threat of removing him from the group, and then making very difficult demands when, according to Gurdjieff, to lose a school is worse than death. This is a harrowing situation. Also, speaking from inside of someone is a *very direct* way of confronting them. It represents, for the person spoken to, a total loss of personal privacy. Radical methods such as these can motivate, but at the same time they can create fear and anxiety — a kind of negative self-consciousness. Thus, there is a risk involved. Will the motivation so created produce a right result?

The motivation to realize Higher Centers, which is the highest labor of which man is capable, *must be based on a positive evaluation of Higher Centers,* and on a sense of their possibility. If the motivation is not *fundamentally* positive, nothing else can come right. If the *principal* motivation is fear or self-hatred, then the efforts made *will not* produce the desired result. A negative motivation will not engage essence, and essence is needed to make a right connection with Higher Centers.

Having said this, it must be acknowledged that *both kinds of motivation — negative and positive — are needed*. And Ouspensky is not saying that the balance was wrong in Gurdjieff's teaching. Obviously, Gurdjieff's intervention at the Finland dacha produced an ultimately positive result for Ouspensky. What Ouspensky is questioning is something in the overall tone or atmosphere of the teaching, which affects all the students. There is a certain kind of trust that must exist in a group attempting this difficult work.

In the weeks following the crisis at Finland, Ouspensky found himself 'seeing' sleeping people in the street.

> After this there followed a strange period of time. It lasted about three weeks. And during this period from time to time I saw "sleeping people." This requires a particular explanation. Two or three days after G.'s departure I was walking along the Troitsky street and suddenly I saw that the man who was walking towards me was *asleep*. There could be no doubt whatever about this. Although

his eyes were open, he was walking along obviously immersed in dreams which ran like clouds across his face. It entered my mind that if I could look at him long enough I should see his dreams, that is, I should understand what he was seeing in his dreams. But he passed on. After him came another also sleeping. A sleeping *izvostchik* went by and two sleeping passengers. Suddenly I found myself in the position of the prince in the "Sleeping Princess." Everyone around me was asleep. ... I at once made the discovery that by trying to remember myself I was able to intensify and prolong these sensations for so long as I had the energy enough not to be diverted .... When attention was diverted I ceased to see "sleeping people" because I had obviously gone to sleep myself.[1]

In the winter of 1916 Gurdjieff returned to Moscow. The Great War, now in its second year, was creating ever greater difficulties for Russia. In October Ouspensky was drafted into the Guards Sappers, who perform engineering duties, such as demolitions and the laying and clearing of mine fields. The regimental headquarters was quite near his apartment on Troitskaia, allowing him to remain active with the St. Petersburg group. In the winter of 1916-1917 Sophia Grigorievna Maximenko entered the St. Petersburg group.

Sophia Grigorievna and Peter Ouspensky — who were both the same age — formed an immediate connection, and she moved, with her daughter, into Ouspensky's apartment. (Ouspensky and Anna Butkovsky had already parted ways.) The nineteen-year-old daughter, Lenotchka, had just been widowed by the war, and was pregnant with her deceased husband's child. This move was the beginning of a lifelong connection between the three people.[2]

---

1. *Ibid.*, p. 265.
2. Sophia Grigorievna Volochine, b. 1878, had, at the age of sixteen, married a university student and had a son and a daughter by him. The son died. She divorced the student and married a mining engineer, by the name of Maximenko. At some point she left Maximenko. At the age of thirty-eight she appeared in the St. Petersburg group. Sophia Grigorievna's daughter Lenotchka had been married to a young man by the name of Savitsky, who was killed in the war.

In January of 1917 Ouspensky was discharged from the Guards Sappers, due to his poor vision. By this time the pressures of the war were creating acute supply problems throughout Russia, and general social unrest was developing. In February of 1917, just before the abdication of Tsar Nicholas II, Gurdjieff made his last visit to St. Petersburg. During that visit he spoke to Ouspensky about leaving Russia and waiting out the end of the war in a neutral country – but Ouspensky had no definite plan at that time.[3]

Almost immediately on Gurdjieff's return to Moscow, on 1st March 1917, the Tsar abdicated, and Alexander Kerensky formed a provisional democratic government. This opened a period of acute social unrest and general confusion. Gurdjieff left Moscow to make contact with his family in Alexandropol, in the Southern Caucasus. He felt that they were threatened by a possible Turkish invasion, which did in fact occur. He promised his students he would return to Moscow by Easter, April 8th, which – in the way the events played out – he was not able to do. He asked Ouspensky, in his absence, to continue directing the work of the St. Petersburg group. This was a difficult period for Ouspensky, as he found himself between two stools. It was every day more apparent that he would have to leave his native country, and he had no idea what the future held in store for him.

> I had no illusions about the revolution and I realized that the days of Russia were numbered. I decided to go abroad, wait for the end of the war in one of the neutral countries, and afterwards continue my work in London where, on my way back from India, I had made some preparations for publishing my books.[4]

In early June of 1917 Ouspensky received a telegram from Gurdjieff in Alexandropol: "If you want rest come here to me." He was inviting Ouspensky to join him while he assessed the situation. In Alexandropol Ouspensky had the opportunity to meet Gurdjieff's family. At the end of two weeks Gurdjieff asked Ouspensky to return to Moscow and St. Petersburg, and ask every member of the group who could, to join him in Essentuki for

---

3. See Taylor, Merrily E. (compiler & editor), *Remembering Pyotr Demianovich Ouspensky*, Yale University Library, New Haven, CT, 1978, p. 28
4. *Ibid.*, p. 12.

group work. In mid-July Ouspensky arrived in Essentuki with fourteen people, including Sophia Grigorievna and her daughter.

For six weeks, from mid-July to August of 1917, Gurdjieff conducted the *first Essentuki workshop*. He worked with his students "day and night for six weeks of unparalleled intensity."[1] The Essentuki workshop was the fulfillment of five years of Gurdjieff's teaching in Russia, and an indication of all that might be possible on that foundation. As we noted in Chapter 2, Ouspensky saw, in these intensive teachings, a plan for the whole development of the Work. During the workshop he had an altered experience of time, later saying that the six weeks at Essentuki contained a full six years worth of experience.

At such a point the door between worlds is open. We can understand this with reference to the idea of *kairos time*: an intersection of the horizontal line of time with the vertical line of the sixth dimension — the dimension in which all possibilities are realized.[2] Such moments occur in every life, and in the life of every school. This does not mean that, for one who enters such a moment, all possibilities are realized, only that they are all open. In the *kairos* moment something entirely new can enter the life of the individual or the school. Outside of the *kairos* moment no amount of effort will produce such a result. When people move close to the moment of all possibilities, there is an elongation of time. Everything is of greater significance, and minutes can seem like hours. The atmosphere of *kairos* time is represented clearly in the gospels of the New Testament.

The *kairos* moment of Essentuki in August of 1917 was formative for Peter Ouspensky's vision of the Work, and a timeless moment in the history of the Fourth Way. It suddenly made things possible, at many different points in time. Ouspensky was often to refer back to this moment in his later life. What doors did it open? Personal doors for each of its participants, certainly. Ouspensky clearly felt that doors had been opened for the creation of a great Fourth Way school. Gurdjieff may have felt the same, but, as a teacher, the experience revealed to him certain limitations in the

---

1. Bennett, J.G., *Gurdjieff: Making a New World*, Turnstone Books, London, 1973, p. 120.

2. This is Ouspensky's definition of *kairos time*, with which Gurdjieff concurred.

Figure 31. Sophia Grigorievna Maximenko.

group he was presently working with. He ended the experiment suddenly, holding the group responsible for a dispute which had arisen between two of its members. Gurdjieff did not feel that *the next step* for his group would be a direct continuation of the work of August 1917. Perhaps certain things needed to be worked out before the Work could continue.

Whatever the case, the workshop ended on an ambiguous note. As Ouspensky put it:

> For a reason that seemed to me to be accidental, and which was the result of friction between certain members of our small group, G. announced that he was dispersing the whole group and stopping all work. (Was he putting us to a test?) I considered the moment most inappropriate for "acting," and if what G. said was serious, then why had the whole business been started? ... And I have to confess that my confidence in G. began to waver from this moment.[3]

---

3. Ouspensky, P.D., *In Search of the Miraclous,* Routledge & Kegan Paul, London, 1977, p. 367-368

Following the closure of the workshop Gurdjieff went with Andrie Zakharov to Tuapse, and soon after Julia Ostrowska and the de Hartmanns went to join him there. Ouspensky returned to St. Petersburg to retrieve some of his belongings. In the month to follow (September) Gurdjieff contacted Ouspensky, with an invitation to spend the winter with him in the Caucasus. In mid-October Ouspensky left St. Petersburg to join Gurdjieff.

Just after Ouspensky's departure from St. Petersburg, on 25th October 1917, the Bolsheviks overthrew the provisional government. The Red Guards seized the Winter Palace and Lenin immediately announced an armistice with the Central Powers. But in their negotiation with the Central Powers the Bolsheviks were unable to reach an agreement on territorial boundaries – and from that point forward the revolution and the war proceeded simultaneously.[1]

From November through January Gurdjieff and his five companions moved between Tuapse, Uch-Dere, and Olghniki. In February the group returned to Essentuki, where Gurdjieff — in anticipation of a second intensive workshop — rented a house and property. In the third month of the Russian Revolution, on 12th February 1918, Gurdjieff summoned all of his Moscow and St. Petersburg students to Essentuki. About fifteen people were able to come. By March a total of forty people had assembled, more than half of whom Gurdjieff had recruited locally.

The *second Essentuki workshop* was much different from the first. The people who had been recruited locally were complete novices to the Work. It was not a matter, then, of taking a prepared group of people through to a new level of work. Nor was there any sense of a long-term plan. The themes that had been broached in the first workshop were not taken up again.

In March, after about a month, Ouspensky separated himself from the group. He left the house that Gurdjieff had rented, took rooms in the town nearby, and recommenced work on his manuscript for *A New Model of the Universe*.[2] This was not a casual decision on Ouspensky's part; it was a

---

1. The Brest-Litovsk treaty between the Germans and the Russians was not signed until the 3rd of March 1918.
2. This book, which outlines the history of esotericism and its place in the history of the human race, was first published thirteen years later, in 1931. While

decision to work independently from Gurdjieff. It marked a fundamental moment of division between the two men, and so we need to look at it carefully.

WHY DID OUSPENSKY LEAVE GURDJIEFF?

The first Essentuki workshop challenged students who had been trained intensively in relation to their deepest areas of identification. They were challenged in relation to the standards of the Inner Circle of Humanity. The second workshop created challenges that were — in the words of Ouspensky – of a more "banal and workaday" nature. Ouspensky wrote that "the new directions which G.'s work had taken were somehow aimless and led nowhere." The 'search for the miraculous' had, in Ouspensky's view, become submerged in "mere submission and obedience."[3]

On a deeper level Ouspensky felt that – over a more extended period of time – Gurdjieff ... "demanded from people to accept what they did not believe and to do what they did not understand."[4] In the first Russian draft of *In Search of the Miraculous* Ouspensky wrote.

> He (Gurdjieff) confused and muddled people so much that they finally lost all sense of the right and the left side. This was the system. And sometimes G. even explained it. He said that a man ought to be so sure of his right and his left sides that it should be quite impossible to confuse him. And so long as he could be confused, he must be confused. But it was strange that in many cases he evidently could not stop himself and continued to "act" even when his "acting" had become too obvious and produced results directly opposed to the ones he expected.[5]

We suspect that Ouspensky's objection to Gurdjieff's compulsive acting was more central to his decision to leave than his frustration with the "banal and workaday" nature of the workshop. Yet neither of these reasons would, in themselves, have caused

---

adhering exactly to system principles, it uses the vocabulary of teachings known to history, and in so doing fleshes out the stark categories of the system. While the book reads easily it represents a careful interpretation of many different teachings. From one point of view, it is a very understated acknowledgement of the place of C Influence, or Higher School, in history.

3. From the 1926 Draft of *In Search of the Miraculous,* from the Ouspensky Papers, at the Yale University Archive, Sterling Library, Folder 1688.
4. From the typescript of a meeting given in London on 13th October 1937.
5. From the 1926 Draft of *In Search of the Miraculous,* from the Ouspensky Papers, at the Yale University Archive, Sterling Library, Folder 1688.

Ouspensky to leave. What forced matters to a head in March of 1918 was that Ouspensky "did not find it possible to accept certain demands, which were either directly made upon me as a condition of my further work with G., or followed from his actions."[1] Ouspensky added that, "I can say nothing about the demands which determined the character of my subsequent relations with G. because any attempt to describe these demands or to explain why I refused to accept them would inevitably acquire a character of self-justification and a desire [to assert] that G. was in the wrong ... neither the one nor the other enters my intention."

In sum, Ouspensky at different times emphasized: being asked to do something out of obligation without understanding; being asked to act on faith rather than on verification; and the aspect of violence, which he felt was not useful.

In considering Ouspensky's response to Gurdjieff's demands, we know that he had already accepted some very difficult demands, and that he knew the value of working with difficult demands from a teacher. He stated that he "realized perfectly that everything I received from G. was only due to my submitting to his demands."[2] So we must leave Ouspensky with his 'justification,' whatever it was. This refusal to gossip became a permanent aspect of his character.

What we see at work behind these statements is the equanimity of an awakened being. He does not need to prove himself. Something has become independent of the functions. The decision to leave the workshop was neither reactive nor impulsive, yet it was probably the most difficult decision of his life.

> When I decided to leave G. I knew no other school and no other G. More than that, I knew for certain that I would never find anything of its kind; or even if I ever happened to meet something like a school, it would be after many years, in quite different surroundings, in quite different circumstances, which I could neither foresee nor foretell. Consequently, it was not at all easy for me to leave G. and I did not deceive myself with false expectations and hopes. I knew that something had failed.[3]

> My leaving G. and everything I said at the time as well as later did not and does not show any distrust of G. or any doubt in him [i.e. that he was awake]. I did not see anything actually negative and did not look for it.[4]

---

1. *Ibid.*, Folder 1688.
2. *Ibid.*, Folder 1688.
3. *Ibid.*, Folder 1688.
4. *Ibid.*, Folder 1688.

I understood from the very first that a critical or negative attitude toward G. himself and his ideas would be essentially wrong.[5]

There are certain points in a relationship that is not working — whether between a man and a woman or between a student and a teacher — when a person stands alone. Certain things have been said and done, and neither person can ever completely go back on that. This is not to deny all the best that has been in the relationship, but it is not to ignore the worst of it – or to naively presume that the worst will not recur. Having been forced to stand outside of the relationship, while still in it, one can only go forward on a new basis. Ouspensky decided to go forward outside of the formal teacher-student relationship that had been agreed upon in the Moscow café in 1915. But the relationship itself was too deep to be dismissed ... on either side. And so it was to continue on a different footing, independently of the will or choice of either of these two men. And this was the context in which the Fourth Way was to develop.

We shall never know what Gurdjieff's aims for the second Essentuki workshop were, whether those aims were realized, or how Gurdjieff saw the future of his group at that time. Nor shall we ever know what Peter Ouspensky might have gained by complying with the demands that Gurdjieff made upon him. When John Bennett later came to a similar crossroads with Gurdjieff, Ouspensky advised him by telling him a story of a knight on a quest.

> There is a Russian fairy tale of a knight who sets out on a great adventure. He arrives at a place where the road divides into three. Unable to decide which to choose, he sees an old man, who tells him that if he goes to the right he will lose his horse, if he goes to the left he will lose himself, while if he takes the road in the center he will lose both himself and his horse. He reasons with himself that a knight without a horse is useless, and a horse without a knight is useless, so he might as well risk losing both. He chooses the middle path, and after desperate adventures, in which the old man's prophecy is fulfilled, he finally reaches his goal. You are now in that position. But I might as well tell you that if the knight had chosen either of the other two paths, it would have been the same in the end. It was only necessary that he should persist and never give up. That is the only condition.[6]

This was certainly Ouspensky's story. He never gave up. He knew that, once the knight had made his choice, he must be able to go ahead, positively, without knowing

---

5. *Ibid.*, Folder 1688.

6. Bennett, J.G., *Witness, the Story of a Search,* Dharma Book Company, NY, 1962, p. 136.

whether he had done the right thing or not — because it is vanity that needs to know that we are right. At the level of the Ray of Creation we occupy, we are bound to make mistakes, and it nevertheless remains true that everything *is* at stake. Taking responsibility for this uncertainty — not from weakness but from strength — was Ouspensky's outstanding contribution to the Fourth Way.

And so Peter Ouspensky worked independently of Gurdjieff from this point in time: independent of but inescapably connected to. He was to cooperate with Gurdjieff at later points in his life, without expectation. He saw himself as owing a debt to his teacher, and as being, together with Gurdjieff, the servant of an emerging esoteric movement in the West. In that regard he had an obligation. He was to provide significant support to Gurdjieff in Constantinople, and even greater support later in Paris. In each case he brought Gurdjieff many new students, both through direct recruitment and through the books he published. Over the next three decades the two men were to define different forms of the Work, not each on their own, but in a field of tension and reciprocal influence.

Having reviewed Ouspensky's decision we return to the narrative of events. When Ouspensky left the house used for the retreat, he took rooms in the village nearby. Gurdjieff continued to visit him from time to time, and the two men continued to converse.

After the workshop Gurdjieff, with fourteen students, undertook the two-month journey through the Caucasus to Sochi that was described in the previous chapter. From Sochi the group travelled to Tiflis, the capital of Georgia, to create a new base of operations. Ouspensky remained with his family in Essentuki through the winter months, during which time the city was occupied by the Red Army. Ouspensky first took work as a porter, then as a schoolmaster, and finally as a librarian. In this way he managed to support Sophia Grigorievna, Lenotchka, and her newborn baby Leonidas. Between September and December 1918 the family suffered cold, hunger, and the ravages of typhoid fever. In January 1919 Essentuki was liberated by the White Russian army, but it was clear to Ouspensky that this liberation was temporary. He continued to take different kinds of work, travelling between Essentuki, Ekaterinodar, Rostov, and Novorossisk. At the beginning of June 1919, he moved his family into an apartment in Ekaterinodar. Here — on top of all his other activities — he began to give lectures on the system.

In the five months following the move to Ekaterinodar three things happened: 1) Ouspensky began to teach his first group, 2) a caste of characters important to Ouspensky's future made their appearance, and 3) a new degree of uncertainty entered Ouspensky's life, perhaps corresponding to a new level of being. We feel the hand of fate: the future is somehow alive in the present.

During the autumn of 1919, as part of his ongoing attempt to earn money, he sent five articles to A.R. Orage, the editor of the *New Age,* whom Ouspensky had met on his visit to London in 1914.[1] Orage, on becoming aware of Ouspensky's material situation, recommended him to Major Frank Pinder, the head of the British Economic Mission to the White Russian army. Major Pinder promptly employed Ouspensky to write the Mission's press summaries. In the autumn of 1919 (September-October) Ouspensky went with Major Pinder to Rostov, leaving his family in the apartment at Ekaterinodar. In Rostov he resumed public lectures on the system, and was soon joined by Andrei Zakharov, one of the original Petrograd group. In mid-December of 1919 Ouspensky's London contact for the *New Age,* Carl Bechhofer-Roberts, arrived in Rostov. Seeing the general situation of the White Army in the region, he encouraged Ouspensky to relocate to London.

By the end of December 1919, the Red Army had reached the outer perimeter of Rostov. Andrei Zakharov left for Novorossisk, where he died of smallpox. Bechhofer-Roberts made his way back to London. Ouspensky returned to Ekaterinodar, and then brought his family across the Crimea to Odessa, from whence he embarked for Constantinople.

Having traced Ouspensky's final two years in Russia, we must now re-examine the period from August 1916 (the retreat at the dacha at Finland) to December 1919 (the departure from Russia) from the standpoint of awakening.

---

1. These have been republished as *Letters From Russia 1919,* Penguin/Arkana, 1992. They are dated from 25th July to 25th September, with two undated letters.

Ouspensky's Awakening: 1917–1919

Sometime in the aftermath of the second Essentuki workshop, in June or July of 1918, Ouspensky underwent a fundamental change. This change was not sudden; it came gradually. He spoke of the change a year later, in June 1919, in response to a question asked at one of his lectures in Ekaterinodar. The question must have been something like, "What have you gotten out of the system for yourself?"

> Remembering all I had experienced during the preceding year, particularly after G.s departure, I said that I had acquired a strange confidence ... it is a confidence in the unimportance and the insignificance of *self*; that self which we usually know. But what I am confident about is that if something terrible happened to me ... then it would be not I who would meet it, not this ordinary I, but another I within me who would be equal to the occasion. Two years ago [in June 1917, at the beginning of the first Essentuki workshop] G. asked me whether I felt a new I inside me and I had to answer that I felt no change whatever. Now I can speak otherwise. And I can explain how the change takes place. It does not take place at once; I mean that the change does not embrace every moment of life. All the ordinary life goes on in the ordinary way, all those very ordinary stupid small 'I's, excepting perhaps a few which have already become impossible. But if something big were to happen, something which would require the straining of every nerve, then I know that this big thing would be met not by the ordinary small I, which is now speaking, and which can be made afraid, nor by anything like it — but by another, a big I, which nothing can frighten and which would be equal to everything that happened. I cannot describe it better. But for me it is a fact.[1]

This experience of "another I within me" was not a fleeting glimpse of Higher Centers, of the kind that Ouspensky had described in *Tertium Organum*; it was an understanding that he existed *in a relationship* to Real I.

---

1. Ouspensky, P.D., *In Search of the Miraculous,* Routlege & Kegan Paul, London, 1977, p. 379-80.

While it had not yet become continuous in him, he understood that *it was what he really was*. Something had come into existence *behind* the Peter Ouspensky who gave the lectures, who wrote the articles for the *New Age*, and who provided for his family. And he saw that he could, in a certain way, rely on that something.

Having undergone this change he noticed that he had the ability to see other people ... "as he himself had been." In other words, he could see where their sense of self-importance was lodged, and what their personal obstacles were. This was the quality that he had so much admired in Gurdjieff, and it had come to him as a function of this new feeling of 'I.' So with the diminution of his own sense of self-importance, there came a greater compassion for others, and a greater ability to see the obstacles that kept them from Real I. These are the defining characteristics of a teacher.

Let us review the trajectory of Ouspensky's awakening. As he noted, the process of awakening "does not take place all at once."

August 1916 The incident at Mme. Maximovitch's dacha in Finland ... "but I had found something else". From this moment begins the diminution of the extreme sense of individuality, and the growing sense of connectedness to others.

Late 1916 Documents recording conversations in the final months of Ouspensky's life, suggest there may have been a second such incident, in St. Petersburg, involving Gurdjieff and Sophia Grigorievna.[2]

March 1917 The altered reality of the first six-week intensive workshop in Essentuki, where "G. unfolded to us the whole plan of the work."

October 1917 The Russian Revolution brings a permanent heightening of tension and uncertainty in Ouspensky's life. He is, from this point forward, 'a man without a country.'

March 1918 The second workshop at Essentuki, where Ouspensky decided to work independently from Gurdjieff. This decision coincides with Ouspensky's first grounded realization of Real I. With his decision to

---

2. Collin, Rodney, *Last Remembrances of a Magician*, c. 1948.

work separately begins the sore trial of crystallization, which parallels what Gurdjieff underwent at the oasis at Yanghi Hissar, sixteen years before.

June-July 1918 The beginning of the internal change that Ouspensky described a year later, in June of 1919: the emergence of a "strange confidence" as something new begins to stabilize within him.

August 1918 Gurdjieff sets out on an expedition through the Caucasus to Sochi, and Ouspensky is left to his own resources, with his new family, in the midst of Bolshevik Russia. The internal changes Ouspensky is undergoing are now complemented by greater external uncertainty. The world he had known was passing away forever, and now both he, and those closest to him, were in some degree of physical danger.

June 1919 At the end of the first Essentuki workshop, Gurdjieff had asked if he felt a new sense of I inside of himself? Ouspensky had answered no. He could now tell a student: "Now I can speak otherwise."

It is characteristic of such a transition that, for the entire period — the better part of three years — Ouspensky was kept in a state of extreme uncertainty. He was in physical danger for most of this time, he lost all of his possessions, and his personal relationships were in a state of flux. In this period his learned identity began to come apart, and a higher level began to open up behind it. This is the tremendous pressure of making the transition to man number five. The confluence of circumstances required to produce such a transition requires careful engineering, of a kind that is quite beyond human capacity. The skill required of a master-jeweler to cut a flawless diamond is nothing compared with the skill required to produce a permanent Self out of unstable molecular matter in the coarse medium of organic life.

We pointed out, in the Introductory and Overview chapters, that awakening brings critical insights related to the person's role. With Real I comes the inner conviction that it should be exercised in a certain way and in a certain direction. Self-consciousness combines with an awareness of the responsibilities that it entails — and this is unique for each individual. While we cannot know just what this was for Ouspensky, we can reconstruct something of his situation.

We know that in the Petrograd group, in the spring of 1916, Peter Ouspensky sensed the future of a Great Teaching, and that this was heightened by his experience of the first Essentuki workshop, where six years of experience were compressed into six weeks. He had found a system that was exactly appropriate to the needs of humanity in its hour of atheist materialism, freshly divorced from traditional wisdom, and freshly empowered by the promethean byproducts of the first industrial revolution. And so the deepening contact with his Real Self combined with a sense of task, or duty. While for Ouspensky this sense would have been simpler and more profound than what we can here describe, it would have included:

1. No violence. This was later to take the form of a commitment to control the expression of negative emotions.

2. No unquestioning acceptance of 'ideas' pertaining to a higher level – as in a religious teaching. The student must always be moved to connect with *the reality of a higher level,* at whatever level they can experience that.

3. The conviction that the Work itself must be based on positive motivation — which poses the practical problem of finding a right balance between positive and negative motivation.

4. A sense of urgency to establish a new teaching in a world that was fast becoming divorced from the great teachings of the past.

5. Above all, for Ouspensky, there was the sense of the hidden source from which the system had sprung — Higher School — and the will to reconnect with that source, in order to present the system in all its depth and profundity.

Our contention here is that it was his commitment to the hidden source — not willfulness or ambition — that drove Ouspensky to work independently of Gurdjieff. After having experienced a number of restarts with Gurdjieff's Work, he had the underlying feeling that it would not produce the hoped for connection to the source of the system. This intuition was not something fixed and permanent, but at the same time — having been given something of his own — Ouspensky couldn't wait indefinitely, through innumerable restarts, to see what results might come.

Having said this, we must emphasize that Ouspensky still felt that something might come from Gurdjieff's Work. He even *expected* that something would. But would that 'something' be Great School in the West? Or would it be a series of challenging experiments that produced useful results for a few, and confusion for many. Ouspensky retained a profound respect for Gurdjieff throughout his lifetime. He was to work actively with him again in Constantinople, and later in Fontainebleau. He helped Gurdjieff to finance his endeavors and to attract students until 1924, when Gurdjieff closed the Institute. Ouspensky always, and under all circumstances, acknowledged Gurdjieff as a very highly developed being, to whom he owed a great debt.

And thus, from July 1918, Gurdjieff and Ouspensky worked – partially connected, partially separate – for the remainder of their lives. Let us look briefly at the connection between the two men and their respective 'ways.' In the literature of the Fourth Way this division has been both dramatized and exaggerated: we hear of villains and traitors, of good guys and bad guys. Why? Simply because the two teachers were contemporary to one another. But why should this produce confusion?

A teacher is by definition grounded in Worlds 6 and 12, and the students rightly look to their teacher for guidance. Each teacher tries to create a special context for their students to help them bridge the dimensional difference between the human world and the worlds beyond. There are certain 'do's and 'don't's, certain core texts, certain exercises, certain images, certain art forms, and a certain myth of awakening to encompass it all. The context is something *on this level* that helps to orient the student to *a higher level*. It inspires and motivates, while at the same time bringing out the resistance to awakening that is in the students. The students rightly take this context as sacred because it is the means their teacher has given them for making Higher Centers central to their lives. And this is something that humanity, taken as a whole, is unable to do for itself.

Given that the student accepts the context created by their teacher, another teacher – who is equally grounded in Higher Centers – may create a different context, or choose a different point of emphasis in their teaching. We keep in mind that the context not only inspires, but also creates the necessary denying force for the students. It brings them up against their mechanicality. For both these reasons, the exposure to an alternative context may represent a temptation. You escape the denying force that makes your own life difficult, and you are exposed to an alternative inspiration. Farther fields are greener. To the extent that the alternative context does create a temptation it has the effect of de-sacralizing the original context. There is, therefore, a strong tendency for students to discredit a competing context as 'wrong.' Perhaps for the students of the first teacher, this is true – for they need to *use* the context created by the teacher they have chosen.[1] So there is a tendency for the students of each teacher to discredit the other teacher, and this tendency is clearly expressed in the secondary literature on Gurdjieff and Ouspensky. Underneath the tendency to discredit lies fear, but the differences between these two men cannot be understood in terms of fear.

From the summer of 1918, Gurdjieff and Ouspensky worked separately, while in a wider context they remained connected to one another. They were briefly reconciled in Constantinople in 1920, in London in 1922, and then between 1922 and 1924 Ouspensky helped to finance the Prieuré at Fontainebleau and actually encouraged his students to spend time there. In 1924 Gurdjieff and Ouspensky went their separate ways again, yet they continued to visit and communicate with one another until the German occupation of Paris made that impossible. When the war ended Gurdjieff made an overture to Ouspensky, but by that time he was in the final months of his life.

In sum, what is often reported is the discord between these two men. In the eyes of the students – each circle wanting to feel conviction in its own work – one of the two men is wrong and the other right. But the underlying tension can be viewed in a different light. We can try to establish perspective by reconstructing how Gurdjieff, as a teacher, viewed Peter Ouspensky.

---

1. Who the "right" teacher is, is ultimately a matter of fate.

GURDJIEFF'S RELATION TO OUSPENSKY

At some point Gurdjieff realized that Peter Ouspensky had the potential to awaken, and that, beyond this, he had a real ability to teach. Gurdjieff was probably open to the possibility of Ouspensky teaching under him or independently of him, depending on how things worked out. And Gurdjieff had a very high tolerance for uncertainty! Gurdjieff's commitment as a teacher was to ensure that when and if Peter Ouspensky began to teach, he would have a clear sense of how his features might affect his relationship to students.

Every teacher carries, from the moment of their awakening, aspects of their features into their teaching. It is part of the 'play' of the developing teaching to work these features out. When Gurdjieff discredited Ouspensky on his first visits to London in 1922, it was because he saw a young teacher's vanity feature at work. He knew that Ouspensky could assimilate the rebuke and take direction from it.

Gurdjieff was more advanced than Ouspensky. He had come to Moscow at a level close to a man number six. Ouspensky never claimed to be on a higher level than Gurdjieff – it was simply that he saw that something in the way Gurdjieff was proceeding was problematic. Gurdjieff was, of course, aware that there were problems with his own group, although he saw these in a different light. He would have had no trouble understanding Ouspensky's reservations about his own approach to the Work. He would also have understood the kind of decision Ouspensky faced when he pressured him to leave the group, at Essentuki, in March 1918.

Most importantly Gurdjieff would have understood that, while Ouspensky had reservations about his own approach to the Work, he valued the Fourth Way teaching itself. He saw the invisible source of that teaching as existing on a different scale from any disagreements that might exist between the two of them. The teaching of the Fourth Way was a C influence dispensation to humanity in its hour of need, and the Higher Source would be watching the experiment unfold. Ouspensky's commitment to this Higher Source would always override his personal reservations about Gurdjieff's approach to the Work. So Gurdjieff played his hand with a fairly clear idea of how his student would respond. Having said this, we acknowledge that many of the actual exchanges between the two men may have been difficult on both sides.

Finally, Gurdjieff knew that Ouspensky was in a live relation with his own Real I and was strong enough to go deeper with it. After parting ways with Gurdjieff, Ouspensky showed as much deference and respect for Gurdjieff as his independent position would allow.

The Young Teacher: 1919–1921

When Gurdjieff left Essentuki in August 1918, Ouspensky did not see him again for nearly two years. Ouspensky could not now return to Moscow or St. Petersburg, and he was struggling hard to support his wife Sophia, his stepdaughter Lenotchka, and her child Leonidas.

At the beginning of June, the Ouspensky family was able to relocate to Ekaterinodar, which was safer, more stable, and offered a better vantage point for travel. When Orage arranged the contact with Major Pinder, Ouspensky began to move between Rostov and Ekaterinodar. During this time he came more and more in contact with the English who were supporting the White Russians, and at this point he began to consider a long term plan of relocating to Britain.

By December 1919 the Bolshevik forces were approaching Rostov, and the prospects for the White Russian forces were bleak. Ouspensky returned to Ekaterinodar, gathered his family, brought them across the Crimea to Odessa, and from there embarked for Constantinople. For Ouspensky it was now true externally as it was internally that "the son of man hath

Figure 32. Gurdjieff and Ouspensky c. 1918.

nowhere to lay his head." He was entering a state of exile from which he would never return.

In January 1920 the Ouspensky family arrived, destitute émigrés, in the city of Constantinople, which was now filled with Allied forces and Russian refugees. Ouspensky was able to find rooms on Prinkipo Island, just offshore from the city, and immediately began to support himself by teaching mathematics to children, and English to other Russian émigrés. In March of 1920 he began to give lectures on the Work ideas in the European quarter of Constantinople, in what is called the Péra district. One of his students was acquainted with an Englishwoman, Winifred Beaumont, who owned rooms in the Péra, and she allowed Ouspensky to make use of these rooms for his lectures. He quickly attracted twenty or thirty students. Winifred Beaumont and her husband, John Bennett, a young British diplomat, both became friends with Ouspensky at this time, although they did not become part of his group.

On the 7th June 1920 Gurdjieff and his entourage, having been forced to leave Tiflis, arrived in Constantinople, and immediately took apartments in Koumbaradji Street in the Péra district.

We can imagine Gurdjieff and Ouspensky meeting one day, early in June, perhaps in the Péra district. The two men, on seeing one another, must have realized the degree to which their fates were connected. Gurdjieff offered to include Ouspensky in his Work, and Ouspensky accepted, and — following a pattern that was to repeat in the future — introduced all of his students to Gurdjieff.

> I was very glad to see G. and to me personally it seemed then that, in the interests of the work, all former difficulties could be set aside and that I could again work with him as in St. Petersburg. I brought G. to my lectures and handed over to him all the people who came to my lectures, particularly the small group of about thirty persons who met upstairs in the offices of the "Miyak."[1]

---

1. Ouspensky, P.D., *In Search of the Miraculous*, Routledge & Kegan Paul, London, 1977, p. 382.

From June through August the two men worked, together with Thomas de Hartmann and Alexandre de Salzmann, on *The Struggle of the Magicians,* creating script, sets, music, and choreography. While they worked they studied the performances of the Mevlevi dervishes, whose main *tekke*[2] was close by. Constantinople was, at this time, still the capital of the Ottoman Empire, and still the greatest center of activity for the Sufi Orders of Islam. This study of the dervish dances of several of the great Sufi orders must have been a 'golden hour' in the lives of the four men.[3]

> It was a very interesting time for me. G. often came to me in Prinkipo. We went together through the Constantinople bazaars. We went to the Mevlevi dervishes, and he explained to me what I had not been able to understand before. And this was that the whirling of the Mevlevi dervishes was an exercise for the brain based upon counting, like those exercises that he had shown to us in Essentuki. Sometimes I worked with him for entire days and nights [on choreographing the ballet or translating Dervish songs for use in the ballet]. ... I saw G. the artist and G. the poet, whom he had so carefully hidden inside him, particularly the latter.[4]

In September Gurdjieff rented, as a new location for the Institute, the first three floors of an office building at 13 Yemeneci Abdullatif Sokak – quite close to his apartment on Koumbaradji Street. At the same time, he rented space for the performance of the movements in a synagogue, known as the Grand Rabbinate, which was immediately adjacent, at 21 Yemeneci Abdullatif Sokak. After a few weeks the Institute began to give regular Saturday performances at this venue. Ouspensky gave talks at #13, attended the movement classes, and was involved with the theater.

However, with the passage of time, the same differences that had come up in Essentuki re-surfaced in Constantinople. In October 1920 Ouspensky

---

2. Lodge or center.

3. Ouspensky was to return to this experience many years later, inviting the Mevlevi dervishes to London in 1939.

4. Ouspenksy, P.D., *In Search of the Miraculous,* Routledge & Kegan Paul, London, 1977, p. 382-3.

disassociated himself from the Work of the Institute. In his later references to this event Ouspensky was not specific about what the differences were, but this second parting of the ways was not a crisis for him – for he had gone into the situation knowing its limitations.

In his 1926 draft for *In Search of the Miraculous* Ouspensky made some notes on his work on *The Struggle of the Magicians* in Constantinople. These notes shed light on what the differences between the two men were. As we recall from our description in the previous chapter, two of the dance sequences represent the invocation of magic, and are intended to be complementary. In the first sequence the Black Magician casts a spell on Zenaib to make her fall in love with Gafar. This spell is, effectively, a deprivation of will. Later in the play the White Magician casts a counter-spell which neutralizes the effects of the Black Magician's spell, and so frees both Zenaib and Gafar from identification. Ouspensky comments:

> The ceremony of the White Magician was too much like the ceremony of the Black Magician. In both cases, allowing for slight differences in ritual, it was what is known as "envoutement" — deprivation of will power ... "Envoutement" could be practiced in the school of the White Magician only as an experiment. In the school of the Black Magician it could be practiced for the purpose of attaining a certain definite object.[1]

The choreography for the enactment of the two spells ran parallel. The Black Magician takes control of Zenaib, and the White Magician takes her back. Ouspensky remarks:

> From the standpoint of a rightly understood idea of "school" it would have been much better for Zenaib if she were left in the hands of Gafar to go through all the consequences of the spell, and later through repentance, regret, and the realization of her fall to

---

1. From the 1926 Draft of *In Search of the Miraculous,* from the Ouspensky Papers, at the Yale University Archive, Sterling Library, Folder 1688. Technically, envoutement is the occult practice of using the image or likeness of a person to influence his or her actions or destiny, usually with malevolent intent.

return unaided to the right path, perhaps even bringing Gafar with her.[2]

Ouspensky parallels the methods used by the White Magician to certain aspects of Gurdjieff's teaching.

> Gurdjieff began by demanding consciousness in work, and passed to the demand of submission. He lowered the standard of his demands, becoming satisfied with mechanical submission.[3]

This hearkens directly back to Ouspensky's comments on the second Essentuki workshop. After having ended his formal involvement with Gurdjieff's Work, Ouspensky withdrew to the island of Prinkipo, and resumed his own lectures in the Péra. But, it must be emphasized that this move *did not involve a break in the communication between the two men.*

> In order not to hinder G. or to give rise to discord among those who came to my lectures, I put an end to my own lectures [at 13 Yemeneci Abdullatif Sokak] and ceased to visit Constantinople. A few of those who came to my lectures visited me in Prinkipo and there we continued the talks begun in Constantinople.
>
> Two months later when G.'s work had already become consolidated I again started to give lectures at the "Miyak" in Constantinople and I continued them for another six months. I visited G.'s Institute from time to time and sometimes he came to me in Prinkipo. The inner relation between us remained very good. In the spring he proposed that I should give lectures in his Institute, and I began to give lectures there once a week in which G. himself took part, supplementing my explanations.[4]

The continuity of their friendship is revealed by an incident recorded by John Bennett, which occurred *before* Bennett and his wife knew Gurdjieff. As we noted, John Bennett and Winifred Beaumont knew the Ouspenskys

---

2. *Ibid.*, Folder 1688.
3. *Ibid.*, Folder 1688.
4. Ouspensky, P.D., *In Search of the Miraculous,* Routledge & Kegan Paul, London, 1977 p. 383.

as their tenants, and were on visiting terms with them. By a remarkable coincidence – in a city of 900,000 people — John Bennett happened to meet Gurdjieff socially. One of Bennett's diplomatic connections, Prince Mehmed Sabahaddin, knew Gurdjieff and introduced Bennett to him. This introduction occurred in January 1921, *after* Ouspensky had decided to work on his own. On the basis of this brief introduction, Bennett decided to attend a performance of the Sacred Dances at the Grand Rabbinate. He was completely surprised to find his tenant, Ouspensky, attending the performance and speaking casually with the performers after the show. This shows that the connection between Ouspensky and Gurdjieff was not something that can be labeled or pigeon-holed at the level of logical mind. Ouspensky, while not being able to work under Gurdjieff's conditions, was not in any way denigrating him as a teacher. While Ouspensky had decided to work independently, he wished Gurdjieff well, and expected and hoped that results would come from his Work. It also shows a certain respect by Gurdjieff for Ouspensky's projects.

However, the series of remarkable coincidences which brought Gurdjieff and Ouspensky together in Constantinople had not come to an end. At just this point, two things happened simultaneously.

Through a connection of Alexandre de Salzmann's, Gurdjieff received a letter of invitation from Émile Jaques-Dalcroze in Geneva, inviting him to make use of the Dalcroze Institute site at Hellerau, in Germany. Gurdjieff accepted this invitation, without the immediate means of transporting his entourage of thirty or so people, or of feeding and housing them in Germany. With the collusion of his recent British acquaintance, John Bennett, he was able to make an extraordinary business deal, buying and selling a British naval vessel. This gave him the capital he required. On the 13th August 1921, Gurdjieff and his circle left Constantinople, travelling by train to Berlin.

In November of 1920 Ouspensky, to his complete surprise, had received a substantial royalty check from his publisher Nikolai Bassaraboff. This payment was for the English translation of *Tertium Organum*, which Ouspensky did not know existed. Then, at the same time Gurdjieff received the invitation to Hellerau, Ouspensky received an invitation from a Lady

Rothermere to lecture in London – with the promise of covering his personal expenses. In May 1921 Ouspensky received a cheque of £100 from Lady Rothermere, and in mid-August he left for London.

Gurdjieff left Constantinople on the 13th of August, and Ouspensky in mid-August! The two men must have left the city within days of one another. Thus, Gurdjieff and Ouspensky were suddenly and simultaneously taken to different parts of the world, but they were separated in just such a way as to set them up for the next shared scenario of their lives. This is the same kind of celestial engineering we saw with respect to Gurdjieff in Yanghi Hissar in 1902 and with respect to Ouspensky in Essentuki in March of 1918. It is a kind of engineering that requires the ability to prioritize matter in the electronic and molecular state (Worlds 6 and 12) over matter in the cellular state.

The parting of Gurdjieff and Ouspensky in Constantinople in August 1921 was unlike the parting that had occurred in Essentuki three years before in one important way. Ouspensky's family — Sophie, Lenotchka, and Lonya — went with Gurdjieff, while Ouspensky went alone to London. Sophie Grigorievna had decided to remain with Gurdjieff, as her teacher, in an arrangement which must have been talked through by the two men – for Gurdjieff took full responsibility for supporting the two Savitskys. The Ouspenskys parted amicably, and she was to rejoin him again as his wife (at Gurdjieff's request) in the summer of 1928. Lenotchka remained eternally grateful to Peter Ouspensky for supporting the family through the tumultuous years of the Russian revolution, and she was also to rejoin him with her child Lonya in 1928. From that time forward the three remained with Ouspensky until his death in 1947.

In moving to London, Ouspensky was not just placing distance between himself and Gurdjieff, but following through on the aim that he had established for himself in Essentuki in 1919. Since that time, he had twice begun his own independent work, and from the outbreak of the Russian Revolution he had considered London to be a natural destination.

In anticipation of their second parting, Ouspensky, with the scrupulous good householder that was characteristic of him, spoke with Gurdjieff about the agreement that they had made, in April 1915, concerning the permission to write about the system. The original condition of writing had been that Ouspensky understand — to Gurdjieff's satisfaction — what he was writing about. More explicitly, an analogy was made to a research group making scientific experiments. This group had "made it a condition that no one would have the right to speak of or describe any experiment unless he was able to carry it out himself." Gurdjieff had then agreed that "There could be no better formulation."[1] Now, six years later, Ouspensky asked Gurdjieff for permission to write about the teaching he had received.[2]

> I told him (Gurdjieff) in detail of a plan I had drawn up for a book to expound his St. Petersburg lectures and talks with commentaries of my own. He agreed to this plan and authorized me to write and publish it.[3]

By giving his permission Gurdjieff was saying that *he felt that Ouspensky was now able to carry out the experiment by himself*. He could write about what he knew how to do. Gurdjieff also knew that, if given permission to write, Ouspensky would publish, and that if he published he would teach. Ouspensky must have begun writing soon after his arrival in London, because the oldest surviving manuscript of *Fragments of an Unknown Teaching: In Search of the Miraculous* is dated 1925, only four years later.

Early London Years: 1921-1924

While Gurdjieff spent time testing the ground for his Institute in Germany, Ouspensky was able to establish himself in London immediately.

He arrived in August 1921. His patron, Lady Rothermere, provided him with a room in a Bloomsbury hotel on Taviton Street, and a place in which to hold meetings at Circus Road, St John's Wood. She distributed copies of *Tertium Organum* to a wide circle of her friends, while her associate A.R.

---

1. *Ibid.*, p. 14.
2. Taylor, Merrily E., (compiler & editor), *Remembering Pyotr Demianovich Ouspensky,* Yale University Library, New Haven CT, 1978, p. 28.
3. Ouspensky, P.D., *In Search of the Miraculous,* Routledge & Kegan Paul, London, 1977. p. 383.

Orage organized recruitment for Ouspensky's first presentations. The list of attendees included Clifford Sharp, editor of the *New Statesman,* Rowland Kenney, editor of the *Daily Herald,* the poet T.S. Eliot, the author Katherine Mansfield, various members of the London *Theosophical Society,* various members of the *Quest Society,* and a number of Jungian psychiatrists, including Dr. Maurice Nicoll and Dr. James Young. It was a highly literate and relatively well-to-do crowd.

One of the Russian émigrés who been part of Ouspensky's lecture group in the Péra district of Constantinople was able to follow him to London. Madame Eugenie Kadloubovsky became a founding member of the London group. This unassuming but very competent Russian lady, with an excellent background in publishing, became Ouspensky's private secretary. She organized the publication of all his books, kept the records of all his meetings, and remained close to him through the final months of his life. She became an important part of what made the London group what it was for the next twenty-six years.[4]

And now another coincidence. Just as Ouspensky's meetings at Circus Road got under way, in September 1921, John Bennett and Winifred Beaumont returned to London from Constantinople. They were surprised to discover that their Russian tenant at Péra was giving lectures in St. John's Wood, and — after attending several of these lectures — decided to join his group. And so the Gods assembled the cast for the next act in the unfolding drama of the Fourth Way.

Ouspensky soon supplemented his formal lectures with a question-and-answer period, and then with personal interviews and instruction. Step by step, he began to create the circumstances for second and third line of work. The one record we have of Ouspensky's teaching in this period is in the published letters of his student Rosamund Bland, written in 1921.[5] From these letters we can see that Ouspensky spent private time with his students and coached them carefully in the work. Ouspensky's English

---

4. See p. 145 of *The Bridge,* No. 12, Autumn 1997 (ed. Eadie, Peter McGregor), © The Study Society, Colet House, Talgarth Road, London, 1997.

5. Bland, Rosamund, *Nine Letters by Rosamund Bland,* The Stourton Press, Cape Town, 1952.

followers were attracted to — as one of them put it — "good wood:" a person that is solid, purposeful, and trustworthy. Ouspensky was fundamentally understated, never making himself into something he was not, and at the same time he was shaken by nothing. This was the perfect approach for the English. Although Ouspensky was modest in his presentation, he had his sights on the highest aims, and never deviated from them.

Soon a nucleus of seriously interested people formed around him. Maurice Nicoll was to be Ouspensky's best known — and certainly most published — student. By the end of October Ralph Philipson, a coal magnate and patron of the arts, had joined the group. He became Ouspensky's principal financial backer, proving more stable over time than Lady Rothermere. He made both his home at 74 Portland Place and his villa at Sandgate available to the group, and over the years helped Ouspensky to secure important properties in the London area. In September of 1922 he became the principal source of finance for the purchase of the Prieuré. He remained with Ouspensky, as a central member of his group, until his own death in 1928.

With growing resources at his disposal Ouspensky was soon able to make provisions for group work. He moved from his hotel room on Taviton Street to a flat on 55a Gwendwr Road, in West Kensington. This was to become his residence for the next fourteen years. At the same time Ouspensky was able to rent a large meeting room at the Theosophical Hall at 38 Warwick Gardens, South Kensington. Here, in October 1921, he began to hold meetings three and four times a week. Ouspensky later said of this time that he "found himself with the beginnings of a School on his hands".[1]

In the meantime, Gurdjieff, in Germany, had begun to see that the Weimar Republic was not going to provide stable ground for the Institute. Legal issues beset the promised property at Hellerau, and Gurdjieff was becoming ever more aware of the precarious situation in that country. The economy was unstable: the pre-war industrial export business had been lost, there was a general shortage of supplies, and unemployment and inflation were rampant. The German Communist Party — the KPD — was the

---

1. Taylor, Merrily E. (compiler & editor), *Remembering Pyotr Demianovich Ouspensky,* Yale University Library, New Haven, CT, 1978, p. 32.

Figure 33. Eugenie Kadloubovsky and J.G. Bennett.

largest in Europe, and was working in close connection with the Russian Communist Party. Gurdjieff had the multi-lingual Olga de Hartmann research other options, in both London and Paris. In January 1922, probably as a result of Olga's initiatives, Ouspensky invited Gurdjieff to London and prepared to introduce him to his circle of students. This gesture represented a considerable sacrifice on Ouspensky's part, for he knew that everything he had developed over the last seven months would suddenly become shared property.

Gurdjieff made two visits to London, in February and March 1922, and Ouspensky's fledgling group was significantly impacted by them.

Gurdjieff first arrived in the city on 13th February 1922, with Olga de Hartmann and Frank Pinder. We have John Bennett's record of the meeting that he led (described in the previous chapter). Gurdjieff conveyed a clear sense of leadership in the Work, and gave the impression of being Ouspensky's senior — which, of course, he was. He also gave the impression of being ready to begin practical work on a very large scale in the near future.

Effectively, he was integrating all that Ouspensky had achieved in London into the pattern of his own Work, and treating Ouspensky as his lieutenant.

After Gurdjieff's departure Ouspensky's group began to research suitable property for Gurdjieff in Hampstead, and Lady Rothermere began to use her influence at the Home Office to secure permanent entry permits for Gurdjieff's people. While Ouspensky must have had a range of different internal reactions to the developing situation, he was in his outward behavior totally accommodating, totally ready to surrender all that he had created, and totally ready to help. Whatever internal 'I's clamor for expression it matters only that one place the higher level over the lower level and act upon the 'I's that correspond to it. This affirms the higher level within us, and so enables real change. Ouspensky's behavior during Gurdjieff's move to France and establishment at the Prieuré suggests a mature man number five. It reflects Ouspensky's dedication to "the source of the system," which — at this point — commits him both to 1) Gurdjieff, as its first chosen agent, and 2) to the particular form of the Work which his own crystallization had committed him to.

Gurdjieff returned to London one month later, on 15th March 1922, for a visit of three weeks — during which time he led a number of meetings. He reaffirmed his intent to launch the *Institute for the Harmonious Development of Man* on a large scale for the long term. An incident occurred during one of the meetings, when Ouspensky corrected Gurdjieff's translator, Frank Pinder, on a point related to the Work. Gurdjieff cut Ouspensky short, emphasizing that Pinder was translating for him, not Ouspensky.

When Gurdjieff returned to Berlin in June 1922, two related events determined the direction of his future work: he lost a court case in Germany to secure the property at Hellerau, and the Home Office in London, despite Lady Rothermere's intercessions, refused Gurdjieff a permanent entry permit.

The shock of this refusal affected Ouspensky as much as it did Gurdjieff. Ouspensky's people had made every preparation to host Gurdjieff in London. Had Gurdjieff established himself in London, he would have been the leader of the Work. Ouspensky had been poised, on Gurdjieff's arrival, to move abroad. "I had decided for myself that if the Institute opened in London I would go either to Paris or to America."[1]

The Home Office refusal of Gurdjieff's permit made two things clear to Ouspensky: that he would remain in London for the time being, and that he would remain open to cooperating with the 'Gurdjieff-side' of the experiment, which would recommence somewhere in France.

Gurdjieff determined to move to Paris, where the indomitable Olga de Hartmann had already begun to make arrangements. Ouspensky let Gurdjieff know that his people were prepared to back him to secure an estate in the greater Paris area. With this assurance Gurdjieff made the legal arrangements to relocate in France, and, on 14th July 1922, brought his entourage to rented accommodation in Paris. By October 1st they were able to secure a 100-acre estate at the Prieuré des Basses Loges in Fontainebleau-Avon, one hour and forty-five minutes drive south of Paris. It was only 250 miles away from Ouspensky's group in London.

Ouspensky's students immediately became the first paying residents at the Prieuré: Katherine Mansfield, A.R. Orage, Maurice Nicoll, James Young, Rowland Kenney, Eric Adam, and Lady Rothermere all arrived in the first month. Ouspensky himself visited in November. We may remark that Ouspensky's visits would have included a welcome reunion with Madame Ouspensky, Lenotchka, and Lonya, who were installed at Le Paradou.

Throughout 1922 and 1923 Ouspensky's group provided the financial backing for the Prieuré, and Ouspensky himself went many times to Fontainebleau. He was consistently positive in his references to Gurdjieff, and advised his students to take full advantage of Gurdjieff's teaching.

John Bennett, speaking as a new student in Ouspensky's group, reported, "Gurdjieff regained Ouspensky's confidence and affection to such a degree that throughout 1923 Ouspensky spoke about the Prieuré as a unique opportunity for those who could go to it."[2] What Bennett was seeing was Ouspensky's aim to endorse and to support Gurdjieff's project before his

---

1. Ouspensky, P.D., *In Search of the Miraculous*, Routledge & Kegan Paul, London, 1977, p. 385.

2. Bennett, J.G., *Gurdjieff: Making a New World*, Turnstone Books, London, 1973, p. 141.

students. What he did not see was that Ouspensky was intentionally acting out a role. In line with his commitment to the invisible source of the system, Ouspensky was doing everything he could to give the French incarnation of the Institute a chance.

In order to appreciate the situation that was taking form we must consider something of what it means to be a teacher.

> ### ON THE REQUIREMENTS OF BEING A TEACHER
>
> To be effective, a teacher must: 1) exercise a certain authority and 2) create trust. The teacher must create trust because he must make demands on his students considerably beyond the demands made by job and family in the normal course of life. There will be a temptation for any teacher to identify with this authority and to fear the inevitable threats that will come to it. To the extent the teacher identifies with his authority, he will not be effective. And so the teacher must not identify with the role, *while actually creating that role in the form most beneficial to the students.*
>
> In London, in 1921, Peter Ouspensky was challenged in both of these areas: creating a role and not identifying with that role. Gurdjieff's discrediting of his authority in London would have made that identification visible to him, and so helped him to struggle against it. Gurdjieff was pressuring Ouspensky to find confidence in himself on the level of Real I, rather than in his sense of identity as a teacher.
>
> It also challenged Ouspensky to find a deeper level in himself *to teach from*; it challenged him as a teacher to put his own presence before any presentational, organizational, or administrative skills he might possess. In this new phase, when Gurdjieff challenged Ouspensky, Ouspensky responded not by fighting back, but by going ever deeper into himself.
>
> We recall that Ouspensky's first decision to work independently, in March of 1918, was very difficult for him. To have remained open to further involvement with Gurdjieff shows a certain greatness of mind. What has seemed to some to be vacillation is in fact Ouspensky's constancy in relation to a higher level; it is relativity about *himself* in light of something higher than himself. Thus, Ouspensky remained true to his instinct to work independently, while remaining open to: 1) the possibility that his own Work might develop differently than he expected, 2) the possibility that Gurdjieff's Work might bring useful results, and 3) the possibility that the Work of both men might be part of a connected plan of Higher Forces.

So, with Gurdjieff's teaching only two days to the south, and with a commitment to giving his students full access to that teaching, Ouspensky continued his Work in London with complete, though understated, dedication.

> I still expected a very great deal more from his [Gurdjieff's] work and I decided to do everything I could to help him organize his Institute and the preparation of his ballet. But I did not believe it was possible for me to work with him.[1]

We noted that, on Ouspensky's arrival in London, he felt that he had "found himself with the beginnings of a school."[2] He was indeed trying to establish a school, yet those plans would have to remain tentative while the Institute was taking form. In the meantime, he determined to create a nucleus of work around himself. Once a group of dedicated people had been formed, other things would become possible.

The London group met regularly at Warwick Gardens, where they were to continue for seventeen years. Almost from the beginning there were people who were to be a part of the future of the Fourth Way, such as John Bennett, Alfred Orage, Maurice Nicoll, and Kenneth Walker. Stanley Nott said of Ouspensky's meetings at Warwick Gardens, "I became more and more impressed with the breadth and clarity of his massive and powerful mind."[3] J.G. Bennett said of this same period, "We were greatly stirred by the magnificent sweep of Ouspensky's exposition."[4] These statements show us that Ouspensky continued, with the full force of his being, to implement the Work that was his own.

What became unique in Ouspensky's Work was a firm resolution to combat negative emotions and to control their expression. This was related to his credo that good results could not come from violence. Ouspensky

---

1. Ouspensky, P.D., *In Search of the Miraculous,* Routledge & Kegan Paul, London, 1977, p. 384.
2. Taylor, Merrily E. (compiler & editor), *Remembering Pyotr Demianovich Ouspensky,* Yale University Library, New Haven, CT, 1978, p. 32.
3. Nott, C.S., *Journey Through This World,* Routledge & Kegan Paul, London, 1974, p. 103.
4. Bennett, J.G., *Witness, the Story of a Search,* Dharma Book Company, New York, New York, 1962, p. 131.

taught that negative emotions are not natural to us, but are learned. They represent a wrong connection between the instinctive center and the emotional center. They are directly connected to chief feature, comprising the very ground of its existence. The control of negative emotions is a requirement for purification of the emotional center from imagination, and the development of essence. The motivation to awaken had to be, on balance, positive. The emotional center and essence are the bridge between the lower centers and the Higher Centers.

As the new people came, and the group became larger, Eugenie Kadloubovksy began to compile records of Ouspensky's meetings. At the same time she helped him to work on the manuscripts for *A New Model of the Universe* and *In Search of the Miraculous*.[1] Thus, on the London side of the channel, and independently of Gurdjieff, a circle of people was forming around Ouspensky who would remain connected with him for the rest of their lives. There is something of chemistry and of fate in such a bond. Madame Kadloubovsky, for example, for all her study of the system, never even considered working with Gurdjieff.

From the opening of the Prieuré in October 1922 Ouspensky's students went back and forth to France, putting together Ouspensky's firm grounding in the system with the experiential intensity of Gurdjieff's Work. In 1922 Maurice Nicoll returned from a lengthy visit to the Prieuré to become one of Ouspensky's most solid students, eventually taking a teaching role. Ouspensky himself visited the Prieuré regularly. He found the work at the Prieuré very interesting but did not accept Gurdjieff's invitations to live there, because he felt "elements of instability in the organization of the Institute."

> In my opinion, some had been in far too great a hurry to give up their ordinary occupations in England in order to follow G. I could have said nothing to them because they had already made their decision when they spoke to me about it. I feared that they would meet with disappointment because G.'s work seemed to me not sufficiently rightly organized and therefore to be unstable. But at

---

1. The meetings recorded in *The Fourth Way* begin from 1921.

the same time, I could not be sure of my own opinions and did not want to interfere with them because if everything went right and my fears proved to be false then they would undoubtedly have gained by their decision.[2]

Presumably he began to see some of the same things that he had seen in Essentuki and Constantinople. He would then have placed all the more value on his Work in London. If Gurdjieff's Work at the Prieuré suddenly disbanded, as it had at Essentuki and Constantinople, what would be left of the Fourth Way?

When John Bennett and Winifred Beaumont expressed interest in work at the Prieuré, Ouspensky encouraged them, and they both went: Winifred in July-August of 1923 and John in September.

On Winifred's return she had questions for Ouspensky. John Bennett's record of Ouspensky's answers provides a good picture of Ouspensky's scrupulous standards. Winifred asked Ouspensky his opinion of Gurdjieff.

> She said, "I can see that Gurdjieff is an extraordinary man, but I cannot tell if he is good or bad. He seems to be both together." Ouspensky categorically assured her that Gurdjieff was a good man and that she should be confident that I (John Bennett) would receive benefit from being with him, providing I remembered that Gurdjieff had said that we must believe nothing that we had not verified for ourselves.[3]

John Bennett did indeed "receive benefit" from Gurdjieff. As we recorded in the previous chapter, Gurdjieff worked directly and intensively with Bennett, to create a peak experience for him: a glimpse of what would be possible with many years of dedicated effort. Having created this experience, Gurdjieff offered to include Bennett in his Work on a full-time basis. Bennett, who was at a transitional point in his career, felt that he needed to take some time to straighten out his business affairs. And, at the same

---

2. Ouspensky, P.D., *In Search of the Miraculous*, Routledge & Kegan Paul. London, 1977, p. 385.
3. Bennett, J.G., *Gurdjieff: Making a New World*, Turnstone Books, London, 1973, p. 147.

time, he had an underlying question about the offer itself. In September of 1923 Bennett left Fontainebleau for London, where he reconnected with Ouspensky's Work and strove to bring some order to his life.[1] While trying to straighten out his business affairs, Bennett examined his ambivalent feelings about the Work at the Prieuré. Winifred, hearing her husband's reservations, again asked Ouspensky for an opinion about Gurdjieff, and whether or not her husband should return to work with him. Ouspensky replied, "I can assure you that Gurdjieff is a good man. But Bennett was right to come away: he is not yet ready for that work."[2]

In August of 1923 Madame Ouspensky sent a telegram to Peter Ouspensky, asking him to come to the Prieuré immediately, on Gurdjieff's request. He did so, and a meeting with Gurdjieff followed. After a long silence Gurdjieff told Ouspensky that he was very dissatisfied with the Work and the attitude of several people in the Institute. He said that the momentum of the Work was such that he could not control it. We do not know what Ouspensky's response was, but this was a moment of sincerity between the two men. Gurdjieff is here simply seeking a response from the person most advanced in his Work. He is, perhaps, gathering data for a decision.

That there were problems at the Prieuré, both Gurdjieff and Ouspensky acknowledged, but neither of them have left us with an exact record of what they perceived to be wrong. However, John Bennett, who was generally supportive of the Work at the Prieuré, has left us with his impression.

> ... there was something not right. It was too frenzied, we were all in too much of a hurry ... Few, at that time, were ready to accept that the process of transformation takes time and that each stage must be completed if the next is to go forward properly. ... Looking back, it seems that Gurdjieff was still experimenting. He wanted to see what European people were capable of. He discovered that they were prepared to make efforts that few Asiatics will accept ... it may

---

1. Bennett, J.G., *Witness, the Story of a Search,* Dharma Book Company, New York, New York, 1962, p. 129.
2. *Ibid.,* p. 131.

be that Gurdjieff misjudged the capacity for effort, and took it for ability to accept the need for inward change. As I see it now, we did not really grasp the profound change of attitude towards oneself that is needed before the process of the Work can act freely in us ... The British people in 1922 still had that puritanical streak that makes us believe that what is good for us must necessarily be hard and even unpleasant. So one could see men and women accepting with alacrity the most absurd demands and outrageous behaviour on Gurdjieff's part.[3]

Certainly Gurdjieff was making experiments, as he had made experiments in Essentuki and in Constantinople. In Essentuki in 1918 he gave up on a certain approach with a group of Russians, and in Constantinople in 1921 he gave up on another approach with a group of Turks.[4] How, then, would the French and the English respond to his teaching? And what kind of teaching would they best respond to? Perhaps Gurdjieff had determined to use their 'active' side to pressure certain individuals to breakthroughs, as he did with Bennett at the Prieuré. The problem is that one can have such breakthroughs without being able to integrate them into the daily practice of one's Work. In fact, the unprepared student may be worse off after such an event than they were before, because they can now — from the level of the functions — enter imagination about the 'special experience.' It becomes something external to them that they want to repeat, and it may make them feel unique in relation to other people. In other words, these glimpses of a higher level can become yet another source of identification.

It is clear that the new English students did not come to the Prieuré with the foundational experience needed to accurately distinguish the level of consciousness from the level of the functions. This needs long years of work on self-observation, self-remembering, and internal separation. It needs a purification of the functions themselves. It is one thing to recognize a source of consciousness outside of oneself, in the form of a conscious

---

3. Bennett, J.G., *Gurdjieff: Making a New World*, Turnstone Books, London, 1973, p. 156
4. Gurdjieff's dissatisfaction with the students who joined at Constantinople apparently preceded his decision to leave the city.

teacher, but it is quite another to understand the relation between consciousness and functions *within oneself*, and to train the lower level to serve the higher. When you are able to make this distinction, you are able to learn in quite a different way from your conscious teacher. When the teacher speaks to you, he can speak directly to the corresponding 'conscious part.' In other words, he can speak directly to the latent Higher Self, encouraging it to *separate itself* from the functions.

If such a base of Work has *not* been established, and an external source of consciousness makes active demands on the student, that student can become — as Bennett put it — "frenzied." In effect, it is the machine that is trying to wake up, but the machine *cannot* wake up. The Work must begin on the level of the functions because it cannot begin anywhere else. The functions must be brought out of imagination, connected correctly, and observed accurately. Features must be studied, and finally the student must begin to understand how the illusion of 'I' is sustained. As this process continues the conscious part within the student comes nearer and nearer to the surface and begins to know itself for what it is. Over time it begins to exist independently of *both* the desire to awaken *and* the disappointment at not being able to awaken. As this separation develops the student becomes able to respond more intelligently to the external requirements of the second and third lines of work.

Indeed, the entire middle section of Bennett's book *Witness* describes Ouspensky trying to educate Bennett in this separation of levels, while Bennett — having had a smattering of Gurdjieff's master classes — has difficulty accepting the need to master the basics. His machine wants consciousness, as though that were something external to him.[1] Neither Bennett nor Orage, who had both experienced significant breakthroughs under Gurdjieff, appear to have had a right foundation laid down in the first years of the Work. Orage was always wanting Gurdjieff to give him another 'initiation,' so that he would have something to teach to his own students. Bennett, to the end of his days, sought out spectacular experiences. In these examples there is a disparity between the external and the internal.

---

1. Bennett, J.G., *Witness, the Story of a Search,* Dharma Book Company, New York, New York, 1962, chapters 11 through 14.

❦

But to return to the situation at the Prieuré. In late 1923 Peter Ouspensky was having an extended visit at the Château. On 16th December he went with Gurdjieff to Paris to attend the performance of the Sacred Dances given at the Théâtre des Champs-Elysées. Two and a half weeks later, on 4th January 1924, Ouspensky went to the dock at Le Havre to see Gurdjieff and his company set out to give demonstrations in New York, Philadelphia, Boston, and Chicago. From Le Havre Ouspensky returned to London. On the surface there was an achievement to celebrate, but something Ouspensky had seen during this stay changed his relation to the experiment at the Prieuré. Ouspensky sensed disaster.

> I could not fail to see, as I had seen in Essentuki in 1918, that there were many destructive elements in the organization of the affair itself and that it had to fall to pieces.[2]

On his return to London, he informed his students that he was separating his Work from Gurdjieff's and would in future operate independently. This was just six months before Gurdjieff's auto accident and seven months before the closure of the Institute. It represented a turning point in Ouspensky's life and a turning point in the history of the Work.

Alfred Orage, who was also at the Prieuré in December of 1923, felt that it was Gurdjieff's near rape of a student who was suffering from mental illness (and who some years later committed suicide) that decided Ouspensky to go his own way. But Ouspensky had known this side of Gurdjieff for much longer than Orage, who may himself have been upset by the incident.[3]

Ouspensky's decision to make his Work independent — *for the third time* — was not based on a particular incident but on the accumulation of

---

2. Ouspensky, P.D., *In Search of the Miraculous,* Routledge & Kegan Paul, London, 1977, p. 389.
3. For a different perspective on this episode see Howarth, Jessmin and Dushka, *It's Up to Ourselves*, Gurdjieff Heritage Society, New York, New York 1998, p. 68.

experience over many years. One factor in determining the need for a break was the lack of a boundary between what was, increasingly, two different groups of people practicing the Work. The notes and records of the students of Gurdjieff and Ouspensky in the early 1920s shows us two separate-but-related groups easily forming a "Work knowledgeable crowd." They can share opinions, compare teachers, and decide — on the basis of their own wisdom — what they think is best: "Ouspensky says this, Gurdjieff says that, I'll take a bit of both." But a Work knowledgeable crowd is not a school! A real school confronts each student with his or her denying force in a context in which they can work with it. When the teacher begins to interact with the student, helping them to come to terms with their denying force, the teacher becomes responsible for managing the process. And it is a process that cannot be 'double managed.'

Going it Alone: 1924–1934

In January of 1924 Ouspensky gathered ten of his students at Ralph Philipson's flat in Portland Place. The group included Maurice Nicoll, John Bennett, Rowland Kenney, and Kenneth Walker. Without preliminaries he stated:

> I have asked you to come because I must tell you that I have decided to break off all relations with Gurdjieff. This means that you have to choose. Either you can go and work with him, or you can work with me: but if you remain with me, you must give an undertaking [pledge] that you will not communicate in any way with Gurdjieff or his pupils.[1]

Ralph Philipson asked what the reason for this was. Ouspensky replied:

> Gurdjieff is a very extraordinary man. His possibilities are much greater than those of people like ourselves. But he also can go in the wrong way. I believe that he is now passing through a crisis, the

---

1. Bennett, J.G., *Witness, the Story of a Search*, Dharma Book Company, New York, New York, 1962, p. 134.

outcome of which no one can foresee. Most people have many 'I's. If these 'I's are at war with one another, it does not produce great harm, because they are all weak. But with Gurdjieff there are only two 'I's; one very good and one very bad. I believe that in the end the good 'I' will conquer. But meanwhile it is very dangerous to be near him. We cannot be of any help to him, and in his present situation he cannot be of any help to us. Therefore, I have decided to break off all contact. But this does not mean that I am against him, or that I consider that what he is doing is bad.[2]

Someone said: "If it does go the wrong way, what could happen?" Ouspensky answered: "He could go mad. Or else he could attract to himself some disaster in which all those round him would be involved."[3] Thus, just six months before Gurdjieff's motor accident, Ouspensky predicted that Gurdjieff "could attract to himself some disaster." And in that disaster "all those round him were involved."

Ouspensky himself continued to visit the Prieuré until 1931. When the disaster did occur, on 8th July 1924, Ouspensky was deeply affected. He went immediately to the Prieuré to see Gurdjieff, who was still in serious condition and not accepting visitors. He then went to the site of the accident itself, accompanied by Boris Mouravieff. According to Mouravieff, Ouspensky, on seeing the scene of the accident, made the following statement:

> Georgeivanitch's Institute was established to escape from the influence of the law of accident under which men spend their lives. Well, see how he himself has fallen under the influence of this very law ... I wonder whether it's really a pure accident?[4]

In the days and weeks that followed, Mouravieff repeatedly pressed Ouspensky to speak further about Gurdjieff, but he would not. At one point, in

---

2. *Ibid.*, p. 134.
3. *Ibid.*, p. 134.
4. Webb, James, *The Harmonious Circle*, Shambhala, Boston, 1987, p. 294, quoting an untranslated publication by Mouravieff.

the midst of a social evening, Mouravieff directly asked Ouspensky why he avoided such a discussion.

> Suddenly, his expression changed. I had the impression that before me was *another man,* and no more the one with whom I had spent the whole of a pleasant evening in the most interesting discussions. He turned abruptly back to me and said in a strange tone of voice: "Imagine that a member of the family has committed a crime. In the family, one doesn't talk of it!"[1]

What does this tell us? Why does Ouspensky use the word "crime"? Ouspensky was deeply concerned about the future of the Fourth Way. It was not a good omen that the person who was its first agent, and who had devoted his life to realizing it, had been suddenly struck down. Yes, Gurdjieff, with his habit of erratic driving, had laid himself open to the accident. The accident was a 'crime' in the sense that Gurdjieff had placed something of great value (not only to himself but to humanity) in jeopardy. But, beyond this, Ouspensky related the event to Gurdjieff's acknowledgement, less than a year before, that "the momentum of the work was such that he could not control it." Whatever the causes were, something rare and precious had come to the end of its life. *And this crisis had occurred within Peter Ouspensky's spiritual family*. His fate was connected to Gurdjieff's fate, *and the family still had to make good*. For Ouspensky this was not an abstract question, it directly concerned everything he placed the highest value on. What was the plan of the Gods for Great School in the West?

The accident and the closing of the Institute were seminal events for all concerned. In what circumstances did they find Ouspensky?

If we accept that Ouspensky awakened sometime in 1917, he was in his seventh year as a conscious being. In the previous two decades he had clearly observed the decay of the traditional cultures of Central Asia and the Far East — where the Work had been most deeply established. He had also observed the decay of European civilizational order as he had known it. In 1916 he had enlisted to serve in the First World War, and immediately upon his discharge, went through the brutal experience of the Russian

---

1. *Ibid.*, p. 295.

Revolution. He had seen the rise of Communism in continental Europe, and the simultaneous expansion and development of the mass media. He saw the European culture that he had known and respected being supplanted by an ersatz popular culture. By the time of Gurdjieff's auto accident, in 1924, he was anticipating a second general European war – and he considered that this war might be an 'Armageddon' for humanity. When he was presented with the "whole plan of the work" in Essentuki in 1917, he immediately recognized that *this synthesis, appearing at this moment in time, was pure magic.* It was a vision of the Work that transcended the mystery of its ancient sources and became part of the historical present. By August of 1924 Gurdjieff's attempt to implement this vision at the Institute in Fontainebleau had foundered.

As we noted, following the initial split with Gurdjieff, Ouspensky had continued work in London with a circle of about fifty students. While the Institute was formally closed in 1924, the Prieuré was still inhabited, and Gurdjieff continued to work with students, particularly the Americans. Ouspensky stated that after 1924 he continued to keep the scale of his teaching small because he did not want to compete with any further effort that Gurdjieff might make to expand or develop his teaching. There may have been another reason for this. In 1924 Ouspensky found himself surrounded by a core of people who could respond to his instruction. He did not want to suddenly draw in a large outer circle, because new understandings that were just being fixed might become diluted.

Ouspensky was trying to create a foundation that he felt had been missing in the Institute. The Institute – from its forerunners in Essentuki, Tiflis, and Constantinople – was constantly in crisis, forming and reforming itself, with a high turnover of students. These upheavals meant that the new students did not have *the stable ground needed to distinguish consciousness from functions.* In attempting to provide this foundation and this stability Ouspensky was creating his own template for the Fourth Way. He put together self-remembering, self-observation, and a detailed understanding of human types and features, with three stable lines of work. Only with these elements in place can you gain a right understanding of the doctrine of the many 'I's and a practical understanding of different levels that exist within yourself.

On the basis of his teaching experience in London Ouspensky produced a series of *Psychological Lectures,* that were later published as *The Psychology of Man's Possible Evolution.* These lectures were, in effect, a statement of how his group worked, of the particular way that he followed. According to the *Psychology* what is needed to awaken is simple: a conscious teacher; rightly motivated students; the system; sufficient pressure; a social context that will allow the system, the teacher, and the students to come together in the right way (that is, not Weimar Germany or Bolshevik Russia); C Influence.

Ouspensky could more or less provide the first four, but with respect to the last two he could only hope for the best.

Let us examine the implications of this more closely. From before the time he began to study Gurdjieff's system, Ouspensky had been possessed of the vision of School *and the hope of making a connection to Higher School.* In the *The Fourth Way* Ouspensky is recorded as saying, "Without the connection to some kind of higher school a school has no meaning."[1] What does this mean? It does not mean an endorsement from some other, more developed organization on the planet's surface, that has been certified as competent. It means a connection *in the present* to School on a Higher Level, creating a lift-on-lift connection through higher levels of Creation. This is directly related to the idea of the Inner Circle of Humanity. With the hope of making a connection to Higher School Ouspensky embarked, in January of 1924, on a seven-year period of focused experimentation with a group of fifty people: closed meetings, secrecy, special exercises, projects of different kinds.

John Bennett recalls one of Ouspensky's statements of aim from this period. In the summer of 1928, in a small work group at Gwendwr Road, Bennett remarked: "I am sure that this work can lead to the attainment of consciousness and immortality, but I am not sure if I can reach it myself. The more I learn about myself, the less do I seem able to achieve anything.

---

1. Ouspensky, P.D., *The Fourth Way,* Vintage Books, New York, New York, 1971. p. 167.

In fact, in the last year I have gone back rather than forward."[2] Bennett then describes Ouspensky's response.

> He stood with his back to the gas fire, peering at me as usual through his powerful pince-nez. He sighed deeply, and said: "You say that you are sure that this work can lead to consciousness and immortality. I am not sure. I am sure of nothing. But I do know that we have nothing, and therefore we have nothing to lose. For me it is not a question of hope, but of being sure that there is no other way. I have tried too much and seen too much to believe in anything. But I will not give up the struggle. In principle, I believe that it is possible to attain what we seek — but I am not sure that we have yet found the way. But it is useless to wait. We know that we have something that has come from a Higher Source. It may be that something more will come from the same Source."[3]

This is a very understated claim to the best life has to give. On the one hand Ouspensky says, "I am sure of nothing" and on the other he states that, "It may be that something more will come from the same Source." In speculating that something may come to us from the "same Source" Ouspensky has expressed the hope of connecting to the Circle of the Gods in eternity. And behind this, certainly, there was the hope to create, out of that connection, the foundation for a new Inner Circle of Humanity. In the way Ouspensky makes his statement, it is honest and shows an absolute minimum of mythical construct. Bennett says of his response, "I was deeply stirred by this sincere confession that Ouspensky himself was still not sure of the way. It gave me far more confidence than any positive affirmation."[4] No human being is "sure of the way" — because surety in such matters is not given on this level. The apostles were in a state of complete uncertainty in the wake of Jesus' crucifixion. With respect to humanity uncertainty is a higher state. Ouspensky was including his students in his own uncertainty, in such a way

---

2. Bennett, J.G., *Witness, the Story of a Search,* Dharma Book Company, Inc., New York, New York, 1962, p. 137.

3. *Ibid.,* p. 137.

4. *Ibid.,* p. 137.

Figure 34. Ouspensky and Granddaughter Tania Savitsky.

as to include them in his own level of Work. What reassured Bennett was not Ouspensky's 'sincere confession' but a glimpse of the world as seen by Ouspensky's Higher Centers.

In considering Ouspensky's statement of aim, we keep in mind that he believed that everything is connected, and that the more conscious it is, the more it is connected internally to consciousness on a higher level. Becoming more conscious is thus, potentially, attracting higher consciousness. Ouspensky's aim to make a connection to Higher School *was not an aim of physical search,* but a matter of hoping you are destined to reconnect with the Source, and acting as if you were. And indeed, on every level, the Work is a matter of acting "as if."

On June 26th 1926, Gurdjieff's wife, Julia Ostrowska, came to the end of her life. Her funeral in July brought Ouspensky back into contact with both Gurdjieff and Madame Ouspensky. Madame Ouspensky, on having been asked to leave the Prieuré in mid-October of 1924, had moved to the suburb of Asnières in the north of Paris. She lived there with Lenotchka and the young Leonidas, now about eight years old. She would meet with

Gurdjieff when he visited Paris, and spent time with both the de Hartmanns and the de Salzmanns. In the summer of 1928 Madame Ouspensky visited Ouspensky in London, and stayed for several months.[1] This became the first of a series of summer visits.

From about 1926 Ouspensky had drawn closer to Maurice and Catherine Nicoll. Pogson, reports that, "A very deep personal relationship developed between himself [Maurice Nicoll] and Ouspensky. Other members of the group have told me that Dr. Nicoll was apparently the only one of the group with whom Ouspensky could really relax, and, more than anyone else, Dr. Nicoll could make him laugh.[2] At Ouspensky's meeetings, Nicoll would take the questions at the beginning, and respond to specific questions when Ouspensky asked him to.

From 1927 until 1933 Ouspensky spent every other weekend at a cottage rented by Nicoll in Sidlesham, known as Alley Cottage. He was preparing Nicoll for greater responsibility.

Ouspensky and his students also made weekend visits to the large Italianate villa owned by Ralph and Maya Philipson, just east of Dymchurch on the south coast.

Ralph Philipson died in 1928, but Maya continued in the Work and Ouspensky remained in close contact with her, through the war, until her death in 1945. An obituary in the *Times* noted that Ralph Philipson "was known for his wide circle of literary friends, and was a remarkable host, both at Portland Place and in his jewel-like country house at Sandgate over the sea. Harassed since the War by the difficulties of large colliery interests, he was nevertheless remarkably generous ... He was a happy combination of the robustness of Northumberland and the code of Eton."

Between 1928 and 1931 Ouspensky's group took a number of houses outside of London — at Wendover, Bledlow Ridge near High Wycombe,

---

1. She must have stayed several months, as Bennett comments that during this time: "I was teaching her English while she was teaching me Russian." See Bennett, J.G., *Witness, the Story of a Search,* Dharma Book Company, New York, New York, 1962, p. 137.
2. Pogson, Beryl, *Maurice Nicoll: A Portrait,* Fourth Way Books, New York, 1987, p. 94-5.

and Trotscliffe, Kent. For Madame Ouspensky's now annual visits he rented a cottage called the Red Spire in Dymchurch.

In October of 1930 Ouspensky decided to let his Work become more widely known.[1] Given that the group had worked in secrecy up to this time Bennett asked: "What about your relation to Gurdjieff as your teacher?" Ouspensky replied:

> I waited for all these years because I wanted to see what Gurdjieff would do. His work has not given the results he hoped for. I am still as certain as ever that there is a Great Source from which our System has come. Gurdjieff must have had a contact with that Source, but I do not believe that it was a complete contact. Something is missing, and he has not been able to find it. If we cannot find it through him, then our only hope is to have a direct contact with the Source. But there is no chance for us to find it by looking, of that I have been convinced for nearly twenty years. It is much better hidden than people suppose. Therefore, our only hope is that the Source will seek us out. That is why I am giving these lectures in London.[2]

Ouspensky reaffirms that he is hoping to attract direct help from C Influence. This was not just an idea for him, it was central to what he was. This is the second recorded statement that we have of his aim as a teacher, and we will argue in these pages that it was ultimately realized — although not, perhaps, in the way Ouspensky envisaged it in 1930.

The following year, 1931, was a watershed year for Ouspensky's Work. In that year *A New Model of the Universe* was finally published, and Ouspensky's public lectures began to attract hundreds of people. A marked sign of the development occurred on 9th September 1931. Ouspensky asked his most trusted student, Maurice Nicoll, to come to his study. There was a silence, and then he said, "Nicoll, you had better go away." After a long

---

1. Bennett, J.G., *Witness, the Story of a Search*, Dharma Book Company, New York, New York, 1962, p. 161.
2. *Ibid.*, pp. 161-162.

pause he added, "Go away — and teach the System."[3] Nicoll did, from that point, begin his own teaching, but the two groups remained connected. From time to time some of Nicoll's students were invited to attend Ouspensky's meetings in Warwick Gardens, and occasionally Ouspensky would lead one of the meetings of Nicoll's group. Ouspensky was "putting someone in his place," and so creating a lift-on-lift upward movement.

Figure 35. Clockwise from left: Maurice Nicoll, Catherine Nicoll and daughter, Mme. Ouspensky, Mr. Ouspensky, two other students, c. 1927.

While Ouspensky's own teaching continued to grow, relations with the Prieuré became more distant. It was sometime in the middle of 1931 that Ouspensky came to visit, and Gurdjieff finally refused him access to the property. (This was consistent with the 'banishment' and 'remove from my eyesight' aims that Gurdjieff had at that time.) The two men had their last conversation in the Café Henri IV in Fontainebleau. Shortly after this meeting Gurdjieff asked Madame Ouspensky, who had been visiting London regularly in the summers, to rejoin Ouspensky in London. There was

---

3. Pogson, Beryl, *Maurice Nicoll: A Portrait*, Fourth Way Books, New York, 1987, p. 109.

something enigmatic about the request, for Madame Ouspensky was, with Jeanne de Salzmann, one of his most devoted students. In 1921 she had chosen Gurdjieff over Ouspensky as her teacher, and had gone with him from Constantinople to Berlin rather than to London. Gurdjieff almost certainly knew that Sophia Grigorievna would be a valuable complement to Ouspensky's teaching, and he also knew that these two people were important to each other. It was exactly as if Mikhail Fokine, as the head of the Imperial Russian Ballet in 1910, was to send Tamara Karsevina to Diaghelev's *Ballets Russes*. What would she do there? Sending Madame Ouspensky to London was a complementary action to closing the doors of the Prieuré to Ouspensky.

Nicoll left Ouspensky's teaching in September and Madame came to it in October. Ouspensky could see the phenomenon of replacement taking place. Nicoll was in some ways similar to Ouspensky. Madame was unlike Ouspensky but complementary to him. Complementary and dissimilar influences in the inner circle of a School produce a deeper dynamic, bringing in more parts of centers and more different kinds of people. In the complementarity of Peter Ouspensky and Madame Ouspensky we see an image of the complementarity between Ouspensky and Gurdjieff. With Madame came a certain expansion of the second and third lines, and this fitted with the expansion of the School.

Madame Ouspensky settled permanently in London in October. In preparation for the move Ouspensky rented The Dell at Sevenoaks, about 20 miles southeast of London. Madame took full responsibility for the move, committing herself to a new form of the Work. She made the rules of Ouspensky's teaching her own, and she asked his students to leave when they did not obey those rules, which included not speaking about Gurdjieff's Work. In other words, she acknowledged that Peter Ouspensky was attempting to open up a new way, and she committed herself to supporting that way. She had the experience and the ability, not only to teach, but to arrange a demanding schedule of work for Ouspensky's students. And she was careful never to present herself as the 'teacher.' John Bennett, who was with Madame Ouspensky during her move, observed:

Throughout all this Madame Ouspensky never changed her attitude. Neither approving nor disapproving, taking sides with no one, her sole aim at all times was to promote unity without sacrificing the basic principles of the Work. Of all the remarkable people I have met in my life, Madame Ouspensky stands out uniquely for her singleness of purpose and her unwavering pursuit of her aim. Her self-discipline has been an inspiration to all who have known her. She would never undertake anything beyond her own understanding and powers.[1]

In some circles she acquired a reputation for severity, but this was largely a reflection of her ability to give new students the observations that they needed. Her observations were generally both accurate and penetrating. It is true that at times she may have been a martinet, but this was simply the wrong expression of a tendency — not what she was in herself.

Bennett gives us a snapshot of Madame Ouspensky at the Prieuré, at the age of forty-three. He had been asked to wash the floors in the kitchen, and, having soaped and sluiced them, found the kitchen in a sea of dirty water. He was at a loss what to do next:

> At that moment, Madame Ouspensky, a majestic figure dressed entirely in black, and with dark chestnut hair and flashing eyes, appeared standing in the doorway, a high step above the floor. I had not seen her since we had met on the Island of Prinkipo more than two years before. She laughed like a young girl, snatched up a couple of kitchen cloths, and went down on her knees to mop up the water and squeeze it into the pail.[2]

Another addition to Ouspensky's family arrived at this time. In the early 1930s someone made him a gift of two Siberian cats, Vashka and Josch, each of which grew to an enormous size. Ouspensky retained a lifelong

---

1. Bennett, J.G., *Witness, the Story of a Search,* Dharma Book Company, Inc. New York, New York, 1962, p. 333.
2. *Ibid.,* p. 115.

attachment to them.[1] Rodney Collin recalled that Ouspensky often had scars on the back of his hands from playing with the cats. They were with him at his death.

In this same watershed year of 1931 Ouspensky began a series of experiments, using what he called 'methods of repetition' with his students. These methods were used to develop and reinforce an emergent steward. John Bennett gives us a record of one of the workshops.

> The next evening Ouspensky introduced a new theme that was to have a great influence on my life for the next twelve years. He spoke about methods used in esoteric schools throughout Asia and Eastern Europe for fixing the attention and preventing the mind from wandering in vain imaginings. These are based on the fact that memory can work only in a single track. If we remember one thing, we forget others. By exercising the memory we exclude random thoughts. This can be done either by memorizing or by repetition.[2]

Ouspensky went on to speak about repetition. He described the prayer of the heart — that is the constant repetition of the invocation: "Lord Jesus Christ, Son of God, have Mercy upon me." When this was introduced more than a thousand years ago into the monasteries of the Greek Orthodox Church, it had produced spectacular results, thousands of monks and nuns attaining to states of illumination by following literally the injunction of St. Paul to pray

---

1. Siberian cats came originally from the taiga of Siberia. They have been domesticated for at least 1,000 years, and are spoken of in old Russian folk tales. They grow to a great size, and the appearance of physical mass is enhanced by a long, thick, protective coat. An adult male can reach 25 pounds without being overweight. They are highly intelligent, playful and affectionate, but very quiet. They have a calm disposition. Despite their size they are quite athletic and have a superb sense of balance. After Ouspensky's death Rodney Collin made a painting of his teacher, as he was in the night-vigils of the last months of his life, with one cat sitting on either knee. See Collin-Smith, Joyce, *Call No Man Master*, Gateway Books, Bath 1988, p. 43.

2. Bennett, J.G., *Witness, the Story of a Search,* Dharma Book Company, New York, New York, 1962, p. 169 (reference dated 1931).

without ceasing. He said that the prayer of the heart in its original form is suitable only for monks, but a form of repetition less disturbing for the emotions might be useful for us.[3]

Following this introduction Ouspensky then gave a number of his students exercises of repetition, using material from The Lord's Prayer, The Prayer of the Heart, and The Sermon on the Mount.

Nikolai Rabeneck provides a later account of an experiment with 'methods of repetition,' in his description of the meetings of the Russian Group which began at Madame Kadloubovksy's London flat in 1931.[4] In their first meetings Ouspensky created a relaxed atmosphere, reviewed the main ideas of the system, and spoke particularly about the problem of memory. From September of 1932 the Russian Group began to meet at the new house in Gaddesden, and at these meetings Ouspensky introduced the exercises of repetition. At the first Gaddesden meeting Ouspensky gave a survey of the group work undertaken by Gurdjieff in Essentuki in 1917, emphasizing its nature and intensity: "Some exercises that no one could do were mentioned and others that were within our possibilities were described and demonstrated by Ouspensky."[5] Nicolai Rabeneck continues:

> At the first meeting the reading was about the exercise of 'repetition.' The Lord's Prayer was recommended, and the advantage of repeating it not in the habitual language, which for Russians is Church Slavonic. The Latin or Greek texts were to be preferred, as closer to the original. The possibility of repeating the Lord's Prayer in two or even three languages simultaneously (i.e., line by line) was discussed. Ouspensky spoke of his own efforts to get this triple practice going; the great and prolonged effort this demanded exhausted one to the limits. He also talked of the monastic tradition coming from Mount Athos of uninterrupted 'mental prayer;' the

---

3. *Ibid.*, p. 170 (reference dated 1931).

4. See article by Nicolai Rabeneck, *The Russian Group*, in *The Bridge*, No. 12, Autumn 1997, (ed. Eadie, Peter McGregor), © The Study Society, Colet House, London, 1997, pp. 145-148.

5. *Ibid.*, p. 147.

inward reciting of the short 'Jesus prayer' for hours and hours each day and night was the way to make it permanent.[1]

Thus, in a casual atmosphere, Ouspensky is clearly suggesting *another level of work* to a circle of his students. He raised the question as to what might be involved in making self-remembering a permanent state, and he returned to the first Essentuki workshop as a point of reference. In so doing he was returning to a *kairos* moment in the history of the Fourth Way – in order to develop the potentials that were contained within it. He continued the experiments with repetition with different groups of students, and with individual students, throughout the later 1930s.

Methods to enable self-remembering *all the time* can only be applied when the student is capable of separating out the different levels of themselves, so that they can make a continuous effort to *further* that separation. You can't separate what you can't see. Constant effort, by itself, tends to fix the part that makes the efforts — which is not the Higher Centers. This kind of effort will thus actually displace the Higher Centers. But with the right training, and the right method, this apparently insuperable obstacle can be overcome: the necessary relation of effort to non-effort can be achieved. Eventually the steward learns to bow to the Higher Centers and come active in the moment that they pass.

When Ouspensky moved to America in 1941, he dropped the work on repetition, as the American students were quite new. Individuals in London almost certainly continued to use the method. After Ouspensky's death Eugenie Kadloubovsky (the host of the Russian Group meetings) edited and translated into English (with G.E.H. Palmer) all of the Greek *Philokalia* material bearing on methods of repetition — a legacy of 1,100 years of intensive practice by the monks of Mount Athos.

Nicolai Rabeneck noted that Ouspensky's habitual farewell to the members of the Russian Group was:

"Don't forget ...," in Russian "*Ne zabuyvayte*," ... In colloquial Russian a usual good-bye to a visitor is "Don't forget ... drop in again" ... In Ouspensky's usage "Don't forget ..." meaning, of course,

---

1. *Ibid.*, p. 147.

"Remember." This reminder ... was somehow always present in all he said, in fact in the whole of his bearing and being.[2]

Ouspensky himself had experimented seriously with the *Prayer of the Heart* from the earliest days in Moscow and St. Petersburg, and that he was familiar with the orthodox literature on this subject.

Moving from first line to the second and third lines, the 1931 expansion saw a new set of arrangements for the group as a whole. Ouspensky now worked to create an internal hierarchy, in order to secure different levels of Work for different levels of understanding, and so create opportunities for all of his students. We have already noted the place he created for Maurice Nicoll in the preceding period. From the time of the 1931 expansion he did this, in different ways, for all his older students. He had created a cadre of students who could competently teach and guide new students in the Work. He could now, safely, open the doors of his teaching. Additionally, Ouspensky gave special attention to those students capable of responding directly to his Higher Centers. This might occur, for example, at the late night sessions that have been described by Francis Roles, John Bennett, and Rodney Collin. Finally, Ouspensky created special groups for work in different areas, which the senior students might lead or which he himself might lead.

He distinguished more clearly between the formal meetings, called lectures, which he led, and the special groups. In response to a question about present and proposed groups he responded:

> These [the present meetings] are not groups: these are lectures. Groups should be, first of all, much smaller; maximum thirty people, better less. And sometimes (I do not say necessarily always) a group must be selected in a special way. It wants a variety of types.

---

2. From the article *Nicolai Rabeneck's Ties with Ouspensky*, by Katie Hager, in *The Bridge*, No. 12, Autumn 1997, (ed. Eadie, Peter McGregor), © The Study Society, Colet House, London, 1997, p. 143.

If all people are of the same type, then it will not work. Then special tasks are given, one to one group, another to another.[1]

Some groups were for acclimatizing newer people and some were for more advanced students, moving toward the inner circle. If students were attending lectures and appearing consistently on the weekend work projects, they were invited to join such a group.

Within his teaching Ouspensky created a space where people could find themselves, and have as much or as little of what was being offered as they needed. He did not put great pressure on people who were not capable of making use of it. He did provide opportunities for people who could. While, as a mature Teacher, Ouspensky might have seemed formidable and commanding, there was something in him of a very fine, light temper. A student accustomed to dealing with a figure of authority might suddenly find sensitivity and warmth. When questioned or criticized Ouspensky would never defend himself; he was imperturbable, unassuming, and self-contained. Yet, while understated in his presentation, he played for the highest stakes.

In September 1932, with the expansion of the group, Madame Ouspensky's property in Sevenoaks was released and the Ouspensky's took a large Victorian mansion on seven acres of land at Little Gaddesden, in Hertfordshire, some thirty miles northwest of London. And here we see Ouspensky's consideration of Sophia Grigorievna: "the large drawing-room was filled with beautiful Russian prints, ornaments and ikons."[2]

In 1933 Gurdjieff finally lost the Prieuré, as the mortgagees moved to foreclose the property. This released the final brake on the development of Ouspensky's teaching. He had been committed to continuing his Work on a smaller scale while there was still the possibility of another stage of the Work at the Prieuré.

---

1. Ouspensky, P.D., *A Record of Meetings*, Arkana (Penguin Group) London, 1992, p. 130.
2. Nott, C.S., *Journey Through This World*, Routledge & Kegan Paul, London, 1974, p. 95.

The Prime Years: 1934–1941

From 1933 to 1935 Ouspensky's teaching grew from a few hundred people to over a thousand. From this time we sense, in Ouspensky, the greater mass and more concentrated energy of a man number six. He was possessed of greater authority, faced with more difficult decisions, and there was an increased pressure of work.

By 1934 a second edition of *A New Model of the Universe* was released. At the same time Ouspensky produced a lucid précis of the system: *The Psychology of Man's Possible Evolution*. It was a set of introductory lectures which could be read to a new group of people, and also applied to many different levels of Work. Awakening does not need more knowledge than can be found in the 128 pages of the *Psychology*, but it needs great experience in the application of that knowledge. The principles outlined in the *Psychology* can be understood again and again in different ways, at different levels of the work.

In the spring of 1935 Olga and Thomas de Hartmann visited the Ouspenskys at Gaddesden, and stayed with them a few days.[3] This must have been a precious reunion for half of the surviving membership of the original Petrograd Group. (Of the others, Leonid and Elisaveta Stjernvall were now running a hotel in Normandy and Petrov was a high school principal in what was now the U.S.S.R.) The de Hartmanns and the Ouspenskys were also veterans of the first Essentuki workshop.

In the months following her move to London, Madame Ouspensky had invited Jessmin Howarth to teach the movements at Little Gaddesden. Jessmin had lost her job at the Prieuré when the Institute closed in 1924, and was making her living — as she had done before meeting Gurdjieff — as a self-employed Dalcroze movements instructor.[4] She was, in 1931, working between Paris and New York, but was prepared to move her studio

---

3. *Ibid.*, p. 95.
4. More specifically, while touring with Gurdjieff in 1923 she had become pregnant with Gurdjieff's child. He left her in New York without return fare, to fend for herself. Whatever plans he may have had for her future were cancelled by the auto accident of 1924.

to London for the opportunity of once again teaching the movements to students. In 1934 a move to London became possible, and between 1934 and 1939 Jessmin, and her accompanist Rosemary Lillard, taught the movements — first at Little Gaddesden and later at Lyne Place and Colet House. On the year of her arrival she would have been 42, in the prime of her teaching years.

By mid-summer of 1935 Ouspensky had more than 1,000 students. The two-acre property at Little Gaddesden had become inadequate to support the weekend work projects and activities, and the meeting hall at 38 Warwick Gardens was becoming too small. With the help of financial backers Ouspensky purchased Lyne Place, an imposing Regency house twenty-three miles southwest of London, near the town of Virginia Water, on ninety acres of farmland. The permanent residents included the Ouspenskys, Lenotchka Savitsky, with her two grown children, Lonya and Tania; Madame Kadloubovksy; several St. Petersburg pensioners; and the team of English students who managed the household and grounds. Practical work was arranged for the host of students that came every weekend.

The Lyne estate was situated on ninety acres of cultivated parkland: there was a lake, a ravine with a water garden, and a farm that supported both dairy and agriculture. The property had been last owned by Rufus Isaacs, who had been at different times the Attorney General, the Ambassador to the United States, and the Viceroy of India. The house itself was of Georgian origin, rebuilt in Regency style during the 1840s, extended in the early 20th century, and then remodeled extensively by the previous owner. It was therefore immaculate, but it needed adjustments to fit the needs of Ouspensky's group. In this regard it was a source of intensive third line work. By 1938 twenty people lived permanently at Lyne and on the weekends another forty came to work each day. On the weekend, workday meals were provided for the visitors and Madame Ouspensky would hold a meeting at teatime. In the evening there might be a formal dinner and concert. Ouspensky himself spent the week in London and the weekends at Lyne. The introductory meetings were usually held at Lyne. One of Ouspensky's aims was to use the property to make the group self-sustaining, for he anticipated a second world war even at this early date.

The Ouspensky Today website provides a student's description of Ouspensky:

> Let me describe him. He was a man of perhaps five feet nine inches, very broad, robust and thickset, about forty-five when I first met him in the early 1920s. Short grey hair, pale, heavy face, with pale blue eyes behind thick-lensed glasses. His eyes were remarkable for their capacity to hide at will all sign of feeling and thought. He could make himself look heavy, almost stupid; or a sudden charming smile could light up and humanize his whole face. You could not be with him a minute without being aware of his strength and power. When he wished, he could hold any gathering by his rich vocabulary and great range of ideas. ...
>
> What marked Ouspensky out from most other teachers, I think, was his capacity to take into account not only the question but the questioner ... this is how I remember him. A man, first of all, of the most complete and unswerving spiritual integrity. ... A man of the very highest intellectual powers, with a superb memory ... A dominating man, though he did not, I think, consciously seek dominance. Yet, for all the force that resided in him, a man who commanded, in many individuals and over long periods, the deepest loyalty and affection. I think this was not so much because of his personality — for to many he seemed cold and inscrutable — as because you felt that in some way he represented the best and highest part of yourself. To be disloyal to him was to betray the God in yourself ... he stood for something in man that is great and noble.[1]

Membership continued to swell. In the autumn of 1936 the burgeoning school attracted Rodney and Janet Collin-Smith. Janet was an heiress, and was able to support Ouspensky in certain of his projects, as Ralph Philipson had done in the 1920s. The addition of this couple to the group was the seed of things to come.

Once the group had settled into the estate at Lyne, Ouspensky announced a two-pronged project: first the property itself was to become

---

1. Quotation presented anonymously, as coming from "one of Ouspensky's close associates."

Figure 36. Lyne Place about 1940.

self-supporting, and second a larger meeting facility in London was to be secured. Making Lyne self-supporting would involve a host of different projects that would be ongoing. Ouspensky was clearly opening up the third line of work, creating a context in which the bonds that support the second line could grow stronger. He was also anticipating the shortages which might occur in a second European war. The action on the second aim, on securing a new meeting facility, took a little more time. At the end of October of 1938 the Theosophical Hall at 38 Warwick Gardens was let go, and the group acquired Colet House, at 46 Colet Gardens (now 151

Figure 37. Partial view of the main dining room.

Talgarth Road). It was within two blocks of the original Gwendwr Road apartment, which the Ouspenskys retained. The hall, which had been constructed in 1885 as an adjunct to St. Paul's School, was an imposing building with meeting facilities capable of accommodating 500 people. It was the largest single studio in London at that time.

Figure 38. View of the entrance hall from the front door.

The choice of Colet House was not accidental. The building was owned by one of Ouspensky's students, Nadine Nicolaeva Legat (1895-1971), who had used it to host the Legat School of Ballet. Her decision to base the Legat School outside of London coincided exactly with Ouspensky's need for a new location within the city.

The availability of Colet House, and the appearance of Nadine Legat, brings our attention to another developing area of the group's work: dance and the movements. Jessmin Howarth and Rosemary Lillard had been teaching the movements to Ouspensky's students since their arrival at Lyne Place in mid-1935. Colet House offered a venue that was both more convenient for rehearsal and more suitable for performance. The practice of

Figure 39. Colet House in the 1960s.

the movements thus accelerated from the time the group acquired Colet House.[1]

The movements developed as part of the group's work not through the single decision the Ouspenskys made in 1934 to bring Jessmin to London — but through the action of an interwoven tapestry of lives, running back into pre-revolutionary Russia.

THE MOVEMENTS UNDER OUSPENSKY

Jessmin Howarth had been one of the central figures in Gurdjieff's final orchestration of the movements at the Prieuré, in 1923. At that time a set of twenty-seven complementary movements were finalized, and treated as a working whole. All the students learned every movement in precise detail. Later, when Gurdjieff recommenced teaching the movements after the war, they were broken up into sets, and specializations developed. But in 1923 the focus was on the result that the complete program produced in each student, and that program was viewed as sacred. It was a very strenuous regimen, and it was this totality that Jessmin Howath — with Madame Ouspensky's full support — introduced and taught in London. While Ouspensky had never been enthusiastic about Gurdjieff's early moving-centered exercises (in the 1910s), he did understand the dance as a form of objective art. He had made serious study of the

---

1. We note the strange anomaly that Ouspensky, who was not himself a teacher of the dance, was surrounded, throughout his teaching life, by accomplished dancers, while Gurdjieff, who was not a man of letters, was surrounded throughout his teaching life by professional writers and literary critics.

dervish dances in the great tekkes of Ottoman Constantinople, in the company of Gurdjieff, Thomas de Hartman, and Alexandre de Salzmann. He fully appreciated their esoteric value, and saw them as a profound cultural statement. Additionally, he had helped Gurdjieff with the choreography of his own ballet.

Nadine and her husband Nicolai Legat were expatriate Russian dancers who had established the Legat School of Ballet in London in 1923. They had purchased Colet House in 1931. Nadine had been prima ballerina for both the Russian Imperial Ballet and the State Theater Ballet. Nicolai had been a principal dancer for the Russian Imperial Ballet and the Mariinsky Ballet. At the time of the Russian Revolution Nicolai was ballet master for the Imperial Ballet. Nadine and Nicolai Legat were amongst the greatest dancers of their generation. As teachers they were renowned for their rigor, and their uncompromising devotion to art. The Legat School of Ballet trained Ninette de Valois, Margot Fonteyn, Moira Shearer, Natalie Krassovska, and many of the dancers who later worked with Sadler's Wells, the Royal Ballet, and the Ballets Russe. By a remarkable coincidence, Nicolai Legat had produced Thomas de Hartmann's 1907 ballet, the *Pink Flower*, with Vaslav Nijinsky and Tamara Karsavina.

On Nicolai's death in 1937, Nadine secured properties outside of London to teach dancers intensively in residence, in the first ballet boarding school in Great Britain. She then arranged for Ouspensky to purchase Colet House.

Nadine Legat had joined Ouspensky's teaching in the expansion of 1934, at about the same time Jessica Howarth had begun to teach the movements at Lyne. We can be certain that she understood the full value of Jessmin's achievement, for we know that when Jessmin returned to America, at the outbreak of the war, Nadine continued to teach the movements in London for another thirty years.[2] Nadine Legat would have been forty-three years old in 1938, three years younger than Jessmin Howarth, and at the very prime of her teaching life. Her presence would certainly have contributed to the remarkable performances of the movements that were achieved at Colet House in the years immediately preceding the war.

By 1939 the execution of the movements, under the combined influence of Jessmin Howarth and Nadine Legat, had reached a level that was compelling. In April of the same year, with Ouspensky's encouragement, J.G. Bennett wrote to the Hereditary Chief of the Mevlei Dervish Order, who had gone into exile in Aleppo in Syria. He

---

2. See the record of Nadine Legat's lineage of ballet teaching at the website of The Anneliese von Oettingen School of Ballet. The Wikipedia entry for Nadine Legat states that she "choreographed dances based on the Movements Exercises of G.I. Gurdjieff." James Webb, in *The Harmonious Circle*, p. 409, states — on the basis of interviews — that Nadine Legat "had evolved a gymnastic for dancing incorporating Gurdjieffian principles of self-observation".

received a very warm reply, which delighted Ouspensky. Arrangements were made for the Mevlevi Dervishes to perform at Colet House, but the war intervened and the connection was not recovered.[1]

In considering the remarkable flowering of the dance in Ouspensky's teaching (when Gurdjieff himself was in relative retreat), you can see something wanting to happen; some latent unity of things wanting to come into its full existence, whether at Tiflis, or Fontainebleau, or London, or New York. There is something in this beyond either Gurdjieff or Ouspensky.

It would have been in this environment that Ouspensky's student Rodney Collin was first exposed to the movements, and this explains why Rodney himself taught them — as something of unquestioned value — for the remainder of his life. He later incorporated them into the work of this own theater group, The Unicorn Players. Thus, in their different ways, both Rodney Collin and Nadine Legat carried the practice of the movements forward. Rodney taught the set of twenty-seven movements until his death in 1956, and Nadine taught them — probably working in tandem with the historical society — into the nineteen sixties. She herself died in 1971.

In all of this, there is an interesting sideline connection to the Royal Ballet. Nadine Legat's student, Ninette de Valois, was the Founder and Artistic Director of the Royal Ballet, which from 1931 to 1946 was known as Sadler's Wells Ballet. In 1938 her husband, Dr. Arthur Connell, became a student of Ouspensky. (Did Nadine invite Ninette and Arthur to view the movements, and Arthur join on the basis of that contact?) Arthur Connell remained a core member of Ouspensky's group — and its successor, the Study Society — until his own death in 1980. After Ouspensky's death Madame Ouspensky took possession of Colet House and used it for Gurdjieff Foundation activities. In 1954 Madame Ouspensky leased Colet House to the Royal Ballet (then still Sadler's Wells Ballet), and once again it became a school for ballet. When, in 1957, the Sadler's Wells Ballet was granted the Royal Charter, and the company became centered in Covent Garden and Baron's Court, Arthur Connell then arranged that Colet House be returned to the Study Society, under the leadership of Ouspensky's student Dr. Francis Roles.

While the movements classes accelerated, the preparation of Colet House showed the level of third line of work that had become a part of the school: a main staircase was carpeted; the large meeting room in the top studio was equipped with plush red tip-up seating; smaller studios were set up where senior students could lead groups.

---

1. See Bennett, J.G., *Witness: The Story of a Search*, Dharma Book Company, Inc., New York, New York, 1962, p 185.

And Colet House was more than a venue for meetings and the movements. The acquisition of the building made possible the formation of the non-profit Historico-Psychological Society. This gave external form to the developing organization of the school: a constitution was drawn up and a governing committee established, including the Ouspenskys, Francis Roles, Kenneth Walker, and John Pentland. At this point Ouspensky created a set of internal rules for the Society: members should not converse together before strangers, members should not speak to anyone who had left the group, members should not address one another by their Christian names. The reason for these exercises was not simply to produce friction, but to teach members to place a right value on the bond that existed between them — for the standards of society at large are not sufficient to support the process of awakening. Ouspensky was, step by step, sectioning his students out of society, and relating their work to the standards of the Inner Circle of Humanity.

Ouspensky hoped to finance these new developments by publishing new material. He planned to produce an English edition of his novel *Strange Life of Ivan Osokin,* and a new edition of *Tertium Organum,* with terminology consistent with the terminology of *New Model*.[2] Ouspensky had his student Fairfax Hall, a printer by profession, set up the Stourton Press in the basement of Colet House. The first publication of the Historico-Psychological Society was, then, *Psychological Lectures* — a hardbound version of the five lectures Ouspenky's group used at their introductory meeting series. (These were published after the war as *The Psychology of Man's Possible Evolution*).

And all these different lines of effort were having their effect. Ouspensky's presence was slowly but surely penetrating the British culture of his time. In John Buchan's 1932 novel, *The Gap in the Curtain,* Ouspensky was characterized as Professor August Moe. In J.B. Priestley's 1937 play, *I Have Been Here Before,* he was represented in the character of Dr. Görtler. His influence is clearly apparent in Aldous Huxley's 1937 book, *Ends and Means*. Amongst those attending Ouspensky's lectures were T.S. Eliot,

---

2. Ouspensky, P.D., *A Record of Meetings,* Arkana (Penguin Group) London, 1992, p. 126-7.

D.H. Lawrence, Algernon Blackwood, Christopher Isherwood, Gerald Heard, and Aldous Huxley. Both Heard and Huxley spent weekends at Lyne. Ouspensky's books were read by many, including the young Denis Healey, one of the most prominent Labour politicians of the postwar era. Richard Guyatt, a seminal figure in British graphic design in the postwar period, was a student of Ouspensky's from 1933 until his death. Having said this, Ouspensky made absolutely no attempt to court eminent people.

We provide a few quotations to show the impression that the mature Ouspensky made on those around him.

> Chiefly my recollection from the first meetings I went to is of Ouspensky's great strength and authority; he was very impersonal and succinct in his replies to questions, but he had much humor and charm as well ... If you spoke with him alone about some personal problem he was always helpful, benevolent and kind. But he could be merciless to pretense and artificiality. ... The accepted image of cold intellectualism is absurdly incomplete. It ignores attributes such as warmth, kindness, innate honesty, a keen sense of humor, and extreme modesty.[1]

> His control over his moving center was absolutely marvelous; he made no unnecessary movements and he answered no unnecessary questions.[2]

> Although his answers were as always precise and short, his manner and tone created a relaxed atmosphere.[3]

> He was unfailingly courteous, but when it was absolutely necessary he could also 'shout in Moscow fashion' as he called it. This was a

---

1. Taylor, Merrily E., (compiler & editor), *Remembering Pyotr Demianovich Ouspensky,* Yale University Library, New Haven CT, 1978, p. 38.
2. Article by Arthur Connell, *Memories of P.D. Ouspensky,* p. 146, *The Bridge,* No. 12, Autumn 1997, (ed. Eadie, Peter McGregor), © The Study Society, Colet House, London, 1997, p. 123.
3. Article by Nicolai Rabeneck, *The Russian Group,* p. 146, *The Bridge,* No. 12, Autumn 1997, (ed. Eadie, Peter McGregor), © The Study Society, Colet House, Talgarth Road, London, 1997.

sound which could truly 'split the air' and shock into awareness the daydreaming pupil who might be meandering around in a state of 'waking sleep.' This shouting was done in a controlled and detached manner ... for one of the tenets of his teaching, which he himself strictly followed, was the denial of the expression of any 'negative emotions.'[4]

Self-advertisement did not exist for him ... he 'was silent,' he never disputed nor did he try to convince anyone about anything.[5]

This last quality, of never defending himself, would have a marked impact in British culture, where the cut and thrust of intellectual debate was an accepted norm. Thus, the intellectual atmosphere of the Enlightenment met with the much deeper intellectual current of Hermetic teaching.

We have discussed Ouspensky's expansion of the second and third lines of work, and his experiments with methods of repetition. While all of this was based on mastering and applying the principles presented in the *Psychology,* Ouspensky taught in a different way to the circle of his most advanced students. He might invite some of the older students to an after-dinner gathering; he would sit at the great kitchen table, with a lavish spread of hors d'oeuvres and assorted bottles of port, brandy, and claret. The topics of conversation would be varied: Russian literature, the art of target shooting, dressage, Moscow stories, the current state of European culture ... "but it was in the early morning hours that he would expand on the Ideas of the System."[6]

And he would do more than "expand on the Ideas of the System." Following a long day of physical work on the property at Lyne, Ouspensky would create in his guests an atmosphere of relaxed presence: the pleasant, positive energy that engenders trust. This would be the prelude to the direct sharing of Higher Centers. The mixed topics of conversation were a preliminary to entering the regions of the Self. John Bennett has left us with

---

4. Taylor, Merrily E., (compiler & editor), *Remembering Pyotr Demianovich Ouspensky,* Yale University Library, New Haven CT, 1978, p. 39.
5. *Ibid.,* p. 40.
6. *Ibid.,* p. 37.

the report of such an evening from 1933. At this time Bennett was staying in Shoreham. He had made a trip into London on business, returning to Shoreham by way of Gaddesden, where Ouspensky then resided. Bennett decided to drop by and Ouspensky invited him to dinner. There was only the two of them. Towards morning, after they had drunk several bottles of claret, Bennett was holding forth.

> I was speaking and expressing my opinion about some question — I have completely forgotten what it was. But as I spoke I went quite outside myself, and heard my own voice and even watched my own thoughts as if they were going on in someone else. I saw myself as completely artificial: neither my thoughts nor my words were my own. 'I' — whoever at that moment 'I' might be — was a completely indifferent spectator of the performance. Quite suddenly, the spell broke, and I was back 'inside' myself. I said to Ouspensky: "Now I know what self-observation really is. In all these years I have never seen Bennett as he really is, until this moment." He replied very seriously, saying: "Was this worth sitting up all night for?" I said: "Yes, indeed, or for twenty nights if necessary." He continued: "If only you can remember what you have just seen you will be able to work. But you must understand that no one can help you in this. If you do not see for yourself, it is impossible for anyone else to show you." Soon afterwards he went off to bed, and I took my car and drove to Shoreham as the sun was rising. The intense beauty of the summer morning filled me with a joy that I had rarely known before ... I watched the swallows skimming over the morning fields and said to myself: "One vision does not make a conscious man." Nevertheless, at this seminar I got further than ever before in reaching a sense of unity with those I worked with.[1]

We note here, that although a lot of alcohol was consumed, Ouspensky does not appear to have been in the least inebriated. A remark on alcohol is in place, as both Gurdjieff and Ouspensky used it as a teaching tool.

---

1. Bennett, J.G., *Witness, the Story of a Search*, Dharma Book Company, New York, New York, 1962, pages176-177.

Figure 40. Formal dinner at Lyne.

TEACHING AND ALCOHOL

Generally, alcohol has the effect of weakening both the intellectual center and the intellectual parts of the moving, instinctive, and emotional centers. You do not balance your accounts or make rendering drawings after taking a few drinks. But, at the same time, it weakens the artificial control of personality, making people less rigid and more spontaneous. The positive effect of this is that it can, in the right circumstances, bring people closer to essence. But there can also be negative effects. The loosening of control weakens the mechanical brakes on the direct expression of features — and can lead to the explosive release of coarse instinctive and emotional energies. The alcohol in itself causes neither the moments of essence nor the outbursts of temper; it can liberate lower things or higher things depending on the kind of third force that is present in the situation. A practiced teacher can use the release of mechanical inhibitions to show students things about themselves. In the special atmosphere where Higher Centers are active, there is a greater potential for the release of higher things: first essence, and then Higher Centers. When lower things come out they can be made visible — often for the first time — to the person giving expression. Additionally, when Higher Centers are active, they themselves can stimulate the intellectual parts of centers, even when a significant amount of alcohol has been consumed. Thus, a teacher can teach to a more open and receptive audience, and in an atmosphere of intimacy. Having said this, such teaching is an art, and one not easily mastered. Ouspensky used alcohol in this way, to enable a deeper level of communication.

We note that, in the instance described by John Bennett, Ouspensky communicated a full experience of Higher Centers in a very understated way. Ouspensky, like Gurdjieff, possessed powers, but he made a more subtle use of them. With Bennett he enabled a state and made a promise, "If only you can remember what you have just seen you will be able to work." But in fact Bennett was not able to remember this; the penchant to be a teacher was too strong in him. He was unable to follow the exercises that Ouspensky later gave him to limit this form of mechanical expression, in such a way that he might get behind himself as he had done that morning at Gadsden.

Rodney Collin remarks on Ouspensky's teaching in this area.

> I often think of the last years with Ouspensky. He would have two or three people sit with him, not doing anything, just sitting, smoking, occasionally making a remark, drinking a glass of wine, for hours on end. At first it was very difficult — one racked one's brains what to say, how to start a conversation, thought of all kinds of imaginary duties elsewhere. Many people could never bear it. But after a while, these became the most interesting times of all. One began to feel — everything is possible in *this moment*, let the past and future take care of itself. Some kind of momentum slowed down, and sometimes quite new ideas, a quite new connection with time and one's surroundings, seemed to form. One was shown what it meant to be more free.[1]

In sum, in the late 1930s Ouspensky's group began to acquire depth. It had produced one mature teacher in the form of Maurice Nicoll, and others were seeding. Ouspensky tried to create roles for his students to develop

Figure 41. Ouspensky's Table.

---

1. Collin, Rodney, *The Theory of Conscious Harmony*, Watkins, London, 1976, p. 64-5.

Figure 42. Ouspensky's Table.

into, roles that would make the right kind of requirement on the one who played them.

Ouspensky's students were coming to lead a shared life; the meetings at Colet House, the development of the property at Lyne, the special events at Lyne, the movements, the late-night teaching sessions, the many special projects, and the battery of exercises and disciplines which covered all parts of the day. In this context the formal balls and dinners at Lyne were not simply another theater of work, they were also the celebration of a way of life. They were special events in the lives of the participants. Madame Kadloubovksy, who had been with Ouspensky since his first groups in the Péra, remembered her teacher at one of these events:

> There came a day when we stood together side by side at the top of the long staircase at Colet House watching the crowd of people streaming down it; he said, in his quiet Moscow way: 'Vse Ya sam'. (All this I did myself.)[2]

The acceleration of activity did not seem to plateau. Madame Kadloubovsky noted: "One measure of the increased pace of activity from April 1938 to the outbreak of the war in September 1939 is the number of volumes of typescripts of meetings; there are 13 volumes for these 16 months, and for

---

2. Taylor, Merrily E. (compiler & editor), *Remembering Pyotr Demianovich Ouspensky,* Yale University Library, New Haven CT, 1978, p. 43.

Figure 43. Ouspensky in 1938.

the rest of the 25 years from 1922 to 1947 there are 21 volumes."[1] This corresponded to a new kind of authority in Ouspensky himself: the depth and concentration of a man number six. But a man number six, with his greater presence, also faces greater uncertainty. And great uncertainty certainly came to Ouspensky in 1939. That fateful year brought disruption to all that Ouspensky had labored for over eighteen years in London.

In July of 1939 Madame Ouspensky became quite ill, suffering from the onset of Parkinson's disease. Stanley Nott was convinced that Gurdjieff could help her, and — with Ouspensky's consent — he asked Gurdjieff for his assistance. Gurdjieff agreed, and arrangements were made for a visit to London, but only a few days before Gurdjieff's scheduled trip, the war broke out. Madame Ouspensky did slowly recover, and in January of 1941 she was able to go to America, but she remained partially invalid for the remainder of her life.

---

1. *Ibid.,* p. 34.

From 3rd September 1939, when Britain declared war on Germany, the British government implemented conscription, rationing, evacuations, and nightly black outs. The effects of these measures eventually made the continuation of the Work impossible. From 1937 Ouspensky himself had been under Home Office surveillance. Now, in order to avoid being interned, he had to live permanently at Lyne. Madame Ouspensky had already prepared the property to receive evacuees from central London, and a circle of students gathered there to wait out the war. Ouspensky continued to lead small meetings. Maurice Nicoll's entire group was evacuated to Gloucestershire. At the same time J.G. Bennett and Kenneth Walker continued to hold meetings at Colet Gardens.

On 10th May 1940 the German armies began their invasion and conquest of the Netherlands, Belgium, France, Denmark, and Norway. On 29th May 1940 the British Expeditionary Force was evacuated from Dunkirk. The Battle of Britain began in August of 1940, and almost immediately there was damage to the flat on 55a Gwendwr Road.

Ouspensky's students reacted with the same concern that every other person in the British Isles felt. He reminded them, "Man cannot do, everything happens." Uncertainty is the environment of school work, and presence is the only thing that is real on this level. At the same time, these events touched Ouspensky's most sensitive chords: his abhorrence of violence, and his fear of a society dominated by criminals. Ouspensky was concerned that Germany might win the war, and that the victory of a criminal regime would be followed by the Communist overthrow of Fascist government in Europe, making school impossible for the indefinite future. On 6th September 1940 the Luftwaffe bombed the London docks within twenty miles of Lyne. The blaze was spectacular. The residents at Lyne stood silently on the rooftop watching.

The fall of Western Europe convinced Ouspensky of the need to find a more secure base for his teaching. He had been considering America for some time; *Tertium Organum* had sold well in the U.S., and *A New Model of the Universe* was selling better in the U.S. than it was in Britain. The time appeared ripe.

Ouspensky announced his intention to emigrate at his last wartime meeting at Colet Gardens, on 25th January 1941. At this meeting he compared the present situation to his experience in the Caucasus in the 1910s, and told his students that "Quite possibly they were witnessing the end of one particular historical period and the beginning of another."[1] He sensed the approach of a *kairos* time. Ouspensky asked those students who could, to emigrate with him. He asked all those who could not to maintain both Lyne Place and Colet Gardens as best they could. It would be a strong affirmation of the Work if they could sustain some level of activity under the conditions of total war. He would keep in contact and advise by mail.

The Mendham Years: 1941–1946

On 4th January 1941 Madame Ouspensky, Lenotchka, and Lonya left for the United States, where they were received by Ouspensky's friends. Ouspensky arranged that Janet Collin-Smith and her daughter Chloe should follow within a week. Janet's husband Rodney had hopes of eventually relocating in New York through his wartime work assignments with the British Purchasing Commission. In March of 1941 Ouspensky himself sailed from Liverpool to New York on a troop ship. By an amazing coincidence he happened to be on the same ship which the British Purchasing Commission was using to send Rodney to Bermuda via New York, the S.S. Georgic. The two separated again at New York, but, as we shall see, the thread of their lives was woven tight together.

Madame Ouspensky arranged a reception for her husband in New York. The two of them then — with Lenotchka and Lonya — took rooms in the city. Once established they began to search, with the help of Janet, for a larger property that would substitute for Lyne Place. While this search was underway, Ouspensky rented a studio apartment on East 78th Street, where he began to conduct meetings. His audiences numbered between thirty and fifty. Irmis Popoff describes her response to Ouspensky's first lecture in New York.

---

1. Webb, James, *The Harmonious Circle*, Shambhala, Boston, 1987, p. 440

> I walked out of Ouspensky's apartment feeling that I carried within myself a hallowed cathedral, and the services that would charge it with life, music, and meaning were about to begin.[2]

In October 1941, with the backing of Janet Collin-Smith, the Ouspensky's purchased Franklin Farms in Mendham, New Jersey. This was a substantial three-story mansion on a 400-acre estate. It had been the former residence of the Governor of New Jersey. Once the estate was secured, Ouspensky began to invite people from the New York meetings to spend weekends there. The acquisition of Franklin Farms was announced at Lyne Place on 1st November 1941, and Ouspensky asked all those who could to join him there. The Mendham estate made possible all the different lines of work than had been undertaken at Lyne. Madame Ouspensky organized the practical work – farmwork and housework – and a regular schedule of social events was set up. While Madame remained permanently based at Franklin Farms, Ouspensky stayed at the original New York apartment during the week, giving meetings and organizing workgroups. After both the New York meetings and the social events at Mendham Ouspensky would often teach late into the night.

In the month after his arrival in America Ouspensky met with a number of Orage's followers resident in New York. He carefully distinguished his own teaching from that of Orage, and made clear the conditions for anyone wanting to work with him. He did not require that they not speak of Gurdjieff, he only asked that they not ask questions about *Beelzebub's Tales* at the meetings. Ouspensky accepted all the people who accepted his conditions, but refused their money, insisting that it be sent to Gurdjieff in Paris.[3]

As the year progressed several London students were able to emigrate to the United States, including Jessmin Howarth and Rosemary Lillard.[4]

---

2. Popoff, Irmis, *Gurdjieff: His Work on Myself with Others for the Work*, Eureka Editions, Utrecht, 2001, p. 18.
3. Nott, C.S., *Journey Through This World*, Routledge & Kegan Paul, 1969, p. 159.
4. Rosemary had become Rosemary Nott, on her marriage to Stanley Nott. Both had emigrated at this time.

Jessmin and Rosemary began to teach the movements at Franklin Farms shortly after it opened. John Pentland and his family were also able to relocate in New York. Gradually Ouspensky's American following increased from 50 to 150, principally residents of New York. He had quickly generated a nucleus of people, and a certain level of activity. Still, these were almost all new students, and the rate of turnover was high.

Stanley Nott said of Mendham:

> It was as if Lyne Place had been Americanized and transferred to New Jersey; not only the house and park, gardens and grounds were similar, but many of the same people were there and already the atmosphere of Lyne was being created. There was the same kind of magnificence and the same kind of work, and the same rules were being established.[1]

> At the big dinners students wore formal apparel: tuxedos and gowns. After a strenuous day of work on the grounds, or a demanding session of the movements, faces would be flushed with a glow of excitement, and tempered by the gentle reserve that presence brings. Ouspensky might invite a smaller group to continue into the small hours of the morning. The lives of the Ouspenskys were of a high order.[2]

From time to time members of the London group were able to visit Mendham, linking the two phases of Ouspensky's Work.

Rodney Collin, whom the British Purchasing Commission had placed in New York following his Bermuda assignment, was very active in an understated way. While working full time in the city he was able to spend his weekends at Mendham, where he put in long hours maintaining the grounds. During his weekdays in the city, he drove Ouspensky to and from all the New York meetings. Rodney was able to respond directly and deeply to Ouspensky's Higher Centers. Thus, in the midst of all the difficulties

---

1. Nott, C.S., *Journey Through This World*, Routledge & Kegan Paul, London, 1974, p. 164.
2. *Ibid.*, p. 165.

Ouspensky faced, a student with the potential to become fully conscious suddenly appeared.

An unassuming portrait of Ouspensky was given by the commissionaire of his favorite restaurant in New York, Longchamps. When, in a period of Ouspensky's absence, he saw students gathered at a table, he brought a bunch of flowers to the table and said, "I thought he must be ill as he hasn't come lately. I can't understand his books, but Ouspensky is the only really *kind* man I have ever met."[3]

In the first years at Mendham, Ouspensky was able to clearly formulate certain cosmological principles that he had been developing since the late 1930s. Specifically, his theory of the six cosmic processes that form a cosmos, at any level of the universe. This is a significant achievement that his teaching added to the Fourth Way tradition. It was reported to the students, as a completed theory, at Mendham in 1943.[4]

THE SIX COSMIC PROCESSES

According to the system, the visible universe is a Macrocosm comprised of a hierarchy of cosmoses, each lower cosmos contained within a higher cosmos until you reach the cosmos of cosmoses. Ouspensky stated that every cosmos, on every level, was comprised of six complementary processes. The names that apply to these processes on the level of the cosmos of man are: Crime, Growth, Digestion, Healing, Destruction, and Regeneration. While, as we noted, the substances that comprise the six processes

---

3. Taylor, Merrily E. (compiler & editor), *Remembering Pyotr Demianovich Ouspensky*, Yale University Library, New Haven CT, 1978, p. 39.

4. The first sketches of this theory can be found in the records of the 1937 London meetings. See Ouspensky, P.D., *A Record of Meetings*, Arkana (Penguin Group) London, 1992. See p. 160-164, entry for 8th November, 1937. The six cosmic processes (triads) are depicted, and then described summarily. There is an emphasis on the process of regeneration. By 1943 the theory was complete. The Mendham meetings for March and April of 1945 show a developed conception of the different triads. See Ouspensky, P.D., *A Further Record: Extracts From Meetings 1928-1945*, Arkana (Penguin Group) London, 1986. See p. 173, the entry for 21st March 1945 (in New York). The six processes are depicted, along with the activities connected with them. There is mention of a seventh process, possible only for the Absolute. The meeting following on 11th April 1945 adds more on the theme, classifying the different 'activities' as they exist on different levels of creation.

vary at every level of the Ray of Creation, the processes themselves always work the same way. This theory is based on the principle of triads, or the Law of Three, which Gurdjieff had used to explain the links between the different levels of Creation. A triad is comprised of three forces:

1. The Active Force — initiates the process.
2. The Passive Force — receives the action and provides the resistance.
3. The Neutralizing Force — context that determines the outcome.

Any human activity of any kind is the result of the combination of these three forces. For each force (active, passive, neutralizing) the other two forces can change their place, and this results in six different combinations. In other words, these three forces, in all their possible combinations, yield six different triads.

The condition of a triad is such that, at whatever level of the Ray of Creation a triad takes place, each of the three forces is represented by a substance: a composite of hydrogens whose vibrations are carried within the 'matter' of that substance. In other words, the force — active or passive or neutralizing — acts through a cosmic substance. The vibrational levels of the substances will vary at each level of the Ray of Creation, but there is always a highest substance, a middle substance, and a lowest substance. The vibrational levels of the three substances can never be the same, otherwise there would be no interaction.

Sometimes the active force is on the highest vibrational level, sometimes it is on a lower level than *either* the passive force or the neutralizing force, and sometimes it is on a lower level than *both* the passive force and the neutralizing force. These different positionings determine whether the triad will raise or lower the overall hydrogen level of its constituents. A triad with the first force on the lowest level and the third force on the highest level will leave a resultant substance on the middle level. This is the process of Digestion: it ends on a higher level than where it began.[1]

There is, then, a seventh process, which is all six processes at once. All forces act in the same place at the same time. Ouspensky says of this process that it is only possible for the Absolute, and so we do not study it here.[2]

We provide in Figure 44 a diagram of the six processes that emphasizes the *level* of the active, passive, and neutralizing forces in each triad. In other words, it shows,

---

1. Ouspensky very clearly marks each process as either ascending or descending. See Ouspensky, P.D., *A Record of Meetings,* Penguin/Arkana, London, 1992, p. 161.
2. See Ouspensky, P.D., *A Further Record,* Arkana, London & New York, 1986, p. 193, and Collin, Rodney, *The Theory of Celestial Influence,* Watkins, London, 1980, p. 154. Collin describes the seventh process as one where "all three forces (active, passive, neutralizing) work simultaneously at all points."

for each triad, which of the three forces operates through the highest, the middle, or the lowest substance. This clarifies the essential nature of the process and shows its action in the line of time. The neutralizing force (or the third force) always appears as the resultant force. This diagram has been taken from a more comprehensive diagram circulated privately by Girard Haven.[3]

Haven's original diagram included the names given by Ouspensky for the processes as they exist on different levels of the cosmic scale. We have used here only the terms that apply on the human scale. Haven shows the forces embodying the higher vibrational level, the middle vibrational level, and the lower vibrational level with the letters **H, M, L** which appear alongside each box.

The terms Higher, Middle, and Lower are not very descriptive. Rodney Collin, in his publication of the research he did with Ouspensky, gave names to the three levels which make some intuitive sense on all levels of the Ray of Creation. The Higher is Life, the Middle is Form, and the Lower is Matter.[4] These terms are shown for each process on the diagram, and we have used them in the descriptions to follow.

Sometimes a person can recognize that they are subject to a particular cosmic process by the quality of energy involved. The process of destruction, for example, can often have a coarse, violent energy. The process of healing, a sensitive and sympathetic energy. The study of the processes begins with the intellect but becomes, over time, the ability to directly recognize the different qualities of energy involved in every human activity.

The diagram shows how each process leaves the average hydrogen level of the three substances at either a higher or a lower level. All processes are needed for the cosmic order.

These are the six processes, on the human scale, as they relate to the Work:

Growth: The higher level acts on the lower level to produce the middle level. A descending process. Higher Forces (the higher level) act on mankind (the lower level) to raise it, by awakening an individual or by creating a school. The result is a middle level between Higher Forces and humanity. In this way humanity is infused with a certain amount of conscious life.

---

3. Haven's diagram was based on a study of all the material published on the cosmic processes by Gurdjieff, Ouspensky, and Collin. Collin and Ouspensky worked together on the study of the processes at Mendham in the late 1930s. Their work of collaboration is described in the chapter on Rodney Collin. The results of their work appear in *A Record of Meetings, A Further Record,* and in Collin's book *The Theory of Celestial Influence.*

4. Collin, Rodney, *The Theory of Celestial Influence,* Watkins, London, 1980, p. 54-57, 172-203.

Destruction: The higher level acts on the middle level to produce the lower level. A descending process. A teacher (the higher level) makes a student (the middle level) aware of their chief feature (the lower level), and a certain false idea that the student has of themselves is destroyed. *But if nothing higher is put in the place of the feature* the student is simply worse off than they were before. (In the work, the destruction of what is false must be followed by the process of regeneration. Both processes are necessary, but in the right order.)

Digestion: The lower level acts on the higher level to produce the middle level. An ascending process. Intellect and emotion (the lower level) assimilate a higher state of consciousness (the higher level) that has occurred in the past and has been retained in memory. They work together to create new attitudes (the middle level) that more closely conform to the higher state. The attitudes (the middle level) are less than the higher state itself, but we are better off than we were before.

Crime: The middle level acts on the higher level to produce the lower level. A descending process. A student in a school (the higher level) develops doubts about the teacher (from the middle level), and becomes cynical, losing their work entirely (so reaching the lower level).

Healing: The lower level acts on the middle level to produce the higher level. An ascending process. The middle level, which has been diseased or damaged, rediscovers its original form to produce a state of good health. A student suffers an emotional wound, through the loss of a spouse or a child. They become subject to grief and depression in their emotional center (the middle level), and this disrupts both their personal work (the higher level) and their bodily health (the lower level). The student then puts the middle and lower levels in order. He or she observes and separates from the distressed emotional center; takes in positive rather than negative impressions; finds new activities; promotes constructive thought; ensures good instinctive habits (diet and sleep). Over time the lower level returns to its normal state. The psychological anxieties (at the middle level) are relieved. The student's work (the higher level) is then able to proceed as it did before.

Regeneration: The middle level acts on the lower level to produce the higher level. An ascending process. The middle level (the steward) acts on the contents of the four lower centers (the lower level) to put them in a condition where they can enable the Higher Centers (the higher level). And then the Higher Centers actually appear. This is the emulation of the higher level by the middle level, and it is what makes transcendence possible. Thus, regeneration is unique in that it prepares the ground for transcendence, which comes from a higher level.

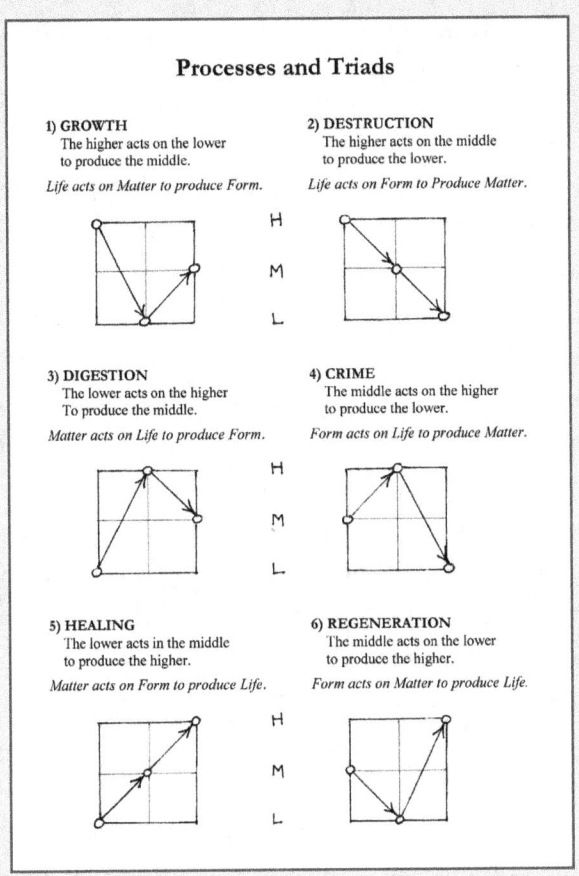

Figure 44. Processes and Triads (Girard Haven).

The theory of the six cosmic processes represents an achievement of Hermetic science. It relates the theory of triads to different densities of matter and can be understood in relation to consciousness. It is, at the same time, an elucidation of the cosmic laws depicted in the enneagram and can be related directly to the law of three and the law of seven as shown in the enneagram. Above all, it has direct, practical implications for the Work. It allows us to place and prioritize the processes in relation to our work. Above all it relates the practice of self-remembering to the cosmic process of regeneration. The triad of regeneration describes the process of transcendence, or change of level. It brings out the difference between making the effort to self-remember and experiencing a state which transcends effort. And it shows how those two are rightly related. In other words, it gives the possibility of understanding self-remembering not just as

> effort generated from the functions, but in relation to a presence *that is not of* the functions. The theory of the six cosmic processes thus represents an accurate development of the system Ouspensky received, on the foundation that had been given.

By mid-1942 Ouspensky had established a second base of teaching in New York. Colet House was requisitioned by the British Navy for the war effort, so the London meetings could only take place at Lyne, and attendance there was limited by the restrictions of the blackout. At Lyne the residents remained firm in their practice of the exercises Ouspensky left them.

Even though opening the teaching in America was a great achievement, we must emphasize that these were difficult years for Ouspensky. Madame Ouspensky's illness persisted, and he himself began to suffer from a kidney disease. He saw clearly that both his time and his energies were limited. He had only a few years left. Knowing the amount of effort that it takes to bring a group of people to a certain level of Work, he must have questioned what was possible in the time that remained to him. Yes, he had managed to re-create the London Work at Mendham, but most of the American students were still quite new, and his Work in London had been significantly disrupted by the war. There must have been moments when – like Gurdjieff in the dark years following the motor accident – he questioned whether his life's work would produce an enduring result. The penumbral aura of the Inner Circle of Humanity — the invisible source of the system — must, in certain moments, have seemed very distant.

In early 1944 there came further cause for concern. London students reported to Ouspensky that John Bennett had begun a series of lectures expounding his own ideas, and that he intended to publish a book elaborating the material he was presenting in his lectures. This book was eventually published in 1956, in four volumes, as *The Dramatic Universe*. Bennett had submitted a draft of *The Dramatic Universe* to Ouspensky in December of 1943. Ouspensky, after reading the draft, counseled Bennett that "nothing new can be found by intellectual processes alone … there is only one hope: that we should find the way to work with the higher emotional center."[1]

---

1. Bennett, J.G., *Witness, the Story of a Search,* Dharma Book Company, New York, New York, 1962, p. 204.

What did Ouspensky mean by this? Let us say that the Higher Emotional Center is *presence fully self-aware*: fully independent of the operations of the intellect and fully self-sustaining. Once a person has achieved this state, the world looks very different, and the intellect can be used to record and to describe certain aspects of what one sees. These records would be a *direct report on experience*: the ordering of concepts in conformity with the insights of the Higher Centers. Additionally, as this state deepens, one may see certain things about the nature of the cosmic order, and these insights too can be given intellectual expression — although this is a more demanding task. If successful, these records might constitute a contribution to Hermetic science. Ouspensky's presentation of the six cosmic processes would be an example, for to understand these rightly they must be seen from a higher level. But if a student writes compulsively, striving for ever wider intellectual syntheses, hoping for a transcendent "Eureka," then the intellect itself is occupying the space of the Higher Emotional Center, and, at the same time, disabling the steward.

A student's efforts need to go directly into enabling presence and to pursuing the three lines of work. *The Dramatic Universe* is not without value, but had Bennett been able to concentrate his energy on his internal work he might have left us with something more profound. If Ouspensky had not taken responsibility for Bennett as a student (and if Bennett had not taken it upon himself to present these ad hoc teachings to Ouspensky's other students), the publication of this material would have done no harm. Speculative works of this kind abound. But in the context of schoolwork things are not the same. We will recall that Ouspensky had always been most scrupulous with the teachings he received from Gurdjieff and asked his permission to publish anything related to them.

More generally, it is clear that Bennett was unable to understand that Ouspensky *had established a way*. Ouspensky knew the sequence of steps that lead to awakening, and knew some of the things Bennett needed to let go of in order to take the next step. After 1941, with Ouspensky's stabilizing influence at a distance, Bennett's difficulty in mastering the practice of self-remembering, combined with his fixation on 'peak experiences,' led to deviations in his personal work. He forgot what Ouspensky had shown him that morning at Gaddesden in 1933, when he counseled: "If only you can remember what you have just seen you will be able to work."

And Bennett's problem was not just a problem for himself, but for the group. When one student presents material that promises to reveal hidden things, he engages other students in his speculations. But what the other students need in order to take the *next step* in their own evolution is not speculation. The priority is *to get behind the ideas they have already been given*; for example, to remember the real experience of self-observation, to understand what it means that imagination is a continuous state, to understand what it means that negative emotions are 'not real.' And more practically, in 1941-1945, to follow the very demanding exercises that Ouspensky had given his students.

There is an analogy here to sports disciplines. An Olympic athlete must figure out exactly what to do to win an event: what muscles to develop, what supporting exercises to employ, what to eat, how long to sleep. And then focus just on that. The athlete will never win without the capacity to simplify and concentrate. And above all he or she must have a sense that winning is possible. The same process of concentration and simplification applies to the Work. In the monastic schools of the Middle Ages very little information was given; the entire effort was to *get behind* a small amount of information in just the right way.

Ouspensky had given Bennett a leadership role in the group. He had been given responsibility to teach a system given from Higher Mind to engage Higher Centers — and he had been asked not to mix this teaching with his own speculations. Because he lacked confidence in his ability to use the system, he kept adding other things to it. Thus, before having mastered the system, he began to teach his own material to other people still struggling to master the same system. The effect of this was to dilute a teaching that works, if properly applied. In early 1944, Ouspensky asked Bennett to stop lecturing, and issued instructions curtailing Bennett's authority within the group. Bennett continued to teach and to lecture. In continuing after he had been asked to stop, he was compromising both his own evolution and the Work of the London group. In the spring of 1945 Ouspensky instructed the London students not to communicate with Bennett.

Ouspensky needed people under him who understood, from their being, the core principles of the Work. He needed people who could apply the methods of the Work to engage Higher Centers *within themselves*: people who understood – from direct experience – what the obstacles to engaging Higher Centers were. These are not just people who can quote the right work idea on the right occasion, but people who have actually begun to separate out the different levels within themselves, and make the lower levels serve the higher levels. And, in a school of regeneration, this development of the first line must find expression in three lines of Work. Was such an organization coming into existence at either Lyne or Mendham?

Ouspensky had concerns about the new students at Mendham, concerns about the older students at Lyne, concerns about his personal health, concerns about his wife's health, and concerns about the continuance of the Work. He was navigating deeper waters, *and this placed a greater pressure on him to read the pilot lights*: from his first glimpses of Higher Centers in St. Petersburg, to the vision of the Great Work in Essentuki, to whatever intuition he had of 'the source of the system,' to the aims he had shared with the small group at Ralph Philipson's apartment in 1924.

Ouspensky had *already seen* the destruction of the conditions for Work in his native Russia, in the Caucasus, in Constantinople, and in wartime London. He believed that the teaching he had been entrusted with had come from Higher Mind, and he sought to serve Higher Mind in keeping it alive. In short, he was trying to do everything he could to keep the link to Higher School open. He was aware of both the potentials and the limitations of a sleeping Mankind, and in the 1940s that Mankind was showing its dark underside. A large portion of the human race was now living under either Fascist or Communist regimes. Sixty million people were being slaughtered in the global conflict that was raging all around him, and the traditional religions and cultures that had once supported the Work were being rapidly displaced. Ouspensky's ever-growing awareness of the limitations of his situation, was complemented by a clear sense of the possibilities he had been given. And with all of this he had just been diagnosed as terminally ill.

It must have seemed to him that — after the so-promising expansion of the 1930s — he had come to an impasse. Thus, in early 1944, he entered the same twilight realm that Gurdjieff had entered in 1924 as a result of his automobile accident.

Suddenly, in the very depths of this impasse, Ouspensky was given an insight into what was possible for him in the remaining months of his life. This was not a vision of how he might found a non-monastic way in the West, or of how he might produce an ark to seed a new civilization, or of how he might center the many threads of the Gurdjieff work. The possibility that he saw was *to actually reconnect with the Source of the System*. And this spoke directly to the aim behind his many aims. From this formative experience — which probably occurred in the spring of 1945 — Ouspensky's course was set.

Ouspensky's being at this point could be likened to a shard of calcium carbonate, which, under extraordinary heat and pressure, has begun to crystallize into a transparent diamond.

Rodney Collin, who was in close contact with Ouspensky from April 1945 until the end of Ouspensky's life in October 1947, expressed it in this way. It was as though Ouspensky had discovered the script of a play, generated from Higher School, that had been enacted at various times and in various places over the centuries. In this play the teacher uses his own death to effect a transfiguration, linking energies on different levels of creation, and so linking Mankind to the Gods. The script is an archetypal drama, existing outside of time and space, that can be realized at several points in time. Collin made an analogy to the performance of a piece of music. The authors of the play of transfiguration — the Gods — are like the authors of a symphony, and the person effecting the transfiguration is like the conductor of that symphony:

> A man writes a symphony. A conductor collects an orchestra of many instruments and gives a performance. The music is actualized in one place at one particular day and hour. The manuscript may then lie lost in a drawer for years, even centuries. One day it is found. Another conductor collects another orchestra. The music is again actualized, in another place and at another moment in

time, which bears no relation to the first at all — and yet if it is the same music, it produces the same emotions in players and audience. And the number of times and places in which it may be played is infinite, but the result is always the same or similar. The symphony itself somehow exists outside time and space, but it can be evoked again whenever the right players with the right conductor get hold of a copy of the score. In some way, I feel that the 'score' of our work exists, somewhere outside time. Ouspensky got hold of this score, and without many people realising what was happening he got his players together and after coaching them for a long time in the theory of music, he actually put on a performance.[1]

Before going further we must ask, what reason is there for placing this formative insight, where Ouspensky received the 'script' of his play, in the spring of 1945? James Webb provides the following information, drawn from his many interviews with Ouspensky's students:

> In 1945, near the end of the war, the couple superintending Lyne were able to visit Mendham. It was clear to them that Ouspensky was not in good health. He seemed much older. He told them that he had little time left to live. He instructed them to return to England and "derequisition Colet Gardens from the Navy" and restore it for his return.[2]

The war ended in Europe on the 8th of May 1945, so this conversation might have occurred in March or April. Webb came to the following conclusion, based on his conversations with the anonymous couple:

> It is clear that Ouspensky's return [to London] was long premeditated and part of a deliberately conceived plan.[3]

---

1. Collin, Rodney, *The Theory of Conscious Harmony*, Watkins, London, 1976, p. 146. Note: in the text Rodney's letter is dated April 3, 1939. This is surely at typo. The date must be 1949.
2. Webb, James, *The Harmonious Circle*, Shambhala, Boston, 1987, p. 447.
3. *Ibid.*, p. 447.

The couple superintending Lyne were Francis and Elizabeth Roles. Ouspensky communicated to them his intention to return to England, and the approaching end of his own life. These two students clearly felt that Ouspensky had a plan in mind, although they did not know what it was. We know that Bennett's refusal to stop lecturing in the spring of 1945 (probably March) was the nadir of Ouspensky's Mendham years, and immediately preceded the vision of what was possible in the remaining two years of his life. Ouspensky would, then, have had the 'script' of his play of transfiguration in hand when he gave the instructions to Francis and Elizabeth Roles in late March or early April 1945.

On the basis of his formative insight of March-April 1945, Ouspensky risked all that he had worked for, from the time of his arrival in London in 1921. Success in producing this 'play of transfiguration' would have direct implications for all those around him, and – in some unknown way – for the future of the Work itself. But to succeed in producing this play he would have to destroy the existing forms of his own Work: the limiting *status quo* which inevitably develops in any group of people practicing the Work. For it is only through the destruction of form on a lower level that the Gods can open a glimpse of the cosmic vastness that lies beyond. Ouspensky saw that a few of his people were in a position to support him in this remarkable effort, and that the others, when the dust settled, would have to make of it what they could. The result for them, whatever it was to be, would be better than what would have happened otherwise. And in some unknown way this event would affect the future — for the effect of an act of transfiguration is not linear, it is vertical. It is a movement from the temporal to what is outside of time. A play of transfiguration may affect the past and the future at once, while appearing to have little effect on the present ... that is, the weeks and months immediately following the event. So it was with the transfiguration of Jesus Christ.

On his return to London Ouspensky opened up a *kairos* moment for those closest to him, just as Gurdjieff had opened a *kairos* moment for those closest to him at the first Essentuki workshop. Rodney Collin became Ouspensky's principal partner in this play, at first unknowingly, and then drawn into the very vortex of the maelstrom. Looking back, Collin saw how all

Ouspensky's actions culminated in a climax that no one but he could have anticipated.

With the allied victory in Europe, Ouspensky's plan became possible. In the summer of 1946 Ouspensky announced to the students at Mendham that he would be returning to England, and Madame Ouspensky would organize the Work in America in his absence.

The Final Months: 1947

Ouspensky sailed from New York on 19th January 1947 with a small entourage, including Aubrey Wolton, Basil Tilley, his secretary Miss Quinn, and his nurse Randi Romer.[1]

The group arrived at Southampton on 23rd January, and were driven immediately to Lyne Place, where Ouspensky – obviously very ill and in a wheelchair – was reunited with his London students. The atmosphere was one of restrained but intense emotion.

At Lyne Ouspensky was daily attended by Miss Quinn (from Mendham) and his physician Francis Roles (from London). The other residents would have included Madame Kadloubovsky and probably a few other English and Russian students. Rodney Collin was to remain in Mendham until mid-April.

Once settled at Lyne the apparently decrepit Ouspensky surprised his students by beginning to walk without the wheelchair, and then doing so for longer and longer periods of time. They found his efforts painful to watch, but he would not desist. Soon he was asking his attendants to help

---

1. Randi Romer joined Ouspensky's Work in London, and went with him from London to New York in 1941. Nick Roles writes of Miss Randi Romer "who spoke with a Danish accent. She dressed like a nurse and was always the height of efficiency." (See *The Bridge*, No. 12, Autumn 1997 (ed. Eadie, Peter McGregor), © The Study Society, Colet House, Talgarth Road, London, 1997, p. 114.) At Lyne she would help Ouspensky on the stairs and bring him his food. She was a member of the Historical Society and remained in London, with Francis Roles' group, long after Ouspensky's death. We have been unable to find the first or given name for Ouspensky's secretary Miss Quinn, and so, although she plays a central role, references to her remain formal.

him walk up and down stairs. Then, one day, Miss Quinn saw him out on the lawn, walking by himself. He was quite weak, taking one step after the next, and struggling to maintain his balance. Then he began to lose his balance. He stopped walking, steadied himself, and stood firm. He looked up. It was as though he was experiencing a great infusion of life ... and then he continued to walk much more normally. He had achieved a kind of breakthrough, an independence from the shrunken and pain-filled body and a certain mastery over it.

While Ouspensky made remarkable demands on himself, he was at the same time testing the people around him — determining their responsiveness, that he might create a circle of people capable of carrying through a great esoteric experiment. As notes made during that period record:

> Before leaving America, he had written to Lyne saying that he was coming to see certain people "whom he would choose." On the very day of his arrival he did in fact invite one or two people to come and sit with him or to dine. But curiously enough, after the first invitation, nearly all these people found themselves too busy to respond. Some had unavoidable duties on the farm or business in London, which they regarded as work—and so were never available when called for. Others came once, but finding that nothing was said or done, innerly felt it rather a waste of time. Unaccepted invitations were not repeated. In this way it happened that W. [Aubrey Wolton], Miss Q. [his secretary], Miss R. [Randi Romer], and later CS [Rodney Collin] became almost his only companions.[1]

To the list of close companions we can add, with hindsight, Francis Roles, Eve Pryor and — in a slightly lower profile — Eugenie Kadloubovsky.

---

1. Collin, Rodney, *Last Remembrances of a Magician,* unpublished work, circa. 1948. This is a composite work of rough notes taken by the people around Ouspensky in the last months of his life. There are several different versions of it, and each version was added to in different ways. Parts of it have been published online at different times. We have made our best attempt to assemble the pieces and to cross check references. In the remaining text we shall refer to these notes simply as *Last Remembrances.*

After about two weeks, on 6th February, Ouspensky summoned Francis Roles and Eugenie Kadloubovsky to his room, and asked them to gather three hundred people for a meeting in the large studio at Colet Gardens. The Yale Notes record the conversation thus:

'Collect 300 people.'
'How long have we got?'
'Say three weeks.'
'What shall we say to them?'
'Why say anything? Ask them what they want.'[2]

To gather the 300 people Kadloubovsky and Roles were obliged to ask each student to bring three acquaintances. These would be people unfamiliar with the Work. Additionally, everyone attending the meeting was asked not to use Work terms. Why, we may ask, did Ouspensky have his students invite non-students to these last climactic meetings? Perhaps because he intended to break the pattern established in the pre-war meetings. The students would see the mechanical reactions of the non-students to what was going on and become aware — in a different way — of these same reactions in themselves. They would thus be better able to distinguish the state the meeting was creating in them from their own mechanical reactions to the words spoken. The sometimes bizarre questions from the non-students, and the surprising replies from Ouspensky, would have the effect of paralyzing formatory mind. Certainly, the ambiguous situation would heighten the tension in the room, which would help anyone trying to connect with the depth of presence that Peter Ouspensky had achieved in the previous months. And perhaps some of the new people would begin to understand the real work.

Kadloubovsky and Roles succeeded in gathering the required number of people and a series of six meetings followed – with more than 300

---

2. Taylor, Merrily E., (compiler & editor), *Remembering Pyotr Demianovich Ouspensky,* Yale University Library, New Haven CT, 1978, p. 40.

people attending each. These meetings were to continue over a period of four months, between February 24th and June 18th.[1]

THE SIX MEETINGS

On 24th February Ouspensky appeared on the platform of the large studio room at Colet Gardens with Miss Quinn and Aubrey Wolton. Miss Quinn was used as a filter for the questions. If she could not understand them, they would not go to Ouspensky. Some of the questions were submitted in writing in advance, as was done before the war, and some came directly from the floor. Francis Roles, who was seated in the front row, was asked to read out the written questions. The effect of these meetings was momentous. Ouspensky's replies were abrupt, curt, and sometimes difficult to understand. Students were thrown back on themselves. People were repeatedly asked what it was they wanted. It became apparent that he was pressing people back to a new starting point.

There was certainly an element of destruction in this: the destruction of the fixed idea of the Work that had developed over a period of more than twenty years. But there was also encouragement. The answers were always *to the individual*. In other words, they addressed the state of the individual who had asked the question. They penetrated through to what is real in the person who asked the question. For this reason, answers to different people were sometimes contradictory. For the answer is whatever helps the student to move from the place they are in. For many there seemed no context for what was happening. There was no ground to stand on. At the fifth meeting Kenneth Walker sought clarification: "Do you mean, Ouspensky, that you have abandoned the System?" Ouspensky responded: "There is no System." An invisible boundary line had been crossed.

Speaking of his own experiences of the last three of these meetings Rodney Collin wrote:

---

1. The meetings occurred on February 24th, March 5th, March 12th, May 7th, May 21st, and June 18th. The transcripts of these are available in Ouspensky, P.D., *A Record of Meetings*, Arkana (Penguin Group), London, 1992. The material was assembled anonymously by Ouspensky's students and published in a limited edition by the Stourton Press in 1951.

It is impossible to convey the impression made by this question and answering. For he seemed to hold up a mirror to people in which their desires could be seen reflected, whether true or false. And as CS [Rodney Collin] sat listening, there suddenly came into his mind the exact formulation of his own aim that he had been groping for, for so long. For him this simple phrase was to act almost as a charm. From this moment on, everything began to fall into place for him, his life arranged itself, so that he later came to think that the true formulation of one's aim is in very fact the magic "sesame" by which a certain door can open.[2]

Rodney here draws attention to the invisible substance of the meetings, which was almost entirely independent of the written record of the words exchanged.

We provide a few excerpts from each of the meetings, to suggest something of their impact and something of the trajectory of the series. In trying to make sense of the material, we keep in mind that communication from the level of World 6 (the level Ouspensky is teaching from) is more an attempt to bypass rational mind than to connect with it. In these meetings Ouspensky is transmitting his state to those capable of responding to it, rather than trying to transmit information. Where one might expect a substantive reply, Ouspensky might simply say: "Continue in this way." "Very good." "We may see something from that." Or "Quite right." In these moments, the student has momentarily achieved the state, and Ouspensky is affirming the state itself rather than responding to the question. He is jumping a level. We note a progression in the six meetings. The first meetings contain a stronger element of negation: there are contradictory things stated, or remarks to which the student may not be able to attach meaning. They produce a state where the student — wanting to reconnect with his or her teacher — does not know what is going on. From the standpoint of a teacher stationed in World 6 the student then becomes accessible. As the group begins to center around its new point of reference, the meetings begin to bring affirmation. But the affirmation is again the affirmation of

---

2. Collin, Rodney, *Last Remembrances of a Magician,* unpublished work, circa. 1948.

a state, not the affirmation of information. By the final two meetings Ouspensky has broken his audience out of the paradigm of meaning that had been established before the war.

The meetings took place in the upper studio at Colet House.

First Meeting: 24th February 1947. This is the initial confrontation of the transformed Ouspensky with his old London students; answers often take the form of a direct negation.[1]

> Q. Do you wish us to continue with the programme you gave us in 1940?
> Mr.O. Programme? I don't know programme. Which programme?
> Mr. A.W. Programme which you gave in 1940.
> Mr. O. No, I don't remember.
> Q. We have been trying to follow out the teaching you gave us years ago.
> Mr. O. I have no teaching.
> Q. Where can we begin to work now?
> Mr. O. I will see what you want to know and where you want to begin, and then we will see first step, and perhaps we will find second step. We don't know first step, that is the question. That you must remember.

At the same time Ouspensky does open a door.

> Q. What is wrong with us?
> Mr. O. I didn't say that anything is wrong. May be quite right. But necessary to start, to begin.
> Mr. O. First question is what you want. Only on the basis of that, something can be done.

Second Meeting: 5th March 1947. Here we see a more formative interaction between teacher and student.

---

1. All of the material quoted from the six meetings below comes from Ouspensky, P.D., *A Record of Meetings*, Arkana (Penguin Group), London, 1992. See pp. 585-643.

Mr. R. You have given me glimpses that the world and I are quite different from all I have ever believed, and I feel I need your help to extend these glimpses.
Mr. O. What kind of glimpses?
Mr. R. Glimpses that the world is not as I had believed it.
Mr. O. Necessary to begin with that.

Mr. O. Aim. First of all, necessary to know your aim.

Mrs. J. Can one learn in one's own case?
Mr. O. Yes, certainly. Only in your own case.

Mr. O. [Closing remark, summing up] If we continue in that way we may find some method — not method — way — to come to certain conclusions, that we can speak about this, and not about that. Well, I may come another time.

Third Meeting: 12th March 1947. In the third meeting there are more examples of the affirmation of a state.

Mr. O. Only necessary to start alone [each person] and come to something. Six or seven years ago we came to definite conclusion. We tried to avoid all usual questions, and we had some kind of system that we talked about, and then we came to the conclusion system would not help. So that is how we began at that time, and I think we came to something now.

Mr. A.N. I want to live well and fully in the present.
Mr. O. Well, continue in the same way. If you ask this, it is interesting, and then there is material to begin with.

There is an apparent contradiction in next two responses.

Miss T. How can we understand better what you want from us?
Mr. O. Simple things.
Mr. V. Can you teach me to be more simple, less complicated?
Mr. O. I don't teach simple. It does not work.

The student must find simplicity within himself or herself, Ouspensky cannot find that for the student. But from another point of view that is what he is actually doing here.

At the end of the meeting Ouspensky rises to his feet and addresses the room.

> Mr. O. I hope to see you, if you want to see me.
> MANY VOICES. Please do come. We want you to come.

Rodney Collin returned from Mendham to London on or about 18th April, in time for the fourth meeting. He immediately observed that Ouspensky was different than he had been before his departure from Mendham. Rodney stated that he was "more than ever impressed by a certain indefinable but very definite power."[1] Ouspensky went through a health crisis on April 26-27th, just before the fourth meeting, taking him into the zone that is near to death. He recovered the following morning and immediately scheduled the meeting.

Fourth Meeting: 7th May 1947. In this meeting we see something beginning to come together. There is definite encouragement towards the end: "Begin in that way." "Quite right." "Go on." or "Perhaps we may come to something." When the students connect with Ouspensky's state, they enter a higher current of the Work. The frequent reference to "continue" refers to the continuance of the state Ouspensky has created in his students.

> Mr. J. I have knowledge of certain moments when I seem to understand a category of thought quite different from my normal thought, and I feel my difficulty is that I try to approach many things I really want from my ordinary thought.
> Mr. O. Well, that is the whole thing. Continue in the same way. Perhaps you can come somewhere.
>
> Mr. N. Have we to break something before we can begin?
> Mr. O. Better, certainly, if you can begin that way.

---

1. Collin, Rodney, *Last Remembrances of a Magician*, unpublished work, circa 1948.

> Mr. P. I believe that when I want something I only want it because I am selfish and possessive. I need an aim which is outside myself.
> Mr. O. Right. Very good.
>
> Mr. H. How can I make my will come into action as quickly as my desire?
> Mr. O. Very good. We may see something from that.
>
> Mr. O. (in response) Quite. You can begin in this way. Try something! Try.

That night Ouspensky returned to Lyne to rest. His colleagues, according to Rodney, "were struck by the fact that although physically exhausted, there was much more firmness, more keenness in his face, more external interest apparent than for months." Miss Quinn congratulated him on the meeting, "It was wonderful." He turned away with a gesture, half of impatience, half of recognition. "No, it was not wonderful," he said. Then gently: "Well, we may speak of it later." …[2] It was more than wonderful, it was an objective linking of different levels in the universe.

Fifth Meeting: 21st May 1947. Here Ouspensky speaks again about remembering and self-remembering. There is some assimilation of what had gone before.

> Mr. P. Can you give us more methods of remembering ourselves?
> Mr. O. I just begin to say "Quite right.", because it is necessary to start from "to remember."
>
> Dr. R. If one tries to remember one finds that certain things stop it. One just thinks about it instead of doing it.
> Mr. O. Quite right. One remembers if one tries to make oneself remember.
>
> Miss Q. The important thing is, why does one forget, why does one not remember?
> Mr. O. You begin quite well, but please, there is no continuation.

---

2. *Ibid.*

Mr. B Are our questions too personal?
Mr. O. Cannot be too personal. You came here because you want to ask something. You must ask something that means something to you. When I was told about things that have no meaning for me, I could not answer them [in the earlier meetings], so now they brought certain examples of memory, and I say I will take that.

Mr. O. We tried several times [in the previous meetings], and on the whole we can say that it becomes a little better; we have more material each week.

Mr. C. Why do we say "remember ourselves"? Surely it is other things ...
Mr. O. I have such a strange idea of calling it that. Maybe whoever doesn't like won't follow, or maybe who follows must understand what I mean by that.

Mrs. V. How can I learn to remember myself?
Mr. O. Find what is missing. Maybe it will be sufficient.
Mrs. C. Is it good to try to recapture what goes with a better state?
Mr. O. Probably. This is what I have said last time — that if you try to recover — how I said this? — try to remember, it may help.

Sixth Meeting: 18th June 1947. In the final meeting there is clarification, and the trace of a synthesis. There are some moments of actual empowerment, referring not just to the state, but to the student's work to sustain the state.

Mr. D. Do I understand rightly that the rules do not exist anymore?
Mr. O. I don't know what means rules. In any case all that could be called rules never could exist for a long time. Question is what you want.

Miss Q. People don't seem to know how to approach this matter of remembering which is so apart from their usual way of living.
Mr. O. We have to begin. If it is more difficult to begin, how can it be easier.

Mr. O. Each one must find chief thing for himself — why one cannot remember.

Miss Q. Would you say it is necessary, Mr. O., to know what it is one wants to remember more than anything else?
Mr. O. Yes. *Why* want, *what* wants, and so on.

Mr. O. Words mean nothing at all. We can replace one kind of words with another, and so on. You must find what you want and so not forget it.

Miss R. I want to learn to be more present. Now I realize that I am not present nearly all day.
Mr. O. Well try and avoid all sorts of difficulties. Go on. Perhaps we may come to something.

Mr. N. Even in complete solitude when trying to remember, after a short time my mind wanders. Are there any physical aims that will keep my mind on what I want and what I am trying to remember?
Mr. O. Yes, it is necessary to insist, to do something definite.

Mrs. S. I have often thought that many years of preparation were necessary in order to come to some understanding... Have you the right to demand what you want?
Mr. O. One has right to everything. One does not spend time wondering about has one the right or not. One has right to everything.

Mr. C. Have we to realize that we are powerless before we can begin at all?
Mr. O. Who is?

Miss. R. I have tried on several things, and I find that very helpful, but it is difficult to set oneself a task.
Mr. O. Yes. Try to observe. Try this way, that way — variation. There are many things that you want [to make use of]. Necessary to try one, another, and so on. Pass from one to another. Sometimes you don't know, sometimes you know more definitely what you want.

We come to the last lines of the sixth meeting.

Mr. O. Necessary to be able to say clearly what you want — what direction. Try to remember it — this moment — that moment.

Mr. A. It changes because that moment is reliable; one feels quite different; false things stop for the moment. I can discriminate between the opposite times, but at that time I cannot get further.

Mr. O. Well, you may continue. Sometimes it needs a longer time. We can go, and then if you can find something I may come again. I may still. I still may have some time.

Mr. P. What is it that one must try to remember?

Mr. O. You can try. Anybody can try to remember.

Mr. A. You asked us to formulate our wishes. I want to notice things, more things which are beautiful and interesting. Other people do, and point them out to me, but I cannot do it myself. How can I learn to do it myself?

Mr. O. Well, if you can. Time. Occasions. Patience.

And so the cycle ends. At the final meeting Ouspensky emphasized that everyone must begin from what he or she really wants. Honour Hammond provides us with a summary of her experience of the six meetings:

> Those of us who were fortunate enough to be able to attend the last meetings of Ouspensky in 1947 will probably remember some things with particular vividness. We were all asked to bring three new people, and we were told not to use system language. When Ouspensky arrived on the platform, it was evident that he did not have long to live. At the same time, his presence was enormous. Impossible to forget how he looked at us. It seemed clear he knew us all, and his look contained many emotions all at once. There was this knowledge of us, compassion, and something which could be called scorn. Other things I would not try to find words for. None of this was personal. It was something much larger.[1]

---

1. Hammond, Honour, *Memories of P.D. Ouspensky*, from the periodical *The Bridge*, No. 12, Autumn 1997 (ed. Eadie, Peter McGregor), © The Study Society, Colet House, Talgarth Road, London, 1997, p. 128.

This impersonality, combined with penetrating insight, is an indication of World 6. The "scorn" is not in Ouspensky; it is how a cellular being may feel in the presence of World 6. Honour said the meetings were "impossible to forget." The series of meetings permanently marked her life, creating a window to another world. The winnowing of the London students that had preceded the meetings resulted in a circle of people capable of responding to the last phase of Ouspensky's teaching: a circle of people like the well-named Honour. She took away one particular gem from the meetings:

> I remember him saying in a very definite voice, "I never expected to find school, but I found school."[2]

This discovery summed up the last quarter century of Ouspensky's life — the search for the Source of the System. James Webb reports a similar observation by another student:

> To the pupil who had organized the restoration of Colet House, it appeared that sometimes Ouspensky could overcome his physical disabilities and make contact with a deeper and more powerful sort of knowledge than ever before.[3]

LIFE AT LYNE DURING THE SIX MEETINGS

Throughout the course of the meetings Ouspenksy continued his daily routine at Lyne with Miss Quinn, Randi Romer, Eve Pryor, Aubrey Wolton, and — after April of 1947 — Rodney Collin.[4] Francis Roles saw him daily, as his doctor, and Eugenie Kadloubovsky and several others were also part of the pattern. It was quiet, but with a quietness that contained great freedom and light. Rodney Collin noted that they would ...

> ... sit over lunch or supper at the long refectory table in the paneled dining-room, its French windows looking out across the lawn to the ravine and the cedar-tree. It was spring, and the whole scene

---

2. *Ibid.*
3. Webb, James, *The Harmonious Circle*, Shambhala, Boston, 1987, p. 451.
4. Lonya Savitsky returned with Rodney Collin, and was involved peripherally until June 4th when — after the 5th meeting — he returned to Mendham.

PETER OUSPENSKY

seemed bathed in a mildness and beneficence which was very striking after the harshness of America.[1]

For many hours at a stretch they became used to sitting in the Green Drawing Room with him, saying nothing, doing nothing. One's eyes fell with pleasure on the bright spots of Persian and Indian miniatures against the restful green and gold walls, or on the chestnut-tree beyond the window, on which day by day buds gave way to flowers, and these to clusters of nuts. Nothing else was apparent. And yet in some way one's whole attitude of life changed at such times, all impatience vanished, and one became content to exist definitely in the present. This, it later became clear, was a very definite preparation.[2]

As we noted Ouspensky experienced periodic health crises during this period. These might leave him unable to move for a day or two. But as soon as movement became possible, he began to make his body do the things he normally did, such as getting dressed or climbing stairs. To the observer it seemed that he was asking the weakened husk of a body to do the impossible, yet, at the same time he would make light of the matter. He would take the edge off the situation by making casual remarks and observations. There was a great intensity of Work with no trace of morbidity.

An interesting episode occurred before the final meeting in June. Ouspensky became aware that a man who had been a close childhood friend (referred to as 'F') was presently in Paris. The two men had had a second contact in Constantinople in 1920, and it may have been that the man was briefly a part of Ouspensky's expatriate Russian group. However it occurred, once the contact was made Ouspensky invited the man to Lyne. He accepted, arriving on the 11th of May. He was, according to Rodney Collin, "a quiet man with the sensitiveness of one who had lived in many countries and conditions, adapted well and was able to talk easily to him." In some inexplicable way the entire relation between the two men was related to

---

1. Collin, Rodney, *Last Remembrances of a Magician,* unpublished work, circa. 1948.
2. *Ibid.*

Figure 45. Lyne Place Today.

Ouspensky's study of recurrence, and the creation of memory within the time body. 'F' was able to attend the final meeting of the series of six, and following it ... "He kept repeating that never in any church or law court had he experienced anything like it." Rodney Collin adds ...

> That night [after the last meeting] when supper was over, O. drew himself up very strongly and looked F. absolutely straight in the eyes for a few seconds as he shook hands in farewell. F. took both his hands very warmly and said, with real emotion: "Goodbye, my old friend." The next morning he left for Paris.[3]

AFTER THE MEETINGS

After the final sixth meeting Ouspensky retired to Lyne for the rest of the summer. He was now attended by eight people that we know of: from the original London group Eve Pryor, Eugenie Kadloubovsky, and Francis Roles; from the Mendham group Miss Quinn, Randi Romer, Aubrey Wolton, and Rodney Collin. There was a total of about fifteen residents at Lyne, who were all to be involved — in varying degrees — with the drama of transfiguration that was about to take place. And there were Vashka and

---

3. *Ibid.*

Josch, Ouspensky's two enormous Siberian Cats, who had become a definite part of the picture.

In the immediate aftermath of the six meetings Ouspensky hardly spoke, and the atmosphere was strangely charged. But the initial awkwardness soon passed. Ouspensky remained in his room for much of the time; on fine days he might sit on the lawn under the cedar trees, and on wet days spend time in the Green Drawing Room. And then he slowly began a kind of wordless teaching, which could only occur in an environment of total receptivity. Rodney Collin describes:

> He hardly spoke at all even to the people who were eating and sitting with him. Yet one had the sense that everything that was done was a kind of demonstration, and gradually an atmosphere developed which can hardly be described. Looking back, this seems the happiest and most vivid period of my life. He showed the few who were with him, without explanation, what it means for a man to pass consciously into the realm of the spirit.[1]

> I noticed one day that Ouspensky was showing us an exercise ... But he did the exercise without words or explanations; it was almost invisible. ... One sits comfortably in a chair. Then for a definite time — say half an hour — one moves, slightly and naturally. *But without stopping for a single moment.* For example, one puts out one's right hand to take a cigarette, one lights it, crosses one's legs, rubs one's cheek, turns one's head, knocks the ash off the cigarette into the ashtray etc. etc. *But all in slow and continuous movement.* After half an hour of this one begins to realize the true nature of movement. And at the end, for a short time, one has the possibility of remaining completely still, without any movement at all. From this immobility further realizations can come.[2]

James Webb interviewed a student who, some thirty years later, remembered sitting with Ouspensky in the Green Drawing Room when a powerful

---

1. Collin, Rodney, *The Theory of Conscious Harmony,* Watkins, London, 1976, p. 179-180
2. *Ibid.,* p. 68.

presence suddenly impinged upon the group. No one spoke. Ouspensky said: "You notice?"[3] Rodney Collin records a similar impression:

> Among the many extraordinary impressions at the time of Ouspensky's death there was — particularly at one period — the immensely strong feeling of some great power or being, some Christ-like being, as far above Ouspensky as Ouspensky was above us, presiding over all that was being done.[4]

Returning to the themes of the six meetings someone made a comment about "abandoning" the system. Ouspensky replied, enigmatically, "Yes, I said abandon, not destroy." The following exchange touches the same area:

> Q: What should we do when you are no longer with us?
> Mr. O.: Dismantle the system.
> Q: What, to destroy everything?
> A: No, not destroy, dismantle. Keep the form, but let a dozen people from within the organization reconstruct everything.[5]

The issue was raised again when a student asked "how they could live without the ideas and ideals they had come to rely on to guide them through life?" Ouspensky replied simply, "The System is greater than any man."[6]

Here Ouspensky replies by shifting scale: he is not referring to the system that is presented in *The Psychology of Man's Possible Evolution*; he is speaking about a certain understanding of the laws that govern human evolution in any age. He is speaking about the structure of the universe itself and the place of man in it. To integrate truth on this scale you must have and remember experiences of Higher Centers — and make that level of yourself a permanent point of departure. Then you can 'own' the system

---

3. Webb, James, *The Harmonious Circle*, Shambhala, Boston, 1987, p. 454.
4. Collin, Rodney, *The Theory of Conscious Harmony*, Watkins, London, 1976, p. 152.
5. Collin, Rodney, *Last Remembrances of a Magician*, unpublished work, circa. 1948.
6. Hunter, Bob, *Don't Forget: P.D. Ouspensky's Life of Self-remembering*, Bardic Press, California, 2006, p. 196.

and use it consciously. This was the 'new beginning' that Ouspensky was trying to create for his students.

The little group at Lyne had entered a world under different laws: they had come onto the line of their fate. The pattern of life they had shared through the period of the six meetings changed:

> ... a curious change began to come over the pattern of their lives. O. seemed to find it difficult to sleep long, and after two or three hours rest would wake again about 9 or 10PM, take breakfast, coffee, rise, and begin another day. This would mean that Miss R. must serve "lunch" sometime after midnight, after which they might sit together for an hour or two, and then go back to bed again. Next day O. might wake at 10AM, there would be a second lunch at 2PM, supper at 6:30PM, he would retire once more, and so on. In this way, two complete days became compressed into 24 hours.
>
> As always when O. began a new experiment, they were at first deceived into thinking him at fault, and would naively demonstrate that it was night outside the still-closed shutters. At this he would laugh and say, "I don't believe it." Afterwards it seemed extraordinary to them that they could ever have imagined one whose instinctive time-sense was so preternaturally acute to be so mistaken. But this was a definite aspect of his experiments: their very originality ensured that they should always be taken as his foolishness.[1]

All fixed patterns began to dissolve. After one of the midnight lunches Miss Romer and Miss Quinn dozed off. Rodney Collin recalled how he, for some reason, remained alert, and ...

> ... was filled with a strange awareness, sitting there, the whole house asleep in the curious pause of the small hours, facing O. for hour after hour, the two of them quite silent and quite still. O.'s eyes were shut, asleep or apparently asleep; suddenly they would open, shoot a piercing glance which took in the whole room, and as quickly close again. Awareness mounted and mounted in the silence, and

---

1. Collin, Rodney, *Last Remembrances of a Magician*, unpublished work, circa. 1948.

then suddenly gave out, drowsiness falling till the dawn whitened the cracks in the shutters, hours later.

It was strange, too, falling completely out of step with ordinary life: and curious when early or later ceased to have meaning, because there was nothing to measure by. Was a meal late lunch or early supper, and were they late retiring on Friday or early to bed on Saturday? All such ideas, and in fact all ordinary ways of looking at the routine of life and passage of time were revealed as simply habits of thought. If a man were strong enough to create circumstances which broke such habits, quite new points of view became possible. Like everything else that summer, it was preparation. But for what?[2]

Under these circumstances an extraordinary sensitivity began to develop amongst the circle close to Ouspensky:

> O. would say little or nothing, but from time to time point to the cats, as though directing attention specially to them. Sometimes he might ask for something, or wish a dish set aside or a pie placed by his soup. But with such economy of words that 'Go,' 'Take,' and 'Put' seemed to cover almost all eventualities. If something were not required, the rest had learnt to remain still, both outwardly and innerly curbing any impulse to move, suggest or interfere—until the solution showed itself.[3]

And eventually those close to Ouspensky began to understand the things he wished or intended without being told. They began to see his single words and gestures as filled with meaning. Everything seemed to point towards some impending denouement, where the different threads of meaning would be drawn together and explained. But — from another point of view — responding to words and gestures put each person on their own. You never knew if your neighbor understood the same thing that you did. Everything had an immense possible range of meaning, which no one interpretation could exploit. Thus, while one became aware of the immediate

---

2. *Ibid.*
3. *Ibid.*

possibility of higher things, one also became aware of the quite definite limitations of embodiment.

TURNING POINT AT SOUTHAMPTON

The pace was accelerating, but the drama had not yet reached its climax. In mid-July Ouspensky suddenly announced that he was returning to America. The circle of people he was working with were asked to make all the necessary preparations, and passages were booked on a ship leaving from Southampton on September 4th. Aubrey Wolton was assigned to coordinate packing, arrange shipboard facilities, and anticipate all the difficulties that might arise along the way. In one way or another everyone at Lyne became focused on Ouspensky's departure, while everyone at Mendham was focused on his arrival. The whole future of the Work seemed centered on this proposed move.

In the early morning of September 4th Randi Romer brought all the baggage for Ouspensky's party down to the customs station at Southampton and had it processed through by midday. The group itself arrived at 3:30PM, and it was arranged — through the ship's medical officer — that the car carrying Ouspensky should drive straight to the foot of the gangway. "From everything that happened at this time the impression arose that nothing could go wrong, that some special influence was at work to enable all material arrangements to be fulfilled with unusual and almost incredible ease."[1]

When Ouspensky finally arrived at the dock, just a few hours before the boat was due to sail, he said quietly, "I am not going to America this time."

It was like the 'stop' exercise on the scale of the whole Work. A stop was made in many lives, everyone's personal plans were turned upside down, and a space made in the momentum of time where something quite new could be done.[2]

---

1. *Ibid.*

2. Collin, Rodney, *The Theory of Conscious Harmony,* Watkins, London, 1976, p. 179-180.

Ouspensky then came up to each person individually and said, "I cannot go in these conditions." The reservations and special accommodations were cancelled, the luggage removed from the customs, the explanations made to officials, and the residents at Lyne and Mendham alerted. Some of the students, who had already made arrangements for new jobs in New York, went to America anyway. As Ouspensky's Daimler left the dock at Southampton to make the sixty-mile journey back to Lyne, he leaned forward from the back seat and said, so that all four people in the car could hear, "You know I never intended to go to America—not for a minute." The stage was now set for the final act of the play.

THE FINAL MONTH: 4 SEPTEMBER TO 2 OCTOBER

At some point after the series of six meetings Ouspensky had asked the people around him to record their experiences. These records, made principally by Rodney Collin and Francis Roles, were cross-checked with the records of Randi Romer, Eve Pryor, and Miss Quinn. They were then consolidated and put into a pamphlet. This document did not get beyond the rough draft state — far from the standard of Rodney Collins' published writings. For example, in the text, there are multiple authors each writing in the third person. As a result there are points at which it is impossible to know what is going on. The document itself was titled *Last Remembrances of a Magician*. Rodney Collin and Francis Roles each kept their own version, and each made later additions as they remembered other bits and pieces. Thus, several versions of *Last Remembrances* exist, and — not surprisingly — some of the material is contradictory. The people involved were under extraordinary pressure, with a 'double day' schedule that was subject to change at any moment. They occasionally worked right through a night into the following day. As a result, there is some confusion about whether Ouspensky's presentation of the plan for the reconstruction of the system was given in one or two sessions, whether it occurred in the car or in the house, and on what day(s) it occurred. We have done the best we can to make sense of these records and to present a sequence of events that has no contradictions. We have a parallel record of part of this period from a letter Francis Roles wrote to Madame Ouspensky on the 18th of September, summing

Ouspensky's plan for the reconstruction of the system. Excerpts from this letter are included in the narrative below. A much more complete assimilation of these experiences appears in different places throughout Rodney Collin's published works: *The Theory of Eternal Life, The Theory of Celestial Influence,* and the posthumous collection of his letters *The Theory of Conscious Harmony.*

In the last month of his life Peter Ouspensky was directly preparing his people for the climax that was to occur immediately after his death on October 2nd. On his return to Lyne, Ouspensky began a series of the most extraordinary day trips. As Rodney Collin describes it:

> ... in the last month of all, when his death was clearly a matter of days, his weakness extreme, and the severest pain continuous, this man began to undertake without any explanation a series of feats of endurance quite inexplicable from any ordinary point of view. Medically prescribed complete rest, he required to be driven day after day for long excursions across the country to all those houses in which he had lived during his years in England. On these excursions he neither ate nor drank, and on his return would often remain all night sitting in the car in the darkness and cold.[1]

Ouspensky would travel, in the company of two or three students, to different parts of England where he had lived, or which he had visited frequently. Destinations included Ralph Philipson's villa on Encombe Road, the house at West Wickham, the house at Wendover, the cottage the Ouspensky's had rented at Dymchurch, the Dell at Sevenoaks, the house at Gaddesden, and Maurice Nicoll's cottage at Sidlesham. These were round trips of between eighty and one hundred and forty miles, made on the rough roads that existed in postwar England. Rodney Collin would drive, there might be one or two passengers, and Ouspensky would bring his two enormous Siberian

---

1. Collin, Rodney, *The Theory of Eternal Life,* Watkins, London, 1974, p. 101.

cats — which had become the strange double-image of the Magician's cat in *Ivan Osokin*.

These trips have been represented as an attempt by Ouspensky to escape recurrence, by introducing memory into moments where memory had not originally been created. Yes, the group did always visit places that Ouspensky had known, but he often showed no interest in the place itself, and on arrival made the most extraordinary physical efforts without any apparent reference to his immediate surroundings. Whatever interest in recurrence Ouspensky may have had, the trips were used principally to impact the group in such a way as to enable the drama of transfiguration that was to follow. Additionally, these destinations were places known to both the driver and the passengers, so they could simply drive without having to guess which way to go, which was a great advantage in the situation they were in.

This last phase of the Work began immediately with the group's return from the dock at Southampton. When they arrived at Lyne Ouspensky refused to get out of the car. Eventually he got out with Miss R., climbed up to the hall, took off his hat and coat and then very deliberately walked back to the car again and got in. "This is not the right Lyne," he said, "let's go and find another." The group was nonplussed. After a time he said, very pleasantly, to Rodney Collin, "Well what is the matter?" Collin replied that he couldn't think of anywhere better to go at the moment. Ouspensky simply said, "Let's go anyway." They went to Chertsey and returned after twenty minutes.[2]

The day trips would often continue late into the night, and when the group arrived at Lyne in the small hours of the morning Ouspensky might extend the effort with a silent vigil until dawn. The Daimler would remain in the parking lot and Ouspensky would sit in the back seat with one Siberian cat on each knee: the three sphinx-like figures staring silently into the night. Rodney would remain motionless at the driver's seat. The other passengers might or might not return to the house. Thus, the shrunken husk of a man, in the last months of his life, generated a line of effort that exhausted

---

2. Collin, Rodney, *Last Remembrances of a Magician,* unpublished work, circa 1948.

the young and healthy people around him. Ouspensky was remembering himself *all the time.*

The circle around Ouspensky entered a 'white heat' of work: minutes might seem like hours and hours might seem like weeks. The effects of the law of accident were diminished and the law of fate came more directly into play. Ouspensky's circle had re-entered the alternate time that Ouspensky himself had known in Essentuki in 1918 — with its great compression of meaning and significance. They came into contact with the dimension of "all possibilities."

Ouspensky now began to communicate to his students internally, without word or gesture, just as — thirty years before — Gurdjieff had communicated to Ouspensky at Madame Maximovitch's dacha in Finland. He made telepathic suggestions to help his students realize their roles in the play of transfiguration that was unfolding around them. One of the students, struggling to separate the telepathic communications from her own imagination, asked Ouspensky to speak aloud. He did as she asked. Ouspensky signaled Rodney Collin to *stay at his side,* so that the younger man's physical presence would remind him of what might be expected of a young and healthy body. He signaled one of the women at Lyne to meet his retinue on their late return from the day trips. And so, as Ouspensky and his companions pulled up the driveway, they would find a light on in one of the windows above, revealing the silhouette of a woman, motionless, with an open hand raised.

Wordless suggestions came which might touch the hearer deeply. There might be an invitation to realize a very special possibility; there might equally be a temptation connected to the secret desires of chief feature. In enacting these suggestions, one might be exposed as a fool or one might realize some hidden potential in one's nature. In either case one could only find the true course by connecting to a deeper level of awareness. Everything seemed possible, and, at the same time, nothing was certain. The world became plastic, molten, responsive, and alive:

> One felt the happenings of another world very immediately, not as we usually suppose far away, but as *very close,* pervading us and

everything, *creating something new*. In some way, Ouspensky forced the door between this world and another at that time.[1]

Higher School had Lyne Place in its grip, and Ouspensky pressed his students to respond:

Move, move, you must move from the place where you are.[2]

This phase came to a first of climax on the days of September 16, 17, 18. The people involved were Francis Roles, Rodney Collin, Randi Romer, and Eve Pryor.

After a lengthy day trip, the group arrived back late to the mansion at Lyne. The car pulled into the driveway in the small hours of September 16th. But Ouspensky did not get out, and so neither did anyone else. He and the other passengers spent the whole night and all of the following morning sitting in the car. Finally, towards midday, Ouspensky decided to enter the house for lunch — but even then he would not rest, having Miss Romer help him to repeatedly climb up and down the stairs that led to his bedroom. He did not do this in a negative way, but with a simple certainty which conveyed an extraordinary impression of will. Finally, on the evening of September 16th, he rested. But on the morning of the 17th he was up early again and ready to go. They must all "drive somewhere." At 8:30AM the group set out in a hired car for Dymchurch on the southeast coast, a distance of almost one hundred miles. And from 8:30AM to 8:00PM Ouspensky never gave them a moment's rest.

He would have them stop at different points along the road, get out of the car, and walk with him up and down the road. Then they would all return to the car and get in, except Ouspensky. He would shut the car doors and totter off down the road. When everyone started to get back out of the car to help him, he would shout at them. This created a rising tension and ambiguous feelings. As the process repeated itself it became torture. The group finally returned to Lyne at 8PM. The car stopped, and there everyone

---

1. Collin, Rodney, *The Theory of Conscious Harmony,* Watkins, London, 1976, p. 181.
2. *Ibid.,* p. 78.

sat. There had been no pause, and no break for a meal, for twelve hours. People were hoping that Ouspensky would take dinner and rest. But when this was suggested, he "laughed at them and appeared very cheerful and continued to sit where he was."[1] He was not being cynical, he was in high spirits, as though he didn't have a thought on his mind. And so they all sat in the car, one hour after the next, stiff and cold, reaching the very depths of indignation. As midnight approached things gradually began to change. It was as though the future and the past dissolved, and they were all just sitting there. At about two in the morning Ouspensky broke the silence. He explained that he had put them through all of this so that they might understand his plan for the continuation of the Work. Something had to die in them before something new could enter. He affirmed that it was possible to come to Real I. He explained to them that they already knew it sometimes, and that the whole point was to prolong it by demanding that of themselves. "I will show you how."[2]

Then he began to outline his plan for the Work:

> I had to move you from where you were. Now I can speak. Begin with a few people ...People only must know to some extent what they want and must have courage. Courage to experiment. Get material from people. From this material, real facts, real questions, we begin to reconstruct ... Something *changed for you*. You have got something ... System as I learnt it was Gurdjieff's. But what you can understand in your own experience is yours. No one can take it from you. From this you can reconstruct.[3]

This is certainly not a detailed project plan, and we have no hope of understanding the mass of it, outside of the special circumstances in which it was given. But these records do make clear what Ouspensky's intention

---

1. Collin, Rodney, *Last Remembrances of a Magician,* unpublished work, circa 1948.
2. This episode has been adapted from the letter Francis Roles wrote to Madame Ouspensky, which is quoted in full by Beckwith, Gerald de Symons, *Ouspensky's Fourth Way,* Starnine Media & Publishing Ltd., Oxford, 2015, p. 50.
3. Collin, Rodney, *Last Remembrances of a Magician,* unpublished work, circa 1948.

was through the period of the six meetings. It was to move people towards a new beginning. And this moment, in which he announces the reconstruction, was just the beginning of the beginning. He was later to give them more, but in quite a different way.

He later gave a further practical guideline to Francis Roles: "You must go and find a method by which you can remember yourself at will. If you find that method, you may find the source."[4] In speaking of the source Ouspensky is not referring to an organization or esoteric school, but to the source of the system itself: to things that pertain directly to higher levels of consciousness. We note that he made this remark to Francis Roles and not to Rodney Collin. Perhaps he sensed that, after his passing, Francis would be reliant on methods, while Rodney was developing something within himself that transcended method — in which case he would adapt the method of his choice to the people he was teaching.

Rodney Collin has left us with some general comments, summing up his understanding of the period through to September 27th:

> So Ouspensky aroused vexation in those with him — in one from compassion with his suffering, in another that the carefully prepared supper should spoil, in a third from physical impatience at the enforced immobility. It was at this time that he seemed to begin to do all he could to be 'unreasonable,' striving in every way to make his companions vexed with him and set them against him. For this was a test of them, and to bring them to a state where they could give up every impulse of self will, and accept all. Only when one observed, it was seen that every 'unreasonableness' and every test was at the cost of his own suffering. But this he completely hid. As through all the rest of those weeks, so great was his self-control that one could be close by him yet under the impression that he was quite at ease. Only by a definite effort of imagination and sympathy could one come to realise what he must, for purely physical reasons,

---

4. *The Bridge*, Number 12, P.D. Ouspensky Commemorative Issue, The Study Society, London, 1997. p. 230.

be suffering. And when one did, one had to accept this also, and not rebel against it.[1]

When almost unable to set one foot before the other he would make his dying body walk step by step for an hour at a time through the rough lanes; force it to rise in the small hours, dress, descend and climb long nights of stairs; turn night into day; and require of his companions, in order to remain with him, such feats of endurance as they in full possession of health and strength were scarcely able to accomplish.[2]

Somewhere in the course of this extraordinary regimen, Ouspensky turned to Collin and said:

Now do you understand that everything has to be done by effort or do you still think that things come right by themselves?[3]

At one point near the end he said simply, "More aim, more effort." Ouspensky is not speaking here of making more and more efforts along the line of time, or of increasing the intensity and frequency of a certain kind of effort. He is speaking of another *kind* of effort, connected to another *kind* of aim. It is an effort coming from a different part of yourself, expressing the life of that part. Collin recalled that, in a critical moment of the last days, Ouspensky said, "People must not be afraid to take second step."[4] Collin understood the second step as graduating from a series of efforts to self-remember to permanent attention: remembering all the time. The Self knowing its Self.

Each of the people who recorded their reminiscences in *Last Remembrances* felt that Ouspensky had brought out the chief weakness of his or her personality in an inescapable way: brought it so directly into their view

---

1. Collin, Rodney, *Last Remembrances of a Magician,* unpublished work, circa 1948.
2. Collin, Rodney, *The Theory of Eternal Life,* Watkins, London 1974 p. 101.
3. Collin, Rodney, *The Theory of Conscious Harmony,* Watkins, London, 1976, p. 6.
4. *Ibid.,* p. 181.

that they were able to see that they themselves were *not it*. It existed outside of what they really were. And, at the same time, they found themselves on the other side of any kind of negativity. He made it clear that this very weakness was also the individual's opportunity, his or her way of understanding. We could call it their innate tendency. In the service of false personality, it is a negative force; in the service of the latent Self, it is the student's way forward.

LAST WORDS

Suddenly, on 27th September, all the expeditions, teachings, and demonstrations stopped, and Ouspensky retired to his room. In the early morning of October 1st the front door bell at Lyne rang repeatedly. The person ringing the bell was actually holding it down for periods of time. The residents came quickly down, one after another, to find Peter Ouspensky, fully dressed in suit and tie. He had put on his clothes and come down the stairs without assistance. He was not wearing his glasses, yet he could apparently see perfectly. As each person approached him, he met their gaze. There was a benevolence radiating from him that created a bond with each person and with the group as a whole. They all moved to the Green Drawing Room and sat there for some period. A few words were exchanged. The bond between them continued to concentrate and deepen. Ouspensky then spoke briefly to each person, and in so doing "he was able to communicate many ideas in such a way that each perceived in them the solution to their own problem."[5] They had the sense of being together in a presence that transcended individual identity. After having spoken to each person Ouspensky paused, looked at them all, and said, "Now you must reconstruct everything, from the very beginning."[6] A long silence followed, that was eventually broken by Ouspensky's words …. "How beautiful … all people together. Tomorrow different, different …"[7] He was then carried upstairs,

---

5. Collin, Rodney, *The Theory of Eternal Life,* Watkins, London, 1974, pp. 101-102.
6. Collin, Rodney, *The Theory of Conscious Harmony,* Watkins, London 1976, p. 180.
7. Collin, Rodney, *Last Remembrances of a Magician,* unpublished work, circa 1948.

and put to bed. He fell asleep promptly and at seven the next morning drew his last breath. Yes, tomorrow was to be "different, different ... " as different as finding himself incorporated into the living body of Higher School.

In the afternoon of 2nd October Ouspensky's students took his body out of his room and prepared it for burial at Holy Trinity Church in Lyne.

CRESCENDO

The completion of the drama described above occurred after Ouspensky's heart had stopped beating. Having died in his cellular body he became manifest, simultaneously, in several different physical locations, communicating openly with his students. In some cases, he did this in what appeared to be his physical body, with the tactile sense of his actual presence. This is the deed of a Master; it is what Jesus accomplished in his appearances to the apostles after the crucifixion. The apostles felt his physical presence. The record we have of this miracle is from Rodney Collin:

> Of my own teacher I can only say that he also produced among his friends a play, of which they unwittingly but perfectly played their parts, and whose plot was his own death. ... Lying in bed in Surrey, he possessed with his own mind a young man flying over the Atlantic, whom he had already rid of an illusion. That morning dead, he walked with a traveler - crossing London Bridge; and to another at the wheel of a car showed the nature of the universe.[1]

These manifestations were outside of time as we know it, in a direct connection to higher worlds. Just as the eight months since Ouspensky's arrival at Southampton compressed the previous twenty-four years of his Work, so these last hours compressed the eight months of intensified Work at Lyne. And they constitute a *kairos* moment in the history of the Fourth Way. Looking back, we can see the anticipations of this great compression, but we cannot see its reverberations looking forward. They are nevertheless there. A great transfiguration of this kind resonates deep into the collective life of humanity, changing possibilities in both the past and the future.

---

1. Collin, Rodney, *The Theory of Eternal Life,* Watkins, London 1974, p. 116.

Figure 46. Oupensky's gravestone,
Holy Trinity churchyard, Lyne.

In relation to the vision of school that had possessed Ouspensky in 1916-1917, his Work fell short in many ways, yet in the end he succeeded with his highest aim: reconnecting with the source of the system.

Ouspensky's Work

When considering Ouspensky's approach to the Fourth Way, we keep in mind that in the first decades of the twentieth century the teaching of the Fourth Way developed in relation to stories of high adventure, spectacular experiments in consciousness, and emphasis on the dire consequences of failure. The 'dire consequences' were particularly brought out by the confrontational style Gurdjieff sometimes adopted. Objectively the work does open up great possibilities, and failure can have dire consequences. But the problem of placing a strong emphasis on the extraordinary possibilities and the dire consequences is that, over time, the machine will take these things *on its own terms*. In other words, it will attach to them its own hopes, fears, and ambitions. There is, then, ambition related to awakening and fear in relation to failure. All of this is quite mechanical, and a denying force to awakening itself. As the Work took form in the Western European countries, these tendencies needed to be addressed. In addressing them Peter Ouspensky relied on three understandings:

1. Spiritual development includes visions and higher states of consciousness, but *it is the machine* that takes these to be of earthshaking importance, and things that other people should hear about.
2. Spiritual development includes seeing difficult things about yourself, but *it is the machine* that indulges in extremes of self-deprecation, remorse, and despair. This is simply the other side of self-importance.
3. The point is to keep making the efforts you are already making, without expectation and without identifying with making them.

Ouspensky's aim was to make the Work practical. He emphasized that all that was needed was readily available. The desire for the exotic and the spectacular was romantic imagination, and this kind of imagination weakens the will to master the basic tools of the Work. Ouspensky produced a template of the basic tools in *The Psychology of Man's Possible Evolution*. Given this bundle of tools, what is needed is *focus* on the part of the student, *guidance* on the part of the teacher, and enough *pressure* to bring out the best in both parties.

Ouspensky understood that a student must have a foundation in the Work based on a clear understanding of the difference between consciousness and functions. In the twenty-five years before the turning point of April 1945, he did everything he could to create that foundation in his students. He tried to make them competent in threading back through triumph and despair, to the eternal Now.

Because the moment of Now is always here, and the latent Higher Centers are always close to it, the Work is always the same. You don't start thinking you are a demigod or a prophet, and you don't entertain the idea that you are eternally damned. What you need to know is simple. But it is not easy to understand and to apply this simple knowledge in the right way.

The student must expect to make years and decades of slowly cumulative effort. It is this that produces a mature man number four.

But how, having created the groundwork, how do we move from the work of a mature man number four to a man number four attempting to become a man number five? In this phase of the Work the student's very foundations are shaken: a person is forced to "move from the place that you are." The machine can no longer be your home. These foundations cannot be shaken before they exist, but once they are in place the shaking can begin.

In August 1946 Ouspensky suddenly launched this second level of Work and based his every action upon it. This did include spectacular experiences, super efforts, and the use of powers. But he did not add the second level of Work to the first, he simply changed direction and forced a number of his students to catch up with him. Those few students already had the right foundation, and he — without their knowing it — built on that. In his teaching he simply dropped the first level of Work, the form that he had developed over the previous twenty years.

In the great Sufi Orders of Islam, and the Orders of Tibetan Buddhism as they were in ancient Tibet, what we have called the second level of Work ran parallel to the first level. But in August of 1946 Ouspensky did not have time for that. We might say that he introduced the second level before his group was properly ready for it. He took a gambler's risk and won. The decision, of course, was not his. He was presented with a 'play of transfiguration,' which his entire life had prepared him for — and he took the opportunity. Here was the taste of Higher School.

When we think beyond the Work of a man number four striving to become a man number five, and we consider the great schools of the past, what would be added to the work of Ouspensky's group as it was in the late 1930s? There is an indication of three influences:

1. A task given from a higher level than the group itself, which is then the measure of that group.

2. The direct and continuous involvement of C Influence with the group itself.

3. Means and techniques for developing the work of the steward within the students.

Ouspensky discovered a trace of the first influence at Mendham in March-April of 1945 and some part of the second influence on his return to Lyne, from January-February of 1947. He had attempted details of the third influence in the late Thirties with the exercises of repetition, but found his students not quite ready. Probably the small circle of people he worked with at Lyne had internalized these or comparable disciplines.

GURDJIEFF AND OUSPENSKY: TWO DIFFERENT TEACHERS

One further point of comparison between the two teachers must be drawn. It derives from the very character of the two men and the different roles they were given to play.

Gurdjieff worked quickly to sort out the different levels of his students. This was an alchemical process; he tested them to determine each student's capacity to respond to his own Higher Centers, and he directly challenged each student to deal with the internal resistance that he or she had to deal with. We note that he modified this approach after 1935.

Ouspensky did not initially pressure his students in this way. As a teacher he played less the role of first force and more the role of third force. From one point of view this is a slower process, but it is more conducive to the development of a tiered organization. Ouspensky's focus was on creating a stable context in which many people could work together, and which would at the same time support a range of different approaches to the Work. We note that he modified this approach after 1945.

From one point of view Gurdjieff's approach was the more compassionate, in that he directly communicated the perspective that a higher level has of a lower level. From another point of view Ouspensky was the more compassionate, in that he recognized that the Work is long and that the aspirant needs real and permanent reference points. In these pages we have, perhaps, emphasized the value of Ouspensky's approach. But awakening is not a rational process. The long period of preparation is necessary, the tremendous pressure that Gurdjieff applied is necessary, the unexpected shocks and turnarounds are necessary, deep and ancient magic is necessary.

While these two men were different in their approach, *the vision of School* in the hour of humanity's greatest need was the same for both. And they both strove with every fiber of their being to realize it. While working independently, each of them — in the most surprising ways — extended himself to the other at critical moments. In the end neither George Gurdjieff nor Peter Ouspensky was able to realize the vision of the Great Work in its connection to the Inner Circle of Humanity. Yet there can be no doubt that, in each of these men, in different ways, that vision always burned — whether their students realized it or not. And the vision itself endured. It found expression in the Work of Rodney Collin, Alexander Francis Horn, and Robert Earl Burton. In examining the recrudescence of this vision, in different forms and in different contexts, we hope to make it ever more clear.

CHAPTER 4

Rodney Collin

Early Life and Marriage

Rodney Collin was born in Brighton, England on 26th April 1909. His father, Frederick Collin-Smith, was a successful wine importer who had lived in different countries in Europe, and in Egypt, before settling in Brighton.[1]

There he met and married Kathleen Logan, the daughter of a local hotel proprietor. The couple had two sons: Rodney, the elder, and Richard. Frederick died while the boys were still quite young, but he left the family with an ample inheritance. Rodney had the Christian upbringing that was standard in upper middle-class England in the 1910s, but his outlook was affected by the fact that his mother was an ardent member of the local Theosophical Lodge. She had a strong service work ethic and undertook voluntary work transcribing theosophical books for the blind. There were always many books on religion and philosophy in the house.

As a boy Rodney was active, creative, and a voracious reader. He took long walking tours in the local countryside, and habitually browsed the used bookshops and old antique stores around Brighton. He attended Brighton College Preparatory School and later boarded at Ashford Grammar School in Kent.

In 1926, when he was seventeen years old, Rodney spent his summer holidays with a French family in the Chateaux country. From that year until

---

1. Rodney's full family name was Collin-Smith, but we have here used the name he was known by among his students and in his published works.

Figure 47. Rodney Collin at 20.

1930 he spent each summer on the continent, making use of the facilities of the Youth Hostel Association and the Toc H Hostels. Sometimes he simply found what lodging he could at local inns and farmhouses. In 1927 he completed a three-month walking tour of Andalusia, and from that experience wrote his first book, *Palms and Patios,* published in 1931. It represents a remarkable achievement for an eighteen-year-old. During this trip he learned enough Spanish to be drafted into the Ministry of Information during the Second World War.

After graduating from Ashford Grammar School, he entered the London School of Economics, where he earned — in only three years — a Bachelor of Commerce. The London School of Economics was, and is, one of the most distinguished universities in Britain. While studying for his commerce degree, he lived at the Toc H Hostel in Fitzroy Square, in the Marylebone district of London. Rodney's connection to the Toc H was not casual. The organization was an International Christian movement that gave assistance to disadvantaged groups — particularly veterans — through acts of service. The name came from a WWI code abbreviation for Talbot House, which had been used as a center for the recovery of wounded soldiers. After the war Toc H organized holidays for the disabled, provided entertainment for the residents of care homes, and promoted youth travel. In 1929, at the age of 20, Rodney visited Austria, Hungary, and Czechoslovakia on Toc H related expeditions.

After completing his Bachelor of Commerce degree Rodney embarked on a career in journalism, writing articles for some of the best-known periodicals in the country, including *The Evening Standard, The Spectator,* and *The New Statesman.* While continuing to write articles for these publications, he found full-time work as part of a team researching the *Daily Express Encyclopedia.*

His writing career developed in tandem with a career in public service. He joined a number of public service non-profits, including the Youth Hostel Association, the Peace Pledge Union (a pacifist movement that appeared in the buildup to WWII), and — of course — Toc H. For a period of time he was secretary of the Youth Hostels Association and editor of their journal, *The Rucksack.* He was also the assistant editor of the *Toc H Journal.*

We see in Rodney someone who had a remarkable ability to attempt many things at once and to produce results in each area. He made contacts easily and networked extensively without losing his direction.

On a Toc H pilgrimage to the Passion Play at Oberammergau in 1930, when he was 21, he met his future wife, Janet Buckley.

Janet was ten years older than Rodney, and the heiress to a considerable fortune. Her father, Wilfred Buckley (1873-1933), was an influential figure in the dairy industry. He had been the British Minister of Milk Production during the First World War. He was also an authority on Venetian glass and bequeathed the Buckley Collection of Venetian glass to the Victoria and Albert Museum, where it is still on display. Janet's mother, Bertha Buckley (née Terrell), was an American by birth, and had inherited a family fortune of her own. The family thus had assets on both sides of the Atlantic. Janet herself had been raised principally in England.[1] Janet had a developed in-

---

1. Wilfred (b. Birmingham) and Bertha (b. New York) were married in New York in 1898. In the 1930s Wilfred began writing *The Art of Glass,* based on the study of his collection, which Bertha completed after his death. She herself died in 1937 and the book was published posthumously by Phaidon Press in 1939.

Figure 48. Rodney and Janet.

terest in spirituality and was well read in the spiritual literature of her time. From the moment Rodney and Janet met they were seldom apart: she became an essential player in his life. She never failed to support him, through many trials, from their first meeting in 1930 until his death in 1956. Both had a passionate love of travel, and Janet's resources gave them the freedom to actively pursue this interest. While they both worked throughout their lives to serve charitable and spiritual purposes, they always combined this with a remarkable range of travel. To understand them one must understand that they were both accustomed to purchasing a plane or train ticket on a moment's notice and visiting many different places in rapid succession.

In the same year that Rodney met Janet, and at her suggestion, Rodney read Ouspensky's *A New Model of the Universe*. Janet and Rodney were married in London in March of 1934. In 1935 they attended a series of lectures by Maurice Nicoll, which seems not to have made a strong impression on them. Shortly after attending Nicoll's lectures, they left for a six-month motor journey across the United States, returning along the Mexican border. On their return one of Rodney's connections at the Peace Pledge Union — Robert de Ropp — introduced them to Ouspensky's lectures.

Rodney Meets Ouspensky

Rodney's first thought on meeting Peter Ouspensky was, "This is the most interesting man I have ever encountered. But I'm not ready for him."[1] Janet was ready. She immediately joined Ouspensky's group. Seeing the effect of the Work on her over time, and speaking to her about it, Rodney soon decided to join himself. Rodney and Janet were part of the tide of incoming students that brought Ouspensky's group to 1,000 in the year 1936. Once he joined Ouspensky's Work, Rodney realized that he had found what he had been searching for in all his studies and travels. Toc H, the Peace Pledge, and the Youth Hostel Association all disappeared, and Rodney dedicated his time to Ouspensky's teaching.

In 1937 Rodney and Janet had a daughter, whom they named Chloe. In that that same year Janet purchased a house in Virginia Water, adjacent to Lyne Place, and Rodney, Janet, and Chloe moved in. Rodney kept his full-time job with the *Daily Express Encyclopedia,* commuting every day to Fleet Street and back. Rodney and Janet spent most of their weekends at Lyne, working in the gardens or on the property. They also practiced the Gurdjieff movements with Jessmin Howarth and the rapidly developing movements group at Lyne.

Rodney worked hard at everything he did, imposing upon himself the most rigid disciplines. In his spare moments he spent time at the British Library, integrating his past reading and study with the new system he was being taught.

In 1938 Rodney participated in a series of public demonstrations of the movements. These demonstrations had been made possible through the co-operation of Jessmin Howarth, her pianist Rosemary Lillard, and the ballet principal Nadine Legat. The combination was electric. After experiencing

---

1. Collin, Rodney, *The Theory of Conscious Harmony,* Watkins, London, 1976, p. viii.

this level of performance, Rodney, with characteristic impulsiveness, went straight to Damascus to see the turning of the Mevlevi Dervishes. The movements became a permanent part of Rodney's life, and he taught them himself, from the time of his arrival in Mexico in 1948 until his death.

The Outbreak of War and the Move to Mendham

In September of 1939 the war came, and in July of 1940 the Battle of Britain began. Requisitions and blackouts made the Work in London increasingly difficult. The Ouspenskys prepared the property at Lyne as a retreat for students living in London. In August of 1940 Ouspensky's flat on Gwendwr Road was damaged in the bombing. Colet House was requisitioned by the Royal Navy, as was Janet and Rodney's home at Virginia Water. Janet, Rodney, and Chloe moved into the mansion at Lyne Place. After the move, Rodney, with his extensive language skills, was drafted into the Ministry of Information where he worked on censorship. Each day he went to the University of London campus (the large Senate House building) and each night he worked with the local Air Raid Defense.

The conditions created by the Battle of Britain soon made it impossible for Ouspensky to continue to teach in the London area. He considered a move to America. He began to network with different contacts and publishing connections to arrange a move to New York. He encouraged those of his students who could to make similar plans. Almost certainly Ouspensky talked with Janet about the planned move. Janet had significant assets in the U.S. through an inheritance from her American mother's estate. Ouspensky wanted to 1) rent space in New York City, where he could arrange meetings and recruit new students, and 2) secure a second property in upstate New York which would become the base for the group's activities.

Madame Ouspensky, Lenotchka, and Lonya sailed to New York on 4th January 1941. Janet and the four-year-old Chloe followed them within a week. Ouspensky was able to book a passage on a troop ship, the S.V. Georgic, in March.

And what, then, of Rodney? He was a drafted employee of the British Government, in what was fast becoming a global war. In February of 1941 (just after Janet and Chloe had left for New York) the Ministry of Information decided to transfer Rodney to Bermuda, by way of New York. By an amazing coincidence Rodney was scheduled to travel on the Georgic, on the same voyage as Ouspensky. Both men were in the midst of a major transition in their lives. On the voyage Rodney connected with Peter Ouspensky in a way he had not done before. While the external formality of teacher and student remained intact, something changed under the surface. From that point forward Rodney had a different awareness of the level of his teacher, and Ouspensky was aware of certain possibilities that existed within his student.

As soon as Ouspensky arrived in New York he began to rent suitable property, give lectures, and recruit students. He was networking actively with Janet. By September of 1941 Ouspensky was — with Janet's backing — making plans to purchase a 400-acre estate in Mendham, New Jersey, within driving distance of New York City. Once the estate was secured, Ouspensky asked all students at Lyne who were in a position to do so to join him. At the same time, he began to invite people from his New York lectures to spend weekends at Mendham. Ouspensky himself would spend most of the week in New York City, returning to Mendham for the weekend. Jessmin Howarth and Rosemary Lillard were able to move to Mendham, and the practice of the movements began afresh. Ouspensky's American following soon grew to 150.

At this time Rodney's life was in quite a state of flux. In August of 1941, after six months in Bermuda, he was shifted to the British Purchasing Commission, which worked internationally but was based in New York. What was the British Purchasing Commission? By 1941 Britain was locked in a life-or-death struggle with the Axis powers, fighting on land, sea, and air. The British war effort was completely dependent on convoys of ships continuously bringing supplies and armaments from the New World. The Axis forces were focused on destroying those convoys. If the convoys failed, Britain failed. The Battle of the North Atlantic suddenly became a major theater of the war. The Purchasing Commission arranged for both the production and the purchase of the armaments that were to be carried by the convoys, paying its many suppliers directly from Britain's gold reserves. As it was illegal to transport war materials direct from U.S. ports, most of its purchases were shipped from Halifax, Canada.

Almost as soon as he transferred to the Purchasing Commission, Rodney was sent on a special assignment to Mexico, and then, after a short period, was assigned to the central location in New York. He arrived in New York City in September of 1941, joining Janet and Chloe at Mendham. He then began commuting daily into the city. Thus, Rodney, Janet, and Chloe were together again at Franklin Farms under the sphere of influence of Ouspensky. Here we see the same series of fateful coincidences that impacted the relationship of Gurdjieff and Ouspensky — from Essentuki through Constantinople to London and Paris.

At the time of Rodney's arrival in New York the British Purchasing Commission would have been operating in a state of emergency. To give perspective, between 1940 and 1945, the Battle of the North Atlantic saw the loss of 3,500 merchant vessels, 175 allied warships, 47 German warships, and 783 German U-boats. It was Britain's struggle for survival. We recall that, in addition to his wartime work, his responsibilities at Mendham, and his demanding commute between the two locations, Rodney was a husband and parent. In his first months at Mendham, he could not even find time to attend Ouspensky's weekday lectures at New York. He attended what meetings he could at Mendham, and he was active in third line of work — both in the gardens and in the maintenance of the property. When Ouspensky's entourage returned to Mendham after the Friday lecture in New York, Rodney would lie awake in his bedroom until he saw the lights of the big Packard coming up the driveway and passing across the wall of his room. The car doors would close, and he would hear Ouspensky's party enter the house and pass into the kitchen. There — he knew — they would open a bottle of wine and begin to discuss the Work in a different context. Because of his experience with Ouspensky on the Georgic, Rodney had a clear idea of the kind of exchange that might be transpiring. He was aware of this, yet he was not a participant.

On the Georgic there had been just enough personal exchange between Rodney and Ouspensky for a transmission of World 12, and for both parties to understand the significance of what had happened. But when they arrived in New York they were still on the same footing they had been on at Lyne. And, once in New York, both were immediately engaged in a host of activities. A tension accumulated within Rodney day by day. Joyce Collin-Smith, Rodney's sister-in-law by her marriage to his brother Richard, has left us with a vivid description of how the tension reached its climax:

> One night it occurred to Rodney with a sudden sense of revelation that he went to bed instead of to lectures for a very different reason than he supposed. It had been easy to say that, after a day's work with the Purchasing Commission and the evening digging potatoes, he was too tired. Now he saw that ... he was again shirking some inner demand of his nature. ... He told me, "I leapt out of bed, flung on my dressing gown without even bothering to fasten it and tie the cord, and ran downstairs and flung open the kitchen door with a crash." ... He quite expected to find a number of people sitting drinking wine together. He was still a junior member of the household and would not usually have joined them uninvited. It so happened Ouspensky was quite alone, sitting at the end of the long table with a bottle and a glass of wine. Rodney said, "Before I lost courage and before I could control my words, I shouted at O., 'Why am I afraid of you?' O. looked at me calmly and said, 'Why do you say 'I'?' "[1]

A deep moment of Higher Centers united the two men, and from this point communication came naturally. Rodney spoke of his many ideas concerning the Work while Ouspensky listened. At some point during the conversation Rodney said, "I am a journalist. I want to write." Ouspensky replied, "You have nothing to write about. But stay with me and later we shall find you something to write."[2] We note that this is the same claim that Ouspensky made to Gurdjieff twenty-six years earlier, and the

---

1. Collin-Smith, Joyce, *Call No Man Master*, Gateway Books, Bath, 1988, p. 41.
2. *Ibid.*, p. 42.

answer — stay with me and we will find you something — was equally fateful. At the end of the conversation Ouspensky asked Rodney if he would like to trade the gardening duties to be his chauffeur on the drives to and from New York. Rodney immediately accepted, and from that time forward he attended all the New York meetings, joining Ouspensky's party at restaurant dinners afterward. As the weeks went by Rodney became a frequent visitor to Ouspensky's study at Mendham. He could come and go without making an appointment. He now had a privileged relationship with his teacher, which — because of his unassuming nature — was invisible to the other students.

Unknown to his colleagues Rodney became an active foil for Peter Ouspensky's thoughts on Man and the universe. Their exchange covered such areas as the law of three, the law of seven, the six cosmic processes, and the history of School. In the first year at Mendham Ouspensky's theory of the six cosmic processes came to its finished form, allowing him to share it with the London students as a completed understanding, and as an achievement of their group.

While Rodney collaborated with Ouspensky in their areas of mutual interest, he continued with his own writing. In late July 1943 he realized that his personal writing was beginning to take an unforeseen direction. He felt that he had come into contact with a set of master ideas, or 'broad abstracts,' that took form and developed in different ways. These broad abstracts did not in any way seem to be his own. It was as though he had access to them, and they took form in relation to the contents of his own mind. But he felt that he could not lay claim to the streams of thought that developed out of them. When he spoke to Ouspensky about this, it was as if Ouspensky already knew. This is not surprising, because Ouspensky had experienced the same phenomenon thirty years before — as he described it in *A New Model of the Universe*.[1] What Rodney called broad abstracts, Ouspensky had called 'moving hieroglyphs.' At a certain moment in his experiments of 1911, Ouspensky recorded that he began to see forms, moving hieroglyphs, which communicated a more concentrated meaning than it is

---

1. Ouspensky, P.D., *A New Model of the Universe,* Alfred A. Knopf, Inc., New York, 1969, pp. 336, 337.

possible to receive through words or concepts. Each hieroglyph seemed to reveal a thousand relationships and correlations all at once. Ouspensky felt that he was seeing directly into the signatures of things.

It was during this period, in contact with the broad abstracts, that Rodney took down the notes that were to become the first draft of *The Theory of Celestial Influence*. This work is deeply imbued with 1) all that is implicit in *A New Model of the Universe* and 2) all that is implicit in the theory of the six cosmic processes. It also demonstrates a thorough understanding of the material presented in *In Search of the Miraculous,* which was not published until 1949. Ouspensky had no doubt shared the draft manuscript with him. Rodney, in his introduction to the *Theory of Celestial Influence* (which was finally published in 1954), asked that the reader read *In Search of the Miraculous* first.

There is something more to be said about the so-called broad abstracts, or moving hieroglyphs. Such concentrations of meaning do not exist in a void; they arise out of a relationship between those in need of instruction and the source of that instruction. They appear when someone on a lower level seeks higher understanding, in the right way. *They are the response to a need.* The broad abstracts came close to Rodney because of the relationship that he and his teacher had to the larger body of Ouspensky's Work. Such understandings hover behind every teaching, and the Work of every great school, becoming the characteristic or formative understandings of that group. They find expression in its sacred texts, its works of art, its architecture, drama, music, or even codes of law. They are reflected in all the contributions that mark that school in the line of time. Thus, the traces of school that are known to humanity at large, are the partial traces of something much more real and alive, that determined the activities of the school in question. Some members of the school had direct contact with the broad abstracts, while many others knew them in a degree only, through participating in the school's general field of activity. Any documents or sacred texts would be partial expressions of the broad abstracts. Teachings and schools are always imperfect approximations of something that can only be complete on a higher level, for the level that we inhabit cannot contain something of such depth and dynamism.

Rodney's work with the British Purchasing Commission proceeded apace. We noted that on hiring Rodney, the Commission first sent him to Mexico. As the war reached what Churchill later called the Hinge of Fate phase, Rodney was sent frequently to Halifax, Canada — the port from which the convoys sailed. Nevertheless, during his short periods of leave, for reasons known only to himself, Rodney would return to Mexico. This was an interesting development. Why, when so many demands were being made upon him, and when he had a young family to support, would he travel to Mexico? Clearly he was responding to some deeply felt intuition, and clearly both Ouspensky and Janet — in their different ways — were accepting of this.

By 1943, with the allied victories in North Africa and the invasion of Italy, the tide of the war had begun to turn. Yet it remained a desperate struggle.

The last years at Mendham — 1944-45 — became more difficult for the Ouspenskys. Madame Ouspensky was increasingly affected by Parkinson's disease, and Peter Ouspensky was diagnosed with terminal kidney disease. We do not know what Rodney's thoughts were concerning this period. He spent time with Ouspensky, he continued to make exceptional demands upon himself, he continued to visit Mexico on his short leaves, and he continued to elaborate the notes that were to become *The Theory of Celestial Influence*. Ouspensky's health deteriorated slowly, and, as it did so, he seemed — more and more — to like to have Rodney near him.

As we noted in the previous chapter, Ouspensky went through a crisis in March or early April of 1945 which brought him into contact with Higher School. This was probably around the time of his terminal diagnosis. He was given the vision of a 'play of transfiguration,' which was to condense and encapsulate all his years of teaching and culminate in his own death. On having recognized the archetypal form of this play, and the potentials contained in it, he became the director of the actual performance. His role was to coach each of the other actors to fulfill the potential that was in his or her role. Rodney was one of the actors, and he was just as much an unknowing player as any of the others. The close friendship that existed between the two men continued; it was simply that one of these two men was now directly connected to a higher level, and had to respect — in a new way — the requirements of that level.

The play of transfiguration was to be enacted in England. In April 1945 Ouspensky told some visiting London students of his intention to return to Lyne. From this moment onward the tension began to build. Rodney never doubted Ouspensky as his teacher, and yet he would certainly have been concerned about the decline in Ouspensky's health, and would have — like everyone else — been in a state of wonder about Ouspensky's intention to return to Lyne.

The Return to Lyne: Ouspensky's Last Eight Months

Ouspensky left for England with a small entourage on 19th January, 1947. A few months later, on 5th April, Rodney sailed from New York to Portsmouth to join him. Rodney, Janet, and the ten-year-old Chloe travelled together. They spent a week in Paris before arriving in London, on or about 18th April. As their house at Virginia Water had been commandeered by the Royal Navy, and a gun emplacement set up in the front garden, they moved into a caravan on the property at Lyne Place. During the stay at Lyne, Janet was obliged to make several voyages back to New York to manage her assets there. It was fourteen months that was to change their lives forever.

This fourteen month period has been already covered in the chapter on Ouspensky. We will add here material to show how Rodney was personally affected by the drama of Ouspensky's death. This would include his work on chief feature and the discovery of his personal aim.[1]

Rodney arrived just before the fifth of the series of six meetings that Ouspensky gave at Colet Gardens between February and June of 1947. As we noted, in these meetings Ouspensky often challenged his questioners,

---

1. The original records of these events, often made in haste or based on later interviews, may give different dates for the same incident. The author has tried to use the dates that are most consistent with the other dates given.

helping them come to a deeper level of themselves. As Rodney listened to the questions, heard Ouspensky's responses, and saw the change in the questioners, "there suddenly came into his mind the exact formulation of his own aim that he had been groping for, for so long" ... "and from this moment on, everything began to fall into place for him."[1] To know one's personal aim is to be able to see both the higher level of oneself and the lower level of oneself, and — seeing the difference between these two — make consistent efforts to 1) serve the higher level, and 2) to displace the lower level. Such an aim, when it comes to you, is best expressed in a few words only.

The final meeting in the series was on 18th June 1947. In the days following the smaller circle of students around Ouspensky at Lyne began to experience nonverbal contact with their teacher. This occurred in two ways: through Ouspensky making gestures, which seemed to have an immediate and profound significance, and through students actually hearing Ouspensky's voice inside of themselves. Suggestions and tasks might be given by either means. A remarkable openness developed amongst the group, and *everything* seemed to become significant. There was a heightened responsiveness to higher influence; at the same time, hidden hopes and fears might suddenly come to the fore. Everything seemed to have a great range of meanings and possible interpretations, and in this atmosphere one's secret desires were ever poised to find expression.

On the one hand higher possibilities might be realized, and on the other hand a person's features might become directly visible. Ouspensky worked both sides of this equation.

Rodney was quickly and completely integrated into this group, and the nonverbal communications that were part of it. It was important to interpret Ouspensky's suggestions and tasks rightly, as he was communicating individually with each person and the suggestions to an individual

---

1. Rodney writes of this, describing himself in the third person, in *Last Remembrances of a Magician*, an unpublished work, c. 1948. More generally, our knowledge of the period from April 1947 to October 1947 has been supplemented by notes taken from conversations with the late Mervyn Brady, who, for a period, was in contact with Rodney Collin's student John Grepe, and was given access to all Rodney's papers in Mexico.

might — at the same time — relate to the group itself. Different individuals might understand things in different ways. The students had to work together.

Ouspensky was expert at making suggestions that touched the deepest chords in a person's being. They might connect with hidden potentials in a person's essence or the suppressed desires of false personality. Rodney worked in both areas. He found that — in face of one of Ouspensky's suggestions — he had three alternatives: 1) he might identify with the suggestion, and let false personality take it for its own; 2) he might resist that temptation, and not act out his response at all; or 3) he might see the temptation, and, still seeing it, act out the suggestion according to his best understanding. He found that following the third alternative allowed him to find his true course.

One of the suggestions that Ouspensky conveyed to Rodney defined Rodney's relation to this entire phase of the Work. Rodney understood that it was his duty to provide an example of how a young and healthy body would respond to the exceptional stress that they were all under. In other words, the responses of Rodney's young and healthy body would give Ouspensky a measure to assess the reactions of his own diseased body, and so to provide a third force for him to resist those reactions.

At a certain point Ouspensky, in the presence of the entire group, gestured towards Rodney and said, "Do as he says." Rodney had been designated as the leader, or chief interpreter, of Ouspensky's terse and often wordless communications. If a member of the group found themselves confused, they might speak with Rodney.

As Rodney became more and more involved in the drama at Lyne Place, Janet found herself again obliged to return to the U.S. to deal with her assets. When she left, Rodney moved from the caravan that they shared to the big house, to occupy Ouspensky's now unused study. Now more integrated into the group, he began to find himself under a white heat of pressure. At times he felt Ouspensky was infusing his whole being, displacing his learned identity with another kind of identity.

On September 24th Rodney felt an impulse summoning him to Ouspensky's room. There he found Ouspensky seated in an armchair with several other students around him. Rodney took a seat himself, and the group remained together in silence for some time. Then Ouspensky began to move in a rhythmic manner. At a certain point, this tiny, aged man stood, shouted, and laid hands on the six-foot three-inch Rodney, shaking him vigorously. He then butted their foreheads repeatedly and forcefully together. It could not have been a greater shock for Rodney, yet he accepted the experience as it came. He did not at any point react. He sensed that Ouspensky's action was breaking a barrier between the two of them. He felt that, from this point forward, there was some permanent connection between himself and Ouspensky. He felt in continuous communication with his teacher.

Joyce Collin-Smith recorded what Rodney said of this some years later:

> ... Rodney said that O. had invaded his being in some way. That he felt his presence and thought he was being given direct messages of an extraordinary power and depth. Nothing mattered except that he attend to the inner experience consciously, minute by minute.[1]

But there was more to the head-butting episode than just establishing a permanent connection with Ouspensky. Rodney felt that he had actually died to the person who had walked into the room, and had been reborn another person. But who or what was this person? He was not sure. The only thing he was sure of was that he had lost his old self, and there was no possibility of its return.

Three months later, looking back on the episode, Rodney drafted an analysis of the in-between space he had entered.[2] He stated that awakening involves both 1) the destruction of the old personality and 2) the creation of a soul. But these "are two separate processes, not necessarily following from one another." After the destruction of the personality, the aspirant

---

1. Collin-Smith, Joyce, *Call No Man Master*, Gateway Books, Bath, 1988, p. 45.
2. The finished analysis appears in *The Theory of Celestial Influence*. Rodney produced a preliminary draft of this book in November-December of 1947, just before departing for Mexico. This was only three months after the head-butting episode. The chapter on The Work of Schools clearly reflects what Rodney himself had been through a few short months before.

... "finds himself without anything and without any past. It is as though his body were placed naked on a desert island where it had no previous connections of any kind." Then ... "quite separate from the death of the old personality, though it may take place at the same time, is the conception of a conscious soul in him."[3]

Rodney knew from his own experience that there could be a gap between the destruction of the personality and the fixing of the soul, and he knew it was a dangerous place to be. He elaborated:

> ... quite different school methods and exercises are involved in the two processes, though they may and should go on together. If they do not, it may happen that the old personality is destroyed without a soul being acquired, resulting in some form of possession by another or in insanity.[4]

For Rodney, when he was caught in this intermediary state, there manifested either a very great self-confidence — when the connection to Ouspensky was strong — or the uncertainty of an infinite void. The state of self-confidence, when it was there, was not based on anything real. Here we must add that, in this intermediary state, World 12 does begin to show through, but it is not aware of itself as such. (World 12 self-aware is what the *Theory of Celestial Influence* calls the soul.)

When Rodney entered this vulnerable condition, a number of quite specific thoughts and plans began to run through his mind. Some concerned the future of the Work, while others were related to particular people. He took these thoughts to be Ouspensky's.

The first specific thought came in relation to his wife, Janet. Rodney felt that he had been so significantly changed that he needed to reaffirm his marriage with her. She happened to be at Lyne at that time. He went to her directly and told her that the man she had married was dead, and that she might marry him again, meaning as he now was. She accepted the new Rodney, as she had accepted so many extraordinary things from both

---

3. Collin, Rodney, *The Theory of Celestial Influence,* Watkins, London, 1980, p. 322-323.
4. *Ibid.,* p. 322.

Rodney and Peter Ouspensky. She understood that Rodney was in a significantly altered state and was trying to find his way. She could not have been a greater support.

The second thought about a particular person came in relation to his teacher's wife, Madame Ouspensky. It seemed that the disabled Sophia

Figure 49. Dr. Francis Roles.

Grigorievna, who had been so central to the teaching up to this point, had to be included in the play that was unfolding at Lyne.

And so immediately after leaving Janet, Rodney went to Ouspensky and told him that he must now go to Madame, to include her in what was happening. In the same way that Ouspensky had said, six years before in the kitchen at Mendham, "Why do you say I?," he now shouted "Who goes to Madame?" In other words, who is doing it? And with these words he hit Rodney full in the face with his open hand.

There was a moment's pause, and then Ouspensky, in a clear voice, asked Rodney what had just happened. Rodney replied, in a matter-of-fact tone, that a man had just been killed. Then Rodney went over to Francis

Roles, who was in the room, and gave him a terrific buffet on the side of the head with his open hand.[1] Perhaps Rodney had hoped to include Francis in the state that he himself had just entered, but that was not how Francis took it. Rodney, for his part, was overwhelmed by gratitude for Ouspensky, who — in delivering the blow — had completed some important stage in the destruction of his old self. Yet the new self was not yet in place. Rodney was still in the state of possession described in *The Theory of Celestial Influence*.

After having freed Rodney from at least one degree of illusion, Ouspensky did give his approval to Rodney to visit Madame at Mendham. We do not know the words he used. Rodney immediately made a flight reservation for New York. Regular Trans-Atlantic flight service between London and New York had been established two years before, in 1945. Rodney, being an experienced — and even compulsive — traveler, went directly to London Airport (now called Heathrow).

With respect to the impulses that came to Rodney at this time, we do not know whether they came directly from Ouspensky, or whether they came from Rodney thinking himself to be Ouspensky. Almost certainly it was some combination of the two.

Shortly after Rodney left Lyne for the airport, Ouspensky asked Eve Pryor to contact Rodney, to tell him that he was excused from having to visit Madame. When Eve telephoned the airport with an urgent request, she was informed that Rodney Collin had already passed through customs, but that she could leave a message. She turned to Ouspensky, who was beside her, and asked what message was to be given. Ouspensky said, "No message." Eve then told the airport clerk that there had been a mistake and that there was no message. And so we see Ouspensky's half-affirmation of Rodney's impulse to speak to Madame. He was reading the signs. If it had gone this far, let it go through to completion.

The still-possessed Rodney flew to New York, took a taxi from the airport directly to Mendham, and entered the great house. Ignoring the surprised greetings of friends and colleagues, he went straight upstairs and confronted Madame in her room. She was not well and had not wanted to receive guests. Rodney, on entering, assumed the full authority of his

---

1. Webb, James, *The Harmonious Circle*, Shambhala, Boston, 1987, p. 456.

master, in a way that was quite disorienting for her. As James Webb put it, "He considerably scared Madame Ouspensky by assuming the manners and voice of her husband."[1] She asked Rodney, quite directly, what it was he wanted. He replied simply that Ouspensky needed her help, and that she must come. She pointed out that she was very ill. How could she come? And then she spoke firmly to him, saying that no one could come between her and Ouspensky in that way.

Madame Ouspensky could not accept the things Rodney was saying, and, even though badly shaken, she challenged and denounced his arrogance. This was not what he had expected. On realizing that this kind of communication was not working, he kissed her hand, blessed her, and left the room. But his implacable self-confidence had been shaken. In the wake of this shock, and during the train ride back to New York, he felt that he had lost his contact with Ouspensky. He entered a period of great uncertainty.

Rodney was able to get a return flight to London that evening. The sense of Ouspensky's presence reentered him during the flight, and he was back at Lyne the following day. On his arrival he went promptly to Ouspensky's room. Ouspensky looked at him and asked how it had gone. "Quite wrong," he replied. Madame had understood nothing. Ouspensky did not seem perturbed in the least. He had viewed Rodney's trip as an experiment, and he seemed to feel the outcome was a natural thing.

This was the last conversation Rodney was to have with Peter Ouspensky, for he now ceased to be involved with the care of the dying man. He felt that the inner presence of Ouspensky had displaced the old external relationship. In separating from the physical presence of Ouspensky, Rodney had passed a certain point of no return. He was now on his own with respect to distinguishing higher influence from subjective illusion.

In the period after his return from Mendham Rodney had a difficult incident with Francis Roles. Roles was Ouspensky's doctor and saw him every day. He had a different relationship to Ouspensky than Rodney did, the more so after Rodney's physical separation from Ouspensky. When Ouspensky had earlier designated Rodney as the leader of the group by saying "Do as he says," Rodney had understood this in an esoteric way, that he was

---

1. *Ibid.,* p. 456.

a conscious leader. But Francis had understood it in a more practical way, that Rodney was a group coordinator. After the head-butting episode Rodney had ceased to act even like a coordinator, and Ouspensky continued to make demands on Francis. Francis forgot about Rodney's special role.

At some point Rodney had asked Francis to take care of Ouspensky's luggage, which had been put in a room, still unpacked from the return from Shoreham. Francis had said that he would do this, and then forgot about it. At a certain point Rodney confronted Francis in the room where the luggage was stored. He asked him — in front of other people — to move the boxes. Francis, doubtless offended, did not acquiesce. He simply turned away, saying calmly that he didn't have time to move boxes and that he was "going to Ouspensky now." Rodney threw a cup of hot tea at him, called him a traitor to his face, and told him to get out of the room.

In a way both men were right. Francis was refusing to acknowledge Rodney's leadership, but he himself was under great pressure, and Rodney was behaving strangely. On his side, Rodney felt the importance of his role in the process of transfiguration. In this exchange Rodney clearly saw his own feature coming to the fore: coming over him, as something not himself.

To understand this incident better, let us consider one of Rodney's greatest strengths: his ability to interpret, integrate, and record. Ouspensky skillfully brought out both the mechanical and the conscious side of this strength. In so doing he encouraged Rodney to the point where he sometimes overreached. Rodney saw that when his feature gained control, it gave rise to intense pride in his exclusive way of interpreting things, and to an exaggeration of his own self-importance. He saw himself beginning to act with extraordinary arrogance, something like a cross between and Indian Rajah and the Grand Lama.[2] This subjective character flaw, this arrogance, is exactly what was behind his abusive exchanges with Francis Roles.

Considering the tension between Rodney and Francis, we keep in mind that a teacher often plays two students off against one another, to show up features — just as Gurdjieff had done with Ouspensky and Leonid Stjernvall at the dacha in Finland. It is almost certain, in retrospect, that

---

2. See Beckwith, Gerard de Symons, *Ouspensky's Fourth Way,* Starnine Media & Publishing Ltd., Oxford, 2015, p. 38.

Ouspensky saw that after his death Rodney was going to leave London for Mexico and Francis was going to stay.

More generally, one cannot awaken without making mistakes, and in a way one awakens because of them. It is the machine that makes the mistakes, and the machine cannot not make mistakes. It is a very limited tool. The Self separates itself from this, but it can only do so when the mistake is seen and acknowledged for what it is. It is this acknowledgement that creates the space in which the Self can distance itself from its planetary vehicle.

Let us consider the incidents that occurred after the head-butting episode, in light of what Rodney later wrote in *The Theory of Celestial Influence*. There he stated that, in the critical moments of awakening, there are two related processes: the destruction of the old personality and the birth of the Higher Centers. These two processes must occur in harmony.

Following the head-butting episode Rodney had entered this difficult in-between space: he had lost the unity and cohesiveness of the personality that he had, without anything of his own to put in its place. There were different impulses coming through, some from a higher level, some from a lower level. There was consciousness — much more than before — but not a sufficient concentration of consciousness aware of itself. In the confusion of being possessed by Ouspensky, Rodney was not himself and not what he was to become.

Three months later, writing of this interval — after having bridged it — he stated that, in order to bridge the interval, the aspirant:

> ... strives to eliminate from his organism everything that he does not want to keep permanently ... the pupil has to learn how to make himself do difficult things and how to carry out certain painful or repetitive exercises, which will ... be necessary to fix a certain state in him.[1]

At some point, after returning from the visit to Madame, Rodney realized that he had to consolidate the new state that had begun to appear in him. He had to affirm something that appeared between the illusion of

---

1. Collin, Rodney, *The Theory of Celestial Influence,* Watkins, London, 1980, p. 323.

Ouspensky's presence and the pending sense of an unlimited Void. He had to affirm World 12 self-aware.

RODNEY'S VIGIL

Janet arrived back from America on 28th September. She did not join Rodney in his room at Lyne Place, understanding that Rodney was involved in special Work with Ouspensky's immediate circle. She returned to the caravan adjoining the main house, where she and Rodney had stayed before the trip. While unpacking her things she received a remarkable intuition. On the basis of this intuition, on the morning of 29th September, she went up to Rodney's room — in his absence — and supplied it with several gallons of water, fruit, biscuits, and a chamber pot.

On the afternoon of 29th September Rodney — with the aim of stabilizing a clear World 12 — went to his room, barricaded the door, and locked himself in. He was still receiving suggestions directly from Ouspensky, and he believed that he was acting on these. After locking the door and placing the barricade, he saw the provisions that Janet had left him — and saw that the stage was set for the next scene of the play. He was now alone, with provisions. In the silence of the barricaded room, he established a regimen of exercise, prayer, meditation, and writing that would cover every hour of every day for seven days. This included slots of unstructured time for simple, total receptivity.

He refused to respond to any attempt at communication. He remained in this room (Ouspensky's old study) for six days, until 4th October — two days after Ouspensky's death. We note that Rodney was not with Ouspensky when he died.

What were the others to make of Rodney's sudden isolation? He had, after all, been the senior student and the lead interpreter. In the heat of events, each student had their own take on this. For some he had gone off track, for others he was going through some process on his own.

Ouspensky's last day came, as we have already recorded, on 1st October. In the morning he called his inner circle together — save Rodney — and addressed each one of them individually. He then retired, and died at dawn on 2nd October. In the afternoon of the 2nd his body was taken out of the house and prepared for burial at Holy Trinity Church in Lyne. His room was now empty. Rodney remained in retreat.

Days passed without a sound coming from Rodney's room. It was known that the room had no water faucet, and how long can a person go without water? All attempts to open the door, or to gain Rodney's attention, failed. Concern grew. Was Rodney still alive? At one point Francis Roles arranged that a ladder be put up to the window, and someone started to climb up. Suddenly the window flew open and a hand shot out, thrusting the ladder down. Francis was ready to take further measures, but the ever-supportive Janet persuaded him to leave Rodney to his vigil.

At 5:00AM on 4th October, two days after Ouspensky's death, Rodney put his retreat room in order, slipped quietly into Ouspensky's vacated bedroom, and locked the door — thus ensuring a seventh day of retreat. At the end of that day the servant's bell, installed in the room for Ouspensky's use, began to ring loudly and continuously. Janet was sent to respond to the call. Joyce Collin-Smith later recorded Janet's memory of the event. The squared brackets are the author's insertions:

> He [Rodney] was seated cross-legged on Ouspensky's bed, unshaven, emaciated, dirty ... he had neither eaten nor drunk during his long vigil and she [Janet] maintained there was no water in the dressing room. ... At any rate he was extremely thirsty. He asked for lime juice and Janet brought it to him. [Janet told me] "He looked very strange and childlike. I had difficulty in communicating with him. I told him he must wash and shave. I brought him a comb and put it in his hand. He sat looking at it for a long time, turning it this way and that. He said, "This is the most beautiful comb I have ever seen."[1]

AFTER OUSPENSKY'S DEATH

Eventually Rodney collected himself, bathed, shaved, changed his clothes, and had something to eat and drink. Later in the day he asked to address the household. When everyone was assembled he recounted his experience

---

1. Collin-Smith, Joyce, *Call No Man Master*, Gateway Books, Bath, 1988, p. 45.

over the preceding days. There is no record of what he said, but it appears that he spoke directly from a significantly altered state. As Joyce Collin-Smith stated: "There have been several versions of this event, which aroused excited interest in some and bewilderment or distaste in others. Clearly from the accounts he was still 'high.'"[2]

Some were able to respond to Rodney's address in the spirit in which it was given, while others were confused or even repelled. The mixed response showed Rodney that this was not the time or the place to attempt to communicate what he had understood. He may also have sensed that he was no longer the leader of this group. It was the first clear post-Ouspensky indication that his future Work was not to be in England.

In the weeks to follow Rodney and Janet remained based in their caravan, and had little contact with the others. They began to make their own plans for the future, and took several trips into London.

These are the events in the line of time, but the most important events that occurred in the wake of Ouspensky's death were outside the line of time: the climax of the process of transfiguration. As we noted in the previous chapter, after Ouspensky's death he manifested himself simultaneously in several different physical locations, communicating openly with his students. See page 334.

The man "at the wheel of a car" was Rodney himself. Having completed the two related processes, of the destruction of the personality and of the birth of the soul, he had a vessel that could receive such a revelation.

LATER RECORDS OF THE TRANSFIGURATION

As we noted, there is a chapter in *The Theory of Celestial Influence,* called The Work of Schools, which is Rodney's digestion of the experiences recorded in *Last Remembrances*. In this chapter Rodney breaks awakening into four stages: 1) the loosening of the personality and the purification of the lower centers, 2) the death of the personality, 3) the implanting of the soul, and 4) the fixing of the soul and the attitudes and understandings which characterize it.

---

2. *Ibid.,* p. 46.

We have already spoken of stage 2) the death of the personality and stage 3) the implanting of the soul. These two processes do not follow one another in a necessary order, and they must be coordinated by School. If not, the old personality can be destroyed without a soul being acquired, or a soul can be acquired without the old personality being destroyed, which creates a cosmic aberration.[1] The important point is that the aspirant cannot synchronize the two processes by himself. They are entirely dependent on a right external third force. Let us look at Rodney's experience in light of these four stages:

1. The loosening of the personality and the purification of the lower centers. This, for Rodney, would have been all his Work prior to the return to Lyne, in August of 1947.
2. The death of the personality. This begins with Rodney's arrival at Lyne and his integration into the group around Ouspensky. It reaches a climax in the head-butting episode of September 24th. This event was a significant moment in the displacement of Rodney's personality.
3. The implanting of a soul. This begins from the same head-butting episode and continues through to the end of Rodney's seven-day vigil on 5th October. In Rodney's case it includes, particularly, conquering the state of possession he had entered into at the time of the head-butting.
4. The fixing of the soul and the attitudes and understandings characteristic of it. This begins with the seven-day vigil and is completed in the vision of the universe given Rodney by Ouspensky (probably around 6th or 7th October). This vision was the final seal that showed the new conscious being his place in the living universe. Once Rodney was through the vigil he was clear, and the final fixing could take place. As he himself remarks, "The suggestions continued to come from Ouspensky, but I now no longer WAS them, they came to me and I acted on them." In other words, there was a space in which Rodney could receive and process the suggestions. His invisible Self had come awake.

---

1. See, Collin, Rodney, *The Theory of Celestial Influence,* Watkins, London, 1980, p. 322-323.

For Rodney there was period when stage 2 had been largely accomplished, but stage 3 was not yet complete. During this period, he was badly confused in his dealings with both Francis Roles and Madame Ouspensky. It was as though he didn't know who he was, yet at the same time he was functioning at a high level of intensity. There was consciousness, but it was not consciousness fully self-aware. By the time he came out of the seven-day vigil that phase was over.

The vigil was important. We speculate that in the period before the vigil Rodney saw particular things in his being that he did not want fixed, like the extraordinary arrogance that overcame him on the visit to Madame Ouspensky and the exchanges with Francis Roles. With great discipline he inwardly disengaged from these impulses. We speculate that in the latter part of the vigil, he learned to "exist without the help of anything on earth." Again, Rodney gives us his own direct reflections on this part of the process. The square brackets contain the author's insertions:

> Once the soul has 'taken in' the pupil's essence, the time comes for all to be fixed. ... Perhaps the pupil feels in himself an irresistible call to go away alone, in conditions of special difficulty, without food or drink. ... Alone in his retreat he is thrown upon his own resources. Suggestions may be conveyed to him by his teacher ... But the way he carries them out, the methods he uses, and the conclusions he comes to, all derive from his own essence. ... In general, pain and repetition are fixative agents [The exercise regimen for Rodney's vigil was very demanding.] ... What is important is the *attitude* which accompanies them. For these experiences may indeed fix permanently in a man a certain attitude towards God, towards his fellow men, towards his duty. And if they are sufficiently intense, such attitudes will remain with him for the rest of his life. [But]... not only the general attitudes aroused in him by the situation and his suffering will become fixed, but also any casual thoughts, longings, regret, fears and ambitions still left over from his personality ... If during the fixing experience, he thus finds arising in him regrets, longings or imaginations apart from the understanding he wishes to fix, he must seriously consider whether he is willing to live with such thoughts or feelings for the rest of his life.

> ... during fixation is set the future course of the man's life and work. ... certain basic ideals and attitudes are established in him which he can never go back on, and upon which his understanding may grow infinitely in the future.[1]

Rodney came out of the vigil corrected: a balanced man number five. Certain attitudes had been made permanent in him. There are two attitudes that distinguish Rodney Collin from many other conscious beings: 1) a tendency towards extreme physical effort and 2) a permanent remembrance of his teacher. Ouspensky's use of the technique of super-effort through the last months of his life gave Rodney a permanent relationship to that tool. Also, Rodney's experience at Lyne of giving immediate response to suggestions coming from a higher level was to return to him strongly in his last two years in Mexico.

The final act of the transfiguration — the setting of the seal — came on October 16th or 17th, when Ouspensky brought the now stabilized Rodney to a vision of the living universe. This imbued in him a certain direction and certain ideals that were to find rich expression in all his later Work and writings.

In this vision, Rodney saw the intersection of the four worlds that together comprise the cosmic context of human existence. He saw this in terms of what the system describes as the four levels of matter: mineral, cellular, molecular, electronic. Rodney and Peter Ouspensky had worked together studying this area during the years at Mendham. The vision showed Rodney the entire cycle of human life and death in relation to the four levels of matter. He made an attempt to describe the vision in his book *The Theory of Eternal Life,* which was drafted in the two months immediately following the vision.

Under Rodney's direction the artist Richard Guyatt — one of Ouspensky's students and a personal friend of Rodney's — painted a representation of what Rodney saw. The electronic world is the golden globe at the top, the mineral world is the dark globe at the bottom. The cellular world is the

---

1. *Ibid.,* pp. 324-325.

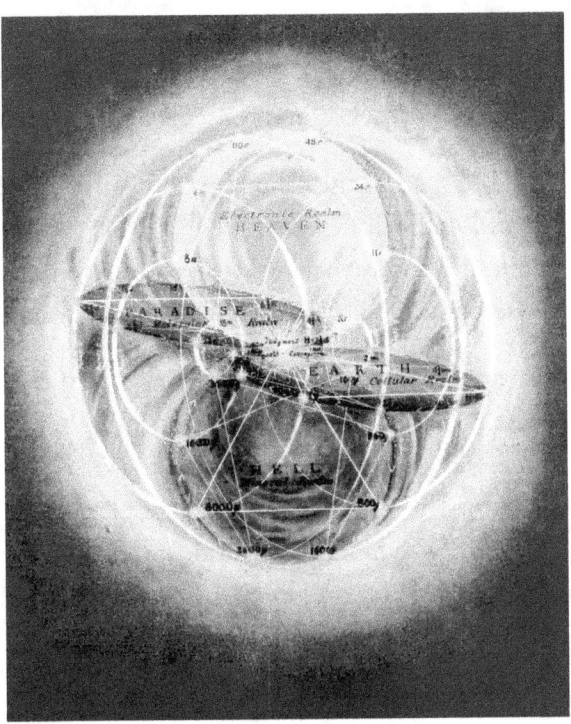

Figure 50. The Four Worlds by Richard Guyatt.

green disc nearest to us, on the horizontal plane, and the molecular world is the blue disc most distant from us on the horizontal plane.[2]

We provide a brief summary of what Rodney wrote of this in *The Theory of Eternal Life*. He perceived the four worlds as four connected and interpenetrating energy fields. They represent the range of worlds depicted in the table of the hydrogens and the step diagram. Rodney saw the universe as sentient, and these worlds as "worlds of experience." Two worlds given in the step diagram are not included in Rodney's presentation. These worlds are the two extremes of the Ray of Creation, the world centered in H1536 (cosmic waste) and the world centered in H1 (the Absolute as He is in himself). The four worlds are, if you will, everything else. Interpreted in terms of the table of hydrogens, the four worlds are as follows:

---

2. A painting in the possession of Joyce Collin-Smith. A black and white reproduction appears on p. 116 of *Theory of Eternal Life*.

Mineral World: This world is centered in $H384$ (minerals) and $H768$ (metals). From the human point of view the material of this world is extremely concentrated, dark, dense, and resistant to any change. It is Hell.

Cellular World: The span of the cellular world embraces $H192$ (plants), $H96$ (invertebrates), and $H48$ (vertebrates). This is the world of tissue, flesh, organs, stimulus response networks, and the experience of life itself. This scale comprises most of what Man is, in his physical embodiment.

Molecular World: The molecular world is a fineness of energy that is, either actually or potentially, independent of physical embodiment. It is part of the human experience, but it is so fine that it is usually not recognized by humans *as it is in itself*. The molecular energies are a harbinger of what Man was created to become. The molecular world embraces matter centered in $H24$ (human essence) and $H12$ (the Higher Emotional Center).[1]

Electronic World: The electronic world is of an intensity and fineness of vibration that is, for all intents and purposes, beyond human reach. It embraces $H6$ (the Higher Intellectual Center) and $H3$ (the Eternal Unchanging). The cycle of human experience touches the electronic world at the time of death, and this is the reason death is not remembered. Yet the most developed exemplars of our species have entered into and participated in this world.

These four interpenetrating worlds describe the round of human life that includes death and rebirth. Only a small part of this completed round is part of our everyday experience. Rodney recorded that, in a later phase of this same experience, he had a vision of a building based on the enneagram. This vision was to become the basis for the Planetarium at Tetecala, Mexico.

---

1. The study of molecular fields, as they relate to the cellular body, is relevant to the study of human thought and emotion. Additionally, the energies of the central nervous system (instinctive) are largely molecular. Jung's theory of the collective unconscious touches on this area. The relation between molecular and cellular, as that relates to the human experience, and to organic life generally, has been further explored by Rupert Sheldrake in his studies of morphic fields. See his *Morphic Resonance* and *A New Science of Life*. See also recent researches in cellular biology.

❦

In reviewing the period from his arrival in London on April 7th to the final vision of the four Worlds shared by Ouspensky, Rodney found he could relate what had occurred to other records in esoteric literature. He found previous reports of transfiguration in the traditions of Gautama Buddha, Jesus Christ, and Jetsun Milarepa.[2] Generalizing from all of these, he speaks of transfiguration as a ...

> ... tremendous birth pang, involving all parts of the universe ... a crack has been produced through all levels of matter, and through time itself by the direct intervention of electronic energy. Through this crack the perception of ordinary men may for a short time see into higher worlds and into the past and future. And through it, for all beings, there now lies a way of escape which did not exist before.[3]

From the standpoint of the actors who are being lifted up through the crack between worlds ...

> ... this dénoument of the drama, brings perhaps the greatest test of all. The disciples may have passed many other tests, made great efforts, and understood much. Now all depends on whether they have positive attitude, or in religious language, faith towards their teacher. For only with complete faith and purged of fear can they follow him to the electronic world.[4]

For those who pass through the crack ...

> ... a quite new connection with their teacher becomes possible. For by virtue of his electronic body he can reach them anywhere and at any time. By the nature of electronic matter, which penetrates all things, he can possess them and make them do his will, as long

---

2. Collin, Rodney, *The Theory of Eternal Life*, Watkins, London 1974, p. 114.
3. *Ibid.*, p. 113.
4. *Ibid.*, p. 115.

as they so wish. By the nature of electronic matter, which surpasses time, he can come to them in the future, and perhaps even in the past. He has become not only omnipotent but eternal in relation to them. And he can exercise his power of creating souls, not only among them, but among all men who believe in him, as long as electronic matter endures. His indeed will be *conscious immortality*.[1]

It was on the basis of such a connection that Rodney moved forward, coming out of the vigil and disengaging himself from the group at Lyne.

From Lyne to London

A new chapter of Rodney's life had begun. Janet, in her introduction to *The Theory of Conscious Harmony*, comments:

> The experiences that Rodney went through at this time profoundly affected his whole being. During the week following Ouspensky's death, he reached a perception of what his future Work was to be. He realized that, while attached to his teacher for and through all time, he must reconstruct in himself what Ouspensky had given him and thereafter take the responsibility of expressing it according to his own understanding.[2]

This perception of future Work had two sides:

1. An assimilation of all that had happened in the previous nine months, and a re-formulation of the basic principles of the Work.
2. A conviction that he would begin again in Mexico. This was not just an impulse; it had had a long gestation. We recall that Rodney had — with his teacher's permission — visited Mexico frequently in 1942, 1943, and 1944.

---

1. *Ibid.*, p. 115.
2. See Janet Collin-Smith's introduction to Collin, Rodney, *The Theory of Conscious Harmony*, Watkins, London, 1976, pp. ix-x.

On a different note, Rodney's discovery of his personal aim in May enabled many things. Through August and September, amidst everything else that was happening, Rodney found himself able to pull together his Mendham writings, and — in the light of the new understandings that were coming to him — give them order and unity. He made a very rough draft of what was to become *The Theory of Celestial Influence*. Then, beginning from mid-October — on the basis of the vision shared with him by Ouspensky — Rodney drafted *The Theory of Eternal Life* (which was published in 1949). Finally — in 1948 — Rodney created a proper draft for *The Theory of Celestial Influence*, which was to become his best-known work.[3]

The Theory of Celestial Influence integrates earlier writings Rodney had done at Mendham, in the attempt to record his impression of the broad abstracts. We will provide a brief overview of this work, as it was one of the bases on which Rodney moved forward.

THE THEORY OF CELESTIAL INFLUENCE

We could say that *The Theory of Celestial Influence* is "a series of presentations of the connectedness of things" in a sentient universe that is ultimately sourced in the identity of the Absolute. The principal points of reference are 1) the microcosmos man, 2) the physical universe known to Man through science, 3) the total Macrocosm of Creation (including the celestial hierarchy within it), and 4) a transcendent divinity. The book is a Renaissance synthesis, in that it is centered in the experience of the microcosmos man. Each different aspect of the human experience is taken and expanded in its relation to the whole. And this synthesis includes much that modern man has forgotten. It is a Renaissance synthesis that both absorbs and transcends modernity.

---

3. This longer work was first published in Spanish in 1953 as El Desarrollo De La Luz and then published in English the following year by Watkins as *The Theory of Celestial Influence*. In *The Theory of Celestial Influence*, Watkins, London, 1980, p. XIX, Rodney writes, "And the outline of the present book was written in the two months immediately before his (Ouspensky's) death, in October 1947, as a direct result of what he was trying to achieve and show at that time." His notes reveal that the 1947 synthesis was based on notes produced from 1943 onward.

As Rodney put it, such a model "must not only display the inner form and structure of the universe, but must also reveal man's relation to it and his present and possible fates within it."[1]

The book begins cosmologically, and then rises up from the mineral world and through to nature and then to man. Rodney relates the perception of the six dimensions described by Ouspensky to the hierarchy of cosmoses comprising the Macrocosm of Creation. There is a brilliant analysis of the seven periods of the periodic table of elements in relation to 1) the perception of dimensions and 2) the formation of the hierarchy of cosmoses. That some of the science is now dated does not affect the power of the synthesis. Rodney then proceeds to examine the six cosmic processes (that he and Ouspensky were able to elaborate in 1942) in relation to man. He shows how the six processes find expression in man's inner life, and externally in the history of human civilizations. In this context he looks at the Work of schools through history. Finally, he looks at Man in eternity: death, recurrence, and beyond recurrence.

While the material of *The Theory of Celestial Influence* is often abstract, and draws for analogy on known science, it is filled with the most remarkable personal understandings. The work is not structured by guiding intellectual principles, but by the broad abstracts themselves; but at the same time it is not in any way automatic writing. It is a matter of Rodney seeing energetic/symbolic phenomena and finding the terms in which to describe them. His struggle to rightly express what he saw must have been considerable. Sometimes he sees the inner truth of something known externally and expresses it artistically. But more often it is a matter of trying to put some entirely new insight into words. Rodney brings relevant bits of science and myth into alignment and hopes the reader may catch a glimpse of what he has seen.

Two months after Ouspensky's death, on December 1st 1947, Rodney moved, with Janet and Chloe, to a mansion flat on St. James's Street, within half a mile of Buckingham Palace. It was here, in a state of relative retreat, that he produced the finished draft for *The Theory of Eternal Life*. While he was working on this project certain of his friends would seek him out. A number of those who had been at Lyne sensed that Rodney had gained a new presence and authority. Something in him had changed. In the beginning he responded to each person individually. Eventually weekly meetings were held at the flat on St. James's Street. Many of those attending were later to join Rodney in Mexico. Rodney never sought disciples, people were

---

1. Collin, Rodney, *The Theory of Celestial Influence,* Watkins, London, 1980, p. XI.

simply attracted to him. He retained, for the rest of his life, something of the childlike spontaneity that had come over him during the vigil.

THE CIRCLE AT LYNE GOES ITS OWN WAY

With Rodney in relative retreat at St. James's Street, Francis Roles took leadership of the remnants of Ouspensky's group. His first instinct was to preserve the energy field that Ouspensky had created. He made a list of proscribed books, banning the works of Nicoll and Bennett. He also produced a list of people to whom students were not to speak, which soon included Rodney. The ban on Rodney is not hard to understand. Francis had heard of Rodney's intention to teach in Mexico, and was worried that people would follow him, and that the group would be dispersed. There were other cleavages within the London group. Madame Kadloubovsky determined to publish Ouspensky's meeting material from the previous decade. Francis Roles forbade her to do so, saying that Ouspensky had asked that his work not be published. Madame Kadloubovksy simply went ahead, and accepted the ban that followed. Her record of the meetings was published in 1957 under the title *The Fourth Way,* which became — in the 1960s — the single best known work of the Gurdjieff tradition.[2]

---

2. In 1957 Madame Kadloubovsky had *The Fourth Way* published simultaneously in New York (by Alfred Knopf) and in London (by Routledge & Kegan Paul). She had been part of Ouspensky's first group in the Pera District of Constantinople, and she stayed with him until the day of his death. After having been his personal secretary for 26 years she pursued a career in publishing. In 1950 she published a re-translation of *Tertium Organum* (Capetown, Stourton Press), which she had done under Ouspensky's supervision. As Ouspensky's principal assistant in the experiments involving methods of repetition, she shared his interest in the Orthodox prayer of the heart. After his death she went on to edit and translate *Writings From the Philokalia on the Prayer of the Heart* (with G.E.H. Palmer), *Early Fathers from the Philokalia* (with G.E.H. Palmer), and *The Art of Prayer, an Orthodox Anthology* (with G.E.H. Palmer and Timothy Ware). Many of the archive notes in the Yale University Library's publication *Remembering Pyotr Demianovitch Ouspensky* (ed. Merrily E. Taylor) are the work of Eugenie Kadloubovsky. Always understated, Madame Kadloubovksy is an example of someone who kept the inner spirit of her teacher's teaching long after his death. Gurdjieff had two disciples who were cast from the same mold: Elizabeth Gordon, who was mentioned in the

The formal exclusion of Rodney from the Lyne circle marks a third interval in the relationship between Rodney and Francis. The first interval had occurred when Rodney had called Francis a traitor, after his refusal to move Ouspensky's luggage. The second interval began with Rodney's vigil and his address to the assembled company. Some of those who heard the address felt threatened by Rodney's new level, while others simply failed to recognize it. This situation was exacerbated by Francis' concerns on finding himself alone, the leader of the London group, with Gurdjieff teaching just across the channel — and Madame Ouspensky at Mendham actively recommending Gurdjieff's Work over the Work of the London group. We will recall that Francis had been asked by Ouspensky, in the strongest terms, to recreate the system and the teaching. One can certainly understand the pressures that were working on Francis. At the same time Francis and Rodney remained bonded by their experience of Ouspensky's last months. Once Rodney had become established in Mexico, and Gurdjieff had passed away, they met and were reconciled.

In the last months of his life Ouspensky had asked Francis Roles to search for a direct method for self-remembering. In 1960 Francis found a form of meditation which he thought satisfied this task: the Maharishi Mahesh Yogi's version of transcendental meditation. But this was something far short of awakening.

The Move to Mexico

In June 1948 Rodney, with Janet and Chloe and a few followers, left for New York en route to Mexico to make their new beginning. They stayed the first six months in Guadalajara. Here Rodney made a final draft of *Theory of Eternal Life*, a final draft of his play *Hellas: A Spectacle with Music and Dances*, and brought the draft of *The Theory of Celestial Influence* closer to

---

previous chapter, and Ethel Merston, whom Gurdjieff had always asked to manage the practical affairs of the Prieuré in his absence. All three were understated, quietly dedicated, and consistent. They were permanently formed by their experience of their teacher. A soldier so dedicated would receive a Victoria Cross, an Iron Cross, or a Medal of Honor.

final form. Each of these three works are profound, each is perfectly coherent, and each complements the others. The level of activity Rodney sustained throughout the period of all this writing demonstrates an unusual capacity for concentration.

Over 1948 and 1949 Rodney formed a theater group, the Unicorn Players, to perform *Hellas,* with the first performance taking place in Mexico City. The play represents the involvement of Higher School in the civilization of ancient Greece.[1] Rodney called his work "a return to the form of myth." This form allowed him to express many things he could not express in another way. *Hellas* reveals many of Rodney's hopes for his own group and conveys, in artistic form, his sense of what civilizational order is. This is important, because Rodney felt that part of his role was to participate in a renewal of civilization. A civilization is merely human, but at the same time a real civilization has its source in a higher level. There are links — however faint — between the human social order and the celestial order that lies beyond it. When these links break, civilization becomes simple society, which can then easily pass into a state of barbarism. In none of Rodney's other writings is there such direct representation of the relation between civilization and school. In giving form to his myth of civilizational order Rodney combined music, dance, and drama. The dance sequences in the play are based on the Gurdjieff movements, which Rodney knew well. As Rodney put it, "The choreography is described from actual dances (once a true expression of ideas), brought from the East, and reconstructed some years since in Europe and America."[2] It is, in some cases, possible to determine which Gurdjieff movements were intended for which scene. Beyond this, the potential for the involvement of the visual arts in the staging is practically unlimited.

The play captures Rodney's feeling for what a civilization is. Rodney saw himself and his group as being in the interstice between two phases of a civilization. Modern western civilization was, at the time *Hellas* was first performed, emerging from a global conflict of unprecedented violence, and

---

1. See Collin, Rodney, *Hellas, A Spectacle with Music and Dances in four acts,* The Stourton Press, Cape Town, 1951.
2. *Ibid.,* Preface.

a new balance of power was being established between principal players. In this interval Rodney is relating civilizational order to its source in Higher Worlds. The understanding of this linkage was a significant part of Rodney Collin's legacy as a conscious being.

The play is important for all these reasons, and also because it shows something about Rodney himself. When a dramatist creates dialogue he reveals himself — even if he does not present a character similar to himself. We also see something of Rodney's approach as a teacher, and we see what a multi-faceted teacher he was. And finally, we see the seed form of the plays of his student, Alexander Francis Horn. Alex Horn adopted and developed Rodney Collin's use of the cosmic context. Additionally, the feminine character of Hellas (the spirit of Greece) appears as a link between the human and the divine, and this feminine link reappears — in a similar way — in the character of Grace in Alex Horn's final play.

The small company of the Unicorn Players rented the theater, produced the sets, costumes, scenery, and props, and did all of the promotion. In this way it was an echo, thirty years after, of Gurdjieff's production of *The Struggle of the Magicians* in Tiflis and Constantinople.

In January of 1949 Rodney's group moved from Guadalajara to Mexico City, and after a few months purchased an old hacienda in the suburb of Tlálpam. A number of Ouspensky's London students then came to join them. Janet and Rodney rented additional space in the city center where meetings could be held, at first in both Spanish and English, and then — as the English became conversant in Spanish — in Spanish only. The nucleus of a permanent group had formed.

From the new base in Tlálpam Rodney initiated one project after another: lectures, movements classes, meetings, theater rehearsals. To complement this activity Janet established a daily routine for the large hacienda where most of the students lived. She had helped Madame Ouspensky to establish and organize the routine at Mendham, and so she had experience in this area. Three meals were served each day, the lights went out at 10:00PM, and — at a time when the use of tobacco was at its apogee — there was a ban on smoking.

The year 1949 — the year of Gurdjieff's death — was to be a turning point for Rodney's group. Once based in Mexico City it acquired a certain critical mass and began to take in new students.

PUBLISHING ACTIVITIES AND THE PLANETARIUM

We note that, by the end of his first six months in Mexico, Rodney had drafted *The Theory of Celestial Influence,* completed the *Theory of Eternal Life* (published by The Stourton Press in 1950) and completed *Hellas* (published by The Stourton Press in 1951). But Rodney had many other publications in mind. To facilitate his publication projects he created his own publishing house, *Ediciones Sol*.[1] In the spring of 1949 *Ediciones Sol* began to publish Spanish translations of Ouspensky's books. By 1951 Rodney was using it to publish a series of journals, written by himself and others, for his own group. Between 1949 and 1956 *Ediciones Sol* brought out fourteen titles, including Spanish translations of the works of Maurice Nicoll. Rodney had begun to publish the reading list for a new civilization.

In 1949 Rodney and Janet purchased land in the mountains outside of Mexico City, with a view to constructing a building, based on the enneagram, which would reflect the vision that Rodney had seen during his vigil at Lyne. He had seen it originally, in the broad abstracts, as a three-dimensional image, simultaneously expressing many cosmic laws. The site for the building was 9,000 feet above sea level and 2,000 feet above Mexico City.

The structure was called at different times, the planetarium, the cathedral, and Tetecala — which in Aztec means 'the stone house of God.' Its dome was to function as a planetarium, and it was formally christened as Tetecala. Rodney began the project by making a series of design drawings, which were detailed and completed by students with architectural skills. In 1951 Rodney's group laid the foundations for the structure. It became a focal point and a symbol for the group.

The Planetarium was based on two interlinking circular chambers, below ground level, which were sculpted out of the lava rock on which the whole structure was to stand. The larger circle was called the Chamber of

---

1. There is no equivalent English name for this publishing house.

the Sun and the smaller circle was the Chamber of the Moon. Between the two circles, in the interlinking space, was a great upturned shell, standing on a pedestal, which — on the day of the summer solstice — received the sun's rays through an aperture on the level above. Round each of the underground chambers ran a narrow curving passageway, the walls of which were

Figure 51. Rodney and Janet's home at Tetecala.

decorated with mosaic designs. These depicted, in graduated sequence, all of the life forms that lead up to (and are combined in) the microcosmos man. The final mosaic represented conscious (or cosmic) man.

Rodney himself designed, cut, and placed all the mosaics. The upward continuation of the Chamber of the Sun was to be a lecture hall, which could also be used for ritual dancing, the Gurdjieff movements, or theater performances. The dome of the Chamber of the Sun was the planetarium, onto which a moving image of the constellations could be projected. The upward continuation of the Chamber of the Moon was to be a library, to house Rodney's ever-growing collection of books.

The whole was designed like the famous mosque of Qaytbay in Cairo, such that walking through its interiors, in their intended sequence, could

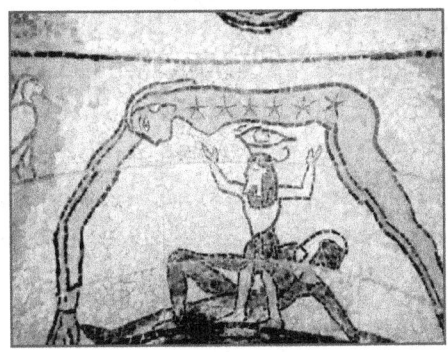

Figure 52. Mosaic of Nut, the ancient Egyptian sky goddess.

evoke a range of emotions in a person, emotions which, experienced with sensitivity, could reveal the person to themselves on a deeper level.

The architectural perspective drawings for the completed building still survive. They show the marked influence of the Frank Lloyd Wright school of architecture. Definite plans for its completion were never drawn up, and now little exists above the foundation level.

OTHER PROJECTS

As more and more people from Mexico City joined the group, Rodney initiated a range of other projects. In Mexico City he established an English bookstore, the *Libraria Britannica,* which carried the publications of

Figure 53. Mosaic of Ouspensky.

Ediciones Sol and the run of Work books then in print. In the mountains above the city Rodney acquired a mine, which yielded silver, salt, and nitrates. He asked a group of his Mexican students to weave colored Aztec blankets and serapes, which were then sold to the tourists. Janet, recognizing a lack of basic healthcare in the area, established a clinic and dispensary, and employed a full-time doctor. A garden was put in on the Planetarium site and an irrigation system installed. Vegetables were planted in terraced rows, interspersed with small trees which gave shelter from the sun. While all of this was occurring, many of the students who had initially settled around Tlálpam, in rented property, began to build more permanent homes in the area of the Planetarium. The main teaching house at Tlálpam remained, and many students kept apartments in the city.

Alongside all of this work, the group regularly practiced the movements. From his arrival in Mexico, through to the end of his life, Rodney led classes in the movements. We will recall that he had received his own instruction directly from one of Gurdjieff's principal movement teachers, Jessmin Howarth, and from her colleague, the Bolshoi trained repetiteur Nadine Nikolai-Legat. All of the dance scenes in *Hellas* are derived from the movements, and many can be traced to particular movements from the set perfected by Gurdjieff in 1924.

Word of Rodney's Work spread, and old Fourth Way associates from London and New York would fly in to see him and to connect with his Work. As Joyce Collin-Smith put it, "There were in fact continual visitors flying in from all over the place, and Rodney would be closeted with various people talking privately. In the evenings the household and guests would usually go out somewhere to dine around eleven or midnight. There might be any number from four of us to twenty."[1] Parallel to this Rodney kept up an extensive correspondence with people all over the world.

In this ever-widening sphere of activities, we sense a greater purpose than the attentive student at Lyne and Mendham had suspected. As Rodney expressed it:

---

1. Collin-Smith, Joyce, *Call No Man Master*, Gateway Books, Bath, 1988, p. 64. Joyce is describing a scene from 1954.

> My own aim is to live permanently in this miraculous atmosphere; or at least permanently in the knowledge and memory of it. At such times it is less and less the need of *personal work* I feel, and more and more the urgency of acting as a pure and understanding instrument of the realization of a great plan.[2]

The more than personal side of Rodney's Work focused on the connection to the Inner Circle of Humanity.

> All Work for the creation of groups on earth is concerned with the building of arks to be navigated from a higher level.[3]

Rodney As Teacher

Rodney engaged easily with others and had a natural gift for making connections. In the wake of the profound changes he had undergone in October of 1947, he acquired a peculiar lightness and self-assurance: a boyish quality. He did not have an assertive manner, yet he possessed a tremendous natural authority and a remarkable energy. He could and did make severe demands on himself and on others. He could shock, with the deft certainty of Gurdjieff, but he did so without making an issue of it. He attracted many people to himself.

Joyce Collin-Smith, who had known Rodney in England before the war, gives a first impression of meeting him in Mexico. She had first met Rodney on one of his visits back to Europe, after he had relocated to Mexico. Joyce noted that *The Theory of Eternal Life* and *The Theory of Celestial Influence* were both in print at that time, so the meeting in Mexico must have been, at the earliest, 1954. Joyce had been a student of Francis Roles when she met Rodney. Not being satisfied with that teaching she decided to visit Rodney and Janet. She then spent most of 1955 and 1956 with Rodney:

---

2. Collin, Rodney, *The Theory of Conscious Harmony*, Watkins, London, 1976, p. 157. November 15th, 1951.

3. *Ibid.*, p. 165. September 24, 1955

Figure 54. Rodney Collin in 1953.

I remembered him personally only as the mild and amiable man I had known for a few weeks on his visit to England a couple of years previously. Whether through flight fatigue, altitude or the tequila, I began to feel within an hour in his company here in Mexico that I was dealing with someone totally different from my recollection. He was wearing a vivid blue shirt open at the neck and hanging outside his trousers. The sun-browned skin accentuated the now greying, longish hair that curled up and away from his face. He seemed exceptionally tall. His eyes ...were of an exceptional blue ... Rodney had round him a group of those English men and women who had followed him from London, but these were now outnumbered by the Spanish-speaking Mexicans. As a result, he lectured mainly in Spanish, and almost all group meetings were in that language too.

At the time of my visit, work at the planetarium was gradually taking over from all the other projects. We drove up there most days. Rodney's creative drive and imagination, and his manual skills, were considerable, and his energy seemed boundless. He was also so much in demand to answer comments and questions and deal with matters of a philosophical nature, that it was difficult to get a word with him at all. To do so one must pick up tools or implements and work with or beside him on whatever was then demanding his attention. I felt that I wanted to learn from him. There was a quality of dignity and authority in him.[1]

What centered all of these activities was something Rodney had inherited directly from Peter Ouspensky — the single-minded aim to reconnect with Higher School. Rodney had begun to teach in Mexico in the faith that he had the connection with C Influence needed to raise group work to the level of school work, and then — on that basis — to make the connection to Higher School. He referred to this connection to Higher School as "The Great Work" or the "Work of Works." In order to give his students the certainty they needed, he sometimes acted as if he already had this connection. He had, after all, been formed in the atmosphere of Ouspensky's last great effort: he always played for the highest stakes.

As a teacher Rodney created a milieu in which his students could speak easily about their personal work and their understandings. He humanized Ouspensky's expression of the Work, and gave his students greater freedom. At the same time, he made a tremendous demand on himself and trusted his students. Indeed, he gave his life to them.

THE IDEA OF A NEW AGE

In 1952 the idea of a New Age became prominent in Rodney's Work. He believed that the role of his group might be to provide an ark of spiritual understanding to inseminate the age to come. This was not an idea that he had invented. Both Gurdjieff and Ouspensky had considered their Work to be the possible basis for an ark. It was a natural assumption, given that they had begun their Work together in the midst of the Bolshevik revolution, developed their respective teachings through the First and Second World Wars, and finally saw the creation and deployment of the atomic bomb. Both men had considered the possibility of a pending demise of humanity.

---

1. Collin-Smith, Joyce, *Call No Man Master*, Gateway Books, Bath, 1988, p. 58.

Both saw an ark as a vessel, culling the real understandings of a dying civilization, and transmitting them forward to the civilization to follow.

Rodney was considering a different possibility. He did not presume the death of the old civilization, but considered an ark that would inseminate new life into the already existing civilization — giving birth to a New Age. By the mid-twentieth century, religion in its various forms had become divorced from the Work of School. Rodney's Work, through forming a connection to Higher School, might reconnect religion to the Work of School, enabling a renewal of religion itself — and so bringing harmony to the New Age that was to follow. The principles of the Fourth Way would reinvigorate the inner life of the Christian religion, and the principle of harmony would bring a new balance to the relationship between religion and civilizational order. The innocence of Mexico, Rodney felt, lent itself perfectly to this task.

In 1952-53 Rodney and Janet travelled to America, England, and France with the aim of establishing right connections with the people of the Gurdjieff Work. From one point of view Rodney was reconnecting with old friends and colleagues, and healing misunderstandings that might have been created in the past. At the same time, he was keeping a sharp eye open for signs of the New Age.

Rodney's open, buoyant nature and his natural charm helped him to sidestep the inter-group rivalries that had developed between the followers of Ouspensky and Gurdjieff, and between the sub-groups that had formed within each group after the death of their respective teachers. Rodney and Janet first visited Mendham, where Madame Ouspensky still lived, but found the students there lacking in any real feeling for the miraculous. Rodney was then invited by Maurice Nicoll to speak at Great Amwell House, about ten miles north of London. He made a very promising connection with Nicoll's group, but Maurice himself died in August of 1953, just a few months after Rodney's visit. On the same trip Rodney renewed his contact with Francis Roles and the old Ouspensky circle in London. Rodney and Francis were able to cancel old accounts, and to compare their notes on the final months of Ouspensky's life. Rodney and Janet also visited Paris, where they made connections with the Gurdjieff Foundation. While in

Paris Rodney visited the *Librairie Véga* where he purchased a large private library of occult books to be housed in the Planetarium. The only prominent figure in the Fourth Way community that Rodney did not connect with was John Bennett (who was then based in Coombe Springs). This was a direct result of the sharp severance of communications that had occurred between Ouspensky and Bennett in early 1944.

THE PACE ACCELERATES

After the return from Europe, in 1953, the Work continued, developing themes and forms connected with the New Age. But from mid-1954 the pace increased. In May of 1954 Rodney met Toby and Mema Dickins. Toby was an Englishman who worked for Kodak in Mexico City; his wife Mema was a devout Roman Catholic and a natural medium. The couple had three sons. A few months prior to their meeting, Mema had begun to receive visitations from a man who instructed her to "go to the philosopher Rodney Collin."[1] Shortly after this she heard Rodney's name mentioned, and learned that he lived at a house in Tlálpam. She made an appointment to meet him. When she was first shown into Rodney's study, she immediately noted the large painting of Ouspensky that hung on the wall. She exclaimed, "That's the man who sent me!"[2] Rodney was immediately receptive. Mema then began to deliver a series of messages from Ouspensky. Later there came messages from Gurdjieff, and then from other conscious beings throughout history.

The fact that Rodney gave these messages credence created an upheaval in Tlálpam. Janet and a core of followers — principally Mexican — took Mema very seriously and recorded all her messages with great care. Others were repelled, and a number of the original English followers — who found mediumship or prophecy at odds with the Fourth Way — left Rodney at this time. The developing connection with Mema also placed the other Gurdjieff-Ouspensky groups at a greater distance. They too were suspicious.

---

1. Collin-Smith, Joyce, *Call No Man Master*, Gateway Books, Bath, 1988, p. 72.
2. *Ibid.*, p. 73.

It is possible to make both too much and too little of this. Mema did indeed become the connective thread binding three developing themes in Rodney's Work: 1) the direct connection to Peter Ouspensky, 2) the Idea of the New Age, and 3) the Christian religion. Yet those three themes were there, independent of Mema. And, following Mema's entry into the group, Rodney continued to meet with his students and deal with their needs and concerns just as he had before. The connection with Higher School that he had experienced in 1947 remained at the core of his being. He continued to teach the system that Ouspensky had taught, he continued to lead his group in the movements, and he accelerated his work with the theater. His interest in the world around him grew, unabated.

It was at this time that the idea of harmony became central to Rodney's Work. It was an idea that had been important to Ouspensky in the last months of his life, although it was not, at that time, clear to his followers what he meant by it. The idea, nevertheless, continued to be important for Rodney. If we can understand what it meant for Rodney in 1954-1956, we can understand how he saw the different aspects of his Work fitting together. In 1954 Rodney published, through *Ediciones Sol*, a pamphlet called *The Herald of Harmony*.

THE HERALD OF HARMONY

The booklet describes the connection between Christianity, the idea of the New Age, and Peter Ouspensky's act of transfiguration. Rodney begins by stating that Christ brought a new vision of the cosmic hierarchy to the world: "With the coming of Christ, Mankind stood straight and recognized the light."[1] But this vision brought a severe break with all that had gone before: a sharp severance of the old from the new. As Christ stated, "Do not think that I came to bring peace on earth. I did not come to bring peace but a sword."[2] However, what Christ and his Apostles understood internally, with respect to the separation of the different levels *within* man, the Christian Church understood externally, in relation to human behavior. One result of this was a denial of man's sensual nature. Another was sectarian strife, as factions split over doctrinal differences. A third was the dismissal, by many, of the pre-Christian world.

---

1. Collin, Rodney, *The Herald of Harmony*, Ediciones Sol, Tlálpam, Mexico, 1951, p. 7.
2. Matthew 10:34 NKJV.

Different kinds of extreme thinking invited persecution, first under Nero and then Diocletian. The church was eventually centralized by Constantine, but a major cleavage then occurred between Catholic and Orthodox factions. Parallel with this cleavage the Christian Church entered into an acute external conflict with Islam. Then, in the sixteenth century, came the Protestant reformation. The wars and persecutions of the counter-reformation brought the tension between Christian and Christian to a climax. Through all of this period of struggle there were partial resolutions. The Italian Renaissance synthesized the Christian vision of Man with the Classical feeling for beauty, helping to reconcile Man with his sensual nature. In the early 19th century there came a vision of the unity of all religions, with the translations of the great Buddhist and Vedantic texts by Max Mueller, the advent of the Theosophical teachings, and the teachings of Ram Mohan Roy. But Mankind was not yet ripe for the New Age.

Then, in the 20th century, there came two chosen messengers from Higher School: a Greek-Armenian, George Gurdjieff, and a Russian, Peter Ouspensky. Both men were fully awake, both taught the same system that prioritized the old internal truths, but each had a different approach. A tension developed between the two teachings, which created a kind of magnetic field. The death of Peter Ouspensky, and the act of transfiguration which followed it, directly connected that magnetic field to Higher School. Rodney believed that Christ was at the top of the hidden hierarchy which comprises Higher School. Thus, the ultimate result of the connection of this magnetic field to Higher School was to be the re-establishment of Christ's leadership of Mankind through a renewal of the church. A New Age would be initiated under the hierarchy led by Christ. Gurdjieff's death, in October of 1949, marked the actual beginning of this New Age.

In the New Age each faith will find its own truth, distinguishing the inner meaning from the outer meaning, and from that there will come harmony. Buddhists, Muslims, Vedantins, and Jews will each discover the essence of their faith and reconcile that with a broader, all-inclusive view. Rodney emphasized that the leadership of the New Age comes not from men, but from the "hidden hierarchy" of Higher School. The Fourth Way is the means of realizing harmony between different faiths. The system gives us the keys to distinguish the inner meaning of each religion. Additionally, it clearly distinguishes the Work of school, from the work of religion, from the work of civilizational order. This understanding makes possible harmony between school, religion, and civilization. It also neutralizes Christianity's sharp severance of Man from his sensual nature and the factionalism between the different churches and religions. We see, then, how the system is the missing link: ecumenic, impartial, relative, and precise. The figure of Ouspensky appears as a vanguard of the New Age, and he has — on a higher level — a central role in steering the ark.

We see here the 'ascended' Ouspensky playing a role considerably beyond anything imagined by the participants in the events of September-October 1947. Rodney had taken Mema Dickins to be a direct conduit to Peter Ouspensky. He felt that — through her communications — he had direct access to the intentions of Higher School. Consequently, he increased his pace to the level of effort he had achieved in Ouspensky's last days.

Here we note that the work of a medium is by nature imperfect. A medium picks up on the presence of molecular fields, which are beyond the range that human beings normally perceive. But the medium can also pick up on the hopes and fears of the people around them, and be unable to distinguish these from other, more objective, sources. And then there are the promptings of their own subconscious mind. Well-known mediums include Helena Blavatsky, Edgar Cayce, the authors of the Urantia Papers, Gitta Mallasz, and Jane Roberts. All are of interest, but all are skewed — and some significantly so. The medium may have a connection to a source beyond humanity's normal understanding, but the reportage is always muddied to a degree. The one true connection between a higher level and a lower level must always be consciousness: depth of presence. Sensational mediumistic communications can actually distract from this.

Perhaps Rodney was too reliant on the strong link to Ouspensky, as that was secured through Mema? His increasing reliance on her transmissions was the reliance on a connection he had not secured through his own Work. In other words, it was not a direct conscious link. The extreme efforts and the treks of his last years, which climaxed in his early death, were based on a complete confidence in her transmissions.

In considering these matters we are questioning Rodney's judgement. The author acknowledges that, in doing so, he is questioning the judgement of a being higher than himself. In questioning Rodney's judgement, we affirm that he was possessed of a level of understanding beyond our own. We keep in mind, however, that — in the higher reaches of the way — things become more difficult. Our consciousness is amplified and our illusions diminished, but every illusion that we retain is magnified by the presence of Hydrogen 12. The distortion in the lens of perception can produce effects which are then attributed to a higher scale. Additionally (according to Ouspensky) there may be more than one future branching out from a single present moment, and one may have intuitions of something that is going to happen, but will not happen in the line of time that we are in. And so it is very easy to make mistakes. Rodney himself said, in his letters, that it is necessary for a student to forgive the mistakes of a teacher. There are no teachers who do not make mistakes.

But to return to the narrative, we note that the New Age was — according to Mema Dickins — to have been initiated with the "second messenger's ascent," that is, with Gurdjieff's death in October 1949. This was three years before she revealed the idea to Rodney. The year 1949 had indeed been a signal year for Rodney's group: they had purchased the land intended for the Planetarium, and Rodney published both *The Theory of Eternal Life* and *Hellas*.

Rodney described the moment of conception of the New Age:

> The guiding constellations wheeled to place. Cells on another scale paired, merged, split, multiplied, the spiritual chromosomes resolving ecstatically to the new age's shape, to pattern as of yet unmanifested harmony. The clock of new creation began to tick ... The web and weft of an age in embryo went knitting up: its organs sketched in: its understanding glimpsed. Its interdependent parts — now single men, now groups — later must grow to nations, beliefs, whole races and their destiny.[1]

This New Age vision came to Rodney (from Mema) in 1952, but according to Mema's prophecy it was already underway since the time of Gurdjieff's death.

Here we see what was behind Rodney's openness to the work of the other groups: Maurice Nicoll's Work at Great Amwell, the Gurdjieff Foundation's Work in New York and Paris, Francis Roles' Work in London. And the work of scattered individuals throughout the world. He saw, in all of this, the seeds of the New Age.

---

1. Collin, Rodney, *The Herald of Harmony,* Ediciones Sol, Tlálpam, Mexico, 1951, p. 19.

We note that, in *The Herald of Harmony*'s hidden hierarchy, the figure of Jesus Christ is at the top, reflecting Rodney's Christian orientation. But this hierarchy also reflects and accommodates all faiths. Rodney's teaching was resolutely Fourth Way in this respect. It was a teaching of the techniques of self-development, and each student might keep their own religious orientation. Religion was a matter of individual choice. The Work was not.

Rodney's Work acquired an occult or psychic dimension at this time. Rodney had a predilection for the occult, and it found expression in this phase of his teaching. Joyce Collin-Smith provides us with an example. She describes a talk with Rodney that occurred shortly after her own arrival in Mexico in 1954. Joyce had been taken aback by the intensity of the group's activities and the new Spanish language standard. She managed to make a private appointment with Rodney at his office apartment on Rio Nazas, in Mexico City. When she arrived Rodney was seated at his desk, which was covered with papers, letters, and manuscripts. On the wall hung a large painting of Ouspensky, seated, with a Siberian cat on either arm of his chair. The rays of the late afternoon sun cut through the white Venetian blinds, striping everything in the room with light and shadow. Joyce pressed her question on Rodney:

> 'I don't understand anything! I am waiting to get some sort of revelation of what your Work is actually all about.' ... The blue eyes regarded me benignly. 'Joyce, nothing can happen until you are quiet,' he said. ... We remained in silence. Suddenly the room began to swim ... I thought the slatted light and shadow might be about to give me a migraine headache. ... I said shakily: 'Could you close the blind, Rodney?' He reached behind him and pulled the cord. The lines of black and white disappeared and the room became marginally dimmer. Still we looked at one another and nothing was said. Then slowly Rodney's face began to change in shape and type. I couldn't understand what was happening. 'You look like an old man,' I blurted out. 'There's a growth of a bit of beard —' ... 'It's only because I haven't shaved for a few days,' came a voice out of Rodney's mouth that was not Rodney's voice at all.

Frightened, I glanced about the room in confusion. Then I looked back again. The face of the man in the chair was the square, heavy-jawed, bespectacled visage of Piotr Demianovitch Ouspensky. 'You are Ouspensky!' 'I was called that,' answered a different, guttural voice. In a few moments, the Ouspensky face faded completely, and like a television program in which one picture is panned in over another, an oriental face appeared. 'You're Chinese now.' 'Tibetan,' he answered.

Then with great rapidity, a series of different faces superimposed themselves one on another — dark-skinned, middle-eastern, Mediterranean, northern European, of several different apparent ages and types, some wearing headgear of one kind or another. My heart thumped as I watched. 'Who are you?' I asked at last. 'All these and many others too,' answered the voice of Rodney Collin, and his sunburned, grey-haired, blue-eyed twentieth century face appeared as normal as if it had been there all the time. 'Your other lives?' 'The curtain of time grows thin,' he answered me.[1]

In the spring of 1954, it was decided that Rodney's group would leave the main house at Tlálpam, and that the Planetarium would become the central focus for the group's activities. Rodney himself would continue to make use of the office apartment on Rio Nazas, near the *Libraria Britannica*. Some students moved from Tlálpam to the site of the Planetarium, while others took individual homes in Mexico City or apartments near Rio Nazas. Rodney felt that the house at Tlálpam had now played its role. The new phase of the Work was to be many-sided. From this point there was a marked re-focus on the development of the Unicorn Players. Twelve public performances of Ibsen's *Peer Gynt* were given in Mexico City, in which Rodney himself played the part of the Button Moulder.

JOURNEYS TO EUROPE AND THE NEAR EAST

As Mema Dickins began to function more and more within Rodney's sphere of influence, she began to receive transmissions from historical

---

1. Collin-Smith, Joyce, *Call No Man Master*, Gateway Books, Bath, 1988, excerpts from pp. 61, 62.

figures connected with school. It seemed possible, then, to collect material concerning the great schools of the past, and to create a history of school. Such a history had already been sketched in *The Theory of Celestial Influence*. Increasingly Mema spent time with Rodney's group, with the consent of her family, who were proud of her powers of clairvoyance and felt she had found a genuine outlet. In the summer of 1954 Rodney decided to make a tour of Europe and the Middle East to follow up on the records of Mema's transmissions, which were fast accumulating. The plan was that Rodney, Janet, and Mema would visit Paris, Seville, Athens, the Greek Islands, Rome, Egypt, Syria, Lebanon, Istanbul, Persia, Rome again, and then come back to Mexico via London. According to Joyce Collin-Smith, Rodney's notes from this period contained a great deal of material on Cosimo de Medici, the House of Lorraine, and Leonardo da Vinci. In his letters from this time Rodney spoke often of the 18th and 19th century 'School of Rome,' which perhaps influenced such figures as Shelley, Knut Thorvaldsen, Hans Christian Andersen, and Jean Dominique Ingres.

In a trance session that Mema had in Mexico before leaving on the journey, she had mentioned the name Ivan Ivanovitch, as being "one of the teachers of Gurdjieff." While Rodney was travelling in Europe, Joyce wrote to ask him if they had been able to make further verifications in this area. Mema had, indeed, given more information about Ivan Ivanovitch. Replying in a letter, Rodney wrote:

> Ivan Ivanovitch, we have been told, was a mysterious figure who came from Tibet early in the 19th century, who moved unseen behind the schools in Sicily, in Florence and in Rome, who inspired Ibsen and Stevenson and Nietzsche, who returned to Russia about 1885, gave Krilov his fables, helped Philemon translate the Philokalia, moulded the Russian ballet, and disappeared whence he came on the eve of the 1914 war.[1]

We note that the essence of this insight is that there is a Russian, with a background in school, travelling through Tibet and Central Asia in the early 19th century and then returning to Europe. To have been Gurdjieff's

---

1. *Ibid.*, p. 79.

teacher — on the basis of the information given in *Meetings with Remarkable Men* and on Ouspensky's early conversations with Gurdjieff — this man must have been in Central Asia in the years 1898-1907. Perhaps Mema's well-traveled Russian returned to Central Asia for a period of time at the turn of the century. Mema's transmission fits, in a very general way, with the hypothesis of Gurdjieff's teacher that we have previously advanced.[2]

However, none of this material ever came to final formulation, and the references to this research in *The Theory of Conscious Harmony* — which covers the same period — are much more modest. We take all of this, then, under advisement. There are certainly many unknown dramas and connections in the history of school, and perhaps Rodney did have access to some of them.

On his second stop in Rome Rodney was received into the Roman Catholic Church, a move he had contemplated for several years. It was not that he became a practicing Catholic, but that he felt himself a Christian, in the universal sense. He felt that Christ was at the head of the Celestial Hierarchy (at least in relation to Mankind) and that his conversion expressed his particular connection to that hierarchy. He retained his ecumenic view that the same truth exists at the heart of every great religion, and his belief that each person should find the truth of their own religion. He believed that, for the most part, people do not choose the religion that is their own.

RETURN TO MEXICO

It appears that The Unicorn Players were most active in the years 1954-56 — between Rodney's move to Rio Nazas and his death in March of 1956. This stage of his Work attracted young people from the centers of theatrical activity in Chicago and New York. Rodney, as we have noted, had kept

---

2. It fits in a general way, but it is by no means an exact match. The seamless fusion of ancient Mesopotamian teachings with Masonic cosmology is a life's calling, requiring a very high degree of focus. It is unlikely that this kind of focus would be relevant to helping with the Philokalia, or counseling Shelley, or coaching ballet dancers. The energy would be better invested closer to its sphere. Still, the idea of a Russian, as the vehicle for fusing the Eastern and Western currents, is of particular interest.

up his connection with both the Ouspensky people in New York and the Gurdjieff Foundation. There was, by this time, a substantial Fourth Way subculture in New York that Rodney connected with when he visited that city. Young people attracted to the Gurdjieff Foundation, and to Bennett's groups, soon heard of a burgeoning Fourth Way theater in Mexico City, and some travelled south to visit. The most prominent of these visitors was Alexander Horn, who became Rodney's student, and who was to later initiate *The Theatre of All Possibilities* in San Francisco and New York. He became the most artistically innovative American playwright of his generation.

We know that The Unicorn Players produced Ibsen's *Peer Gynt* in the spring of 1954. In the autumn of 1955 they produced Jean Anouilh's *The Lark* — depicting the life of Joan of Arc — with Rodney in the role of Bishop Cuachon. They likely produced Rodney's own play, *Hellas,* for we see the marked influence of this drama on the later dramatic works of Alexander Horn.

The *Ediciones Sol* also remained active. In 1954 *The Theory of Celestial Influence* was finally published in English. It has remained in print ever since and is the principal source through which Rodney's Work is known.

At the Center of the Maelstrom

The pace of Rodney's Work was blistering. He expressed this in his own way, in a letter written in 1953:

> I am sure that the possibility of big change depends on one's nearness to Big School. It is like a great whirlpool with what Ouspensky was and is and what stands behind him at the center. Beyond this vortex of esoteric energy the water is still. On its edge the water begins to swirl, slowly here and there changes are possible. The nearer the center the faster the torrent, the quicker and more complete the transformation of an individual life. Nearer the middle, it seems to me, everything is in flux, anything is possible.[1]

---

1. Collin, Rodney, *The Theory of Conscious Harmony,* Watkins, London, 1976, p. 156.

Figure 55. Rodney on pilgrimage.

Rodney was certainly at the center of a vortex of change. On top of all his other activities he regularly initiated day trips or expeditions which were marathons of endurance. He would select a destination, often a cathedral or a 'sacred site,' and make it the object of a pilgrimage. The group would walk long distances in the heat, sometimes for several days, sometimes without rest or water. Rodney was usually attended by John Grepe, one of his original English students, and a core of others — both old students and new — who were dedicated to his mission. These trials exhausted their participants but generated transcendent states, where the sense of past and future dissolved. They also earned Rodney the nickname 'Sledgehammer Smith.' We note in passing that Rodney's student, Alexander Horn, also arranged such treks as part of his own teaching in the 1960s and 1970s. It is likely that this came from first-hand experience of the treks with Rodney.

Here we must emphasize another aspect of this phase of Rodney's Work, which was the expansion of his teaching to other Latin American countries. As a result of the circulation of the *Ediciones Sol* publications, groups were started in Peru, Chile, Uruguay, and Argentina. In January of 1955 Rodney visited the groups in Argentina (Buenos Aires) and Peru (Lima and Cuzco). In Peru he visited Maccu Picchu to study the remains of the Incan civilization. How these visits blended with the work on the theater, the movements, the marathons, the research work at Rio Nazas, the travels to Europe and New York, the work on the Planetarium, and the charity work, we can only imagine.

In the meantime, through the early 1950s, Chloe grew into a beautiful young lady, obedient and adoring of her father. Mema and Janet thought that Chloe should marry Mema's eldest son, Tony. In 1954, when Chloe was 18, the two were placed on what might be called a 'schedule of engagement,' which began with Chloe spending two years in a convent in France. She was there when her father died in 1956. She did later marry Tony Dickins.

In 1955 Rodney began to show signs of exhaustion. He experienced a number of blackouts later that year, after the marathon walking treks. In January of 1956 he led an all-night pilgrimage from the Planetarium to the shrine of Our Lady of Guadalupe in the main square of Mexico City (a thirty-mile trek). When they arrived at the Cathedral, the group attended Mass at the Basilica. Rodney fainted during the mass, and did not recover for nearly twenty minutes. It is likely that this was the first in a series of heart attacks.

In 1955 Joyce accompanied Rodney on a journey to Teotihuacan (which Rodney believed to have been the center of the ancient Mesoamerican Civilization) and on a journey to the great volcano at Popocatepetl. Joyce remembers standing on the rim of the volcano with Rodney:

> If one speaks of peak experiences, mine was a peak indeed. I felt that nothing more could be desired, but to live and work beside my beloved brother for evermore. I did not realize at all that I was getting into a state of increasing euphoria. The strange experiences of the last months, together with the continual effect of the Mexican air, was putting me gradually into a perpetual 'high.'[1]

---

1. Collin-Smith, Joyce, *Call No Man Master*, Gateway Books, Bath, 1988, p. 66-8.

Joyce was unaccustomed to such experiences. She was not on an artificial high, she was simply closer to reality. We may take this as an indication of the states produced in Rodney's students by the pilgrimages.

In March of 1956 Rodney focused on putting his business affairs in order and paying all of his debts. When Janet commented that he seemed to be excessively preoccupied with these things, he replied, "All debts must be paid before moving on to something new. And I know that something new has to begin. We have to be prepared." He expected great things to come, but he had no idea what.

On the 24th of April 1956 Rodney, Janet, Mema, John Grepe and one or two others flew from Mexico City to Lima, Peru to visit the group there. In Lima Rodney held daily meetings, lead long hours of movements practice, and had innumerable private conversations with students. On the 2nd of May Rodney's group took a small aircraft to fly up to the ancient mountain city of Cuzco. During the flight they had to take oxygen from tubes several times. On arrival in Cuzco, at an altitude of 11,800 feet, Rodney admitted to feeling strange. Contrary to his established habit of avoiding medicines, he took several doses of coramine.[2]

The group rested to recover from the altitude change and then toured the city, making arrangements with a guide to take them to the Inca ruins in the surrounding hills. They visited Cuzco's Cathedral of Santo Domingo and there Rodney saw a crippled beggar-boy who lived in the cathedral's bell tower. Suddenly the boy made eye contact with Rodney. Rodney exclaimed to Mema, "I've seen the boy."[3] Apparently Mema had had a premonition of encountering such a boy, and had spoken to Rodney about it. When the group turned away from the Cathedral square to go back to the hotel, the boy followed them, hobbling on his crutches. When they went into the hotel, he simply took up a position outside and waited.

After taking lunch at the hotel the group decided to rest in preparation for the afternoon's tour. Rodney went out again, telling the others he would be back by 3:30PM, in time for the tour guide's arrival. He then sought out

---

2. Collin, Rodney, *The Theory of Conscious Harmony,* Watkins, London, 1976, p. 187.
3. Collin-Smith, Joyce, *Call No Man Master*, Gateway Books, Bath, 1988, p. 83.

the boy, whose name was Modesto, and took him up to the great statue of Christ that stands on the hill overlooking the city. There he prayed that the boy might be healed. Then the two of them went to the public baths, where Rodney washed the boy before taking him to a garment shop to buy new clothes. A crowd gathered outside the shop, curious that a foreigner should take such an interest in an Indian beggar boy. Rodney said to the crowd:

> "This boy is your responsibility. He is yourselves. If you pray to Our Lord to make him well, he will be healed. You must learn what is harmony; you must learn to look after each other; you must learn to give — to give." Someone in the crowd said: "That's all very well for you — you're rich." Rodney answered: "Everyone can give something. Everyone can give a prayer. Even if you can't give anything else, you can always give a smile; that doesn't cost anything."[1]

Rodney then went with the group on the afternoon tour. Late that night, after Rodney and Janet had retired, Rodney had a premonition:

> In the middle of the night, Janet, who had been sleeping soundly, was wakened by Rodney, who seemed to be in a state of distress. In answer to her anxious enquiry whether he was ill, he said: "I've done the wrong thing. It seemed to me so important that Modesto should be healed that I have been offering my own life in his place. Now I realise suddenly that I have been prepared for other work." ... Janet said, "If there is other work to do, you will be shown it." Rodney replied, "I invoked the Trinity. If you do that, what you ask is done."[2]

On the next day, May 3rd 1956, after breakfast, the boy came to take Rodney to the belfry of the cathedral, to show him where he was allowed to sleep, in a corner under the bells. There was a steep climb of ninety-eight steps to reach the belfry. After this visit Rodney rejoined the rest of the group, and together they went on a tour of the Inca ruins in the mountains adjoining the city. Following the tour the group took lunch and again rested:

---

1. Collin, Rodney, *The Theory of Conscious Harmony*, Watkins, London, 1976, p. 187.
2. Collin-Smith, Joyce, *Call No Man Master*, Gateway Books, Bath, 1988, p. 84.

After lunch, again while the others were resting, Rodney went out. He climbed to the cathedral belfry to find the boy and sat on the step below the low containing wall, below an arch. He told the boy that he was going to arrange with a doctor to operate on his twisted leg. While talking he was looking at the statute of Christ on the mountain opposite. Suddenly he got up with a gasp as though his breath had failed, staggered forward onto the top of the low wall, grasping the two wooden beams that were supporting the arch. Then he fell forward, striking his head against one of them. His body fell onto the wide cornice that juts out below and slipped off, falling to the street below. He lay where he fell, his arms out sideways in the form of a cross, his eyes open as though looking up at the sky, smiling.[3]

Janet's conclusion was that Rodney had a heart attack (perhaps the final in a series of heart attacks) while he was looking at the statue of Christ. This seems likely. From a different point of view, Rodney had been working at a pace that his body could not sustain: he had worked himself to death. And from yet another point of view, Rodney had a particular, preordained role, and this is how that role completed.

Rodney's remains were brought back to Mexico City and his ashes were interred in the wall of the church, Mary Hope in the Resurrection of the Lord, on the southern perimeter of Mexico City (Adolfo López Mateos 430, Parques del Pedregal, 14010 Ciudad de México, CDMX, Mexico). On a memorial plaque is inscribed a prayer that Rodney wrote one month before he died.

> *I was in the presence of God,*
> *He sent me to earth,*
> *I lost my wings,*
> *My body entered matter,*
> *My soul was fascinated,*
> *Earth drew me down,*
> *I reached the depth.*
> *I am inert,*

---

3. Collin, Rodney, *The Theory of Conscious Harmony*, Watkins, London, 1976, p. 187.

Longing arises,
I gather my strength,
Will is created,
I receive and meditate,
I adore the Trinity,
I am in the presence of God.

Aftermath and Final Thoughts

Modesto disappeared for five weeks. He was then seen hobbling across the cathedral square, on the way to his nest in the belfry tower. When the police questioned him he was terrified. They asked why he had not come home. He replied, "Because the God-man said he would heal me, and then he died. They will say I killed him."[1] Rodney's students raised money for an operation on Modesto's leg, which, while not completely restoring the leg, allowed him to walk normally.

After Rodney's death Mema proposed different members of the group as leaders, but no one was able to replace Rodney. The *Libraria Britannica*, the work on the site of the Planetarium, and the other activities of the group continued on a more casual basis. The New Age was left to take care of itself.

Janet Collin-Smith was then only fifty-five years old. The two central figures of her adult life, Rodney and Peter Ouspensky, had passed away. She had supported Ouspensky in a central way at Lyne and at Mendham. She was true to Rodney at every stage of his life: bringing him to Ouspensky's teaching; standing by him through the trials of Ouspensky's last months; and going with him to Mexico to start everything anew. In Mexico she had applied all that she had learned in the management of Mendham to the work at Tlálpam and Rio Nazas. When Mema came, Janet supported her. Janet's poetry shows evidence of a sensitive nature and of higher states. And then, suddenly, she was left alone. She did not glorify herself or pretend to be a teacher. Nor did she complain. For the next fifteen years, until her death in 1971, she engaged in social work, helping impoverished Mexican

---

1. Collin-Smith, Joyce, *Call No Man Master*, Gateway Books, Bath, 1988, p. 85.

children. This while she had a substantial inheritance held in trust. She stands as a tribute to her teacher, her beloved husband, and to the Work.

Rodney Collin died at the age of 47, an age when the other Fourth Way teachers documented in this book were just beginning their essential Work. Higher Forces 'timed Rodney out' in May of 1956, with his Work

Figure 56. Plaque marking the spot where Rodney fell, Cathedral of Santo Domingo, Cuzco.

apparently incomplete. He survived his own teacher, Peter Ouspensky, by only nine years. How can we understand this? What were the intentions of Higher School? Rodney's death does not make obvious sense when viewed in the line of time, but his Work was governed by forces that exist outside of the line of time. The common sense of the 21st century, geared as it is to cause and effect explanations, might see this as a poor result. But it can be understood in a different way. We can view it in terms of the Platonic concept of archetype (αρχετυπον). Rodney Collin's Work is the partial realization of a certain archetype of school. It is imperfect, but at the same time it does reflect the archetype. Where the archetype itself is perfect, the medium in which it is realized is always, in greater or lesser degree, imperfect. The result is a balance between the two. You can see the archetype in it, and you can see the imperfection in it. Though incomplete, the partial realization of the archetype does make other things possible for the future; it inseminates the collective unconscious of our species. It makes Mankind a more fertile ground for similar experiments in the future. In this way we may compare it to Peter Ouspensky's play of transfiguration. As an event, Ouspensky's death reflects the archetype of transfiguration with great purity: all the pieces were in place, all the people around him were properly prepared. With respect to Rodney's teaching, the people around him were not all equally well prepared. Mema Dickins was an effective medium, but what was her capacity to distinguish consciousness from functions? Did Rodney respond naively to Mema's promptings: did he take what he felt *should be true* for the actual truth? With more than sixty years of hindsight it is clear that the New Age was not what either Mema or Rodney anticipated it to be. And there are other questions that can be raised. Were Rodney's English students able to properly value him as a teacher? Did his Mexican students have sufficient preparation in the Work? Did Rodney drive himself too hard in circumstances that were not yet ripe? Perhaps, seeing the limitations of Rodney Collin's circumstances, Higher Forces ended his role rather than allowing the Work of his group to descend. Perhaps the archetype would be more clearly revealed by a brilliant terminal shock, without the obscuration of a later, lesser phase. With respect to all these matters we can only speculate.

Rodney worked himself beyond his capacities in a prayer for direct connection to Higher School. He created, for a period of time, his own world: at Tlálpam; at the site of the Planetarium; at the Libraria Britannica; at his office in Rio Nazas; and amongst all of those close to him. With his death in 1956 that world came to an end, for Rodney had no successor within it.

That world, so full of promise, was like the world of the Preiuré, in that, in some mysterious way, while existing only for a few years, it sounded a note that was to resonate forward to other places and other times. Rodney's Work directly seeded the Work of Alexander Francis Horn. And beyond this, all Work is connected in ways that are invisible to us. Rodney's vision remains important. His understanding of the relation of school to civilizational order is exceptional.

We have seen the developing vision that drove Rodney's Work. We note that this was, in part, based on external things. In the 1940s it was based on the physical presence of his teacher. From the first week of October 1947, it was based on the molecular presence of his teacher. In the years after 1954 it was based on Mema's oracular transmissions and on the anticipation of a New Age. Relative to all of these things the Self is internal. When we look, by comparison, at the intensity of the Work of Jesus Christ or Muhammad, we sense that their intensity is related to *who they actually are*. Yes, there are dramatic external circumstances, and yes there are great prophecies and great visions, but Christ and Muhammad are simply "doing what they do." Their Work is integral to what they have become. The archetype of the prophet is expressed completely and leaves a deep mark in the Mind of Man. Christ and Muhammad changed the world, and their like is rare in the life of humanity.

Rodney's achievement, by comparison, is little known or remembered. But it was significant; it still lives, and it is something that we cannot properly measure or assess on this level. Rodney himself succeeded in all that is most important: he made permanent entry to the electronic world. He joined his teacher in eternity and became one of the small company who have transcended the medium of organic life on earth. He has indeed been called to the "other kinds of work," in which he is now engaged.

CHAPTER 5

Alexander Francis Horn

Alexander Francis Horn was born in Chicago at the Mt. Sinai Hospital on 14th August 1929, just before the start of the Great Depression. His father was a 46-year-old Russian Jewish immigrant and his mother, Louise, a 21-year-old Italian immigrant. According to the U.S. Social Security records his father worked as a salesman. We know little of Alexander Horn's early life because he spoke very little about it. On 9th February 1935 the *Chicago Tribune* reported that the five-year-old Alex spread the alarm for a fire that broke out in his home. This bold act anticipated his adult role: in the fully awakened state he sounded the fire alarm for sleeping humanity.

Alex had a positive relationship with his parents, in circumstances that must have been difficult, as both parents were immigrants and the depression years were hard. His father, for whom he had a great deal of respect, died in 1939 when he was only ten years old. His mother was unable to care for him at that time and placed him in the Marks Nathan Jewish Orphan Home in Chicago.[1] Whatever the ten-year-old Alex may have gone through on entering the Marks Nathan home, in his adult life he cultivated a positive relationship with his mother, sometimes inviting her to the performances of his plays, and always treating her with respect.

---

1. There are discrepancies about dates given from different sources for Alex's entry into the orphanage. It seems likely that Alex Horn's father died when he was ten. The 1940 Census Record shows "Horn, Alexander, Inmate (of the Marks Nathan home), aged 10. Born Illinois. Residence, as of 1st April 1935, in the state of Illinois." The balance of the recollections of those who knew him is that he entered the orphanage at that time.

Figure 57. Marks Nathan Jewish Orphan Home.

Alex dedicated his 1972 play *The Fantastic Arising of Padraic Clancy Muldoon* to his father, his mother, and his wife. The dedications to his father and mother read:

To my father, who taught me never to be ashamed of what I love.
To my mother, who taught me to fight.

The Marks Nathan Jewish Orphanage was a privately funded orphanage, in an era before the government funding of child welfare. It was in operation from 1906 to 1948. In 1939 it was based in the 300-bed facility shown above, on 1550 South Albany in the Lawndale Community of Chicago. It was run by a Reform Jewish organization. The children were educated at an adjoining public school, but they were also given a Hebrew education at the Marks Nathan. All children were required to spend an hour in the orphanage library every day before going out to play. The orphanage encouraged sports and fielded both baseball and soccer teams. Recently arrived immigrants tended to place children at the Marks Nathan, as its religious customs were closer to those of the old world. The orthodox Jews who managed the home were serious about raising the children in a proper, healthy Jewish environment. This left a lasting impression on the young Alex — who retained a marked respect for, and profound knowledge of, his Judaic heritage. The home itself had high academic standards and many of its children were successful in later life.

Years of Apprenticeship: 1947-1956

Following the 1940 census report, we hear nothing of Alex Horn until after World War II. We know that he entered the University of Chicago in or around 1947 and acquired a Bachelor of Arts degree. This is, minimally, a four-year program, so he must have been involved with the university until at least 1952, and probably a few years after that. Since he began undergraduate work at the age of 19, he must have made a fairly direct transition from the Marks Nathan home to the University of Chicago campus lodgings. He probably had some support from his mother to get started.

At the university Alex had a wide circle of friends and became involved with acting classes outside of the regular curriculum. Unlike most undergraduate students he took his studies very seriously in relation to his life. Outside of class he would discuss his current reading material with friends. We are told that his favorite works included Werner Jaeger's *Paidea: The Ideals of Greek Culture,* Constantine Stanislavsky's *An Actor Prepares,* Leo Tolstoy's novella *What Men Live By,* and — most importantly — Peter Demian Ouspensky's *In Search of the Miraculous.* Alex must have read widely because these works, drawn from different fields, complement one another perfectly. This selection of works suggests a young man who was fast forming a coherent world view.

More generally, in the years 1947-1956 Alex took full advantage of one of America's top universities, got a good start in the theater, and — most importantly — made contact with his Fourth Way teacher, Rodney Collin.

It all began from the University of Chicago campus. Alex was a diligent student, who connected with many of the most progressive influences of his time. While attending university classes he was involved with the Gurdjieff Foundation in Chicago and on the East Coast. He told a classmate that *In Search of the Miraculous* was his favorite book. With respect to the theater, his exposure was not limited to the University of Chicago. What, then, did it involve? This needs a word of explanation.

Before the war the University of Chicago had no drama department. In the 1930s there was a Dramatic Association and there was a strong initiative for student performances. As a result, experimental theater groups formed in the university area, attracting many students. In 1946 a University

Theater formed, with an emphasis on classical drama and, at the same time, an openness to innovative technique. Shortly before Alex's arrival a Department of Theater and Performance Studies was finally established. It attracted new and interesting people from different parts of the country, aware of the achievements of the Moscow Art Theater and of the innovative work of people like Michael Chekhov and Viola Spolin. The new department existed *in conjunction with* the Drama groups that had already formed in the area, and these groups continued to develop, also receiving direct stimulus from the advent of television. It was to this mixed environment that the undergraduate Alex was attracted, and he immediately saw a connection between the theater and his Fourth Way studies. Alex continued to work both within the university and with the experimental theater groups in the university area. Some of these groups eventually achieved national stature. When Alex graduated, in 1953 or 1954, he remained in the University area for the next ten years, working with the different theater groups.

All of these influences were happening at once, but the most important influence, the influence that pulled all of the others together, was the pursuit of the Fourth Way.

Understanding the formative context of Alex's student years is necessary to understanding the aims of the mature teacher and the dramatist. In discussing Alex's involvement with Rodney Collin, we will see how drama and the Fourth Way interpenetrate — for Rodney was both a playwright and a director.

ALEX HORN AND RODNEY COLLIN

We know that by his early twenties Alex was actively seeking esoteric truth. During his years at the University of Chicago he connected, at different times, with the Gurdjieff Foundation in New York City, Willem Nyland's group in upstate New York, and John Bennett's group in the U.K.[1] He did not find the answers he was looking for in any of these places.

---

1. Alex had contact with Willem Nyland during the time he was involved with the Gurdjieff Foundation, but he was never a student of Nyland's, as some rumors have it. Willem Nyland became independent from the Foundation in 1960, four

Through his Gurdjieff connections Alex would have heard of Rodney Collin. As we know Rodney had been teaching independently in Mexico since 1948. Though his group was based in Mexico, Rodney continued to visit New York State and network with his colleagues from Lyne Place and Franklin Farms. Many of these people, following Madame Ouspensky's advice to "go to Gurdjieff," were now connected with the Foundation. At some point, in the course of these visits to New York from Mexico, Alex had the opportunity to meet Rodney. While Alex had mixed feelings about the Gurdjieff Foundation, he at once recognized Rodney as a man who was fully awake. At some point in the late 1940s or early 1950s he began to liaise with Rodney Collin's group, visiting their property in Tlálpam.[2]

We have it from two sources that in 1954 and 1955 Alex took colleagues from the off-campus theater groups to visit Rodney Collin's Unicorn Players. A first source is David Daniels, one of Alex's friends at the University of Chicago. Daniels graduated from the University of Chicago in about 1953 and then went to New York for a year. On returning to Chicago in 1954 he found Alexander Horn leading an acting class. In an online posting Daniels wrote: "The group (Alex's acting class) took an 'esoteric' trip to Mexico, on account of Horn's interest in Ouspensky biographer Rodney Collin, who had settled there." What gives Daniel's posting credence is that he did not himself know who Rodney Collin was, and so he could not have had a personal agenda to connect the names of the two men. We note that Alex must have had a prior connection to Rodney Collin, in order to gain Collin's permission to invite selected people to his teaching.

A second confirmation of the 'esoteric trips' to Mexico comes from the annals of the Compass Players. A recent anthology of the works of playwright George Birimisa includes comments on his life by some of his contemporaries. The actress Caty Cook Powell contributed a recollection

---

years after the death of Rodney Collin, when Alex was 31. By this time Alex was steering by a different pilot star.

2. In an online blog (which has since been removed) a student of Alexander Horn's, under the name *Moishe 3rd*, responded to the question, "Who was Alex Horn's Teacher?" He speculated "… was it John Bennett, very briefly, as others say, or was it Rodney Collin, as he told us once, but only once, and very much in passing." It appears that *Moishe 3rd* heard correctly.

which includes an anecdote about a trip that George Birimisa took to Mexico with Alexander Horn. We note that Powell refers to the "charismatic and controversial director, Alex Horn." This makes it clear that Alex had already begun to make his mark in the theater, and this would certainly be related to his first-hand experience of a conscious theater in Mexico. Powell writes:

> In 1954 or '55, anyway in the middle 50s, George [Birimisa] entered — or, more like it, catapulted — into my life. I was then a neophyte actor living on the South Side of Chicago and helping to start Compass Players, the first glimmer of an improvisational movement that led later to SNI, and Second City. A young and impoverished Elaine May was our teacher, and we developed ideas for performance based on methods she had learned as a child in Viola Spolin's Children's Theater. Elaine knew charismatic and controversial director Alex Horn from earlier days, so throughout the summer she told us about the doings of some "real" New York actors who had gone to Mexico with Alex planning to work for a year on their craft with no interruption and then create the greatest theater ever seen.[1] In those days one could live in Mexico forever on a pittance. Of course, we all wanted to be there working with the "real artists." However, the artists only lasted in Mexico for a few months due to fights or backers backing out, though they reportedly did do some wonderful work.[2] Toward the end of summer one day, into our workshop like a tornado blew George with Jerry Cunliffe, both bronzed from the tropical sun, wearing Mexican worker pants and sandals, having hitchhiked, I romantically presumed, all the way from Chichen Itza. Elaine turned the class over to them and they put us through a series of newly developed acting exercises. I was smitten. Turned out that George and Jerry were the

---

1. Elaine May came to the University of Chicago from Los Angeles in 1950 to study drama. She would have been in class with Alex for most of his undergraduate years, and on her graduation she worked with him in the Playwrights Theater Club.

2. It appears that Elaine and a few others went back to Chicago after the first "few months" while the rest of the group — including Alex — stayed on.

vanguard of the Mexico group, now down to a handful but still coming on like an army of conquering heroes. Alex, Anne Rain and Charles Bennett soon arrived [back from Mexico] and set up a collective, living together, pooling their money for the eventual theater, working assorted shit jobs and taking just carfare and cigarette money each day. Well of course I had to go and leave the offer of an actual paying job as an actor — what was I thinking? — to go join these nuts.[3][4]

So we know that Alex was a student of Rodney Collin, and that in the year 1954 he had been with Rodney for some years. Let us say that Alex had begun to visit Tlálpam in 1950, in his third year of university. At that time he would have been 21 years old and Rodney Collin 41. In 1956, the year of Rodney Collin's death, Rodney would have been 47 and Alex 27. This would give a significant overlap in the lives of the two men, and the timing would be right for a good relationship between student and teacher.

While Alex learned about acting and drama from his colleagues at the University of Chicago, his orientation towards theater was more broadly based. Almost from the beginning, he sought out the teachers that he needed. He took all he could from the innovative theater developing in Chicago, and he carefully studied and drew deeply from the core theatric traditions of the West. We single out three particular sources of influence:

- Francis Fergusson's theory of drama.
- The Tragedy with Transcendence of Greek theater.
- The acting of the Moscow Art Theater.

---

3. Birimisa, George (Author), Baugniet, Larry (Editor), Sagan, Paul (Editor), *Birimisa: Portraits, Plays, Perversions,* Sweetheart Press, San Francisco, 2009, p. 14.

4. Elaine May, three years younger than Alex, worked under Maria Ouspenskaya in Los Angeles before the latter's death in 1949. It is not impossible that the young Alex — through Elaine May — had some contact with Maria Ouspenskaya and that she was the inspiration for the character of Natasha Ravenskaya in *The Legend of Sharon Shashanovah.*

FRANCIS FERGUSSON AND THE MAJOR SCHOOLS OF DRAMA

Francis Fergusson (1904-1986) was the preeminent drama critic of his generation.[1] He defined the three principal schools of drama in the western tradition as: 1) the school of classical Greece, 2) the school of the Medieval Passion Plays, and 3) the Shakespearian school. He saw each of these schools as representing man in a cosmic context. Alex's teachers at the University of Chicago would have brought his attention to Fergusson's writings, and Alex himself referred to Fergusson as an authority on theater in the 1987 introduction to his published plays. While Alex was at the University of Chicago, Francis Fergusson lectured at Princeton, Rutgers, and the University of Indiana. For the precocious young Alex, who was given to travelling on impulse, all of these institutions were within reach.

There was more to Francis Fergusson than just drama theory. In the late twenties and early 1930s he was connected with the diaspora of the first Moscow Art Theater. These were Russians who had emigrated to America in the wake of the Bolshevik Revolution. In 1922 Stanislvasky's students Richard Boleslavsky and Maria Ouspenskaya formed the American Laboratory Theater to teach the Stanislavsky method. Fergusson became involved with the American Laboratory Theater and worked with it until the depression forced its closure in 1933. Later, while teaching at Bennington College, Fergusson made contact with Michael Chekhov, one of Stanislavksy's most gifted students. Chekhov was to exercise a great influence on American film and theater through the 1930s, 1940s, and 1950s. Thus, Francis Fergusson connected with original impulses from the Moscow Art Theater, which were later simplified into 'method acting' of the 1950s.[2]

---

1. Fergusson authored four seminal works on drama: *The Idea of a Theatre*; *Dante's Drama of the Mind*; *Trope and Allegory: Themes Common to Dante and Shakespeare*; and *Shakespeare: The Pattern in his Carpet*.
2. A student of Boleslavsky and Ouspenskaya, Stella Adler developed this simplified form of the Stanislavsky method. She, along with Robert Lewis and Cheryl Crawford, opened the Actor's Studio, in 1947.

One of Fergusson's achievements as a critic was to emphasize the social space in which drama takes place. He explored this in relation to each of the three great dramatic schools.

Greek Drama occurred in a public space that was continuous with the life of the *polis*. This public space included the Eleusinian, the Dionysian, and the Orphic Mysteries. The entire population of the city, including slaves, participated in these events, and they occurred at the same time each year. The Mysteries represented the cosmic context of human existence. Before the backdrop of the Mysteries, the Tragedies explored the fate and destiny of the individual human soul. The first tragedian, Aeschylus, was actually prosecuted (unsuccessfully) on a charge of revealing the content of the Eleusinian mysteries.

Medieval Passion Plays presented and explored a Christian vision of the universe. Both the actors and the audience were born, lived, and died within the Christian Church. The Christian view presented heaven above and hell below, with the earth spliced in-between. In medieval times these regions were seen as coexistent in the present. Fergusson argued that the cosmic vision of the Medieval Passion Plays — particularly the way in which the three levels were co-present — was best exemplified by Dante's *Divine Comedy*.

Shakespearian Theater found its subject matter in the life of the court, seen as a microcosm of the nation, in which all walks of life were represented. Fergusson argued that Shakespeare's plays drew directly on the cosmic context of the medieval passion plays, with heaven, hell, and earth coexistent in the present. The Elizabethan audience understood this context and Shakespeare exploited it to the full — in ways that are not apparent to a contemporary audience.

Neither the Greek tragedies, the medieval Passion Plays, nor the plays of Shakespeare present a linear view of time. Gods, Men, and Demons coexist and interact. Heaven, hell, and earth all exist at the same time. Since Shakespeare's time we have experienced the Age of Enlightenment, the development of the sciences, the first industrial revolution, and the rise to power of the business classes. What has followed from this, throughout the western world, has been a progressivist materialism with a purely linear view of time. In this general reconfiguration Western drama lost its cosmic context. The aim is no longer to educate man about his place in the universe, but to influence, to stimulate, and above all to make a profit. More specifically, in the years since World War II, the theater has become specialized in creating the impacts and effects that will hold the attention of a general audience. In short, Western drama has ceased to search out and to reveal the measure of man in a living universe.

In his critical works Francis Fergusson used the cosmic context of Dante's *Divine Comedy* to interpret the Passion plays. This same context, he argues, is implicit in Shakespearian theater. We shall explore the cosmic context of Dante, because all of Alexander Horn's mature plays re-introduce exactly this context in a post-Christian frame of reference.

THE COSMIC CONTEXT OF DANTE'S DIVINE COMEDY

The *Divine Comedy* presents us with a pageant of human lives; each life a particular kind of drama, and each life appearing as an element in a cosmic drama. Within this pageant of lives there are four different levels: the Inferno, the Paradiso, the Purgatorio, and the lives of those who inhabit the Earth. These four levels all exist at the same time, and there is an invisible staircase connecting them, with both upward and downward movement.

Inferno The *Inferno* is a lower world, which (for its inhabitants) has lost connection to the *Paradiso*, and so to the living whole. The drama of an infernal life may be represented in the stage-set of hell, or as it was enacted on the planet earth. The lives of the Inferno are determined by driving fixations or passions, which close off the person in question from any real understanding of other human beings. Each infernal life has its own dead-end finality.

Paradiso The *Paradiso* completely transcends the human level. For this reason it does not provide us with any very substantial material for drama, and Dante himself represents it to us as a poet can. Yet the lives of the *Paradiso* are needed to complete the whole. The *Inferno* and the *Purgatorio* are not complete in themselves, and the significance of the infernal and purgatorial lives can only be grasped in relation to the *Paradiso*.

Life on Earth We must be sure to add the level that Dante Alighieri — as the protagonist of the Divine Comedy — is centered in: *Life on Earth*. This is the world of humanity as we know it. The Earth is the midpoint between the *Inferno* and the *Purgatorio*. It nevertheless has its own direct connection to the *Paradiso*. What is unique about *Life on Earth,* is that 1) it determines a person's movement to the Inferno, the Purgatorio, or the Paradiso, and 2) it can be — and often is — lived in complete forgetfulness of these three other levels.

Purgatorio The *Purgatorio* refers to the period of purgation which can follow life on earth and precede entry into heaven. It is life lived with the unbending aim to separate out the different levels of one's being, and to affirm the higher levels over the lower levels. It is what life on earth ought to be. The people of Purgatory have an aim which they never forget, and they are intensely aware of both the inferno below and paradise above. They may err, and they certainly suffer, but they never forget. In sum, the purgatorial life is immediately and consciously connected to lives on the levels one above and one below, and this on a moment-by-moment basis.

In the moments when embodied mortals, in the midst of life on Earth, find their aim and live by it, they rise to the level of the Purgatorio, and may even glimpse Paradise … just as Dante did. They live in an awareness of all the other levels, and they understand that they contain those levels within themselves. If they use their time well (if they experience the Purgatorio while still on Earth), they can go directly to the Paradise. It was the aim of both the Passion Plays and of the Shakespearian theater to create a Purgatorial consciousness within the audience.

According to Francis Fergusson, placing man in the cosmic context gives him *heroic stature*. The great dramatic artists of the western tradition — such as Aeschylus, Sophocles, and Shakespeare — centered their dramatic works in the human level. The protagonist is raised to the purgatorial level whenever his being is challenged and the cosmic context remembered. This awareness of co-present levels forces the protagonist to bear the full weight of his humanity, with all its implications. He becomes the hero. This is the very opposite of the one-faced heroism of the Hollywood leading male. The conscious hero shows us several faces, and can easily slip down into hell or up into heaven. He is also the opposite of the more recent anti-hero, in that — despite his failings — he remembers what he must become.

It was Alexander Horn's stated aim to recover both the cosmic dimension and the heroic context for modern drama. No other playwright or dramatist of his generation was focused on these aims. This is how Alex himself put it in his 1987 essay *Theater and the Esoteric Tradition*:

The modern theater founded by Ibsen, great as he is, is also a partial perspective, which culminates in Chekhov, the pathetic modality, and which is inferior to heroic man seen in the round, as part of the universe and part of divinity. Modern theater lacks cosmic dimension. Hebbel, Ibsen, Chekhov, Brecht, Miller, Williams, Strindberg, Shaw, Cocteau, Anouilh, O'Neill, Ionesco all remarkable, each a partial perspective. For theater to become truly great again, it must be restored to its cosmic dimension, lost to it since the theater of Shakespeare. The mirror has cracked, the great mirror of Man which in Hamlet is held up to the world to reveal all the multiple facets on various levels of Man, the microcosmos that reflects his entire society and the great world, the macrocosm.[1]

We move, then, from Dante's cosmic context to a second formative influence of Alex's student years: Greek tragedy. We shall examine the Greek principle of Tragedy with Transcendence, and the theater of the Classical Greek school.

GREEK THEATER: TRAGEDY WITH TRANSCENDENCE

There is a dimension of Greek drama which Alex made his own, and which is apparent in each of his six plays. The greatest of the Greek tragedies do not present us with the absolute destruction of the hero, but show him rise, phoenix-like, from the ashes of a ruined life. This effect is intended to produce a purgation of emotion in the audience. The Greek word for this is *catharsis* (κάθαρσις). Such a tragedy, in its highest expression, reveals something of the final separation of consciousness from functions that occurs at the end of a human life.

In this kind of tragedy a person of noble character fails in certain of the critical tests of life, and is made aware of this failure, and of exactly how the flaws in their character have brought it about. The suffering is so intense that the tragic hero loses the very justification for their existence. At the same time, and almost unbeknownst to them, something deep within their

---

1. Horn, Alexander Francis, *In Search of a Solar Hero*, Element Books Ltd, Shaftesbury, Dorset UK, 1987, p.ix.

nature transcends the tragic moment and is renewed to continue on another plane. The aim of Greek tragedy was to evoke this depth of experience in the audience, producing an epiphany (*epiphaneia*: ἐπιφάνεια).

In order to have something within themselves pass through to a higher plane of existence, the tragic hero must lose their usual sense of 'I.' This was called, by the Greeks, *kenosis*: κένωσις: the act of 'emptying out' so as to become receptive to the divinity. In the manner in which the protagonist bears the tragic moment, he or she makes (or fails to make) the payment to enter into existence on a higher level. The measure of the dramatic artist is, then, the extent to which they can reveal the great uncertainty of the tragic moment — the infinite abyss of 'I' and 'not-I' — and so allow the audience to participate in a transcendence that goes beyond the four lower centers.

In the Greek theater this movement towards transcendence is represented in the four terms: *catharsis, kenosis, thaumazai,* and *epiphanaia.*

Catharsis (κάθαρσις) is the purification of emotions through art. Aristotle compares the effects of tragedy to the effect of a medical cathartic on the body. It eliminates the poisons.

Kenosis (κένωσις) is the act of emptying oneself, so as to become entirely receptive to the divinity.

Thaumazai (θαυμάζαι) is to gaze with shocked wonder and amazement: to honor, to admire, and to worship.

Epiphany (ἐπιφάνεια) is to experience a sudden realization; the moment when one becomes conscious of something that is important on the scale of a lifetime.

The movement towards transcendence is not arbitrary but subject to fate, and under higher laws. How did the Greek dramatists understand this? Fate was seen to be comprised of three aspects:

1. Momentums created by the protagonist's past actions, in combination with the influence of the web of surrounding human lives.
2. The protagonist's sense of his microcosmic potential, or the divine seed within him.

3. Submission to the Gods.

Greek Theater examined these three aspects of man's fate in relation to *hubris,* or the protagonist's tragic flaw. The tragic flaw in a person's character stands directly in the way of realizing their microcosmic potential, and every person has such a flaw. People do not know they have hubris, and they are driven by it. It is the part in man that defies or ignores the Gods. (It is the same thing Gurdjieff referred to, in a different context, as chief feature.) A man cannot change the first aspect of his fate (past karma); change is only possible with respect to the second aspect (realizing potential). And with respect to the third, he can only hope for the favor of the Gods. To realize the divine potential that exists within oneself, each person must confront his or her tragic flaw.

Every one of Alex Horn's plays explores the relation between fate and tragic flaw. But this does not exhaust Alex's debt to the Greeks. He attempted to adopt the very form and structure of Greek drama, particularly in his later plays. He adhered to the rules of drama outlined in Aristotle's *Poetics*.[1] Let us review the rules of the *Poetics*.

ARISTOTLE'S POETICS

In the words of Aristotle, "Tragedy is the imitation of an action that is serious, complete and of a certain magnitude."[2] "It should have for its subject a single action, whole and complete, with a beginning, a middle, and an end. It will thus resemble a living organism in all its unity, and produce the pleasure proper to it."[3]

By action (*praxis*), Aristotle does not mean just specific deeds or physical activities. *Praxis* includes the motivation from which deeds spring: the trigger to action. And this motivation is inscribed in the character of the tragic hero. By imitation, Aristotle does not mean copying, but capturing the essence of something and accurately representing it. By magnitude, Aristotle does not mean simply size or grandeur. The proper

---

1. Why is Aristotle's essay about epic and drama called the *Poetics*? The Greek verb poiesis — ποίησις refers to the activity of bringing something into being that did not exist before. Drama is viewed in this light.
2. *Aristotle's Poetics,* (transl. S.H. Butcher), Hill and Wang, New York, 1961, p. 65.
3. *Ibid.,* p. 115.

magnitude of a tragedy is that which, according to the action represented, will allow the entire sequence of events to unfold naturally, without being weakened by unnecessary embellishment or artificial foreshortening:

> As in the structure of the plot, so too in the portraiture of character, the poet should always aim either at the necessary or the probable. Thus, a person of a given character should speak or act in a given way, by the rule either of necessity or of probability, just as this event should follow that by necessary or probable sequence.[4]

A tragedy is not a narrative (like a history or an epic) but the representation of an action and its necessary consequences. In this regard it gives expression to the universal. It shows how a person of a certain type will speak or act, according to the law of probability or necessity. When a tragedy achieves universality, we see ourselves in the tragic hero and experience pity and fear as we see his or her destiny unfold. This impact occurs when the drama is a living, organic whole — neither too short nor too long.

By evoking pity and fear the tragedian effects a purgation (catharsis) of those same emotions within us. We are emptied, and enter a receptive state. The climax of tragedy is an epiphany (ἐπιφάνεια), evoking tragic wonder:

> The change of fortune [in a tragedy] should not be from good to bad. It should come about as the result not of vice, but of some great error or frailty, in a character either such as we have described [not preeminently good, but basically well intentioned], or better rather than worse.[5]

Alexander Horn succeeded in realizing the essential spirit of Greek drama in great purity in the three plays, *The Legend of Sharon Shashanovah*, *The Magician*, and '*I*.'

This brings us to a third formative influence on the young Alex.

THE MOSCOW ART THEATER: STANISLAVSKY, VAKHTANGOV, CHEKHOV

Constantin Stanislavsky (1863-1938) was the co-founder of the first Moscow Art Theater in 1898. Alexander Horn practiced the acting techniques which Stanislavsky documented in his three principal works: *An Actor Prepares*, *Building a Character*, and *Creating a Role*. Stanislavksy called his

---

4. *Ibid.*, p. 82.
5. *Ibid.*, p. 76.

approach to acting theatrical realism. It is realism because the actor does not imitate, but strives to experience the emotions he or she portrays, and the audience can feel that they are real, not imitated.

A counterpoint to Stanislavsky's realism was given by Vsevolod Meyerhold (1874-1940), another member of the first Moscow Art Theater. Meyerhold argued that the very essence of theater was not to be 'realistic' but to be 'theatrical.' He would interrupt the narrative of a play with interludes to allow the entire cast to produce a special effect, representing the tension that was building behind the scenes. He called this a 'symbolic' effect. Meyerhold believed that the theater was the place for spectacular, contrived effects, brought off with professional understanding.

The story line of the play might be suddenly interrupted by the whole cast acting out a particular emotional state or representing the energy of a particularly fateful moment. The actors might use gestures, dance movements, or other special effects. With respect to the sets, the house in which a murder had been committed might appear bizarre and sinister, with no real right angles in its structure. In the 'symbolic' interludes of the play the actors might contribute in the manner of a Greek chorus, voicing collective sentiments, but — with Meyerhold — their intervention was usually a little more of a spectacle. He made much use of the moving center, in the sense of learned gestures and learned movements. This was not, in his mind, a contradiction to the idea of the actors producing the appropriate emotions

Figure 58. The chorus expresses remorse.

Figure 59. A spiderweb enmeshes the players in sleep.

within themselves. It related, rather, to the intentional communication of those emotions to an audience by means of theatrical devices.

In Figure 58 the actors interrupt the narrative of the play to create a symbolic representation of a state of guilt.

It was Yevgeny Vakhtangov (1874-1940) who combined the realism of Stanislavsky's theater with the theatrical innovations of Meyerhold, creating an onstage world where fantastic, magical, and fairy-tale events occur, which the actors respond to in a realistic way. This approach was called *fantastic realism*.

In Figure 59 the actors struggle to find their way through a fantastical world.

Stanislavsky, just before his death, called Vakhtangov, "my sole heir." Alexander Horn said that Vakhtangov, "Trained by Stanislavsky ... was the most inspired director to come out of the studio tradition. Vakhtangov worked closely with Michael Chekhov on contributions to the art of the theater and directed some of the most beautiful productions of the twentieth century."[1]

---

1. Horn, Alexander Francis, *In Search of a Solar Hero,* Element Books Ltd, Shaftesbury, Dorset UK, 1987, p. 314, footnote #2 to *The Legend of Sharon Shashanovah*).

Alex immediately saw in Vakhtangov's innovations a means of recovering the cosmic theater of Dante and Shakespeare. He wanted to show Man in his place in the living universe. He aspired to go beyond Vakhtangov's representation of "fantastic, magical, and fairy-tale events," to a full representation of Heaven and Hell — including the beings who inhabit those realms. It was his aim to present the intersection of these worlds — Heaven, Hell, Earth — and the interaction of the beings who inhabit them. To this end he made abundant use of the upper stage, of a wide variety of exotic stage sets and costumes, and of Meyerhold's symbolic techniques. He regularly introduced collective gesture and dance.

The sets in his plays often depicted symbolic worlds that the actors would respond to as real. This evoked in the audience a sense of the actual presence of divine and demonic forces in our own world and in the theater.

We could say that Alex incorporated the techniques of Stanislavksy, Meyerhold, and Vakhtangov to recreate the cosmic theater of Dante.

Alex was also influenced by the acting techniques developed by Michael Chekhov, nephew of the playwright Anton Chekhov and member of the first Moscow Art Theater. In 1928 Michael Chekhov broke with the Soviet version of the Moscow Art Theater (the second theater of 1924-36) and emigrated to the UK. At the outbreak of war in 1939, he moved to America. There he started the Chekhov Ridgefield School in Ridgefield, Connecticut. This school was broken up by the American draft in 1942, and Chekhov relocated to Hollywood where he taught many film stars, including Marilyn Monroe, Anthony Quinn, Clint Eastwood, Yul Brynner, Jack Palance, and Elia Kazan. Chekhov's teaching had a great impact on the American film industry, but in coaching the stars he created a popular version of the realism of the first Moscow Art Theater.

Alex employed many of the training exercises that Michael Chekhov developed, such as molding, floating, and flying in space. In Alex's 1979 play, *The Legend of Sharon Shashanova,* the background character Jacob Shashanov is similar to the background presence of Michael Chekhov in American theater in the 1960s.

Let us now consider what was happening in film during Alex's undergraduate years at the University of Chicago, in order to capture the note that was then sounding. These years correspond to Elia Kazan's prominence as a director, with films such as *Death of a Salesman* (1949) and *East of Eden* (1955). Kazan discovered the actors Marlon Brando and James Dean. Both Kazan and Marlon Brando worked with Stella Adler and method acting. In his early roles Brando showed an electric spontaneity. Some of his greatest performances include *A Streetcar Named Desire* (1951), *Viva Zapata* (1952), *The Wild One* (1953), *Julius Caesar* (1953), and *On the Waterfront* (1954).

Turning to American theater, the two well-known American playwrights of the 20th century — Eugene O'Neill and Tennessee Williams — were both writing and producing their plays during the late 1940s and early 1950s. Eugene O'Neill's *The Iceman Cometh* was first produced in 1946 and *A Long Day's Journey into Night* was produced posthumously in 1956. Tennessee Williams' plays *The Glass Menagerie* and *Streetcar Named Desire* were both produced in 1944, and *Cat on a Hot Tin Roof* in 1955. Both O'Neill and Williams were tragic realists; despairing critics of the American social order, with a real genius for holding the mirror to its face. There is the thread of everyday social exchange with veins of repressed tension running through it, and then, in certain moments, desperation and desire break through. At points these plays are volcanic. O'Neill and Williams cut open veins in the popular culture of their time, going right through to a level of repressed emotion. Alex did the same, and some scenes in his plays resonate with this genre of theater.

While there are moments of catharsis in both O'Neill and Williams, neither show a trace of cosmic context. In 1949 Arthur Miller wrote *Death of a Salesman* in a similar genre, with a little more sympathy for the protagonist. This *was* American theater in the postwar period. All of these writers were winning Pulitzer Prizes for their work.

There was a single exception to this unbroken stream of tragic realism. In 1938 Thornton Wilder, a student of Orage and Gurdjieff, produced *Our Town*. This portrays a cosmic context — worlds above and worlds below — and suggests transcendence. It was commercially successful, and it won the Pulitzer Prize for drama in that year. So perhaps the American public was ready for something more than the a-cosmic pessimism of O'Neill and Williams.

Alex Horn took O'Neill and Williams' 'tragedy of despair' through to Greek Tragedy with Transcendence. His plays give you something to live for. And he went one step further than Aeschylus and Sophocles by making *explicit* the cosmic context (to an audience that did not regularly attend the Eleusinian mysteries). Additionally, in the plays of his King Trilogy (*Adam King, The Magician,* and *I*), Alex follows Aristotle's rule of taking "noted men of noble families" for his characters. Finally, there is an explosiveness and expressiveness in Horn's work that is reminiscent of O'Neill and Williams. Alexander Horn's drama seamlessly integrates the best of American theater with 1) the acting techniques of fantastic realism and 2) the Aristotelian principle that drama should resemble "a living organism in all its unity." And, following Dante and Shakespeare, he presents man once more in full heroic stature. Thus, he draws from each of the great dramatic schools of the Western Tradition in an American context.

PLAYWRIGHTS THEATER CLUB/COMPASS PLAYERS

The University of Chicago in the early 1950s was a good place for a young actor to be. The Drama Department offered advanced programs, and the faculty and graduate students would have had exposure to the traditions of the Moscow Art Theater, via the American Laboratory Theater, the Chekhov Ridgefield School, or the School of Dramatic Art. And Francis Fergusson, while not teaching at the University of Chicago, was well known in the Drama Department. In 1952 he moved from Princeton University to take a post at the University of Indiana, within driving distance of Chicago. A motivated University of Chicago student would have been able to attend some of his lectures and workshops. A particularly motivated student might even have attempted to seek out some of his Russian *émigré* associates.

More generally, we don't know the exact points of contact between the young Alexander Horn and the tradition of the Moscow Art Theater, but the mature Alex does leave us with some clues. In his 1979 play *The Legend of Sharon Shashanovah,* he introduces the characters of Madame Natasha Ilyichna Ravenskaya and Jacob Shashanov. Madame Ravenskaya is an acting coach of great authority. Her character almost certainly owes something to Constantine Stanislavsky's student Maria Ouspenskaya, who was a founder of the School of Dramatic Art. She died in 1949 when Alex was twenty, and it is possible that he met her. The character of Jacob Shashanov is reminiscent of Michael Chekhov, who died in 1955, just after Alex's graduation.

In 1953, at about the time of Alex's graduation, a theater group formed — loosely connected with the university — called the Playwrights Theater Club. It had evolved out of groups that had been active on campus the three preceding years. Alex was certainly active in the precursor groups, and naturally became involved with the Playwrights Theater Club as it developed.

The Playwrights Theater Club was founded by David Shepherd and Paul Sills. Within two years, in 1955, Shepherd and Sills felt the need to recreate it as the Compass Players. The very success of the Compass Players forced a second restart. In 1959 Paul Sills, Bernie Sahlins, and Howard Alk launched The Second City company, perhaps the best-known theater company in America. It continues active to this day. This series of Chicago-based groups generated many of the stars of the 1960s, including Alan Alda, Shelley Berman, David Shepherd, Paul Sill, Mike Nichols, Elaine May, Jerry Siller, Ed Asner, Jerry Cunliffe, and Alan Arkin. Alex was involved with all of these groups and was known to the people in them. Later — in the period after Rodney Collin's death and before he opened his own theater group — Alex maintained a working connection with The Second City.

Both the Playwrights Theater Club and the Compass Players produced plays that were derived from improvisations, worked up out of general outlines. Both theater groups were in the tradition of the Italian *commedia dell'arte,* which made use of theater games to enable spontaneous real-time interplay between actors. The games taught the actors not to think about themselves, but to be aware of the others around them and of what was

Figure 60. Alex Horn, Ed Asner, and a third actor (Playwright's Theater Club 1953).

going on in the room. They developed a live, interactive relationship with the other members of the cast *and* with the audience. This is, we speculate, related to what Alex had been doing in the campus-based groups in his undergraduate years. Certainly the *commedia dell'arte* skills remained with him. As a teacher Alex was *always* intentionally producing an effect on his students, in relation to their state of consciousness. He was *interacting* with them not just to 'engage an audience,' but to engage something deeper and more intimate: the third state of consciousness. Having freed his lower centers from the grip of the second state he had a spontaneity and responsiveness that could be placed at the service of higher centers.

As we noted, during Alex's undergraduate years at the University of Chicago he made contact with Rodney Collin's Unicorn Players. The point to emphasize here is that the theater group work of Alex's 2nd and 3rd years, and the experimental work with the Playwrights Theater Club and the Compass Players that followed, would have *overlapped* with Alex's exposure to the Unicorn Players. Alex would have seen the theater groups *in light* of his understanding of conscious theater. And the work of the Unicorn Players was not at all part of the *commedia dell'arte* tradition which inspired the two theater groups. At the same time Rodney Collin's work would have both reinforced and transcended Francis Fergusson's teaching of the cosmic context. Here, then, we have a strong and formative correspondence. What Francis Fergusson taught, Rodney Collin was actually practicing. The influence of Rodney Collin had the effect of permanently splitting Alexander Horn off from the American theater of his own time. He ultimately refused to play by the rules of the Compass Players or The Second City. He gained experience acting in the Chicago groups, but he learned about great theater from Francis Fergusson and Rodney Collin.

The split with contemporary American theater deepened to include acting as well. As we have noted, interpretations of the Stanislavsky method had begun to circulate in Hollywood under the general banner of Stella Adler's method acting. By 1950 method acting had had been reduced, in some quarters, to techniques used to make an impact on the screen. The typecast stars would remain typecast stars, who used method acting techniques to hold their audience. Alex despised the Hollywood star system, and the destruction of dramatic art that it produced. In his play *The Legend of Sharon Shashanova* the lead character, Sharon Shashanovah, speaks of "the Hollywood commercial machine" ruining "Griffith, Welles, Von Stroheim, my beautiful Michael Chekhov."[1]

Having said these things about American theater culture, we note that the improvisational game-playing techniques used by the Playwright's Theater Club perfectly complement both the Stanislavsky method and the principles of Greek tragedy. These interactive techniques empower the theater to "to hold...the mirror up to nature," as Hamlet put it, "to show Virtue her own feature, scorn her own image, and the very age and body of the time his form and pressure." Improvisational theater technique helps to bring all of this alive in the moment.

In sum, Francis Fergusson, Rodney Collin, and the heritage of the first Moscow Art Theater penetrated Alexander Horn's artistic center. These influences came together seamlessly, drawing an invisible line between his own work and: 1) the typecast performances of the Hollywood stars, and 2) the spontaneous comedics of The Second City. As an actor Alex returned to the world of the young Michael Chekhov.

---

1. Horn, Alexander Francis, *Ponderings of a Citizen of the Milky Way*, Element Books Ltd, Shaftesbury, Dorset UK, 1987, p. 145.

THE IDEA OF A MAGIC THEATER

Another influence on Alexander Horn was the writings of Hermann Hesse. Hesse's major works had all been translated into English by 1956, and they achieved mass circulation in the early 1960s. Hesse's novel *Steppenwolf*, available in English from 1929, would have come to Alex in his undergraduate years. In this novel we see a template on which a twentieth century cosmic theater might be modeled.[1] But there is more to it than this. Hesse's template bridges theater with 'school of theater' — a fine line that the mature Alexander Horn walked for forty years.

The protagonist of *Steppenwolf*, Harry Haller, encounters a Magic Theater through two of its members, who we know only as Pablo and Hermine. They are both magicians. Within the Magic Theater they guide Harry though many different scenarios, which turn out to be playbacks of scenarios existing in Harry's own mind. It is all somehow accomplished through mirrors. These mirrors show Harry all the different stages of his life, drilling into repressed areas to show what actually happened rather than what Harry remembered to have happened. They also show alternative playouts of what might have happened had Harry not followed a repressed negative impulse, or had he actually been able to follow a genuine impulse. Once Harry has *seen* one of these repressed areas in the mirror — seen it as it is — it ceases to act on him. He has integrated that content into who he presently is. If the persona shown in the mirror image no longer has a place in Harry's life, the mirror itself turns gray and charred and opaque, as though it had been burned out. Hermine, Harry's feminine guide, clearly understands Harry better than he understands himself. She is aware of the repressed aspects of his nature, and she is aware of his different personalities.

The interior of the Magic Theater is presented as a long circular hall, curved like a horseshoe. On the outside of the curve are doors that lead into mirror-rooms that portray either different chapters of one's life or different personalities. All around the inside of the curve is a gigantic floor-to-ceiling

---

1. During Alex Horn's years teaching in the Bay Area, he would recommend *Steppenwolf*, *The Glass Bead Game*, and *Journey to the East* as reading material for his students.

mirror. There is a relationship between this all-encompassing mirror and the mirrors of the separate chambers. It is only the clarity of the great mirror image that allows the apprentice actor (Harry Haller) to disengage from the personalities that are revealed in the smaller mirrors of the different chambers. In other words, it is only this mirror that gives continuity to all the different things that are happening inside of all the chambers. As the mirrors in the chambers crumble and char, the great mirror becomes ever clearer. In terms of the Fourth Way teaching, this is a representation of objective memory. Harry Haller's aim, as he understands it, is to achieve awareness of his different personalities, eliminating those that are destructive, and achieving a degree of disengagement from the others that will allow him more freedom to maneuver and more possibility for change. Pablo instructs Harry:

> ... we supplement the imperfect psychology of science by the conception that we call the art of building up the soul. We demonstrate to anyone whose soul has fallen to pieces that he can rearrange these pieces of a previous self in what order he pleases, and so attain to an endless multiplicity of moves in the game of life. As the playwright shapes a drama from a handful of characters, so do we, from the pieces of the disintegrated self, build up ever new groups, with ever new interplay and suspense, and new situations that are eternally inexhaustible.[2]

For Hesse, the understanding of man's lack of unity is the key to opening the actor to the depths of their nature. The goal of the Magic Theater is the dissolution of the shell-personality that is our social identity. The individual is dissolved into 1,000 selves. The disengagement from the illusory selves releases creativity and insight of different kinds; it opens a new world of possibilities. As you get behind the different parts of yourself, you can find altogether new alternatives. You can own certain behaviors rather than simply be possessed by them. Because you can observe these behavior-patterns, you can also see how they affect other people, and how they react to you. As

---

2. Hesse, Hermann, *Steppenwolf*, transl. from the German by Basil Creighton, Holt, Rinehart and Winston, New York, 1963, p. 192.

this capacity develops, you become aware of other people in your past who had a formative impact on you. You can become aware in what way they exist in your present, and you can either accept their influence or reject it. In sum, you can have a deeper awareness of your own time-body.

Yet all these aims fall short of the aim of creating a soul, as that is understood in the Fourth Way. It is true that on the Fourth Way one must learn to break oneself up into pieces, to have an awareness that is independent of all the separate pieces, and to be able to rearrange the pieces in new ways. But the Fourth Way is focused on consciousness fully self-aware; not just the consciousness of this or that aspect of oneself. It is focused on the awakening of the latent Self. When this level comes awake it naturally rearranges the world below it. But the Self arranges the different bundles of 'I's in a form suitable to its own continued existence, and it values sustaining that existence immeasurably more than it values 'more effective performances' in the external world. There are many things in us that are not compatible with the aims of the Self, and there are few that are: and only the Self knows which is which. So while there is some commonality between the work of Pablo and Hermine and the work of the Fourth Way, the latter clearly transcends the former.

In *Steppenwolf* there is a vague idea of a level beyond the level we are on, but one does not feel that any of the characters — Pablo, Hermine, or Harry — are centered in it. Alex Horn, in his maturity, was centered in that level: he had a Self. And from that vantage point he was able to use objective understanding to complete Hesse's *Magic Theater* in the truly cosmic *Theatre of All Possibilities*. We note that the theaters Alex used on Mission Street and Golden Gate Avenue in San Francisco, and the theaters his group later used in New York, had their walls hung with literally hundreds of mirrors. The mature Alex Horn taught his students, much more directly than Pablo and Hermine taught Harry Haller, that their souls were in pieces. He did not train them to play an infinitely creative game rearranging those pieces. Rather he prepared them for: 1) the displacement of the false 'I', and 2) the arrival of the Real I that fills the void created by this displacement. Alex Horn's cosmic theater was reflected both in his direct work with his students and in his creation of the *Theatre of All Possibilities*. He combined a Hesse-like theater of internal development with the attempt to reawaken a conscious theatric tradition in the West.

CONVERGENCE OF THE THEATER AND THE MIRACULOUS

The contact with Rodney Collin was the point at which two major themes of Alex's life — *the theater* and *the search for the miraculous* — converged. Here Alex was not receiving *just* exposure to the theater or *just* esoteric teaching, he was receiving both at once. Rodney was an awakened actor/director/writer, and this is what Alex was later to become. This was, perhaps, the strongest formative imprint of Alexander Horn's lifetime. Let us review what we know of this time.

Rodney Collin's play *Hellas* was written in 1948, just after Rodney established his group at Tlalpham, on the outskirts of Mexico City. (This was the year in which Alex began his undergraduate studies.) The play was probably first performed in that year, at a theater in Mexico City. We do not know what other plays the Unicorn Players produced at that time. In 1951 Rodney's group began to construct the Planetarium, which was located in the mountains behind Mexico City. The new project displaced the group's emphasis on drama, although it did continue in the background. In 1954, with the arrival of Mema Dickens in Rodney's group, the work on the Planetarium was put on hold, and — for some reason — emphasis shifted back to the theater. The Unicorn Players then entered their most active phase, producing a series of public performances which ended only with Rodney's death in May of 1956.

We recall, then, that Alex graduated from the University of Chicago in 1953/54, and this would place him in a position to be directly involved with the most intensive phase of Rodney's work. The Unicorn Players produced Ibsen's *Peer Gynt* in 1954 and Jean Anouilh's *The Lark* in 1955. The group would also likely have produced Rodney's play, *Hellas*. We note that in this play, the character of The Shadow is like Alexander Horn's character of the Tyrant, who appears in each of the plays of the King Trilogy.

In most of Alex's six plays (produced between 1972 and 1981) there is a graphic presentation of contact with the dead, or — more specifically — with deceased conscious beings who are no longer in the embodied state. In each of the King Trilogy plays there is mention of a vow made to such a person in the protagonist's past. These descriptions are so vivid that they seem to correspond to something within the author's experience. Could they be rooted in the contact he had with Rodney Collin? Rodney's unexpected death in 1956, at the age of 47, must have been a terrific shock to Alex. Did Alex sense something of Rodney's continued presence in his life in the years following? In his final play *I* Alex has a God tell the protagonist that, "All men make a vow and then they forget." Did Alex feel that this described something of his relationship to Rodney Collin?

In Rodney Collin's play *Hellas* Alex would have found the 'cosmic context' that he had studied in Shakespearian, Medieval, and Greek drama. *Hellas* was based on the author's firsthand experience of the molecular and electronic worlds, and the play presents people having the experience of both of those worlds. The entire dramatic production was used as a means of producing presence, in both the actors and the audience. Additionally, Rodney Collin saw the theater as embodying a unity of the performing arts. He made a combined use of music, dance, and theater. The mature Alexander Horn did the same. More specifically, the voice and expressions of the characters of *Hellas,* when they come into contact with Worlds 6 and 12, are similar to the voice later used by Alex in that same context. There is the same outspoken simplicity, intensity, and sincerity. In *Hellas* Rodney several times represents — in a unique way — the long body of the civilization of Greece: that is, how it would appear as one phenomenon when seen from outside of time. Alex Horn presents this same vision in both *The Fantastic Arising of Padraic Clancy Muldoon* and *The Journey to Jerusalem*. In *Hellas* Rodney Collin adopts the form of Goethe's drama *Faust,* which begins with a Prologue in Heaven, then returns to the place of the Prologue between each scene and concludes with it in the final scene. Alex Horn used this same device in his last play *I*. Having said this, Alex did not remain an apprentice to his master, he became a master himself. Alex's mature plays have greater dramatic unity and exhibit a wider range of voices than *Hellas*.

While we have suggested a continuity between the work of Rodney's group and the work of Alex's group, there were also significant differences. As we know, in his later years, Rodney was guided by transmissions from a psychic medium, joined the Catholic Church, and anticipated the direct involvement of the entire celestial hierarchy in a coming New Age. As a teacher Alex did not associate with any church, did not make any prophetic predictions, and focused on keeping his students out of imagination. It may have been that he did not want to replicate certain things that he had seen in Rodney's group, just as Ouspensky did not want to replicate certain things that he had seen in Gurdjieff's group. Having said that, Alex did pursue Collin's principal of harmony through all his plays. And he did acknowledge C Influence, although in a more understated way than Rodney had. Alex did not dismiss the idea of an Ark or a New Age, but he did not at all emphasize those themes. His principal focus, as a teacher, was very much to relieve his students of their life-illusions — to connect them to the 'great mirror' on the inside curve of Hermann Hesse's *Magic Theater*.

In summing up Alex's student years, it is clear that he led a very full undergraduate life. His contemporary David Daniels described him as talented, energetic, and in a psychological condition where "he could not be afraid of anything." This latter state suggests some formative movement of Higher Centers, freeing him from the sediment of fear and self-doubt that is at the base of every human psychology.

Journeyman Years: 1956–1965

Alex Horn graduated from the University of Chicago in 1952-1953. Rodney Collin died a few years later in 1956, when Alex was 27. Alex appeared in San Francisco, as a fully-fledged teacher, at the age of 36 in 1965. There is a nine-year period, then, between the death of Rodney Collin and Alex's appearance in San Francisco. These were his *wanderjahre*: the years in which the young journeyman travels, taking different jobs under different masters, developing the skills needed to function as a master himself.[1] These years

---

1. This is the term Goethe used to describe the life of the young Wilhelm Meister.

gave him experience with theater and — more importantly — served as a forcing house for Alex's fledgling Higher Centers.

At the time of Rodney's death in 1956 Alex was one of many aspiring actors and theater people in the Chicago area. Rodney had not — that we know of — designated him as a successor or asked him to teach. Yet the separation of consciousness from functions had well begun. When Alex appeared in San Francisco in 1965 he seemed a man with a mission, just as George Gurdjieff had appeared to his pupils in Moscow in 1912. He had a remarkable presence, floored everyone he met, and launched multiple, connected projects — one after another.

It was probably during the *wanderjahre* that Alex Horn began to have direct encounters with C Influence. Disembodied conscious beings are represented in *every one* of his plays. In Alex's own words:

> The gods ... have always been with us, but man, asleep, has failed to see them. When he awakens to his blindness, his illusions, his self-deceit, his paralyzed state of impotence, and takes the decisive step of dying to himself, he can be reborn as a conscious being in their company — to the heavenly kingdom that lies within him, and which has always awaited him, and inherit the Earth at last.[1]

We submit that, when Alexander Horn wrote these words, he was speaking from direct experience. There may have been an initial contact with the Gods before Rodney Collin's death, which left him a wanderer without a teacher, moving between Boston, Chicago, and New York. Such an initial contact would have given him a pole star by which to navigate the difficult years to come. There were likely critical or formative contacts with the Gods between 1960 and 1965 which gave him his mandate to teach. At the end of this time he did have such a mandate; he was clearly a 'tasked' man, or as Saint Paul put it a 'bondman.' And he gave himself unreservedly to teaching for the remainder of his life — sustaining a pitch of activity over four decades that was unmatched in the previous history of the Fourth Way.

---

1. Horn, Alexander Francis, from the introduction to *In Search of a Solar Hero* and *Ponderings of a Citizen of the Milky Way*, (both) Element Books, Shaftesbury, Dorset UK, 1987, p. xiii.

Thus, Rodney Collin gave Alex Horn the Fourth Way teaching in pure conscious form, and then the Gods undertook to complete his crystallization as a man number five. In attending his crystallization, they gave him some idea of what was expected of him. They may also have given him restrictions. For example, Alex directed and produced plays, but he did not engage any of the media connections he had established in Boston and New York. He never followed the conventional promotional channels of the industry. He never played to a Hollywood audience or even to a Second City audience, and he consistently broke many of the conventions that would have allowed him to do so. At the same time, he felt empowered to work intensively and personally with all his students, directly confronting them with their features, and putting them in touch with their own Higher Centers. He never focused on accumulating money for himself. What he had he spent on his group, on the group retreats, and on the theater projects. He did everything in a certain way and never broke his own rules.

While we know little of Alex's life between 1956 and 1965, we do know he continued with the theater. He was active with both the Compass Players and later The Second City. In the late 1950s Alex began to produce plays in and around Chicago and New York. By 1963-64 he had produced several plays with a theater group under his direction, which he named *The Theatre of All Possibilities* (with the Anglicized spelling).[2] During these same years Alex retained his connection with the Gurdjieff Foundation and with

---

2. *The Theatre of All Possibilities* became a generic name for Alex's theater group in later years. He may, however, have run into copyright problems using that name when he opened his theater in San Francisco in the late 1960s. The incorporated name of the first San Francisco theater group was *Everyman Theatre*, and that name appeared on the first theater Alex used for his performances, at the corner of 3316 24th Street and Mission. Yet Alex Horn's theater, as an artistic venture, continued to be referred to by his students as *The Theatre of All Possibilities*. The second theater Alex used in San Francisco, at 150 Golden Gate Avenue, was named *The Theatre of All Possibilities*. This discrepancy between the two names is reflected in his first publication of his plays: e.g., Horn, Alexander Francis, *Theatre of All Possibilities,* Everyman Publications, San Francisco, 1978. Everyman is given

Willem Nyland's groups. In 1960 he travelled with a small theater group to J.G. Bennett's property at Coombe Springs, just southwest of London. Bennett's group was, at that time, involved in an open field of experimental work, which included theater. There he met Anne Burrage, whom he married and with whom he was to have five children. Alex was 31; Anne, 18.

At the time of Alex's visit, Bennett was working with a Javanese mystic, Bapak Subuh, who practiced a method called the *latihan*. Subuh was the founder of the Subud Religion, which was based on the practice of the Latihan technique. Bennett's group practiced the latihan from 1956, and by 1958 Bennett had dropped the Gurdjieff work in favor of latihan practice, believing that it was, in itself, sufficient to awaken. By 1960 Bennett had determined that the latihan was not sufficient to awaken, and supplemented it again with the Gurdjieff methods. In 1962, after a number of suicides in his group, Bennett dropped the latihan altogether. During Alex's visit the latihan was being practiced as the principal method to achieve awakening.

The method involved spinning on the spot, to stimulate the molecular body and release either expansive states of consciousness or repressed pockets of deep negativity — much as psychedelic drugs do for the unprepared. In Fourth Way terms, buffers are dissolved and both positive and negative experiences follow. You see into yourself and you see many things that you do not normally see. To the extent that you can see these things in yourself, you can usually — to a greater or lesser degree — see them in others. J.G. Bennett speaks of a latihan session which initiated a purgation that lasted for fourteen days:

> This experience was truly purgatorial. A vivid inner light began pitilessly to shine upon my own past. My life stood before me in every detail ... I recalled everything, pleasant and unpleasant — especially those episodes which I had wished to forget. ... all were displayed and made sharply, mercilessly visible in hundreds of episodes that

---

as the publisher and was probably the same business organization as the incorporated theater group.

Figure 61. Poster for *The Magician*.

haunted me like malignant imps. I could not for a moment forget them. At night I could not sleep for remorse and self-loathing.[1]

It is likely that Alex practiced the latihan, but whether he did or not, he had this kind of insight into his own students' lives. This faculty seems to have become fixed in him with the opening of his Higher Centers, so that he did not need any technique to sustain it. He could see others' thoughts and feelings, and he could see things about their past. In a cross-examination he could read responses that were not articulated, and he could read them very clearly. It was impossible to deceive him. This was part of his working repertoire as a teacher.

---

1. See Bennett, J.G., *Witness, the Story of a Search,* Dharma Book Company, Inc., New York, New York, 1962, p. 338-339.

To understand Alex's teaching, we must turn from Alex himself to the world that he inhabited in the late 1950s and early 1960s. America's counterculture was breaking out of the rigid cold war mentality and leaving behind the post-war and post-depression fixation with security and career. All of Alex's plays reflect the atmosphere of this time.

AMERICA IN THE LATE FIFTIES AND EARLY SIXTIES

By 1956 the Beat Generation Movement had reached its acme. Jack Kerouac's *On the Road* was published in 1957 and *The Dharma Bums* in 1958. Allen Ginsberg's *Howl* was published in 1956, and William S. Burroughs' *Naked Lunch* in 1959. Leonard Bernstein's musical *West Side Story* opened in 1957, and the note sounded in Tony's song "Something's Coming" — the tremendous sense of hope and of approaching apotheosis — resonated through the whole decade to follow. Tennessee William's *Cat on a Hot Tin Roof* premiered in 1958, stripping the mask off bourgeois complacency. By the late 1950s Woody Guthrie, Pete Seeger, the Weavers, and the Kingston Trio were making a new kind of music.

In 1957 Martin Luther King Jr. met with sixty black pastors and civil rights leaders to coordinate nonviolent protests against racial discrimination. John F. Kennedy became president in 1961 and, under his leadership, Sargent Shriver formed the Peace Corps. In 1964 the War on Poverty was announced. New social ideals found expression in the music of Peter, Paul and Mary, the Limeliters, the Seekers, Simon and Garfunkel, and Joan Baez. From 1962 Bob Dylan began cutting records.

At a certain point the 1960s took off. In 1962 Michael Murphy and Dick Price opened the *Esalen Institute* at Big Sur, dedicated to the realization of human potential: gestalt therapy, rolfing, Reichian therapy, prenatal psychology, and transpersonal psychology. And there was the conservative reaction. John F. Kennedy was assassinated in 1963 and Malcolm X in 1965. In 1965 the American Ground War began in Vietnam, and the reality of what happened there was televised across the nation daily. In that same year a ground war of another kind began: Neal Cassady, Ken Kesey and the thirteen other Merry Pranksters set out on The Electric Kool Aid Acid Bus to cross the nation, fueling on pure Sandoz LSD-25. A generation of young people began to "turn on, tune in, and drop out." Teenagers from the east coast packed their bags into colorfully painted Volkswagen vans and headed across the continent to California. The full flowering of the 1960s came with the music of The Doors, The Grateful Dead, The Mamas and the Papas, Jefferson Airplane, and The Mothers of Invention. San Francisco's Haight-Ashbury district became a legendary center of psychedelia. Alterative views of 'the Establishment' became general in the rising generation. The standard undergraduate reading material of those years included Marx's *Critique of Political Economy*, Lenin's *Imperialism, Highest Phase of Capitalism*, Herbert Marcuse's *One Dimensional Man*, and Hermann Hesse's *Steppenwolf*. A whole generation reached a sudden conviction that the future was not going to be anything like the past.

These were the years in which Alexander Francis Horn awakened and began to teach. There was an explosive openness and a feeling that anything was possible. As a teacher Alex harnessed this energy with a clear sense of aim in relation to man's highest possibilities, and a firm discipline in relation to that aim. He took the 'psychedelic' through to the legitimate experience of Higher Centers. He translated the ideals of the counterculture into the ideals of the Great Work. He took breaking social conventions through to breaking the hold of features and formatory mind, and the consequent release of man from the bonds of imagination. He took the inchoate desire for experience through to a liberated Eros. And he gave a generation determined to "break on through to the other side" a real destination.

To repeat, we know little of Alex's doings from 1956 to 1965. He was involved in theater activities, he participated in group work of different kinds, and he became the father of a fast-growing family. But in 1965 he suddenly appears at a party in the San Francisco Bay Area as a fully formed teacher.

Alex as Teacher: 1965–1988

Alex Horn and Anne Burrage arrived in the Bay Area in early 1965 with a growing family.[1] They rented a large Victorian house in the Haight District, and then — using Anne's money — purchased property in Sonoma County, on the rim of the Valley of the Moon. The house in the Haight was a family residence, which could be used for prospective student meetings. The property in Sonoma, which had a residence and outbuildings, gave the group the space and privacy it would need for its activities.

How did it all begin? Alex had a few contacts in the Bay Area, including Ron and Alexa Russel. It may be that Ron and Alexa had worked with Alex in the theater on the East Coast. They were themselves part of a much wider social circle, which was principally comprised of hippies; the children

---

1. In 1965 Alex was 36 and Anne 23. They were to have five children: Maurice, Elaine, Matthew, Mary Ellen, and Benjamin.

of middle class families who had dropped out of what was appropriately called the 'American dream.' When Alex let Ron and Alexa know that he was coming to the Bay Area, they invited him to a party at their house, off Sonoma Mountain Road, introducing him to their friends as a spiritual teacher from New York.

On arrival at the party Alex found a group of young people happily smoking pot and listening to rock music. They were, perhaps, expecting a 'love and light' Sufi, or a new version of the Beatle's Maharishi Mahesh Yogi — who would affirm their 'tune in, turn on, and drop out' lifestyle. Alex entered the party quietly and observed what was going on. We might imagine Barry Mann's song, *There's a New World Coming*, playing: "There's a new day dawning, the one that's for you and me ... and I saw another Heaven ... and its just around the bend." During a momentary lull, while someone was changing the records, Alex spoke out, in his clear, crisp baritone voice: "You think you're in heaven, but you're really all in hell, and I'm the only person here who can tell you how to get out." This attracted a number of different responses. Alex held forth, "answering every question with unwavering nerve and charisma — thus transforming the loose gathering into a core group of proto-followers then and there." Alex's presentation drew a sharp dividing line in the group, separating those with a definite interest from those who had none. The impact of Alex's presentation permanently separated couples at a single stroke.[1]

Shortly after the party a 'Gurdjieff Weekend' was arranged at the Sonoma property. Activities began on Friday afternoon and lasted until late Sunday night. That weekend helped to consolidate the group and established a pattern for weekends to follow. After the initial party a more formal meeting was held at the San Francisco Victorian house, where Alex outlined the plan of his work. Committees and sub-groups were created, related to the different projects he envisaged. In the beginning each student was asked to pay $150 a month, and occasionally extra payments were asked. The fledgling group soon launched a small vineyard on the property at Sonoma.

---

1. These words, from an online posting, were reported to Dave Archer by Ron Russel.

From the very beginning there were meetings several times a week, retreats at the Sonoma ranch, and construction projects of different kinds. The recruitment of new students also became an ongoing third line activity. Alex presented the group to prospective students as a fast-moving train. If you did not board the train NOW, you would miss your chance at the miraculous. All students were required to have a full-time job, and students who were independently wealthy were also expected to take jobs, just to comply with the task. In the beginning Alex lead all the prospective student meetings, but soon other students were involved.

We have learned just enough about how Alex's work began to describe the form of his teaching. It is necessary to present this form before we run though the history of the group, because the events themselves would have little meaning without reference to it. As the form did not reach maturity until the early 1970s, we shall have to run a bit ahead of ourselves. The first area in which we shall 'run ahead' is in introducing Sharon Gans. As we noted, Anne Burrage had been Alex's partner in the first years of the teaching, but she was never herself a teacher. Very few accounts of that time mention her name. Alex's second wife, Sharon Gans, whom he married two years after his separation from Anne, was both a partner and a teacher. She helped Alex to define the form of his group. Thus, we will here present the form of the group as it was after Sharon's arrival in 1972.

THE FORM OF THE TEACHING

A student of the San Francisco years, Thomas Farber, has left us with a record of how Alex himself presented his teaching. The following record is from 1967. Thomas describes Alex addressing a group of prospective students:

> We are a group doing the Work. Many of our teachings come from George Gurdjieff. We learn also, as he did, from any Higher Man. We have a ranch, and each weekend we work on the ranch. We have a fourth-way school, that is not the way of the yogi, the monk, or the fakir, but a school in life, a school to build being. It costs two hundred dollars a month for each person to work, payable in advance. If there is something you want from us, you may come, but

do so only if you intend to get your money's worth. Otherwise, you will only waste your time and ours.

You know, I am sure, that we can all read the words of Christ and other inspired men. Many of us do. Yet after all has been read, we do not act on these words. We aspire to something finer but do not approach it. Our premise here, then, is that we must first confront the worst in ourselves, our mechanicality, our sleeping state, and then, perhaps, hope to find our way to love. It is of course our obligation to care for others. Yet here, now, we cannot, even as we try — we do not know how to begin. With luck, with Work, we will be perhaps more than part-time liars, cheats, and fools. With the help of others in this Work, we may be able to remember ourselves, to work, to work to our finest part, but we can do nothing before confronting, fighting, and accepting what we are now. We begin at the beginning.[1]

Thomas recorded that after having attended the meeting, which ran for over an hour ...

I could focus only on the man himself, his clarity, directness, and control, and concede that I had in fact never seen anything like him in my life. True, I had been shocked, but what stayed with me was the intentionality of the effect he had produced, the obviously purposive staging of the whole evening.[2]

What was striking about the speaker's response [to questions] was the overwhelming softness of his words in their simplicity and directness .... After the meeting I drove across the Bay Bridge, moving smoothly above the water, lulled by the steady procession of lights, easing past the toll booth and off the freeway to home. I kept thinking about his remarkable display of energy and purpose, his overwhelming control and intensity. Though I had met my share of committed individuals, I had never seen anyone whose faith

---

1. Farber, Thomas, *Tales for the Son of My Unborn Child,* Pocket Books (Simon & Schuster, Inc.), New York, 1973, p. 113-114.
2. *Ibid.,* p. 111.

translated so directly into palpable energy, whose beliefs seemed to yield such presence, such authority, such power.[3]

The young Thomas Farber had received a transmission from Alex's Higher Centers. In such a transmission there is something behind the words that words themselves cannot convey; they just keep coming out of this integrated higher space, servants of a nameless master. In such a transmission there is a tremendous sense of purpose and almost limitless force — for the words are expressing a state that is sustaining itself through time. It is the state that speaks, not the man.

An experience of such depth and significance can transform one's life, but one must acknowledge it while it is occurring, remember it, and make it a reference point. The state from which the words come is connected to one's destiny; to receive such a transmission is part of one's fate. In a room of fifty people only those who have a right affinity, or a right preparation, will receive the transmission. The others will receive only the information. Of all those who do receive the state, only a few will be able to make it their life's purpose.

Involvement with the group very easily took all of a person's waking hours, if one includes the mandatory full-time job. Meetings took place on the theater stage, with everyone sitting in a large circle. Alex would teach during the first half, and in the second half he either asked students questions or asked how they were doing with their tasks. Students were asked personal questions, but they were not singled out from the group. The meetings might run for two or three hours, but they could also go on all night, depending on the state that developed amongst the people involved. In the San Francisco years meetings were held on Thursday and Saturday nights, the Thursday meeting focusing on knowledge and the Saturday meeting becoming more personal and going directly into student's work. Alex called the Saturday meetings 'being' meetings. With respect to the knowledge

---

3. *Ibid.*, p. 116.

meetings, Alexander Horn was a teacher who had internalized the cosmology of the system and he taught that cosmology as objectively true.

New students usually started with the group by attending the Thursday night meetings. If they showed a strong interest over time, they might be invited to a Saturday meeting. At the Saturday meeting Alex would interview the new student, asking him or her personal questions and on the basis of their reactions and replies assign a task. This task would target the student's particular area of weakness. Alex would not give a student a task until he was sure they were ready for it. A second interview might be based on questions about the student's progress with the task. When a task was worked through to successful completion, another task might be given. Everyone at a Saturday meeting was expected to contribute something, but one or two students might undergo lengthy questioning. This more intensive questioning was called "being on the hot seat." To this we shall return.

Alex was drawing mainly from counterculture people and instilling in them a discipline comparable to the discipline of the medieval monastic orders. While he did not take away all their countercultural diversions, and even encouraged a certain sense of adventure, the discipline was no less exacting.

In the 1960s and 1970s students were introduced, in the prospective student meetings and in the first few meetings thereafter, to the ideas presented in *The Psychology of Man's Possible Evolution*. These preliminary introductions gave new students an orientation that would allow the ideas to take hold in the right way.

It was easy to lose connection with the group, because of the level of pressure and the difficulty of the tasks assigned. People might be asked to leave for missing payments or for failing with a task. But it was also easy to come back; there would be a contact number that a person could call at any time. Alex actually expected many of the people that he asked to leave to come back. Sometimes a period of time was needed for a student to digest a particularly difficult lesson and to extract the value from it.

In speaking of the group's work, or of his own role in the group, Alex was always understated. He never presented himself as a Great Teacher; he just was what he was. He sometimes spoke of the Real Work or the Great

Work as a distant goal. Yet in certain moments he would speak of Higher Forces or C Influence as if they were present.

All of his students were under a vow not to speak about the group or about their work, except to other students or to people who might be interested in joining. There was no publicity. People found the group through open meetings, through direct contact with students, or through exposure to his public theater performances.

In the late 1960s Alex began to travel to Europe regularly, often taking a group of students with him.

THE BEING MEETING

At the Saturday meetings students were given tasks or questioned about their progress with tasks. Alex could, as we noted, read others' thoughts and feelings, and he could see things about a person's past. In his questioning he was immediately aware of responses that were unspoken, and it was impossible to deceive him. When a student was asked to report on the completion of a difficult task, Alex would know when they were being straightforward and when they were hiding something.

A student would sit on a chair at center stage of the theater, and Alex would ask them questions: "What do you do for a living?" "Well, I am a carpenter." "Are you doing that now?" "Oh, I don't have a job just now." "How did that come about?" The questioning followed an unerring line. Most of these interactions were, in the end, uplifting for the student. But if Alex sensed evasion, or if a person lied, he immediately knew it. And the questioning quickly brought it out.

When there was resistance to Alex's questioning, it might turn into a 'hot seat' situation. Alex was expert in bringing out the contradictions between what a student was saying and what he himself could see inside of them. In his cross examination he would reveal the student to themselves and to all the others in the room. It was as though they were being made objectively transparent. It was a kind of surgery. It was not easy to experience, and it was not easy to watch. But often the student came out of it on the higher side of themselves and was thankful for having been given the opportunity to separate from all the rest. And all the other students in the room got to see buffers in action and to consider if they wanted that kind of thing happening to them. One student described the process as a sacred act.

Alex did not perform this kind of interrogation out of cruelty, but because he insisted people be sincere with themselves and acknowledge things exactly as they were. He would quickly bring out contradictions deep in a person's nature, of a kind that people go through their whole adult lives without acknowledging. If a person was cooperative and truthful, he would be compassionate; but when someone was resistant, or tried to get smart with him, he could be severity itself. Some people would be on the hot seat for twenty minutes, others for up to four hours.

Everyone in the room was deeply affected by what went on, and it was demanding for all concerned. Each person saw himself or herself in the person being questioned. Sometimes a person would repeatedly deny things that everyone else in the room knew to be true. The only person not to acknowledge the truth would be the person on the hot seat, who had been pressured directly on their blind spot. And we all have such a blind spot. To see the blind spot in human nature is to see something universal. To some this seemed black magic. The hot seat provided a direct view of the mechanics by which chief feature defends itself. As students gained experience, they learned to reside more in presence itself — rather than in their defense mechanisms. They would then try to respond from presence, allowing Alex to help them see themselves more objectively. Alexander Francis Horn was a master at this technique. Some of his students said that he had told them things about their previous lives in a way that made their blood run cold. Some likened him to an exorcist.

One student remembered having been questioned about his father, who had been a fireman, and who had twice received awards for heroism. The student was proud of his father and spoke favorably of him. Alex suddenly asked, "So, why do you hate your father?" The student faltered. Sharon — acting as fair witness — interjected, "I don't think he hates his father?" But the student saw that Alex was right. His father had left his mother for another woman, leaving both his mother and him with no support, which had created great hardship for them both. The student remarked, "Alex knew things about me that I did not know about myself."

The result of such questioning would likely be a task, related to a perceived area of weakness. The tasks that Alex gave were not easy. A student who had left his job was asked to go back and beg to be rehired by the very manager who had let him go. Students who were at odds with a parent might be asked to return home to reconcile with them. There might equally be a task to stop having contact with one's family. A student might be asked to beg in the street, at a determined location, for a set period of time. One student was asked to walk across Times Square in his underwear. In these 'public' tasks, other students might be sent as observers to see how the task was executed.

What was important was not that you succeed with your task, but that you try your best, and Alex would know if you had not tried. He would also know how sincerely you had tried. If you did not complete a task, you would get fined, and each time you failed to complete the task the fine would double. He was a forcefully compassionate man.

Alexander Horn directly confronted false personality. He could use a term like "vile" to describe a deceptive action or an evasive response. He once explained to a student, "When you feel enough disgust, you really break it." He could be very challenging, but you also felt in him a fundamental concern. He wanted to get you past your identifications; he was, ultimately, a fatherly figure.

Alex changed people, and real internal change in an adult human being is rare. One student commented, "It was awesome to see Alex actually change someone in a matter of hours, just to watch it. It wasn't pretty and you didn't want it to happen to you. If a person consistently lied or was insincere, he might simply say, 'You can't come back for a month.' If this behavior continued he might say, 'Go, I am finished with you,' or simply, 'You can't help me.'" Another student said of his own experience, "I really felt that, in the course of this questioning, I was being worked on by something higher. I was experiencing the miraculous; the miracle of change. Alex Horn knew your mechanics. It was all about fear and love and the inevitable pain of internal change."

OTHER ASPECTS OF THE TEACHING

Alex Horn had an almost limitless ability to conceive events, expeditions, and adventures of different kinds. He was at the center of the dynamic social life of his group. He had an ability to use the backdrop of mid-twentieth-century California to create events and spectacles that people would never forget. The ranch site in Sonoma was beautiful and life was lived to the full, with both harsh trials and moments of joyous transcendence. There was a general feeling that the future was going to be entirely unlike the past.

In the San Francisco period all men had to play sports on Saturday mornings. During basketball season men had to play basketball at a local gym. During football season men played tackle football on the Marina green, with no equipment. There were times when all men had to take up boxing. There was the excitement, effort, and teamwork of the game, but beyond this Alex had a keen eye for aggression, fear, poor sportsmanship, and the identification with winning or losing.

Relationships were also an ongoing area of work. In the early years Alex was trying to transition his students from a hippie/communal lifestyle to conventional family relationships. Some students were asked to get married, or — if married — to have children, or to end a relationship. But this kind of direct intervention diminished as time went by. There was casual sex amongst members; indeed, the intimacy of the Work lends itself to this. But Alex did emphasize that "easy sex does you no good," and specific personal tasks might be given. In later years Sharon was more active in suggesting that students begin or end relationships, but these were suggestions. Some took them and some did not.

In the early years Alex used violence as a direct method to promote awakening. Reticence in a hot seat situation might bring a sharp slap, to wake the student up to what was happening. It was not punishment, but a shock expertly administered to break them out of themselves. On one occasion, at a banquet on the Sonoma property, Alex asked one of the students, who had a chief feature of fear, to kill a goat. In the general intensity of the Work disagreements arose between students that might come to blows. Alex sometimes seemed to encourage this, but he would also keep it from going too far. These outbursts were seen as a means of overcoming fear, or of standing up for yourself, or of directly confronting the realities of life. Like Gurdjieff, Alex had a challenging physical presence. He sometimes struck his students, not to injure, but to sting or shock them awake. One student remembered Alex giving her a slap, in passing, at a party. She happened to turn just as he slapped her and noticed his eyes. There was no malice. He was simply saying, "Hey, wake up!" In all of this, the aim was to be in the moment. As one student put it, Alex simply did not have time to be brutal for the sake of being brutal. He had a finite amount of time for each student, and he had to use that time to the best advantage.

Yes, Alex could be confrontational, and indeed outrageous, *but he was always acting.* In other words, there was always a side of him that was not outrageous. He liked to see people shaken up, because it created a certain kind of openness in them. In some cases that openness could not be created in any other way. Violence certainly brings people into the moment — rivets them to the moment — and then you can try to turn that energy toward consciousness. In the early years, naturally aggressive males tended to imitate Alex's confrontational style, but they did not have something behind it that could keep it under control. The effects, then, were harmful — to the other students, but particularly to themselves. One student recalled a prospective meeting led by a group of males who, after an introductory presentation, called for questions. As the questions came, they began to verbally assault and abuse the questioners, even picking up and smashing their personal belongings. At a certain point the leader of the meeting said, "This is the way your life is; we live for something else." But the meeting leaders had begun by taking advantage of their audience to produce a spectacular effect. Violence can create such effects, but over time the results become their opposite — because violence activates parts of the instinctive center that understand nothing of the Work. In the early years, Alex accepted violence for its impact and for its power to penetrate, to break down buffers. But he later recognized the detrimental effects it had on the students who were using violence against others. This was, perhaps, the primary cause of the downsizing of the group that was to come in 1969. The confrontational phase, where disagreements might come to blows, passed as Alex reached deeper levels of himself.

ALEX HORN AS A MATURE TEACHER

Alex was about five foot ten and heavily built. In the 1960s he would have weighed about 225 pounds. Yet he was compact, light on his feet, and could move very quickly. He had a rich baritone voice — clear and resonant — which could be either loud or soft. He normally spoke in a quick and measured way, with the neutral non-dialect accent that some actors learn. His tone radiated authority and he seemed tireless. One student said that, over a period of years, he never saw Alex yawn, stretch, or look even the slightest bit tired. Another said, "Merely being in the vicinity of Alex Horn was to feel a man alive in the moment, fully present yet confidently disinterested, as if focused beyond the horizon."

Given this formidable presence, Alex would accept observations and photographs from his own students, and he would apologize when his features showed. If Sharon questioned his decisions at a meeting, he would graciously accept a change of direction. If he felt the observation came from the wrong place, he might demonstrate that at another time — often by the role-playing technique. But he would acquiesce in the moment. He was always concerned to show how serious the work was.

As a teacher, Alexander Horn worked directly with everyone who came to him, to the extent that they were able to receive his help. He could intervene deeply in student's lives, in a surgical way. He knew the hidden alchemy of human energies, and he could read people's lives as the fortuneteller reads the lines on the palm of a person's hand. His sense of the theater was based on this same insight, a sense of the pattern of a human life.

And here we must emphasize one aspect of this alchemical work: the teaching of Right Eros. Through all his plays Alex used the term Eros in its exact Platonic sense: it was the Eros of the *Symposium* or of the Eleusinian Mysteries. Eros is what you love, what moves you. Man's Eros is corrupted in the medium of everyday life, where love is colored by lust and possessiveness, and desire to awaken is colored by ambition and greed. We can only truly work if we love what we are working for. In the Work, we must be moved by the love of what is higher. Eros must, then, be raised in stages from the things we are naturally drawn to, to the actual love for higher centers. We cannot invent or suddenly 'turn on' our love for what is higher. It must be salvaged from the corrupted Eros which presently moves us. Many of Alex Horn's most difficult tasks targeted a bent or broken Eros, in order that the student might see it — just as it was — and, in the moment of seeing it, have something more. This is the raising and transmutation of Eros. We cannot work well unless our Eros is straight and true.[1]

Alex applied this principle both in his work with students and his work with drama. As a teacher Alexander Horn was a conscious actor, transforming his student's lives from the unthinking patterns of earthly existence to the purgatorial struggle that takes place in the full awareness of heaven and hell. One of his students, who was with Alex in the years 1996-1997, said of him, "He was hard. At times he would more break you than make you" ... *pauses, and with emotion* ... "He was a great teacher, a really great teacher. Of all the teachers I have had, there was never another like him. He was an amazing master of the transmission of energy." Nobody could forget him.

Alexander Horn taught his students as an actor and directed his plays as a teacher. It is a challenge to imagine the combined effect. We present an example of Alex's ability to turn a student's life into conscious theater.

A CONSCIOUS THEATER SCENARIO

One of Alexander Horn's San Francisco students joined his group while serving in the navy. He immediately entered into the life of the group and was, in very short order, given several tasks, which he succeeded with. After he had been with Alex for more than a year, he received notice from his naval base that he was to be relocated to Hawaii at the end of the month. The new posting would be for a period of three years. The student spoke with Alex about his situation, to see what his response would be. Alex referred him to his sub-group, or to the circle of students with whom he worked regularly. Most of the people in the sub-group told him that he had found a golden opportunity that would never repeat, and so they advised him to go AWOL. The student spoke again with Alex, mentioning that, on a previous visit to Hawaii, he had seen the bookmarks of another Gurdjieff group. Alex's reply was surprisingly open, "You have found a real school, and if you go looking for another one you will know it when you find it."

---

1. In the terminology described in the Overview of the Work, the 'raising of Eros' is the development of the nine of hearts.

As the days and weeks slipped by, the student, still struggling with his decision, found himself packing his bags and preparing to leave for Hawaii. As the end of the month approached, he determined to speak with Alex, hoping to establish a bond that might survive the three-year posting. At his last Saturday meeting he asked Alex if he might come and see him at his home on the following afternoon. The flight to Hawaii was to depart that same evening. Alex replied, "Come over around 11:00AM and ring the doorbell. If I am available at that time I will answer."

The student arrived at Alex's house at exactly 11:00AM. Sharon answered the door. She told him that Alex wasn't up yet. "Come back in an hour." At 12:00 noon the student returned, and again Sharon told him to come back in an hour. That would be 1:00PM. His heart sank: 1:00PM was the time he had calculated he would need to leave San Francisco to make his pre-flight check-in. But having gone this far he was not going to back out. At 1:00PM he knocked again with his heart in his mouth. Sharon opened the door and told him that Alex was in. She invited him into the kitchen, and there he saw Alex, in his bathrobe, in the middle of preparing a meal. Alex looked up at the student and immediately invited him in for breakfast. Sharon asked him what he wanted. Suddenly there was *no 'teacher act' at all*. Alex's eight-year-old daughter ran up to him full of affection, and he took her in his arms. He showed himself a loving father. Alex then queried the student, in a friendly way, about his areas of interest: the music of Bach, and his recent studies of Shakespeare's drama.

Even in the complete informality of his home Alex's every movement was intentional. Every time he lifted the coffee cup and put it to his lips, every time he turned his head, every time he lit a cigarette, he did so consciously. There was an unbroken presence behind every movement and every word.

The student asked if he might write letters. Alex told him that he did not read his letters; Sharon might read some of them. He added lightly, "Don't bother." The student then asked if he could come back at the end of the three years. Alex said yes, he could, but he himself did not know what he would be doing in three years. He might or might not remain in San Francisco. He said this in a very matter of fact way, neither pressuring nor intimidating.

The student had come to the Marina house filled with the tension that had built in him over the previous month. That tension had been heightened each time he knocked on the door and Sharon told him to come back in an hour. When he finally entered the kitchen there was a sudden transition: he felt himself "on the inside." C Influence was there. The energy behind the tension was suddenly transmuted into something finer and higher. When the student questioned Alex about the future, and Alex responded, that same energy was taken one step further — to the impartial objectivity of a longer-term view of his life. It was a moment of objective consciousness. It was as though the student had been taken into the inner chamber of his own life and been given a

> completely neutral view of the whole. Looking back on this moment, the student always felt that he would somehow reconnect with Alex. That moment was always there: the episode became an indelible part of him.

Alex here used an actor's instinct and an actor's timing to create a mirror for his student, in which he could view himself from without. Alex always saw life as a play and viewed the work of his group as theater. It was a theater that not only *represented* a higher level to an audience *but could actually give access to it*. Alex's teaching — taken as a whole — could be viewed as an alchemical retort for separating out the different levels of energy within his students. He raised their lives from the unthinking treadmill of earthly existence to the purgatorial level, which exists in a live relationship to heaven. Alex pressured his students to access the deepest parts of their nature, and then to access *what lies behind human nature itself*. From that point of view his *Theatre of All Possibilities* was a theater within a theater.

Having said this, it is also true that Alex hoped to make a contribution to American drama in his lifetime, and he probably took this to be a dimension of his role. But it is now difficult to reconstruct his vision, because Alex was unable to make that contribution, and the time in which he might have made it has now passed. His vision probably included some further stage of integration of his group work with the developing theater. Having said that, his failure to realize this vision was more a failure of the American public than it was a failure of the conscious dramatist. Alex would never compromise his artistic principles to get good reviews; his service was to art as he knew it. This is not to say the *Theatre of All Possibilities* was without flaws. Sometimes the script was labored, sometimes it was a little too much 'in your face,' sometimes impact reigned over art. But in trying to understand Alexander Francis Horn, we must remember that during the 1960s, 1970s, and 1980s the potential to bring a cosmic dimension to American theater still existed. And such a potential is a sacred thing. It was a third force acting on Alex and affecting all his decisions. Passages in *The Legend of Sharon Shashanovah* describe the passion for a conscious theater vividly.

And Alex's group was like a theater. People were suddenly drawn into it and suddenly cast out of it. But they might reappear in a later scene, in a different role — the new performance being that much closer to the magical

Tragedy with Transcendence. One thing was for sure, Alex's performances in the role of teacher left an absolutely unforgettable impression. Perhaps there were times when — like Gurdjieff — Alex acted a bit too much. But 'too much' is hard to assess, for conscious acting, when pursued relentlessly, becomes a negation of external reality. It breaks the rigid relation that exists between the unending series of external events and our inner life. It is for the student to absorb this teaching and these impacts and to make something of it for themselves.

How Things Went Forward: 1966-1978

Having introduced the principal characters and sketched in the form of Alex's teaching, we shall return to the chronology of events. But before doing so, we must provide a brief overview of what was happening in the United States between 1968 and 1973 — because these events were the backdrop for both Alex's teachings and his six plays.

AMERICA IN THE LATE SIXTIES AND EARLY SEVENTIES

Beginning from about 1966 thousands of teenagers began to simply leave their homes: leave their families; leave their schooling; leave the lives they had led. These young people gravitated to the great countercultural meccas that were appearing across the nation: Greenwich Village in New York, the Haight-Ashbury District of San Francisco, Laurel Canyon in Los Angeles. Collectively these young people were known as the 'runaways.' More than ten thousand of them flocked into the Bay Area in 1967, and this became what was called the 'Summer of Love.' That was the beginning; the pressures that drove these young people out of their homes continued to mount, as did the countercultural reaction to them.

In January 1968 the Viet Cong launched the Tet Offensive, radically escalating the Vietnam war. In April of that year Martin Luther King was assassinated in Memphis. In May Robert Kennedy was assassinated in Los Angeles. In July 1969 Ted Kennedy's presidential aspirations were terminated by the Chappaquiddick incident. The tragedy of the Kennedy family — the twentieth century House of Atreus — had worked its way through to a conclusion. In March 1969 Richard Nixon began the unannounced carpet bombing of Cambodia and Laos, nations on which American had not declared war. In August of 1969 the countercultural volcano, known as Woodstock Nation, erupted.

> On 4th May, 1970 the students at Kent State University demonstrated against the bombing of Cambodia and National Guardsmen opened fire on them. The students were unarmed; four were killed and nine were wounded. By 1973 the era that was later known as "the sixties" had come to an end. The magical openness that had been so perfectly heralded in Leonard Bernstein's 1957 hit 'Something's Coming' was gone forever.
>
> Both the openness *and the exact tension* of those times is reflected in Alexander Horn's plays. As he put it:
>
>> The theater — a reflector of reality, a celebration of life, the conscience of the nation, the conscience of the world ... The murders of John Kennedy, Robert Kennedy, Martin Luther King ... The sixties, Vietnam, the peace marches, the Kent State shootings ... These plays begin here.[1]
>
> And they also ended here. Alexander Horn's plays do not go beyond that time; he continued to live in the dynamic idealism of those years.

We noted that there were two meetings a week and regular retreats at the Sonoma ranch. To this list was soon added work on the vineyard at Sonoma, and participation in the various sports activities. From the very first meeting of the group there had been a strong focus on students getting jobs and settling down: moving from a hippie-commune lifestyle to conventional famuily relationships. All students in the group, except single mothers with young children, were required to hold a full-time job, whether they needed to work or not. The teaching payments soon went from $150 a month to $200 a month, and if you could not make your payment, you were out of the group! There was consideration for special circumstances, and, given the severity of the exercise, Alex often found himself making exceptions. For the whole group there was unrelenting pressure, and students were never to speak about what they were doing to anyone outside of the group.

Every Friday afternoon students from all over the Bay Area carpooled their way to the Sonoma ranch, where they worked in the vineyard, erected outbuildings, and constructed a sauna. After a long day's work there would be parties that might continue into the following day. The parties

---

1. Horn, Alexander Francis, *In Search of a Solar Hero,* Element Books Ltd., 1987, Author's Preface.

Figure 62. The vineyard at Red Mountain Ranch.

themselves often had themes, and students might be asked to wear certain costumes or to play certain roles. On long weekends the parties might be connected with special events, and continue for several days. In the less inhibited environment of Sonoma many different aspects of the students came to light, and different kinds of connections between them formed.

Figure 63. The winery at Red Mountain Ranch.

After a year the group had raised enough money to purchase a larger ranch with a substantial house and swimming pool on Red Mountain, on the opposite rim of the Valley of the Moon. The group moved the makeshift winery to the new location and planted a forty-acre vineyard. The property became known as the Red Mountain Ranch, and within a year the group grew to three hundred students.

THE VOYAGE OF THE GOODWILL

By late 1966 all of the students in the newly enlarged group had full-time jobs, and some were independently wealthy. Alex had the idea of purchasing a private offshore island, which necessitated purchasing a ship. A student was asked to do some research. One night, on a Red Mountain Ranch weekend, after a dinner under the stars, Alex asked the student to share what he had found. The student announced to the group that a very promising schooner was for sale in Hawaii at a good price. It was a 161-foot ocean racing yacht called the Goodwill. It had been built in 1922 for the A.G. Spaulding sporting goods family, and it had twice won the Transpacific Yacht Race from Los Angeles to Honolulu. It was moored in Hawaii and was being sold there by the owner of a large tool and die company.

Alex promptly entered negotiations with the owner. It was decided that members of the group would make a trial run of the ship from Hawaii to San Francisco before agreeing to the purchase. A crew of four students was recruited and an experienced sailing master, the brother of one of the students, flew to Hawaii to man the ship. At the beginning of the cruise the sailing master required each crew member to wear a life preserver *at all times*. He warned them that when you go overboard in the open ocean, you almost immediately become invisible behind the waves. Your chances of rescue with a life preserver are small, but without a life preserver they are non-existent.

Fifteen days out of Hawaii, somewhere in the mid-Pacific, a student named Mike Watson noticed a free bit of line had tangled in a starboard ladder. He climbed down the ladder to clear the line when the rotten ladder gave way. Suddenly Mike was off the ship floating free in the Pacific Ocean. Mike couldn't swim. The cry, "Man overboard" went out. The sails were dropped, the engine turned on, and the sailing master began to bring the ship around in a huge circle. The crew looked out into the vast, churning sea for any trace of Mike. Nothing was visible. Then an albatross, that had followed the ship all the way from Hawaii, was seen circling over a specific point in the waves. And soon someone spotted a bobbing black spot in the water just beneath the circling bird. It was Mike's head. Mike, for his part, had suddenly taught himself how to swim. He could be faintly heard crying out, "I can't stay up." The sailing master immediately stripped down, put on rubber flippers and a life preserver, took another life preserver in his arm, and plunged in. As he reached Mike the crew put out a lifeboat with a line to the Goodwill. Not one person was thinking about themselves. The lifeboat, manned by amateurs, made an odd looping path through the high wind-furrowed ridges of waves, miraculously connecting with Mike and the sailing master. One observer called it "nothing less than full-out magic."

Later, in a group discussion about the experience, Alex stated that this was an intervention by C Influence. The albatross was a symbol of good fortune, or divine mercy. It was a circumstance that instilled maximum presence in everyone involved.

As the Goodwill finally approached San Francisco Bay, the crew radioed ahead to the members of the group to let them know of the ship's location. Every student who was not at their mandatory full-time job immediately headed to the Golden Gate Bridge. As the ship entered San Francisco harbor the crew could see them, running from both ends of the bridge like tiny ants, waving down to the Goodwill. When the ship finally docked at the Trident Restaurant in Sausalito the entire group came onboard to celebrate.

In the subsequent dry-dock survey the ship was found to have twenty thousand electrolysis holes in her hull, and many major repairs would be necessary to make her seaworthy. Alex, without batting an eye, decided to pass on buying the ship.

It was a great adventure, but there was so much to do in San Francisco that students hardly noticed the passing of the private island project. At some point Alex and Anne moved from the Haight District to a Victorian house at 350 Page Street.

THE CHANGE OF DIRECTION

In November 1968, at the age of 39, Alexander Francis Horn crystallized as a man number six. One of his students, Robert Burton, noticed that there was a change in his bearing, and a bright and steady flame behind his eyes. Robert reported that, "I could see his starry world." From that time forward Alex was visibly less subject to inner impulse or outer impact. Thomas Farber recorded the effect of Alex's change of level on the group:

> In the same period [after the episode of the Goodwill] he [Alex] announced a redefinition of his role. He was no longer a group leader — he was a Teacher of the Work, like Gurdjieff. He had new responsibilities to us, and we to him. He needed us, he said, but only those of us who were really prepared to do the Work. It was a kind of spiritual trading, in which we were to give him a certain material that he would use and transmute, he in turn providing us with a good return on our investment so that we also could progress, and on we would go. We were told that the Work would be more difficult, and we were given time to gauge our desires. At one meeting, taking a reading of our determination, he asked if we were ready to join him. Hands went up around the circle, person after person, testifying to a desire to push ahead, whatever the price.[1]

These developments were attended by a crisis in Alex's personal life. Anne Burrage had been Alex's original partner in the teaching, and the two of them were raising a family of five in this challenging environment. The explosiveness of the group work and the pressure Alex brought to bear on a generation of young hippies created enormous tension. Anne could take the pace for only so long. At about the time Alex became a man number six she split from the group, and quite a number of students went with her. The custody of the children went principally with Anne, although one or

---

1. Farber, Thomas, *Tales for the Son of My Unborn Child,* Pocket Books (Simon & Schuster, Inc.), New York, 1973, p. 127.

another of them were seen with Alex throughout the San Francisco phase of his teaching.

Anne pursued her own line of work, with the other students who left with her, for at least a few years. The original property in Sonoma was in her name, and it went with her out of the group. The Red Mountain Ranch property remained with Alex, along with the 40-acre vineyard and winery.

And so Alex reached a point of transition. He had achieved a new level, but Anne and a substantial portion of the group left him. The challenge that Alex had made to his students in November was now being reinforced by external events. With hindsight we can see the results that came from Alex's change of direction, but we can only guess what occurred at that turning point — for we have no reports or commentary from any member of the group from April 1969 to early 1972.

What, then, are the results that we know of? There was a downsizing of the group; the psychological work became more focused; there was a partial correction of the tendency towards violence; there was a reduced emphasis on the activities at Sonoma; and there was a growing emphasis on drama. This last change was indicative of things to come. The dramatist in Alex was emerging.

The departure of students with Anne in late 1968 had been the first major 'breathing out' of the group since its inception in 1965. The following March 1969 Alex himself intentionally downsized the group. He made a general announcement to the group that he was ending his work, but he met privately with a small circle of students who he felt were dedicated and doing the work. He gave each of these students a personal task, and then re-created the group out of those who succeeded with their tasks. Probably many other students eventually gravitated back. This was, one could say, a second phase of the first breathing out, and reflected the change in Alex's level of being. For Alex a group of three hundred relatively new students had proven too large. It did not allow him to give the attention to each student that he felt they needed. Alex also used the breathing out to change the tone of his teaching. In the rapid expansion to three hundred something had begun to go wrong. As we have noted, a group of males had become overly assertive; there was bullying, and incidents of violence that were not controlled. Many of the self-assertive males were winnowed out of the group. We do not know the number of students that remained with Alex in his re-start of April-May 1969, but by 1972 the group comprised about eighty people.

The biggest change in the form of the new teaching was the place that the theater was to take. We do not have a clear picture of how the theater work got underway. In late 1969 the group would have been too small to produce a play. There was, perhaps, an initial phase of rehearsal and training. The group made experiments with scenes from Shakespeare, Chekhov, Ibsen, Brecht, O'Neill, and Williams. Then at a certain point the group began to produce plays. Alex was picking up on the dramatic work he had done on the East Coast. If Alex had written any plays of his own at this time, we have no record of them. The group rented a gymnasium at the corner of 3316 24th Street and Mission and proceeded to transform the building into a theater. They put in seating, stage, upper stage, backstage area, and proper theater lighting. It was named the *Everyman Theatre* — taking the incorporated name of Alex's theater group. The Theater on 24th Street became a total experience. The walls were covered floor to ceiling with one-foot square mirrors, making it strangely reminiscent of Hesse's Magic Theater. To enter the theater, off the somewhat seedy sidewalk of 24th Street, was like entering a magic box. Everything inside was exceptionally clean, with the students receiving theater goers politely and respectfully.

Figure 64. *Everyman Theatre*, at 3316 24th Street.

Once the theater had been completed the group held its meetings there, with a circle of chairs set up on the stage for each meeting. We do not know the first plays performed, but, after 1972, they were principally Alex's plays.

The plays would be performed on Saturday night. Setup began midday Saturday. The play would run from 8PM until 10PM, or later. People attending the performance would be asked to join the company for wine and hors d'oeuvres after the play. There they might be asked how they had enjoyed the performance. Did the play connect with experiences in their own lives? Did it help them to understand their lives? Would they be interested to pursue these understandings? And if they were interested, they might be invited to a Thursday night meeting to see something of how the group worked. The wine and hors d'oeuvres party was immediately followed by the Saturday Meeting. The second half of the Meeting — which included the 'hot seat' scenario — would begin around midnight and could go as late as 3 or 4AM.

With the preparations for the performance beginning midday Saturday, the Saturday morning sports activities had to shift to Sunday. So on Sunday morning, after a long day and a very late night, all of the men had to turn out to play football or basketball. During football season Alex would shift from one position to another during the course of the game. But if his team was losing, he would play quarterback. On one occasion a student tackled Alex very hard and broke his leg. Witnesses to this event said that Alex took it quite gracefully.

This intense period of integrating and training up new students was capped and completed by the arrival of Alex's life-partner and collaborator Sharon Gans. Her arrival confirmed the group's emphasis on drama and reinforced the movement away from violence. And, for most students, she made Alex a little easier to live with.

ALEX HORN AND SHARON GANS

Alex met Sharon Gans sometime in 1972. She was 37 years old — an accomplished actress and a beautiful lady. In 1966, at the age of 31, she had won an Obie Award for Best Actress for her performance in *Soon Jack November*.

Figure 65. Alex and Sharon in 1972.

As an actress she is best known for playing the role of Billy Pilgrim's wife, Valencia Merble, in the 1972 film version of Kurt Vonnegut's *Slaughterhouse-Five*. She was working on this part when she first met Alex.

The two married within a year of their first meeting. Sharon was born in New York on 29th July 1935 and grew up in the Bronx. Both of her parents were members of the Gurdjieff Foundation in New York, and she was raised with the Work ideas. She moved to Berkeley in 1954 to attend the University of California, graduating in 1959 at the age of 24. In that same year she married Ezra Kulko, an army officer. The couple moved back to New York, where they had two children: David, born in 1961, and Ilsa, a year later. Ezra and Sharon separated in March of 1972, and Sharon returned to California. Initially custody of the two children was shared, but after a time both children insisted on remaining in California with their mother. Sharon did eventually gain full custody of the children, but because she had moved out of state, she received no support from her ex-husband.[1]

---

1. See Kulko v. California Superior Court, 1978, No. 77-293.

Alex saw in Sharon a partner in the deepest sense. From 1972 until the end of his life he worked in collaboration with her and treated her as a fellow teacher. While, over those 35 years, Alex and Sharon worked in different relations to one another, Sharon became a permanent part of the alchemical field of energy in which Alex operated. Alex allowed Sharon to act as an advisor, a colleague, and a mirror to himself.

As a couple Alex and Sharon were also at once parents of an active family. There were Sharon's two children from her first marriage, and Alex had partial custody of his five children with Anne Burrage. Alex's students of the 1960s and 1970s have memories of these children being around. Alex and Sharon also moved from the house on 350 Page Street to a large house in the Marina District.

At the meetings Sharon would act as a 'fair witness' to Alex, and they would often role-play during a meeting. When Alex suddenly challenged a student on the hot seat, Sharon might question the challenge before the student could respond: "Why do you say that?" This would give the person time to think and to find a neutral place in themselves. Once, at a meeting on the stage of the *Theatre of All Possibilities,* Sharon said something to challenge Alex. He did not reply, but left his chair and walked slowly up into the bleacher seats of the theater in the darkness. She was left alone. His action said, "Do you want to run the show?" They would play out disagreements and reconciliations. There are different opinions as to whether these were purely staged, or whether Alex and Sharon were acting out real disagreements. As the years went by Sharon became more involved in organizing the group's activities, and often counseled students about their personal situations.

One of Alex's San Francisco students said, many years later, that he could never imagine Alex and Sharon apart. They were "naturally together." He saw no disagreement between them during his time with the group, and he imagined that any disagreements in the years to follow would have been role-playing. (Others took some of the disagreements to be real.) Many students said that, in the group, Alex and Sharon seemed to represent the ideal relationship between a man and a woman: of how a mature couple would be together. This was particularly true of students who knew them in the last decade of Alex's life. The two of them together always conveyed something special.

We noted that, in 1969, Alex reduced his group to a small core of people, in order that the teaching itself might take a new form. Sharon's arrival consolidated that change of form. She was a moderating influence: a feminine intelligence and a feminine voice.

DEVELOPMENT OF THE THEATER

Alex had probably planned to introduce theater work from the onset of his role as a teacher, but at a certain point he found that the first group demanded a different set of priorities. Sharon reinforced the original emphasis on the theater. She was an accomplished professional, and she entered the group just as Alex was producing his first play, *The Fantastic Arising of Padraic Clancy Muldoon*. She arrived after the play had been written, but while it was being first staged. The timing was perfect.

Previously Alex had worked with his group on fragments of Shakespeare, Chekhov, and others, and perhaps the occasional complete play. This was the first time the group was to produce the teacher's own play. Alex was not only the writer, producer, and director, but the principal acting coach *and* the lead actor. One man cannot do all of these things and do them well, whatever his level of being. You need to have a competent, experienced person outside of yourself, whom you trust, who can say to you, "Look, this is really good material and needs to be developed, but you can't do it that way. You've got to change certain things, in order to get what you really want." Sharon was that person, and Alex immediately felt it. He was no longer alone with a group of amateurs who did not have an outside perspective on the work being done, and who could only learn from him.

Writing of his plays, at a much later date, Alex said:

> Their real history began the day I met the woman who was to become my wife. It may be a pardonable offense against the spirit of our times for a man to love his wife: to also sing her praises as teacher, actress, director, producer is surely unforgivable.
>
> Yet the truth must be stated. If ever a playwright had a teacher, she has been mine: if ever a work has been a collaboration, these

plays have. For me, writing has been the most difficult of tasks, and I am grateful to have such a comrade by my side.

Socrates had his Diotima, Dante his Beatrice, Shakespeare his Dark Lady of the Sonnets, and I, my Sharon. I cannot compare myself to these giants in greatness, they outdistance me as the stars the earth; yet I hold myself their equal in grace and fortune, for I have been blessed with a love that completes my life and my work.[1]

From this point forward he felt that he could really develop as a dramatic artist. The second play — *Adam King* — was a major step forward, and his other plays followed one after the next. In the San Francisco period there

Figure 66. Adam King Playbill.

came *Journey to Jerusalem,* and at least the first few performances of *The Magician.* In the early 1980s in New York came *The Legend of Sharon Shashanovah* and *I.*

These plays were reintroducing the cosmic theater of Dante and Shakespeare in twentieth century America. We have noted how Alex integrated

---

1. Horn, Alexander Francis, *In Search of a Solar Hero,* Element Books, Dorset 1987, from the Author's Preface.

Vakhtangov's fantastic realism, in his attempt to recreate the cosmic context. To enhance the 'fantastic' effects he created special sets, and his use of the Elizabethan upper stage was an aspect of this. He added an upper stage to each of the theaters he occupied, and in each of his plays he made quite specific use of it.

In Elizabethan times, characters might appear and perform on the upper stage, accessing it either through backstage stairs or by climbing stairs on the stage set itself. In Shakespeare's plays the upper stage was often used to represent ghosts, disembodied beings, or divine beings.

At both San Francisco venues — the Everyman Theatre and the Theatre of All Possibilities — Alex installed an upper stage that was accessed by stairs from the main stage. This allowed for a visible transition between the different levels represented in his plays.

There are two further points to be made about the content of Alex's plays. Firstly, all of them represent *the purification of Eros*. They show the movement of desire, from something that binds the lower centers to the external world, to something that may serve both the Higher Self and the Gods. In each of his plays a bent or broken Eros is exposed to a series of shocks and impacts, interspersed with guidance from a higher level, that allow it to rediscover its own inner truth. With the discovery of right Eros, and only with the discovery of right Eros, man becomes a living microcosmos. Secondly, all of Alex's plays combine the cosmic theater of Dante and Shakespeare with *the heroic stature of the protagonist,* who is called upon to address life on a cosmic scale, and to deal with the flaws in his or her nature which were obstacles to addressing that scale. Here Alexander Horn broke with twentieth century theater, which was either 1) stuck in role-model heroism, or 2) playing with the idea of the anti-hero.

In Alex's group not all students acted in the plays, and not all the actors were students. Alex and Sharon hired non-student professional actors to stand in as needed, and they were treated in a purely professional way. For the students involved, the theater did function as a Fourth Way theater. Students were sometimes intentionally miscast, or casting was set up so that a student could see a different side of themselves. But this kind of Fourth Way work was always subordinated to the art of the theater. The work of school is regeneration, and the art of the theater is regeneration. Better that these two disciplines work together, than that the latter disrupt the former. Sharon did all the choreography.

The plays also served as a vehicle for attracting magnetic centers to the group. It was a third line task for many students to go about the city selling tickets for the shows. At the end of every performance, the audience members who wished to remain were invited to a formal prospective student meeting, which presented basic ideas of the Work and the activities of the group. Alex often attended these meetings.

THE SAN FRANCISCO PLAYS

We shall discuss the San Francisco plays in the order of their first formal production: *The Fantastic Arising of Padraic Clancy Muldoon* in 1972; *Adam King* in 1973; *Journey to Jerusalem* in 1976; *The Magician* in 1978.[1]

Alex's first play, *The Fantastic Arising of Padraic Clancy Muldoon*, was a bold experiment in introducing the cosmic context to twentieth century theater. The drama is modelled after the Kent State shootings, which had occurred two years prior. Padraic Muldoon, the protagonist, is a university professor, who has reached a state of unhealthy resignation. He has lost the ideals of his youth. His passive self-preoccupation is violently disrupted when he loses his son in a university shooting. This affects everyone around him. As he struggles desperately with the contradictions so created, his experience expands to include the Gods and the entire cosmic context of his existence. Padraic's broken Eros passes through a series of violent shocks to rediscover its true form. His son's death produces multiple effects on all of the characters, and provides the context for Padraic's rebirth — which is *both* the re-establishment of right Eros *and* the opening of a connection

---

1. The first three of these plays were first published in Alexander Horn's book *Theatre of All Possibilities,* Everyman Publications, San Francisco, 1978. These plays were updated in minor ways as they were performed. We have used the versions published in *In Search of A Solar Hero,* Element Books Ltd, Shaftesbury, Dorset, UK, 1987, and *Ponderings of a Citizen of the Milky Way,* Element Books Ltd., Shaftesbury, Dorset, UK, 1987. With respect to all Horn's plays, we have accepted the production dates Horn gives in *In Search of A Solar Hero* and *Ponderings of a Citizen of the Milky Way.* There may have been earlier versions of these plays.

to a higher level. We see Padraic as part of all humanity, and as part of the awakened cosmos of man. Throughout the play the Gods are present on the upper stage, sometimes listening, sometimes coming down to the main stage to intervene in the action. Thus, the higher level is built in structurally, with the middle and lower levels co-present on the main stage.

Alex's second play, *Adam King,* was produced in 1973. It is the first drama of the King trilogy, an allegory based on the American tragedy of the Kennedy family. It is placed in a context of Heaven, Purgatory, and Hell. Here Alex follows Aristotle's counsel to take the story of a 'great house' (or family) known to the audience and explore its cosmic dimension. Aristotle's advice worked well. No one in the audience would believe this is the real Kennedy family, but at the same time everyone can accept this is "what might have been." And the representation of higher and lower worlds is all the more vivid because it is connected to our experience of actual people in the life that we know.

All three plays of the King trilogy develop Alex's idea of the *cosmos of man,* which he inherited from Rodney Collin.[2] He emphasizes the deep separation in modern society between the *line of the priests* (men of contemplation) and the *line of the kings* (men of action). The separation of these two lines makes mankind less than a living cosmos. In a true cosmos the process of regeneration must govern and orchestrate the other five processes. Alex tells us that it can only do so when the priests become men of action, and the kings become contemplatives. This, then, is what the appropriately named King trilogy is about.

In *Adam King* we see much more clearly than in Alex's first play, entities on a higher level monitoring life on this level. We see on stage both embodied conscious beings and disembodied conscious beings of different levels. Alex introduces the character of Tyrant. This is the voice of what we have called the Black Queen. There is a Tyrant in each one of us, and there is a collective Tyrant alive in our social order. We can relate this character

---

2. See Collin, Rodney, *The Theory of Celestial Influence,* Watkins, London, 1980. On pp. 227-235 he describes the six processes that comprise a civilization. Alex's use of the Kaballistic myth of Adam Kadmon, in several of his plays, conforms exactly to Rodney Collin's vision.

directly to Alex's personal teaching. In the hot seat scenario of the Saturday night meetings, he made his students see the Tyrant at work within themselves. From the moment you become aware of the Tyrant internally, you are forced to make decisions that will result in either the Tyrant taking you out or you separating yourself from the Tyrant. Final separation from the Tyrant is an act of self-transcendence.

The plays of the King trilogy work through the drama of the King family over several generations. In the performance of these plays Alex always played the role of Tyrant.

Alex's next play, *Journey to Jerusalem,* came three years after Adam King, in 1976. The play is set, from the very beginning, on a cosmic scale — and is filled with beauty, terror, wisdom, and things eternal. It is a more symbolic play, and it takes place across many different time frames simultaneously. We begin with Adam and Eve at the very nadir of their existence, in an incarnation in present day New York. We then see them with different names in different times and places throughout history, from ancient Egypt down to the present. The healing of their Eros is the healing that attends regeneration. The darker side of their nature must be brought to light and acknowledged before the Self can become free of it. In the resolution of the play the couple discover the original form of Adam Kadmon, the GREAT MAN of the Kaballah, who exists outside of time. Adam and Eve transcend themselves as a part of humanity transcending itself. Their own struggle is individual, but because the result of this struggle is outside of time, it is also part of the regenerative dimension of humanity. The play shows us in which way we are cells in a living whole.

In *Journey to Jerusalem* Alex emphasizes the development of the cosmos of man, with conscious school as the vehicle of regeneration. This is how he saw his own group, and the potential that was in it. If he were to achieve conscious theater in America through his group, the theater (representing the process of regeneration) would crown, or at least complement, the other five cosmic processes that comprise American life — thus bringing the nation closer to becoming a living whole.

The last of the San Francisco plays, *The Magician,* was produced in 1978. It is the second play of the King trilogy. It represented a dramatic breakthrough for Alex, opening a deeper vein of his work. There is greater dramatic intensity than in his previous plays, more convincing character development, and less random explosiveness. The relation between levels is represented more clearly and with greater dramatic impact. The play had just opened at the Golden Gate theater when Alex and Sharon were forced to leave the city. The disruption of the production must have been a considerable shock to Alex as an artist, but it eventually had its full run in New York, the very city it depicts.

The group's dramatic repertoire was not limited to Alex's own plays. The *San Francisco Examiner* of Wednesday, March 13th 1974 reported:

> The Everyman Theatre at 24th and Mission Streets is continuing its children's show of stories adapted from the works of the Brothers Grimm and Hans Christian Andersen: "Little Red Riding Hood" and "The Gallant Tailor," "Sleeping Beauty" and "The Emperor's New Clothes." The show is presented every Saturday and Sunday at 1 p.m.

We must always keep in mind this dimension of Alex's theater.

In the fall of 1976 the Everyman Theatre burned to the ground. The *San Francisco Chronicle* reported:

> After a fire gutted the Mission district theater in the fall of 1976, the Horns moved their operations to a new and as yet unbuilt theater in the Syufy building at 150-160 Golden Gate Avenue. ... The group then embarked on a two to three-month refurbishing project, estimated to have cost $350,000. Most of the labor was volunteer.[1]

We can only imagine the pressure this created and the demands that were made on all the students. The theater was renamed *The Theatre of All Possibilities*, and the new address at 150 Golden Gate was five blocks east of the San Francisco City Hall.

Alex's third play, *The Magician*, premiered at *The Theatre of All Possibilities* in 1978, just after the refurbishment was completed.

---

1. *San Francisco Chronicle,* December 23rd, 1978, p. 2.

Figure 67. *Theatre of All Possibilities*, at 150 Golden Gate Avenue.

All was going well for Alex and Sharon, both in their teaching and in their theater work. With the development of the theater the focus of the group's activities was gradually shifting away from the property at Sonoma and the vineyard. Sometime in early 1978 Alex and Sharon purchased property in Condon, Montana, to be used as a retreat for the group. This unusual move seems to have been a premonition of things to come.

On 8th November, 1978 an event occurred which completely disrupted the Work of the group. The *Peoples Temple* cult, under the leadership of Jim Jones, committed a mass murder/suicide in Jonestown, Guyana, taking the lives of 918 people, including 304 children. The group had been based in San Francisco for many years, until it relocated to Guyana in 1977. The group itself had been well known in San Francisco, and the event sent a shockwave through the city. Other "cult" groups immediately came into the crosshairs of both press and police. On 23rd December the *San Francisco Chronicle* published an article on Alex's group, taking every opportunity to draw close parallels to the *Peoples Temple*. Alex and Sharon had become aware, before the publication of the article, that police, journalists, and social welfare investigators were interviewing former students. By the time the article came out Alex and Sharon had dissolved the group, relinquished their properties in the Bay Area, and moved — with a small circle of followers — to the newly purchased property in Montana. From their distant retreat they began to make plans to recreate both their teaching and their theater on the East Coast.

We note that this violent shock came only two years after the fire that destroyed the Mission Street theater, triggering the group's move to the Golden Gate address and the $350,000 refurbishment project. The *People's Temple* incident came *at the very moment* that Alex's finest play to date — *The Magician* — was opening. At the end of 1978 the pressure on Alex Horn increased considerably, and he was suddenly faced with the challenge of completely recreating his group and his personal life.

What, then, of the property in Condon, Montana, which was to become a permanent part of the teaching? It was a ranch, in a remote location, in the foothills of the Rocky Mountains. The group came to know it as the Falls Creek Ranch. The property itself was isolated and gorgeous. Condon is a small hamlet of a few hundred people located in the Swan Mountain Range, a part of the Rocky Mountain system. The valley in which the Falls Creek Ranch was situated was known as Swan Valley, and the lake on Alex's property Swan Lake. At an elevation of 3,700 feet, it has cold winters and warm summers, with temperatures into the eighties. The forested land is beautiful. While they had not planned it so, the Falls Creek Ranch was to become a reference point for Alex and Sharon for the remainder of their lives.

New York and Boston: 1979-2007

Reviewing their situation at the Falls Creek retreat, Alex and Sharon decided to start groups in New York City and Boston. This was to be a new beginning. A small inner circle of students was prepared to support them in this endeavor.

In 1979 they took an apartment in New York and began recruiting new students. The group met regularly, both at Alex and Sharon's apartment, and at different students' homes. Eventually they rented a theater in lower Manhattan where they could produce Alex's plays. The Falls Creek Ranch served as a retreat for more intensive work, including a series of major construction projects. In 1986 Alex and Sharon began to recruit in Boston, and a second group was formed there.

Over the next twenty years Alex and Sharon rented and purchased a network of properties in New York State: Manhattan, Long Island, and upstate New York. Shortly after they left San Francisco they acquired a country house in Mahopac, about 40 miles north of Manhattan. In 1989 they purchased an 18-acre property with three large houses on it, within just a few miles of the Mahopac house, on Croton Falls Road. Between 1989 and 1999 students would meet at the Croton Falls Road property one weekend a month for work of different kinds.

In 1998 Alex's group purchased a 20-acre property in Pawling, New York, at 361 Old Route 55. It was intended as a retreat that would be accessible to everyone in the group at any time. It became the group's main site for work on drama. It was named *Fountain Ridge,* and connected to a nonprofit organization called the *Hudson Valley Artist's Foundation*. Alex and Sharon created a host of other organizations around these properties: the *New York Playwright's Association,* the *Odyssey Study Group,* and *Everyman Inc.,* among others. Initially there was a single large house on the property. Alex's people constructed five additional buildings on the grounds. Alex also had a teaching venue on 248 Blank Lane, Watermill, New York.

During their years in New York City Alex and Sharon rented a number of town houses. Their primary residence over most of this period was a large apartment at 59 West 12th St.

The meetings that took place on the East Coast had a different form from the meetings that had taken place in San Francisco. There was a Wednesday meeting for newer students and a Saturday meeting for more intensive work, and for the assignment of personal tasks. After the first year all meetings and gatherings took place in spacious rented rooms.

There might be sixty people at the Wednesday meeting for newer students. Students would arrive at 8:00PM and begin with a full hour of warmup exercises: a basic exercise to start, then other movements added (revolving, rotating, etc.), then all movements would go double time; then stop; then a second round of exercise, with movements added and so forth. (Exercises like this are often used by theater groups to break down personal boundaries.) After an hour, when people were drenched with perspiration, everyone would change and shower for the formal part of the meeting. The first part of the formal meeting would be led by an older student. There would be personal questions: What are you doing in your life? What do you really want to be? What are your essence impulses? How or in what ways were you derailed? Students were encouraged to find out who they really were. In this context they were encouraged to be free of any fears or concerns, and simply speak their minds. Work language was not used in this part of the meeting because the newer students were not yet able to use Work terms to describe their personal experience. After an hour or so of discussion, Alex and Sharon might arrive; if they did, the meeting could go on until two or three in the morning. In this scenario the new students would get some quality time with both Alex and Sharon.

The Work ideas were given to students as they acquired the experience needed to understand them. Ideas related to human mechanicality were not given until a person had a real sense of the contradictions that existed within themselves. In this way the Work ideas, when they came, could be properly fixed to create a firm foundation. Sincerity was emphasized at all times.

In New York, recruiting new students became a substantial third line effort. The group did not advertise in newspapers or any public forum (as was the case in San Francisco). People met the group through direct contact with students. The aim, then, was to train students to recruit in the right way, and to position themselves so that they would interact with people who had a genuine interest. The process of recruitment, and the training to recruit, was more involved and more carefully managed than it had been in San Francisco. The best opportunity for recruitment was, of course, the gatherings that occurred after the performance of the plays, when audience members were invited to share wine and hors d'oeuvres with the actors. But contacts were also made at bars, museums, concerts, bookstores—wherever one was likely to find a person with a magnetic center. The appropriate sites were chosen by the recruiting team. Individual students were tasked with joining other B Influence organizations to meet people who might be interested in the Work: yoga classes, study groups, meditation centers, and so on. Students would initiate conversations with potential members: "What do you really want out of life?", "What do you feel is your potential?" and "Are you achieving that?" If the response was positive, the ideas of the Work were then introduced, with reference to Plato, Shakespeare, Moses, Buddha, Jesus. "If there was such a school in existence today, would you be interested in studying there?"

Gradually there developed different circles of students: new students, older students, students with different levels of responsibility within the group. Some students lived together, but this was not the rule. And, at the same time, the group began to publish. In 1987 Element Books published all of Alex's plays in two volumes: *In Search of a Solar Hero* (the Adam King trilogy) and *Ponderings of a Citizen of the Milky Way* (the other plays up to 1987). The Adam King trilogy, which began in San Francisco in 1973 with *Adam King*, followed by *The Magician* in 1978, was completed in 1981 in New York with Alex's play *I*.[1]

From about 1987 Alex began to challenge his students more directly, and for many he became more difficult to understand. This led to a major schism in the group in 1988. There is no record of the details of what happened: we only know that the group ended up divided along certain lines, with Alex and Sharon acting separately as teachers. It may have been that Alex was not satisfied with the response of certain of his students, and he decided to work in a different way with those amenable to his methods. It may have been that he wanted to prepare new people in a different way. There was, certainly in the beginning, the appearance of a radical break — of a kind that would allow both sides to rethink their Work, and so to create a new beginning.

Alex and Sharon remained in touch after the split and their work remained connected, although in the first months that connection was quite invisible to others. As actors, they may have amplified the break, but as teachers they hoped to develop the work in different ways and see how the different experiments worked out.

---

1. Alex co-authored a final play with Sharon in 1993, *The Infinite Lives of Giordano Bruno: A Play in Three Acts*. It was published only in limited edition for the use of the group.

At the time of the break Alex announced his intention of continuing his own work in Manhattan. The great majority of the students, including most of Alex's old inner circle, remained with Sharon. Alex also taught a group of twenty or thirty people in Boston, and whether this was the already existing Boston group or whether Alex opened a second Boston group we do not know.

In 1988-1989 Sharon introduced her son, David Kulko, as a successor. He had been raised in the group and was familiar with the Work from his childhood. He became a full-time student with the group after finishing high school and college. At a certain point Sharon felt David was ready to take the reins, as a male counterpart and a co-teacher. David was active in both New York and Boston. But in the year 2000, in a class he taught for newer students, he openly renounced Sharon as his teacher. Sharon immediately asked him to leave the group. He later opened a wine store in Brooklyn. David had been very much an experimental leader, and after his parting Alex and Sharon worked more openly together. The two groups did not fuse, but they became more connected than they had been before.

Both groups travelled extensively, and their travelling was often connected with the theater. Of Alex's group we know little. His theatrical troupe regularly performed in Europe and in Israel. But Sharon's travels have left us with some traces: a publication and a film. Both were produced by the *Hudson Arts Foundation,* and both related to time the group spent in Russia.

In 1993 *Applause Theater & Cinema Books* published a book recording a performance by Sharon Gans and Jorden Charney at the Moscow Art Theater: *A Chekhov Concert: Duets and Arias from the Major Plays of Anton Chekhov.* It was reviewed by *Contemporary Theater* (a Moscow publication) and an English translation of the review was printed on the back cover of the book. The *Chekhov Concer*t was described as:

> A tapestry of plays, stories and letters artistically woven together to form a beautiful new work worthy of Chekhov's own heart and hand. The American artists Sharon Gans and Jordan Charney have reconceived Chekhov in their duets and arias with sensitivity and

passion of the finest dramatic caliber. The true wonder and character of Chekhov shines through ... enlightening![1]

In 2001 Sharon starred in a documentary film, *Artists and Orphans: A True Drama*. It was made by her group while in Russia and was nominated for an Academy Award. The film records the activities of an American theater troupe traveling in the Republic of Georgia *en route* to an international arts festival. They discover that the country is undergoing a humanitarian crisis, in the wake of the Georgian civil war. The troupe is introduced to a group of orphans living in Tbilisi, who are undergoing deprivation.[2] They live in a mental hospital that had been bombed during the civil war. The building lacks heating, food, electricity, and water. With winter approaching the artists attempt to gather funds and supplies for the make-shift orphanage. They then help to prepare the orphanage's building for winter. Andy Sywak reviewed it as "short, gritty and brilliantly scored."[3] At the 74th Academy Awards it was nominated for Best Documentary Short Subject.[4]

Here we have some taste of the kind of adventure that always attended the work of Sharon and Alex. But how did things develop between them following the departure of David Kulko? We know that from 1996 Sharon was working with Alex in his groups in Boston and New York, and that Alex had at least a shadow presence in her groups. The two branches made shared use of the ranch at Condon, Montana. What, then, of the many theater groups that sprang up in the 1990s? Were some or all of these joint efforts? These remain open questions.

In Manhattan Alex worked with several small groups of ten to fifteen people, meeting one night a week. It is likely that a single third-line

---

1. From the back cover of the book, quoting the review.
2. Tbilisi (previously Tiflis) was where the Institute for the Harmonious Development of Man was founded.
3. Sywak, Andy "Film Festival Reviews," *Daily Nexus,* University of California, Santa Barbara, March 8, 2001.
4. The film won Audience Choice Award for Best Documentary at both the 2001 Santa Barbara International Film Festival and the 2001 Lake Arrowhead International Film Festival. It also won Best Short Film at the 2001 Florida Film Festival.

recruiting system — between the two groups — fed some students to Sharon and some to Alex. Alex's groups began with questions, role playing, exercises, and then, after a time, students were introduced to smaller groups where they were directly instructed in the system. The students of the smaller groups would later have the opportunity to help with recruiting. In the small groups Alex made a full use of his acting skills. We keep in mind that a live conscious actor is beyond anything one might see on stage or screen. A student from one of these groups, who has chosen to remain anonymous, noted that Alex could be at one moment formidably angry and in the next, compassionate, open, and even vulnerable:

> "Through all the extremes there was the sense of a strength that came from beyond the self. ... He was an amazing teacher; an amazing master of the transmission of energy. Sharon appeared at some of the meetings and made occasional interventions. She was courageous, free, sometimes opposing. She was powerful, good. I really appreciate both of them. She was sometimes trying to check me out. Checking weak spots. Being tough. Being generous and real like she was. She used the power that she had."

This same person recognized the love between Alex and Sharon: "Sacredness, deep, profound, long lasting." Alex could be hard: "At times he would more break you than make you. For him everything was I, I, I; the breaking of the I, but it should be through to something more; to love, to the place of the heart."

In rounding out the scattered impressions we have of the 1980s, the 1990s, and the early 2000s, we emphasize the place of special events. From the 1960s through to the 21st century Alexander Horn showed a dramatist's genius for arranging events and gatherings: Christmas parties, theme parties, costume parties, theater parties. The events in New York and Boston involved a more mature group than had existed in San Francisco. In the course of these events participants might take vows for life or set personal aims for the coming year. The events involved an affirmation of the aims of the group, and — in effect — of each participant's lifetime of Work. They were very special for the people involved.

THE NEW YORK PLAYS

Alex continued to write, direct, and perform. He dates his fifth play, *The Legend of Sharon Shashanovah,* to 1979, and the sixth, *I,* to 1981. These plays show the deeper thematic unity that we first saw in *The Magician.* The timing is more precise than in the earlier plays, and the effects less forced.

With *The Legend of Sharon Shashanovah* Alex opens a direct window into his own work as a playwright, dramatist, producer, and director. He reveals to us something of his aims as an artist, and in so doing pays tribute to the Moscow Art Theater. The play itself was dedicated to Sharon Gans, who played the lead role in the first production.

The heroine of the play is Sharon Shashanovah, a young lady, born into the theater, whose entire life is fatefully caught up in that milieu. At a certain point she finds herself trying out for a part in a strange theater, that turns out to be very like Hermann Hesse's Magic Theater. But in Alex's play the Magic Theater is the Puppet Theater, because in this theater, the players begin to realize they are not real men and women, but only mechanical dolls caught up in a network of stimulus and response. From that realization — and *only* from that realization — can they cease to be puppets. The theater offers them a way out of their mechanical existence.

Sharon's audition is the beginning of the play, and the part she is trying out for turns out to be the role of her own life!

There are three levels represented in the play:

1. The general mill of life on the planet, which could be viewed as mechanical theater, in which everything just happens.
2. The Puppet Theater, which, as a special 'theater within a theater,' takes one out of the mill of life. The plays of the Puppet Theater are based on scripts written in Higher School, by an unknown author, called simply the Maestro.
3. Finally, on the highest level, there is the Maestro himself, who orchestrates *both* the Puppet Theater *and* the great mechanical play of life.

The work of the Puppet Theater allows you, ultimately, to enter ... "a much greater Theater, of which this little theater is but a mirror."

Through the play we see Sharon's discovery of right Eros. We see the damage done to her nature, both before the play begins and through the action of the play. We see the entry of different influences that allow for healing, and for the formation of permanent ideals that transcend the narrow confines of her life. These ideals include service to art, service to humanity, and service to the Maestro himself. In this context Sharon achieves right Eros. There is a final resolution in Sharon's forgiveness of the other players of the Puppet Theater (who are also the 'other actors' in her own tragic life) and in her willingness to serve them.

As in the tragedies of Sophocles, Sharon fails utterly in relation to the externals of her life. But eventually something deep within her transcends all her limitations.

The second New York Play, and the final play of the King trilogy, was called simply *I*. In the first two plays of the trilogy the negative character of the Tyrant is neutralized, but not defeated. In the final play Tyrant loses; he is both neutralized and transcended. This transcendence, however, is achieved only by certain individuals. The regeneration of American society — wherein the priests become men of action and the kings become contemplatives — is left unresolved. But the right relation between the two lines is discovered: the union of contemplation and action is a regenerative *justice*, which orchestrates all the processes of the cosmos of man. This is the cosmic *dikaiosyne* (δικαιοσύνη) of Aeschylus.

The final play of the trilogy brings out the need to directly confront, and ultimately acknowledge, the darkest aspects of one's nature. What one has not seen acts upon one, beneath the level of awareness. The acceptance of the dark side is necessary to neutralize its effects, and to enable Higher Centers. This path leads to the narrow gate of I and not-I. Only by seeing the evil that is within oneself — the shadow-identity that has built up around the Black Queen — can one transcend it. It may be remarked that Alex's practice of these principles, as a teacher, was shown in his remarkable capacity to reveal, to each of his students, their own dark side. This line of work produced a sometimes frightening impartiality in him.

The drama of *I* depicts the ultimate confrontation between what we have called the Black Queen and the White Queen. It is a depiction of what the Christian monastic tradition calls "The Dark Night of the Soul." It is the final trial of awakening, in which the protagonist passes the last barrier to "rejoining the Gods in eternity." To represent this, the play goes more deeply into Hell (Worlds 384 and 768) than any other of the plays.

In this play we have one of the great understandings of Alex's last years. His original teaching of right Eros is now completed by his teaching of Grace. Grace is, if you will, Alexander Horn's version of Dante's Beatrice. She appears in *I* as a Goddess.

The character of Grace can only be understood in relation to Higher Centers. To clarify: we can make the efforts to awaken, and we may make significant payment, but when the Higher Centers come, they come only by grace. Permanent entry into Worlds 6 and 12 is something we can never deserve, for we are comprised of lower matters. It is, ultimately, by grace alone that we are ever allowed to enter higher worlds. Grace thus refers not to particular experiences of Higher Centers, but to something intrinsic in the unity of the higher level that is behind them and allows these experiences to take place. Something that exists on the scale of your life. To know this grace is to directly experience one's acceptance by a higher level. So, as one progresses, one sees the traces of the goddess in one's life. One sees the traces of something *one cannot deserve*. This can give each of us reassurance in the darkest moments of our life.

In 1993 Alex co-authored, with Sharon, a seventh play, *The Infinite Lives of Giordano Bruno*: *A Play in Three Acts*. It was published in limited edition and the author has, at the time of writing, been unable to obtain a copy. In its content we see a departure from the mid-20th century America context of the other plays. Did Alex no longer feel contemporary with the America of the 1990s?

The Passing of Alexander Francis Horn

In June of 2007, terminally ill with cancer, Alexander Horn returned to the Falls Creek Ranch in Montana, which had served him as a retreat for twenty-nine years. A few students joined him there, and Sharon visited him regularly. He spent the summer in the forested solitude of the Rocky

Mountain foothills. When he saw that he had only a short time to live, he asked to return to New York for his funeral and interment. And he got his wish. He was flown back from Kalispell on a chartered private jet and transported to Sharon's 12th Street apartment in an ambulance. He died within hours of his arrival. A student who visited later that day witnessed Sharon in her bed, with Alex's dead body beside her. Michael Horn was seated by the bed, next to his father. Sharon was still speaking to Alex as though he were alive. And of course, in a way, he was still alive.

Alexander Francis Horn died on the 30th September 2007, just a few days after his 78th birthday. Sharon had previously asked Alex to "find me a Rabbi" for the service. He had done so, and his friend Simon Jacobson presided over the funeral. The pieces played during the ceremony were Johann Sebastian Bach's *Air on a G string,* Wolfgang Mozart's *Laudate Dominum,* and Hector Villa-Lobos' *Aria cantilena*. The reading for the funeral was taken from *The Infinite Lives of Giordano Bruno*:

> The Promethean spirit of man, through countless ages, has labored to break the fatal embrace of Earth which has kept us chained to the wheel of life, prisoners of a gravitation that denies us the grace of Heaven. But we are children of the starry world, and not even our mother, Earth, shall keep us from our birthright.

Alex is buried in East Hampton, Long Island in Shaarey Pardes Accabonac Grove Cemetery, a beautiful location that exudes peace and solitude.[1] All the gravestones lie flat and are placed along a winding paved walkway. Alex's plot is located in Section C, on the inner circle of the section, the fourth gravestone in.

The salutation "O Nobly Born" precedes each of the invocations given in *The Tibetan Book of the Dead:*

> O Nobly Born, O you of glorious origins, remember your radiant true nature, the essence of mind. Trust it. Return to it. It is home.

---

1. Address: Shaarey Pardes Accabonac Grove Cemetery, 306 Old Stone Hwy, East Hampton, NY 11937.

Figure 68. Alexander Horn's gravesite, East Hampton, NY.

We can say that the phrase "O Nobly Born" is a reference to our latent Higher Centers, carried from life to life. They pre-exist our present lifetime. Alex — in his life — acknowledged this birthright, realized his Higher Centers, and returned to the source.

In the period after Alex's death Sharon, and a core of close students, sought to connect with his field of influence, as Rodney Collin had connected with Peter Ouspensky's field of influence. It is our hope that they succeeded. Sharon was to follow Alex some thirteen years later, on 22nd January 2021.

What, then, became of the Magic Theater? What became of Alexander Horn's work, his aims, and the alchemical transformation of energies that he effected — with an unceasing dynamism — for forty-two consecutive years? We do not know. But *certainly it all exists* ... as Tony sang to Maria in *West Side Story*... "Somehow, Someday, Somewhere." He is happening now in some other reality that's beyond our own, and if we too "break the fatal embrace of Earth" we may see him there.

CHAPTER 6

Robert Earl Burton and The Fellowship of Friends

This chapter will be unlike the previous five, which are developed around the lives of Gurdjieff, Ouspensky, Collin, and Horn respectively. The chapter on Robert Burton's teaching, the Fellowship of Friends, will focus rather on the development of the school that he created and the form and methods of the Work he made possible. The Fellowship, in its maturity, became a larger organization than the teachings of Gurdjieff, Ouspensky, Collin, or Horn. It operated over a longer period of time, and it operated on an international scale. In this context certain things became possible. But a full history of the Fellowship would be a larger endeavor than can be undertaken in these pages, and the biography of Robert Earl Burton must be the work of other writers. Having said this, the Work of the Fellowship can certainly be represented in a way that will make clear both its relation to the teachings of Gurdjieff, Ouspensky, Collin, and Horn, and its difference from them. The first-person pronoun will make its appearance in this chapter, as the author of the book is a student of this school, and is reporting on the basis of experience.

Early Years and Work with Alex Horn: 1967–1969

Robert Earl Burton was born in May of 1939, in Little Rock, Arkansas, to Edgar and Velma Burton (neé Schach). Robert was the youngest of four children. His father died when he was only two years old. Two years after his father's death, in 1943, his mother moved the young family to Oakland,

California. There Robert went through grade school, and, on completing the twelfth grade, entered San Jose State University, where he eventually completed a degree in speech pathology. While at the university he developed a serious interest in tennis. After graduating, he decided not to make a career of speech pathology, but to become a schoolteacher. For some years he taught the fourth grade at Springhill Elementary School in Lafayette. During these years he continued to play tennis, reaching the level of semi-professional player and achieving a certain level of success in match play.

One afternoon he was sitting on the balcony of his apartment, looking down at the apartment's swimming pool. He saw that he had a fine dwelling, a good job, a car, and money in the bank ... and that it all amounted to nothing. Having fulfilled the requirements of middle-class life, he was himself unfulfilled. He did not know what he wanted to do, but he determined to break the pattern that he found himself in — then and there. He did not wait until the end of the school term, but put in his resignation at the spring break, leaving the school in March of 1967. "I did not know what the truth was, but I knew I had not found it."

About five months after leaving Springhill School, Robert was hitchhiking from the Berkeley Tennis Club to his new apartment in San Francisco. He was picked up by a doctor, and conversation developed between the two of them. It turned to spiritual topics. At a certain point the doctor asked him, "Do you want to go to a meeting?" Robert replied, "Yes," and found himself — on September 5th 1967 — at one of the prospective student meetings given by Alexander Francis Horn, at his home on 350 Page Street, San Francisco. On hearing Alex present the aims of his Work — just as they have been presented in the previous chapter — Robert felt that ... "I could give my life to this." And, in fact, he did. He went back to work, in order to make the teaching payments that Alex's group required. He did not go back to teaching, but took whatever jobs he could find. He applied every discipline and every exercise that his teacher gave him, even adding disciplines and exercises of his own. Late one evening in December 1967, during a gambling party in San Rafael that Alex had organized, Robert found himself alone, gazing into a fireplace. It was a natural pause. As he watched the flames quietly pulsate, his presence deepened in stages, until suddenly the Self was there, in the full awareness of itself. As Robert put it, "It was the first time the Higher Emotional Center came out, and it was delighted to be there for the first time." Upon this first appearance two 'I's came in quick succession: "Who is that?" "What right does it have to be there?" But Robert sidestepped these 'I's, staying on the side of the emergent Self.

This was a turning point in more ways than one; it was the beginning of a new level of Work for Robert, and — from that moment forward — his life became more difficult. The different part-time jobs began to disappear, and he had more trouble making his teaching payments. Alex Horn had spoken of C Influence working in a specific way with himself (as the teacher) and in a general way with his students. Suddenly Robert realized that C Influence was working in a specific way with him. One day, while driving through Modesto in his Volkswagen bug, he stopped at a red light and signaled to turn left. When the light turned green and he began to make the turn, he suddenly heard the loud blast of a horn behind him. He thought, "This couldn't be for me." He woke up in the hospital with a doctor putting stitches into his head. A truck had lost control approaching the intersection and broadsided his car; as he found out later, his car was pushed under a truck. The doctor put in nearly a hundred stitches. After the surgery, Robert was wheeled out into the corridor and simply left there. Without speaking to anyone, he got up and went directly home from the hospital and slept heavily. The next evening was the meeting with Alex, and he determined to attend despite his injuries. On arriving at the Mission Street theater, he went to the washroom to clean up. Alex came into the washroom and approached him from behind; on seeing the bandages on the back of his head, Alex said simply, "Your scars are precious." It was an acknowledgement, on the part of his teacher, that the bandages were the result of a C Influence intervention, and not the poor judgement of a student.

A few months after this incident Robert noticed a change in Alex, remarking that, "I could see his starry world." Alex had crystallized as a man number six. After the Wednesday meeting, while students were putting the chairs back in place, Robert stepped forward to offer Alex his congratulations. Alex replied, "Thank you, Bob." This was Alexander Horn's transition to the level of man number six, a transition that Robert recognized in Alex and would himself experience later in his life.

Alex began to work more closely with Robert: "During my time with Alex Horn, he openly spoke about my role and his role as being conscious roles. Also, Influence C did not reveal themselves to anyone else in his group." Despite the close working relationship with his teacher, Robert sometimes felt confused or challenged. As the contacts with C Influence began to grow more definite, they were not always in alignment with the directives coming from his own teacher. Indeed, they sometimes seemed to make it difficult to be a student in his teacher's group.

After Robert had been with Alex for about eighteen months, Alex suddenly announced that he was disbanding the group. He called a meeting for the ten students whom he felt were worthy of continuing the work and gave each of them a task. Robert, one of the ten, put everything he could into his task, but C Influence — in the most disarming way — gave him a series of checks that prevented him from fulfilling it. In the end, Robert was out of the group. We keep in mind that, with Alex, being 'out of the group' was not necessarily a final thing; he would often pick up connections with ex-students at a later point in time. Nevertheless, in April of 1969, Robert was alone ... and he was beginning to follow the beat of a different drummer. He knew that he was now ultimately accountable to Higher Forces, but he had no idea of how to connect this to the pattern of his external life. You can no more demand clarification from the Gods than you can squeeze water from a stone. A cellular being is without influence or leverage of any kind in the molecular world. At the same time Robert had just lost a teacher who did clarify the conditions of Work, who did make very firm demands on his students, and who always established a high standard. Yet it appeared that the Gods themselves had taken Robert out of this more structured environment. Would he now return to the mire of imagination, or would he somehow connect with an impossibly distant source? He felt himself ... in the words of the old song ... "to be without a home, like a complete unknown, like a rolling stone."

Robert travelled, by himself, on a very limited income, throughout the United States for seven months. It was a difficult time, yet through these

Figure 69. Robert Burton at age seventy.

months the prompts from C Influence kept coming. They wanted something of him. He set aims to separate his emergent Higher Centers from the many 'I's: "When I was driving, I tried to remember myself one telephone pole to the next; when I reached one pole, I would try to have no thoughts until the next one. Then I would put a tape cassette in my mouth and sit too far forward or too far back in the seat — anything so as not to yield to imagination while driving. The first thing I did when I opened my eyes in the morning was to turn the blanket intentionally aside. I began the day with an intentional movement designed to help me self-remember." Robert was struggling to keep his infant soul alive in a strange new world. And in this new world everything always hung in the balance. There was no certainty. Yes, there was a new level of Work, but there were also moments of despair. It was during this period he came to know that he was going to be a teacher — but he had no sense of when or how this might occur.

The Beginning of the Fellowship:
New Year's Eve 1969

Soon after his return to the Bay Area, Robert was invited by friends to a New Year's Eve costume party in Lafayette. It was the New Year's Eve of 1969. At the event a young lady, Bonita Guido, recognized that Robert was in a completely different state from anyone else at the party. She was in a good position to see this, as she was under the influence of mescaline. When she spoke to Robert he responded directly from his Higher Centers. It was a unique experience for her. In her own words: "There was such intensity to our conversation that at times everything and everyone else just seemed to disappear. I had entered a new, wondrous world, full of hidden portent." She later remembered that when, during the conversation, she mentioned the reservations she had about certain of the spiritual teachers of that time, Robert replied simply: "I know a God who has no feet of clay." She realized that this person was different from anyone she had ever met. She asked Robert if she could speak to him again, after the party, and he agreed. Robert met with Bonita the following day, January 1, 1970, at the Copper Penny, a coffee shop on University Avenue in Berkeley.

A few days after this first meeting Robert met with both Bonita and her husband, David, at the same restaurant. Robert presented the basic principles of the Work to both of them in an ordered way. He had, without in any way trying, attracted his first two students. After a few meetings both Bonita and David committed to working with Robert under the conditions that he specified, which included making monthly teaching payments. The three of them then met six days a week. The first two students had an intensive course! Bonita had a wide circle of friends, and, with Robert's permission, she spread the word to them, one by one. The ringing of the crystal glass, which had begun at the fireplace in San Rafael, was now extending outward to a wider circle.

Robert interviewed each prospective student individually. Each one had to call Robert by themselves, and he would then set up a meeting with them at a coffee shop. He admitted each student personally, in this way, for the first year of his teaching. One of the reasons for this personal screening

Figure 70. Where the teaching began.

was that he would not accept anyone studying with Alexander Horn, out of respect for his former teacher.

Robert began teaching from Ouspensky's template, as given in *The Psychology of Man's Possible Evolution* and *The Fourth Way*. And these two works became the Fellowship "bibles." Robert emphasized Ouspensky's principle of the non-expression of negative emotions, and it became a school exercise. It was the right template for that time and place. The teaching grew, very gradually, to fourteen students in the first year.

Robert was working with what was, in effect, a circle of friends. Those who joined the group in the first year were the trusted friends of the first students. Robert was creating a base. As it was centered on a shared valuation for first things, and as the teacher's relationship to each individual was direct and personal, it became like a family.

In the beginning Robert held six meetings a week! By mid-year, with a larger number of students, there were usually three meetings a week, supplemented by other activities. For the first six or seven months meetings were held in coffee shops in the East Bay, at David and Bonita Guido's home, or — as the group grew larger — in small halls or high school auditoriums. Robert explicitly did not encroach on the San Francisco peninsula, which he considered to be his own teacher's territory. By the fall of 1970, more students had joined, and some of these had homes that were suitable venues for meetings: Anna Gold in the East Bay, and Donald and Rosemary Macdonald in Vacaville.

In early 1971 Donald introduced Robert to Don and Klair Birrell of Vacaville. Don Birrell was the design director for the Nut Tree complex in Vacaville, and he was able to advise Robert on many practical matters. The Birrell's home was a short walk from the home of Yorgos and Kerrie Savides. Robert led meetings in the Birrell's home in the first months of 1971, then in April Robert moved from his home in Walnut Creek to Yorgos and Kerrie Savides' home on Buck Avenue, along with Miles Barth, Linda Kaplan, and James Chisholm. This later became known as "the first teaching house." Robert also spent a lot of time at Donald and Rosemary's farm, where he was able to schedule work octaves for the group.

Many of the first students were older than Robert: professional people, schoolteachers, musicians, doctors, psychologists. Yet they accepted him immediately and respected him as a teacher. He had the natural authority that consciousness brings. This first generation of students were fortunate, not only for themselves, but for the school. They provided a mature base for the younger generations that were to follow.

Robert had awakened in the awareness of C Influence, and in the awareness that he was accountable to them. They had brought him into being, as a conscious being, because they had a task for him. Thus, from the very beginning, he was given what Ouspensky and Gurdjieff had struggled so hard to find, the direct connection to C Influence. Viewed on the scale of the Fourth Way, Gurdjieff, Ouspensky, Collin, and Horn had made the payment for Robert to begin with a direct relation to what Ouspensky called the "source of the system." When Robert said to Bonita Guido, "I know a God who has no feet of clay," he was introducing a theme that was central to his teaching. There was always the sense of Robert as a connection to something beyond Robert. That vision, and the tasks that were to develop out of it, defined the whole character of his teaching.

In relation to this, Robert had a significant shock in his first year as a teacher. He found that C Influence were working not only with himself, but also working directly with his students. Robert would offer photographs or observations to his students, which they — being new to the Work — did not always properly understand. But, Robert noticed, the photographs were often followed by timely shocks, or difficult events in the students' lives, which brought home the point. Robert said that this had never been the case in Alexander Horn's group.

Understanding this difference allowed Robert to re-think his own approach to teaching. Where Alex had forced each individual student to confront their own chief feature, Robert could allow C Influence to confront students with their features and support them in their attempts to work with the friction this created. In this way he could act more effectively as a third force. It is a great limitation for a teacher to have to act as first force. We note that a direct attack on chief feature is a direct attack on the instinctive illusion of unity that is behind chief feature. For the machine this is annihilation. Robert later taught us that you cannot confront the instinctive center directly, in this way. It is simply too strong, and the effect on the student can be shattering. Direct confrontation with the instinctive center comes in later stages of the way, and it comes to each student out of the fabric of their own life: it is a moment of their destiny. The level of the student's work attracts the defining trials. With respect to Alex's sometimes brutal methods, Robert said that, "to use violence to awaken inevitably becomes mechanical." Reflecting on the short period of time he had spent in Alex's group, Robert said that it had been arranged that way by C Influence, so that he would not be too much influenced by his own teacher's methods.

Having made these qualifications about direct work on the instinctive center, Robert ensured that there would be — from the very first day — indirect work on the instinctive center: reducing its space, neutralizing it, separating from it. When we work against the instinctive center on a regular basis, we can bypass it in certain moments, connecting directly to Higher Centers. The cumulation of these moments prepares the student for the direct confrontation that will occur in their final and permanent transition to a Higher Level.

While Robert did not confront or 'corner' the instinctive center, as Alexander Horn had done, he certainly did give penetrating observations of chief feature. In a thousand ways he made you aware of your 'mechanicality,' of the difference between the functions of your machine and consciousness behind it. One sensed that he had the capacity to annihilate you, but that he chose not to do so. Robert understood that, in the Work, destruction, healing, and regeneration must follow one another in a cycle. The student must be able to digest, to recover, and to understand what is happening to them.

In the Fellowship, work against chief feature and the instinctive center was reinforced by the study of the system of body type, chief feature, and center of gravity that had been developed by Rodney Collin.[1] The Fellowship took this system and developed it to the level of an applied science. Everybody studied type and feature, and everybody gave and received observations in this area. Such shared observations were called 'photographs.' One was under an obligation to always accept a photograph, even (and especially) if you didn't agree with it. Most students knew their body type and center of gravity within two weeks of joining the school, and their chief feature within a month — even if it took them another few decades to understand it on a deeper level. Verifying the body type information was, at the same time, verifying that humanity exists in the state of sleep. Everything happens mechanically, according to type and feature. Understanding the difference between consciousness and functions in this way, students understood that there is actually no need for consciousness on this level. Life goes on very well, in the way that it does, without it. At the same time consciousness is the only thing of enduring value that exists on this level. As Robert often reminded us, "It is the only thing you can take away with you." Supported by all of these understandings, we were — as Keats put it — "Awake forever in a sweet unrest."

---

1. See Collin, Rodney, *The Theory of Celestial Influence,* Watkins, London, 1980, pp. 165-173, Types: Endocrine and Astrological. This system was also used by Robert's teacher, Alexander Horn.

At the end of the first year the preparatory stage of Robert's teaching was done; a certain bond had been established between the members of the group, a certain standard had been established, and introductory or 'open' meetings could now begin — allowing a larger number of people to come in. It was, for the new people, like joining a family, and then seeing that family expand and develop. You would see how each new member fitted in, and what they had to add.

At the same time Robert determined that the group should now have its own property. On the first birthday of the school, on January 1st 1971, Robert announced — at a New Year's party at Donald and Rosemary Macdonald's — that he intended to look for property to purchase. A week later, at a dinner at Anna Gold's, he made clear to the group that he was thinking practically. At the end of the evening he asked that everyone present take from their wallet what they needed to get home, and then donate the rest to a collection for a down payment on the property. The total collected that night was $185.00, the exact amount in the end of the price per acre of the property that was eventually purchased. Over the next six months several ranch donations were asked of the entire group. It was a challenging time, with some people having to take second jobs or borrow money.

Initially Robert looked for property in Big Sur and along the nearby Pacific Coast. But soon, in response to negative shocks he received from C Influence, he began to focus on properties in the Sierra Foothills. He, Rosemary Macdonald, and Klair Birrell worked as a team researching properties in the foothills. They used Highway 49 as a baseline for their search. They were looking for land above the fog line, below the snow line, and near a river. Klair would research the properties for sale, contact the real estate agents, and arrange the appointments. Rosemary and Robert would then go out early each morning to meet the real estate agents and to survey the land. They would return in the late afternoon or early evening.

One morning, in May of 1971, after having viewed nearly forty properties, Robert and Rosemary set out to visit a property in Yuba County, in the tiny rural community of Oregon House. They took Highway 20 until it turned into Marysville Road, and then followed the unpaved and pothole-ridden Rices Crossing Road into Oregon House. Finally, they came to the access road to the property, which was a hard left off Rices Crossing Road, just before Richards Ranch. They drove over a wooden bridge across a stream, and came out into a large property, with both field and forest. There was a single pioneer house, dating from 1860.

After several hours surveying the house and the property, Robert and Rosemary took a picnic lunch in a meadow near the back gate to the property. Robert had brought sandwiches and a thermos. Rosemary later remarked that Robert made the most delicious sandwiches. They sat there quietly eating their lunch and looking out over the meadow. At one point, they turned to each other, and Robert said, "This is it." Rosemary replied, "Yes, this is it."

Robert made the real estate agent an offer of $185 an acre, the exact amount collected at the first Ranch donation, at the dinner at Anna Gold's. The offer was accepted in mid-June. The property itself comprised 917 acres of land, with one existing residence (the pioneer house) and a large barn. Oregon House had been a well-known stop on the Oregon Trail in the years before California entered the Union. That was its heyday. It was now, 120 years later, "nowhere in particular." There was one post office and a general store with a gas pump. So the school had a real retreat!

On the property owner's acceptance of Robert's offer, there was a celebration at Anna Gold's house, and Robert announced that all would go out to visit the property on the coming July 4th weekend.

The Founding of the Ranch: 1971

The weekend of July 4th 1971 was the first Ranch Weekend for the school, which now comprised more than sixty people. There was a celebration, and at the same time work began on the property and on the existing house, now permanently called "the lodge." People brought their sleeping bags, and in the evenings either found a place in the lodge, or simply slept under the stars. Ranch Weekends followed on a regular basis. Each weekend was an intense experience, so condensed and concentrated that one student remarked, "It was as though time slowed." The school now had its own place, where work on consciousness could become a real priority.

Figure 71. Robert Burton in 1971.

Robert organized everything. Each morning he gathered everyone together, reviewed the progress of the major projects, and delegated work to each person. There was food preparation, cleaning, painting, and structural work on the lodge itself. Much of the floor was rotten and had to be torn up and replaced. The second floor was uninhabitable, and had to be rebuilt.

Robert made the new property his base of operations, and from the 4th of July until the end of October he did not move from the Ranch. In June, after five weeks of living at the lodge, Robert had a tent delivered to the property. It was erected just above the lodge. Once he had moved into the tent many other students followed his example, and for some years many of the students residing on the property lived in tents. Once the second level of the lodge was complete, near the end of the 1971, Robert moved back into the lodge.

Along with initiating projects on the property, Robert gave many exercises. During the work on renovating the lodge, there was an exercise not to speak to the students you were working with, while you were working. Then came: no coffee for a week; no television; no laughing. The most common exercises were the word exercises. Do not use the word "I," or the word "OK," or the word "oh." They were usually given for a month, although some ran for a much longer time. The exercise not to use contractions ran for many years, until it produced a kind of Fellowship patois — at which point it was dropped. Once an exercise was given, every student had the responsibility to photograph those who couldn't keep it. Photographs would take the form of a brief shutter motion of the finger, as though you were taking a picture with a camera. To go through the day in a hail of shutter motions was a great spur to self-remembering.

It was clear that Robert made unlimited demands on himself, and he did not hesitate to make more demands on his students than they would ever make on themselves. But he did this in a warm and friendly way, as though he were helping members of his family. Demands were a privilege: an acknowledgement of your potential. There was not one pharisaical, censorious, or self-righteous bone in Robert Burton's body. It was all interesting; it was all part of how the school was developing. And failure was part of the game. If you did not fail, you had not made enough demands on yourself. Robert once said that "The way I became conscious was by separating from the disappointment of seeing that I did not remember myself."[1]

After a few months' work at this pace, the old makeshift structure that we called the "lodge," became *The Lodge* — the unquestioned center of the group's activities. Most evenings Robert taught there informally, with students gathering in the large living room to discuss their work. Robert was continuously available to all those around him. Some took the maximum advantage of his presence, while others came and went during the day. Robert worked most intensively with those who worked with him.

Yorgos and Kerrie Savides relocated to the property at the same time Robert did. As permanent residents they managed the property, putting in extensive vegetable gardens, with the idea of eventually making the retreat self-sustaining.

---

1. Ruth-Mueller, Guinevere, *Bread Upon the Water*, G&G Mueller, Gujrat India, 1999, p. 35.

As the weeks turned into months the entire Lodge was renovated. The living room was made into a venue for meetings, the second floor of the west wing was entirely rebuilt, and the kitchen and dining facilities were much enlarged. Poultry and livestock were brought onto the property, and a vegetable garden was begun. Additionally, daytime accommodation was made available for the six or eight children who were staying on the property. A single wide trailer was brought in and labelled the 'Children's House.' Over the months, the students delegated to oversee the Children's House developed it into a kindergarten-cum-elementary school. From the very beginning Robert had a concern with the children as *part* of the Fellowship. Children were both third line of work, and potential future students. The school had to think of how it wanted to raise children, and who they might become. Within a year the property, initially called 'the Ranch,' was renamed — more poetically — 'Via del Sol,' The Way of the Sun. But most people just continued to call it the Ranch.

In September of 1971 an entire Ranch Weekend was held in silence. At the end of that weekend Robert announced that he would himself continue in silence indefinitely. The explanation he later gave for this decision was that, "When I spoke, the light went off." He also said, "I realized that if I could not listen, I could not teach." While this may have been an

Figure 72. The original lodge.
The cabin in the foreground dated to 1860.

Figure 73. Some of the first residents of the Ranch.

overstatement with respect to Robert himself, it was something that he had observed in his students. He was teaching us all to value states over words. Robert did continue to lead meetings and he still took questions from students. As the hands went up, and the questions came, he would write the answers on a piece of paper and give them to an interlocutor who would read them out. The interlocutor became adept at interpreting Robert's responses, and over time the two of them developed a kind of sign language.

More generally, with respect to such radical course changes, *Robert never explained himself.* He just did it. The inspiration might come to him when a glass broke while he was speaking, or when an unusual sequence of events occurred, or because he overheard someone saying certain words just as he was getting out of a car. Robert felt that these were shocks from C Influence. His extreme responsiveness to what was happening in the moment introduced a wild card into our lives. It also taught us respect for Influence C, as they might — through him — change our lives at any moment.

At the time Robert entered silence he asked that the meetings be recorded. Notes were taken during each meeting, weekly transcripts printed up, and the transcripts disseminated to all students. This was the start of the weekly Via Del Sol journal. It contained notes from recent meetings, and current news from around the school. Robert made written comments on the angles given by students and would add some thoughts of his own at the end. It became a new channel of communication.

At a Sunday breakfast at the Macdonald's ranch (in October 1971), Robert asked Rosemary about the Esalen Institute, a community based in Big Sur that was dedicated to exploring human potential. Donald had an association with this community through his experience with their rolfing therapy. Would the Esalen people be interested in the Fellowship? Could Rosemary ask Donald to set up a meeting? Yes, she could. In the same conversation Rosemary told Robert about a friend of hers — Sheila Wallace — who had a magnetic center and who lived in the town of Carmel on the Big Sur coast. Something clicked, and Robert asked, "Can we arrange a meeting with her too?" Calls were made. A meeting was scheduled with Sheila on Monday and another meeting with the Esalen people on Tuesday. It was decided that Donald would go down to Carmel Monday morning and bring Sheila back to Vacaville. On Tuesday, he would host the Esalen people at the Nut Tree for a dinner (which Robert would not attend) and bring them over to the Macdonald's ranch for a meeting with Robert afterward. We must note here, that, throughout this episode, Robert kept his vow of silence, so these exchanges would have taken place either through notes or through Robert signaling an interlocutor who would then interpret his hand signals.

Donald brought Sheila to the ranch on Monday evening, and it was somehow decided that she, being an experienced chef, would prepare the Tuesday evening dinner for Robert and the other students. This dinner would take place *before* the Esalen people came over from the Nut Tree for their meeting. In the course of setting all this up, Shiela — who was English-born — had to reschedule a flight to London. It seemed as if everyone was operating on double time.

Thus, on Tuesday Sheila, with Rosemary as sous chef, prepared a dinner for Robert and others, and then, after the dinner, the Esalen people arrived for their meeting. But, as it turned out, the dinner was no side event. Sheila produced a meal at a very high level, which made a deep impression on Robert. The Esalen people then came over, but in the exchange that followed it became clear that there was no real point of contact between the two groups. The electricity was simply not there. A school requires a different kind of commitment than that of a human potential group. And so Esalen and the Fellowship went their separate ways. However, Sheila — who had made significant personal sacrifices during her brief stay at Vacaville — joined the school. With her entry new seeds were sown, as we shall soon see.

As we noted, from the July 4th weekend through October Robert lived continuously at the Ranch. Towards the end of October, a couple from Vacaville gave him a car for a present, and he began to travel — his favorite destination now being Carmel and visits with Sheila Wallace. Sheila's apartment in the center of town was elegantly furnished, and she served her meals on fine china, with George Jensen silver and Baccarat crystal. Robert made a connection between this level of visual impression and the presence created at the meals. This immediately had implications for the future. Very soon her apartment in Carmel became a center of activity. Sheila introduced Robert to a fashionable men's clothing store in Carmel, and this changed the level of his wardrobe. Sheila would travel with Robert on his shopping expeditions to guarantee the quality and authenticity of the shops — for clothing, glassware, silver, and antiques.

After October 1971 Robert was still at the Ranch on weekends, but during the week he moved between Carmel, Vacaville, the East Bay, and Lake Tahoe. He developed a vision of the school as having more than one major location, with one base at the Ranch, one at Carmel, and one at Lake Tahoe. (The Bay Area was still considered Alex Horn's territory.) For the students living in these locations, most weekends were still Ranch Weekends, and they would travel to the Ranch to help with the work there and to attend the meetings.

Since Robert was off the property much of the week, his second in command, Yorgos Savides, developed a more active role in managing activities at the Ranch. In January of 1972 Robert announced that Yorgos was going to awaken. Thus, Yorgos was not just the ranch manager, but the first student in the Fellowship that Robert said was definitely "going to awaken." In August of that same year Robert stated that there were now three students in the school fated to awaken: Yorgos Savides, Donald Macdonald, and Miles Barth.

Yorgos and Kerrie developed extensive gardens on the property, and for a time the diet was vegetarian. They had what might be called an 'organic' approach to the Work. Under their leadership there was a tendency for life on the property to become communal; people had very little money and they helped each other to get by, one way or another. Sexual relations were casual. During the periods of Robert's absence, the use of soft drugs was commonplace. Yorgos himself was dedicated and determined, while always showing a gentle and forbearing nature. He worked tirelessly on the agriculture, producing real results with an intermittent and often unskilled labor force. He was tolerant and, at the same time, firm and persevering. The group who lived and worked on the property throughout the week felt that they were doing the Work as it had originally been conceived by Robert. They were an increasingly self-sustaining community, focused on the Work and freed from the distractions of life.

This was the beginning of a polarization in the school, for by now parallel lines of development were underway. In the East Bay and Carmel, Robert had no difficulty in dealing with students who were professional people on their own terms. He seemed to have no expectation that they would stop being professional people, nor did he feel that the kind of work they were doing was a denying force to their evolution. He was also increasingly attracted to refined impressions: works of art, examples of good design, fine garments, and gourmet cooking. These impressions are normally part of an urban environment.

On January 2nd of 1972 Robert moved from the Ranch to Carmel.

The Move to Carmel: 1972

Robert, with a select group of students, rented a house on Whitman Circle in Carmel. This, naturally, became known as the 'Whitman House.' He continued to visit the Ranch on a regular basis and to lead meetings in the East Bay and at Donald and Rosemary's ranch in Vacaville. With fewer teaching activities based in Oregon House, other centers of Fellowship activity began to appear in other parts of the state.

More important than the changes taking place in the form of the school were the changes taking place in Robert himself. He was acquiring a more profound grasp of his task and of its requirements. This change had begun in late 1971 but came to its fruition in Carmel in 1972 and 1973. It was — of course — based on new input from Higher Forces. Robert had known, from the time of his lonely year of travel, that he was to teach, but now the Gods gave him to understand that he was *to create a school that would seed a new civilization*. This affected the scale of his thinking. From this time he was always preparing for and anticipating things to come. He would make sudden moves or decisions, watch very carefully to see how things developed, and then adjust course according to the feedback from C Influence. It was never just a matter of interacting with the circle of people around him. He was in the business of laying foundations. With Robert one had to be ready for the unexpected, and the unexpected was always just around the corner.

From another point of view the Gods were using both Robert and his students as the foundation for a finished product that only they could understand. And they were creating it out of the human material that was available to them. It sometimes seemed that we — the students — were not the foundation, but the raw material for the foundation: the rough-hewn stones that had yet to be cut, scoured, and polished.

Robert was also given new direction in relation to the nature of the new civilization. It was to be founded on a rediscovery of the culture of the Italian Renaissance and of Renaissance Europe. There was to be a rediscovery of great art. *The Fellowship of Friends was to explore deeply the relationship between art and awakening.* And there were to be several stages to this. It was not limited to the art of the Renaissance, but was to include all of the classical culture that had been rediscovered in the Italian Renaissance.

There was to be an assimilation of conscious art and literature, principally from the Western Tradition, reaching back to classical times: Plato, Aristotle, Petrarch, Leonardo, Shakespeare, Bach, Vivaldi, Montaigne, Goethe. Robert referred to the Fellowship, at that time, as a "Western Path." With relation to esotericism he said, "The West knows of esotericism in the East, but the East does not suspect the esotericism of the West." Detailed study of Eastern teachers and Eastern art did not come until several years into the 21st century.

In outlining Robert's new understanding we have the advantage of hindsight. For Robert himself the clarification came over several years. One trigger for this change was the influence of Sheila Wallace. She possessed the quality of personal refinement, and she educated Robert in the value of fine impressions: quality materials, good workmanship, and an appreciation of the arts as a way of life. Robert saw a direct connection between the refinement of impressions and presence itself. He expressed this in his teaching of work on *alchemy*. Part of living in the present is refining the alchemical level of one's environment. One is continuously interacting with and refining the contents of the moment. And this deepens one's experience of the present itself. From the time of Robert's move to Carmel his interest in painting, poetry, and classical music developed apace. He began visiting museums and took a marked interest in French (not organic) cuisine. During this period he encountered Johann Peter Eckermann's book *Conversations with Goethe*; it is the record of a conscious being — Goethe — giving discourse on the arts, and on the art of living itself. It could not have had a greater impact on Robert. He later said of it that it changed his vision of the school.

YORGOS SAVIDES' DEPARTURE

As the months passed it became apparent that the Ranch was no longer the central location of the School. Many of the residents who managed the gardens, tended the animals, and did the harvest work moved away to the centers. Yorgos was hard pressed to maintain the property.

At a certain point Yorgos became dissatisfied with the direction the school was taking, and many of the students still residing at the Ranch were influenced by him. He spoke with Robert about his concerns, but there was no chance of deflecting Robert from the new direction. At one of the Vacaville meetings, during the interval when announcements were given, Yorgos asked students to start coming to the Ranch at weekends to help with the harvest. Robert followed Yorgos' request by saying to the group: "Do not identify with the ranch. We may even sell it." He was speaking principally to Yorgos, with whom he had already discussed this subject. In response to Yorgos' further questions, Robert asked him to enter a period of silence.

Yorgos believed himself to be fully awake, felt himself ready to teach, and felt the countercultural way of life he had adopted was the way of the future — as did many people of his generation. He conspired, then, with a number of his associates, to take a large body of students out of the school. This group was to serve as the foundation for Yorgos' own teaching. He planned the event to take place at one of Robert's meetings.

On November 7, 1972 Robert was scheduled to lead one of the regular meetings in the East Bay, at a newly rented space in the Berkeley Hills. Yorgos travelled to attend the meeting, along with a number of other students from the Ranch. At this time Robert — still in silence — was leading meetings through his interlocutor. Another student, other than the interlocutor, would read out the general announcements during the refreshment break. Yorgos made a prior arrangement with the student making the announcements, who was one of his personal friends. He gave that student a note, to be read out in his own name, after the last announcement. The note explained certain things that were wrong with the school, and then outlined an alternative path of awakening. The note concluded: "I am C Influence. Those who wish to follow me, can leave the room with me now." After the note was read, Yorgos stood up and walked out of the room. Thirty-seven students walked out with him. Robert just sat there, keeping his vow of silence, in a state of complete alertness as to the intentions of C Influence. He both maintained his silence and accepted what was happening.

Yorgos began teaching his new group in the Bay Area, but, within a year, there was a scandal — ending in the suicide of one of its members. The group dispersed in late 1973. Thirty-two years later, in 2005, the man who had once been the Fellowship's senior student took his own life.

For most students the sudden departure of so many members was a tragedy, but — seen in a longer time frame — it was part of a natural process of growth. A group of people, who had been an essential part of one phase of the school's development, were deemed by C Influence to be unsuitable for the next. It was as though their departure enabled a new wave of entrants.

A few days after Yorgos and his followers had left, Robert put the property at Oregon House up for sale. The residents, aside from a maintenance crew of three or four, moved elsewhere in California. This represented a direct turn away for the organic way of life. Robert was not so much rejecting the experiment at Oregon House, which had initially been intended as a retreat, but seeing what would happen if he placed it in question. He was asking Higher Forces for an indication of which way to go. As it happened there were no takers to purchase the property.

Robert probably expected that the experimental developments at the Ranch, at Carmel, at the East Bay, and at other locations would eventually come together in some way. But the way in which they actually did come together in the line of time often involved unexpected shocks or dislocations. Yorgos and his people were gone, leaving a vacancy at the heart of the school. But while Yorgos had been proselytizing at the Ranch, Robert had been sowing new seeds in the emerging centers, and those seeds were beginning to sprout.

The official label of 'center' was the formal recognition of a group of students living together in a certain location. Each new center began with a house, rented by the students moving into the area, which was then used for meetings and events. This was the advent of the 'teaching house,' as part of the form of the school.

The Lake Tahoe and Honolulu centers formed spontaneously in mid-1972 after students moved there for employment. The Los Angeles center opened at Robert's request in November 1972 after one person joined the school there. In May-June 1973 Robert asked students to open centers Sacramento, Santa Barbara, and San Diego, and Seattle followed shortly after.

For the latter four centers Robert specifically sent a man and woman — not as a couple — to act as co-directors. This was the beginning of a tradition.

In the period following Yorgos' departure Robert began to give Donald Macdonald a certain space and authority. He was a mature man, in his sixties, and — after Yorgos' departure — he functioned naturally as the senior student in the school. Donald eventually became the center director for the entire Bay Area: the East Bay, San Francisco, and Marin. When Robert led meetings in the Bay Area, there would always be four (and eventually six) other people who sat at the front with him. Donald was always one of them. When Donald spoke, his words were always respected.

We noted that, in August 1972, Robert had predicted that Miles Barth, one of the original residents of the Vacaville House, would become a man number five. Sometime later Robert included a Los Angeles student, Girard Haven, in the list of those who would awaken.

On Christmas day 1972, during a party at the Whitman House, Robert ended his silence, which seemed to complete the transition through to a new stage of the school.

As we noted, when Yorgos left and the Ranch was put up for sale, the salaried residents were reduced to a skeleton crew. As the months passed, the opening of the new centers increased the population of the school. Things seemed to be coming together in a certain way, but with Robert's ever clearer understanding of his task, more radical changes were in the offing.

Sometime in the summer of 1973 Robert received an indication that the property was to be central to the future of the school. The many different centers were not enough. There was a relationship between the task of the school and the property at Oregon House. Robert did not tell us what, exactly, this was; he simply took action.

Return to the Ranch: 1973–1975

In October of 1973 Robert made a permanent move from Carmel back to the Ranch, which he renamed Mount Carmel.[1] He renewed his earlier efforts to develop the property, and — in quick succession — plans were made for a vineyard and winery, a larger poultry complex, and a considerable expansion of the vegetable garden.

During the first phase of development of the Ranch, in mid-1971, a single-wide trailer had been brought in and set up on the hillside below the Lodge. This was used as a day school for the children. But with the downsizing of the Ranch it had gone out of use. On Robert's return it was used to house a number of his new projects: a small publishing operation to produce the Mount Carmel journals (which replaced the Via Del Sol journals), and an architectural office to support new constructions on the property. A hairdressing salon and a gift shop were later crowded into the trailer. It was first called the Lower House, to distinguish it from the Lodge. Then, as it developed, it was re-named the Franklin Complex, after Benjamin Franklin.

More visitors began to come to the property on weekends. By late 1973 the population of the Ranch had begun to increase again. It reached a point where the Lodge, now dubbed the Lincoln Lodge, acquired a permanent full-time kitchen staff. On his return to the property Robert had moved back into his upstairs room at the Lodge, but when the Lodge began to serve three meals a day, six days a week, and two meals on Sunday, he was eventually forced out. He had an airstream trailer brought onto the property as his new home and placed it on the footpath between the Lodge and the Franklin Complex. Robert soon decided that airstream trailers might be a solution for the ever-growing housing problem. He brought together landscape designers, architects, and builders to plan an airstream trailer park. A location was decided, twenty trailer pads were poured, a bath house was constructed, and the trailers installed. This trailer park was dubbed the Court of the Caravans.

---

1. A vivid depiction of this phase of Robert's teaching is found in Guinevere Ruth-Mueller's book *Bread Upon the Water*, G&G Mueller, Rajkot, 1999.

Larger developments were in the making. In November of 1973, the Fellowship invited a wine consultant to determine whether a vineyard and winery could be established on the property. The consultant was Karl Werner, the founding wine master at Callaway Vineyards in Temecula, California.

Prior to World War II, Karl's family had owned the Schloss Vollrads wine estate in the German Rheingau, which had been in continuous production for more than 800 years. His family had lost the estate during the war, and Karl had emigrated to America to make a new start. Karl found that the soil on the Fellowship property was indeed conducive to growing grapes. The high altitude would force the vines to struggle hard to produce a relatively small number of grapes, but these grapes would yield wines of great character. Yes, grapes could be grown on the property, but the terroir would be a labor-intensive "mountain vineyard." And thus we had a very Fourth Way situation! Extra effort would be required to produce world class wines. Karl's first visit lasted the entire weekend. On the morning of his departure, Robert asked Karl for the bill for his consulting services. Karl looked directly at Robert and said, "A dollar." Robert handed him a dollar. Some initial experiments were made, and Karl became a regular visitor to the property. And so began a 350-acre vineyard and winery.

These developments were the beginning of a new phase of the school, and this new phase was not limited to what was happening on the property. It was a development of the whole, and accordingly Robert reoriented himself to the whole. Let us review the situation in the school at large. Prior to Robert's return to the property, he had led weekly meetings in Carmel (where he lived), in the Bay Area, and in Los Angeles. During the Carmel period he did not lead meetings at the Ranch. From October of 1973, on his relocation to the property, Robert led a Saturday meeting at the Ranch, a Tuesday meeting in the Bay Area (which the Carmel students were expected to attend), and a Thursday meeting in Los Angeles (for all of Southern California). Given that he was now more engaged with developments on the property, Robert continued to make a concerted effort to remain connected to the centers.

But the student population in the Bay Area continued to grow. In the fall of 1974, with the continuing growth in the region, the Bay Area Meetings moved to a larger venue: the Skyline Community Church. The Skyline Church was located on a high ridge overlooking the city of Oakland; the site itself was beautiful and the view spectacular. Some sense of the sacred attached to this new place, and the Skyline Church entered the essence of the Fellowship, as it was at that time.

The location was immediately accessible to all students in the Greater Bay Area. It was a three-hour drive from Oregon House, and a two-hour drive from Carmel. It was an overnight journey from either Seattle in the north or Los Angeles in the south. All the Ranch residents who could go would go; for them it was a great 'day out.' They would network with those students who had cars to find rides, perhaps spend the day in San Francisco, and then arrive at the church *en masse*. And so people converge on this church from all over Northern California. The resident minister at Skyline, noting the remarkable focus of activity, commented to Robert, "You are getting a better crowd than I do!"

After the higher states evoked by a Skyline meeting, and the pleasure of reuniting with old friends in the Bay Area, the Ranch residents would then make the long drive home. The return drive would be punctuated by a ritual stop at the Coffee Tree Restaurant in Vacaville, where the key angles of the meeting would be reviewed and talked over. Home, then, by midnight and up again at five in the morning.[1]

On a meeting night you would find as many as ten or twelve booths filled with students. On any Friday night students travelling from the Bay Area in to the Ranch for the weekend would stop here, and at 8:30PM you might find two or three tables of students.

We note the intensity of the stage-change that began in October of 1973: the explosion of activity on the property, while sustaining rapid growth in the centers. It was an acceleration of the pace of the school, an acceleration what was sustained for many years.

---

1. In the earlier years it was the Coffee Tree on the way in and Howard Johnson's on the way back — but eventually the Coffee Tree became an unofficial hub of Fellowship activity.

Donald Macdonald was a central figure in the Fellowship at this time. We have charted how he and his wife Rosemary were among the earliest students, how they had advised and counseled Robert in many of the important decisions that he made for the school, including the location and purchase of the property. Their home had been one of the first sites for Fellowship meetings, and their young daughter was now a student. After they divorced, they both remained close to Robert and active in the school. And after Yorgos' departure Donald had become the senior student, and Robert appeared to acknowledge him as a conscious being. But by 1975 Donald had, in some ways, moved away from Robert's view of the teaching. Donald and Robert had spoken of this privately, but Donald never spoke of this with other students. To the rest of us Donald and Robert seemed completely aligned and Donald Macdonald seemed to be on the cutting edge of the teaching.

In March of 1975 Robert opened a Friday night meeting at the Skyline Church with the announcement that "Donald Macdonald has left the teaching." Robert mentioned that when Donald came to him, to tell him that he was leaving, he had said that "their methods of teaching had diverged." We know from Donald's friends that this was not an easy decision for Donald, and that the departure was painful on both sides. Robert went on to speak of Donald as though he had left the school as a man number five, calling him "a flower of the teaching" and stating that "he can now live for himself." Robert showed greatness of heart — yet he was concerned about what Donald would do next. Would there be a competition for Fellowship students, as there had been with Yorgos Savides? But what Donald did next was simply to leave Vacaville and settle with a new spouse in Vallejo. There he started a new family and continued his medical practice. He did not recruit students. Rosemary moved to the Ranch, where she continued to make her own very significant contribution to the school.

It was as though Donald's move triggered a latent impulse. As we noted, in the previous six months many things had begun to change at once: Robert's return to the property; the idea that we might all eventually be based there; an increase in the donations; a shift from American to European culture. These were difficult things for many people to accept. Many students in the centers were happy with the life that they had, and were put off by the sense of strange, new, and ever-increasing demands. Donald was a trusted figure. If it was OK for Donald to leave it must be OK for the rest of us. This was not a mass departure as with Yorgos. A number of people filtered out over the months to follow, each going their own way. It was a form of passive resistance. C Influence simply subtracted the resistant element. It was as though, at any stage of the school's development, it had an optimum size. In relation to that size, it could only change its content through some people leaving and others replacing them. Robert described the difference between the people who left and the people who stayed by quoting a remark from one of his students: "You begin to enter the Way when you stop fitting the teaching into your life and start fitting your life into the teaching."

We note that both Yorgos Savides and Donald Macdonald had been designated as people likely to awaken. This highlights a danger in the Work. It is very hard to not identify with the idea of becoming a 'conscious being' or a 'teacher.' In a school of the Fourth Way a teacher is not just someone who knows more than the students, but someone who is also more spiritually advanced. This desire to be a teacher can reinforce the feeling of being unique or special, in a way that almost nothing else can. It does so more effectively than the acquisition of great wealth or the wielding of great power. And the danger of it is that *it is the machine that feels special*. Higher Centers do not feel special at all. They simply see themselves in other people and attempt to serve their like in other people. They serve the Gods above and sentient life below: they are happy to be the house-janitors of this level of creation. It is because of the marked tendency of the machine to take credit for the movements of Higher Centers, that — the further on you go — the more humiliation you experience. Not one shred of the machine's self-aggrandizement is acceptable to the Gods.

This capacity of the Lower Self to take credit for the emergent Higher Centers was to give Robert great friction in the years to come. He would scrupulously prepare a 'place' for a student who showed real potential, only to have that person deceived by their Lower Self at the eleventh hour. They would then self-destruct and take others with them. Yet these trials forced the development of the school, removing those who no longer had a place and providing sharp tests for those who stayed. Higher Forces always placed the development of the school over the development of any one individual.

So the 'stage change' that began in the autumn of 1973 was soon reflected in a change that would entirely alter the character of the school.

DEVELOPMENTS ON THE PROPERTY

Let us follow more carefully the developments that were occurring at the Ranch. On Robert's return, there were few students in salaried positions. Many residents had accumulated enough money to stay on the property for a year or two, while others were able to collect unemployment for long periods of time. A few students with essential skills were given salary: a few managers, some of the carpenters, and some of the heavy equipment operators. However, as the different projects multiplied and increased in scope, more and more people came on salary. And this growth, in its turn, made very specific requirements on the kitchen and the Lodge. As staffing needs grew the Ranch gradually became a salaried population, with about 20% unsalaried visitors at any given point in time.

The intimacy and intensity of living on the property was the same as it had been in 1972, but there were more people. Then, in July of 1975, our wine consultant, Karl Werner, joined the school, and he moved to the Ranch in the summer of 1976. With Karl came the host of new vineyard staff who were needed to work alongside a world class winemaker.[1]

At this time some students were still living at the Lodge and sleeping in sleeping bags on its long, unroofed balcony. The Court of the Caravans did ease the accommodation problem, and, at the same time, students with

---

1. Karl's decision to join the school was not as surprising as it might sound. Robert was the second conscious being in Karl's life. Rainer Maria Rilke, a conscious poet, had been part of a reading group which included Karl's mother, when Karl was just a boy. The reading group met at Karl's family home, and Karl remembered Rilke being "around the house." This contact may have helped Karl to recognize Robert on his first visits to the property.

Figure 74. Enlarging the original Lodge.

capital began to buy property in the area and either build a house or purchase existing homes. Thus, increasingly, the Lodge sleepers became the ever-growing population of visitors.

The Fellowship also continued to make additional purchases of land that adjoined the property. The original section of Fellowship land backed onto Rices Crossing Road on the north side, and included the little access road that connected the property to Rices Crossing Road, but not the strip of land running along Rices Crossing Road, west of the entrance road. This comprised four lots, which the school bought up, as circumstances allowed, over the next five or six years. On one of these lots a nice two-bedroom house was adapted for Robert as his home and new base of operations. This also became an opportunity to develop a living environment suitable to a teacher: a residence with a level of visual impressions that would encourage consciousness in the students and fit with the Worlds 6 and 12 of their teacher. We will recall Robert's teaching of alchemy: part of living in the present is to continuously refine the alchemical level of the environment, and in this way to deepen one's experience of the moment. When the Fellowship finally purchased the lot and the residence, Robert had the grounds landscaped and the interior of the house renovated, under the guidance of Sheila Wallace. The renovated house was then called the Blake Cottage,

Figure 75. The refurbished Lodge, a center of school activity for many years.

after the conscious being William Blake. It was not just a teacher's retreat. Robert used it to hold meetings about the many ongoing projects on the property, to give consultations, and to review the school's business affairs. There was a constant ebb and flow of visitors.

Later, in 1978, the Fellowship purchased property further west along Rices Crossing Road, which was named the Whitman Glen. It later became the site of the Fellowship Office and a large tennis court.

Many other projects were initiated. The interior of the Lodge was again renovated, the service upgraded, and the dinners themselves served on fine china. Tiled showers and bathroom facilities were put in, sufficient to serve both the residents and the permanent population of visitors. Extensive land clearing began, and there was a continuing development of the vegetable garden.

And beyond all of that there was the vineyard! The surveying and terracing began in 1975, and the planting of vines commenced in 1976. In the ten years that followed more than 175,000 12-inch holes were drilled into the granite soil and filled with compost, and in each hole a vine was planted. By the end of that time there were 103 miles of contoured terraces on elevations ranging from 1,700 to 2,300 feet. The terraces were planted with clover, annual grasses, and other native ground cover, to prevent erosion on the slopes.

A Global School Begins: 1976

Many of those who came to Mount Carmel in late 1974 and early 1975, in the second phase of the development of the property, felt that they were retreating to a spiritual haven for the remainder of their lives. They were the privileged few, going to pursue the Work under special circumstances. But in late 1975 all of that was to change. Robert appeared at the Lodge one morning with a long list of students' names. He went in turn to each student on the list, asking them if they would like to go out and start a center in one of the major cities of America. Suddenly he would be in front of you asking, "Would you like to go and teach in Boston?" Most students simply answered "Yes." This "yes" was the sudden acceptance of a need to give rather than to receive, and it was the beginning of a new phase for the school. A few said, "Can I have some time to think about it?" Robert would reply, "Yes, you can think about it ...(pause) ... Have you decided yet?"

Robert designated a group of seven students to start each center: one lady and one man as co-directors, and five supporting students, also a mix of men and women. For the center in New York, and later on in London, ten students were sent. Robert also networked with students in the already existing centers to get a full roster of volunteers for each of the planned centers. And so the students based in centers were also part of the great exodus of 1976. All the students going out to open new centers were asked to make a commitment for two full years. At the end of two years, all of the original "teams" of students returned to California and were replaced by new groups of directors and supporting students. No one from that first phase was allowed to remain behind in their city, though this requirement was later removed.

It was time for the school to grow. With the conviction that C Influence was monitoring his students, Robert trusted them to work at a distance.

Starting in January 1976 there were three waves of students sent out to open centers. The first wave went out on 1st January. It included Seattle,

San Diego, Newport Beach, Honolulu, Minneapolis, Denver, Pittsburgh, Washington D.C., Atlanta, Phoenix, and Miami. The second wave in June included Boston, New York, Philadelphia, New Orleans, Detroit, Chicago, and Houston. The third wave in November included Buffalo, Cleveland, St. Louis, Cincinnati, Dallas, and the first foreign center, Vancouver.[1] Robert controlled every step of each wave; it was a precise, intentional drama with ongoing support.

It was understood that the first wave would leave on 1st January, from the property at Oregon House and from multiple centers in California. At the Skyline Church meeting that preceded the exodus, Robert had each departing student stand, give their name and the name of the city they were going to. After everyone stood up there was a long moment of silence, and then a student read from Matthew 4:18-19: "And Jesus, walking by the sea of Galilee, saw two brethren, Simon called Peter, and Andrew his brother, casting a net into the sea: for they were fishers. And he saith unto them, Follow me, and I will make you fishers of men."

When the time came to leave, those of us living on the property gathered to watch the several cars drive off. The West Coast-centric Fellowship was no more.

This exodus started the program of 'travelling teachers.' Chosen students were sent out each month to each of the many centers. In the beginning these were principally students resident at the Ranch and in regular contact with Robert. But it later included qualified students active in the centers. One aspect of the travelling teacher program was to keep the parts connected to the whole, and another to compensate the limited or unbalanced situations that might develop in the centers. The traveling teacher program was divided into four circuits: West Coast, Midwest, South, and Northeast.

From this point forward the population of the school grew rapidly, and the new students were of a younger generation. These were the classic baby boomers. Another important effect of the expansion was that it gave a very

---

1. Some of the cities mentioned were reopenings of previously existing centers, such as San Diego and Seattle.

large number of students the opportunity to teach the system and to represent the school.

The 1976 movement out was very different from the 1972 movement out, when Robert relocated from the Ranch to Carmel. The property at Oregon House remained the center of development, and Robert remained in residence there. With the new focus on the arts and on European culture, Robert changed the official name of the property from Mount Carmel to Renaissance. It was, then, the 'place to go' for all students in all centers.

We noted that in July 1975 our wine consultant Karl Werner joined the school and soon moved permanently to Renaissance. From the time of Karl's arrival, the vineyard grew by leaps and bounds. In the spring of 1975, a D8 Bulldozer was purchased to clear the new slopes that were being selected for cultivation. You could hear it rumbling up and down the surrounding hills from sunrise to sunset and often through the night, six days a week. And there was an ever-growing number of salaried positions related to vineyard work and winemaking. Students were sent, first to Callaway Vineyards, and then to Europe, to study viticulture and winemaking. The year 1976 was a good year for Karl in many ways. It was the bicentennial of the American Declaration of Independence, and in July President Ford invited Queen Elizabeth II to dinner at the White House to affirm the continued friendship between the two nations. One American red wine and one American white wine were selected for the dinner. The white wine chosen was one of Karl's Callaway Dry Riesling vintages.

THE SCHOOL AND ITS TASK

All of these developments were somehow — we were not quite sure how — an expression of Robert's new understanding of the task of the school. It seemed a strangely bigger world. The idea of a new civilization, based on a rediscovery of the relation between art and awakening, and a retrieval of conscious influence through history, was making steady inroads.

However, to address this task fully the tide of young people streaming into the school had to be able to relate to it. In other words, they had to have a positive understanding of the priorities involved. There was an apparent contradiction here. Most of us came from the counterculture, as it was in the 1960s. We recall that, in the mid-seventies, California was still close to the world of Bob Dylan, Jefferson Airplane, and the like. The ideals of the 1960s had only just begun to fade. Psychedelia had raised questions in a generation, and America had been flooded with the writings of eastern teachers and the Gurdjieff literature. An entire generation of young people was looking forward to a future quite unlike the past. This was, in itself, good — for these were people willing to accept major change. If some of these people could exchange the transient pop culture of their own time for a timeless 'high culture' that was more conducive to higher states of consciousness, and — at the same time — to exchange a composite of New Age teachings for an objective teaching that produced objective results, then the contradiction was only apparent. From the standpoint of the Gods, it was the task of the Fellowship to capture that segment of the baby boomers that was ready to take a sharp step upward.

As the Fellowship centers multiplied and flourished, a form developed that would instill discipline and infuse new students with the values of the school. This included two weekly meetings, substantial teaching payments (necessitating a regular job), a culture of formal dress and formal dining, word exercises that changed every month, a host of center activities (concerts, presentations, visits to galleries), regular prospective student meetings, and exercises concerning relationships. This latter exercise was for a time an abrupt about face for many.

Such a transition sounds almost impossible, but we must keep in mind that the baby boomers had war generation ideals and war generation discipline just under their skin. You needed only to scratch the surface to find it. The war generation had been raised during the depression and had known the insecurity of the war years. The fear of want, instilled in youth, lasts a lifetime. The war generation had discipline and desired security and prosperity. The postwar generation grew up in an age of unprecedented prosperity. They grew up feeling they could have anything they wanted. They had no fear. On entering adolescence, and looking at the world around themselves, they renounced the values of their parents. To the boomers it appeared that their parents were living only to augment their income, to move into ever nicer homes, and to secure a good pension. The boomers determined to, in the words of Jim Morrison, "break on through to the other side."

Those of us that came to the Fellowship soon realized that we could no longer ride on the tide of an imagined New Age. Effort and sacrifice were necessary. And it did not take much to touch the war generation values that were there, just under the surface. We were being given a new and a higher reason to live, and the discipline that our parents had tried to instill into us was needed to support that. But we could not simply forget the 1960s by returning to the lifestyle of the 1940s or 1950s. The emotional openness of the Summer of Love was amplified by the greater openness of Higher Centers, and in that way the Summer of Love continued to develop in us. We all knew, somewhere inside of ourselves, that to make our 'highs' permanent we had to pay. Robert Burton showed us how to do it.

He certainly challenged us with three full lines of work. The development of the property at Oregon House, the opening up of the new centers, the meetings, the open meetings, the instruction of new students, and the constant travelling between centers kept us busy all the time. And all of this activity made the school more. The better balanced one's three lines of work were, the more one could see oneself in the school and see the school in oneself. The three lines of work made the work practical and were of tremendous assistance in threading presence through the many activities of the day. To serve a Higher Level externally involves the same triad as serving a Higher Level internally — but it can be learned in a much shorter period of time. And practice in the former speeds the latter. This was the permanent environment of the Fellowship of Friends. The school now embodied three *completely integrated* lines of work. The principle of the three lines of work was not used to such effect in any other of the Fourth Way teachings.

ROBERT'S TEACHING OF THE THREE LINES OF WORK

Robert taught us that "self-remembering has no momentum of its own and is always an uphill battle."[1] As he put it, "Self-remembering never lies behind us, as a point taken" ... and at the same time ... "No one puts enough pressure on himself to awaken." It is the three lines of work that add the momentum and supply the needed pressure.

> "When one meets the system, one is expected to work primarily on the first line. One is intended to receive support from others. Later, one can share information with one's fellow students, which is second line of work. Still later, third line of work begins as one starts contributing to the school. Steadily, the amount of third line work required of one increases. ... The longer one is in the school, the more is expected of one."[2]

> "As one begins to work more efficiently, one balances the three lines of work: work for oneself, work for others, and work for the school. One needs to observe one's relation to the three lines of work periodically to ensure that one's position is relatively balanced."[3]

And in this way ... "The system teaches us to go beyond itself." The three lines of work become a single, unified labor of service to a higher level. In seeking the right balance in the three lines we followed Rainer Maria Rilke's counsel, "to hold always to the difficult." One can get stuck in any of the three lines: in the first line one's efforts seem to stop producing any results; in the second line one's relationships with others become habitual; in the third line one becomes weary of one's responsibilities and finds oneself "just trying to get through." But progress in any one of the three lines helps the others. Progress in the line where progress is possible takes one past sticking points in the other two lines. Effort in the third line, for example, can have sudden and unexpected effects on the first line. In the Fellowship centers the emphasis was on the second line, at Renaissance on the third line, and the first line — remembering oneself — was always and everywhere.

---

1. Burton, Robert Earl, *Self Remembering,* Globe Press Books, New York, 1991, p. 71.
2. *Ibid.,* p. 191.
3. *Ibid.,* p. 189.

THE CHANGING TEMPO OF LIFE

Following Donald Macdonald's departure, and in the heat of the activities of 1975 and 1976, the other two students for whom Robert had predicted conscious roles became more prominent: Miles Barth and Girard Haven. They had not been selected without reason. They distinguished themselves by internalizing the system, and then connecting the service of their emergent Higher Centers to the service of the school. In them, the three lines of work were a unity. They were increasingly able to provide a bridge between Robert's level of understanding, and the questions that were being asked by the new students flooding into the school. The Fellowship was, step by step, recreating Jacob's ladder. And, at a time when we had some need of role models, Miles and Girard provided excellent examples.

Additionally, there was now more of a reciprocal relationship between Renaissance and the centers. Students based in centers took their holidays at Renaissance — re-entering the small intimately connected community that virtually shimmered with emotion. Students coming off salary, with little or no resources, accessed the professional expertise of the students living in the centers, and networked with their friends to find employment. Students with jobs in the Bay Area, who were building homes at Renaissance, hired salaried students to do the landscaping on their property in their off hours. It went on and on.

Living at Renaissance was viewed as a privilege, but there was certainly a corresponding payment. The salary was still just enough to get by on. Most residents left the property only twice a month: once for the meeting at Skyline Church, and once — on payday — to drive twenty-eight miles into Marysville to deposit their paycheck, and buy a few necessities: some underwear, a packet of razor blades, a bottle of perfume, or a roll of duct tape to repair leaking raingear. To pay the dental bills or to own a car you had to find extra work. Eventually Sunday became a free day in which students could earn $10 an hour clearing land or providing whatever service they had to offer. There was a definite element of the way of the fakir in life at Renaissance.

Under these conditions the vineyard expanded steadily, a huge concrete winery was begun, and multiple construction and landscaping projects undertaken. Three large structures were erected to support these activities. They were labelled, imaginatively, Shop One, Shop Two, and Shop Three. Shop One was the site for woodwork, Shop Two the site for metalwork, and Shop Three — the largest — contained the vineyard office and housed the vineyard equipment. It also contained a large auto shop, which did everything from small engine repair (for the weed whips and chain saws) to the repair of students' cars, to the repair and maintenance of the D8 and the massive crane for placing concrete. And new construction was not limited to the property. Students continued to settle and build in the area. Robert actively encouraged those students who had careers to build houses at Oregon House and to take in boarders as needed. Increasingly the visitors coming from outlying centers would make arrangements to stay at student's homes. The unroofed balcony of the Lincoln Lodge had lost its attraction!

By 1976 the inside of the Lincoln Lodge was filled — from early morning until late at night — with the music of Bach, Vivaldi, Haydn, Handel, Mozart, and Beethoven. And the enthusiasm with which that music was received replaced the enthusiasm with which Jefferson Airplane and the Moody Blues had been received a few short years before. There would be commentary and comparison with the performances of the visiting artists, or of other known artists and conductors. Eric Clapton was replaced by Herbert von Karajan. Poetry selections were read aloud before every meal, and often from memory.

And here we must make specific mention of the Fellowship institution of the vineyard: the band of fifteen to twenty-five hardy souls who (at any one point in time) were the vineyard workers. Taken together they were — for many years — a distinct organ in the larger body of the school. They worked six days a week, planting vines, putting in trellises, fertilizing, removing rock, pruning, post hole digging, tending the irrigation lines, cutting out the manzanita, and removing the buckbrush. In the winter the rainstorms would come in, one after the next, each lasting for two or three days. The rain came down in sheets, and you were out in it from before dawn until sunset. Even with good raingear, when the wind came up, the rain would work its way in. It would come in through the gap between your gloves and your rain jacket, or it would get in under your rain cap when you stooped to clip the canes. Starting from the back of your neck the water would work its way down your back, and when it got there you would be wet and cold through and through. Many techniques were used to keep the water out: putting a towel across your back, bringing a change of clothes to work and changing during the break. In the winter the vineyard workers would carry the little Fisherman's Friend cough drops, or packages of beef jerky, and take one every couple of hours to keep their spirits up. When a storm came in there might even be a belt of whiskey to get you out on the slopes. And with summer came the long days when the temperature soared to 105 degrees. There was the seemingly endless heat of the high afternoon, when you might feel giddy or weak at the knees. But you certainly saw all of the 'I's come and go; the dark legions trooping through, one after another.

From one point of view, when you came on salary you brought your whole life with you out into the vineyard, and then — in the long days on the quiet, empty slopes — it paraded before your eyes. You transformed what you saw because you had to; there was no option to do otherwise. And when those dark legions of 'I's passed through and out, you were just empty: the clouds cleared to reveal an endless expanse of blue. Sometimes you felt cleaned right out, just a part of nature. The sunrises and sunsets became things of miraculous beauty. When the first rays of the morning sun hit the water droplets hanging along the trellis wires, they became thousands of little rainbow prisms of light. When the fading sun burned blood red into the dark silhouette of the foothills, you felt the relief of coming darkness. The vineyard was not wanting in World 12 experiences. And the companionship with one's fellow workers went deep; everyone knew you couldn't stay in the vineyard without working. The vineyard workers supported one another in a very basic way. When students in the centers had a bad day at the office, or felt isolated in a distant city, they would remember the vineyard workers steadily pushing on, and remember that they would be joining them on their summer break.

Month by month and year by year Robert Burton was making the inner life of the school independent of the world of the late 20th century by creating a set of alternative standards that his students recognized and acknowledged. And the foundational standard for all other standards was being awake over being asleep. This was the standard to which all the other standards referred: standards of the non-expression of negative emotions, standards of intentional movement, standards of alchemy, standards of the appreciation of the arts, and standards in dining. Prospective students sensed what was behind these standards, and new students continued to surge into the school. Due to the level of demands that were made on students the turnover was high, but the numbers increased, first to 500 and then to 1,000.

Having reached this point we must emphasize something that was unique to Robert Burton's teaching: the focus on essence. Robert taught that, as personality becomes more passive, essence develops naturally — responding ever more deeply to the world around it. We think of a child gazing in wonder at the night sky. As essence can respond deeply to the impressions of nature, so it can be trained to respond to the impressions of great art. When great art is understood for what it is, it evokes essence — for it was created from essence. A great ballet prima must dance from her essence, a great violinist must play from their essence, a great actor must act from their essence — or their performances will not be art. And this is *most* true of the greatest art of all: that of bringing the latent Higher Centers into life. As essence can be trained to respond to great art, it can be trained to respond to presence itself — for presence self-aware is the most beautiful thing in creation, and essence is capable of recognizing this. And with this recognition essence can respond directly to the World 12 that is in great art. As Higher Centers begin to function, essence fuses with presence, and this is what carries something that originates from the machine and continues "from here to eternity." Robert taught us that awakening is, from one point of view, "essence aware of itself." In the technical terms of the system this is the fusion of the most refined part of essence with Higher Centers.

ROBERT'S CRYSTALLIZATION

From the time he returned to the Ranch from Carmel in late 1973, Robert began to predict that his Higher Centers would fuse and that he would crystallize as a complete man number six. At a certain point he predicted that this would happen on March 15th, 1976. The fifteenth day of March for the ancient Romans was the Ides of March: the day Julius Caesar was assassinated. Robert equated Caesar with false personality and took this as an omen that on March 15th his own false personality would come to its end. He chose Phoenix, Arizona as the place to crystalize, being symbolic of the phoenix bird (Higher Centers) rising from the ashes of the lower self.

So Robert planned to leave the Ranch and journey to Phoenix for the event. This would break the momentum of his many activities on the property and allow students to engage with him directly. His entourage was to go with him, the Phoenix center would receive him, and visitors would come from both Renaissance and the nearby centers for scheduled dinners. As to why the event was so public, an indication came when Robert at one point commented, "After Gurdjieff and Ouspensky crystallized they went into a period of dormancy." In encouraging students to be around him Robert was placing pressure on himself to address the school. He knew that Higher Centers are not there for one's own enjoyment, but to serve other people. His mission of service was the core of his life, and he believed that it was the reason he had been given consciousness. Thus, he wanted to engage students from the beginning. The atmosphere was one of quiet celebration.

Another aspect of the expedition out to Phoenix was that it highlighted the approaching unknown. Everything was going to change, and we didn't know how. When Robert left Renaissance, it was a tremendous stop exercise for the school. Everything was going to be different from what it had been before.

Robert arrived in Phoenix on the morning of March 15th, with his secretary and an entourage of three or four. Other students were going to drive directly down from the Ranch, arriving later in the day. And the students of the Phoenix center were certainly going to be part of the activities. On arrival Robert signed in at the Arizona Biltmore Hotel, renting a cottage on the grounds large enough to accommodate both himself and his entourage.

The Arizona Biltmore was designed by a pupil of Frank Lloyd Wright just before the great depression. It was a statement in tasteful opulence and understated grandeur. It was an architectural statement of a kind that is no longer attempted. The Frank Lloyd Wright/Art Deco style is reminiscent of classical Islamic architecture: something out of the Arabian Nights.

Robert had stayed at the Biltmore when he was on the pro tennis circuit, about ten years earlier, and the hotel had made a distinct impression on him. It had a large room with gold leaf covering both the walls and the ceiling. The so-called Gold Room had the second largest gilded ceiling in the world. Many of the walls and ceilings in the other rooms were also gilded, creating a space of enchantment.

Within the main lobby, which was framed as an atrium, there was an indoor balcony that allowed guests to overlook the interior space. On one of his early tennis tours, Robert had found himself alone in this room. He happened to look up at the balcony, and saw a couple there with their young daughter, who was dressed all in white. The little girl looked down on him. Suddenly there was the image of a little girl in white in a golden room—a living symbol of World 12. Later, after he had been given the information that he was to become a man number six, he took this timeless image as an indication of the place where he would crystallize.

All through the day there was a quiet sense of watching and waiting, which Robert enhanced by being present to each simple moment and each simple activity as though there were nothing else on earth. Robert later said that he could feel his astral body "breathing" through that day. He was moving in an Arabian Nights environment: the Gold Room, the boutiques, the specialty shops, the immaculate lawns and gardens. Nothing in particular to do or say. It all had a dreamlike quality, lifted out of normal reality. The students with him were in suspense, but Robert was simply in a deep, continuous display of receptivity.

This same sense of quiet waiting was taking place at Renaissance. The day was quiet, and the stillness was heightened by the anticipation that everyone felt, but no one expressed. The sky was cloudless, with that depth of cobalt blue you sometimes see in the foothills. At about 11AM an extraordinary impression suddenly appeared in the seemingly endless depths of blue just above the Lodge: a rainbow globe about the size of a full moon, like a thick halo, that shimmered intensely with all the colors of the spectrum. There were radiant bands of yellow, blue, orange, green, purple, red. The outer edges of the halo were a bit fuzzy, as though defining the border to another dimension. This phenomenon is called a circumhorizontal arc, or more colloquially, a fire rainbow.[1] The colors of such an arc are more intense and brilliant than those of a rainbow. To have one appear in a perfectly formed global halo, with radiant bands of color defined against a stunning depth of blue, is not only rare, but unique. For the students who saw it on that day, it was first taken as a sign that Robert had crystallized. Later everyone felt something of the relation of what they each were going through to events taking place on a higher level.[2]

Meanwhile, students were beginning to arrive in Phoenix from Renaissance and other locations in California. Robert met everyone for dinner at a restaurant in nearby Scottsdale. He conveyed a warm personal ambience throughout the meal, but he spoke little. After dinner everyone bade Robert goodnight and returned to their respective lodgings. Robert went back to the cottage at the Biltmore to wait for his crystallization to occur. He sat for a good part of the night on a bench in the garden just outside the cottage. Second by second, minute by minute, hour by hour, he remained centered in his conscious Self. He was with his personal secretary, who reported that Robert was quiet, gentle, almost childlike. After a few hours he said, in a matter-of-fact way, "Well, I guess it is not going to happen." And they each returned to their rooms.

The next morning Robert met with students for breakfast at the Biltmore's Orangerie. He announced to the group that the crystallization had not occurred as expected, and that he was going to return directly to Renaissance. He suggested that everyone who had travelled down from Renaissance do the same. And so everyone left.

When people saw how graciously Robert accepted the failure of his prophecy, it made them more aware of his role, and of his vulnerability. Yet they saw in him no disappointment, or any sense of an anticlimax. Conscious beings and conscious beings.

---

1. See Robert MacIsaac's article 'The Globe in the Sky,' in the March 2000 issue of the *Fellowship Forum* for the author's description of this event. Technically, a circumhorizontal arc is formed by hexagonal, plate-shaped ice crystals in high-level cirrus clouds. In certain conditions the ice crystals act as prisms, splitting light. They are very rare and occur only at certain latitudes.

2. Robert later interpreted this event as a portent that 1) he was to crystallize at Renaissance, and 2) the school was to become an international, global school.

Robert's entourage then drove the 826 miles directly back to the Oregon House, arriving late in the evening of March 16th. The next day was business as usual: no predictions, no interpretations, no discussion. When Robert came to dinner that evening, an exceptional quiet fell over the Lodge. He smiled and was considerate to everyone, as he always was, yet there was the distinct feeling that something was incomplete or unfulfilled.

On the evening of the following day, March 18, Robert retired to the Blake Cottage at an early hour. He awoke suddenly, at 4AM March 19, feeling a tremendous presence, quite beyond his own. As he later described it: "It was upon me, and my World 6 rose immediately to meet it. It was very much like having someone come up to you with a gun and shoot you right between the eyes while you watch unperturbed. And when it was over, World 6 was exactly like the Sphinx — except that it was reality rather than a symbol — totally unmoved, totally undisturbed by the incident." His Higher Emotional Center and his Higher Intellectual Center had locked, fused permanently and forever. The first 'I' he had after he crystallized was, "It worked."

He had accepted the timing of the Gods and he had passed the test.

Immediately after crystallization occurred, Robert woke up one of the residents in the Blake Cottage and asked him to call everyone at the Lodge, and then all the centers in the school. Within the hour every student in the country had received the news. However, beyond the calls out to the centers, Robert made no special plans. There were no changes to the regular schedule of events. He was simply being a man number six!

But a very great deal happened without his asking for it. As soon as the regular workday of the 19th came to an end, students went spontaneously into action. They pulled up the sward of rough turf that grew by the front entrance to the Lodge, and worked through the night to lay down layers of fresh green sod to make a new lawn. They put in a new garden around the lawn. They created a walkway of triumphal arches, by bending lengths of plastic pipe in half circles, and covering them with flowers and greenery. Additional plastic piping was installed and hung with lanterns along the road leading up to the Lodge. The result the following evening was an enchanted walkway of light, and a floral arcade along the entrance way to the

Figure 76. Crystallization celebrations, March 19, 1976.

Lodge. Magic lanterns hung from the center of each arch, and the long row of lanterns looked like so many 19th century streetlamps.

Many students in the outlying centers spontaneously journeyed to Renaissance to join the celebrations, with emotional greetings as though they had not seen each other for years (though they had only departed for these centers two months ago). A banquet was prepared at the Lodge that evening the arcade was completed. This was not an enthusiastic riot of activity, but a sacred moment being marked and affirmed. For two more days the party continued, and the inner magic of the school blazed forth in a spontaneous external demonstration.

This moment changed us all; the Fellowship was a different school thereafter.

On the first morning after the crystallization, and throughout the day, Robert was still a bit at one remove from his students, just as he had been in the gardens at the Biltmore. But gradually the locked Higher Centers engaged with teaching. They began to do the job they were created for. Soon after his crystallization Robert began traveling and teaching across America, visiting the many new centers that had been opened since the exodus of January 1st, 1976. He had created it all, step by step: opened the centers, travelled out in the anticipation of crystallization, returned to actually engage his Higher Centers, and then journeyed out again to the newly created centers at a higher level. Both he and the school had reached a new level.

From the morning of March 19th Robert Burton had an unquestioned mass and authority: his molecular field was simply more concentrated.[1] This was the 'Robert' that the author knew, and I hope that here personal testimony will be excused. I found Robert Burton to be different from any other person I had ever met. Not that he had exceptional charisma, or that he was faultless in all things, or that everything that he said or did was wonderful. Simply that there was: 1) presence — sustained, unbroken, and penetrating, 2) an emotional center that was *always awake,* and 3) the natural authority that comes from direct contact with a Higher Level. He was able to touch people deeply and had an ability to elicit their deepest allegiance. This, because he was a living measure of man's potential. He made you aware of an entirely different order of existence. Just his 'being there' challenged you in the best way.

You could see that Robert had *a valuation for the present itself*: recognizing it, fostering it, and placing it above all other things. I had never and have never seen this so constant in another human being. He valued the very moment of NOW over making a deadline, catching an airplane, or tasting the first bite of a gourmet dinner. He saw the loss of the present as a loss which invalidates every other gain. It is remarkable to see someone who actually lives this way.

He took a deep interest in people and had a keen eye for both their potentials and their shortcomings. It is to his exceptional credit that, from

---

1. Robert later stated that the crystallization as a man number five occurs in stages, there is not a defining moment. The crystallization as man a number six, by contrast, is immediate. He also said that, while a man number five — if he continues to function at that level — will achieve immortality, he can still lose all that he has gained during the period that he is still embodied. A man number six cannot lose what he has gained.

his first years as a teacher, he attempted to create opportunities for other people; to create 'roles' for them; to push them one rung higher on the ladder of being. He consequently had the natural ability to create a community around himself.

After Robert's crystallization you could see that something had opened inside of him. There was something unfathomable — vast and uncontained. Yet he was not threatening; there was a pervasive warmth. There was something joyous or celebratory about his presence. At the same time, he could be quite severe. And you never knew what he was going to ask of you, or what he would do next.

This man, with infinite patience, taught us the system. But what he excelled in was the direct transmission of higher states of consciousness. Robert was a master at bypassing the barriers that are inscribed so deeply in human nature.

Looking back to the time of Robert's return to the property in 1973, we note that the remarkable intensity of work that began at that time was sustained through 1974 and 1975. Then, in 1976, there came Robert's crystallization and the expansion out to the centers across America. The heightened pace of October 1973 through March 1976 was that of a man number five working to become a man number six. Once Robert crystallized as a man number six the pace changed again. From March of 1976 we moved to the internationalization of the school, the expansion of the vineyard to 350 acres, the development of a Performing Arts Organization, the emergence of a school for children, and — more generally — the beginnings of a permanent self-sustaining community in and around Oregon House. This is the expression of the work of a man number six.

In 1974 a small elementary school had been created on the property. It was first known as the William Blake school, and then, in 1976 — following an internal change of direction — became the Lewis Carroll School. The foundation for the school had been laid with the 1972 Children's House, which had briefly become a school, and then closed with Robert's move to Carmel. What was common to the three stages of this school was an underlying concern for the children: to develop their essence along with their education, and to create the possibility for some of them to eventually take the decision to join the school. The aim was to create as few barriers as possible and to open as many doors as possible. The staff of the Lewis Carroll School adopted the Montessori method of teaching, not because Maria Montessori was Peter Ouspensky's student, but because, examining the alternatives, this method best conformed to the Fellowship's understanding of what the education of a child should be: emotional openness and a right connection of the lower centers to the present.

The Goethe Academy and Europe

Shortly after his crystallization Robert asked us to take Johann Wolfgang von Goethe as a model in the study of the arts, and as a guide to the art of living itself. Robert said of Goethe, "He changed my vision of the school." Copies of Johann Peter Eckermann's *Conversations with Goethe* were printed for every single student. Even Robert's residence took Goethe's name. The Blake Cottage, in which Robert had been living, was moved to another location off the property, and a much more substantial residence — the *Goethe Academy* — was built in its place. It was inspired by French baroque architecture, and in every way bore the stamp of European culture. The *Goethe Academy,* as the name implies, was more than a residence. It was a center of events for the school: meetings, dinners, receptions weddings. It

Figure 77. The Goethe Academy under construction.

Figure 78. The completed building.

was, if you will, the teaching house of all teaching houses. It also contained the Fellowship's growing art collection. As Robert's house became increasingly the center of events on the property, he lived an increasingly public life. He was as completely available to his students as he could be.

Another, more general, expression of the recent changes in the school was the opening of centers in Europe. The London Center opened in 1977, and the Paris Center (the first center in a non-English speaking country) in late summer 1978. Soon the school had a presence that extended throughout Western Europe: England, France, Germany, Italy, Spain, Greece, Holland, Belgium, and Denmark. Numbers rose past 2,000. This corresponds to the era of the teaching house estates, where properties with a sizeable residence, additional acreage, and outbuildings were leased in the centers with large urban populations. By the early 1980s there were teaching house estates in London, Frankfurt, Amsterdam, Paris, Rome, Copenhagen, and Madrid. This more elaborate teaching house experience was where the founding students of the center resided, where students who joined the center would come to engage in the three lines of work, and where regularly hosted events for the surrounding centers, and occasionally for all of Europe, took place—all of this activity not unlike the experience that Gurdjieff had tried to create at the Prieuré.

The Fellowship had initially helped support the Hall Farm and the Paris Château, but increasingly the European centers managed to fund large

Figure 79. Students gathered at Hall Farm, Chorleywood, England.

teaching houses from their own resources. In the beginning the center directors were sometimes put on salary, but soon they too were expected to work full time and to make regular teaching payments. Their service, then, became their own gift to the school.

Similar teaching house estates gradually appeared in centers across the United States. Many students were entering a phase of their lives where their careers made demands on them. They nevertheless wanted to be part of the school's main direction, and they now had resources at their disposal. As a result, there were significant teaching house properties in Los Angeles, San Francisco, Silicon Valley, Washington D.C., New York, and New Orleans.

Each of these teaching houses was a focal point in the lives of many people, and they became bywords and destinations within the Fellowship.

Some of the centers grew quickly, to fifty or even close to a hundred students. Most of the inner circle of each center sought to live in the main teaching residence, and the residence and surrounding grounds became a hive of activity, a miniature of Renaissance. An entire culture of teaching house life developed. The combination of living together and sharing the work ideas maximized the cultural exchange in the European and larger American centers, as each side learned from the other. If you went to live in a European center, you had to learn the language. At a certain point meetings might be given in the language of the center's host country, or there might be an exercise for students not to speak English in the teaching house.

Each teaching house became a center for the study of the arts: libraries were assembled; students specialized in the study of different art forms; presentations and tours of the galleries of the city were arranged; guest artists were invited to perform at special events. And all of this was spliced with third line projects of repainting, repair, and gardening.

In 1978-79 Robert began reading the works of Western literature. He would allocate two hours of the afternoon to the study of Homer, Plato, Milton, Montaigne, Goethe, Keats, Tennyson and others — focusing particularly on authors whom he deemed to be conscious or to be in the process of awakening. He would overline his reading copy in pencil, and the overlinings would then be typed up and prepared for publication. Robert would add his comments to the passages selected, and the chosen excerpts plus the comments published as a journal and circulated throughout the school. Having a special interest in the visual arts, Robert studied particularly the works of the art historian Bernard Berenson, whose writings

Figure 80. Students gathered at Château de
Fontaine-les-Nonnes, France.

seemed a development of the works of Goethe. Berenson saw that the works of the great masters could teach you how to look at the world. Beyond that they could train you to enter a wordless state of 'looking,' in which you became one with the object of your attention (or with the work of art under study). Berenson connected 'looking' with direct perception and a 'state of consciousness.' We all began to study the works of the old masters with Berenson's categories in mind: tactile values, space composition, color composition, motion, significance, and form.

The Centered Whole: Renaissance, Community, and School

In the meantime, developments continued apace at Renaissance. The vineyard, under Karl's supervision, grew to 365 acres of beautifully contoured terraces, and our wines placed well in competition. We shall take this opportunity to sketch the development of Renaissance Vineyard and Winery, or, as we called it, RVW. With an outstanding terroir we chose to let the land speak for itself. We constantly tested the grapes in each of its many microclimates, to determine which varietals did the best on which slopes. There was an overall aim to avoid artificially fined and 'corrected' wines created for an uneducated palate, for such wines convey nothing of the terroir. We followed the Bordeaux production method, which corrects only by balancing wines with other wines made from grapes grown in different microclimates *on the same estate*.

In other words, we relied only on growing the right grapes in the right location with the right viticulture — processed under the direction of an experienced and discerning winemaker. We paid very close attention to the ageing of the different varietals, which resulted in a timed-release strategy.

In 1990 the renowned wine writer Robert Balzer wrote the following review of RVW:

> It took a decade for the only vineyard in North Yuba County to get its wines on the market, but for Renaissance Vineyard and Winery the wait has been worthwhile.

Since its initial releases in October 1988, Renaissance has been winning international awards left and right, giving credence to the winery's philosophy of not releasing wines for general sales until they are deemed to be outstanding. The most recent award was in May from Wine Magazine's International Challenge in London. Four thousand wines were entered in the competition, but in the Bordeaux Style Wines category, only two gold medals were awarded. One went to Renaissance 1984 Cabernet Sauvignon.

This medal is the latest in a series of victories that began in June 1989, when I first heard about this winery. At VINEXPO, the most formidable wine exposition in the world, the Renaissance 1985 Special Select Late Harvest Riesling was the only American wine to come home with a gold medal. It also won two of the three other awards that American wines received: a silver for its 1982 Late Harvest Sauvignon Blanc and a bronze for its 1987 Dry Riesling.

In October, *Gault Millau*, a well-known European wine publication, rated 70 of the world's luscious dessert nectars. The Renaissance Late Harvest Riesling was ranked in the Top 10, the highest rating for any American wine and the highest rating for any Riesling in the world.[1]

In all of these labors we tried to relate our aim of making world class wines to the first, second, and third lines of work. RVW staff tried to apply the principles of the Work to all their practices and all their business processes. Because RVW recruited students as permanent employees, most applicants had to be trained to fill the positions they were hired for. The staff studied each other's tasks and functions so that there was backup support for one another, in case of absence or turnover. We tried to act as the connected cells of a living whole. We attempted to use the management principle of integrating the work of the different business departments (vineyard, winery, shipping, accounting, sales and marketing) to produce an awareness of the whole in each individual member. This is a core principle of Deming management, which we applied and further developed in relation to our

---

1. Balzer, Robert Lawrence, *Steps to Success: Renaissance's Terraced Vineyards Are Leading Its Wines to Medals*, Sacramento Bee, September 23rd, 1990.

Fourth Way aims. How? By employing the principle of external consideration: by placing one's awareness in the awareness of others; by not thinking about ourselves, but being present to the moment-by-moment unfolding of the whole operation. For example, at the quarterly staff meetings representatives from each department would describe the aims of their group, and the challenges that they faced, letting the rest of us know at which points they would benefit from additional resources. There would be complete silence while each manager spoke, and for most, this was the silence of the third state of consciousness. The executive officer would then comment on each contribution, putting it in context. When he had finished, the other managers might contribute. The delegation of resources was then decided, and it was always tailored exactly to the needs of the whole.

We all understood that, even if we didn't get what we wanted, the whole would benefit — and so would we as part of it. The aim was that each person should understand in exactly what way their contribution was needed to produce a world class winery. It was one great process of alchemical refinement, both externally and internally. We tried to work consciously; we tried to produce world class wines in a state of presence.

Looking back over those years, one of my best memories was working with the mix of different people, thrown suddenly together, with very different backgrounds and very different skill sets. We were trying to cultivate vines, make wine, and sell the wines we made, with only a few of us having professional experience. We all had to work together to get the job done, knowing that we didn't know quite enough. We had to make the fullest use of those people who did know something, and we all had to be open to learn. For everyone involved, it was a matter of recognizing other people's strengths and helping them to develop those strengths. And we were always trying to think how to do things in the best way with limited resources. It was rewarding to see people discover that they could perform a function they were not trained for and perform it well. We made tours of the other wineries in Napa Valley to see how things were done in the industry. There were strong bonds of mutual support running throughout the organization: we were certain of the potential of our terroir; certain that we could produce world class wines; and certain that we wanted to do all of this in the present, moment by moment.

Having said all of this, it must be admitted that the day-to-day reality of RVW did not always match this vision. It had its fair share of discord and personal rivalry. But it did occasionally touch upon its own vision, and in this it permanently marked at least one participant, so that when he later made on-site studies of the Athenian Parthenon and the Hagia Sophia, he saw, in both of these monuments, a full and complete expression of the kind of organization he had glimpsed at RVW.

In the mid-1970s a professional bookbinder joined the school. This was just when Robert became interested in acquiring fine leather-bound books. He hoped to see leather-bound copies of the classics, and of the works of conscious authors, in centers all over the school, and in each individual student's personal library. In 1977 he asked the architect's office to design a bindery, where the bookbinder could work and share his craft. The architects drew up plans, and within months the construction team began to pour the foundations for a building.

But as Robert watched the progress of construction and reviewed the entire site, he decided that the building should be enlarged to include a stage. At that time, we had concerts at the Lodge in the crowded main room every weekend. It had poor acoustics, and the building was stressed to support its ever-growing audience. Suddenly the so-called 'bindery' was recognized as a room large enough for a stage and audience seating. The bindery operation, then, with all its equipment, was shifted into office space on the opposite side of the building. The next requirement from Robert was that the new concert hall double as a meeting hall and be supplied with chairs that could be stacked and removed. A storage room was created for the chairs…and it went on and on. People hardly knew what they were doing from one day to the next. But when it was completed, we had a public building: a meeting hall, a performing arts center, and a civic center. In the end it was called, simply, the Town Hall. Here we had our weekly meetings on Wednesdays, and our concerts or performances on the weekends. Here the Renaissance Chorus, the Renaissance Orchestra, and the Renaissance Drama Octave rehearsed and performed. And of course, it was also used as an office and a bindery. This was an example of how Robert proceeded; he always considered the whole in relation to newly developing areas, and he adjusted moment by moment.

Due to the level of activity that the completed Town Hall sustained, the hardwood floors had to be resurfaced regularly. One was reminded of the stone stairs of ancient monasteries, worn smooth by centuries of constant use. In 2012 the building was renamed the Apollo Festival Hall, dedicated to Michael Goodwin, our premier conductor, who had passed away early that year.

Innumerable other construction projects were launched in the late 1970s and early 1980s, and the pace was set at the level of Gurdjieff's Prieuré—not just for 23 months, but *year in and year out indefinitely*. Most students slept only four or five hours a night. In the summer the salaried students put in a full twelve hours of heavy physical work, before the evening's meetings, dinners, and concerts. And all of this six and seven days a week. There would be all-night work octaves about every second month, and this

Figure 81. Inflatable dome housing the winery under construction 1982. It acquired the nickname "Beelzebubble."

Figure 82. The vineyard facing east, with the completed winery on the knoll to the right.

meant working straight through to the end of the following day. On some occasions it went to three days.

If you had worked in the hot sun all day, and then had been up late washing dishes the night before, you might — on taking your seat at the evening concert — find yourself inadvertently nodding off. Amongst the vineyard and construction workers there was a fraternal system of gentle prods and whispers. We all understood that "there but for the grace of God go I." Robert originally believed, from his own experience, that you had to work physically with this intensity to awaken. Later on he modified this view, particularly with respect to sleeping for only a few hours a night, or working the night through. As families appeared and a community took form, different kinds of work — other than physical work — took center stage: a school system was being developed; art collections and libraries were assembled; publications were launched; and centers opened all over the world. And most of us began to sleep more than three or four hours a night. If you didn't sleep at night, you couldn't be successful with these other kinds of work!

We note in passing that the annual vineyard harvests were an extraordinary experience. In our peak years 700 tons of grapes went into the crush to produce some 40,000 cases of wine. A normal vineyard hires teams of seasonal laborers to come in for the harvest. We hired a few, when necessary, but most of the work was done by students. The students working in the Fellowship office, or in the garden, or on the construction team, or in maintenance, stopped their work to become harvesters. All meals were prepared for the harvesters, and the midday meal was brought out to them on the slopes. The only thing you did on your own was sleep. And every harvest year many students came from outlying centers to help, especially from the centers overseas. There might be sixty or seventy visitors, and they all had to be accommodated. The harvest would begin in late August with a two-week spurt to bring in the whites (riesling, sauvignon blanc, chardonnay). Then came a pause as the reds came ready, and then another two-week push for the cabernet and syrah — this to be followed by another month of scattered days for the late harvest whites.

Each morning a hundred people would gather in the pre-dawn light for a morning meal, and — as the first rays of sunlight came over the hill — went out in trucks and tri-motos to the different slopes.[1] People worked until a little past sunset, which was 8PM at the beginning of the harvest, shortening to 7PM in September. In the midst of a searing hundred-degree-plus afternoon you might find yourself stumbling occasionally or feeling weak at the knees. After 3PM the conversation between harvesters would drop off, and people would just quietly clip the grapes from the vines. In the long silences that emerged, the boundary between the self and the other might suddenly dissolve — and you would see a hundred different versions of yourself quietly picking grapes on the slope. By 4PM you might feel a bit giddy, but you determined to push through to the relief of early evening. The last few hours of the day were always easier. Each evening, after you finished picking your last row, you would go up to a dinner prepared at the winery. Trucks would bring in the harvesting teams from the other parts of the vineyard, and the different groups would gradually merge into one. When you finally arrived at the winery, the Renaissance wines of harvests past stood before you on the tables, and the intimacy that had grown through a long day was suddenly shared. Conversation and gentle laughter continued late into the night. At 11PM you went home for a shower and

---

1. The three wheeled tri-moto was the original all-terrain-vehicle, until it was replaced by the safer four wheeled quad in 1987. The vineyard workers labelled the more pedestrian quads 'quasimodos.'

drop onto your bed. The alarm went off at 5AM the next morning and it began all over again. There were the same bright faces at the breakfast table, at the lunch break, and again at dinner; the faces of Paris, Frankfurt, London, Madrid, and St. Petersburg — who are suddenly the faces of your fellow travelers in the greatest of all adventures. The effect was to create an alternate time: the future and the past disappear, and you enter an eternal harvest. I can remember once wishing, at the end of a long day, as I made my way to the dinner on the winery cap, that I might continue in just this way until I awakened — however many centuries that might take.

From its inception the Town Hall was hosting classical concerts by professional performers on most weekends, and, at the same time, the Renaissance orchestra and chorus had begun to give regular performances. Often the orchestra would back a professional vocalist, pianist, or violin player. Cuisine and dining were modelled after French culture, while evening wear tended towards the Italian style, with an emphasis on fine fabrics and workmanship. All of this was combined with the roughness of the rural setting and the intensity of physical work that was integral to it. You would see heavily callused hands polishing a beautiful pair of secondhand Gucci shoes. To students it sometimes seemed a list of impossible and contradictory demands, but all that mattered, in the end, was that the effort and the suffering was transformed into presence.

When you were on salary Robert seemed either infinitely distant (when you were in a lower state and by yourself) or intimate and intense (when he was right in front of you). There was nothing in between, because there was not one casual bone in Robert Earl Burton's body. When his attention was on you, he cut to the quick, with insight, affection, correction, inspiration, guidance, and discipline. The intimacy of his school was not less than the intimacy of a family, though even deeper and more resonant — for Higher Centers are the most precious possession of every man and woman. Where a family brings forth children, which are sacred to life on this level, a school brings forth the birth of conscious souls, which are sacred to the universe. In a school there is a shared valuation for first things, which is rare in human history. This intimacy was enhanced by Robert's emphasis on the development of essence at the expense of personality. But, given that the average age in 1977 was 26, Robert had to ensure that this intimacy did not lead us back to the casual sex of the 1960s and early 1970s, or to the more communal lifestyle that Yorgos Savides had encouraged. What was encouraged instead was courtship, marital life, and family life.

In September of 1978 Robert, to the complete surprise of his students, suddenly stopped leading meetings. He had driven to the Bay Area to lead a meeting, the car that was carrying him pulled up to the meeting place, but Robert did not get out of the car. He asked another student to lead the meeting, and he gave that student a two-part message to be read to all of us. The gist of this message was: (1) I have decided to stop leading meetings, and (2) I understand the implications of my decision. He then instructed students to teach in his stead. In this way he challenged students to articulate the work for themselves. Indeed, the culture and the level of center meetings had grown, and the regular circulation of travelling teachers throughout the centers had become an established pattern. Robert himself did continue to teach at weekly dinners and in all his daily contacts with students. Robert did not begin leading meetings again until 22 years later, in the fall of 2000.

The space created by Robert's stepping back gave a particular opportunity to Miles Barth and Girard Haven. They were now under a much greater pressure to distinguish consciousness from functions within themselves, so as to enable the direct experience of Higher Centers for others at the meetings. You cannot do this simply by making a 'good performance' at the meetings, you have to make your whole life an example of service to presence. In another way Robert's stepping back made us all teachers: all people that were responsible for communicating the Work, and so accountable to C Influence for controlling our features while we were doing it.

Robert worked carefully, unselfishly, and tirelessly to create and fill the different roles that emerged in relation to his own role. He created an organization, and he created spaces for people to evolve within it. This involved both 1) roles for potential conscious beings, and 2) an ecumenic open space where students could form a relationship to C Influence through service.

Miles proved particularly gifted at leading meetings, and many of his meetings were quite electric. He had a remarkable degree of control over his speech, his movements, and his emotions, and sometimes the Higher Centers took over and you could literally see them teaching through the machine. He had what seemed an unshakeable sense of duty. In his mature teaching years, he slept only a few hours each night, and if he had a pain threshold it was not visible to the rest of us. He would master each new school exercise on the day it was given, and he remembered the name of every student he met. He was widely sought for counsel in many areas, including particularly the area of 'relationship friction.' He could be quite gentle when circumstances required, but he could also be quite severe. He was, for many of us, a role model. At a certain point Robert asked four students, over a single weekend, and independently of one another, to inform Miles that he had awakened. This was a way of letting both Miles and the school know at the same time. There was the joyous feeling throughout the school that "another one of us has made it."

In the period when Miles' awakening seemed imminent, Robert had asked him to lead a series of monthly meetings at the First Unitarian Church in San Francisco. They became known as the Bay Area Meetings. In this new series you could feel the resonance of the old Skyline Church meetings, which were still inscribed in Fellowship memory. As with the Skyline Church meetings, many people would travel in from Renaissance in the east, from the Pacific Northwest, and from Los Angeles in the south. And the Renaissance attendees, on their return journey, always gave the Coffee Tree in Vacaville some extra late-night business.

In January of 1979 Robert had an unexpected surprise. He was visiting Paris, staying at a hotel near the Louvre, when he received a call from Alexander Horn. He had not spoken a word to Alex in ten years. We keep in mind that this was before the age of cellphones. Alex had been given the phone number of Robert's hotel, and for all Robert knew he might be at a hotel close by. Robert had been reminded of Alex only a month before, with the publication of the negative article in the San Francisco Chronicle, and the news that Alex and Sharon had been forced to leave the city. This was Robert's teacher, and it had been a matter of some concern to him. Indeed, he had circulated the Chronicle article through the school when it was published. Suddenly, there he was talking to the man himself, the only conscious being he had ever known, and a full man number six. Alex, who had been rethinking the plan of his Work, was calling Robert to suggest that they work together, "for the future of the Fourth Way." He asked if they might meet. Robert's initial response was "Yes," but he asked if he might call back in an hour, to which Alex agreed.

Robert then reflected on all that had occurred since April 1969, when he had last seen Alex. He realized that the trial of the lonely transitional year had changed him forever. He had followed the will of Higher Forces, and the result was something different from the Theatre of All Possibilities. Reflecting back, he did not see how the two approaches to the Work could fit together. He felt that he had to continue with the task he had been given. When Robert called Alex back, he spoke lovingly but declined to meet with Alex, and instead requested that they not meet again "in the flesh, in this lifetime." Robert spoke very little of Alex after that, although he continued to have a case of Renaissance wine sent to Alex every year at Christmas time. Basically we — the student body — never thought of him. But after Alex's death in 2007, nearly thirty years later, Robert spoke freely of him, and celebrated his success in passing through to a Higher Level. We can only guess what suffering the separation of the two men caused on either side.

By the early 1980s the Fellowship had become a truly international organization, and we found that there was a great value in this — for it is good to have a variety of people in the Work. It gives you more of an outside perspective on yourself. In relation to the Work, every particular ethnicity has its limitations and its strengths, but — at the same time — all are equally microcosmoses. This creates a more complete and vivid mirror effect. You see yourself in a larger and more objective frame of reference. Throughout the 1980s and 1990s centers continued to open all over Eastern Europe, the Middle East, the Far East, and South America. The Fellowship opened, in the course of its history, a total of 154 centers all over the world.

One can imagine what an effort it would be to travel to a distant country, get a job, become proficient in the language, open a center, attract a core of people, and instruct them in the Work as you yourself had been instructed. You then had to encourage this group of people to accept all the disciplines of the school, which meant, effectively, reprioritizing their entire lives. Many of the centers developed individual identities and produced successive generations of students over time. Thus, as the centers matured, you had many alternate realities within the Fellowship.

We learned much from the people who came to us, and we learned much from the cities in which they lived. Fellowship students filled the concert halls of London, Paris, New York, and Milan. We regularly frequented the great galleries of the world: The Uffizi, the Pitti, the Louvre, the Vatican, the National Gallery of London, the National Gallery of Washington, the Archaeological Museum of Athens, and the Hermitage of St. Petersburg.

Imagine yourself as a student, living at Renaissance. The teacher, knowing that you speak Spanish, suggests that you go out and help with the Madrid center. The Fellowship provides you with the plane fare and with a few months of additional salary to get you started. You arrive in Madrid to find yourself surrounded by a circle of mature and considerate students who help you to find your footing in the city and to get a job. And, at the same time, you meet a generation of new students who have just come to the school and who are interested to hear about everything you have seen and done. Once established in Madrid you have the freedom of Europe; you can visit London, Paris, Rome, Florence, Athens, Milan, Moscow, St. Petersburg, Bucharest — and in each city find yourself surrounded by a similar circle of students, to whom you are already connected by shared aims. These students can give you tours of the museums and historical sites and advise you on the best concerts, operas, and theater performances. Wherever you go, you find friends pursing the same path and you sense that it is all opening up into something greater. Immersion in Europe came easily!

At Renaissance, the Fellowship's performing arts center arranged an almost unbroken series of concerts, operas, and theater performances. This organization was later formally titled Apollo Performing Arts, and later yet — as its activities expanded — simply Apollo Arts.

Both Renaissance and the centers continued to develop at pace, but the general complexion of things began to change. By the late 1980s, the students who had joined in the 1970s were well into mid-career and family life. The great majority of students worked off salary, and many of us found careers in the software industry, where we could develop 'portable' skills. For some decades, in software companies all over the world, there were student employees setting alerts to be present, putting post-its on their monitors to remind themselves of daily aims, and installing screen savers of Leonardo, Titian, and Giorgione. Additionally, there was, by this time, a significant intermarriage of people from all over the world. An international multilingual community was taking form. Because Robert spoke only English, every student understood the need to learn English, but often you would hear Spanish or Hebrew spoken in the vineyard, Italian in the kitchen, French at the winery, or Russian among the landscaping crew. It seemed that there was no nationality that could not accept Robert as a teacher: as a person capable of asking them to realize their deepest possibilities and providing the necessary guidance.

In this situation the Lewis Carroll School continued to grow and develop. The children could enter into 'apprenticeships' with students — at the Fellowship office, at the winery, at maintenance, at the press, and at Apollo Arts — in order to give them a picture of the world awaiting them after school. More generally, we all knew one another's children; they grew up with us. Local markets developed and a local economy took form, with students providing services to one another. The many different crafts and trades found expression every weekend at the Sunday Grand Bazaar.

With the rapid growth of the centers in Rome, Milan, Florence, and Venice, there was an increasing influence of Italian and Mediterranean culture in the school. In support of this development, Robert renamed the *Goethe Academy* the *Galleria Apollo*. Robert had had a positive experience of the Galleria Vittorio Emanuele II in Milan, with its great mall. He was also thinking, perhaps, of the *Galerie d'Apollon* in the Louvre. The name 'gallery' implied both a reflection of the growing art collection, and a public space with general emotional openness and interaction. It was more intimate than an academy; it was a space where you could spend time with other people in the best way.

In March of 1985 came the greatest shock for Robert since the school's inception. Miles Barth, who had now been the senior student in the school for more than a decade, and through the entire period when Robert had ceased to lead meetings, visited Robert one afternoon to inform him that he was leaving the school. Miles said: "I am leaving you, as you left your own teacher." Robert then asked that Miles not take Fellowship students with him. Miles replied, "Each student will have to decide that for themselves." This implied both that Miles was going to teach, and that he was going to accept Fellowship students into his teaching. Miles had been given access to a generation of Fellowship students by Robert's grace and on Robert's trust. Robert told Miles that he was making a mistake. Miles replied, "If I can verify that I will return on bended knee." In the moment Robert first replied, "You will be accepted." But sometime later, as events unfolded, Robert commented to other students that "We are already on our knees, and this is something that Miles did not understand."

The play of Yorgos Savides repeated itself, though on a different scale. In the special role that Miles had been given, his machine had come to feel itself unique, and — in an invisible struggle — the lower self had succeeded in taking credit for the emergent Higher Centers. The 'teacher identity' then took the nascent Higher Centers out of the school. Miles' Higher Centers had indeed been intermittently active, and Robert had encouraged Miles by telling him that he was awake. In a way this was true. It is the author's impression that Miles was, for a period, functioning as a man number five — but only in a context that had been carefully created by Robert. And when that context was removed, with the process of crystallization incomplete, the lower self took the reins. In telling Miles that he was awake Robert was helping Miles to grow into the role that he had created for him. Playing the part of a man number five is a high wire act without the safety net, and there are points at which the aspirant needs to feel that someone is behind them.

In the month after Miles' departure, while many students were struggling with their 'I's, Robert made the effort to dine with as many students as possible. At these dinners he said, "I do not misunderstand — I am helping you to understand." He also emphasized that, "One does not take another teacher's students." He himself had been most scrupulous with the students of his own teacher. When Robert first began meeting with prospective students in the Bay Area, he made it clear that he would not accept a student of Alex Horn. He would always say to such a person, "You have a conscious teacher." In his view that person should rather go back to Alex and make better use of the teacher they had.

After his departure Miles circulated a letter amongst many members of the Fellowship, telling them that he would lead a meeting at the First Unitarian Church in San Francisco, where he would outline his plans for the future. This was the same church where he had been leading the Bay Area Meeting series. About 150 Fellowship students attended. Miles also networked with the many ex-students he had known over the years, and there were about 200 ex-students and assorted others present as well. Seventy Fellowship students left the school after that meeting. Miles' group — The New Being Institute — began to operate in June of 1985 with about 120 people, and lasted for some 20 months. Those students who later returned to the Fellowship reported that it lacked the kind of emotion you needed to connect with Higher Centers. It did not stir the deepest parts of their being. And it failed to attract a new circle of students, outside the sphere of the Fellowship.

But in March of 1985 the impact of Miles' departure on the Fellowship was tremendous. We will recall that, at this time, Robert had not been leading meetings for seven years, and for many people Miles had the role of relating the terms of the system, and the practice of the Work, to the experience of Higher Centers. One student said that, on hearing the news of Miles' departure, he felt like a passenger in an airplane who was happily looking out the window, studying the cloud formations, when he saw the pilot bailing out of the plane.

Miles had been in the school for fifteen years, since 1970, and the bonds of friendship, allegiance, and obligation ran deep. He had been trusted, and he evinced trust. His departure cut directly through close personal friendships and family ties. Students who decided to go with Miles, and those who decided to remain in the Fellowship, would never see or speak to each other again. People whom you thought you would spend the rest of your life with were suddenly strangers. It was a hard test.

But what kind of a test was it? Let us compare Miles' departure with the two previous tests. Yorgos Savides had split off an active 'new age' branch of the school, which did not fit with the way the school was developing at that time. Donald Macdonald had removed a passive "let's keep the life we have" branch. Miles split off a branch of people who wanted something for themselves: personal perfection, a flawless articulation of the system, an inspiring role model, or awakening "for themselves" alone. It was a choice between the desire for perfected form and the actual recognition of a Higher Level. The people who stayed were people who somehow sensed the heat and light of C Influence, and with this the direction of the school itself. They were not asking for something but were preparing to serve under whatever conditions were given. It was a test on a Higher Level than the previous two trials, and it was a test for people who had been longer in the Work.

It was Girard Haven who then stepped in to fill the void left by Miles. Girard, now a father of three, had quietly played second fiddle to Miles for many years. He was a more modest and a more unassuming man, who never made claims for himself, but who served faithfully — and was to serve ever more faithfully from that point forward. He took responsibility for working with the situations that continuously came up in the centers. He led meetings at Renaissance and visited centers throughout the world, travelling much more extensively than Miles had ever done. He began a school newspaper, *The Fellowship Forum,* and — over many years — published the series of books that are listed under his name in the bibliography to this volume. He was an example to us all, not because he inspired emulation, but because his life naturally expressed his work. He was the words he spoke, and so the teaching and the counsel that he gave were not forgotten.

Girard's growing presence in the school was considerably reinforced by the fact that, sometime in the late 1980s, Robert made the transition to the level of man number seven. This is a more gradual transition than crystallization as a man number six. At certain points a man number six finds himself functioning as a man number seven, and then again not. It may take years to stabilize. The process began in 1987, and Robert, according to what he shared with us, was functioning permanently as a man number seven by 1989.

In 1997 Robert changed the cultural emphasis of the school from the European Renaissance to Classical Antiquity, with a particular focus on the golden age of Greece. Renaissance was renamed Apollo, and the Apollo University was created to help introduce the school to the culture of the Greek city-state in the fifth century B.C. This was not a matter of 'play acting' the classical, but of understanding the nature of the Greek city-state and the Greek myths. We studied the principles of Greek philosophy, of Greek drama, of Greek sculpture, and of Greek architecture — and applied them to our lives. Tours of the principal classical sites in Greece were arranged on a regular basis, and many students studied Attic Greek. This did not displace the studies of the arts of Renaissance Europe, but rather

Figure 83. Aerial view of the Galleria and grounds.

Figure 84. Galleria rear balcony and gardens.

deepened those studies — as the Renaissance itself had its source in a revival of classicism. Robert gave Apollo University the mission to "bring the miracle of Greece to Apollo." This required the assimilation of the different experiences of travel, art, and study that students were having, both in relation to the Work and in relation to our previous understandings of art and culture. On this basis the University was to present courses and to publish books and pamphlets. Soon Apollo University was able to offer a full range of courses in both the arts and sciences, and conscientiously relating all of these disciplines to awakening.

At one point Robert said that Plato's *Republic* was the template for our school, and that Plato himself (or the disembodied being that Plato now is) was guiding the school through this phase of its development.

It was at just this time that the school began to open up in Russia. This had not been planned. An American student who was travelling in Russia had the impulse to give prospective student meetings in Moscow, and there was an immediate response. Soon centers appeared in both Moscow and St. Petersburg. To everyone's surprise they each quickly grew to nearly one hundred students. In the fall of 2000 Robert visited Russia for the first time. He visited both Moscow and St. Petersburg, and he met and dined with as many students as possible. On the evening of October 7 in St. Petersburg, Robert conducted his first formal meeting since September 1978. The meeting took place in a hall on the Liteyny Prospekt, the same street where Ouspensky made his first attempts to remember himself, as related in *In Search of the Miraculous*. Robert mentioned this at the conclusion of the meeting, saying, "It is very poetic that we are having this meeting here tonight, because out of Mr. Ouspenky's first attempts to remember himself a great School has arisen, and this School is for people from all the nations of the world."

Additional centers soon opened in Nizhny Novgorod, two hundred miles east of Moscow, in Kiev in the Ukraine, and in Novosibirsk in Siberia. Robert had particularly wanted a center in Siberia because of the amount of suffering that has occurred there. Russia had been the place where the Fourth Way had first been introduced to the Western world, and so we had come full circle. Many of the Russian students were able to visit Apollo, and quickly entered into the deepest currents of the Work. The Russians seemed able to take up all the themes of the Work that had been elaborated up to that time, for their own culture included the legacy of orthodox monasticism, the Masonic and Rosicrucian teachings, and all the highest forms of art. There was actually a degree of cultural fusion at this time; part of what the school had become was Russian. With the expansion of the centers in Russia and Eastern Europe our numbers reached about 2,500.

With the rapidly growing Russian population, ballet became a center of interest. It was not just that the Russian students wanted to see the ballet, but that the rest of us, when we visited Moscow and St. Petersburg, were transfixed by the performances of the Bolshoi and Mariinsky ballet companies. For a person trained in the pursuit of presence the ballet absolutely minimizes the denying force to sustaining presence. There is simply no reason to be in imagination before the great art of the Bolshoi and the Mariinsky. The school had had a general interest in the ballet before, but this was art on a different level.

Robert had a special open-air theater constructed — called the θέατρον, or 'Theatron' — for drama, music, and ballet. Every summer the Theatron hosted events for all the performing arts, culminating in the Ballet Galas, with a selection of pieces from different ballets. We invited performers from the greatest ballet companies in the world. This included such artists as Farouk Ruzimatov, Galina Stepanenko, Igor Zelensky, Mariana Ryzhkina, Nikolay Tsiskaridze, and Maria Alexandrova. Indeed, it was

Nikolay Tsiskaridze (later the Rector of the Vaganova Academy) who was consulted on the original dimensions and stage design of the Theatron.

Having said this, the Theatron — once in place — became the site for theater performances, for orchestra, for choir, and for opera. There were events all summer long.

While life at Apollo was no longer as brutally physical as it had been in the 1970s, it was actually *more* intense. With the salaried staff stretched to carry out their regular duties, arranging the summer schedule of Theatron events (including hosting all the visiting ballet dancers) constituted a super effort. Curtains and stage backdrops were created that were exact copies of those at the Marijinsky Theater in St. Petersburg. When opening night finally arrived, and the curtains parted, an evening of total enchantment unfolded. In the face of such consummate beauty the denying force to being present almost disappears.

Before moving on, we must pay tribute to the landscaping crew at Apollo. A team of ten to fifteen students was active over more than thirty years, following through on one landscaping project after the next. It was little short of a miracle that the landscaping crew was able to execute all the new projects Robert asked of them, while maintaining the extensive gardens already created. In the early 1980s Robert invited Russell Page as a landscaping consultant to review the work done and to advise on future developments. Russell Page had been a student of Gurdjieff, and had married one of his daughters. Mr. Page's clients had included Edward the VIII of England (as the Duke of Windsor), King Leopold III of Belgium, Oscar de la Renta, and the Frick Museum. The rows of cypress trees that now feature prominently on the property were placed at his suggestion. When Mr. Page departed, the student who drove him to the airport reported that he wept over what he had witnessed at Apollo, remembering the same atmosphere of the Work that he had known with Gurdjieff many years ago.

On New Year's Day 2001 Robert led a meeting in the Galleria Apollo. The room was filled to overflowing. From this day forward Robert led meetings on a regular basis—first weekly, then gradually increasing to what is today an average of 8-10 meetings per week.

We have presented the form of the school and its teachings up to the year 2001, but the most radical developments were yet to come.

The Inner Work Changes: 2004

In the year 2004 the teaching was 34 years old, and our numbers were about 2,500, yet the work principles applied were still those of the *Psychology* and the *Fourth Way*. As Robert had awakened using these tools — and he was very much awake — we never questioned them, but only our own use of them. On the foundation of *The Psychology* and *The Fourth Way* Robert had introduced:

- A full development of the three lines of work across the school, based on tasks given from C Influence.
- An emphasis on the development of the King of Hearts and on the central place of emotion in awakening.
- An emphasis on the non-expression of negative emotions. Non-expression was sharply distinguished from 'suppression,' and was presented as a first step in the transformation of negative emotions into the positive emotions of the Higher Emotional Center.
- An emphasis on the development of essence. This was connected with the idea that the Self is essence aware of itself. The Self cannot emerge on a foundation other than essence, and the completed astral body carries something of our essence within itself.
- A deep understanding of the relationship between art and awakening, and a priority of the use of impressions in awakening.

We had made an active use of the tools for awakening developed to that time. It seemed to us that we had been given all that one could wish for, but Robert's own work was taking him to new places. Something began to change. From the time he began leading meetings again, Robert had begun to register more accurately our response to his teaching, and the progress of the students who attended the meetings. These observations sowed the seeds for developments to come.

THE THIRTY WORK 'I'S AND THE KEYS

In 2004 Robert, who had, for thirty-four years, used the word self-remembering as a mantra, began to challenge his students with the single syllable "BE," to be followed — when presence wavered — with "HOLD BEING." More and more often he spoke of *prolonging* presence. He also advised us to use simple, direct, and well-targeted Work 'I's. In that regard he often reminded us of a work 'I' that he had used in the difficult year after he left Alex Horn and before he founded the Fellowship. In a moment of great confusion an 'I' suddenly came: "Trust no 'I's; be present."

Such an 'I' does not struggle with our confusions and concerns, by observing, correcting, or analyzing. It simply displaces them. It does not acknowledge their content at all. This is the kind of work 'I' that comes from Higher Centers.

Robert had determined, after careful study over many years, that imagination was the principal obstacle to awakening. The other obstacles could not be surmounted unless this obstacle was addressed. In the new approach Robert was experimenting with, all of the tools of the Work were brought to bear with this priority in mind.

In September 2004 Robert published a short booklet of his own most-used Work 'I's. All of these were concise. While some of them might be a sentence long, they were thoughts you could apply in a moment. The first time I saw this list it affected me profoundly. I realized that my teacher was working in a different way than I was. Here are a few examples:

- Be present. Live the moment.
- Now is the moment to make the work practical.
- Self-remembering first; everything else thereafter.
- Do your work now.
- Employ the looking exercise.

These are highly condensed and focused Work 'I's, aimed at the ever-encroaching world of imagination, negative emotions, and identification. Even when they are a full sentence long, they can be applied at a single stroke. Each has been tried and tested many times. The great advantage of such Work 'I's is that they are *not discursive,* and so escape the context of 'me thinking about myself.' They are not dependent on somehow rising out of the mire of self-reflection and having their brief moment before being swept away. They are invoked in the service of presence. And the more you use them the more you can use them. From another point of view these 'I's are closer to the minimal, focused communications of Higher Centers themselves. We can see why Robert would want to use them. The list was both a turning point and a signal of things to come.

Looking back to this time, it is clear that a change was needed. For all of our enthusiasm in applying Robert's teaching, our relation to the actual practice of the Work was largely discursive. We talked about it all the time. Robert had determined to move us from that place.

There followed an effort to reduce all of the essential Work 'I's to thirty single-syllable words. The requirement of the single syllable Work 'I's was to emphasize that they were not to be used discursively, but to be applied in a single moment, at a single stroke. Robert worked out this list of thirty from indications given him by Influence C, at a time when he was making frequent visits to Egypt. Influence C sometimes instructed him through the Egyptian symbols, and he sometimes found what he had already discovered existing in the patterns of Egyptian art. These symbols he called the "keys," and he began to discover them in art through the centuries. Symbols are closer to the language of Higher Centers. He made a total of thirty visits to Egypt. His aim at this time was "to understand Egypt:" to understand the teaching of the ancient Egyptian school. He felt that in so doing he was rediscovering something known to many of the great schools of the past, presented in different times and places through different images and symbols.

In addition to elaborating the thirty Work 'I's, Robert began to study the polarity between what we called in the Overview the *Black Queen* (the emotional part of the king of clubs) and the *White Queen* (the emotional part of the king of hearts). In examining the role of the Black Queen in relation to the many 'I's, Robert began to speak of the *Lower Self*. He used this

Sufi term to refer to the denying force to awakening, rather than emphasizing false personality or chief feature, as Ouspensky had done. Yes, false personality and chief feature are components of the Lower Self, but the Lower Self is understood in its overall function as the denying force to awakening. Robert's use of the term Lower Self was derivative of his understanding of the role of the Black Queen. Only in light of the role of the Black Queen can we see how all the elements of the Lower Self work together. We note that the Black Queen can even use Work 'I's to further her own ends.

THE BLACK QUEEN AND THE WHITE QUEEN

The nine of clubs is the division of the instinctive center designed to defend the physical organism against external and internal threats. It is behind both the working of the immune system and the sudden access of energy and awareness that comes to us in times of danger. It is the control center of the physical organism, and the foundation for the sense of unity on which imaginary 'I' is based. Higher Centers, when they begin to emerge, threaten the imaginary 'I.' They represent a threatening intrusion into the instinctive center's world, like a foreign body or a flu virus. The nine of clubs begins to defend herself against such intrusion; that is, to actively resist the Higher Centers. And she is a formidable opponent, for she is sleeplessly active, day and night. She is the strongest thing in us, until we develop something stronger. When she is activated in resistance to the Higher Centers, she becomes the Black Queen, the Lower Self.

We recall that the Nine of Hearts is the seat of *objective memory*, that is, the memory of moments of Higher Centers. As the Nine of Hearts becomes able to remember presence itself, independent of the circumstances in which it appears, objective memory becomes cumulative. The more you remember, the more you can remember. With training the Nine of Hearts becomes able to make — with accuracy — two different kinds of perception:

1. Positive perceptions of the presence of the Higher Centers.
2. Negative perceptions of what it means to live under the control of the Lower Self.

These perceptions are, respectively, the perceptions of the negative and positive halves of the White Queen. The White Queen is unique in that the two halves can be trained to work together, in the changing circumstances of external life, to produce a consistent line of effort.

By acquiring these capacities, the Nine of Hearts becomes the White Queen. Robert saw the White Queen as the force behind the steward. Its development is critical to the development of the steward.[1]

THE LOWER SELF

In considering the roles of the Black Queen and the White Queen, Robert found it more appropriate to speak of the Lower Self than of false personality.

False personality is a constantly changing facade, that adjusts its behavior to the behavior of other people and to external circumstances. It preserves the illusion of identity, but it is, in itself, a composite. It develops differently in relation to different *external* situations. The Lower Self, by contrast, is adjusted *internally* by the Nine of Clubs attempting to defend herself. It is what is *behind* the different personalities. The Lower Self, under the leadership of the Black Queen, becomes the foe of the steward, under the leadership of the White Queen.

The term Lower Self takes the focus off the many-headed hydra of features, of 'I's, of sensations, and of emotions that keep us from the present. It puts the focus on what lies behind the 'I's, and on what defends this entire confused and murky world. The 'I's are not wrong in themselves, but in service to the Black Queen they become wrong.

Robert saw the Work as, ultimately, a life-or-death struggle between the Black Queen and the White Queen, between presence and sleep. From the moment a man recognizes this fact he lives in a divided house; his being becomes a war between two opposing forces. In order for the White Queen to win, she must be able to organize and deploy those pieces on

---

1. As we struggled to learn the art of the steward, Robert often surprised us by saying that "The steward does not exist." What he meant was that the steward is a means, not an end. It is still on the level of the many 'I's. Relative to the result produced — Higher Centers — it is not real.

the chessboard capable of serving her and to neutralize those that cannot. And for her, in a strange way, victory is surrender. She bows to the Higher Centers that are above her. When the Higher Centers are there, they transcend struggle; but until they are complete, struggle on the lower level must continue. Having said that, it *is* possible to struggle intentionally, with a minimum of identification. It is possible to make an effort without being identified with making an effort and without being identified with achieving any desired result. This, then, is the Master Game. On the basis of this understanding Robert developed a new sense of how thirty one-syllable Work 'I's [*see list below*] ought to be used and of how they rightly work together.

THE SEQUENCE

Robert realized that something more was needed than the simple application of each of the Work 'I's in a given circumstance. The thirty Work 'I's were not to be used randomly, but in a certain sequence. We are too much subject to stimulus-response reactions to be successful with a random usage. Our line of effort tends to be determined by external stimuli rather than by internal priorities. Robert saw that the initial Work 'I' 'Be' had to be reaffirmed in a special way. It had to be combined, in a certain order, with whichever one of the thirty Work 'I's was best fitted to the external moment. As Robert experimented in his own work, he began to receive guidance; he felt he was learning something that had been known and perfected long ago. He found immediate support for these ideas in his studies of Ancient Egypt and of the Tarot deck, as it was conceived in Egypt.

Soon he presented us with a six-step sequence, comprised of single syllable Work'I's that can be used in all situations in life.

In a single sequence, 'Be' sounded three times in three quite different ways. In preparation for launching a sequence, one Work 'I' of the thirty was selected to stand in the place of THEME (such as 'Look' or 'Hear'), as dictated by the circumstances of the moment (either externally or internally). Robert's shorthand notation for the sequence was, then:

Be—Hold—**THEME**—Back—**THEME**—BE

The capitalization of the final BE signals the end of the sequence, followed by prolonging presence with what he called the "Four wordless breaths." He then distinguished the six Work 'I's of the sequence where effort is made, from the four wordless breaths where no effort is made.

Let us take an example of using the sequence. When driving on the highway in a scenic environment, apply the Work 'I' 'Look.' This, then, would be the THEME of your sequence. The sequence is preceded by the selection of its theme (Look), and then implemented during the sequence in this order:

1. An initial **Be**. (Be present.)
2. Then, as **Be** flags, there comes the second 'I,' **Hold**. That is, HOLD PRESENCE (this is the reappearance of Be).
3. Then, as **Hold** flags, there is the first application of the theme: **Look** (with presence).
4. As **Look** flags there is a second Be, which is a return to the beginning of the sequence. This second Be was eventually called **Back**. The thinking was that if the initial **Look** is sustained past a certain point, the Black Queen will find some way to insert herself, and imagination will re-enter. **Back** means return back to wordless presence.
5. Then comes a repetition of the chosen theme: **Look**. In other words: "Look again, as you are in the circumstances that lend themselves to looking."
6. The sequence ends with **BE**, also known as "Long BE." Long BE is followed by the four wordless breaths (four inhalations and four exhalations). Just as you are beginning to be drawn into what you are experiencing externally, you are drawn back to BE ... and then presence is extended by the four inhalations and exhalations. In a successful sequence something beyond the sequence makes its appearance. The complete sequence, then, is ten: six Work 'I's plus the four wordless breaths. The six is the effort and the four is non-effort. The four wordless breaths are an interval in which the steward withdraws, or "dies." It is the invocation of a higher level. In this space, in one lucky sequence out of many, the invisible Self may make its appearance.

When Robert first taught the sequence, he presented the four wordless breaths as the transcendence of the sequence. With the four wordless breaths we entered a space beyond the functions. Of course, for most of us most of the time, this does not occur. We are present through the four breaths, and then there is the next assault of the Lower Self. But when the sequence does evoke Higher Centers, it is best to stay with Higher Centers. In other words, don't initiate another sequence until you feel Higher Centers waning.

After a certain amount of experimentation Robert felt that each 'I' used in the sequence — with the exception of Long BE — should take place over three seconds (the time of an inhalation and an exhalation).

COMPLETING THE THIRTY: THE INDIVIDUAL WORK 'I'S

The sequence is composed of six Work 'I's, two of which are the single Work 'I' that is the chosen theme. The theme is drawn from the remaining 26 Work 'I's. The 26 Individual Work 'I's are used to address the needs of the many different situations in which a student finds themself. They can be used as themes in a sequence, or they can be used as a single, one-syllable utterance. For example, the Work 'I' Act is often used as a single utterance by itself.

The description of each Work 'I' in the list below may not be immediately meaningful, as the original requirement was that they be one syllable only. They were intended to reproduce the actions of the essential Work 'I's of the System. Repeated practice helps one to get behind them in the right way, to eventually make them your own.

The 26 individual Work 'I's:

Still	Control the impulse to move. Invoke absence of movement.
Turn	Stop imagination.
Act	Engage presence. Do not be passive to imagination.
Pax	Avoid the entire spectrum of negative emotions.
Leave	Leave identification. Do not identify.

Kneel	Do not resent friction. Accept what the moment presents.
Drop	Do not judge or hold accounts.
Use	Use the tool of voluntary suffering.
Wit	Avoid wit.
Now	Think neither of the past nor the future.
Look	Look with presence.
Hear	Hear with presence.
Feel	Feel with presence.
Taste	Taste with presence.
Smell	Smell with presence.
Move	Move with presence.
Talk	Speak with presence.
Think	Think with presence.
Read	Read with presence.
Write	Write with presence.
Child	Remain in essence.
Serve	Serve a level higher than yourself.
Scale	Employ scale and relativity.
Aim	Remember your aim. Complete your octave.
Time	Remember the brevity of life.
Gods	Remember the Gods.

With the hindsight of twenty years, the author finds he uses some of the individual Work 'I's more than others. For example, I do not use Read or Write sequences. I try to bring presence to those activities in other ways. And I do use one-syllable Work 'I's that are not on this list — just as Robert still uses Work 'I's from his original list of 36.

When you become familiar with these 'I's, and familiar with the sequence, both the selection of the theme and the deployment of the sequence ceases to be discursive activity. In other words, these actions are not the outcome of linear thought about the Work. They become simply a relationship to the ever-changing moment of NOW. And there is no identification with the result of the sequence; there is simply effort without identification.

As a person develops experience using the sequence:

- One becomes more adept at selecting the right theme for the moment;
- One becomes better able to sense the Black Queen's countermove, and to use **Back** to place her in checkmate;
- One becomes better able to recognize a transcendent **Long BE** and to see it as the permanent background of the whole process;
- As a consequence of this, one becomes generally more able to use the sequence in service of one's higher Self.

And it all comes together in the moment. Starting a sequence with the appropriate theme becomes the same as invoking a single Work 'I.' Getting the whole process right is like rubbing Alladin's lamp such that the magical genie appears. If you rub and polish without expectation, there comes, in a certain moment, a unified, transcendent consciousness that knows itself for what it is.

A key to understanding the sequence is to understand that *it creates a context in which the White Queen is able to confront the Black Queen*. In other words, in a successful sequence, the White Queen initiates, the Black Queen reacts — and so becomes visible. Her visibility makes the application of the remaining five 'I's more precise and accurate.

Before the sequence, the use of Work 'I's was more random, either as they came to mind or as they were evoked by external circumstances. When one uses random Work 'I's, the struggle to awaken *takes place on ground that is already controlled by the Black Queen*. We struggle, but 'just struggle' is victory for the Black Queen. With the use of the sequence the terrain changes. The steward can anticipate the Black Queen's reactions and counter them. The steward — under the leadership of the White Queen — is then able to take the initiative from the Black Queen and preempt the Lower Self.

Thus, where the Work described in Ouspensky's *Psychology* is reactive and battles on the terrain of the Lower Self, the work of the steward preempts the Lower Self. It attempts to displace her and to create an open, transparent space in which the Higher Centers may make their appearance.

When the sequence is rightly used it enables a certain hydrogen of impressions to enter the machine — and this hydrogen is the natural food of the latent Higher Centers. It attracts the Higher Centers, rousing them from their latent state.

We have shown that, by making use of the sequence the steward is able to address the level below it (the Lower Self). But it must also be able to address the level that is above it (the Higher Centers).

THE STEWARD AND HIGHER CENTERS: EFFORT AND NON-EFFORT

As the steward takes the initiative away from the Lower Self, it must become increasingly sensitive to the emergent Higher Centers and know how to yield to them the moment they appear.

And here there is a problem. *All the efforts that the steward normally makes are initiated from the lower centers.* Yes, these efforts are made under the guidance of the White Queen, with her special insight, but they are still *made from* the lower centers. The problem is, then, that the almost continuous effort required of the lower centers actually takes the space the fledgling Higher Centers need to breathe. The Higher Centers need to take in their own impressions directly.

From the standpoint of the Higher Centers, all the efforts we can make are just part of the chorus of 'I's that continuously arises from the lower centers. They are still part of the second state. The Higher Centers may make more frequent appearances when we are working with the sequence, *but they cannot come into their own* in a space that is dominated by active struggle. A permanent transition through to Worlds 6 and 12 requires something more.[1]

Let us examine the basic dichotomy at work here. With no effort there is only imagination. With continuous effort there is an ongoing struggle that blocks Higher Centers. But with the sequence there is something more, there is timed effort followed by the four wordless breaths *where no*

---

1. Technically, in certain moments, the Higher Centers may initiate a sequence to defend themselves. Robert calls this a "sequence coming from presence." This occurs when the Higher Centers are present, and under assault or starting to fade.

effort is made. Thus, at the close of every sequence, the steward bows to presence itself. Every sequence thus provides *a timed space of non-effort* in which the fledgling Higher Centers can realize themselves. Built into every sequence is the right balance of effort and non-effort.

And there is more to it than this. The Higher Centers may or may not appear in the timed space of Long BE. But the White Queen is watching for them, so that when they do appear they will be recognized for what they are. The steward will then remain passive for as long as they are active, even if that extends beyond the four inhalations and exhalations. If the Higher Centers come, we forget about the number of the breath and remain on bended knee during their presence.

The White Queen stands ever poised to give ground to Higher Centers and to disengage from Work 'I's. She can sense when something higher than herself has emerged and yield to that. She can also sense when this special presence has disappeared and knows the moment to reinitiate efforts to displace the Lower Self. Mastery of the sequence is not just in knowing how to sustain a line of effort, but knowing how to yield to Higher Centers in the moment they arrive—as Robert calls it, "The death of the steward." In kneeling to Higher Centers, the steward unconditionally gives way.

When the invisible Self appears, it can meet a threat from the Lower Self by selecting the Work 'I's it needs to sustain itself. If there is no threat, it can simply sustain itself without Work 'I's or the sequence. The invisible Self is a thousand times more artful than the steward. But, in a man number four, it can last only for so long — as it requires a fuel that is soon exhausted. The White Queen, who has been passively watching, will hopefully remember something of the world of the Self, and use that experience to guide her future efforts. She will rub Alladin's lamp with ever greater skill.

When the Self is able to sustain itself for longer periods, the game changes again, for the Higher Centers work in a different way. This takes us into the work of a conscious being.

In applying the sequence Robert found that the more a person was interacting with external events, the less appropriate the sequence was as a tool.

Better simply to employ individual Work 'I's. For example, you are in rush hour traffic and you need to change lanes several times to make the desired exit. The traffic is quite aggressive; you need to watch carefully and move quickly. A sequence is inappropriate. You are better to strike directly with 'Aim,' or 'Drop,' or 'Now.'

If you are using the sequence regularly in circumstances that *are* appropriate, you are acquiring a discipline that makes your random use of the thirty Work 'I's much more effective. In that regard the sequence is like a forcing house for the development of the steward.

We keep in mind that all use of the sequence develops the White Queen, who alone can recognize and serve presence itself. She is the heart of the steward, and she grows stronger with respect to the Black Queen as we become more competent with the thirty Work 'I's. The steward itself changes as the White Queen develops. Robert reflected on these changes in the form of the steward.

Our ability to make optimal use of the thirty Work 'I's is determined by our ability to apply the six Work 'I's of the sequence. Robert refers to our mechanical 'I's — all of our 'I's that are uninterested in evolution — as "the Ten Thousand." This number is not to be taken literally; it is a way of painting a general picture of our psychology. So if there are thirty Work 'I's at the behest of the White Queen, there are 10,000 at the behest of the Black Queen.

The thirty Work 'I's are sufficient. The steward cannot become too large, or it will lose the necessary speed and focus. The White Queen can use other 'I's if they are compatible, for example from Robert's initial list of 36 Work 'I's. But if the White Queen's retinue becomes too large, she will be defeated because the will of the steward will be split into too many little wills, easily deflected by the devices of the Black Queen. Once a small and disciplined circle of 'I's has been developed in service to the White Queen, it will be much harder for the Black Queen to take possession of any of them.

Robert used the symbol of archer, with his quiver of arrows, to show how the steward works as a unity.

THE QUIVER

The quiver is the container in which the archer keeps his arrows. Robert likened it to the stock of Work 'I's that a student uses regularly. Once one knows the Work 'I's well, then after one shaft is released, the next one is ready.

The steward acts so that exactly one 'I' is implemented in one moment. Within the thirty there is the inner circle of THE SIX, and within the six is the core of Long BE. The inner circle of the six draws a theme from the thirty into the chamber of the nine of hearts, and then launches a sequence. Long BE needs the support of the six and the six needs the support of the thirty.

When one makes good transitions between different external activities, and has the right 'arrows' ready in advance, this can excite Higher Centers. When we are consistent enough, Higher Centers will begin to let us know what works for them. The Work culminates in the modeling and molding of the thirty Work 'I's by the Higher Centers they serve. This is the greatest art and the greatest science known to man.

When the steward is simplified, and focused in the right way, it is not thinking of results or of success or failure. It is just doing what it does. And, with equal skill, when something higher appears, he steps back.

What we are describing is the concentration of the steward. It is reduced in size and enhanced in speed and insight. Eventually it becomes something that has no expectation of the future, no identification with the past, no ambition, no hopes, and no fears. It becomes something that remembers and that is ever focused on the next move.

Mastery of the sequence brings a connection with the field of BEING which is the invisible backdrop of our existence. When we accumulate conscious energy in this way, the invisible screen of awareness, which is the forgotten context of our existence, shimmers into life. Higher Centers begin to become aware of themselves.

Finally, we can connect all of this to Robert's earlier teaching of the place of essence in awakening. Specifically, the fine molecular energies of essence actually unite with the molecular and electronic energies of the emergent Higher Centers to produce a new kind of being in the Universe.

Thus, there is something in essence that can ultimately survive the death of the steward.

As mentioned, while working on the sequence and the thirty Work 'I's, Robert found the most surprising correlations with the teachings of Ancient Egypt. The correlations with Egyptian symbols were so definite that he began to correct or revise his own working principles in relation to these symbolic images, or 'keys.' Over time Robert discovered the keys in other teachings, including the Ancient Mesopotamian, the Vedantic, the Buddhist, the Apostolic Christian, and the Sufi.[1]

Robert felt that the thirty Work 'I's, the sequence, and the keys had only been given to the Fellowship after many decades of payment. We had been prepared in such a way that we could value this gift.

In 1935 Peter Ouspensky said to Dr. Roles: "Something is missing in the system. If man is meant to remember himself there must have been some simple method. But it has been lost. I could never find it. Once in India, I heard an echo of such a method." Robert felt that with the discovery and practice of the Sequence this "simple method" had been found.[2]

Looking back over more than ten-years practice with the sequence, I find that what has happened is a merging of the old Work and the new Work. The sequence is appropriate to certain situations and not to others. The sequence concentrates the steward, and thereby affects one's efforts in the times when it is not in use. Effort becomes more focused and one-pointed, and the principle of surrender to presence emerging is maintained, whether using the sequence or not. The old Work of observation and separation still applies. In situations where there are complex negative emotions that do not simply disappear when a sequence is initiated, previous understandings

---

1. Robert developed an entire teaching of the keys, which we have not recorded in these pages. It was his feeling that this teaching could only be communicated orally, and he did not want interpretations of his teachings in this area to be published.

2. Roles, Francis, *A Lasting Freedom*, Society for the Study of Normal Psychology, London, 1972.

Figure 85. Robert Burton in 2016.

of feature, type, personal attitudes, and characteristic personal reactions are useful and even necessary.

The base of self-observation, and years of practice in separating consciousness from functions, proved helpful training for the 'death of the steward.' They provided a basis both for recognizing the arrival of Higher Centers and for marking the moment of their passing. The latter is a particular challenge, for if that moment is not observed the steward does not automatically re-engage. One is left with vague positive imaginations about "my experience" of Higher Centers.

Not everyone responded to the new teaching favorably; it represented a fundamental change of form. We had to master a challenging new technique, and we now looked to keys and symbols rather than to workbooks. We could not talk about the Work in the same self-assured way that we used to. Indeed, talking about the Work had become, for many of us, a badge of identity. Now it was all a matter of direct application. The sequence showed us that we talked more, and worked less, than we thought we did. Many students left the school at this time.

Having said this, we must emphasize that the sequence is simple when rightly applied. The application of the thirty Work 'I's is more direct, and less discursive, than ruminating about the system ideas in a general way. But direct and simple does not mean easy. The use of the sequence does make the Work more challenging. In short, it brings you closer to reality. The whole school came one step closer to reality.

Created Light and Uncreated Light

In 1997 Robert spoke to us directly, for the first time, of the Absolute, not on the basis of his own first-hand experience, but on the basis of understanding given him by C Influence. In 2016 he shared with us that he had a direct experience of the Absolute and, a few months later, he said he was having a direct experience while leading a meeting of over two hundred students. In these experiences he said that there was no direction being given, no affirmation of a particular aspect of his teaching, no correction. It was just a contact, and a contact that conveyed love. He later mentioned that his first direct experience of the Absolute took place in 2014. This event was witnessed by one student alone, and for almost two years Robert kept the experience to himself. Robert took these experiences as an affirmation to simply do more of what he was doing.

On July 16th, 2017 Robert Burton suffered congestive heart failure. He was transported by ambulance to the cardiac care unit of Rideout Hospital in Marysville. The cardiologist scheduled him for an angiogram two days later, on the morning of Tuesday the 18th. Just prior to the test Robert's heart became so weak that he almost died. He was, however, already in the cardiac unit, and due to the swift action of the staff, they were able to keep him alive. The cardiologist performed the angiography immediately, and he was able to open the clogged blood vessels and insert two stents, which kept the vessels open and saved Robert's life. During the insertion of the two stents Robert felt the closeness of C Influence. He was with them. He had the choice of continuing through to join them or to remain here with his students. For a period of time he had no sense of which would occur. And then he realized that the operation was over and that his condition had stabilized. What followed was a deep sense of happiness. He had more time to be with us, to share his living connection with a Higher Level. We were surprised, and certainly at first concerned, that he continued to lead so many meetings. After a period of time it was clear that he had renewed vigor. Then, on New Years Day of 2018, he determined to accelerate the pace. Whereas he had led three meetings a week, now he led six: a meeting almost every day supplemented by multiple events. In 2020, during the coronavirus pandemic lockdown, when events were not possible, he stepped up the meetings by having them videotaped to eleven a week. His teaching had become continuous.

As he entered into this new rhythm, he began to feel connected to a consciousness that precedes creation. He called this the experience of "uncreated light." He described the experience of Higher Centers that was enabled by the sequence "created light," and what transcended the sequence, existing outside of time and space as we know it, as "uncreated light."

It was as though the Gods had made a gift to Robert after surviving his heart attack and operation. He was able to teach us — over the age of eighty — more actively than he had ever done before.

Robert found uncreated light to be something that — being 'uncreated' — is beyond creation. It was the awareness of a comprehensive and all-encompassing background of consciousness: self-generated and self-sustaining, prior to the cycle of birth and death. And he felt that somehow his experience of uncreated light included all of us, or that we were included with him. Here are a few comments Robert has made about uncreated light:

> With uncreated light, one does not seek reality sequentially, but reality is here. It appears of itself, by itself, for itself.

> Uncreated light is the fulfillment of the system. You abandon the system when you have uncreated light.

> Our loving presence for one another is so strong, that now we have uncreated light.

> Aristotle said that the very best thing for a man is not to have been born at all. This is uncreated light, the very best thing. Not to be born at all is to have the staying power of uncreated light. Influence

C want the best for us — and we have it. The best is uncreated light.[1]

With uncreated light, World 6 and World 12 do not need a protective shield—the nine of hearts. They can handle presence themselves.

[*At a moment during a meeting*] We are not inducing presence now; we are strengthening uncreated light.

All of us are self-contained with uncreated light.

Yesterday it was just like this; today it is just like this; tomorrow it will be just like this. Every day brings uncreated light.

It is so still here now and we are consciously still—quiet uncreated light.

We have distilled our existence into uncreated light.

Something that motivates me is that, when I get to Paradise, I do not want to feel that I could have done more for you. As of now, since we all have uncreated light, mission accomplished.[2]

In this tidal wave of teaching, the entire student body found itself, in certain moments, in what seemed a universal 'containing' space. It was as though we were a unity of like beings, entering an unboundaried domain, that had the taste of eternity and the promise of greater things to come.

The teaching of uncreated light came as Robert entered his 82nd year. The first generation of Fellowship students was already beginning to pass away. One after another, the people who had been involved in the founding of the school were completing their roles. As each person moved on, one had a sense of how each life was a statement of their work on awakening, and — in the atmosphere of uncreated light — there was an unusual feeling of appreciation. You felt the achievement represented in each role, as

---

1. For Robert 'being born' refers to created light, evoking presence through a sequence.
2. All quotations from the Apollo Miracle 8-50, 13th December 2020.

Figure 86. Robert felt that, with uncreated light, we had realized Plato's ideal state.

though it were your own. You appreciated that person's ability to bear suffering, and to pass on with mind and heart open to the present moment. This brought the sense of a common destiny. It was as though these friends were entering a universal field of consciousness, that extends beyond the present embodiment, and that somehow contains the true measure of our existence.

Looking back over the five Fourth Way teachers, the first three — Gurdjieff, Ouspensky, and Collin — pulled together groups and worked intensively with them. They each worked with a larger group for a few years only, at most a decade; otherwise, they worked with smaller groups of people, as the circumstances of life permitted. The majority of the people connected with these groups stayed with their respective teachers for a few years only. Alexander Horn taught for a longer period of time, but with a very high rate of turnover. The thread of his teaching was his theatrical art, but the culture of his time was not ready for that art. Robert Burton started to share his higher centers in 1970 and accelerated his teaching over a period of more than half a century. People remained and worked on themselves decade after decade. It was your life; you thought of your life in terms of evolution. That was the standard, that was the theme. It was a different kind of situation and — consequently — there was a different kind of Work. When it is a life's endeavor you really have to bridge intervals within yourself, and with other people, or you won't stay the course. For it is in the nature of conscious evolution that you go forward or fall back. There are certain transition points in life: changes in relationship or profession, the transition from youth to middle age, the transition from middle age to old age. If you go through these in the Work, the Work goes deeper into yourself. It *is* what your life is about; what gives it continuity.

Postscript

In the winter of 1994, as part of the opening of the Fellowship centers in Russia, the author visited Moscow and St. Petersburg. On the second day of my first visit to St. Petersburg I determined to visit the Hermitage Museum, which was two and a half miles directly down the Nevsky Prospekt from the teaching apartment. It was within walking distance. So I set off early in the morning, in the below zero weather, fascinated by the great city that lay before me. These were truly optimal conditions to be present. It seemed much easier than usual to make efforts, and presence seemed to come more naturally. There were even moments of feeling outside of one's life, as though one were watching a film. I noted the landmarks along the way, to benchmark progress. Suddenly I found myself at the large intersection of Nevsky and Liteyny... Liteyny... Liteyny... There came a memory of Peter Ouspensky's description of his first efforts to remember himself. He had been going to the printers' shop, along Liteyny, and then he turned onto Nevsky. I was just at that intersection. And I realized that I was present *because* Peter Ouspensky had made those efforts so many years before: made them, succeeded with them, and succeeded in making the state permanent in himself. Had Ouspensky not made those efforts, I would not be making the efforts I was making now. A single thread of living presence connected us. It had been kept alive for seventy-nine years, transmitted from one human vehicle to the next. And everyone else around me at the intersection was deeply buried in the same imagination that Ouspensky had seen those seventy-nine years before. The passage of years had not brought one scintilla of presence to the intersection of Nevsky and Liteyny. Ouspensky's 'sleeping people' were all still there, and the enchantment they were under still held secure. I saw something of what is meant by the idea that time is an illusion.

This sudden awareness greatly heightened my valuation for humanity's most precious possession: presence self-aware. And with that came gratitude for all those who had carried the flame down through the generations, from that time to this. In writing this book the author has felt that same thread of presence running back through Horn, Collin, and Ouspensky, to the young Gurdjieff receiving the system from a brotherhood in Central Asia. A single living thread of life. What wonderful people they were! Of course, it is ultimately the Gods who monitor these things and make them happen, but we too have our part in it. And our part in it is the best part that humanity has to play.

Epilogue in Heaven

We see the Archangels Michael, Gabriel, Raphael, and Uriel circling the mid-Heaven: the vast containing space which reveals the life of Mankind through time. We look down with them on that part of the span which contains the cycle of the Fourth Way teachings. Sometimes it seems their labors are the labors of Sisyphus, for the coarse material that comprises the human experience is unstable; it quickly resolves back into its elements. Nevertheless, under the hands of the Archangels, it is intermixed and blended with phosphorescent conscious light. One sees, in the matrices of light that emerge, faint images of great beauty: a Zoroastrian Chinvat Bridge from here to eternity, an Inner Circle of Humanity, a Great Spiritual Tradition, a conscious theater, a Platonic Republic. But these images collapse so quickly, dissolving into the surrounding blackness. Are they chimeras only? Yet as the images rise and fade away, individual sparks of light rise straight up, through the phosphorescent glow, into a world that is invisible to us.

> **Uriel:** There are those in each generation who rise into the Sphere of Sentient Being. And in the longer life of Mankind there is the cumulative work of the schools, which falters but does not die — one generation always enabling the next.
>
> **Michael:** Yet, looking back, we see gaps, and I fear the gaps yet to come — for these threaten the life of the whole. The Work of School is the very nervous system of mankind, and that nervous system seems, at some points, too weak to sustain the life of the larger body.

There is a pause.

> **Raphael:** Their struggles are most touching.

Michael: Yet their errors most consistent and most vile.

Gabriel: The alchemical process is not complete, the final hour has not sounded, the Aeon comes not yet. Our labors may still bear fruit and we shall not desert them.

Turning from the Gods we look down to the level of humanity itself. Suddenly we see humanity as the angels do, in several dimensions more than it sees itself. In the first moments this wider view is discouraging, for we see something that is turned in on itself in an unhealthy way. Humanity appears ignorant of the context in which it exists: of the pantheon of the Gods above, or of the living fabric of nature below. But in the next moment the scenario expands. A regenerate humanity comes into view, arising out of many more humanities than the tiny sampling that exists on our planet earth. This enhanced and expanded humanity is more distinguished than anything that our history has record of. It is humanity's dimension of transcendence: the extended family of its transcended microcosmoses. Robert Burton, the last in the line of the Fourth Way teachers, has described it thus:

> Mankind is immeasurably old. It has existed in different solar systems and galaxies from before the time the earth was created. It is *far* older than the earth. Conscious beings have been created from the microcosmos man for more time than we can comprehend ... from the immeasurable depths of time. There is a line of them, extending back: mysterious, unbelievably ancient. They all inhabit the Celestial City of Paradise — which is truly *The Forbidden City*. The only key to this city is divine presence.

Bibliography

GEORGE GURDJIEFF

Gurdjieff, G.I., *Life is real only then, when "I am"*, All and Everything, Third Series, E.P. Dutton, New York, 1978.

Gurdjieff, G.I., *Meetings with Remarkable Men,* (All and Everything, Second Series), E.P. Dutton & Company, New York, 1963.

Gurdjieff, G.I., *All and Everything, First Series, Beelzebub's Tales to his Grandson,* E.P. Dutton & Co., Inc., New York, 1964.

Gurdjieff, G.I., *The Herald of Coming Good,* Sure Fire Press, Edmonds, Washington, 1988.

Gurdjieff, G.I., Scenario of the Ballet, *The Struggle of the Magicians,* photocopy of a transcription from the original manuscript. No publication information given.

Gurdjieff, G.I., *Views From the Real World: Early Talks of Gurdjieff,* E.P. Dutton, New York, 1973.

PETER OUSPENSKY

Ouspensky, P.D., *A Further Record: Extracts from Meetings 1928-1945,* Routledge & Kegan Paul, Arkana Paperbacks, London, 1986.

Ouspensky, P.D., *A New Model of the Universe,* Alfred A. Knopf, Inc., New York, 1969.

Ouspensky, P.D., *A Record of Meetings,* Arkana (Penguin Group), London, 1992.

Ouspensky, P.D., *Conscience,* Routledge & Kegan Paul, London, 1979.

Ouspensky, P.D., *In Search of the Miraculous,* Routledge & Kegan Paul, London, 1977.

Ouspensky, P.D., *Letters from Russia: 1919,* Routledge & Kegan Paul, London, 1978.

Ouspensky, P.D., *Strange Life of Ivan Osokin,* Arkana (Penguin Group), New York, 1987.

Ouspensky, P.D., *Talks with a Devil,* Turnstone Press Ltd., London, 1972.

Ouspensky, P.D., *Tertium Organum,* Vintage Books, New York, 1982.

Ouspensky, P.D., *The Fourth Way,* Vintage Books, New York, 1971.

Ouspensky, P.D., *The Psychology and Cosmology of Man's Possible Evolution,* Agora Books, Robertsbridge, East Sussex, 1989.

Ouspensky, P.D., *The Psychology of Man's Possible Evolution,* Alfred A. Knopf, New York, 1979.

Additionally, the Stourton Press, under Ouspensky's student Fairfax Hall, published five small hardbound volumes for private circulation, in the years immediately following Ouspensky's death. These are listed below, by date of publication.

Ouspensky, P.D., *Notes on the Work,* Stourton Press, Cape Town, South Africa, 1952.

Ouspensky, P.D., *Memory: Extracts from the Sayings and Writings of P.D.O. about Memory, Self-Remembering and Recurrence,* Stourton Press, Cape Town, South Africa, 1953.

Ouspensky, P.D., *A Synthesis of Some of the Sayings and Writings of P.D.O. on the subject of Negative Emotions,* Stourton Press, Cape Town, South Africa, 1953.

Ouspensky, P.D., *Surface Personality: A Study of Imaginary Man,* Stourton Press, Cape Town, South Africa, 1954.

Ouspensky, P.D., *Self-Will: A Compilation of things said by P.D. Ouspensky mainly about the need to subjugate Self-Will as a preparation for the growth of Will,* Stourton Press, Cape Town, South Africa, 1955.

RODNEY COLLIN

Collin, Rodney, *Hellas, A Spectacle with Music and Dances in four acts,* The Stourton Press, Cape Town, South Africa, 1951.

Collin, Rodney, *The Herald of Harmony,* Ediciones Sol, Tlalpam, Mexico, 1951.

Collin, Rodney, *The Mirror of Light,* Watkins, London, 1976.

Collin, Rodney, *The Theory of Celestial Influence,* Watkins, London, 1980.

Collin, Rodney, *The Theory of Conscious Harmony,* Watkins, London, 1976.

Collin, Rodney, *Theory of Eternal Life,* Watkins, London 1974.

ALEXANDER HORN

Horn, Alexander Francis, *The Infinite Lives of Giordano Bruno: A Play in Three Acts,* 1993. Published only in limited edition.

Horn, Alexander Francis, *In Search of a Solar Hero,* Element Books Ltd., Shaftesbury, Dorset UK, 1987.

Horn, Alexander Francis, *Ponderings of a Citizen of the Milky Way,* Element Books Ltd., Shaftesbury, Dorset UK, 1987.

Horn, Alexander Francis, *Theatre of All Possibilities,* Everyman Publications, San Francisco, 1978.

ROBERT BURTON

Burton, Robert Earl, and Crosby, Dianne, *Awakening,* Fellowship of Friends, Oregon House, CA, 2017.

Burton, Robert Earl, and Grace, Judith, *Fifty Years with Angels,* September 5, 1967–September 5, 2017, Fellowship of Friends, Oregon House, 2017.

Burton, Robert Earl, *Self Remembering,* Globe Press Books, New York, 1991.

Burton, Robert Earl, *The Thirty Traditional Stars,* Vol I, August 2005. Privately printed.

Burton, Robert Earl, *The Thirty Imperishable Stars,* Vol. II, December 2005. Privately printed.

Burton, Robert Earl, *The Thirty Imperishable Stars,* Vol. III, March 2006. Privately printed.

Burton, Robert Earl, *The Six Transcendent Virtues,* Vol. IV, July 2006. Privately printed.

Burton, Robert Earl, *The Six Transcendent Virtues,* Vol. V, September 2006. Privately printed.

Burton, Robert Earl, *The Six Transcendent Virtues,* Vol. VI, December 2006. Privately printed.

SECONDARY SOURCES ON THE FOURTH WAY

Anderson, Margaret, *My Thirty Years' War,* Horizon Press, New York, 1969.

Anderson, Margaret, *The Fiery Fountains,* Horizon Press, New York, 1969.

Anderson, Margaret, *The Strange Necessity*, Horizon Press, New York, 1969.

Anderson, Margaret, *The Unknowable Gurdjieff*, Arkana, Penguin Books Ltd., London, 1991.

Azize, Joseph (compiler), *Gurdjieff's Early Talks 1914-1931*, Book Studio, 2014.

Beckwith, Gerald de Symons, *Ouspensky's Fourth Way*, Starnine Media & Publishing Ltd., Oxford, 2015.

Bennett, J.G., *Gurdjieff: A Very Great Enigma*, Samuel Weiser, Inc., York Beach, Maine, 1973.

Bennett, J.G., *Gurdjieff: Making a New World*, Turnstone Books, London, 1973.

Bennett, J.G. & Elizabeth, *Idiots in Paris*, Weiser Books, New York, 1991.

Bennett, J.G., (compiled by A.G.E. Blake), *Talks on Beelzebub's Tales*, Samuel Weiser, Inc. York Beach, Maine, 1988.

Bennett, J.G., *Witness: The Story of a Search*, Dharma Book Company, Inc., New York, 1962.

Bennett, J.G., *Witness: The Story of a Search*, Bennett Books, Santa Fe, New Mexico, 2007. (including updates made to the 1962 edition).

Birimisa, George (edited by Baugniet, Larry and Sagan, Paul), *Birimisa: Portraits, Plays, Perversions*, Sweetheart Press, San Francisco, 2009.

Bland, Rosamund, *Nine Letters by Rosamund Bland*, The Stourton Press, Cape Town, South Africa, 1952.

Blom, Gert-Jan, (compiler and producer), *Gurdjieff: Harmonic Development, The Complete Harmonium Recordings 1948-1949*, Basta Audiovisuals, Netherlands, 2004.

Blom, Gert-Jan, (compiler and producer), *Gurdjieff/de Hartmann: Oriental Suite, The Complete Orchestral Music, 1923-1924*, Basta Audiovisuals, Netherlands, 2006.

Bukovsky-Hewitt, Anna, *With Gurdjieff in St. Petersburg and Paris*, Samuel Weiser, New York, 1978.

Claustres, Solange, *Becoming Conscious with G.I. Gurdjieff*, Eureka Editions, Utrecht, Holland, 2005.

Collin-Smith, Joyce, *Call No Man Master*, Gateway Books, Bath, 1988.

de Hartmann, Thomas and Olga, *Our Life with Mr. Gurdjieff*, Harper & Row publishers, San Francisco, 1964.

Farber, Thomas, *Tales for the Son of My Unborn Child, Berkeley 1966-1969,* Pocket Books (Simon & Schuster, Inc.), New York, 1973.

Fergusson, Francis, Introduction to *Aristotle's Poetics,* (transl. S.H. Butcher), Hill and Wang, New York, 1961.

Fergusson, Francis, *Dante's Drama of the Mind,* Princeton University Press, Princeton, New Jersey, 1953.

Fergusson, Francis, *The Idea of a Theatre,* Princeton University Press, Princeton, New Jersey, 1972.

Fergusson, Francis, *Trope and Allegory: Themes Common to Dante and Shakespeare,* The University of Georgia Press, Athens, 1977.

Hands, Rina, *Diary of Madame Egout Pour Sweet,* Two Rivers Press, Aurora, Oregon, 1991.

Haven, Girard, *Creating a Soul,* Ulysses Books, Oregon House, CA, 1999.

Haven, Girard, *The Prize is Eternity: Foundations of Inner Work in the Fourth Way,* Ulysses Books, Oregon House, CA, 2002.

Haven, Girard, *The Art of Presence: Perspectives from a Fourth Way School,* Blue Logic, Oregon House, CA, 2010.

Howarth, Jessmin & Dushka, *It's Up to Ourselves,* Gurdjieff Heritage Society, New York, 1998.

Hunter, Bob, *Don't Forget: P.D. Ouspensky's Life of Self-Remembering,* Bardic Press, California, 2006.

Hulme, Kathryn, *Undiscovered Country,* Little, Brown & Co., Boston, 1966.

Kaplan, Linda L., *The Seeds of the Divine Beginning,* Apollo University Press, 2023.

Lannes, Henriette, (ed. Bentley, William and Betty), *Inside a Question: Works of Henriette Lannes,* Paul H. Crompton, London, 2002.

Mairet, Philip, *A.R. Orage,* University Books, New Hyde Park, New York, 1966.

March, Louise Goepfert, (ed. Beth McCorkle), *The Gurdjieff Years: 1929-1945,* The Work Study Association, Inc., Walworth, New York, 1990.

Moore, James, *Gurdjieff: The Anatomy of a Myth,* Element Books Ltd., Shaftesbury, Dorset UK, 1993.

Mouravieff, Boris, *Gnosis, Book One, Exoteric Cycle: Study and Commentaries on the Esoteric Tradition of Eastern Orthodoxy,* Praxis Research Institute, South Brent, UK, 1989.

Mouravieff, Boris, *Gnosis, Book Two, Mesoteric Cycle: Study and Commentaries on the Esoteric Tradition of Eastern Orthodoxy,* Praxis Research Institute, South Brent, UK, 1992.

Mouravieff, Boris, *Gnosis, Book Three, Esoteric Cycle: Study and Commentaries on the Esoteric Tradition of Eastern Orthodoxy,* Praxis Research Institute, South Brent, UK, 1993.

Nicoll, Maurice, *The New Man,* Penguin Books, Inc., Baltimore, 1950.

Nicoll, Maurice, *Psychological Commentaries, Vols. 1-5,* Watkins Publishing, London, 1952.

Nicoll, Maurice, *Living Time,* Vincent Stuart, London, 1952.

Nott, C.S., *Journey Through This World,* Routledge & Kegan Paul, London, 1974.

Nott, C.S., *Teachings of Gurdjieff: A Pupil's Journal,* Arkana, Penguin Books Ltd., London, 1990.

Orage, A.R., *Commentaries on All and Everything,* Two Rivers Press, Aurora, Oregon, 1985.

Orage, A.R., *Consciousness,* Samuel Weiser Inc., New York, 1975.

Orage, A.R., *On Love & Psychological Exercises,* Samuel Weiser Inc., York Beach, Maine, 1998.

Peters, Fritz, *Boyhood with Gurdjieff; Gurdjieff Remembered; Balanced Man,* Bardic Press, California, 2005.

Phillpotts, Dorothy, *Discovering Gurdjieff,* AuthorHouse UK Ltd., Milton Keynes, 2008.

Pogson, Beryl, *Maurice Nicoll: A Portrait,* Fourth Way Books, New York, 1987.

Reyner, J.H., *Ouspensky: The Unsung Genius,* George Allen & Unwin, Ltd., London, 1981.

Roles, Francis, *A Lasting Freedom,* Society for the Study of Normal Psychology, London, 1972.

Ropp, Robert de., *Talks by Madame Ouspensky,* Far Wester Press, San Francisco, 1974.

Ropp, Robert de., *Warrior's Way,* Dell Publishing Co., New York, 1979.

Ruth-Mueller, Guinevere, *Bread Upon the Water,* G&G Mueller, Rajkot, 1999.

Solano, Solita and Hulme, Kathryn, *Gurdjieff and the Women of the Rope: Notes of Meetings in Paris and New York 1935-1939 and 1948-1949,* Book Studio, 2019.

Salzmann, Jeanne de, *The Reality of Being,* Shambhala Publications, Inc., Boulder, Colorado, 2010.

Stjernvall, Nikolai de, *My Dear Father Gurdjieff,* Bardic Press, Dublin, 2013.

Taylor, Merrily E. (compiler & editor), *Remembering Pyotr Demianovich Ouspensky,* Yale University Library, New Haven, CT, 1978.

Taylor, Paul Beekman, *Shadows of Heaven,* Weiser Books Inc., York Beach, Maine, 1998.

Taylor, Paul Beekman, *Gurdjieff and Orage,* Weiser Books Inc., York Beach, Maine, 2001.

The Bridge, No. 12, Autumn 1997, P.D. Ouspensky Commemorative Issue, (ed. Eadie, Peter McGregor), © The Study Society, Colet House, Talgarth Road, London, 1997.

Tonne, Terje, *Rodney Collin, a man who wished to do something with his life,* The Karnak Press, Austin, Texas, 2023.

Tracol, Henri, *A Taste for Things That Are True,* Element Books Ltd., Shaftesbury, Dorset UK, 1994.

Vayesse, Jean, *Toward Awakening,* Far West Undertakings, San Francisco, 1978.

Walker, Kenneth, *Venture with Ideas,* Pellegrini & Cudahy, New York, 1952.

Walker, Kenneth, *A Study of Gurdjieff's Teaching,* Jonathan Cape, London, 1957.

Webb, James, *The Harmonious Circle*, Shambhala, Boston, 1987.

Welch, Louise, *Orage with Gurdjieff in America,* Routledge & Kegan Paul Ltd., London, 1982.

Zuber, René, *Who Are You, Monsieur Gurdjieff?,* Routledge & Kegan Paul Ltd., London, 1980.

Image Credits

Figures 4, 6, 10, 15 — *In Search of the Miraculous* by P.D. Ouspensky, Routledge & Kegan Paul, London, 1977.

Figure 5 — *The Fourth Way* by P.D. Ouspensky, Vintage Books, New York, 1971.

Figure 7 — *Psychological Commentaries on the Teaching of Gurdjieff and Ouspensky* by Maurice Nicoll, Watkins Publishing, London, Vol. 2, 1952.

Figures 8 and 9 — Copyright © 2022 by Hugh James. All rights reserved.

Figures 27, 34, 47, 54 — Petrarch Press archives.

Figure 28 — Photo by Paulina Herrara.

Figures 33, 35, 36, 37, 38, 39, 40, 41, 42, 49 — The Study Society.

Figures — 43, 71, 72, 73, 74, 75, 76, 77, 78, 79, 81, 82, 83, 84, 85 — Fellowship archives.

Figure 44 — Copyright © 2005 by Girard Haven. All rights reserved.

Figures 45 and 46 — Photos by Sharon Gordon.

Figures 51, 52, 53 — Photos by Raul De La Mora.

Figure 56 — Photo by Guadalupe Estrella.

Figures 58 and 59 — *Theatre of All Possibilities* by Alexander Francis Horn, Everyman Publications, San Francisco, 1978.

Figures 62 and 63 — Photos by Patricia Chancellor.

Figure 68 — Photo by Michael Parks.

Figures 69 and 86 — Photos by Leonid Novoselov.

Figures 79 and 80 — Photos by Michael Jackson.

STATEMENT OF FAIR USE

In researching illustrations for *The History of the Fourth Way: School Realized*, the author often encountered uncredited images. Despite efforts to locate the origin of the image, it was often not possible to determine the original copyright holder, or even whether there was a copyright on a given image. As such, this book may contain copyrighted material the use of which has not always been specifically authorized by the copyright owner. All images included by the author have been modified for print production. The author has selected these images only to illustrate concepts and points of narrative contained in this scholarly publication. The author believes this constitutes a 'fair use' of any such copyrighted material as provided for in section 107 of the US Copyright Law.

www.ingramcontent.com/pod-product-compliance
Lightning Source LLC
Chambersburg PA
CBHW072140070526
44585CB00015B/976